AF352511

VERGIL AND ELEGY

PHOENIX

Journal of the Classical Association of Canada
Revue de la Société canadienne des études classiques
Supplementary Volume LX
Tome supplémentaire LX

EDITED BY ALISON KEITH AND
MICAH Y. MYERS

Vergil and Elegy

UNIVERSITY OF TORONTO PRESS
Toronto Buffalo London

Library and Archives Canada Cataloguing in Publication

Title: Vergil and elegy / edited by Alison Keith and Micah Y. Myers.
Names: Keith, Alison, editor. | Myers, Micah Young, 1979– editor.
Series: Phoenix. Supplementary volume ; 60.
Description: Series statement: Phoenix supplementary volumes ; 60 |
Includes bibliographical references and indexes.
Identifiers: Canadiana (print) 2022048872X | Canadiana (ebook) 20220488797 |
ISBN 9781487547950 (cloth) | ISBN 9781487547967 (EPUB) |
ISBN 9781487547998 (PDF)
Subjects: LCSH: Virgil – Criticism and interpretation. | LCSH: Elegiac poetry,
Latin – History and criticism.
Classification: LCC PA6825 .V47 2023 | DDC 871/.01–dc23

We wish to acknowledge the land on which the University of Toronto Press
operates. This land is the traditional territory of the Wendat, the Anishnaabeg, the
Haudenosaunee, the Métis, and the Mississaugas of the Credit First Nation.

University of Toronto Press acknowledges the financial support of the Government
of Canada, the Canada Council for the Arts, and the Ontario Arts Council, an
agency of the Government of Ontario, for its publishing activities.

CONTENTS

Contents vii

ACKNOWLEDGMENTS

It is a pleasure for us to record here the debts of gratitude we have incurred in the preparation of this volume, which originated in a *Symposium Cumanum* held at the Villa Vergiliana in Cuma, Italy, in June 2017, under the auspices of the Vergilian Society. We are grateful to Mina Sgariglia, the manager of the Villa Vergiliana, and to her staff, for the comfortable and convivial setting in which the participants congregated; and to all the speakers and discussants on that occasion, including several whose papers have been published elsewhere – Irene Peirano Garrison, Peter Heslin, Sharon James, Matthew Loar, John Miller, Jim O'Hara, Donncha O'Rourke, Sallie Spence, and Hérica Valladares. This volume also contains papers that were presented at a companion panel on "Epic and Elegy" at the 2017 Celtic Conference in Classics, hosted by the McGill University Department of History and Classics in Montreal. We are also grateful to the other participants in that panel, including Sean Gurd, Don Lavigne, John Schafer, and Bobby Xinyue.

In the preparation of this volume, we have been ably assisted by a quartet of University of Toronto research assistants: Georgia Ferentinou, Don McCarthy, Sheena McKeever, and Karuna Sinha. We wish to thank our contributors for their patience with our slow progress, and to express our gratitude to our families for their unflagging support during the period in which the collection took shape: Sara, Sage, Ella, and Roya Myers, and Stephen Rupp. We are also indebted to our home institutions, Kenyon College and the University of Toronto, for the receipt of funds to defray the subvention costs of publication. Finally, we are pleased to thank the editorial team at the University of Toronto Press for their genial, efficient, and professional treatment of our project in its progress from submission to production. In particular, we are grateful to Suzanne Rancourt, Judy Williams, and Barb Porter.

Alison Keith
Micah Y. Myers

ABBREVIATIONS

CCLE	P. Colafranceso and M. Massaro, *Concordanze dei Carmina Latina epigraphica*. Bari, 1986.
Ernout-Meillet	A. Ernout and A. Meillet, *Dictionnaire Étymologique de la Langue Latine, Histoire des Mots.*[4] Paris, 1994.
Frisk	H. Frisk, *Griechisches Etymologisches Worterbuch*, 2 vols. Heidelberg, 1960.
Halsey	C.S. Halsey, *An Etymology of Latin and Greek*. Boston, 1889.
L-S	C.T. Lewis and C. Short, eds., *A Latin Dictionary*. Oxford, 1879.
LCL	Loeb Classical Library. Cambridge, MA
LSJ	H.G. Liddell and R. Scott, *A Greek-English Lexicon,*[9] rev. Sir Henry Stuart Jones. Oxford, 1940.
OLD	P.G.W. Glare, ed., *Oxford Latin Dictionary*. Oxford, 1968–82.
TLL	*Thesaurus Linguae Latinae*. Leipzig, 1900– .
VSD	*Vita Suetonii vulgo Donatiana*, in J.C. Rolfe, ed., *Suetonius*, vol. 2: 464–83. Cambridge, MA, and London, 1914.

VERGIL AND ELEGY

Introduction

ALISON KEITH

Born in 70 BCE, P. Vergilius Maro came of age during a period of political breakdown and endemic warfare in Rome, across Italy, and around the Mediterranean. The same era witnessed a corresponding ferment of literary experimentalism among Latin authors, including the *floruit* of Lucretius, the leading exponent of Epicurean philosophy in Latin literature, and that of Catullus and his friends Calvus and Cinna, who introduced new Greek verse forms and metres – lyric, short epic, and elegy foremost among them – into the existing repertoire of Latin poetic genres and measures on the model of the poets of Hellenistic Alexandria. In his own earliest poetry, *Bucolica*, Vergil and his pastoral characters explicitly acknowledge the influence of these writers and their verse. In the ninth eclogue, for example, the poetic neophyte Lycidas (perhaps a mask for the poet)[1] disparages his own compositions by reference to contemporary Latin literary masters (*B.* 9.35–6): *nam neque adhuc Vario uideor nec dicere Cinna / digna* ("for I seem yet to compose verses worthy of neither Varius nor Cinna").[2] The names bear witness to Vergil's high regard for the leading proponents of Latin Epicurean and Alexandrian poetry in the 40s BCE: his best friend, L. Varius Rufus, whose hexameter poem *De morte* (c. 44/43 BCE) pursued an Epicurean theme;[3] and the last surviving first-generation "neoteric" poet, C. Helvius Cinna (d. 44 BCE), whose varied oeuvre included an epyllion *Zmyrna*, lyric verse, and elegiac epigram.[4] Over and above Varius and Cinna, Vergil repeatedly expresses his devotion to and literary admiration for the elegist C. Cornelius Gallus in two programmatic eclogues (*B.* 6, 10) dedicated to the writer-soldier-politician and replete with allusions to his poetic projects.[5]

Vergil's extensive engagement with contemporary Latin poets is matched by an equally wide-ranging and assured engagement with the full Greek literary tradition, especially with his paramount generic exemplars: Theocritus in the *Bucolics*, Hesiod in the *Georgics*, and Homer in the *Aeneid*.[6] Across Vergil's hexameter corpus, however, the multi-generic Callimachus emerges as a particularly favoured stylistic model, and Vergil repeatedly draws on his four-book elegiac poem *Aetia* ("Causes" or "Origins") – from the sixth eclogue through the third georgic to the epic *Aeneid* – to articulate his newly refined hexameter poetics.[7] Yet despite the prominence of the elegists Gallus and Callimachus in Vergil's early poetry, his critics have rarely paid sustained attention to his engagement with the elegiac genre across his hexameter oeuvre. It was this striking lacuna in the scholarship that prompted the Vergilian Society in 2017 to convene a *Symposium Cumanum* specifically devoted to Vergil's multifaceted relations with elegy: Vergil's interactions with the genre and its practitioners; the elegists' relationship to, and reception of, Vergil's poetry; and the reception of Vergil's inflection of elegiac modes in subsequent periods. In this introductory chapter, I sketch the contours of Vergil's engagement with Greek and Roman elegy over the course of his career, with a special focus on Gallus and the Hellenistic Greek elegists, as a prolegomenon to the focused studies in this volume.

The sixth eclogue opens with Vergil's rejection of martial epic in favour of pastoral hexameter (*B.* 6.3–5): *cum canerem reges et proelia, Cynthius aurem / uellit et admonuit: "pastorem, Tityre, pinguis / pascere oportet ouis, deductum dicere carmen."* ("When I would sing of kings and battles, Cynthian Apollo plucked my ear and advised: 'The shepherd, Tityrus, ought to fatten his sheep at pasture, but compose slender verse'"). In his Latin verses, Vergil adapts Callimachus' famous statement of poetics in the prologue to the *Aetia* (*Aet.* Fr. 1.21–4):[8]

κανὶ γὰρ ὅτε πρώτιστον ἐμοῖς ἐπὶ δέλτον ἔθηκα
γούνασιν, Ἀπ[ό]λλων εἶπεν ὅ μοι Λύκιος·
'........] ... ἀοιδέ, τὸ μὲν θύος ὅττι πάχιστον
θρέψαι, τὴ]ν Μοῦσαν δ' ὠγαθὲ λεπταλέην·

For when I first put a writing-tablet on my knees Apollo Lycius said to me: "... poet, feed the sacrificial animal so that it becomes as fat as possible, but, my dear fellow, keep the Muse slender."

Vergil's restatement of Callimachus' denunciation of the grand style (cf. *Aet.* Fr. 1.25–8) is closely aligned with his recommitment to Theocritean bucolic, given the pastoral singer's characteristic themes of poetic composition and animal herding.[9] But Vergil transforms the Alexandrian poet's elegiac rejection of epic themes by recasting it as a dismissal of elevated subjects in favour of his humble pastoral subjects. Where the Greek poet contrasts two different genres in respect to their style,[10] his Latin successor contrasts two different hexameter modes in respect to the elevation of their themes.

The didactic elegiac valence of Vergil's Callimachean allusion assumes further significance as the eclogue proceeds to deny hexameter panegyric to its addressee, P. Alfenus Varus (*B.* 6.6–7), and to offer instead a "pastoral composition" (*agrestem tenui meditabor harundine Musam*, 6.8) on aetiological themes.[11] Vergil sets the scene in a Thessalian grotto, where two youthful shepherds discover Bacchus' companion Silenus sleeping off a hangover (6.13–17), restrain him with his own garlands, and press him to sing (6.18–26). Silenus opens with a cosmogony (6.31–40), a theme whose aetiological nature is most clearly illuminated by reference to the opening movement of Ovid's *Metamorphoses* (1.5–437).[12] The song then moves into a series of myths of metamorphosis, many of them with underpinnings aetiological, erotic, or both. Aetiological myths include those of Deucalion and Pyrrha's generation of mankind after the flood (*B.* 6.41–2); Hylas' transformation into an echo (43–5); the origin of the alder (62–3); the menace of Scylla in the straits of Messina (74–7); and the transmutation of Tereus, Philomela, and Procne into birds (78–81). The singer even records the source, or aetiology, of Silenus' song (82–4): *omnia, quae Phoebo quondam meditante beatus / audiit Eurotas … / ille canit* ("He sang all that blessed Eurotas heard when Phoebus Apollo once performed"). The aetiological themes of Silenus' song continue Vergil's homage to Callimachus' *Aetia*, begun in the eclogue's frame, in their implicit reference to the Callimachean source of his own Apollonian poetics.[13]

An aetiological theme also comes to the fore in the praise of Gallus that Silenus offers at the climax of his song (64–73):

> tum canit, errantem Permessi ad flumina Gallum
> Aonas in montis ut duxerit una sororum,
> utque uiro Phoebi chorus adsurrexerit omnis;
> ut Linus haec illi diuino carmine pastor
> floribus atque apio crinis ornatus amaro
> dixerit: "hos tibi dant calamos (en accipe) Musae,
> Ascraeo quos ante seni, quibus ille solebat
> cantando rigidas deducere montibus ornos.
> his tibi Grynei nemoris dicatur origo,
> ne quis sit lucus quo se plus iactet Apollo."

Then he sang how one of the sister Muses led Gallus, wandering beside Permessus' streams, into the Aonian mountains, and how Phoebus' whole choir rose to honour the man; how the shepherd Linus, wearing flowers and bitter parsley in his locks, addressed to him these words in a divine song: "The Muses give you these reeds – look, take them – which they formerly gave to the old man of Ascra; by playing on them he used to lead the stiff ash trees down the mountains. With these reeds, may you recite the source of the Grynean grove, that there be no grove to which Apollo lays more boastful claim."

Silenus situates Gallus at the foot of Helicon, the setting not only of Hesiod's epiphanic encounter with the Muses (*Theog.* 26–8) but also of Callimachus' explicitly Hesiodic dream vision of the poetic sorority at the outset of the *Aetia* (Fr. 2). Inset in his song are the words of the archetypal poet Linus, transformed here into a pastoral singer, who invests Gallus with the rustic reedpipe that once belonged to Hesiod. With this gift, Linus commissions Gallus to compose explicitly aetiological poetry on the implicitly pastoral theme of Apollo's Grynean grove.[14] The two poets, Greek Linus and Roman Gallus, are naturalized in Vergilian bucolic through this literary genealogy, which merges Hesiod's famous account of his investiture by the Muses while pasturing his sheep (*Theog.* 26–30) with Theocritus' pastoral portrait of the old hero Linus teaching the young Heracles to read (*Id.* 24.103–6). Gallus thus enters Vergil's bucolic collection as the legitimate heir to Hesiod's didactic epos, Callimachus' aetiological elegy, and Theocritus' rustic idylls.

Servius auctus (ad *B.* 6.72) identifies the obscure Hellenistic Greek poet Euphorion as the source of Gallus' proposed aetiological composition on the Grynean grove, but many scholars have been sceptical that either poet treated the theme.[15] The exiguous extant fragments of Euphorion and Gallus contain no trace of such a work, though of course lack of evidence is not evidence that neither wrote on the theme. Still, in the case of Gallus, we also have the positive testimony of his elegiac successors Propertius and Ovid, who associate him exclusively with erotic elegy as the founder of their genre.[16] Moreover, as Stephen Harrison has observed, it is rather the late Hellenistic poet Parthenius, Greek teacher to both Cinna and Vergil, who seems to have had an interest in the Grynean grove, as he "certainly used the phrase Γρύνειος Ἀπόλλων, 'Gryneian Apollo.'"[17] Harrison therefore makes the attractive suggestion that Parthenius' lost *Metamorphoses* was the source of the transformation myths that dominate Silenus' song. In this connection, it is worth noting that Gregory Hutchinson has proposed Parthenian authorship, with specific reference to his *Metamorphoses*, of an Oxyrhynchus papyrus containing fragmentary elegiac verses on aetiological and erotic myths of metamorphosis (Adonis, Asterie, Narcissus).[18] Of particular interest is the juxtaposition of aetiology, erotic passion, and metamorphosis in the papyrus' elegiacs,[19] a nexus which points, on the one hand, to the overlap between aetiological myth and tales of transformation and, on the other, to the association of aetiology with elegiac verse, from Callimachus in the *Aetia* to Gallus' Roman heirs Propertius (in *Elegies* 4) and Ovid (in the *Fasti*).[20] The conjuncture of aetiology, erotic passion, and metamorphosis also aligns suggestively with the myths on display in Silenus' song in *B.* 6.

The possibility that Vergil's sixth eclogue implicitly proposed two Greek elegiac models – certainly that of Callimachus' *Aetia* and perhaps also that of Parthenius' *Metamorphoses*, if it was indeed composed in elegiac distichs – for adaptation by Gallus would cohere with the Roman poet's standing as an author of, and authority on, Latin elegiac verse. It is an especially attractive possibility that Parthenius' *Metamorphoses* supplied the Latin poet with another source of elegiac material, in tandem with his prose Ἐρωτικὰ Παθήματα ("Erotic Sufferings"), explicitly dedicated to Gallus for use in hexameter or elegiac composition.[21] The amatory themes of Parthenius' tales of "erotic suffering" seem to have continued in his *Metamorphoses*, if we are correct in identifying the Oxyrynchus papyri as a fragment of that work. Certainly, the metamorphic myths Vergil includes in the sixth eclogue exhibit a striking focus not only on aetiology and transformation, but also on erotic passion. In addition to the metamorphoses of Hylas, Scylla, Tereus, Philomela, and Procne, Vergil includes the amatory myths of Pasiphaë and Atalanta (*B.* 6.45–61). With the myth of Pasiphaë in particular, Vergil develops a negative *exemplum* of pathological love (6.52–60),[22] as Pasiphaë wanders in the pastoral landscape tracking an elusive (not to say illusory) lover, Minos' white bull. The erotic delusions on display in Silenus' repertoire signally validate Epicurean doctrine about the perils of amatory passion and implicitly discredit the posture of erotic obsession that seems to have animated the elegiac lover-poet in Gallus' *Amores*. The suite of metamorphic myths of perverse eroticism thereby reinforces Silenus' proposal of an aetiological, rather than amatory, theme to Rome's leading elegiac poet.

In the tenth eclogue too, Vergil proposes a generic makeover to Gallus. He represents the pastoral landscape and its divinities lamenting Gallus' sufferings (10.11–15), as they had once mourned the bucolic culture-hero Daphnis as he lay dying (Th. *Id.* 1.65–143), thereby shading Gallus in the generic contours of bucolic poetry. Depicting Gallus as an exponent of, and subject to, "troubled love" (*sollicitos Galli amores*, 10.6), Vergil draws him into pastoral by reference to Daphnis, whose death Theocritus commemorates in his first idyll (1.66): πᾷ ποκ᾽ ἄρ᾽ ἦσθ᾽, ὅκα Δάφνις ἐτάκετο, πᾷ ποκα, Νύμφαι; ("Where were you, Nymphs, where were you when Daphnis was wasting away?").[23] Vergil crafts a close imitation of Theocritus' song of the dying Daphnis in application to Gallus (*B.* 10.9–10): *Quae nemora aut*

qui uos saltus habuere, puellae / Naides, indigno cum Gallus amore peribat?
("What groves or what glades detained you, Naiad maids, when Gallus was
consumed by unworthy love?"). Richard Hunter notes that Theocritus' verb,
ἐτάκετο (from τήκω, "consume"), is "often used of the sufferings of unsat-
isfied love," and we may infer that "Daphnis' pangs" (τὰ Δάφνιδος ἄλγεα,
Theoc. *Id.* 1.19) are motivated by erotic obsession, whether that of the
nymph who loves him, of the Sicilian princess who seduces him, or of Daphnis himself, whom Theocritus characterizes as δύσερως (*Id.* 1.85), "perverse
with regard to love" (often with the sense of erotic obsession).[24] This nexus
of potential motivations is implicit in the version of the myth of Daphnis
that Parthenius sketches in his handbook on "erotic sufferings" (no. 29, Περὶ
Δάφνιδος), dedicated to Gallus. Vergil too seems to have understood Daphnis' sufferings as arising from erotic passion, since he explicitly introduces
Gallus as "perishing from unworthy [elegiac] love." By implication, Gallus'
amores, his "troubled" and "unworthy" passions, are elegiac not only in their
thematic focus but also in their poetic form.

Propertius (2.34.91–2) and Ovid (*Am.* 1.15.29–30 et passim) mention
Gallus' desperate love for his mistress, and Servius confirms the image in
his notice (ad *B.* 10.1)[25] that Gallus composed four books of elegiac *Amores*
detailing his erotic obsession with the mime-actress Cytheris, named Lycoris in his verse. Servius even identifies a suite of four lines spoken by the
Vergilian Gallus as excerpted from Gallus' *Amores* (*B.* 10.46–9):

> tu procul a patria (nec sit mihi credere tantum)
> Alpinas, a! dura niues et frigora Rheni
> me sine sola uides. a, te ne frigora laedant!
> a, tibi ne teneras glacies secet aspera plantas!

You, far from the fatherland (let me not be able to believe such a thing!), look on
Alpine snow, alas, and the harsh cold of the Rhine, all alone without me. Alas, may
the cold not harm you! Alas, may the harsh ice not cut your tender feet!

Vergil's commentators have demonstrated that the interjections and excited
rhythm are diagnostic of the lines' elegiac provenance, along with the
hemiepes *me sine sola uides* (10.48) with its pentameter cadence.[26] Moreover, scholars since La Cerda have drawn attention to a four-line Propertian
passage that closely rehearses the elegiac lexicon, neoteric style, and erotic
themes of these lines (Prop. 1.8.5–8):

> tune audire potes uesani murmura ponti
>   fortis, et in dura naue iacere potes?

> tu pedibus teneris positas fulcire pruinas,
> tu potes insolitas, Cynthia, ferre niues?

Can you listen to the rumble of the wild ocean with fortitude, and lie low in a harsh ship? Can you tread the fallen frost with your tender feet, Cynthia, and endure unaccustomed snow?

Although lacking the interjection *a*, associated with Latin neotericism and evocative of Gallus' lovelorn posture in *B*. 10, the lines overlap strikingly with *B*.10.46–9 in their anaphora of *tu* (5, 7, 8; cf. *B*. 10.46, 48, 49); appeal to possibility (*potes*, 5, 6, 8; cf. *sit*, *B*. 10.46); and contrast between harsh travel (*dura*, 6; *B*. 10.47), including unaccustomed snow (8; cf. *B*. 10.47), and the girlfriend's tender feet (7; cf. *B*. 10.48), though the elegist substitutes travel by sea (5) for the pastoral poet's intimations of travel on the Rhine (*B*. 10.47). The convergence of lexicon, style, and theme in the two passages has accordingly led scholars to view Gallus' *Amores* as the inspiration for both.

Vergil briefly alludes to Silenus' proposal of an aetiological theme to Gallus in *B*. 6 with the pastoral gods' inquiry into the aetiology of the love poet's suffering (*omnes "unde amor iste" rogant "tibi?"* 10.21), but the final eclogue expressly urges the merits of bucolic over elegy. Thus Pan, the tutelary god of Vergil's collection, evinces a pastoral disdain for Gallus' erotic obsession with Lycoris (10.28–30):[27] *"ecquis erit modus?" inquit. "Amor non talia curat, / nec lacrimis crudelis Amor nec gramina riuis / nec cytiso saturantur apes nec fronde capellae"* ("'What will be the limit?' Pan asked. 'Love does not care about such things: cruel Love is not sated on tears, nor grass on rivulets, nor bees on clover, nor she-goats on foliage'"). The Arcadian god's pastoral analogies (10.29–30) confirm him as an authority in, and on, Vergil's genre, while his rustic appearance, "rosy from the dwarf-elder's blood-red berries and cinnabar" (*sanguineis ebuli bacis minioque rubentem*, 10.27), aligns him with the Silenus of the sixth eclogue, "whose face and temples the Naiad Aegle painted with blood-red berries" (*sanguineis frontem moris et tempora pingit*, 6.21). In response to this context, Gallus imagines abandoning elegy, and its conventional themes of erotic obsession and amatory suffering, to espouse instead pastoral promiscuity (10.35–41):

> atque utinam ex uobis unus uestrique fuissem
> aut custos gregis aut maturae uinitor uuae!
> certe siue mihi Phyllis siue esset Amyntas
> seu quicumque furor (quid tum, si fuscus Amyntas?
> et nigrae uiolae sunt et uaccinia nigra),

> mecum inter salices lenta sub uite iaceret;
> serta mihi Phyllis legeret, cantaret Amyntas.

And would that I had been one of you and yours, whether the guardian of a flock or the harvester of the ripe grape! Certainly, whether Phyllis were mine or Amyntas – What then, if Amyntas is dusky? Both violets and hyacinths are black! –, or whatever passionate lover lay with me beneath the pliant vine amid the willows, Phyllis would pick garlands for me, Amyntas would sing.

Yet the elegiac poet cannot sustain his assumption of the conventional posture of the peripatetic pastoral lover, as his thoughts revert to Lycoris (42–9; cf. *tua cura Lycoris*, 22) and her faithless attendance on a rival in Gaul (46–9, quoted above). Erotic obsession, it is implied, prompts Gallus to carve his *amores* – both his passion and his poetry – in the wooded pastoral landscape (50–4):

> ibo et Chalcidico quae sunt mihi condita uersu
> carmina pastoris Siculi modulabor auena.
> certum est in siluis inter spelaea ferarum
> malle pati tenerisque meos incidere amores
> arboribus: crescent illae, crescetis, amores.

I shall go and practise the songs which I composed in Chalcidian verse on the Sicilian shepherd's reed. It is surely preferable to suffer in the woods amid the wild beasts' haunts and to carve my loves in the tender trees: as they will grow, so you will grow, my loves.

Gallus' erotic obsession with Lycoris and its elegiac expression in *amores* resist generic transformation in Vergil's pastoral Arcadia. It is thus no surprise that the rustic pursuits of hunting and singing in the woods pall for Gallus (55–68). The tenth eclogue allusively rehearses Silenus' proposal in the sixth that Gallus compose Callimachean aetiology (10.21, quoted above), Parthenian metamorphosis (35–41, quoted above; cf. *non me ulla uetabunt / frigora Parthenios canibus circumdare saltus*, 56–7),[28] and/or obscure Euphorionic verse (*ibo et Chalcidico quae sunt mihi condita uersu / carmina pastoris Siculi modulabor auena*, 50–1),[29] but to no purpose. Just as Gallus enters the eclogue an exponent of unhappy love (6), so he leaves it (69): *omnia uincit Amor: et nos cedamus Amori* ("Love conquers all things: let me too yield to Love").

The concluding verses underscore a strong ethical contrast between Gallus' amatory excesses (and their expression in erotic elegy) and the more circumscribed scope for passion in the eclogue singer's pastoral practice (and its articulation in bucolic hexameter). By comparison with the elegist (10.28, quoted above), the pastoral singer recognizes and respects limits (10.70–1): *haec sat erit, diuae, uestrum cecinisse poetam / dum sedet et gracili fiscellam texit hibisco* ("This will be enough, goddesses, for your poet to have sung, while he sits and weaves a little basket with supple mallow"). He finds satisfaction in the pastoral pursuits appropriate to his genre, metaphorized in the homely task of weaving a rustic basket,[30] from which he may also derive amatory solace (10.72–4): *Pierides: uos haec facietis maxima Gallo, / Gallo, cuius amor tantum mihi crescit in horas / quantum uere nouo uiridis se subicit alnus* ("Pierian Muses: for Gallus you will make my song very great – for Gallus, my love for whom grows by the hour, as much as the green alder shoots up in early spring"). The eclogue singer's great love for Gallus is contextualized within the natural processes of the pastoral world and delineated within the familiar routines of animal husbandry, as the poem concludes with a series of closural images – sated goats heading home as night falls (*ite domum saturae, uenit Hesperus, ite capellae,* 77).[31] The eclogue's quiet conclusion unequivocally reasserts the value of pastoral over elegy in its espousal of restraint over excess.

Especially striking in the bucolic collection is Vergil's named identification of admired fellow poets and his dedication of two eclogues specifically to Gallus and his genre of elegy. In the *Georgics* and *Aeneid,* by contrast, Vergil no longer explicitly identifies literary models by name, alluding to them only indirectly through intertextual appropriation. A particularly concentrated locus of elegiac allusion can be found in the fourth *Georgic,* where Vergil treats apiculture.[32] The project is quintessentially Callimachean in its scope, a learned account in refined style of the bees' miniature society. Vergil closes the book with the failure of the hive and its miraculous regeneration through the Egyptian rite of *bugonia,* "generation from cattle" (4.281–310). Invoking the Muses for the first time in the poem, he asks them to disclose the origin of the rite (4.315–16): *Quis deus hanc, Musae, quis nobis extudit artem? / unde noua ingressus hominum experientia cepit?* ("What god was it, Muses, who hammered out this technique for us? Whence did the strange new knowledge of men take its beginnings?"). Vergil's introduction of the rite suggests a Callimachean source,[33] since he explicitly cites Egypt as the original site of the ritual (4.287–92) and he emphasizes the technical skill (Vergilian *ars* = Callimachean τέχνη) required. He introduces his subject by inquiring into the origins of the *bugonia* (4.316, quoted above)[34] and addresses the Muses directly, just as Callimachus had done in the first two books of his *Aetia.*[35] The tale is marked as "Cyrenaean," moreover, like Callimachus himself (who was born in Cyrene), since the mythical cowherd Aristaeus (*G.* 1.14–15), who first establishes the rite, is the son of the nymph Cyrene (4.321).[36]

The epyllion opens with Aristaeus' lament (4.319–20): *tristis ad extremi sacrum caput astitit amnis / multa querens, atque hac adfatus uoce parentem* ("He stood sadly at the sacred source of the remotest stream, lamenting many things, and addressed his mother with these words …"). Vergil finds literary inspiration in Achilles' two laments to his sea-nymph mother Thetis in the *Iliad* (1.348–56, 18.79–93), but his Aristaeus also resembles the figure of Gallus in Silenus' song, standing beside the river Permessus (*B.* 6.64) at the moment of his initiation into the Hesiodic tradition of poetry (*B.* 6.69–71). It is the nymph Arethusa, moreover, who takes the lead in drawing Aristaeus' lament to his mother's attention (4.351–6), recalling her prominence in *B.* 10, over which she presides like a Muse (*G.* 4.353–6): *o gemitu non frustra exterrita tanto, / Cyrene soror, ipse tibi, tua maxima cura, / tristis Aristaeus Penei genitoris ad undam / stat lacrimans, et te crudelem nomine dicit* ("O sister Cyrene, not vain was your terror at such a great lament; Aristaeus himself, your greatest love, stands weeping sadly at our father Peneus' waters, and calls on you by name as cruel"). Indeed, her lament rehearses Apollo's words in *B.* 10, reminding Gallus that his girlfriend (*tua cura Lycoris*, 10.22) has left him to follow a soldier on campaign. The reminiscences of the tenth eclogue here in the fourth *Georgic* have led scholars to speculate that the passage reworks some of the lost poetry of Vergil's friend and fellow poet.

The intensity of allusions to Gallus in the passage is worth considering in connection with Servius' report that Vergil sang "the praises of Gallus" in the second half of the fourth *Georgic*. Servius (on *B.* 10.1) relates that "Gallus was such a good friend of Vergil's that the fourth book of the *Georgics*, from the middle all the way to the end, contained his praise, which he afterwards changed to the myth of Aristaeus on the order of Augustus."[37] He reiterates this information in his note at the beginning of the fourth *Georgic*, where he specifies the occasion of the change as Augustus' renunciation of friendship with Gallus and the poet's subsequent suicide, in 27 or 26 BCE, two or three years after Vergil had finished the poem.[38] Scholarly consensus rejects Servius' testimony, as it is surely inconceivable that Vergil could have suppressed any part of a poem already in circulation, given the practicalities of literary "publication" in antiquity.[39] Many critics think that Servius either confuses the end of Vergil's poem on farming with the end of his bucolic collection, where the tenth eclogue does indeed contain explicit praise of Gallus, or presents in garbled version an earlier commentary tradition that recognized Vergil's intense interaction with the style and substance of Gallus' poetry in the Aristaeus episode.[40] After all, the passage is cast as a Callimachean *aetion*, the genre proposed to Gallus in *B.* 6.72 (quoted above), and takes the form of an epyllion, with Proteus' account of the myth of Orpheus embedded within the poet's tale of Aristaeus' loss of his bees, in a formal structure that was apparently characteristic of Gallan elegy and neoteric poetry (cf. Catull. *c.* 64).[41] The amatory exemplum of Orpheus' obsessive love for Eurydice, moreover, is undoubtedly the type of mythological tale that appeared in Gallus' *Amores*, if the myths compiled by Parthenius in his handbook on "erotic sufferings" are anything to go by. Proteus' "Orpheus and Eurydice" (*G.* 4.453–527) bears a strong likeness to the herdsmen's strains in the *Bucolics* and doubtless also to Gallus' own amatory elegy, celebrated in the sixth and tenth eclogues.

In Proteus' tale, too, we find numerous points of contact with the style of poetry Vergil associates with Gallus in *B.* 6 and 10. Proteus opens his song by detailing the cause of the nymphs' anger at Aristaeus, Eurydice's flight from his lustful pursuit, and the snakebite from which she died (4.457–9): *illa quidem, dum te fugeret per flumina praeceps, / immanem ante pedes hydrum moritura puella / seruantem ripas alta non uidit in herba* ("She indeed, the doomed girl, while she fled you headlong through the rills, failed to see beneath her feet the huge water-snake hugging the banks in the tall grass"). The pathetic evocation of Eurydice as "the doomed girl" (*moritura puella*, 4.458) recalls the Vergilian Silenus' emotional invocation of Pasiphaë as an "unhappy maiden" in the sixth eclogue (*uirgo infelix*, *B.* 6.47), while the subsequent description of nature mourning Eurydice's death (4.460–3) is also highly reminiscent of the tenth eclogue, where the Naiads take the lead in mourning the dying Gallus (*B.* 10.9–10), and the natural world joins in (*B.* 10.13–15). After describing Eurydice's death, Proteus details Orpheus' distress in equally mannered lines (4.464–6): *ipse caua solans aegrum testudine amorem / te, dulcis coniunx, te solo in litore secum, / te ueniente die, te decedente canebat* ("He himself, solacing his grievous love on the hollow tortoise-shell lyre, was hymning you, sweet wife, you, by himself on the lonely shore – you, when day rose, you when night fell"). Here too Vergil's theme and technique evoke the elegiac precedent of Gallus: Orpheus endeavours to console himself with song (*G.* 4.464), just as Vergil represents Silenus trying to console Pasiphaë in her passion for Minos' bull (*B.* 6.46), and both poets address the subject of their songs directly (*G.* 465, *B.* 6.47; both quoted above), in the style of the neoteric poets.

Vergil relates the tale of Orpheus' exceptional descent to Hades but shows him ultimately unsuccessful (*G.* 4.485–91):

> iamque pedem referens casus euaserat omnis,
> redditaque Eurydice superas ueniebat ad auras
> pone sequens (namque hanc dederat Proserpina legem),
> cum subita incautum dementia cepit amantem,
> ignoscenda quidem, scirent si ignoscere Manes:

restitit, Eurydicenque suam iam luce sub ipsa
immemor heu! uictusque animi respexit …

And now, retracing his steps, he had avoided every mischance, and Eurydice, returned to him, was coming to the upper air, following behind (for Proserpina had imposed this law), when a sudden madness [*dementia*] seized the unwary lover – forgivable indeed, if the shades knew how to forgive: he stopped still and alas, forgetting, he looked back at his Eurydice already in the light, overcome in his purpose …

Orpheus' failure to set a limit to his passion recalls Gallus' elegiac obsession in Vergil's tenth eclogue. Indeed, Eurydice's reproach to Orpheus (4.494–5) – *illa "quis et me" inquit "miseram et te perdidit, Orpheu, / quis tantus furor?"* ("She cried: 'What huge passion, Orpheus, has destroyed me, wretched, and you?'") – rehearses the question posed to Gallus by Apollo in the final eclogue (*B.* 10.22): *Galle, quid insanis?* ("Gallus, why are you impassioned?"). Like Gallus before him, Orpheus acts on his passion rather than setting limits to it. Barred from undertaking a second katabasis (*G.* 4.502–3), he agonizes over how to continue (4.504–5). His anguished deliberations recall, in part, Aristaeus' reproaches to his mother (4.322–5, partially quoted above), but most fully resemble those of the Gallus of the tenth eclogue as he abandons himself to song in a landscape that reflects his emotions (4.507–10). Vergil emphasizes the elegiac quality of Orpheus' lament (4.511–15), drawing on the elegiac lexicon of love, lament, and song developed by Catullus in *c.* 65. But the elegiac tonality of Orpheus' song, in combination with the bard's posture by the side of a river, must especially evoke Gallus' elegiac poetry: the lineaments of the tenth eclogue's Gallus, adapting himself and his lament for his faithless mistress Lycoris to Vergil's bucolic landscape, are discernible behind the portrait of Orpheus' single-minded lament for his dead wife in the frigid landscape of Thrace (*G.* 4.516–20), not least because Vergil's Gallus complains of the cruelty of the love god even should he toil in Orpheus' Thrace (*B.* 10.64–6).

At the end of *Georgics* 4, Orpheus' intransigence provokes the Ciconian women to tear him limb from limb, and Proteus closes his song with the image of the dead bard's head floating down the Hebrus, still singing (*G.* 4.523–7):

tum quoque marmorea caput a ceruice reuulsum
gurgite cum medio portans Oeagrius Hebrus
uolueret, Eurydicen uox ipsa et frigida lingua,
a miseram Eurydicen! anima fugiente uocabat:
Eurydicen toto referebant flumine ripae.

Then too Oeagrian Hebrus, carrying the bard's head, plucked from his snowy shoulders, in the middle of his eddy, rolled it downstream; his voice and cold tongue were calling "Eurydice, ah poor Eurydice," as his spirit fled; the banks re-echoed "Eurydice" over the whole river.

Here too, Gallus has been seen as the primary model for the mannered song, in quintessential neoteric style, of Vergil's decapitated bard. The repeated invocation of Orpheus' dead bride, in conjunction with the interjection "*a*," particularly favoured by Catullus and his friend Calvus at moments of high pathos, is especially reminiscent of Gallus' despairing address to Lycoris in the tenth eclogue, which Servius reports Vergil drew verbatim from Gallus' own poetry (*B.* 10.46–9, quoted above). The Aristaeus episode thus sustains to its conclusion the mannered Alexandrian techniques and erotic material typical of Gallus' elegiac poetry which Vergil integrates into the Homeric style and themes that anticipate the *Aeneid*.

Even in the martial books of Vergil's *Aeneid*, moreover, we may catch faint glimpses of erotic elegy.[42] For example, behind the brilliant figure of Aeneas' son Ascanius encouraging the Trojan troops in battle stands the elegiac *puer delicatus* (*A.* 10.132–8):[43]

> ipse inter medios, Veneris iustissima cura,
> Dardanius caput, ecce, puer detectus honestum,
> qualis gemma micat fuluum quae diuidit aurum,
> aut collo decus aut capiti, uel quale per artem   135
> inclusum buxo aut Oricia terebintho
> lucet ebur; fusos ceruix cui lactea crinis
> accipit et molli subnectens circulus auro.

Look! In their midst, the Trojan youth himself – Venus' most proper concern – uncovered his handsome head, shining such as a gem that parts its tawny gold setting in two, an ornament for either neck or head; or such as ivory gleams when skilfully inlaid in box- or Orician terebinth-wood; his hair spilled out over his milky-white neck, encircled by a torque of soft gold.

The eroticizing description of bare-headed Ascanius gleaming on the battlefield like a bright gemstone or translucent ivory briefly turns the Trojan prince into an elegiac boy-beloved. While most closely associated with Tibullus' oeuvre,[44] the figure of the *puer delicatus* also appears in connection with an author named Gallus, generally agreed to be the elegist,[45] in a Propertian elegy that offers the addressee advice about retaining the affections of a beautiful youth assimilated to Hercules' beloved squire Hylas (Prop.

1.20.5–6). Ascanius is strongly marked as a figure from amatory elegy in this passage, through the accumulation of erotic lexemes, themes, and characters that surround him here. Thus Venus, the tutelary deity of elegy, takes a special interest in him (*A.* 10.132; cf. *mea maxima cura*, 1.678), which the poet articulates in the erotic lexicon of Gallus in *B.* 10.22 (*tua cura Lycoris*).[46] Still a tender youth (*puer, A.* 10.133), Ascanius exhibits the physical and sartorial attributes of the elegiac beloved, whether male or female: milk-white complexion and tender neck, gracefully disordered locks, and golden accoutrements (137–8).[47] Vergil's Ascanius gleams white and gold, like Propertius' "golden Cynthia" (*aurea Cynthia*, Prop. 4.7.85; cf. 2.2.5–6, *fulua coma est longaeque manus et maxima toto / corpore*), with her "ivory fingers" (*digitis eburnis*, 2.1.9). Fashioned from "soft gold" (*molli auro, A.* 10.138), moreover, the torque that adorns his neck bears a metapoetic resonance of "soft" elegy.[48]

Of particular interest in this heavily elegiacizing context is Vergil's highly mannered line comparing Ascanius' shining beauty, as he appears against the dark ranks of soldiers, to the glow of translucent ivory against boxwood or "terebinth," the lustrous dark wood of the turpentine tree (10.136–7, quoted above). Propertius surrounds a similarly callow Roman youth with correspondingly sumptuous luxury items in an elegiac poem roughly contemporary with Vergil's composition of the last books of the *Aeneid* (Prop. 3.7.49–50): *sed thyio thalamo aut Oricia terebintho / ecfultum pluma uersicolore caput* ("But his head has been pillowed on many-coloured feathers in a chamber of citron-wood or Orician terebinth").[49] The shared line ending, *aut Oricia terebintho*, exhibits two rare Hellenizing metrical effects in Latin verse, hiatus at caesura (*buxo aut, A.* 10.136; *thalamo aut,* Prop. 3.7.49) and tetrasyllable at line-end (*terebintho*); and both lines are redolent of the exotic east in their deployment of a series of Greek loanwords (*buxo … Oricia terebintho, A.* 10.136; *thyio thalamo … Oricia terebintho*, Prop. 3.7.49). Vergil is generally viewed as the model, Propertius as the imitator here,[50] even though, as Paolo Fedeli has observed, Propertius does not engage with the later books of the *Aeneid* elsewhere in his third book of elegies.[51] It therefore seems more likely that they share a common source, and both have accordingly been seen as responding to a line by the Hellenistic Greek poet Nicander (πύξου δὲ χροιῆι προσαλίγκιος Ὠρικίοιο, "like the colour of Orician boxwood," *Ther.* 516), which includes both a precious wood and the erudite geographical epithet "Orician." Yet the Nicandrian line has quite a different metrical and verbal shape from the lines of Propertius and Vergil, which seem more closely reminiscent of Catullus' elegiac experimentation with Grecizing effects in his pentameters.[52] For these reasons, Francis Cairns' suggestion of a shared Greek original (by Parthenius?) rendered into Latin verse by a shared intermediary (Gallus?) is attractive.[53]

Vergil's extensive engagement across his hexameter oeuvre with the genre of elegy, in its full array of thematic foci and its wide range of Greek and Roman practitioners, offers an instructive model for his intergeneric compositional methods, in general, and the signal importance of his interactions with elegy in particular. Yet Vergil's critics have rarely paid sustained attention to the poet's engagement with the elegiac genre across all his hexameter works, understandably preferring to focus instead on his hexameter models Theocritus, Hesiod, and, especially, Homer;[54] his espousal of Callimachean poetics from *B.* 6 through *G.* 3 to *A.* 8;[55] his exploitation of tragic themes and tropes;[56] his relationship to powerful friends (including Pollio, Maecenas, and Augustus);[57] his connection to Italy and his Italian homelands;[58] and his abiding interests in Greek philosophy and Roman religion.[59] Even when considering Vergil's representation of Gallus and Gallan elegy in *B.* 6 and 10, his critics tend to focus on the rather different questions of Gallus' biography and lost literary corpus.[60] Yet, as we have seen, Vergil's engagement with the genre of elegy spans linguistic traditions, historical periods, and thematic foci. Contributors to this volume were therefore invited to explore Vergil's relations with the elegiac genre from the *Bucolics* to the *Aeneid* and well beyond. Part I of this volume contains papers which investigate Vergil's poetry in relation to his contemporaries, the elegists Gallus, Tibullus, and Propertius. Ovid's reception of Vergil's hexameter poetry across his elegiac works, from the *Amores* to the *Tristia*, is the focus of Part II. The third part collects papers on imperial Latin poetry and examines elegy through the lens of Vergilian reception and vice versa. Finally, Part IV intervenes in the late antique and early modern reception of Vergilian poetry with a focus on elegiac themes.

John Henkel opens Part I with a metapoetic interpretation of *B.* 1 as an anti-elegiac polemic in response specifically to Gallan elegy, defined tendentiously (by both Henkel and Henkel's Vergil) as "uniquely suited to love poetry and Callimacheanism." Jacqueline Fabre-Serris continues the discussion of Vergil's generic polemic against Gallan elegy, shifting the ground to *B.* 10, in which she suggests that Vergil articulates his generic opposition to elegy through an Epicurean philosophical matrix that represents Gallus' elegiac poetry as unable to provide a remedy for erotic suffering, represented in the Gallan trope of *medicina amoris*. Hunter Gardner, taking *B.* 4 as her point of departure, extends the investigation of Vergil's hexameter relations with contemporary elegy across his oeuvre to consider his shifting presentation of the Golden Age also in *G.* 1 and *A.* 7–8, and Tibullus' elegiac reorientation of the Vergilian Golden Age as a haven for elegiac contentment under Saturn. Micah Myers also explores an epic trope, that of *nostos*, in Vergil's poetry from *B*. 1 to *A*. 12 and its contemporary elegiac reception in Propertius. He documents Vergil's suppression of amatory reunion, which he shows to be a constituent feature of this Homeric theme, in his treatment of *nostos* in the *Aeneid*, and argues that Propertius, in response to Vergil, emphasizes precisely this feature in his elegies 2.14 and 3.12. Eva Anagnostou-Laoutides brings early Greek elegy into the mix with a consideration of Vergil's interest in the elegiac world of Propertius. She demonstrates that Vergil draws on the early Greek elegists Solon and Theognis, as well as on Propertius' contemporary elegiac poetry, in his linkage of the bestial fury of hunting tyrants with the emotional frenzy of elegiac mistresses to delimit the dangers of uncontrolled passion in civic discourse and civil war. Sarah McCallum discusses the elegiac features of the opening movement of *A*. 7, which unites both funerary and erotic motifs in an elegiac program that culminates in the invocation of Erato as the Muse of the Italian war narrative. Part I concludes with Bill Gladhill's discussion of the intersection of elegy and threnody in Horace, and Vergil's reception of this matrix of funerary lament and sung epitaph in the conclusion of the Nisus and Euryalus episode in *A*. 9. In his radical contamination of epic with elegy, Vergil sets the standard for imperial Latin epic.

The papers collected in Part II of the volume treat Ovid's elegiac reception of Vergil's poetry. The contributors to this section are all very much alive to Ovid's unfailing capacity to expose and interrogate some of Vergil's most difficult passages. Thus, Mariapia Pietropaolo opens this section of the volume by considering Vergil's depiction of Pasiphaë's erotic obsession with Minos' bull in *B*. 6 in the light of Ovid's elegiacizing reception of the passage in *Ars* 1. Barbara Weiden Boyd analyses Ovid's engagement with the Aristaeus epyllion of *G*. 4 in his treatment of the festival of the Agonalia in *Fasti* 1 and its relationship to his poetics of exile, and probes Ovid's suppression of Vergil's inset Orpheus episode in his account of Aristaeus' ritual success. Judith Hallett interprets Ovid's elegy *Amores* 3.9, the epicedion ostensibly written on the occasion of the death of Tibullus in 19 BCE, as a double critique of Tibullan elegy and Vergilian epic. Hallett demonstrates that, intertwined with Ovid's reminiscences of Tibullan elegy, there are allusions to Vergil's portrayal of sexuality and piety in the *Aeneid*. Sophia Papaioannou continues the exploration of Vergil's representation of eros in relation to elegiac conventions, with a special focus on the interactions of Dido and her sister Anna in *A*. 4 and Ovid's elegiac reception of Anna in *Fasti* 3. Garth Tissol concludes this section with an analysis of Ovid's self-fashioning as the exile Meliboeus of *B*. 1 in his idealizing fantasies of return to the city of Rome and the Italian countryside in *Pont*. 1.8.

Part III moves from Vergilian reception in the last of the Augustan elegists to the reception of Vergil's poetry in imperial Latin literature. Yelena Baraz treats Calpurnius' engagement with love elegy in his *Eclogues* 2 and 3 as evidence of Calpurnius' emulative response to Vergilian pastoral. She argues that he succeeds, where Vergil had failed in *B.* 10, in depicting the successful embrace of elegy within bucolic. In a similar vein, Giulio Celotto considers Lucan's epic redevelopment of the elegiac trope of *militia amoris* as *amor militiae* in his account of the deforestation of a sacred grove during Caesar's preparations for the military assault on Massilia in *BC* 3. He shows that Lucan alludes to Vergilian epic and Ovidian elegy in tandem to develop a sexual subtext that characterizes the assault on the grove as the rape of a virgin. Jessica Blum-Sorensen explores the integration of amatory elegy into the later martial epic of Valerius Flaccus by focusing on the case of Hylas in *Argonautica* 3. Valerius departs from classical literary tradition, in which Hylas is marked as un-epic by reference to a different generic context (pastoral in Theoc. *Id.* 13; elegy in Prop. 1.20), when he represents Hylas as faithful to the Vergilian epic code through his imitation of the martial models of Hercules and Aeneas. The youth's epic qualities prove his undoing, however, by provoking the nymphs' romantic interest in him and thereby drawing him inexorably into the world of elegiac *amor*. The final paper in this section, by Alessandra De Cristofaro, explores Statius' (mis)application of elegiac conventions to epic in the *Achilleid* and of epic conventions to his epithalamion in honour of the elegiac poet Stella and his bride Violentilla in *Siluae* 1.2.

Part IV traces the impact of Vergil's relations with elegiac poetry from late antiquity to early modern Italy. Nandini Pandey explores the topos of Vergil's experimentation in generic mixing and the ancient reception of his epic achievement in elegy and *elogia*, epitaphs and epigraphs. Giancarlo Abbamonte probes Servius' lack of interest in the elegiac poets in his commentary on Vergil and documents his restriction of quotation from the Augustan elegists to Ovid's non-elegiac *Metamorphoses*. Kenneth Draper reads Vergilian epic through Ovidian elegy in Ausonius' *Cupido Cruciatus*. He argues that while Ausonius, in both preface and *incipit*, cites Vergil's underworld as the source for his register of heroines who died of love and demand redress, Ovid too contributes figures to the catalogue, and in this way Ausonius amplifies the elegiac notes of Vergil's *lugentes campi* ("mourning fields," *A.* 6.441). Three final papers trace Vergil's reception in Renaissance Italy. Giovanni Pontano, the leading humanist of fifteenth-century Naples, is the focus of Luke Roman's chapter, which analyses the reception of Vergil's Italian homeland in Pontano's elegiac collection *Eridanus*, named for the river Po in whose valley lay Vergil's *patria* of Mantua. Lorenzo Miletti treats the representation of Vergil in the antiquarian elegiac distichs of four fifteenth- and sixteenth-century Neapolitan humanists: Francesco Patrizi of Siena, Bishop of Gaeta; Elisio Calenzio, tutor to the son of King Ferrante; Aurelio Serena of Monopoli; and Francesco Peto of Fondi. In the volume's final chapter, Joseph M. Ortiz investigates Vergil's modulation between the registers of epic and elegy in the Nisus and Euryalus episode of *A.* 9 and Ariosto's adaptation of the *Aeneid* in his Italian epic *Orlando Furioso*.

Far from wishing to offer the last word on Vergil and elegy, we hope that this volume will rather stimulate discussion as broadly as possible. Vergil's own relations with the genre and its practitioners were so wide-ranging and iconoclastic that far more authors than the elegists who were his contemporaries responded to his radical contamination of epic with elegy. Even Horace – neither an elegist nor an epicist, though contemporary with specialists of both genres – often triangulates his lyric and epistolary assessments of Vergil's poetry by reference to contemporary elegy.[61] His interventions into the generic polemics of the period foreshadow the continuing vitality of the confrontation of epic and elegy in the reception not only of Vergil's works but of the hexameter modes – pastoral, didactic, and epic – in which he worked.

NOTES

1 Coleman 1977, 264; cf. Clausen 1994: 278 ad *B.* 9.35, "the pastoral illusion is momentarily shattered."

2 I quote Vergil from Mynors 1969; translations are my own unless otherwise indicated.

3 On L. Varius Rufus and his poetry, see Cova 1989 with the reviews of Harrison 1990; Courtney 1993: 271–5; Hollis 1996 and 2007: 253–81. The addressee of *Catalepton* 7 (generally deemed authentically Vergilian), he is coupled with Vergil by Horace (*Serm.* 1.6.55; *Epist.* 2.1.247; *Ars* 55; cf. *Serm.* 1.5.40, 1.10.43–4, 1.10.81) and in the Vergilian biographical tradition (*VSD* 37–42; Probus, *Vita Verg.*).

4 On C. Helvius Cinna, see Wiseman 1974; Dahlmann 1977; Watson 1982; Courtney 1993: 212–24; Hollis 2007: 11–48. For specifically elegiac experimentation amongst the first-generation "neoteric" poets, see Calvus' *Quintilia* (perhaps modelled on Parthenius' *Arete*, on which see Lightfoot 1999: 31–5, 100–5, 134–45); and Catullus 65–8, 76.

5 On C. Cornelius Gallus, see Boucher 1966; Crowther in *ANRW*; Anderson, Parsons, Nisbet 1979; Courtney 1993: 259–70; Hollis 2007: 219–52.

6 On Theocritus in the *Bucolics*, see *VSD* and Serv. ad *B.* 1, with Hubbard 1998 on Hesiod in the *Georgics*, see *VSD* and Serv. ad *G.* 1, with Farrell 1991; and on

Homer in the *Aeneid*, see *VSD* and Serv., with, e.g., Knauer 1964a and 1964b; Barchiesi 2015.

7 The *loci classici* are Clausen 1964 and 1987; Thomas 1983 and 1988a.

8 Quotation and translation of Callimachus' *Aetia* from Harder 2012 throughout.

9 On Vergil's predilection for "proems in the middle," see Thomas 1983; Conte 1992.

10 The precise poetics espoused by Callimachus in the *Aetia* prologue are beyond the scope of this discussion: Harder (2012: 2.55–63) summarizes the *communis opinio* (*contra* Cameron 1995: 104–32).

11 On Vergil's sustained reception of Callimachus' *Aetia* in *B.* 6, see also Clauss 2004.

12 On Ovid's *Metamorphoses* as aetiological poetry, see Myers 1994; cf. Hutchinson 2006b: 77–8.

13 On Apollo in *B.* 6, see Clausen 1976, 1977, and Clausen 1994: 179–80, ad loc.

14 For the programmatic valence of *nemus*, "grove," aligned with *siluae*, the "woods" (*B* 6.2) of Vergilian bucolic, see Harrison 2007a: 36, with n8, and 70.

15 Quoted in Clausen 1994: 203–4. For scepticism, see Harrison 2007a: 56.

16 Prop. 2.34.91–2; Ov. *Am.* 1.15.29–30, 3.9.64; *Ars* 3.334, 537; *Rem.* 765; *Tr.* 2.445, 4.10.53, 5.1.17. While both Latin love poets eventually turned from erotic elegy to the composition of aetiological elegy, Propertius explicitly identifies Callimachus as the inspiration for the reorientation of his elegiac themes from *amor* to *causae* (Prop. 4.1.64): see Hutchinson 2006a; Fedeli et al. 2015.

17 Harrison 2007a: 56.

18 Hutchinson 2006b, building on a suggestion first put forth in Henry 2005. On Parthenius' *Metamorphoses*, see Lightfoot 1999: 112–15 and 164–7.

19 Hutchinson 2006b: 75 et passim.

20 For aetiology in the *Metamorphoses*, see n12 above.

21 On Parthenius' *Erotic Sufferings*, see Lightfoot 1999: 215–558. On the connections between Vergil's representation of Gallus, and his poetry, in the sixth eclogue and Gallus' actual poetry, see Ross 1975: 32, 34–6, 40–3, 118–20.

22 For Vergil's complex intertextual dialogue with Calvus' lost *Io* in the Pasiphaë exemplum, see Coleman 1977: 189–93; Clausen 1994: 194–8; Armstrong 2006: 169–77.

23 On the relationship between Verg. *B.* 10 and Theoc. *Id.* 1, see Coleman 1977: 276–95; Clausen 1994: 288–300.

24 On the different versions of the myth, see Gow 1952: 1–2; Hunter 1999: 63–8.

25 Quoted in Clausen 1994, ad loc.

26 Coleman 1977: 288 ad 46; Clausen 1994: 291, 305–6.

27 For the importance of limiting erotic expression in Vergilian pastoral, cf. Corydon's question at *B.* 2.68 (*me tamen urit amor: quis enim modus adsit*

amori? ("Nevertheless love burns me: what limit should be set to love?") with Davis 2012: 99–111.

28 On *Parthenios saltus* ("Parthenian glades"), as a compliment to Parthenius with metaliterary resonance, see Ross 1975: 85–106.

29 *Chalcidico … uersu* (50) is interpreted by Quintilian as referring to Euphorion, who came from Chalcis.

30 Servius comments on the poetic valence of the eclogue singer's basket weaving (ad *gracili*, 10.71): *significat se composuisse hunc libellum tenuissimo stilo* ("he means that he has composed his little book in the most refined style").

31 On the passage, see also Pandey in this volume.

32 On *G.* 4, see Griffin 1979 (reprinted in Volk 2008: 225–48); Farrell 1991: 238–72; and the commentaries of Thomas 1988a and Mynors 1990, ad loc. My discussion follows Keith 2020: 78–88.

33 On the tradition, see Stephens 2004; Keith 2018, with full bibliography. Antigonus of Carystus (19.23) includes the *bugonia* in his *paradoxa*, while Philitas connects the adjective βουγενής ("cowborn") to the practice of *bugonia* (Fr. 14a Spanoudakis): βουγενέας … μελίσσας ("cowborn bees"); see Spanoudakis 2002, 184–6, ad loc. Callimachus – himself writing in Egypt, at the Ptolemaic court – applies the same adjective to Io's descendant Danaus (Call. *Aet.* Fr. 54.4 Harder) in a passage that introduces the Apis bull (Call. *Aet.* Fr. 54.16 Harder), with which Danaus' ancestor, Io's son Epaphus, was associated: see Harder 2012: 2.400–1 and 412–13 respectively. As Acosta-Hughes and Stephens (2012: 243n102) put it, in tracing intertextual connections between Callimachus' Epaphus/Apis bull and Vergil's *bugonia*, there is "an implied bilingual pun as the cowborn Apis in Callimachus becomes 'cowborn' *apes* in Virgil," through its metonymic relation to Io's son Epaphus, who is himself "equated with the Egyptian Apis bull (mentioned at *Victoria Berenices* 16)." Cf. Stephens 2004: 158–60, who sees in Vergil's description of the Egyptian rite of *bugonia* a resemblance to the famous Egyptian ritual "of the death, mummification, and 'rebirth' of the Apis bull that functioned to insure the fertility of Egypt" (159). She notes (160) that "for Virgil the transformation may have been even more obvious, since the Greek name for the Egyptian bull (Hapi), 'Apis,' was a word that in Latin already meant 'bee.'"

34 Cf. *G.* 4.285–6: *altius omnem / expediam prima repetens ab origine famam* ("I shall expound the whole tale from its first origin, tracing back more deeply").

35 Harder 2012: 1.8–11.

36 Both Apollonius (*Arg.* 2.500–27) and Callimachus (*Aet.* 3 Fr. 75.32–5 Harder) were familiar with the myth of the nymph's rape by Apollo (who thereby fathered Aristaeus) and relocation to Libya, where her eponymous city was later founded (Pind. *Pyth.* 9.39–65).

37 Thilo-Hagen 1881: 118.

38 "We must remember, as I said before, that the last part of this book has been changed: for Gallus' praises were contained in that place which now holds the story of Orpheus, itself inserted after Gallus died, a victim of Augustus' anger" (Thilo-Hagen 1881: 320).

39 On the practical limitations on the printing and circulation of books in classical Rome, see Kenney 1983: 15–23.

40 On the controversy, see Griffin 1979; *contra* Jacobson 1984 and Jocelyn 1984. Nisbet (1987: 189) suggests that Servius misreports a reception tradition that interpreted the Aristaeus passage as allegorical praise of Gallus.

41 The standard history of classical epyllion is that of Crump 1931, who discusses "Catullus and his School" at 114–40. For her discussion of Vergil's Aristaeus episode, see Crump 1931: 178–94.

42 On elegy in the *Aeneid*, see Cairns 1989: 129–50; Harrison 2007a: 208–14; McCallum forthcoming.

43 On the passage, see Harrison 1991: 96–8 ad loc.

44 On the Marathus-cycle of Tibullus' elegies 1.4, 8, and 9, see Nikoloutsos 2007 and 2011; Drinkwater 2012; Zimmermann Damer 2014, with further bibliography.

45 On the identification of the Gallus of Prop. 1.20 with the elegist, see Cairns 1983 and 2006: 219–49; Keith 2008b: 124–5.

46 For erotic *cura*, see Pichon 1902: 120, s.v.

47 On the interchangeability of male and female elegiac beloveds, with particular reference to the beloved's hair, see Ov. *Am.* 1.1.19–20 (*aut puer aut longas compta puella comas*), with McKeown 1989 (in 1987–98): 137 ad loc. For the elegiac valence of a "milk-white neck," see Pichon 1902: 98, 213–14.

48 Cf. Cynthia's "soft" gait (Prop. 2.12.24).

49 Translation adapted from Heyworth and Morwood 2011: 164 ad loc.

50 Both Harrison (1991, 97 ad *A.* 10.136) and Heyworth and Morwood (2011, 164 ad Prop. 3.7.49–50) view Propertius as the imitator; Rothstein (1920 ad Prop. 3.7.49) agrees that one of the two depends on the other, though he leaves the question of priority open.

51 Fedeli 1985: 265 ad Prop. 3.7.49, following Tränkle 1960: 53 ad loc.

52 Fedeli 1985: 265 ad Prop. 3.7.49, citing Zicàri 1978, 218, who adduces Catull. *c.* 66.48, 67.44, 68.58, 76.10, 97.2, and 99.8.

53 Cairns 2006: 158–9.

54 See above, n6.

55 See above, n7.

56 Heinze 1915; Zarker 1969; Wlosok 1976; Harrison 1972/3 and 1989; Panoussi 2009.

57 Pollio: *VSD* and Serv. ad *B.* 3, with André 1949; Zecchini 1982; Néraudau 1983; Cairns 2008; on his poetry, see Courtney 1993: 254–6; Hollis 2007:

215–18. Maecenas: *VSD* and Serv. ad *G.* 1, with Paturzo 1999; Cairns 2006: 250–319; Le Doze 2014; Chillet 2016; on his poetry, see Courtney 1993: 276–81; Hollis 2007: 314–25. Augustus: *VSD* and Serv. ad *A.* 1, with Zanker 1988; Galinsky 1996; Cairns 2006: 320–443; Eck 2007.

58 McKay 1970; Fantham 2009: 3–62.

59 On Vergil's long-standing interest in philosophy and religion, see Feeney 1986; Hardie 1986; Dyson 2001; Armstrong et al. 2004; Miller 2009; Davis 2012; Braund 2019; Keith 2020.

60 Gallus: Servius ad *B.* 6.72 and 10.1; Skutsch 1901 and 1906; Ross 1975; Cairns 2006: 70–249.

61 Cf., e.g., Horace's reception in *Carm.* 2.9 of Valgius' elegiac laments about the loss of his *puer delicatus* Mystes, triangulated through Vergil's treatment of Orpheus' loss of Eurydice in *G.* 4, with the discussions ad loc. of Nisbet and Hubbard 1978: 137–8 and 144; and Harrison 2017: 118–19 and 124–5. For further discussion of Horace's reception of Vergilian epic through an elegiacizing lens, see the chapters of Anagnostou-Laoutides and Gladhill in this volume.

PART ONE

Elegy in Vergil

1

Elegy and Metapoetic Polemic in Vergil's First Eclogue

JOHN HENKEL

Probably few critics would call Vergil a polemical poet. The elegists, on the other hand, practically define their genre by its polemical rejection of hexameter epic.[1] So, it is surprising that our earliest Augustan *recusationes*, which imitate the elegiac polemic of Callimachus' *Aetia* prologue, come not from elegy but two hexameter poems, Vergil's sixth eclogue and Horace's *Satires* 1.10. Most scholars since Clausen (1964) have seen *B.* 6 as carrying the banner of Callimachean anti-epic polemic into the Augustan period; and while this view makes sense of Vergil's career, with its focus on Callimacheanism in the hexameter genres, it fails to explain why Vergil's Callimacheanism would prompt him to reject epic in a hexameter poem instead of an elegiac one like Callimachus himself wrote. The traditional view also neglects the massive influence that Gallan elegy had on early Augustan poetry, including the *Bucolics*: not only do Propertius, Tibullus, and Ovid imitate it later, but Vergil and Horace both seem to answer it in their own early works, writing poems with elegiac features (humble style, Callimachean refinement, erotic subject matter) but in the non-elegiac metres of iamb (Horace's *Epodes*) and hexameter (Vergil's *Bucolics* and Horace's *Satires* 1).[2] The simplest explanation, in my view, is that Gallus had imitated Callimachus by polemically rejecting epic in elegy before Vergil did so in hexameter.[3] Gallus' elegiac program almost certainly resembled that of the later elegists, who see Roman elegy as uniquely appropriate for love poetry and Callimacheanism, and uniquely opposed to the grandeur and panegyric of epic.[4] This is a traditional but parochial view of genre, which makes perfect sense before the *Bucolics* – when hexameter was still largely dominated by panegyric epics on recent history (especially Caesar), mostly of middling quality (cf. Catull. 36).[5]

If Gallus had presented genre – as the later elegists do – as a stark choice between panegyric hexameter epic and Callimachean elegy, then Vergil's own approach to these genres – both in the *Bucolics* and throughout his career – snaps into clear focus: he is answering the challenge of elegiac polemic as a partisan defender of the hexameter tradition.[6] All of Vergil's work is Callimachean hexameter, which itself contradicts elegy's apparent claim to Callimachus, and each major work deprecates the obsessive love that elegy celebrates (*B.* 2, 8, 10; *G.* 3; *A.* 4). More directly, the *Bucolics* feature Gallus himself as a character, but in poems that claim Callimacheanism and love poetry as belonging to bucolic hexameter as well as elegy (*B.* 6 and 10, respectively); one of these even specifically imagines a reader "obsessed with love" or "obsessed with love poetry" (*si quis <u>captus amore leget</u>, B.* 6.9–10).[7] *B.* 10, in particular, has for over thirty years been read as a metapoetic confrontation between bucolic and elegy.[8] My argument in this chapter is that *B.* 1 should be read in this way as well. Taken together, the two poems frame the book of eclogues as a quasi-polemical meditation on the similarities – and true differences – between elegy and hexameter *epos*, a genre that the elegists associated with panegyric military epic, but which Vergil construed broadly to include bucolic and didactic as well as martial epic. Both genres, Vergil claims, can admit love poetry and Callimachean refinement, but where elegy celebrates hopeless love, Theocritean *epos* seeks generally to avoid or console it. I argue this case more broadly in a book project on metapoetic allegory in the *Bucolics*, but *B.* 1 can be read in isolation as a polemical reply to Gallan elegy. This metapoetic approach is not the only way to read *B.* 1, which on the literal level is a moving drama about war and dispossession.[9] My reading, moreover, necessarily requires some speculation about Gallus' lost poetry. The result, however, provides a compelling and economical account of early Augustan poetry that solves problems not only in the interpretation of *B.* 1 but also in our understanding of Roman Callimacheanism.

Unlike the explicit literary polemics of elegy, Vergil's polemics in the *Bucolics* are metapoetic and allegorical. As I have argued in previous articles, Vergilian metapoetics work by doing two big things with metaphor. First, Vergil literalizes and combines literary critical metaphors, so that if other poets, e.g., use herding as a metaphor for poetry, Vergil can write metapoetically about poetry by writing literally about cows and herding.[10] Second, he turns intertextuality into a tool of metapoetics by treating certain well-known narratives, like that of Polyphemus in Theocritus *Idyll* 11 or Daphnis in *Idyll* 1, as metaphors for the genre with which they are associated, so that when Vergil's Corydon in *B.* 2 plays the role of Polyphemus, for example, the effect is to figure him as participating in Theocritean bucolic. When the character in question has his own connection to a different genre, as when the elegist Gallus plays the arch-herdsman Daphnis in *B.* 10, the generic mismatch can be a vehicle of metapoetic polemics. So much is obvious when a poet is himself a character in the poem as in *B.* 10, but polemics are also at play when Vergil uses shepherds as allegorical stand-ins for Gallus or himself. My embrace of allegory may give some readers pause, but what I advocate is poetic allegory rather than the biographical allegory so familiar since Servius.[11] Poetic allegory has a long history in bucolic, where readers equated singing shepherds with the poet at least as early as the reception of Theocritus *Idyll* 7; by the first century BCE, "the equation of poet with cowherd had become … the central metaphor informing bucolics, the overarching means by which it functioned poetically."[12] This kind of allegory was more prevalent in the early years of Vergilian exegesis as well, but Donatus and Servius narrowed the scope of allegorical readings by insisting that Vergil only used allegory to thank Octavian for saving his land from the confiscations after Philippi (*VSD* 66, Serv. ad *B.* 3.20); before their respective commentaries, there was clearly a larger and more diverse range of allegorical readings, many of which resembled what we now call metapoetics.[13]

In the metapoetic allegory of *B.* 1, the herdsmen Meliboeus and Tityrus figure Gallus and Vergil, respectively, and their relationship – which I will argue is somewhat more hostile than most have seen it – figures the polemical relationship between Gallan elegy and Vergil's genre of hexameter *epos*. Meliboeus is a goatherd with no background in Theocritus;[14] he appears in *B.* 1 for the first time in extant pastoral only to depart immediately as an exile from the countryside. The ancient commentators clearly knew a tradition in which Meliboeus stood for Gallus: outside of Servius, all the scholia identify Meliboeus either as Cornelius Gallus or a Mantuan – i.e., a Gaul (*Gallus*) – or a Mantuan specifically named Cornelius or Cornelius Gallus (DServ., Jun. Phil. I, Jun. Phil. II ad *B.* 1.1; Schol. Bern. *praef.* ad *B.* 1).[15] The recovery of Gallan fragments now points in this direction too, since allusions to the elegist seem to appear only in speeches of Meliboeus.[16] Tityrus, on the other hand, was a minor herdsman in Theocritus but now sings in shady repose while Meliboeus is forced into exile. Readers ancient and modern have seen Tityrus as a figure for Vergil (e.g., Serv. ad *B.* 1.1), who we hear likewise escaped the confiscations (*VSD* 19) – but the biographical tradition is least reliable in places like this where it might simply be based on a poet's text. As metapoetic rather than biographical allegory, Vergil's alignment with Tityrus figures him instead as an intertextual imitator of Gallan love poetry.[17] Tityrus in Theocritus was a surrogate goatherd and – to Vergil's eyes, apparently – a singer of other people's love songs. When he first appears in *Idyll* 3, Tityrus receives a herd of goats when the goatherd goes courting Amaryllis (*Id.* 3.1–5); perhaps these goats were just goats for Theocritus, but herds are often metapoetic in the *Bucolics* (see further below), and Vergil himself seems to view the transfer of goats in *Idyll* 3 as a transfer also of the goatherd's love song for Amaryllis (Ὦ χαρίεσσ' Ἀμαρυλλί, *Id.* 3.6), since this is precisely what Meliboeus finds Tityrus singing at the start of *B.* 1 (*formosam Amaryllida, B.* 1.5).[18] Later in Theocritus *Idyll* 7, Tityrus is also the second herdsman in the collection to sing the archetypal Daphnis song, which he frames somewhat more as a love song than had been done in *Idyll* 1 (τᾶς Ξενέας ἠράσσατο Δάφνις ὁ βούτας, *Id.* 7. 73; contrast τὰ Δάφνιδος ἄλγε', *Id.* 1.19). On my reading of *B.* 1, Tityrus once again plays the role of surrogate goatherd when Meliboeus seems at the end to leave his goats with Tityrus before departing into exile at the end of the poem (*non me pascente*, 1.77; see below). If Meliboeus is an allegory for Gallus and Tityrus for Vergil, then this transfer of goats can again be read as a transfer of love poetry: as Gallus departs love poetry for panegyric epic (more on this in a moment), he leaves his flock with Vergil, signalling the latter's initiation into love poetry – a move parallel to the Theocritean investiture of Corydon in *B.* 2 and the Callimachean investiture of Gallus himself in *B.* 6.[19]

In his treatment of Tityrus, Vergil both literalizes metaphors (poems = herds) and adapts a pre-existing narrative to make claims about generic participation: it is Tityrus's Theocritean backstory that allows us to see him (and so Vergil) pointedly as a pastoral character singing someone else's love poetry. This latter type of metapoetics, which I have elsewhere called metanarrative symbolism, is especially potent with well-known narratives seen as archetypes for their genre: thus Gallus, as Conte showed, seems especially pastoral in *B.* 10 because he is playing the archetypal role of Daphnis from Theocritus *Idyll* 1.[20] So also in *B.* 1, Tityrus and Meliboeus seem cast into the iconic metanarratives that Roman love elegy uses for itself and for epic, respectively; at this early date, these metanarratives must be drawn from the poetry of Gallus himself, which means that Vergil has cast himself and Gallus allegorically into Gallus' own stereotypes of genre. Tityrus in his past infatuation with Galatea plays the role of the archetypal elegiac lover (*B.* 1.27–35, see below), a figure that also appears in *B.* 2, 8, and 10: the poet loves a girl and courts her with poetry, but she prefers material gifts and/or the rich lover who can provide them.[21] Meliboeus, by contrast, seems to be cast into elegy's distinctive vision of epic, which I will call the military *recusatio* metanarrative. Although scholars tend to view the *recusatio* as linked to Apollo's speech in the *Aetia* prologue (fr. 1.21–8),[22] I believe (but cannot prove) that Gallus prominently rejected epic in a way based directly on the circumstance that notionally occasions most Augustan *recusationes*: a great man invites the poet to join him on campaign and write panegyric epic about his accomplishments; the poet demurs, often citing his dedication to love and/or love poetry, but promises to comply when his current project is done. I have argued elsewhere that such a pattern lies behind the structure of Tibullus Book 1, where the poet figures panegyric epic as a journey postponed: he begins by demurring from a campaign with Messalla (1.1), later imagines it postponed by illness (1.3), then finally must go at the close of the book (1.10).[23] We glimpse the same pattern in Propertius 2.10, which Lyne saw as concluding its book, when Propertius says he "will sing wars when/since my girl has been written" (*bella canam quando scripta puella mea est*, Prop. 2.10.8).[24] As Propertius and Tibullus did for their patrons, I believe that Gallus promised Caesar an epic when he had finished writing elegy; like Tibullus, he may have connected that epic with his own service on the dictator's future campaigns, including perhaps the campaigns in Parthia, Scythia, and Germany that Caesar had planned at the time of his death (Plut. *Vit. Caes.* 58; cf. Gallus fr. 145.2–5 Hollis), or those of his heir, whom he served as governor in Egypt. The *Bucolics* make no explicit reference to a Gallan military *recusatio*, but this would help explain the military overtones of Meliboeus' exile from the country, which Tityrus connects with Rome's enemies in Parthia and Germany (1.62) and Meliboeus himself links to the theatres of Caesar's real or intended campaigns (Africa, Scythia, Britain: *B.* 1.64–5).[25] And like Tibullus' first book of elegies, Vergil's bucolic collection is structured around the postponement of this journey abroad: when Tityrus offers hospitality at the end of *B.* 1 (*hic tamen hanc mecum poteras requiescere noctem*, 1.79), he creates a generic space that protects Meliboeus from both his journey abroad and panegyric epic, at least for the space of the book. As in Tibullus as well, this journey re-emerges as a motif towards the end of the book, first with the journey out of the countryside in *B.* 9 (different characters, but still a consequence of war and dispossession), then with Gallus' own involvement with foreign war in *B.* 10.44–5. The characters may shift from poem to poem, but the underlying metanarrative remains constant, and the shift from Meliboeus in *B.* 1 to Gallus in *B.* 10 serves to reveal the allegory that underlies the collection throughout.

In addition to the two Gallan elegiac metanarratives that annotate Vergil's practice of erotic poetry in the *Bucolics*, one other elegiac metanarrative structures *B.* 1 in a way that seems to vaunt the collection's Callimachean stylistic refinement: Callimachus' own "Reply to the Telchines" from the *Aetia* prologue (fr. 1), which Vergil prominently adapts in *B.* 6 as well. For Callimachus that passage is a polemical and programmatic defence of his own elegiac poetics against critics who think his poetry should be longer and grander (i.e., more like hexameter epic). Vergil too, as I will argue, uses it to defend a Callimachean poetics of smallness and refinement but travesties its specifically elegiac orientation by locating these stylistic qualities in Theocritean hexameter as well. Broadly speaking, Tityrus and Meliboeus re-enact the "Reply to the Telchines," with Tityrus defending a bucolic-Callimachean poetics of small hexameter against Meliboeus' Telchines-like objection that hexameter should be grand like panegyric epic. There is considerable humour in this reversal of roles, which is made possible by the Gallan military *recusatio*: if Gallus had promised to write epic after finishing his book of elegy, it follows that now – as Vergil and others read and respond to that book – the elegist must be working on the promised panegyric, notionally on campaign with the dictator's heir.[26] Still, the reader's knowledge of his character is based precisely on the elegiac book(s) in which he probably begged off this obligation and figured his own values as directly opposed to those of epic. So, although he is aligned in *B.* 1 with panegyric epic, we must imagine him unhappy or unwilling, like the poet-lover dragged off to war in Tibullus 1.10 (*nunc ad bella trahor*, Tib. 1.10.13; cf. Tib. 2.6). Meliboeus' dispossession from his land figures this forcible transfer of genre in a way that prepares us for his initiation of Tityrus-Vergil into elegy at the end of the poem. But meanwhile, if Gallus had claimed Callimachus for elegy as I believe he did, we notice that Vergil has already appropriated Callimachus for bucolic by casting Tityrus as the Callimachean poet himself from the *Aetia* prologue – a move he will continue more overtly when Tityrus himself encounters Apollo in *B.* 6 (even while Vergil figures Gallus in a Callimachean initiation scene there).[27]

Among other problems it solves, viewing *B.* 1 in this way as intergeneric polemic helps explain why Meliboeus' speech, which opens the bucolic collection, is less obviously Theocritean than many scholars would like.[28] Not only does Meliboeus' name have no precedent in extant Greek bucolic (despite its etymology: see n14), but the most Theocritean elements of his speech seem also to allude to Callimachus and Philetas, whom the Roman elegists revered as generic forebears to their genre (Prop. 3.1.1). So, while many have seen Tityrus' shady repose in line 1 as alluding to the goatherd Comatas in *Idyll* 7 (*Tityre, tu patulae recubans sub tegmine fagi*, *B.* 1.1; cf. Theoc. *Id.* 7.88), scholars have increasingly seen Vergil's *fagi* as an allusion to Callimachus' Acontius, who reclines under φηγοί (*Aet.* fr. 75b.57 Harder) and laments "beautiful Cydippe" (*Aet.* fr. 73.2) just as Tityrus makes the woods echo "beautiful Amaryllis" (*B.* 1.5).[29] Similarly, although Tityrus' song obviously alludes to the goatherd in *Idyll* 3, several scholars have argued that Amaryllis in *Idyll* 3 derives ultimately from the poetry of Philetas, where she seems already associated with echoes and the countryside.[30] These features are only problematic if Vergil meant Meliboeus' speech to be programmatically Theocritean, not if Meliboeus is intended as an elegiac foil to the Theocritean Tityrus. Such an arrangement also provides context for Gutzwiller's argument that Meliboeus' speech alludes programmatically to the opening poem of a collection of Meleager's erotic epigrams (13 G.-P. = *Anth. Pal.* 7.196), while Tityrus' speech alludes programmatically to the opening poem of Theocritus' bucolic epigrams (Theoc. *Epigr.* 1 Gow = *Anth. Pal.* 6.336).[31]

A Metapoetic Reading of *B.* 1

The dialogue of Meliboeus and Tityrus represents a confrontation between elegiac and bucolic perspectives on literature, love, and the poet's relationship to political power. Because Meliboeus-Gallus is an elegiac figure with a rigid sense of decorum and generic loyalty, he objects both to his own conscription into bucolic hexameter (probably because Gallus imagined himself in pastoral settings in his elegies)[32] and to Tityrus' confounding of generic boundaries by writing Callimachean love poetry in hexameters. The poem opens with a speech in which Meliboeus laments his own exile from fields he calls "sweet" (*dulcia linquimus arua, B.* 1.3) – a programmatic term in elegy – before continuing later with scorn for his present surroundings (46–9), where neither he nor his goats have fared well (11–18).[33] Many have seen Meliboeus as felicitating Tityrus in this opening speech, but at least two ancient commentators saw Meliboeus as "spiteful" and characterized his exchange with Tityrus as "contentious" (*inuidens ... contentiose locutus,* Schol. Bern. *praef.* ad *B.* 1; cf. Jun. Phil. I ibid.). Among modern scholars, Van Sickle detects a note of sarcasm, even derision, when Meliboeus says that Tityrus rehearses a "woodsy Muse" on his "skinny oat" (*B.* 1.1–5):

> M. Tityre, tu patulae recubans sub tegmine fagi
> <u>siluestrem tenui Musam meditaris auena</u>;
> nos patriae fines et dulcia linquimus arua.
> nos patriam fugimus; tu, Tityre, lentus in umbra
> formosam resonare doces Amaryllida siluas.

M. Tityrus, you recline beneath the cover of a spreading beech and <u>rehearse your woodsy Muse on a skinny oat</u>; we are leaving the borders of our fatherland and our sweet fields. We are fleeing our fatherland; you, Tityrus, lazy in the shade, are teaching the woods to echo beautiful Amaryllis.[34]

Despite Vergil's use of *tenuis* elsewhere to adapt the Callimachean program of λεπτότης (e.g., *B.* 6.8), Van Sickle shows that "oat" (*auena*) is a more clearly derogative term for Tityrus' pipes than other pastoral equivalents like *calamus* and *harundo*.[35] I would argue that this is no casual allusion to Callimachus: taken together, the terms *siluestris Musa* and *tenuis auena* adapt the most famous moment of Callimachean anti-epic polemic in the "Reply to the Telchines," in which Apollo tells Callimachus to "keep his <u>Muse</u> <u>slender</u> but feed his sacrifice fat" (τὸ μὲν θύος ὅττι πάχιστον / θρέψαι, τὴ]ν <u>Μοῦσαν</u> δ' ὠγαθὲ <u>λεπταλέην</u>, *Aet.* fr. 1.23–4; cf. *B.* 6.4–5). As in Callimachus, *Musa* at *B* 1.2 is a metaphor for Tityrus' poetry – a usage made more elegiac by its identification in line 5 with Tityrus' *puella*, Amaryllis. It is easy to imagine "woodsy Muse" as a compliment in the context of the *Bucolics*, where the woods eventually come to stand for the aesthetic values of the collection itself (e.g., 4.3, 6.2),[36] but in elegy the phrase would be a gibe, since that genre follows Catullus in associating the countryside with boorish inelegance.[37] In this context the combination of "woodsy Muse" with "skinny oat" seems actually to travesty the Callimachean refinement that elegy values; even if *siluestris* and *auena* could have positive associations in the mouth of a Tityrus, coming from Meliboeus they undercut the programmatically elegiac and Callimachean implications of *Musa* and *tenuis*.

Meliboeus' derisive tone continues as he criticizes Tityrus for "lazily" singing in the shade (*lentus*). "Lazy" is the usual meaning of *lentus*, and it makes good sense of the contrast with Meliboeus' own dispossession and exile (*nos patriam fugimus; tu, Tityre, lentus in umbra*, 1.4).[38] I have claimed that this exile is a generic one, and to that end *lentus* helps figure Meliboeus as a spokesman for panegyric epic, since the elegists often characterize themselves as "lazy" for avoiding war and this genre.[39] But the word also helps develop an important criticism of Vergilian bucolic as unoriginal, since its intertextuality recycles and combines the work of other poets. Poetic borrowing is normal in bucolic and central to Vergil's style, but in this dialogue with elegy and its Callimachean emphasis on originality, Vergil seems to acknowledge that borrowing could be criticized as unoriginal.[40] Tityrus himself, of course, is closely tied to questions of ownership and originality, and the pastoral world itself thematizes Vergil's communal approach to poetry, both here and throughout the bucolic collection. Shadows and shade (*lentus in <u>umbra</u>*, 4) are for Vergil a potent symbol of literary influence, and their ubiquity throughout the *Bucolics* is a constant reminder of Vergil's indebtedness to other poets.[41] Here shade is tellingly combined with echo (*resonare*, 5) – itself an important Vergilian figure for allusion – and the literary echo of the goatherd's love song for Amaryllis in *Idyll* 3 (which Theocritus may have lifted from Philetas in the first place); even the phrase *siluestris Musa* alludes to Lucretius' claim that echo was the origin of pastoral music (*DRN* 4.589).[42] Coming from Meliboeus, the combination of lazy shade with these "echoing" allusions reads metapoetically as a criticism not just of Tityrus but also of Vergil's highly allusive pastoral.

Like the Telchines, Meliboeus is a disapproving critic with literary values foreign to the current genre. Because he is an elegist, he judges Tityrus' love poetry for Amaryllis on elegiac terms, criticizing it for its inappropriate rusticity and lack of originality. Tityrus himself, however, insistently characterizes his poetry as bucolic, shifting from the elegiac poet-as-lover conceit to the bucolic conceit of poet as herdsman. This change of metaphor is the most important feature of Tityrus' first speech, which expresses his gratitude that Octavian has allowed him to continue herding and "singing what I wish," i.e., composing pastoral (*B.* 1.6–10):[43]

> T. O Meliboee, deus nobis haec otia fecit.
> namque erit ille mihi semper deus, illius aram
> saepe tener nostris ab ouilibus imbuet agnus.
> <u>ille meas errare boues, ut cernis, et ipsum</u>
> <u>ludere quae uellem calamo permisit agresti.</u>

T. O Meliboeus, a god has made this leisure for us. For indeed that one will always be a god to me, and a tender lamb from our folds will often stain that one's altar. <u>That one, as you see, allowed my cows to roam and myself to play what I wish on my fieldsy reed.</u>

Increasingly, scholars have seen the reference to herding and singing in lines 9–10 as programmatic of bucolic poetry, anticipating the more directly programmatic command below to "pasture your cows" (*pascite ut ante boues*, 45 = βουκολεῖτε < βουκόλος).[44] The central feature of this passage, however, is not Tityrus' herding but his sacrifice of thanksgiving (7–8), which he adapts again from the "Reply to the Telchines" (*Aet.* fr. 1.23–4, above). In that context, the fat sacrificial animal was the non-metaphorical foil to Callimachus' slender Muse, but in Vergil sacrificial animals are a natural extension of the bucolic metaphor that figures the poet as a herdsman shepherding his flock of poems. By promising Octavian a "tender" sacrifice (*tener agnus*, 8), Tityrus casts him in the role of Callimachus' Apollo, multiplying to a divine level the honour Tityrus does his patron.[45] Notably, his poetic sacrifice will not be "fat," like the poetry Callimachus rejected (cf. fr. 398), but "tender" (*tener*) – an elegiac equivalent to Callimachus' λεπτός, which the elegists used polemically to reject "hard" epic.[46] This last point is important because it means the literary-political situation is no longer what it was for Gallus, when panegyric seemed the only appropriate way to honour Caesar. Instead, the point of *B.* 1 seems to be that Octavian will accept oblique poetic tribute in whatever genre Tityrus-Vergil chooses (*ut cernis ... <u>ludere quae uellem ... calamo permisit agresti</u>*, 1.9–10).

Throughout the poem, Vergil's metapoetic drama is driven by this disconnect between what Meliboeus-Gallus expects from hexameter *epos* and what he finds to be the case with Tityrus-Vergil in the *Bucolics*. The next two speeches explore that disconnect with regard to style. Just as Tityrus figured his own bucolic poetry through his cows, Meliboeus now figures elegy as herding goats – an apt choice both for their association with erotic passion and because Tityrus, the symbol of Vergil's elegiac *aemulatio*, is known as a surrogate goatherd. As an exile from elegy, Meliboeus has already arrived in unfamiliar country, but he overestimates its difference from his own genre, since the elegists always associate hexameter epic with grandeur. He sees in this alien landscape only the extremes of stylistic failure, at which too much grandeur is swollen and turgid (as in panegyric) or too little grandeur is naked and insufficient (*nudus*, 15, 47). So even though the *Bucolics* share elegy's Callimachean stylistic humility, Meliboeus says that he and his goats are suffering, just as he later says that Tityrus' herds would be harmed by emigrating from pastoral (49–50).

Meliboeus continues in these lines to play the Telchines, echoing Callimachean polemic against epic and the grand style. His second speech opens with a clear allusion to the "envy" that Callimachus persistently attributes to his critics (*B*. 1.11–18):

M. Non equidem <u>inuideo</u>, <u>miror</u> magis; undique totis
usque adeo turbatur agris. en ipse capellas
protinus aeger ago; hanc etiam uix, Tityre, duco.
hic inter densas corylos modo namque gemellos,
spem gregis, a! silice in nuda conixa reliquit.
saepe malum hoc nobis, si mens non laeua fuisset,
de caelo tactas memini praedicere quercus.
sed tamen iste deus qui sit da, Tityre, nobis.

M. For my own part, I am not <u>envious</u>, more in <u>wonder</u>; everywhere in all the fields there is such turbulence; look at the young goats I am driving straight on, though I am sick myself; this one, even, Tityrus, I scarcely lead. Here among the dense hazels just now, yes, she laboured with twins – the hope of the flock – then left them on the naked rock. Often this misfortune – if my mind had not been foolish – I remember the oaks touched from heaven foretold it to us. But still give us, Tityrus, what sort is that god of yours?

The Telchines are associated with envy in the "Reply" (*Aet*. fr. 1.17), but this passage more closely resembles the *Hymn to Apollo*, where Callimachus personifies Envy herself as a critic who only "wonders" at a poem as vast as the sea (οὐκ ἄγαμαι, *Hymn* 2.106).[47] Wonder is a response associated especially with the grand style, so Meliboeus may be sarcastic when he "wonders" at humble bucolic – especially since the rest of the speech is framed by Callimachus' two best-known images for denouncing epic grandeur: the turbulent river and thunder.[48] Meliboeus protests that he himself is not envious, but his *equidem* (B. 1.11) suggests that others, at least, would resent Tityrus' *otium* because "there is such turbulence everywhere in all the fields" (11–12). Fields are not usually "turbulent," but turbulence might figure the fields of *epos* as a turbid river (*turbatur* < *turbidus*), alluding to the powerful but muddy Euphrates, which Callimachus used for the grand style in the *Hymn to Apollo* (*Hymn* 2.108–12).[49] This metapoetic sense is reinforced when Meliboeus' speech closes with an image of thunder and lightning, which Callimachus uses to disclaim the grand style in the "Reply to the Telchines" (βροντᾶν οὐκ ἐμόν, *Aet.* fr. 1.20).[50] On the other hand, *turbatur* might figure the fields as "crowded" (*turbatur* < *turba*), the opposite of Callimachean literary originality.[51] These two senses would seem to be at odds with one another, but stylistic humility and literary originality are the twin obsessions of Roman Callimacheanism, and metapoetic allegory often combines related concepts in this way.

Meliboeus' discomfiture in hexameter is figured through his own poor health and the recent death of his she-goat's twin progeny, which he laments as having been the "hope of the herd" (*spem gregis, a!* 15). Part of this image is a humorous comment on the difference between elegiac and hexameter metrics, which differ primarily in the "limp" of the elegiac pentameter. Metapoetic limp imagery is best known from Ovid, who figures Elegy as a woman with attractively uneven feet (*Am.* 3.1.7–10), but metapoetic limp imagery is widespread in Tibullus as well and derives from similar imagery associated with the "lame" or "limping" iamb (choliamb/scazon) in Greek poetry.[52] There is every chance that Gallus used metapoetic foot puns as well – I have elsewhere suggested that this is what lies behind subtle foot puns in Vergil, especially in *Bucolics* 6 and 10 where Gallus appears explicitly as a character.[53] But even here, where Gallus appears only allegorically, Meliboeus' sickness and the halting progress of his goats can be seen as figuring the "limp" that distinguishes Gallan elegy from its grander hexameter cousin (*protinus aeger ago; hanc etiam uix, Tityre, duco*, 13). Sickness and hesitation are common ways to figure the metrical limp of both elegy and choliamb, and Meliboeus' line breaks syntax right where elegy limps, at the penthemimeres. Vergil elides through this apparent caesura, but the resulting combination of syllables, *ag-anc*, is so colourfully cacophonous that it seems to make the whole line a pillory of the elegiac Meliboeus' attempt to speak hexameter.

Tityrus's next speech, which remarks on the foolishness of comparing great things to small, clarifies the mismatch between Meliboeus' expectations and the reality of hexameter in the *Bucolics*. Critics since Servius have faulted Tityrus here for his failure to respond to Meliboeus' question about his patron (Serv. ad *B*. 1.19), but as a metapoetic discussion of style these lines respond exactly to the problem raised by Meliboeus throughout his speech: bucolic is a distinctly small subgenre of hexameter, more comparable to humble elegy than to grand panegyric epic (*B*. 1.19–25):

> T. Urbem quam dicunt Romam, Meliboee, putaui
> stultus ego huic nostrae similem, cui saepe solemus
> pastores ouium teneros depellere fetus.
> sic canibus catulos similes, sic matribus haedos
> noram, <u>sic paruis componere magna solebam</u>.
> uerum haec tantum alias inter caput extulit urbes
> quantum lenta solent inter uiburna cupressi.

T. The city they call Rome, Meliboeus, I thought foolishly was similar to this one of ours, to which we shepherds are often accustomed to drive the tender offspring of our sheep. I knew that puppies were thus similar to dogs, thus kids to their mothers, and <u>thus I was accustomed to compare large things to small</u>. But this one lifted her head among the other cities as far as cypresses among the pliant shrubs.

Here and throughout the *Bucolics*, Vergil is defending hexameter *epos* by showing that Theocritean *epos*, at least, has more in common with Callimachus and Roman elegy than with the panegyric epic that elegy defines itself against. A metapoetic reading lets us follow other movements of this passage as well. Tityrus' statement that shepherds drive their "tender lambs" to the market town (*pastores ouium teneros depellere fetus*, 21) hints at an economy of poetic dedication that involves even the "soft" genres like elegy and pastoral. Moreover, the comparison of cypresses to "pliant shrubs" (*lenta uiburna*) as an image for pastoral recontextualizes an adjective that Meliboeus had earlier applied as a taunt. This recontextualizing move is standard part of the metapoetic and conceptual tug-of-war we see throughout the *Bucolics* – and indeed throughout the Augustan period – with the specialized language of intergeneric polemic.

The revaluation of words is a standard feature of politics as well as poetics, especially in periods of revolution (Thuc. 3.82.3), and the connection between these two phenomena is nowhere clearer in *B*. 1 than when Tityrus talks about *libertas*, which has potent associations in both spheres (*B*. 1.26–7): M. *Et quae tanta fuit Romam tibi causa uidendi?* / T. <u>*Libertas*</u>, *quae sera tamen respexit inertem* … ("M. And what reason did you have for seeing Rome? T. <u>Liberty</u>, which looked back late upon the lazy, looked back nevertheless …"). "Freedom" was nearly ubiquitous as a political slogan in the late Republic: Caesar's assassins styled themselves liberators but so too did his heir (*Res Gestae* 1), and Clausen suggests that we read *libertas* in *B.* 1 as part of Vergil's political homage to Octavian (1994 ad loc.). Within the poem's metapoetic allegory, the term also refers to freedom of choice in the matter of genre, which is felt most immediately in the ability of Tityrus-Vergil to demur from panegyric epic. This substantial freedom will become the hallmark of Augustan literary culture, in which the oblique praise of the *recusatio* largely replaces the panegyric so common under Caesar.[54] The later elegists enjoy such poetic freedom that they can turn the concept on its head, figuring themselves as generically unfree because of their figurative "slavery" to their mistresses (*seruitium amoris*). This freedom of choice is a necessary component of Callimachean originality, so there is no little irony when Tityrus concedes that his own *libertas* is "belated" (*quae sera tamen …*) and humorously attributes this fact to the laziness that Meliboeus accused him of above (… *respexit inertem*, 27; cf. *lentus in umbra*, 4).

Read in dialogue with elegy, the implication of these lines is the same as Vergil's provocative opening to *G.* 3, "all is now trite" (*omnia iam uulgata*, *G.* 3.4; see Thomas 1988a ad loc.): others may have written Callimachean elegy to be original, but I am late to that game and must look elsewhere for the source of my own originality.[55] Indeed, the rest of Tityrus' speech can be read metapoetically as a renunciation of Gallan love elegy, which Vergil figures precisely through the elegiac motif of *seruitium amoris*. Lyne argued that *seruitium amoris* appears first in Propertius, and that Gallus had not used it previously, but there are good reasons to detect it in Tityrus' speech and to consider this an allusion to its likely use in Gallus.[56] Such an approach, as Eckerman has argued, in fact solves several problems in our understanding of *B.* 1, including the logistics of Tityrus' manumission and his odd digression on his romantic history (*B.* 1.27–35):[57]

> T. Libertas, quae sera tamen respexit inertem,
> candidior postquam tondenti barba cadebat,
> respexit tamen et longo post tempore uenit,
> postquam nos Amaryllis habet, Galatea reliquit.
> namque (fatebor enim) dum me Galatea tenebat,
> nec spes libertatis erat nec cura peculi.
> quamuis multa meis exiret uictima saeptis
> pinguis et ingratae premeretur caseus urbi,
> non umquam grauis aere domum mihi dextra redibat.

T. Liberty, which looked back late upon the lazy, looked back nevertheless, after the trimmings of my beard began to fall whiter; she looked back nevertheless and came a long time later, after Amaryllis had us and Galatea had left. For indeed I will admit, while Galatea held me, I had neither a hope of liberty nor a care for my savings. Although many a fat victim went out from my folds and many a cheese was pressed for the ungrateful city, my right hand never returned home heavy with cash.

Others have noted that Vergil uses erotic commonplaces in this passage. I would go further and say that he adapts and pastoralizes the basic meta-narrative of Gallan and later Roman love elegy. Like the beloved Alexis of *B.* 2, Tityrus' Galatea resembles the Galatea of Theocritus *Idyll* 11; but unlike in that poem, this Galatea lives in the city and is modelled essentially on elegy's greedy *puella*, whom the elegiac poet-lover must ply with gifts. This seems to be why Tityrus, when he was hers, had no care for his savings and came home from town empty-handed, despite selling "many a fat victim and cheese" there.[58] Following Heyne, the modern consensus takes *pinguis* with *caseus* rather than *uictima*, but "fat victim" – which Servius read – makes better sense both literally and in the Callimachean metapoetic allegory of *B.* 1.[59]

Much like Tragedy and Elegy in Ovid's *Amores* 3.1, Galatea and Amaryllis in *B.* 1 are metaphorical personifications of contrasting types of erotic poetry.[60] Galatea's role is as elegiac foil to Tityrus' current interest in the pastoral Amaryllis, who not only is a symbol for pastoral poetry (*siluestrem Musam*, 2) but her first mention in *B.* 1 is even itself a pastoral love song from Theocritus *Idyll* 3 (*formosam … Amaryllida, B.* 1.5; see above). As Tityrus presents it, he had passed through a phase of elegiac love and love poetry in his younger days (Galatea), but he found no success until he turned to pastoral love and love poetry with Amaryllis. I do not mean to suggest that Vergil himself wrote elegiac juvenilia, but rather that the character's fictive biography is a metaphor for the poet's program, specifically his preference for the pastoral approach to love poetry. It was in those early elegiac days, Tityrus says, that he was "lazy" (*inertem*, 27) – a neat turn on Meliboeus' earlier gibe (*lentus in umbra*, 4). Switching to the bucolic metaphor, he styles these early poems as "fat victims" – precisely the image that Callimachus used as the opposite of his slender Muse (θύος ὅττι πάχιστον, *Aet.* fr. 1.23) – and suggests that they found no patron in the city, since he came home with no money in hand (35).[61] Things are different, however, now that Tityrus' beard grows white: this image of age both inverts the elegiac topos that love and love poetry are for the young and also suggests the posture of Callimachus in the "Reply," who figures himself as an old man.[62] Thus ironically Tityrus himself now plays Callimachus, who speaks hexameters to Meliboeus, his elegiac Telchines.

Throughout the rest of *B*. 1, Tityrus continues his metapoetic repudiation of elegy in terms that reject elegy's erotic metaphors and assert a new generic rhetoric based on pastoral metaphors of sacrifice and dedication. Continuing the *seruitium amoris* theme from his mention of Galatea, Tityrus states clearly that he went to Rome because he could not otherwise leave his "slavery" (*neque seruitio me exire licebat*, 40). The majority of this speech, however, he spends further developing the pastoral/Callimachean theme that he began above: his patron is a god (*nec tam praesentis alibi cognoscere divos*, 41) to whom he as poet-shepherd will regularly dedicate sacrifices (*quotannis / bis senos cui nostra dies altaria fumant*, 42–3). The reference here, as Clausen shows, is to the Hellenistic ruler cult and probably specifically to Theocritus *Idyll* 17, which assimilates Ptolemy II to Zeus.[63] Yet the framing of this speech draws a strong metapoetic contrast between the generic *seruitium* of the Roman love elegists and the paradoxical freedom that Vergil finds in honouring Octavian, who permits the indirect honour of pastoral dedication – "pasture your cattle as before, boys" (*pascite ut ante boues, pueri*, 45) – rather than demanding a panegyric epic. Meanwhile the terms in which Meliboeus-Gallus laments his own exile continue to suggest a departure from more familiar genres, "here amidst familiar streams" (*hic inter flumina nota*, 52), for campaign and panegyric epic, which he figures both through military theatres like Africa, Scythia, and Britain (64–6) and again through the un-Callimachean stylistics of the turbulent river Oaxes (*rapidum cretae ... Oaxen*, 65).[64] Lest we doubt it is genre that is at stake here, the terms in which Meliboeus felicitates Tityrus and recalls his own past happiness (*fortunatus senex*, 46, 51; *felix quondam*, 74) precisely match Vergil's later generic synkrisis between Lucretian didactic and his own agricultural didactic in the *Georgics* (*felix qui ... fortunatus et ille*, G. 2.490, 493): in both cases Vergil describes his indirect generic model (Gallus in *B*. 1, Lucretius in G. 2) as *felix* and his own imitation as *fortunatus*.[65]

The poem's last ten lines, in which Meliboeus gives his goats to Tityrus and Tityrus offers one night's hospitality as a temporary reprieve from Meliboeus' exile, set up an allegorical structure for the rest of the *Bucolics*. If goats are a metaphor for love poetry, as I have claimed, then the transfer of Meliboeus' goats in lines 74–8 can be read allegorically as an initiation of Tityrus-Vergil into the tradition of Gallan Roman love elegy, which the *Bucolics* often resemble quite closely (esp. *B*. 2, 8, 10). When Meliboeus tells his goats to "go, my once happy flock" (74), most readers imagine that he is driving his herd into exile, where they will eat "unaccustomed food" (*insueta ... pabula*, 49) and face the danger of contagion from neighbouring flocks (*mala uicini pecoris contagia laedent*, 50). But this reading requires a contortion of syntax in the final words of Meliboeus' speech (*non me pascente, capellae, / florentem cytisum et salices carpetis amaras*, 77–8), where Coleman, for example, insists we read, "I will be your herdsman, she-goats, but you will not graze on flowering clover and willows," taking *non* with *carpetis* instead of *me pascente*.[66] The more natural reading takes *non* with *me pascente*: "you will graze but I will not be your herdsman"; in the allegory of genre, where Meliboeus-Gallus is already an exile from his own genre of love elegy, the *insueta pabula* and *uicini pecoris contagia* are threats that Meliboeus-Gallus thinks his elegy faces here in the world of hexameter. The phrase *felix quondam pecus* ("once happy flock," 74) is both a felicitation of Gallus' own past literary success and a sarcastic joke about the herd's future prospects with Tityrus; surrogate herdsmen face similar insults elsewhere in both Theocritus and Vergil (*Id.* 4.1–3, 13; cf. *B.* 3.3, *infelix … pecus*). Meliboeus-Gallus is going off to war so will "sing no songs" (*carmina nulla canam*, 77) because the elegists always protest that their poetry is dependent on the inspiration of their *puellae*, whom they must not abandon for war and panegyric epic. Tityrus-Vergil will stay behind and watch his goats as he sings his song, as Tityrus had done for the goatherd in *Idyll* 3 – and this is just where we find Vergil when he appears as the narrator of *B.* 10: he is pasturing goats while singing the troubled *amores* of Gallus (*sollicitos Galli dicamus amores, / dum tenera attondent simae uirgulta capellae*, 10.6–7).[67] Vergil's closing speech in that poem – which serves as the *envoi* to the whole book – ends with a line that closely matches the farewell of Meliboeus-Gallus to his goats in *B.* 1 (*ite domum saturae, uenit Hesperus, ite capellae*, 10.77; *ite meae, felix quondam pecus, ite capellae*, 1.74), as Vergil himself now resigns Gallan elegy at the end of the bucolic collection and returns his flock to Gallus, for whom he hopes that Theocritean hexameter will have proven grand enough (*Pierides: vos haec facietis maxima Gallo*, 10.72; cf. above on *magna satis*, 1.47).

B. 1 closes with an offer of hospitality from Tityrus to Meliboeus, which I have claimed grants Gallus a temporary sojourn here in pastoral, at least through the end of *B.* 10. The first three lines, which invite Meliboeus to stay the night (*hic tamen hanc mecum poteras requiescere noctem / fronde super uiridi*, 79–80) and offer to share a simple country feast of fruit, chestnuts, and cheese (*sunt nobis mitia poma, / castaneae molles et pressi copia lactis*, 80–1), are modelled on the country symposium at the end of Theocritus *Idyll* 7 (133–57) and the Cyclops' invitation to Galatea in *Idyll* 11 (44–9). Like the metapoetic symposium in *Idyll* 7, the feast Tityrus offers reflects metaphorically on qualities of his own poetry, seeming to argue a stylistic similarity between pastoral and elegy that should put Gallus at ease: *mitis, mollis*, and *pressus* are all used in Roman literary criticism to characterize the stylistic simplicity of the plain and middle styles.[68] The allusion to Polyphemus and Galatea helps set up the allegory of *B.* 2, where *Idyll* 11 is the dominant model and the metaphorical relationship between pastoral and elegy is one of erotic pursuit; but this is beyond the present scope. Despite the apparent similarity between these genres, Meliboeus-Gallus' fixation throughout *B.* 1 has been on the stylistic grandeur he associates normatively with hexameter *epos* but does not find in pastoral; the poem's closing two lines seem to demonstrate how Vergilian pastoral achieves a modicum of grandeur (*magna satis*, 47) despite its self-consciously humble primary model. The picture of evening in these lines, with its smoking chimneys and "greater shadows falling from lofty mountains" (*maioresque cadunt altis de montibus umbrae*, 83), alludes to two grander hexameter subgenres, Lucretian didactic (*de altis montibus*, *DRN* 4.1020 et al.) and Apollonian epic (*Arg.* 1.451–2). Shade was a symbol for literary influence that Meliboeus used in the beginning of the poem to ridicule Tityrus' poetry as unoriginal and unambitious (*lentus in umbra*, 4); Tityrus redeems it here, showing how the "greater shadows" of Vergilian pastoral are precisely the influence of these "loftier" hexameter models, such as Vergil adapts constantly throughout the *Bucolics* (and *Georgics*).[69]

Vergil's metapoetic allegory is rich and remarkably thorough: the reading I propose here can be pressed for more detail and extended over much of the *Bucolics*, as I hope to demonstrate elsewhere. Suffice it for now to show that Vergil in *B.* 1 is deeply engaged with Gallus' Roman love elegy, which he admires for its beauty but rejects for its hopeless dedication to love – an apt description too of his treatment of Orpheus in *G.* 4, whom many also see as an allegory for Gallus. Vergil clearly rejects the elegiac caricature of hexameter epic as fawning and un-Callimachean panegyric, and he corrects the record both by his choice of Theocritean bucolic and by his development of that genre into a vehicle for tastefully oblique hexameter praise poetry. Throughout his career, Vergil would continue to redeem the other major hexameter subgenres, didactic and epic; his friend Horace would do the same for hexameter satire and epistles, while he also wrote love poetry in iambic and lyric metres as a riposte to elegy's claim on erotic content. Those actions are themselves polemical, and as metapoetic approaches spread to more of Vergil's and Horace's works, I think we will find more metapoetic program pieces like *B.* 1, which shine light both on elegy's massive influence on Augustan poetry and on Vergil's and Horace's playfully polemical resistance.

NOTES

1 See now esp. Heslin 2018 on Propertian polemic aimed specifically at Vergil.
2 See Barchiesi 1997a on Gallan elegiac influence on early Horace: "La questione che riguarda Cornelio Gallo è forse la più importante. Non abbiamo prove di

un'amicizia come quella che lega Gallo a Virgilio; ma quando H. comincia a scrivere poesia gli *Amores* di Gallo sono verosimilmente già in circolazione. Se l'elegia è una presenza attiva già mentre H. si forma come poeta, diventano più comprensibili molte intonazioni degli *Epodi*, di *S* I, e di *C* I–III, tutti testi in cui si possono cogliere toni di competizione e di dialogo programmatico nei confronti della poetica elegiaca … più ancora che verso singoli colleghi" (42).

3 Lyne (1995: 34–6) also argues for a Gallan *recusatio* but sees it intervening between Vergil and Horace. Cameron 1995 argued that Callimachean polemic focused on elegy but was wrongly understood as anti-epic by the Romans; Harder 2012 sees a likely reference to epic (ad *Aet.* fr. 1.3–5).

4 Heslin 2018: 9–14 cautions against reconstructing Gallus based on Propertius and Vergil, since he believes Propertius is reacting against Vergil as much as imitating Gallus. My own attempt, however, is modest and relies less on Propertius than the consensus of all three elegists, to which I refer throughout my argument.

5 On panegyric epic see White 1993: 78–82, Wiseman 1974: 36–8.

6 Ross 1975 influentially argued that Gallus was a generic universalist and that Vergil paid homage to this fact through the cross-generic intertextuality of *B.* 6 and 10, but Zetzel 1977 and others since have found generic universalism more characteristic of Vergil – a view that I share. On Augustan penchant for genre crossing (Kroll's *Kreuzung der Gattungen* [Kroll 1924]), see conveniently Harrison 2007a.

7 *Amor* is famously ambiguous in both the plural (DServ. ad *B.* 8.22; cf. *B.* 10 *passim*) and singular (Harrison 2007a: 65 on personified Love at *B.* 10.28–30).

8 Conte 1986: 100–29.

9 See, e.g., Nappa 2005: 219–32 on the poem's political overtones.

10 See Henkel 2011, 2014a, 2014b. For the bucolic metaphor, see esp. Gutzwiller 1991: 177–8 on Artemidorus *Anth. Pal.* 9.205, prefaced to the edition of Theocritus probably used by Vergil.

11 See esp. Kronenberg 2016 on metapoetic vs. biographical allegory in the *Bucolics*.

12 Gutzwiller 1991: 177; see more broadly 176–9.

13 On Servius cf. Hamblin 1922: 31–41; metapoetic allegories are preserved sometimes by Servius when he rejects them (e.g., ad *B.* 3.70–1) and at other times by the other scholia, which take a more permissive approach to allegory (e.g., Schol. Veron. ad *B.* 3.40).

14 Although Meliboeus' name suggests cowherding (< μέλει αὐτῷ τῶν βοῶν, Serv. *praef.* ad *B.* 1), Vergil associates him specifically with goats in *B.* 1 and 7 (*capellae* 1.12, 74, 77; *caper … et haedi,* 7.9) and specifically disassociates him from sheep in *B.* 3 (*cuium pecus? an Meliboei?* 3.1); Tityrus, by contrast, appears with cows (1.9, 45), goats (3.20, 3.96, 5.12, 9.23), and sheep (6.5).

15 One sees here the effect of Donatus' and Servius' pronouncement about allegory, since the later commentators seem to have found a reference to Cornelius Gallus but reinterpreted it through the lens of the Mantuan land distributions allegory. Jun. Phil. II is garbled but instructive (ad *B.* 1.1): Cornelius Gallus is both a Mantuan who lost his land (i.e., Meliboeus) and – along with Varus and Pollio (i.e., the three external dedicatees in the *Bucolics*) – one of the land commissioners that allowed Vergil to keep his.

16 Du Quesnay detects the possibility of Gallan influence at *B.* 1.1–5, 64–6, and 74 (1981: 40, 47, 50, 78, 82, 86); indeed, 74 is the parade example of a word pattern named after Gallus, the *schema Cornelianum* which appears three times in *B.* 1, only in Meliboeus' speeches; see Solodow 1986 on the history of this figure.

17 See Kronenberg 2016: 27–31 on biographical allegorical readings of the *Bucolics*, and Horsfall 1995: 1–25 for sceptical reappraisal of the biographical tradition itself. Others have sought the significance of Tityrus in etymology or in *Idyll* 7 alone: cf., e.g., Cairns 1999; Van Sickle 2000, 2004.

18 On the symbolism of herd animals in Vergil cf., e.g., Farrell 1997: 231; Lee 1989: 36.

19 See Hubbard 1998: 64 on *B.* 2.36–9 and Ross 1975: 20–38 on *B.* 6.64–75.

20 See n8 above.

21 See James 2003b on tropes of elegy and the material reality behind them. On elegiac influence on the *Bucolics*, see Kenney 1983, Papanghelis 1999, and Fabre-Serris in the present volume.

22 Cf. Lyne 1995: 32.

23 Henkel 2014b: 462–5.

24 Cf. Lyne 1998a, 1998b; cf. Fedeli 2005 ad loc. on *quando*.

25 See Hollis 2007 ad Gall. fr. 145.2–5.

26 I leave aside the impossible problem of dating Gallus' four books relative to the *Bucolics*. It is clear from Vergil's adaptation that at least one book, which contained the motifs Vergil alludes to, was publicly available to the audience of the *B.*

27 Cf. Courtney 1990: 100 on Vergil's pastoralization of Callimachus in *B.* 6 and further Clauss 2004 on his structural imitation of the *Aetia*.

28 See the exchange between Cairns 1999 and Van Sickle 2000, 2004.

29 See Kenney 1983: 50 on the "learned catachresis" of *fagi* for φηγοί and cf. Wright 1983: 129.

30 Bowie 1985; Spanoudakis 2002: 40–1.

31 See Gutzwiller 1996.

32 Ross 1975; Rosen and Farrell 1986; Cairns 2006: 131–43.

33 On elegiac sweetness cf. Harder ad Callim. *Aet* fr. 1.11; pastoral is also programmatically "sweet": see Hunter 1999 ad Theoc. *Id.* 1.1.

34 Unless otherwise indicated, translations are mine.

35 Van Sickle: 2004: 338–41.

36 See esp. Lipka 2001: 30–1, 67, Harrison 2007a: 32.

37 See Watson 1990.

38 Scholars usually gloss *lentus* as "relaxed" or "easy in the shade," an analogy to plants that Fedeli points out is a neoteric modernism (1972: 287); these positive glosses beg the question of Meliboeus' tone, which I argue is derisive.

39 On *inertia* and the *uita umbratilis* in elegy, see McKeown 1987–98 ad Ov. *Am.* 1.9.43, 1.15.1; Fedeli 1985 ad Prop 3.7.72; Maltby 2002 ad Tib. 1.1.5.

40 See Farrell 1997: 231 on the opening of *B.* 3, which thematizes the issue of literary originality in allusive poetry through the alleged theft of Meliboeus' herd *Dic mihi, Damoeta, cuium pecus? an Meliboei? B.* 3.1); cf. too *B.* 9.21–5, where Lycidas admits having plagiarized the song of Menalcas (*sublegi tacitus*, 9.21).

41 See Henkel 2014a, esp. 40–1 on the close of *B.* 10 (10.73–7) and 53–8 on the problem of shade in *G.* 2 arboriculture (*G.* 2.47–72). Clausen 1994: xxv–xxvi notes that it was Vergil, not Theocritus, who made shade such an important feature of the pastoral landscape.

42 On echo, see Breed 2006a: 95–101.

43 See Du Quesnay 1981: 40–4, Wright 1983 on the motif of Octavian as *deus*; Du Quesnay 1981: 102–9 on the sacrifice motif.

44 Cf. Harrison 2007a: 50; Nauta 2006: 307–9; Wright 1983: 116–17.

45 On the poem-as-sacrifice motif later in Horace, cf. Bowditch 2001: 66n3.

46 Philargyrius ad *B.* 1.8: agnus tener *idest carmen tenue*; on *tenuis*, see Harder 2012 ad *Aet.* fr. 1.24. Gallus seems to have figured his poetry as *mollis* (Cairns 2006 index s.v.), which Vergil tropes (often as *tener*) at *B.* 1.8, 21 (see below) and 10.7, 33, 49, 53. On *mollis* and *durus* in elegy, cf. Fedeli 1980 ad Prop. 1.7.19, Fedeli 2005 ad Prop. 2.1.41–2.

47 Cf. Wright 1983: 130–1 on Callimachean envy in *B.* 1, Brink 1982 ad Hor. *Ep.* 2.1.64 on Latin *mirari* as a term for literary approbation.

48 On wonder and the grand style, cf. Henderson 1955 s.v. *mirabilis*.

49 On the symbolism of this passage, see Stephens 2015: 73 and ad loc. On the rhetorical implications of *turbidus*, see Henderson 1955 s.v. and cf. Gowers 2012 ad Hor. *Epist.* 4.11 (*lutulentus*); on its role in Roman Callimacheanism, see Freudenburg 1993: 158–60 with further bibliography at 158n86.

50 See Harder 2012 ad loc.

51 Cf. Call. *Aet.* fr. 1.25–8, *Epigr.* 28. Augustan poets often use *turba* (*scriptorum*) in this dismissive and derogatory sense, cf. Hor. *Sat.* 1.10.67 and McKeown 1987–98 ad Ov. *Am.* 3.1.6; Propertius later uses the image to figure himself as an object of literary imitation (Prop. 3.1.12, 3.1.21, 4.1.136).

52 On metapoetic limping in elegy and choliamb, see Henkel 2014b: 457–62 with further bibliography.

53 See Henkel 2014b: 474–5 esp. on the binding of Silenus at *B.* 6.18–19 and Lycoris's tender feet at *B.* 10.48–9.

54 On panegyric, see above n5; Horace also makes "freedom" a buzzword of his hexameter poetics, focusing on free speech (=Gk. παρρησία): see Gowers 2012 ad *Sat.* 1.4.5.

55 I argue in Henkel 2014a that originality is also a major metapoetic theme in Vergil's treatment of arboriculture at *Geo.* 2.9–82.

56 See Lyne 1979: 121–2, which must descend to special pleading to discount the apparent evidence of Hor. *Epod.* 11, where the influence of Gallus is likely (see, e.g., Barchiesi 1994). Contrast Du Quesnay 1981: 122n545, 1979: 61.

57 Eckerman 2016.

58 *Pace* Conington 1898 ad loc. (= Conington and Nettleship 2007), Du Quesnay 1981: 122, whose objections are met by a metapoetic reading.

59 Few moderns follow my reading here, but note Du Quesnay 1981: 43, 122n547 and Lee 1984: 109 ad 33–4.

60 On Ov. *Am.* 3.1, see Wyke 2002: 115–54. For another symbolic approach to the women of *B.* 1, cf. Davis 2012: 24–6, who connects them to periods of philosophical felicity and vicissitude, respectively, in Tityrus' life.

61 This transactional image does not resemble the "gift economy of patronage" (Bowditch 2001) so much as its travesty in Horace's description of Choerilus and Alexander (*Epist.* 2.1.233–4).

62 On age as metapoetic for genre in elegy, see Henkel 2014b: 472–3 on Tib. 1.1.69–72; cf. Wright 1983: 132 3 on Callimachus in this passage of *B.* 1.

63 See Clausen 1994 ad *B.* 1.43, with further bibliography.

64 Cf. Wright 1983: 137–8.

65 Keith 2020: 67–8 discusses the philosophical valence of the pair *felix/ fortunatus*; on Lucretius as a model in *G.* 2, see Farrell 1991: 187–206.

66 Coleman 1977 ad loc., who must admit, however, "It is of course probable that he will have to sell his animals before he migrates, and then they will not have him as their herdsman; but this is not the point that concerns him now."

67 Most but not all readers identify the speaker of *B.* 10 with Vergil: see, e.g., Breed 2006b: 354–7 and cf. Thomas 1999: 291–2. *Amores* can mean either "love affairs" (*OLD* 2) or "love poetry" (DServ. ad *B.* 8.22; cf. Prop. 2.1.1) and may have been Gallus' title (Cairns 2006: 230–2; but cf. Gauly 1990: 33–40).

68 On Theocritus *Id.* 7, see Hunter 1999 ad 7.135–47, Lawall 1967: 102–6; on *mitis, mollis,* and *pressus,* see Henderson 1955 s.vv.

69 On Vergil's programmatic alignment with Lucretius at the beginning and end of the *Bucolics,* see Breed 2006a: 97–101; Hardie 2006: 276–8; and Lipka 2001: 66–8, which compares the deification theme in *B.* 1 with the deification of Epicurus in the proem to *DRN* 5; Lipka 2001: 65–80 treats Vergil's allusions to Lucretius throughout the *Bucolics.*

2

Generic Polemic in the *Bucolics:* Vergil, Gallus, and *remedia amoris*

JACQUELINE FABRE-SERRIS

During the first century BCE, Rome conquered the most important Hellenistic courts in which literature and science had formerly flourished. As a result, the gradual transfer to Rome of Greek culture contributed to progressive changes in the landscape of philosophy, poetry, rhetoric, science, and medicine,[1] but at the same time led to a general crisis, political, moral, and ideological, affecting the foundations of Roman identity. The set of rules, beliefs, and values, known as *mos maiorum*, is then at the heart of the debate.[2] The deteriorating political situation and the outbreak of civil wars were attributed to the loss of traditional values. Instead of continuing to practise civic virtues, the Romans indulged in individual passions, such as ambition, greed, and sensual gratification (Sall. *Cat.*10–13). It is also at this time that love became the central focus of a large body of literature. The erotic poets, called *neoteroi*, were particularly interested in the power of love (controlled and limited in Roman moral tradition) and its devastating effects on private and public life. In neoteric poetry, the *Amores* of Gallus was a major literary event. Gallus proposed a detailed exploration of love as an extreme and uncontrollable feeling (*furor*) and he made this exploration more impressive by incorporating it in a new literary genre, characterized by some specific metrical and verbal features. Gallus' concept of *furor* was inspired by Lucretius, who had defined *amor* as a horrendous mental construction with destructive effects. The Epicurean philosopher distinguishes *amor* – as a state of mind in which the lover is constantly obsessed by their beloved, even if s/he is absent (*DRN* 4.1061–2) – from *Venus*, defined as the sexual desire focused on an immediate satisfaction (4.1063–72).[3] *Amor* is a disease that must be vigorously fought. The only way to escape from troubles and anxieties is periodically to change objects of desire. Otherwise, *amor* becomes madness (*furor*) for which there is no cure (4.1069–72):[4]

> Inque dies gliscit furor atque aerumna grauescit,
> si non prima nouis conturbes uolnera plagis,
> uolgiuagaque uagus Venere ante recentia cures,
> aut alio possis animi traducere motus.

Day by day the madness is increasing and the troubles are becoming heavier, if you don't confuse the first wounds by new blows and cure them in time while fresh, by wandering, with crowd-wandering Venus, and if you could not direct elsewhere the impulses of your mind.

In this paper I argue that the outstanding success of Gallus' *Amores* is evidenced by the immediate reaction of another new poet, Vergil, driven by his philosophical commitment to condemn and fight the passions. Because he followed the teachings of the Epicurean philosopher Siro at Naples and was a member of Philodemus' circle at Herculaneum, in the *Bucolics* Vergil engages in polemics with Gallus precisely on the issue: "are there remedies for love?" I will focus on *B.* 10, in which Vergil shows that elegiac poetry is unable to provide remedies for amorous suffering, unlike bucolic poetry written in the manner of Theocritus. My second thesis is that the theme of *medicina amoris* becomes a major elegiac motif because of this controversy, and the elegists, anxious to defend Gallus' positions, give various responses to Vergil.

1. Philodemus' *De musica* and Vergil's Conception of Pastoral Poetry

As he was well acquainted with Epicurean circles on the Gulf of Naples, Vergil knew the *De musica* of Philodemus of Gadara.[5] In this treatise, the Epicurean philosopher discusses the thesis of the Stoic philosopher Diogenes of Babylon that music could have beneficial effects on the soul and the passions. The latter, who refused to distinguish music from poetry, cited as an example the Cyclops Polyphemus by referring to a dithyramb of Philoxenus of Cythera (435–380 BCE). In this poem, Philoxenus showed how the unfortunate lover of the nymph Galatea came to be cured by the music of his flute. On the contrary, Philodemus (4.6.13–26) considers that music is not morally useful. He makes a distinction between words and melody. Unlike poetic texts, melody and rhythms are not a matter of *logos*. As, strictly speaking, music is composed of sounds, it affects only the hearing. Vergil's position is in line, but not in complete agreement, with Philodemus' views. According to him, a remedy for love can be found in some poetic texts, but not all. It is necessary to take into account the genre. The genre of Latin love elegy, as invented by Gallus, celebrated the triumph of erotic passion. Vergil advocates for pastoral genre, arguing that some of its motives could have an effect on reason and provide cures for love.[6] Among the pastoral poets, he chooses as his model Theocritus, possibly because of his treatment of the loves of Polyphemus, the singer of Philoxenus' dithyramb. In *Idyll* 11, addressed to his friend, the physician and poet Nicias, Theocritus argued that only poetry (ταὶ Πιερίδες, 3) could provide a remedy (φάρμακον, 1) for love and gave the Cyclops Polyphemus as an example. In Theocritus' poem, the latter laments his unhappy love for Galatea, fails to convince her to share his passion, and finally decides to give her up and find another object of desire. Vergil apparently felt that this decision could illustrate Lucretius' teachings: as we shall see, *B.* 2, openly inspired by Theocritus' *Idyll* 11, is implicitly proposed as a model of curative pastoral poetry to Gallus in *B.* 10.

2. Vergil's Critical Reading of Elegy in *B.* 10

The dialogic context[7] staged by Vergil in *B.* 10 allows him not only to create a confrontation between the pastoral genre and the elegiac genre but also to differentiate his own practice of pastoral poetry from the point of view on the pastoral genre proposed by Gallus in his elegies. I argue that we can indeed conclude from *B.* 10 that Gallus himself had already confronted, in the *Amores*, elegy and pastoral poetry by referring to a Hellenistic poet other than the Sicilian Theocritus. The Peloponnese and Sicily are the two areas mentioned by the mythographers when they are looking for the popular origins of pastoral poetry.[8] As we will see further on, it emerges from *B.* 10 that Gallus preferred the first location and focused on Arcadia, probably in reference to Philetas' pastoral poems, as Bowie suggests.[9]

In the Qaṣr Ibrîm papyrus, Gallus mentions as among his future readers his *domina*, who is presented as the addressee of his poems: ... *tandem fece-runt c(a)rmina Musae / quae possem domina deicere digna mea* ("finally the Muses have made poems that I could say as worthy of my mistress," 6–7).[10] He also mentions two men, Viscus and (Valerius) Cato,[11] suggesting that they could be potentially hostile critics:[12] ... *atur idem tibi, non ego, Visce / ... Kato, iudice te uereor* ("... the same to you, I do not, Viscus, ... I do not, Kato, fear ..., with you as judge," 8–9). Unfortunately, as the text is damaged, we cannot capture the exact relationship between the three characters. But Vergil apparently plays on this situation in *B.* 10 by putting himself, more or less openly, in the position of an arbiter and friend, to urge Gallus to change both lifestyle and poetic genre.

In the first verse of *B.* 10, Vergil asks Arethusa for an *extremus labor*. Arethusa was a nymph born in the Peloponnese but who immigrated to

Sicily by trying to escape Alpheus' love. She was celebrated as the source of pastoral poetry by Hellenistic poets, especially in the *Lament for Bion* (77).[13] Vergil needs Arethusa's assistance to "say a few verses" for Gallus (*pauca meo Gallo … carmina sunt dicenda*), that are "worth reading" by his beloved, Lycoris (*quae legat ipsa Lycoris*, 2). As observed by critics,[14] he probably refers to verses 6–7 of the papyrus of Qaṣr Ibrîm. It follows from *quae legat ipsa Lycoris* that Vergil's gift will be enjoyed by the female addressee of the *Amores* only if his verses are in accordance with those written for her earlier by Gallus. Vergil's project is complex: with the assistance of Arethusa, he wants to sing Gallus' troubled loves (*sollicitos Galli dicamus amores*, 6), while both paying tribute to him as an (elegiac) poet and advising him, inspired by his own pastoral poetry, to help Gallus heal his cruel disease.

As Conte has pointed out,[15] Vergil models Gallus' *sollicitos amores* on Daphnis' sufferings, sung by Theocritus in *Idyll* 1. Like Daphnis, the inventor of the pastoral genre, Gallus, the inventor of the elegiac genre, is described as dying of love in nature and visited by men and gods moved by his unhappy condition. Since Gallus is put into a situation borrowed from Theocritus, this part of *B.* 10 is only relevant if some descriptive and narrative elements refer also to the *Amores*. The modern reader does not know Gallus' poems, but we can compare Theocritus' idyll with Vergil's eclogue. Everything that is not taken from Theocritus could indeed, *de facto*, come from the *Amores*, once a few hints to the *Lament for Bion* and the *Lament for Adonis* are identified.[16] Compared with *Idyll* 1, the Vergilian poem displays two distinctive features. First, Gallus' sufferings come from a different origin than Daphnis' disease. While the pastoral poet is dying because he refuses to yield to love, the elegiac poet is dying because he is overindulging his passion, which is consistent with the elegiac concept of *furor*. Secondly, the two poets are not located in the same area. The fictional author of Theocritus' *Idyll* 1, Thyrsis, wonders where the nymphs were when Daphnis was perishing – in the Valley of Pineus River, or on Pindus (67), i.e., in Greece? One thing is certain: they were neither in the Anapos River, nor on the summit of Mount Etna, nor in the Acis River, i.e., in Sicily (68–9). Further on (117), Thyrsis quotes the name of Arethusa, apparently as a local place that Daphnis will no longer frequent. Then (123–6), Daphnis asks Pan to come "to Sicily," wherever he may be: on Mount Lycaion, on Mount Maenalus, on the summit of Helike, places all located in Arcadia. In *B.* 10, Vergil also asks where the Naiads were when Gallus was dying of love. They were neither on Parnassus (in Thessaly), nor on Pindus (in Epirus), nor near Aganippe (at the base of Mount Helicon, in Boeotia). As for Gallus, he was in Arcadia: while he was lying under an isolated rock, Maenalus and Lycaion shed tears for him (14–15).

Like Daphnis, Gallus is visited by men and deities, but they are not the same as in *Idyll* 1 and their advice is different. The cowherds, shepherds, and goatherds of Theocritus are replaced, in *B.* 10, by a shepherd and his sheep, the swineherds, and Menalcas. The gods Hermes, Priapus, and Kypris are replaced by Apollo, Silvanus, and Pan, *deus Arcadiae … quem uidimus ipsi* ("god of Arcadia … whom I saw myself," 26). Like the expression *memini, quem uidimus* is to be taken as a standard literary motif, i.e., a word intended to signal that the author is referring to another text.[17] *Vidimus* probably alludes to a poem of Gallus, in which Vergil has "seen" the name and description of the god, and confirms that the Arcadian component of the poem comes from the *Amores*.[18] To Pan are given the place of honour and decisive intervention. The god advises Gallus to change his behaviour and set "a limit" to his love and suffering (*Ecquis erit modus?* 28) because "Love, love cares not for such things, Cruel Love isn't sated with tears, or grass with streams, or bees with clover, or nanny-goats with leaves" (*Amor non talia curat, / nec lacrimis crudelis Amor nec gramina riuis / nec cytiso saturantur apes nec fronde capellae*, 28–30).

Vergil then gives voice to his friend. As a result, the speech attributed to Gallus should correspond to some views already expressed in his own verses. In what is probably the first hint about the *Amores*, Gallus speaks to those around him by calling them "Arcadians": *Tamen cantabitis, Arcades, inquit / montibus haec uestris, soli cantare periti / Arcades* ("However you will sing my suffering to your mountains, Arcadians, who alone know how to sing," 31–3). The "death of the poet from his sufferings in love" is a motif common to pastoral poetry and elegy. In the first part of his eclogue, Vergil treated it by adapting Gallus' situation to Theocritus' *Idyll* 1. In this second part, he shows Gallus performing a pastoral modulation of the same motif, but (necessarily) different in that his inspiration must be identified as Arcadian (33–6):

> … O mihi tum quam molliter ossa quiescant,
> uestra meos olim si fistula dicat amores!
> Atque utinam ex uobis unus uestrique fuissem
> aut custos gregis aut maturae uinitor uuae!

Oh! How soft my bones would rest if once your flute said my loves! Ah! If I had been one of you, the guardian of your herd or a picker of your ripe grapes!

Was Gallus' regret about not being an Arcadian also in the *Amores*? It is tempting to assume from the entire passage that "Arcadian" pastoral poetry was a poetic option that Gallus compared to his own choice of elegy (as offering two different ways of being in love) and finally rejected. In the following lines Gallus indeed contrasts the happiness of the shepherds in Arcadia with his own suffering and failure in love. According to him, pastoral loves in Arcadia are interchangeable (if he had been an Arcadian poet, he could have been in love with a girl named Phyllis, or with a boy called Amyntas, or with someone else), and amorous activity endures until the end of life (37–41):

> Certe siue mihi Phyllis siue esset Amyntas,
> seu quicumque furor (quid tum, si fuscus Amyntas?
> et nigrae uiolae sunt et uaccinia nigra),
> mecum inter salices lenta sub uite iaceret:
> serta mihi Phyllis legeret, cantaret Amyntas.
> Hic gelidi fontes, hic mollia prata, Lycori;
> hic nemus; hic ipso tecum consumerer aeuo.

Certainly either Phyllis or Amyntas, or another object of my passion (what does it matter if Amyntas has a dark complexion? black are violets and hyacinths are black) would lie with me, among the willows, under the supple vine. Phyllis would pick garlands for me, Amyntas would sing. Here are fresh springs, here are sweet meadows, Lycoris, here is a wood, here at your side is the very age that would consume me.

In elegiac poetry lovers are separated. Gallus provides his own example: Lycoris followed another man far from Rome, while he himself was involved in a military campaign (44–9):

> Nunc insanus amor duri me Martis in armis
> tela inter media atque aduersos detinet hostis.
> Tu procul a patria (nec sit mihi credere tantum)
> Alpinas, a, dura, niues et frigora Rheni
> me sine sola uides. A! te ne frigora laedant!
> a, tibi ne teneras glacies secet aspera plantas!

But the insane love of harsh Mars holds me back under arms, exposed to the javelins, facing the enemies. You, far from the homeland (I wish I didn't have to believe such news), you see alone and without me, ah! the snows of the Alps and the cold of the Rhine. Ah! May the cold not harm you! Ah! May the roughness of the ice not cut off your delicate feet!

In these two passages Gallus focuses on fidelity and constancy as means of ensuring happiness in love. Fidelity and constancy are secured in Arcadian pastoral community but changing and uncertain between elegiac lovers. As a result of this comparison that is unfavourable for elegiac poetry, Vergil attributes to his friend the decision to change literary genre. Gallus claims that he now wants to experiment with pastoral genre by taking Theocritus' pipes (50–1): *Ibo et Chalcidico quae sunt mihi condita uersu / carmina pastoris Siculi modulabor auena* ("I will go and the poems I have composed using Chalcidian verse, I will modulate them on the Sicilian shepherd's pipe"). Since Gallus specifies that he will transpose into the pastoral genre his own verses, which were previously composed using the Hellenistic poet Euphorion of Calchis as a model,[19] the reader should expect a mixture of elegiac poetry and pastoral poetry. However, why use Theocritus as a model and choose "Sicilian" pastoral poetry (following Vergil's example) instead of the Arcadian one? The reader understands only at the very moment Gallus acknowledges his failure that he was looking for cures to his passion (60–1): *tamquam haec sit nostri medicina furoris, / aut deus ille malis hominum mitescere discat!* ("As if this were a remedy for my love, or as if this god could learn to become mild towards the misfortunes of men!"). The search for remedies is explained by the intensity of his disease: Gallus was dying of love. At this point in his suffering, he considers practising in the pastoral genre to be preferable to elegiac poetry, no longer by taking fidelity as a parameter, but because of pastoral poetry's stronger capacity to provide remedies for love. In my opinion, the belief attributed to Gallus that Theocritus' pastoral poetry has this healing capacity must be related to Vergil's reading of *Idyll* 11, which he took as a model in *B.* 2. As Gallus cannot totally give up the generic elegiac code, what remains of his prior elegiac inspiration in this new pseudo-Theocritean *carmen*? After disguising Gallus as Daphnis, Vergil portrays him imitating "for real" (and not metaphorically) Acontius and Milanion, whose examples, as far as we know, were used in the *Amores* to illustrate the effectiveness of the *seruitium amoris* in seducing a *dura puella*.[20] Once in the middle of the forest (after leaving the city, the elegiac space par excellence), Gallus tries to adapt different skills previously used in his *seruitium amoris* (to conquer or regain Lycoris) in order to achieve a *renuntiatio amoris*. Without going into the details of how Vergil uses and adapts the Gallan version of Acontius' and Milanion's stories,[21] I will just note that Gallus fails in his attempt to find cures for love. For his part, Vergil had already experimented successfully with the remedy suggested to Gallus in *B.* 2 where Theocritus' *Idyll* 1 is his model. There he presented a shepherd, Corydon, who goes into the forests to give free expression to his vain passion for the beautiful Alexis, and, like the Cyclops Polyphemus, at the end decides not to worry about his beloved since he despises him. Why does Gallus fail where Corydon succeeds? Is it because an elegiac poet cannot become a pure pastoral poet? This is what Vergil sought to show.

However, why and how could pastoral poetry written in the manner of Theocritus provide remedies for love? In fact, the answer given to these questions is not exactly the same in *Idyll* 11 and in *B*. 2, although Vergil took Theocritus as a model. Theocritus explains that the Cyclops "found the remedy" (τὸ φάρμακον εὗρε, 17) "by nourishing his love through singing" (Οὕτω τοι Πολύφαμος ἐποίμαινεν τὸν ἔρωτα / μουσίσδων, 80–1). The verb ἐποίμαινεν assimilates Polyphemus' poetic activity to his main task as a shepherd. Just as he feeds his flock, so too does the Cyclops nourish his love with songs until, if we pursue the metaphor, it is satisfied. At this time, acknowledging his madness, Polyphemus decides to return to "pastoral" tasks he had neglected, in the proper sense of the word, such as weaving baskets or picking up young branches for the lambs. Again using a pastoral metaphor ("milk [ἄμελγε] the one to hand, why pursue the one who flees?" 75), the Cyclops adds that he will find another Galatea, perhaps more beautiful (76). Before attributing to Corydon the same kind of decision, as noted by Servius (ad *B*. 2.63), Vergil inserts a passage taken from another *Idyll* (*B*. 2.63–5): *Torua leaena lupum sequitur, lupus ipse capellam; / florentem cytisum sequitur lasciua capella, / te, Corydon, o Alexi: trahit sua quemque uoluptas* ("The fierce lioness follows the wolf; the wolf the goat; the lascivious goat is looking for the laburnum in bloom, and Corydon for you, Alexis: each one, it is his own pleasure that drives them"). In *Idyll* 10, Theocritus wrote (30–3): Ἀ αἶξ τὰν κύτισον, ὁ λύκος τὰν αἶγα διώκει, / ἁ γέρανος τὤροτρον· ἐγὼ δ' ἐπὶ τὶν μεμάνημαι ("the goat is looking for the laburnum; the wolf for the goat; the crane follows the plough; I am crazy about you"). Vergil drops the example of the crane, which introduces a break in the series of desires (where every time the word put in the complement position is the subject of the following proposition) and replaces it with the lioness driven, like Corydon, by sexual desire. According to Pliny the Elder,[22] the lioness is indeed looking toward males of another species than her own. In Theocritus' *Idyll* the search for food is presented as an equivalent for sexual desire. Vergil frames two cases of search for food by two cases of sexual desire and concludes with a sentence inspired again by Lucretius. *Trahit sua quemque uoluptas* is a variation on *quo ducit quemque uoluptas* ("where pleasure leads everyone," *DRN* 2.258).[23] He thus makes the search for "pleasure," whether it is to satisfy nutritional or sexual needs, a general law of nature in accordance with Epicurean doctrine.

After this observation, another law of nature: the return of evening pushes Corydon to take the same salutary decision as the Cyclops. The shepherd urges himself to watch the return of oxen from the ploughing (which signals the end of field work) when the sun declines, and, noting that his passion continues to burn him, he wonders what "limit" there might be to his love (*B*. 2.68): *me tamen urit amor; quis enim modus adsit amori?* The question:

quis enim adsit modus amori? may be seen as a variation on a verse of Meleager (*Anth. Pal.* 12.117) which was part of his famous *Garland*, known in
Rome at the beginning of the first century BCE: Τί δ' ἔρωτι λογισμός; ("Is
there anything in love that obeys reasoning?").[24] Vergil has substituted for
the notion of reasoning that of *modus*, i.e., of limit, which has a Lucretian
"resonance."[25] The word used by Lucretius to express the concept of limit
is *finis*.[26] Why did Vergil prefer the word *modus*? I argue that this choice
can be explained because *modus* is particularly appropriate to the context.
Modus designates measure both in the musical sense, the mode, and in the
philosophical sense, the right limit. In *B.* 10, the words attributed to the god
of Arcadia, Pan (*ecquis erit modus?* 28), are precisely alluding to this passage
in *B.* 2. Here Corydon wonders if there is a limit to love, which is associated with madness (*dementia*, 69), since the approach of evening imposes a
natural limit on the work of the fields, but not on his burning passion. In *B.*
2, the first way to put a limit on Corydon's love is to return to the pastoral
tasks that have been left aside. Vergil gives as a reason *usus* ("need"). For
having been abandoned for too long, some tasks are now urgent (69–72):

> A! Corydon, Corydon, quae te dementia cepit?
> Semiputata tibi frondosa uitis in ulmo est.
> Quin tu aliquid saltem potius, quorum indiget usus,
> uiminibus mollique paras detexere iunco?

Ah! Corydon, Corydon, what madness did you get? Half-pruned vines await you on
elms thick with leaves. Why not rather resolve to weave from osier twigs and soft
rush something at least your need requires?

The shepherds are supposed to alternate pastoral tasks and rustic songs. The
notion of *usus* employed to justify the return to pastoral activities will reappear, under the variant *urgens egestas*, in Vergil's thoughts on agriculture in
the *Georgics*. After indicating that Jupiter made it difficult to cultivate fields
(1.121–2): *Pater ipse colendi / haud facile esse uiam uoluit*, Vergil comments
on the invention of the *uariae artes* (145–6): *labor <u>omnia uicit</u> / improbus, et
duris urgens in rebus egestas* ("Unrelenting work without respite triumphed
over everything and poverty, oppressing in harsh situations"). This variation on the famous Gallan expression *uicit/uincit amor*, already used in *B.*
10.69 (*omnia uincit amor*), is one of the signs that Vergil has continued to
debate with the elegiac poet on human life and its values. In the *Georgics*,
labor is not only the most important value in farmers' lives but also what
defines the human condition. To return to *B.* 2, like Polyphemus, Corydon
decides to stop singing and chasing the one who flees from him: he is confident that he will find someone else to love (73): *Inuenies alium, si te hic*

fastidit, Alexim. Since Vergil read Theocritus in the light of Lucretius, he saw this decision, borrowed from Theocritus, as illustrating a behaviour actually putting into practice Lucretius' advice to avoid the sufferings of love by regularly changing objects of desire. In Vergil's view, Gallus as a eulogist of a singular (elegiac) love could only fail to find a cure for his sufferings. How did the elegists respond to this portrait of elegiac lover?

3. Some Examples of Elegiac Answers to Vergil

As demonstrated by Tränkle,[27] the *medicina amoris* metaphor, used, for example, in *B.* 10.60 (*tamquam haec sit nostri medicina furoris!*), when the elegiac poet admits his failure, originates with Gallus. If we refer to Horace's *Epode* 11, a poem inspired by and referring to Gallus' elegies, where, on the advice of a friend of his, a lover tries (in vain) to renounce his unhappy *furor* (19–22), it seems likely that the double motif of the attempt (on the suggestion of friends) and the failure of a *renuntiatio amoris* also existed in the *Amores*.[28] I argue, however, that, if the inability to find any remedies for love becomes a major elegiac motif, it is because the elegists have sought to defend Gallus against Vergil's critics. It would take too long to establish this thesis exhaustively. So I will give just a few examples, starting with elegy 2.3 of Tibullus.[29]

Elegy 2.3 may be considered as an answer to *B.* 10. Faced with the same situation as Gallus (his beloved, Nemesis, has left him for another man, and she is now far from Rome, in the countryside), Tibullus claims that he is ready to work in the fields, referring, as an example, to the *seruitium amoris* of Apollo, who made himself the cowherd of his beloved, Admetus. Tibullus underscores his willingness to support *seruitium amoris*, as a technique promoted by Gallus in a love affair, against Vergil's critical reading by referring to *B.* 10. *Pauit et Admeti tauros formosus Apollo* ("Beautiful Apollo also grazed Admetus bulls," 11) is a variation on *et formosus ouis ad flumina pauit Adonis* ("Beautiful Adonis grazed his sheep by the rivers," 18) in *B.* 10. How does Tibullus defend Gallus? Of course, he does not adopt Vergil's point of view. He immediately emphasizes that the *seruitium amoris* cannot help one to recover from love, by using the Gallan *iunctura "uicit amor"* (13–14): *nec potuit curas sanare salubribus herbis: / quidquid erat medicae uicerat artis amor* ("he could not heal his torments by using salutary herbs / Love had triumphed over all resources of the medical art"). Then Tibullus describes at length Apollo's love sufferings and their degrading effects on his body and behaviour. But he also proclaims that Apollo was right to submit to love slavery because it is better to be mocked than to be (even) a god who would not know love (31–2): *Fabula nunc ille est, sed cui sua cura puella est, / fabula sit mauult quam sine amore deus* ("he makes others laugh at him now, but the one who has his mistress in his heart prefers that the others laugh at him than be a god (who would be) without love"). In *B.* 2, Vergil had promoted pastoral tasks as a good way to set a limit to love. Tibullus reports that during his *seruitium amoris* Apollo invented two techniques to make cheese: he added a coagulating agent to fresh milk to curdle it and turn it into cheese, and wove from rushes a small basket which moulded the cheese and allowed the whey to drain off (14–16). By describing Apollo both as an unhappy lover and the first inventor of a pastoral *ars*, Tibullus provides an ironic twofold answer to Vergil. Contrary to Vergil's belief, engaging in useful pastoral tasks does not have any curative effect on love. Nevertheless, love sufferings do not prevent Apollo from inventing *artes* similar to those for which Vergil praises the gods in the *Georgics*. According to Vergil, by revealing *artes* to the first farmers, as did Ceres, for example, by teaching mortals to turn the earth with iron (*Prima Ceres ferro mortalis uertere terram / instituit …*, 1.147–8), the gods have highly improved humanity's harsh way of life. But, as Tibullus points out, that's also what Apollo did for the shepherds and herdsmen during his *seruitium amoris*.[30]

In the *Monobiblos*, Propertius affirms his originality by hardening the elegiac code invented by Gallus. In the first elegy he proclaims that, unlike Milanion, whose *seruitium amoris* was successful (9–16),[31] for him Love is so slow that he "is planning no stratagems, and remembers not to tread, as formerly, his well-known paths" (*In me tardus Amor non ullas cogitat artes / nec meminit notas, ut prius, ire uias*, 17–18). In vain his friends are looking for cures to heal him (25–6): *aut uos, qui sero lapsum reuocatis, amici, / quaerite non sani pectoris auxilia* ("else you, my friends, who too late call back the fallen, seek medicines for a heart that is sick").[32] In elegy 1.5, Propertius argues that, if Gallus would like to experience his own *furores* (3), he will be forced to learn the *graue seruitium* (19) imposed by Cynthia. Propertius adds that he will be unable to relieve Gallus' pains because there is no remedy for his own sufferings (*cum mihi nulla mei sit medicina mali*, 28). However, in elegy 1.10, also addressed to Gallus, Propertius adopts a different position. He presents himself as a *praeceptor amoris*, and claims that, even if he is unable to cure himself, his love experience may be helpful for others (15–18):

> Possum ego diuersos iterum coniungere amantes,
>   et dominae tardas possum aperire fores;
> et possum alterius curas sanare recentis,
>   nec leuis in uerbis est medicina meis.

I can unite separated lovers again; I can open a mistress's reluctant door; I can cure another's recent love cares and the healing power of my words is not slight.

In lines 15–16, Propertius seems to allude to the situation that in *B*. 10 causes Gallus' sufferings and is leading him to death (the elegiac poet and his mistress are separated and she does not want to renew relations with him). Propertius' claim that he can reunite separated lovers is a way of responding both to Gallus and to Vergil. In lines 17–18, he uses Gallan words such as *medicina* and *cura* to assert that he is able to cure loving suffering of others. In so doing he challenges the admission of erotic failure attributed by Vergil to Gallus in *B*. 10.60 (*tamquam haec sit nostri medicina furoris*) with the peculiarity that Propertius' ability to heal does not concern his own case. At the same time, with the expression *curas sanare recentis*, Propertius responds to Lucretius' advice about the only way to cure love's suffering (4.1070–1): *si non prima nouis conturbes uolnera plagis / uolgiuagaque uagus Venere ante <u>recentia cures</u>*. According to Propertius, there are indeed some means to avoid being unhappy in love. His advice is all about the strategic use of words in *seruitium amoris*. Propertius explains that Gallus has to avoid both *superba uerba* and long periods of silence (22), and that he must be careful not to hurt his beloved's pride (23–6) by refusing what she asks for. He presents this *ars amandi* as the result of Cynthia's teaching by using the Lucretian verb *docuit* (*Cynthia me docuit*, "Cynthia has taught me," 19). This position as a lover capable of helping other lovers is very representative of how the elegists explain why they are right to write elegiac poetry instead of bucolic, epic, or satiric poetry. What fundamentally justifies the elegiac genre is the conviction that love is the most shared human experience. Even those who believe that they will always escape from passion, like, for example, Bassus in elegy 1.7, will once be struck by love, and they will need to read elegiac poetry (13–14): *me legat assidue post haec neglectus amator, / et prosint illi cognita nostra mala* ("hereafter let the disdained lover read me avidly and let it profit him to learn of my torments").

The *praeceptor amoris* par excellence is Ovid, who, in the *Ars Amatoria*, putting forward his personal experience (*usus*, 1.29), claims that he has become the master of Cupid (1.17, 21–2): *Aeacidae Chiron, ego sum praeceptor Amoris* ... / *et mihi cedit Amor, quamuis mea uulneret arcu / pectora iactatas excutiatque faces* ("Chiron was the master of Aeacus' grandson, I am the master of love ... Love gives into me, though he had wounded my chest with his arrows and wielded his torches"). Ovid here uses a Gallan *iunctura*: *Amor* and the verb *cedere*, judging from the variations on this phrase in Tibullus (1.4.40), Propertius (1.5.24; 9.28; 14.8), and Ovid himself (*Am*. 3.11a.2; *Rem. Am*. 144, 752; *Her*. 19.172).[33] In so doing Ovid also reverses the admission of failure attributed by Vergil to Gallus in *B*. 10.69 (*Omnia uincit Amor et nos cedamus amori*, "Love triumphs over everything and we too, let us give in to love"), especially since he announces that he will avenge the wounds inflicted on him by love (*facti uulneris ultor ero*, 24). The project of overcoming love becomes more explicit at the beginning of the *Remedia amoris*, whose title is judged by Love as a declaration of war (1–2). Vergil had tried to show that the *renuntiatio amoris* was totally impossible in elegiac poetry. The answer of the last elegist is to write a book for lovers subjected to a mistress unworthy of their love, in which he will teach us how to stop loving in order to prevent anyone from dying of love (*Rem. Am.* 21–2): *Qui, nisi desierit, misero periturus amore est / desinat, et nulli funeris auctor eris* ("If someone is about to die of an unhappy love, unless he put an end to it, may he put an end to it and you will not be the author of any death"). It appears from his ingenious list of remedies that Ovid gives lessons to everyone: Lucretius, Vergil, Gallus, and the other elegists, while completing the triumph of elegy over all poetic genres aimed at preventing or curing the effects of passion.

Conclusion

Without expanding any further on elegiac responses to Vergil's critics, I will end with another example of Vergil's reception: the *Arcadia* of Sannazaro, published in 1504. In this poem, which immediately achieved huge success in Europe, the Neapolitan poet Jacopo Sannazaro freely reworks, with great skill, Roman pastoral texts, especially those written by Vergil. Since, in his time, Vergilian polemic against Gallus was no longer perceived, he reuses some elegiac motifs and expressions referring to the *Amores* to describe the love sufferings of his shepherds, who are obviously modelled on the pastoral characters of the *Bucolics*. The phrase *medicina amoris*, for example, is attributed to a shepherd who sees a beautiful oak tree, "under which, I remember, I once was resting on her chest" (*ove altra volta mi ricordai essermi nel seno di lei riposato, Prosa VIII*). The shepherd sits at the foot of this tree "no more and no less than if it [i.e., the tree] had been a cure for my passion" (*né più né meno come se questa stata fusse medicina del moi furore*) and starts to lament his fate. Gallus himself is reduced to a fictional character, cited together with mythological characters Daphnis and Silenus (*Prosa X*): *aggiungendo a questo la morte di Dafni, la canzone di Sileno e'l fiero amore di Gallo, con altre cose di che le selve, credo, ancora si ricordino e ricorderanno mentre nel mondo saranno pastori* ("adding the death of Daphnis, the song of Silenus and the fierce love of Gallus, along with the other things that the forests, I believe, still remember and will remember as long as there are shepherds"). Thanks to Sannazaro, in a reversal of roles that would have been a great surprise to the poet of the *Bucolics*, for centuries Vergil was praised and imitated as the inventor of the Arcadia as a symbolic place where poets suffer and die of love.

NOTES

1 See Hawkins 2017.

2 Moatti 1997.

3 Traina 1965: 74.

4 I cite the text of Lucretius from Ernout (Les Belles Lettres, Paris, 1966). All translations are mine.

5 See Du Quesnay 1979, 51; Angeli and Rispoli 1996; Delattre 2001 and 2004; Capron and Delattre 2007.

6 Fabre-Serris 2008: 57–8. For a different view on the Epicurean remedy for love sketched in *B.* 2, 6, 8 and 10, see Davis 2012: 99–161.

7 On this linguistic concept ("l'énonciation"), see Ducrot and Todorov 1972, who made the distinction between "le locuteur," the speaker and "l'allocutaire," the addressee. The speaker can be the author or a secondary character, staged by the author.

8 "The bucolics, it is said, were invented in Lacedaemon and developed remarkably … others say that it was in Tyndaris, Sicily, that the bucolics first appeared" (Wendel 1966: 2–3).

9 Bowie 1985: 82–3; Fabre-Serris 2008: 85–6.

10 I understand *carmina … deicere … digna …* in the sense of "saying verses that are worthy" of my mistress, by referring to *B.* 10.2, where Vergil, with the help of Arethusa (like Gallus thanks to the Muses), will "say a few verses such that Lycoris can read them."

11 The *Visci* are mentioned as literary critics by Horace at *Serm.* 1.10.84. He cites the Visci, with Varius, in *Serm.* 1.9.22–3; 1.10.81–4; 2.8.20–1. Kato is probably the poet and critic P. Valerius Cato, who had a great influence on young poets.

12 Anderson, Parsons, and Nisbet 1979: 140.

13 Kennedy 1987: 48.

14 See in particular Hinds 1983; Kennedy 1987: 49.

15 Conte 1984: 18–21.

16 Gagliardi 2014.

17 Cairns 2006: 117 ("the claim to have 'seen' or witnessed someone or something is made sufficiently frequently in Augustan poetry for it to be considered a standard motif"); Fabre-Serris 2018: 39. On the "Alexandrian footnote," see Hinds 1998: 1–5.

18 See Fabre-Serris 2008: 67–8, on the importance of Arcadia, also evoked by Lycoris' name, which echoes the place names and surnames formed on the *lyk*-root, so common in this country. On Gallus and Arcadia, see Kennedy 1987: 56.

19 Propertius' couplet devoted to Gallus in 2.34.91–2 – *et modo formosa quam multa Lycoride Gallus / mortuus inferna uulnera lauit aqua* ("And how many wounds has Gallus, dead for love of beautiful Lycoris, bathed in the water of

the underworld!") – probably refers, as pointed out by critics, to Euphorion's *Hyacinthus* (fr. 43 P): Κώκυτος ‹τοι› μοῦνος ἀφ' ἔλκεα νίψεν Ἄδωνιν ("Only the Cocytus bathed Adonis' wounds"). See Knox (1986: 15–16) on Gallus' use of this Euphorion passage to describe in a metaphorical sense his own death as a result from the incurable wounds inflicted by love. Perhaps Vergil had this passage in mind?

20 Gallus probably presented Acontius' gesture of inserting words on the bark of trees and Milanion's participation in the hunting of Atalanta as two equivalents (in terms of *seruitium amoris*) of writing elegiac poems for the elegiac poet in love with a *dura puella* (Fabre-Serris 2008: 73–4).

21 Conte 1984; Rosen and Farrell 1986; Fabre-Serris 2008: 73–6.

22 According to *Nat.* 8.17, the sexual passions of lions are very violent and females mate with other species, especially with leopards.

23 Fabre-Serris 2008: 53–5; Davis 2012: 108–10.

24 Fabre-Serris 2008: 61n25. On the possible influence of Theocritus 30.12, see Du Quesnay 1979: 58.

25 See also Davis 2012: 99–150, 153.

26 See, for example, *DRN* 5.1432–3: ... *non cognouit quae sit habendi / finis et omnino crescat uera uoluptas* ("[men] ... do not know any limit to possession nor how far true pleasure grows").

27 Tränkle 1960.

28 See Fabre-Serris 2010 and Hardie 2017: 67, who argues that Horace's convivial eleventh *Epode* offers close parallels to the situation in Propertius' 1.1, "perhaps the product of a common model in Gallus: the poet-lover recalls drunken indiscretions about 'Inachia' at an earlier *conuiuium* (with his host Pettius' admonitions), then expatiates to the present company about a new boy-friend, but discounts the remedial efficacy of advice from *amici*."

29 On Tib. 2.3, see also Gardner in this volume.

30 On the use of pastoral settings for elegiac love and *seruitium amoris* in Tibullus, see Fabre-Serris 2005.

31 On Propertius' use of the myth of Milanion, see Hardie 2017: 68–70.

32 About the fact that Propertius moves on to his *amici* and *remedia amoris*, see Hardie 2017: 70.

33 Cairns 2006: 107–8.

3

Elegiac Revaluations of the Golden Age: Saturn's Exile in Vergil and Tibullus

HUNTER H. GARDNER

Vergil's use of golden-age imagery has received a good deal of scholarly attention, especially with reference to the implications of that imagery for a new Augustan order.[1] Elegiac articulations of a Golden Age presided over by Saturn, especially pronounced in Tibullus' poetry, have earned relatively little comment, though Johnston (1980), Newman (1998), and Evans (2008) have made important contributions to the topic. This neglect is perhaps consistent with assumptions concerning the illicit liaisons championed in erotic elegy: as generated from the perspective of a discontented *amator*, elegiac discourse strikes a discordant note with the moral imperatives of Augustus' Golden Age. Ovid's *Amores* acknowledge a former Saturnian age lacking the wealth that drives Rome's sexual economy – an economy that has excluded the poet-lover (*Am.* 3.8.35–44). His *Ars* ironically reduces the returned Golden Age to a reflection of Rome's materialistic impulses (*Ars* 2.277–8). The Propertian *amator* of 2.31–2 pays lip service to the chastity that defined the Princeps' vision of a Saturnian Golden Age (51–2), though the same poem pleads excuses for Cynthia, arguing that such an age is long gone: since Deucalion's flood, chastity is no longer the law of the land.

While elegiac values may prove inconsistent with an Augustan *aurea aetas*, what we have come to recognize as the imagery of that age – the Vergilian-inspired decorative program on the *Ara Pacis* or the prosperity and *pudor* championed in Horace's *Carmen Saeculare* – was the result of a sustained process of negotiation, appropriation, and rejection of cultural currency inherited from the Greco-Roman literary tradition. The present essay demonstrates that elegy, Tibullan elegy in particular, played a significant, if gradually marginalized, role in that process. The Tibullan *amator's* vision of the Golden Age is defined by sexual freedom and lawlessness, conditions granting him unlimited access to his beloved (1.3.43; cf. 2.3.71–8). As Andrew Wallace-Hadrill's work on golden-age imagery of the late Republic and early Principate has demonstrated, an ideal of sexual licence runs counter to contemporary discourses that suggested a Golden Age would only be restored through the "return" of a figure of moral authority, one who would help restrain *scelus* in general and sexual immorality in particular.[2] Tibullus will acquiesce in identifying chastity and marital fidelity as essential to social harmony, though to do so he must implicitly devalue the Golden Age, as he does in poem 2.5: there he celebrates Messallinus' maturity and priesthood, and indicates his own generic evolution beyond the clutches of Nemesis (113–18), evolution that will allow him to sing of loftier themes, such as Messallinus' anticipated triumphs. This turn from idealizing elegiac lawlessness to promotion of imperial expansion mirrors a gradual progression in Italy from a Saturnian Age to an Iron Age governed by Jupiter (*Saturno rege fugato*, 9).

Such linear progress in Tibullan elegy challenges the promotion of some features of a "return" (of both the ruler and the *aurea aetas* over which he presides); it is also a progress whose implications we can better grasp by observing those points where Tibullus' account of Saturn's reign and exile intersects with or diverges from the trajectory of the god's power mapped in Vergil's oeuvre. The present essay initially tracks the evolution of Vergil's *Saturnia regna* as they are prophesied in the fourth eclogue, problematically contextualized in the Italy of *G*. 2, and anticipated in the *Aeneid*'s reflections on a former Saturnian age (7.203–4; 8.319–27) and predictions of Augustus as a second Saturn (6.791–5). I then turn to Tibullus' evocations of Saturn's Golden Age in elegies 1.3, 2.3, and finally 2.5: here we observe the elegist divest Saturn of his authority over sexual conduct, and in the process we view more clearly the "incoherences" (cf. Wallace-Hadrill 1982: 24) that characterize Saturn in Vergil's oeuvre. The elegist's announcement of the god's banishment in poem 2.5 recalls Vergil's use of similar phrasing in *Aeneid* 8 (319–24; cf. 6.792–4),[3] and then expands on the satisfactions of Jupiter's reign, in the process signalling resistance to the notion of the return of a golden-age utopia in the context of Imperial Rome.

To allow for the return of a Golden Age, Vergil had gradually situated Saturn in an agricultural milieu (*G*. 2.532–40), relying on a mythology that imbued the god, whose name, as attested in Varro, Macrobius, and others, implies "sowing" crops (from *sero*), with connotations of productive fields.[4] At the same time, his attempts to divorce agriculture and its characteristic implements, such as Saturn's *falx*, from their connotations of iron-age greed, acquisitiveness, and military conquest are not entirely successful. For Tibullus, Saturn's reign and the agricultural life remain consistently at odds. All the *amator*'s references to the god and the Golden Age (1.3, 2.3, 2.5) stress the impossibility of agriculture under Saturn's reign: as the opening of poem 2.5 suggests, the rustic harmony achieved in the Parilia, the annual celebration of Rome's birthday, occurs in a Jovian setting. I argue that Tibullus' pre-agricultural, irretrievably lost Saturn dialogically responds to Vergil's portrait of the god as it evolved from bucolic verse to heroic epic: the elegist's contestation of Saturn's value, in the context of a revival of golden-age imagery and its incipient moral agenda in the Principate, exposes ideological inconsistencies that mark the god's transformation in Vergil's work. Moreover, by denying the relevance of *Saturnia regna* for the Augustan program, the Tibullan *amator* reserves the Golden Age and its prehistoric temporality for fantasies of static, erotic contentment.

1. Vergil's Saturnian Kingdoms

The Golden Age of Vergil most familiar to readers is perhaps that predicted in the fourth eclogue. References to the god's rule in the bucolic poems relegate Saturn and Jupiter to their own ages and insist on the absence of agricultural *labor* from the imminent *Saturnia regna* (4.4–7):

> ultima Cumaei uenit iam carminis aetas;
> magnus ab integro saeclorum nascitur ordo.
> iam redit et Virgo, redeunt Saturnia regna,
> iam noua progenies caelo demittitur alto.

Now the final age of Cumaean song has come; the great succession of the ages is born anew. Now the Maiden (Astraea) returns, the Saturnian kingdoms return. Now a new lineage is sent down from high heaven.[5]

This age is one in which *tellus* pours forth her gifts *nullo cultu* ("with no cultivation," 9); goats bring home full udders and have no need to fear the lions (21–2). Eventually – after a bit of backsliding, when *uestigia* of a former age have tested the virtue of the poem's *puer* – the full flowering of the Golden Age will render agriculture and its implements obsolete (4.37–41):

> hinc, ubi iam firmata uirum te fecerit aetas,
> cedet et ipse mari uector nec nautica pinus
> mutabit merces; omnis feret omnia tellus.
> non rastros patietur humus, non uinea falcem,
> robustus quoque iam tauris iuga soluet arator.

From here, when your age now strengthened will have made you a man, the trader himself will yield to the sea, the ship of pine will not exchange goods; all the earth will bear all things. The soil will not suffer the hoe, the vine will not suffer the reaping hook, now also the sturdy farmer will free his oxen from the yoke.

In particular, there will be no need for hoe or pruning hook, the *falx* associated with Saturn later in Vergil's poetry, an association that (as we shall see) will endow the golden-age deity with agricultural expertise, an *ars* problematically linked to an Iron Age in which humans must conquer the fields and each other in constant strife.

As Coleman observes (1977: 132), Vergil's allowance for the return of the former age, revising the process of decline that governed the metallic myth of the ages, is apparently unprecedented.[6] Jupiter's rule in the fourth eclogue precedes that of Saturn, and the child who ushers in the age is referred to as Jupiter's offspring (*magnum Iouis incrementum*, 49). The poet here contradicts the order of succession alluded to in *Bucolics* 6.41–2, where *Saturnia regna* occur before Prometheus' quarrel with Jupiter over the theft of fire, a poem which also evokes the strife between father and son through reference to *Dictaeae nymphae* (55–6), the nymphs who hid Jupiter in a Cretan cave before he overthrew his father. In both eclogues, however, *Saturnia regna* are (loosely) preceded by a sturdier race and succeeded by a morally dubious one,[7] charting a temporal flexibility that – despite the exuberant proclamation of an *ultima aetas* – permits the return of a degenerate age as well as that of one whose virtues are rewarded with easy living.[8]

Once Vergil enters the agriculturally oriented world of the *Georgics*, however, he refines his portrait of Saturn and the age he governs so that they conjure a generally prosperous time, in which *labor* has some role, but also signal the containment of conflict. As Evans notes in her analysis of ancient concepts of utopia, the Golden Age in many of its articulations shares with modern notions of utopia a characteristic absence of strife.[9] Hesiod, whose *Works and Days* clearly informed the composition of Vergil's *Georgics*,[10] explicitly distinguishes types of strife (*Op.* 11–26), one destructive and linked to war and battle (πόλεμόν … καὶ δῆριν, 14), the other a more productive variety, a rivalry that compels men to toil (ἔργον, 20) and drives even the rich man to take up the plough (20–4). For the *Georgic* poet, the duality of Hesiod's strife is mirrored through the potential of *labor* to generate and require human *artes*, tools both productive and destructive (cf. *G*.1.143–6). Such mirroring, however, is also the result of a conspicuous distortion: as Gale has stressed, Vergil's famous designation of *labor* as *improbus* collapses Hesiod's distinction and leaves readers to ponder "simply *labor*, with all the ambivalence the word entails."[11]

Despite the poet's best efforts, even the fruitful arts born from *labor*, which keep the farmer from viewing his neighbour's heap with jealousy while scavenging for acorns (*G.* 1.155–9), are not easily contained within a vision of the Golden Age: Vergil's agricultural project is frequently assimilated to the project of war, as humans threaten to convert their struggles against the soil into strife against each other. Still, Saturn's long history with sowing crops and agricultural productivity should allow his farming persona to emerge somewhat organically in the poem. Patricia Johnston has assembled much of the evidence for Saturn's links to farming, including the belief recorded by Varro that farmers were the descendants of the god (*R.R.* 3.1.5).[12] The Greek poet Aratus, moreover, had suggested that farming might be accommodated in the Golden Age, though the age he describes is not ruled by Saturn and explicitly denies the presence of strife (*Phaen.* 108).[13]

Saturn's most prominent role in the *Georgics* is scripted in Book 2, in which the poet celebrates *Italia* as a Saturnian land. Its chief crops are not only the kind intended for eating: there is also the martial variety, intended for fighting. In light of Vergil's bucolic pronouncements of a Golden Age that lacks both military and agricultural *labor*, the collocation of Rome's martial accolades (2.145–8) with golden-age eternal spring and neutralization of hostilities between species (149–56) is striking. It is, moreover, the military virtue of Vergil's *Saturnia tellus* that crowns the encomium, in contrast to cowardice ascribed to its "unwarlike" enemies (2.172). After noting the many warriors Italy has produced – the Marsians, Sabines, Marii, Camilii, and Scipios (2.167–70) –Vergil praises Italy in language that conflates such heroes, including Caesar himself, with agricultural productivity (2.170–6):

> ... et te, maxime Caesar,
> qui nunc extremis Asiae iam uictor in oris
> imbellem auertis Romanis arcibus Indum.
> salue, magna parens frugum, Saturnia tellus,
> magna uirum: tibi res antiquae laudis et artem
> ingredior sanctos ausus recludere fontis,
> Ascraeumque cano Romana per oppida carmen.

[This land also brought forth ...] You, greatest Caesar, who now, a conqueror at the furthest borders of Asia, repel the unwarlike Indian from Roman citadels. Hail, Saturnian land, great mother of crops, great mother of men: for you, I have dared to disclose sacred fonts and approach a matter and art worthy of ancient praise; and I sing an Ascraean song through Roman towns.

While the brief catalogue of Italy's warriors largely reflects a period of external rather than internal strife, mention of Marius conjures not only the Roman commander of the war against Jugurtha but also his conflict with Sulla that resulted in one of the darkest periods of Rome's history.[14] As such, we find already embedded within ostensible praises (*laudes*), in one of the poem's most Hesiodic moments, the problem of directing the inferior kind of strife (that associated with warfare) at the right kind of enemy, an external one.

The problem emerges more forcefully at the end of the same book, which abruptly returns Saturn's age to a remote past,[15] prior to that of Jupiter's reign and military conquest, prior to even the slaughter of animals at an *impius* feast (2.532–40):

> hanc olim ueteres uitam coluere Sabini,
> hanc Remus et frater; sic fortis Etruria creuit
> scilicet et rerum facta est pulcherrima Roma,
> septemque una sibi muro circumdedit arces.
> ante etiam sceptrum Dictaei regis et ante
> impia quam caesis gens est epulata iuuencis,
> aureus hanc uitam in terris Saturnus agebat;
> necdum etiam audierant inflari classica, necdum
> impositos duris crepitare incudibus ensis.

The ancient Sabines once lived this life, so too Remus and his brother; in this way Etruria grew strong, and indeed Rome became the most beautiful of things, and alone surrounded her seven hills with a wall; before even the sceptre of the Dictaean king and before the impious race dined on slaughtered bullocks, golden Saturn lived this life upon the lands; not yet had they heard the war trumpets blown, not yet the swords rattle as they were placed on hard anvils.

Saturn's reign is prior to the time when sword blades rang out on the blacksmith's anvil. But the temporal boundary distinguishing Saturn's Golden Age from its iron-age successor has already worn imperceptibly thin, since the same age is inhabited by Romulus and Remus, about to commit Rome's original sin, and since it appears that *Roma* already has its defensive wall – the *murus* that by some accounts prompted the very dispute resulting in the slaughter of Remus (cf. Liv. 1.7.2).[16]

The Saturn of Vergil's Golden Age conveys mixed messages about the blessings of peace and the virtues of war, offering challenges for the reader who wishes to reconcile them. Perkell and O'Hara both address these inconsistencies as perhaps deliberate prompts forcing the reader to come to terms with "what makes an age golden" or what it means to be "on Jupiter's side" – or Saturn's for that matter.[17] I would push these prompts further and suggest that the poet directs us to consider the slippery slope from peace to war by emphasizing the ease with which the farmer's agricultural implements are converted into military technology. At the end of *Georgics* 1, the poet decries the madness of war (*G.* 1.505–8):

> quippe ubi fas uersum atque nefas; tot bella per orbem,
> tam multae scelerum facies, non ullus aratro
> dignus honos, squalent abductis arua colonis,
> et curuae rigidum falces conflantur in ensem.

[Here] right and wrong are inverted; [where there are] so many wars throughout the world, so many forms of wickedness; nor is any honour given to the plough, fields are overgrown, since their tenants have been led away, and the curved reaping hooks are melted down into rigid swords.

Significantly, it is not just any farm implement that is converted into weapons, but Saturn's *falx*, recognized as the god's "constant emblem."[18] This tool enables the pruning essential to viticulture that will be the subject of the following book, where Vergil signals the god's association with it. When most of the vineyard's leaves have fallen at the onset of winter, the farmer (*rusticus*) is to pursue the remaining vine "with the curved tooth of Saturn" (*curuo Saturni dente*, 2.406). Though reference to the *falx* here is embedded in the more ebullient strains of the second *Georgic*, the tool's potential conversion into weaponry will haunt readers of Book 1, especially in light of the militaristic crop of men celebrated in the *laudes Italiae*.

Vergil's conversion of Saturn's *falx* from agricultural to military implement extends back to Hesiod, whose depiction of Kronos in the *Theogony* grants the god a scythe, a "sickle with jagged teeth" (… ἅρπην καρχαρόδοντα), with which to castrate his own tyrannical father, Ouranos (170–5). This scythe re-emerges in the *Works and Days* (572–3), where the same ἅρπη (sickle) refers to the tools that the farmer, like Vergil's *rusticus*, will use in the vineyard in proper season. Vergil thus depends on a literary tradition already aware that the same artistry used to fashion the scythe might be used to forge the weapons of interfamilial strife. The duality of Saturn/ Kronos and the alternatingly productive and destructive connotations of his signature accoutrement also shape Hesiod's account of justice (δίκη), as the Golden Age in which Kronos lived yields to the succession of ages that allow for Zeus' hegemony. Lamentable as various stages of decline are, they are also a necessary prelude to the δίκη championed by the poet and to Zeus' role in keeping arbitrary violence at bay as he guarantees the social order that allows the farmer a prosperous life (*Op.* 225–47).

In accordance with this Hesiodic meditation on the relative benefactions of Kronos and Jupiter, the Latin poets Catullus and Lucretius exploit the violence latent in the image of the farmer wielding his agricultural implements. Catullus 64 conflates the farmer's *labor* with bloodshed on the battlefield in describing how Achilles will slaughter soldiers at Troy, "just as a reaper [*messor*] hastily gathers closely packed ears of corn" (353–5). Lucretius also, in his account of the gradual peak and inevitable decline of civilization, uses the striking metaphor of soldiers "sowing" deadly wounds (*serebant*, 5.1286). Vergil wants to push back against the rapacity of the farmer-soldier, and uses Saturn to promote an agricultural ideal where the farmer and his tools are uncorrupted by the arts of war. At the same time, as we observed at the end of *G*. 1, the poem demonstrates just how readily the weapons of the farmer are converted into military implements. This conversion is rhetorically facilitated by the most striking use of the farmer-soldier metaphor, which comes just after the well-known theodicy of Jupiter, a termination of the original Golden Age ushering in the necessity of *improbus labor* (146): to aid the farmer in his struggle, the poet instructs him in the use of *arma* (*dicendum et quae sint duris agrestibus arma*, 1.160), without which agriculture would be impossible. Through the figure of Saturn, a revised *Georgic* Golden Age is permeable enough to admit the rustic life and the farmer's tools. But the tenuous boundary between the tenor (agricultural tool) and vehicle (military weapon) of the metaphor – a boundary that Vergil's poem explicitly blurs at the conclusion of Book 1 (506, *et curuae rigidum falces conflantur in ensem*) – suggests this age will eventually accommodate other kinds of *arma* as well, and tarnish it in the process.

If, as scholarship has asserted over the past two decades, the *Georgics* offer a lesson in leadership for Octavian (not yet Augustus), what might these competing models of Saturn and Jupiter, along with their respective ages, instruct?[19] The question becomes more pertinent as we turn to the *Aeneid*, in which the Augustan age is in Book 6 explicitly cast as a Saturnian one. The *Aeneid* mentions Saturn briefly among the images of Latinus' ancestors in Book 7, where the god's *falx* and link to viticulture are curiously transferred to Sabinus in the preceding hexameter (7.180).[20] Latinus boasts to an audience of Trojans that his people once lived under Saturn without the rule of law (7.203–4). This marks a clear departure from Evander's account in the following book, where the Pallantian king stresses the god's imposition of law upon an unruly populace. In this final portrait, Saturn is of the decidedly benign variety, replaying a moment of utopic stasis: he "used to rule" (*regebat*) his peoples in gentle peace, before Latium was swept up into strife and historical change (8.319–27):[21]

> primus ab aetherio uenit Saturnus Olympo
> arma Iouis fugiens et regnis exsul ademptis.
> is genus indocile ac dispersum montibus altis
> composuit legesque dedit, Latiumque uocari
> maluit, his quoniam latuisset tutus in oris.
> aurea quae perhibent illo sub rege fuere
> saecula: sic placida populos in pace regebat,
> deterior donec paulatim ac decolor aetas
> et belli rabies et amor successit habendi.

Saturn first came from Olympus on high, fleeing the arms of Jupiter, as an exile from his seized kingdom. He brought together an unruly race, scattered in the lofty mountains, and gave them laws, and he preferred it to be called Latium, since he had hidden safely in these borders. They say that the ages under that king were golden: thus he ruled his peoples in tranquil peace, until gradually a lesser and duller age followed, along with the madness for/of war and greed.

We are offered no explanation for the deterioration, only a temporal qualification (*paulatim*); greed and the madness of (for?) war simply erupt in an off-colour age. This is perhaps to be expected, however, in light of the *Georgics*' demonstration of the inevitable conflation of the farmer and the soldier in the weapons used by each. *Aeneid* 7, in fact, anticipates Evander's account of transformation and decline in describing the Ausonians' preparation for battle: evoking the *Georgics*' conversion of agricultural tools into military implements, the Ausonians cast aside the honour of the *falx* and the plough, taking up weapons of war instead (*uomeris huc et falcis honos, huc omnis aratri / cessit amor; recoquunt patrios fornacibus ensis*, "to this esteem for the ploughshare and scythe yields, to this all love for the plough has yielded; they fortify their fathers' swords in the furnace," 635–6). The fact that the Ausonians sharpen their *fathers*' swords while disavowing their interest in the fields prompts us to consider a prior generation, as well as a prior poem, and to mark the conversion of tools as cyclical, repetitive, and perhaps inevitable.

In retrospect, the decline that stains Saturn's reign may colour the prediction of Anchises that Augustus will fulfil the role that the god had once performed, presiding over a new Golden Age (6.791–5):

> hic uir, hic est, tibi quem promitti saepius audis,
> Augustus Caesar, diui genus, aurea condet
> saecula qui rursus Latio regnata per arua
> Saturno quondam, super et Garamantas et Indos
> proferet imperium …

This is the man, this is he whom you so often hear promised to you: Augustus Caesar, son of a god, who will establish Golden Ages once again in Latium throughout fields once ruled by Saturn, and he will extend the empire beyond the Garamants and Indians.

The comparison undeniably looks forward to peace and prosperity for Rome. In light of how Saturn's story has ended in the *Georgics* as well as in *A.* 8, however, we are left to question the endurance of that prosperity.

2. Tibullus: Erotic Elegy in the Age of Jove

Vergil uses Saturn as a pivotal figure, who allows us to glance backward at a morally superior age, and forward in two different directions: one recognizes imminent decline as the arts applied to agriculture are appropriated for war; in the other direction we are shown a renewal of Saturn's reign, but one that is hardly static, and thus bound to experience deterioration. Tibullus' poetry, by contrast, insistently forecloses the possibility of Saturn's return. In poems 1.3, 2.3, and 2.5 the elegist recognizes the inevitable conflation of war and agriculture, relegating both to an Iron Age. His Saturn, unlike Vergil's god of the *Georgics* and *Aeneid*, presides over a time before war and agriculture, indeed before the division of property that necessitates both. The god in Book 1 rules a blessed age that needs no private property, labour, commerce, or travel (1.3.35–8, 43–8):

> quam bene Saturno uiuebant rege, priusquam
>   tellus in longas est patefacta uias!
> nondum caeruleas pinus contempserat undas,
>   effusum uentis praebueratque sinum ...
> non domus ulla fores habuit, non fixus in agris
>   qui regeret certis finibus arua lapis;
> ipsae mella dabant quercus, ultroque ferebant
>   obuia securis ubera lactis oues;
> non acies non ira fuit, non bella, nec ensem
>   immiti saeuus duxerat arte faber.[22]

How well they used to live during Saturn's reign, before the earth was laid open in long roads! Not yet had the pine ship defied azure waves, and offered billowing sails to the winds ... Nor did any house have doors; there was no stone that marked off ploughlands fixed in the fields; oak trees themselves used to provide honey. Of their own accord sheep offered udders filled with milk to carefree folks. There was no battleline, no hostility, no wars, nor had the cruel blacksmith forged a sword with pitiless artistry.

The passage invokes the *Georgic* Golden Age verbally and thematically. Lack of property divisions at line 44 echoes the idyllic age before Jupiter's theodicy in *G*. 1 (126–8). The concluding reference to the fabrication of swords brings us back to the context of *G*. 2, where Saturn's rule precedes the clanging of weapons on the anvil (2.540). Tibullus' Golden Age too relies on the absence of *ars*, again the blacksmith's, but perhaps also reminding us more generally of the *variae artes* absent from the Golden Age in Vergil's theodicy (*G*. 1.133–4). The golden pentameter Tibullus uses in verse 48 to convey this point underscores the implicit irony of an elegist's desire for a world without art.[23]

Tibullus' Saturn is in fact doubly removed from art and agriculture as well as historical and imperial progress:[24] the god's reign that would allow the poet's escape from military ventures looks back to the "Saturnian day" keeping the poet in Rome with Delia ("I pleaded the excuse that either unlucky birds or omens or the day sacred to Saturn held me back," *aut ego sum causatus aues aut omina dira / Saturniue sacram me tenuisse diem*, 1.3.17–18). The *dies Saturni* thus proleptically reinforces the absence of travel – and constant presence of the beloved – that Tibullus associates with the Golden Age.[25] At the same time, as Miller has noted, the Golden Age is fundamentally incompatible not only with art but also with the exclusivity and ownership sought through elegy's erotic agenda.[26] Moreover, Keith has demonstrated how the elegiac *puella*'s financial demands, and indeed her very circulation as a figure inspired by courtesans imported from the Greek world, betrays a commitment rather than opposition to iron-age military conquest.[27] Still, the poet-lover's nod to the paraclausithyron (*non domus ulla fores habuit*, 43) clearly conjures a realm where access to the *puella* remains unregulated and sexual behaviours are not subject to scrutiny or censure. Any ideological inconsistency generated from the poet's attitude toward his beloved here does not render the discrepancy between the elegiac Saturn and Vergil's *Georgic* portrait of the god ineffective: rather it underscores a different kind of inconsistency in Vergil's work, one that emerges from the difficulties of lauding some *artes* of Jupiter's age while censuring others. The elegist's Jupiter is credited with none of the human advancement Vergil allows him: for Maltby, the use of *dominus* (1.3.49) to describe the god is pejorative, smacking of the despot rather than the benevolent ruler (*rex*), at least as distinguished by Cicero (*Rep*. 2.47).[28] Tibullus links Jupiter explicitly with "slaughter and wounds" (*caedes et uulnera*) as well as with the "thousand roads to death" (*leti mille ... uiae*) opened up through travel overseas (1.3.49–50); he is the god who may or may not offer mercy to the *amator* hoping to survive his military expedition with Messalla (1.3.55–6).

Jupiter inspires a more benevolent portrait in Book 2, but he is again offered as a foil to Saturn, who remains insistently relegated to a pre-agricultural Golden Age. Such relegation and Jupiter's corresponding ascension are especially pointed in light of the fact that the elegy celebrates the initiation of Messalla's son, Messallinus, into the priesthood of the Quindecemviri; these men were entrusted with the Sibylline books and played a key role in the upcoming celebration of the *ludi Saeculares*, a festival that harnessed the imagery and iconography of a returned Golden Age (2.5.5–10):[29]

> ipse triumphali deuinctus tempora lauro
>   dum cumulant aras ad tua sacra ueni.
> sed nitidus pulcherque ueni: nunc indue uestem
>   sepositam, longas nunc bene pecte comas,
> qualem te memorant Saturno rege fugato
>   uictori laudes concinuisse Ioui.

You [Apollo] yourself come, your temples bound with triumphant laurel, while they pile the altars high for your sacrifices. But come, gleaming and beautiful: now put on the cloak set aside, now comb your long hair, just as they recall you sang praises for the victor Jove after king Saturn had been put to flight.

Saturn's appearance may draw from the less flattering portrait of Euhemerus, in which the god, after being saved by his son, plots to kill him when an oracle predicts Jupiter's succession (Lactantius, *Div. Inst.* 1.14.1).[30] Thus, for Johnston, in Book 2 of the elegies Tibullus picks up on the hostilities in the mythic tradition, in a departure from Vergil, who adopts a more "humane attitude," telling the story from Saturn's point of view.[31] The reference clearly recalls the god's presentation in poem 1.3, the only other mention of Saturn's rule or subsequent banishment in the Tibullan corpus. The couplet describing succession, however, hardly constitutes a hostile portrait – it's really not much of a portrait at all.

I would argue, moreover, that evocation of a lost age of Saturn in poem 2.5 is informed by the god's implicit governance over the age idealized by the elegist in poem 2.3, another elegy in which Apollo plays a prominent role, though in this case as a lover (11–14) and not as poet laureate of the Jovian age. In the poem the venality of the current *ferrea saecula* (2.3.39; cf. 2.3.2) is disparaged in contrast with a simpler age of acorn eating and free love, when an explicit lack of doorkeepers was the law of the land. After bidding the country and agriculture farewell, the poet praises an era that sounds curiously golden (2.3.71–8):

> glans aluit ueteres, et passim semper amarunt.
>> quid nocuit sulcos non habuisse satos?
> tum, quibus aspirabat Amor, praebebat aperte
>> mitis in umbrosa gaudia ualle Venus.
> nullus erat custos, nulla exclusura dolentes
>> ianua. si fas est, mos, precor, ille redi.

Acorns nourished people in the old days and they made love any time and place. What harm is there in not having sown seeds in furrows? Then, for those whom love has inspired, gentle Venus furnishes joys openly in a shady valley. There was no doorkeeper, no door about to shut out grieving lovers. If it is allowed, I pray, may that custom return.

The agricultural view of Saturn is implicitly rejected through reference to sowing crops, *sulcos satos* (72), which had etymologically defined the god and his role in Latium. This anti-agricultural vision is reminiscent of life under Saturn in poem 1.3, and explicitly contrasted with the country life that has subsumed Nemesis. We can sift through lofty ideals to determine one desired effect of this lament. As with the more traditional elegiac *paraclausithyron*, the *amator* decries the barriers that bar his access to his beloved, constituting a program of persuasion that, as James has stressed, deflects attention away from, while implicitly nodding to, the *puella's* social status and profession as a courtesan.[32] The articulation of such an obstacle, here and in poem 1.3, inevitably entangles elegy's sexual politics in a larger program of emergent *Augustan* Golden Age imagery. Who's sleeping with whom, who has access to which houses after hours – these would become increasingly contentious issues as the first Principate evolved and Augustus attempted to pass the legislation concerning marriage and adultery that became known as the *Lex Iulia et Papia Poppaea*.[33]

Tibullus' Saturn plays no role in surveillance or in governing sexual conduct. Where Vergil had briefly sketched a law-giving aspect of Saturn in *A.* 8 (see above), the elegist makes implicit in poem 2.3, as he had made explicit in 1.3, that the Golden Age needed no moral or legal regulation. This is a clear departure from Augustus' Saturnian guise: as Wallace-Hadrill observes of sexual misconduct in the Golden Age of the Principate, "the public political disorder of civil war and the private wrongdoing of the individual are inextricably intertwined – and the emperor as a second Saturn is assigned the role of keeping both at bay."[34] The golden images of 2.3 are cut against the grain of the Princeps' *aurea aetas* and his Saturnian identity prophesied in *A*. 6; and while elegy 2.5's myth of the ages is consistent with saecular evolution elsewhere in the Tibulluan corpus, his vision of Rome's prosperity entangled with the fertility and virtue of its women (2.5.91–2), which ought to align with Augustus' Saturnian kingdoms, is uncomfortably projected within a distinctively Jovian, iron-age setting.

Various scholars exploring the intertextual relationship between Tibullus and Vergil have focused on poem 2.5's echoes of the *Aeneid*, though the priority of either remains an open question.[35] Tibullus' evocation of Saturn's flight followed by observations on Rome's past and present suggests that both poets were interested in charting the progress of empire in a Jovian age. Such loosely parallel structures make Tibullus' decision to deny Saturn a role in his rustic landscape all the more pronounced. Moreover, as noted by Wimmel,[36] Tibullus' mention of Romulus and Remus in lines 23–8 recalls the two brothers poised similarly (just prior to fraternal strife) at the end of *G*. 2 – yet another context that, as we have observed, features Vergil's benevolent Saturn ruling over a Golden Age in Italy. Tibullus' portrait of the siblings captures a moment prior to (*nondum*) the walls that, in the *Georgics*, complicate Saturnian peace by signalling military fortification (2.5.23–8):

> Romulus aeternae nondum formauerat Urbis
>> moenia, consorti non habitanda Remo,
> sed tunc pascebant herbosa Palatia uaccae
>> et stabant humiles in Iouis arce casae.
> lacte madens illic suberat Pan ilicis umbrae
>> et facta agresti lignea falce Pales ...

Romulus had not yet shaped the walls of the eternal city, a city not to be inhabited by Remus as co-ruler; but then cows fed on the grassy Palatine and lowly houses stood on Jupiter's citadel. There Pan, dripping with milk, lingered under the shade of an ilex, and Pales was carved with a rustic pruning hook.

Tibullus conjures the rustic harmony that closes *G*. 2, but hardly allows a moment of calm before the storm: not only is there no Saturnian realm here, there is no moment of concord between brothers – we are directed explicitly to identify the impending walls with fraternal discord (*consorti non habitanda Remo*). Saturn's absence is made more pronounced as his characteristic pruning hook, the *falx*, is appropriated for the deity presiding over celebration of Rome's birthday, set firmly in the Iron Age of Jupiter. The remainder of 2.5 is replete with imagery that anticipates the returned Golden Age about to be celebrated in the *ludi Saeculares*.[37] The poem's emphasis on Apollo, Augustus' patron deity, and Diana, rather than Saturn, in this new age is consistent with imagery in Horace's *Carmen Saeculare* as well as contemporary visual arts (e.g., the breastplate on the well-known statue of Augustus from Prima Porta). At the same time, the reminder of Saturn's reign and relegation of that era to the past is clearly inconsistent with the Augustan/Saturnian connection Vergil has forged in *A.* 6.791–5. So why won't Tibullus grant the Princeps and his new age its Saturnian status? One effect of such a refusal is to underscore a distinction between using Saturn to promote the Augustan era's continuity with the past (as Vergil does) and recognizing a break from the past (as in Tibullus).

In order to speculate on the reasons why the Tibullan *amator* exposes the very fissures that Vergil's poetry papers over, I turn to poem 2.5's final lines. Cairns in particular has demonstrated the ring structure that governs the elegy, a structure that underscores correspondences between the opening invocation and the poem's closure.[38] The *amator* complains of the hardships that Cupid's *ars* has foisted upon him (2.5.109–22):

> et mihi praecipue, iaceo cum saucius annum
> > et faueo morbo, cum iuuat ipse dolor.
> usque cano Nemesim, sine qua uersus mihi nullus
> > uerba potest iustos aut reperire pedes.
> at tu, nam diuum seruat tutela poetas,
> > praemoneo, uati parce puella sacro,
> ut Messallinum celebrem cum praemia belli
> > ante suos currus oppida uicta feret.
> ipse gerens laurus, lauro deuinctus agresti
> > miles "io" magna uoco "Triumphe" canet.
> tunc Messalla meus pia det spectacula turbae
> > et plaudat curru praetereunte pater.
> annue: sic tibi sint intonsi, Phoebe, capilli,
> > sic tua perpetuo sit tibi casta soror.

Upon me especially since I lie wounded for a year now and take pleasure in my sickness, while the pain itself is pleasing. Continuously I sing of Nemesis, without whom no verse is able to discover the right words or rhythm. But you, since poets are protected by the gods, I ask you, girl, take pity on your sacred bard, so that I may honour Messallinus when he drives conquered towns, the spoils of war, before his chariot. He himself wearing laurel, and his soldiers, (heads) bound with rustic laurel, will sing "Io, Triumph" with a loud voice. Then let my Messalla, his father, give the crowd a dutiful display and applause, as the chariot passes by. Assent to this: thus, Phoebus, may your hair always remain unshorn and thus may your sister remain eternally chaste.

These couplets rehearse the thematics of youth and maturity, elegiac torpor vs. epic deeds, as well as orderly paternal succession from father to son. Implicated in that succession is the evolution of the poet, who will elevate himself from love-struck elegist to a poet of Messallinus' military exploits, if only Nemesis will allow him. Under the right circumstances, the Tibullan *amator* will, like Apollo – apparently having moved on from his own erotic *seruitium* to Admetus (2.3.31–4) and celebrating Jupiter's defeat of Saturn – celebrate the martial exploits that secure the stability of the Principate. Yet, as I have argued elsewhere, Nemesis does not grant the poet his reprieve and Tibullus ultimately rejects the poetic evolution promised here.[39] The *amator* of 2.6 is forced to decline Macer's invitation to join the army, or write about military exploits, after he is shut out by the same iron-age doors that have tripped him up in previous elegies. So perhaps the poet will continue to idealize his own version of Saturn's kingdom a bit longer.

As Evans notes, the problem with utopias and Golden Ages is one of teleological orientation: "they provide no opportunity for conflict or narrative development: they are fixed, inert, unable to change – because change would result in a degree less of perfection."[40] Rome's forward momentum, whether articulated as a *felix et satur annus* ("blessed and bountiful year," 2.5.82) or a *saeculum uenturum* ("an age about to arrive," B. 4.52), will bring triumphs but also transformation and inevitable decline. Tibullus' association of erotic contentment with the Golden Age, where he has unlimited, unqualified access to his beloved, allows him to disentangle elegiac love from teleological and degenerative projects, like building an empire. Such contentment is, of course, unattainable, but it allows the elegist a clear alternative to that other Saturnian realm, whose golden veneer was beginning to tarnish even as Vergil was fashioning it.

NOTES

Many thanks are due to the volume's anonymous referees, as well as to Alison Keith and Micah Myers, who organized an especially fruitful conference at Cuma and offered careful insights and recommendations for improving this essay.

1 Wallace-Hadrill 1982, Zanker 1988, and Galinsky 1996 offer general treatments of golden-age imagery in Augustan culture, with some reference to Vergil's contributions. Other accounts of Vergil's Saturnian Age are cited where relevant throughout this essay.

2 Wallace-Hadrill (1982: 26–7) identifies Horace and (to a lesser extent) Vergil and Livy as representing sexual licence as the premier *scelus* in need of

suppressing in order to achieve a restored Golden Age.

3 Scholars have addressed the similarity largely to determine priority; see, e.g., Buchheit 1965, who argues that Tibullus must have been familiar with Vergil's epic and adjusts the elegist's date of death accordingly; contra Della Corte 1980, who is sceptical of Vergil's influence. See Ball 1975 and Maltby 2002: 431, for synopses of the controversy.

4 For ancient attempts to etymologize Saturn's name, see Johnston 1980: 63.

5 Translations are mine unless otherwise noted; the text is that of Fairclough, rev. Goold 1999.

6 Hesiod's statement that he would rather have lived prior to the current Iron Age or be born afterward implies the possibility of amelioration (*Op.* 174–5), though it does not explicitly signal the return of Saturn or a Golden Age.

7 Johnston 1980: 12; cf. Coleman 1977: 187, on the awkward chronology of mentioning the race engendered by Deucalion and Pyrrha (*B.* 6.41) before the theft of Prometheus, who was Deucalion's father.

8 See Feeney 2007: 163–4, on temporal revolutions and cyclical deterioration implied in Roman accounts of the Golden Age.

9 Evans 2008: 2–6.

10 While Hesiod has been acknowledged (e.g., by Servius) as Vergil's predominant inspiration, see esp. Farrell 1991: 27–32, on the limits of Hesiod's influence on the *Georgics*.

11 Gale 2000: 63. On the relationship between *labor* and human *ars*, including poetry and its consolations, see Parry 1972. The past twenty years have shed new light on Vergilian *labor*, especially its propriety for an elite Roman audience (Thibodeau 2011: 48–61) and its integration within the philosophical systems that frame Vergil's approach to farming (e.g., Keith [2020: 62–4] on Epicurean doctrine consistent with the poet's view of *labor* and its rewards).

12 Johnston 1980: 63.

13 Farrell 1991 stresses the predominance of the *Phaenomena* as Vergil's model; cf. Hunter 2014: 21–5, who demonstrates the combined elements of Hesiod (and the "Hesiodic tradition") and Aratus from the start of Vergil's poem; see also Van Noorden 2015: 7–8.

14 See Ross 1987: 109–22, on the falsehoods that dominate the entire *laudes Italiae*; Thomas 1988a: 188–9 notes the uncomfortable realities of Marius' career that most commentators overlook.

15 Mack 1978: 29.

16 See also, in this volume, Boyd, who argues that Ovid's account of the origins of the Agonalia (*F.* 1.337–48), whose ritual sacrifice marks the beginning of an Iron Age, underscores contradictions in Vergil's *Georgic* representation of Italy's "golden-age" characteristics. Just as Boyd sees Ovid's references to the first sacrifice in the Agonalia as "set[ting] a temporal boundary" between Italy

of past and present, I view Tibullan elegy as relegating Saturn's kingdoms to an irretrievable past and responding to or "resolving" Vergil's contradictions about Italy's contemporary status; see further below.

17 Perkell 2002: 8; O'Hara 2007: 101. Cf. Van Noorden 2015: 12, who suggests that one source of such inconsistency is Hesiod's account of racial amelioration in the "better" race of heroes described at *Op.* 158.

18 Mynors 1990: 153.

19 For Octavian's alignment with Jupiter in the poem, see Xinyue 2019, who explores Vergil's projection of Octavian's divination and ascension as a Jupiter figure. Xinyue argues that, by the end of the *Georgics*, the didactic poet falters in his aspiration of shaping Octavian's path to power and approach to governance, an implicit challenge to Nappa (2005: 84–5), who stresses an identification (rather than opposition) between Saturn's land and Jupiter's, especially in the *laudes Italiae*. Nappa upholds that Vergil's "praises" instruct that Jovian *labor* and war are essential for contemporary Italy, as is Octavian, who emerges as "both reassuring and disturbing, but most of all … necessary" (85).

20 Fordyce 1977: 99: "*Falx* is a symbol of Saturn … but this line must refer to Sabinus."

21 The Latin peoples' identity as Saturnian also occurs in Diomedes' response to their plea for help against the Trojans (*A.* 11.252). The epic is riddled throughout with references to the god's role as parent of Juno. For *Saturnia Juno*, see MacKay 1956 and Anderson 1958, who explores the golden-age implications of the epithet. For Anderson, drawing on Deratini 1931, Vergil uses *Saturnia* to track Juno's transformation in the epic as well as the parallel transformation of Italy from the lawlessness implied in Latinus' portrait of Saturn to the benign imposer of law described by Evander.

22 The text is that of Maltby 2002.

23 For the irony of Tibullus' espousal of life without artistic labour, see Cairns 1979: 28.

24 Cf. Lee-Stecum 1998: 113, who emphasizes Saturn's identity as "pre-imperial, pre-republic, outside the familiar Roman social, political, and military spheres."

25 Maltby 2002: 190.

26 P. Miller 2004: 124–5.

27 Keith 2015.

28 Maltby 2002: 199.

29 Zanker 1988: 167–92.

30 Text and translation of Lactantius' citations of Ennius' *Sacra Historia* are included in the Loeb edition of Warmington (1967: 420–3).

31 Johnston 1980: 83.

32 James 2003b: 136–41.

33 For attempts to pass such legislation as early as 28/27 BCE, cf. Prop. 2.7 and
Suet. *Aug.* 34. There is a vast bibliography on the topic; for an overview with
references to the secondary scholarship, see James 2003b: 229–31.
34 Wallace-Hadrill 1982: 32.
35 For the question of priority, see above n3.
36 Wimmel 1961: 238; cf. Ball 1975: 36.
37 See Miller 2009: 260, who offers additional bibliography.
38 Cairns 1979: 206–7.
39 Gardner 2013: 223–32.
40 Evans 2008: 6.

4

Roman Returns: *Nostos* in Vergil and Propertius

MICAH Y. MYERS

Departures and returns feature in the work of Vergil and Propertius from their first poems. *B.* 1 juxtaposes Meliboeus' journey into exile from his *patria* with Tityrus' retention of his land. Tityrus' continued possession of his property has been made possible by a journey to Rome from which he has recently returned. In this manner, Vergil's *corpus* commences with the contrast between the successful homecoming of Tityrus and Meliboeus' journey to distant places. Propertius 1.1 presents a similar juxtaposition, refracted through an elegiac lens. As the poet-lover considers various remedies for his unhappy affair, he asks to be sent to the ends of the earth, while declaring that happy lovers may stay home (1.1.29–34).[1] The poet-lover of course fails to heed his own advice to make such a journey. Elegy 1.3 nonetheless finds him making a poorly received return to Cynthia, although from a night of drunken revelry rather than from a long-distance journey. The opening verses compare the sleeping Cynthia to Ariadne, Andromeda, and a Maenad (1.3.1–6), figures that in turn invoke their male counterparts, including Theseus, Perseus, and Orpheus.[2] Myths surrounding these three heroes relate that each has a *nostos* with a destructive outcome: Theseus causes the death of his father; Perseus drives his grandfather from Argos; Orpheus is torn apart by Maenads. The manner in which 1.3 depicts Cynthia awakening to find the poet-lover returned (35–46) also recalls Penelope in *Odyssey* 23 waking from sleep to be reunited with Odysseus.[3] While Penelope is sceptical and fearful of being deceived when she first sees her husband, Cynthia, in a manner that evokes Penelope's initial anger at being awoken by Euryclea (*Od.* 23.11–24), is furious about the Propertian poet-lover's long absence, and much less forgiving of his philandering than Penelope is of Odysseus' dalliances with Circe and Calypso.

As these examples illustrate, departures and returns are thematized from the outset of Vergil's and Propertius' poetry. This paper will focus on Vergil's *Aeneid* and Propertius 2.14 and 3.12, three poems that include elaborate treatments of *nostos* that are illustrative of some of the broader ways that Vergil and Propertius treat this topic. I posit that Vergil's and Propertius' differing engagements with *nostos* traditions, above all the archetypal *nostos* epic, the *Odyssey*, reveal how these poets each position their poetry in relation to Greek epic, to the Roman context in which they wrote, and to each other's genres. An element of the Homeric model of *nostos* that Vergil's *Aeneid* suppresses is the amatory reunion, precisely the feature that Propertius emphasizes. Indeed in elegies 2.14 and 3.12 *nostos* is distilled into a reunion with the *puella*, who supersedes the other elements of a *nostos* to the point that even the concept of "home" as a place fades into the background. Propertius' reconfiguration of *nostos* in 2.14 and 3.12 is emblematic of elegy as a genre, and we see the focus on the reunion with the *puella* in other elegies as well. For instance, in Propertius 4.8 Cynthia initially assumes the role of a vengeful Odysseus when she comes back from Lanuvium to find the poet-lover with other women.[4] Yet the poem resolves through the rekindling of their relationship according to the terms of elegiac love. Tibullus 1.3, a poem well known for its Odyssean elements, likewise envisions a return for the poet-lover that is hyper-focused on a reunion with Delia.[5] Similarly, Ovid's *propemptikon* for Corinna in *Amores* 2.11 imagines their future reunion as the sole element of her *nostos*.

Although the publication of Propertius' second and third books occurs prior to the publication of the *Aeneid*, in 2.34.61–6 Propertius demonstrates familiarity with Vergil's in-progress epic.[6] This paper shall argue that in 2.14 and 3.12 Propertius responds both to Greek traditions and to the *Aeneid* in his treatments of *nostos*. Propertius does so in a manner that at once distinguishes elegy from epic and also lays claim to the amatory elements in Homeric *nostoi* that Vergil pushes to the margins of the *Aeneid*. While I do not find that Vergil's engagements with *nostos* offer a response to Propertius in particular, the suppression of amatory elements of *nostos* in the *Aeneid* reflects the epic's broader rejoinder to the intense focus on love that is central to elegy.[7] On account of my arguments about Propertius' reception of the *Aeneid* in 2.14 and 3.12, the paper discusses Vergil prior to analysing Propertius. By triangulating Greek *nostos* traditions, Vergil, and Propertius, I aim to elucidate another dimension of the ways that elegy and epic distinguish themselves from one another, while also revealing themselves as fundamentally intertwined.

From Homeric *Nostos* to Roman *Reditus*

In approaching the concept of *nostos*, I follow in particular Anna Bonifazi, who shows that etymologically and in archaic Greek usage *nostos* has a wider sense than just "return home." It can also mean more broadly "a successful journey," or at its root, "surviving danger and attaining safety."[8] Odysseus' *nostos* in the *Odyssey* is paradigmatic and central to the discussion in this paper. Yet *nostos* is a prevalent theme across Greek literature. Even within the *Odyssey* there are references to a number of other *nostoi*, a reflection of the topic's pervasiveness from the beginning of the epic tradition. Sources present *nostoi* with varying outcomes. For instance, Orestes' *nostos* restores social order, while Oedipus' leads to a plague that endangers it.[9] Moreover, the *Nostoi* of the Epic Cycle, Stesichorus' *Nostoi*, the prevalence of *nostos* as a theme in Athenian tragedy, and Hellenistic texts like Apollonius' *Argonautica*, ps.-Lycophron's *Alexandra*, and Lysimachus of Alexandria's prose *Nostoi* reflect the widespread and enduring importance of *nostos* as a theme in Greek literature.[10]

As the *Odyssey* demonstrates, a typical *nostos* contains several elements, which divide between two parts: the external *nostos* and the internal *nostos*.[11] An attempted external *nostos* includes a journey, which can be successful (e.g., Odysseus, Nestor, or Menelaus) or unsuccessful (e.g., Locrian Ajax or Odysseus' crew). The journey's goal is to reach a specific land and places within that land, especially the *oikos*. A typical internal *nostos* involves reuniting with people in these spaces and reclaiming one's role in one's family and community, at the expense of any would-be usurpers (or failing in these efforts, as Agamemnon does). Odysseus' success in all elements of a *nostos* enables his *kleos*. Yet his *nostos* is, of course, not without its problems, and requires the intervention of Zeus and Athena at the end of Book 24 to limit further conflict between Odysseus and his community.

When considered in the context of the period in which Vergil and Propertius wrote, elements of Odysseus' internal *nostos* and other Greek myths about internal *nostoi* have the potential to be especially problematic. Odysseus' use of force to reclaim his place in his community and the narrowly avoided civil conflict at the end of the *Odyssey* might, for Romans in the first century BCE, evoke the series of military figures who brought violence and displacement upon their *reditus* to Italy.[12] Indeed, in this period, a return to community and property and a resumption of one's personal and public roles could be fraught, even a potential challenge to the ruling order. In addition, various social, political, and economic factors drew people away from their hometowns to major cities, especially Rome, or to the repose of places like the Bay of Naples. This sort of migration as well as the practice among Roman elite of possessing multiple houses also could affect notions of "home" and, therefore, of a *nostos*.[13] As Nicholas Purcell observes, however, complications related to the concept of "home" are not unique to the Roman period. Rather, the pervasiveness of mobility, circulation, relocation, and displacement across Mediterranean spaces and times always made the notion of home and *nostos* more complex for certain individuals and communities than the Odyssean model would suggest.[14] Purcell, however, nonetheless concludes that "*nostos*-thinking" was fundamental to how Romans conceptualized their existence, especially the divide between civilian lives at home and military service abroad, two parts of life linked by a *profectio* and *reditus* that were both marked with community rituals.[15] As Purcell's analysis shows, *nostos* was fundamental not just to the literary tradition, but to lived experience in the Roman world as well.

Vergilian *Nostoi*

This section explores some of the ways that in the *Aeneid* Vergil draws on the *Odyssey*'s depictions of *nostos*, recasting them, along with other *nostos* traditions, not just in the first half of his poem, but throughout the epic.[16] In the *Aeneid* the Trojans are of course not headed home in the same sense that Odysseus is in the *Odyssey*. Instead Vergil's epic presents the Trojans' travels as a mix of migration, colonization, and *nostos*, a combination that finds parallels in Hellenistic literature. Apollonius Rhodius uses *nostos* in the sense of "expedition" and "return" and draws on the *Odyssey* during both the outward and return voyages of the Argonauts.[17] Ps.-Lycophron's *Alexandra* includes the wanderings of Trojans alongside narratives about Greek *nostoi*. Similarly, Lysimachus of Alexandria includes Trojan migrants in his *Nostoi*, referring to the descendants of Antenor at Cyrene (fr. 6).[18] Along these lines, Robin Lane Fox, in his discussion of Hellenistic Macedonian narratives about *nostoi*, identifies what he terms a "Virgilian type of *nostos*," which he defines as "a return by people, at first unawares, to lands formerly visited or settled by their kinsmen."[19] From this perspective, the *Aeneid*'s engagement with *nostos* themes in its narrative of Trojan migration to Italy has a lengthy literary and cultural precedent.

One familiar way that Vergil configures the Trojans' arrival in Italy as a *nostos* is through Dardanus' Italian origins, which make the *telos* of the Trojans' journey a return to their ancestral home.[20] Thus, in *A.* 3 the Penates redirect Aeneas to Italy using language that makes it a site for *nostos* (167–8): *hae nobis propriae sedes, hinc Dardanus ortus / Iasiusque pater, genus a quo principe nostrum* ("This is our true home; from here Dardanus sprung, and father Iasius, the origin of our people"). Similar descriptions of the Trojan journey as a return occur several other times in the poem (*A.* 3.94–6; 3.100–1; 7.206–7; 7.240–1; 8.36–7). These repetitions of the notion that the Trojans are returning to Italy add context to Aeneas' recognition in *A.* 7 that his group has arrived at the place that is at once their new home and their ancestral one (7.122): *hic domus, haec patria est* ("this is our home, this is our homeland"). Aeneas' words here befit not just an oecist, but also a hero making a *nostos*.[21] In addition, Aeneas' delayed recognition of his Latin *patria*, a recognition made thanks to his young son Iulus' observation that the Trojans have eaten their "tables," parallels *Odyssey* 13, where Odysseus, after initially not recognizing his home, learns that he has made it to Ithaca thanks to Athena, who has assumed the form of a young man (ἀνδρὶ ... νέῳ, 13.222).[22]

Greek *nostoi* traditions that combine migration and colonization with a return to an ancestral home provide precedent for the *Aeneid*'s construction of the Trojan arrival in Latium as an external *nostos*. In addition, the second half of Vergil's epic, alongside its Iliadic themes, contains resonances with Odysseus' internal *nostos* in the *Odyssey*.[23] The Trojan efforts to settle in Latium parallel Odysseus' endeavours to reclaim his place on Ithaca. Lavinia serves a Penelope-like role, although her differences from Penelope, and Vergil's decision not to depict the completion of the marital elements of Aeneas' *nostos*, will prove critical for the comparison to elegy.[24] To explore the links between the second half of the *Aeneid* and Odysseus' *nostos*, this section of the paper first looks at parallels between Aeneas' slaying of Turnus and Odysseus' slaughter of the suitors. Then it considers the death of Turnus in relation to the end of the *Odyssey* and in relation to the descent of Penelope's suitors' souls into the underworld. Afterwards, I turn to comparisons between Lavinia and Penelope.

Alongside the evocations of the Trojan War in the *Aeneid*'s Italian war, the conflict's culmination with Aeneas killing Turnus, who is among other things a suitor of Lavinia (7.54–6), has similarities to Odysseus' slaughter of the suitors, an essential element of Odysseus' internal *nostos*.[25] Turnus' appeal for Aeneas' mercy at 12.931–8 recalls Hector's entreaties to Achilles in *Iliad* 22 and Priam's in *Iliad* 24.[26] Yet Turnus' speech also evokes Eurymachus' plea to Odysseus to spare the suitors once Antinous is dead (*Od.* 22.45–59). Eurymachus' plea is met with murderous rage from Odysseus, rage that Aeneas' violent response to Turnus echoes. In addition, Aeneas' final speech rejecting Turnus' pleas and condemning him to death for his past actions (12.947–9) parallels Odysseus' response to Eurymachus that there is nothing that the suitors can offer that will prevent him from killing them (*Od.* 22.61–4).[27] Three of the issues that Eurymachus addresses – marrying Penelope, ruling Ithaca, and the attempt on Telemachus' life (22.48–53) – have parallels in the final scene of the *Aeneid* through Lavinia, Latium, and Pallas. Similar to Eurymachus, Turnus tells Aeneas that he is giving up his political ambitions as well as his efforts to marry Lavinia (12.936–7): *uicisti et uictum tendere palmas / Ausonii uidere; tua est Lauinia coniunx* ("You have won and the Ausonians have seen me defeated stretch forth my hands; Lavinia is your wife").[28] Yet the sight of Pallas' baldric reminds Aeneas of Turnus' killing of Pallas – an act of violence against a youth not unlike what in the *Odyssey* the suitors tried but failed to do to Telemachus – and impels Aeneas to further violence. Furthermore, the image engraved on Pallas' baldric is of the Danaids slaying their husbands on their marriage night (*A.* 10.496–9), another myth where suitors meet their death, albeit in different circumstances from the *Odyssey* or *Aeneid*.[29]

Although the *Aeneid*'s abrupt ending with the death of Turnus is a departure from the manner in which either Homeric epic concludes, the end of the *Aeneid* nonetheless contains close connections with the end of the *Odyssey*.[30] The conclusion of the *Aeneid* pointedly lacks a parallel to Athena's final speech, which calms Odysseus' violent intentions (*Od.* 24.542–5), although Athena is on one level present at the end of the *Aeneid* thanks to Pallas, who is mentioned three times in the closing verses.[31] Vergil's epic also omits an equivalent to Athena in the *Odyssey* leading the two sides through peace oaths (24.546–8). Yet, except for these final seven lines of the *Odyssey*, the end of the *Aeneid* possesses significant correspondences with the Homeric epic. Similar to Aeneas' slaying of Turnus, Laertes' killing of Antinous' father Eupeithes brings violence between Odysseus' family and the suitors' relatives into the closing moments of the *Odyssey* (24.521–5). Odysseus' continued enthusiasm to commit violence against his fleeing foes even after Athena's initial admonition to reconcile (24.533–8) finds a parallel in Aeneas' anger at the close of the *Aeneid* (12.946–7). Along with the violent impulses of the protagonists of both epics, each poem contains closing speeches about ceasing from anger: Turnus' final words to Aeneas, *ulterius ne tende odiis* ("don't push your hatred further," 12.938), echo Athena's second speech commanding Odysseus (24.543): παῦε δὲ νεῖκος ὁμοιΐου πολέμοιο ("Cease from the strife of war, common to all").[32] Athena's success where Turnus fails marks the point where the two endings diverge.

The *Aeneid* closes with Turnus' soul descending to the underworld (*A.* 12.952): *uitaque cum gemitu fugit indignata sub umbras* ("And with a moan Turnus' life indignantly fled down to the shades"). This verse recalls the *Iliad*'s description of Hector's and Patroclus' souls departing their bodies.[33] Yet the *katabasis* of Turnus' soul also has similarities to the suitors' deaths and their souls' descent into the underworld in the *Odyssey*, similarities that have not yet been noted, as far as I am aware. In the *Aeneid* Turnus' *uita* flees with a *gemitus*. At the beginning of *Odyssey* 24 the suitors also make sounds as they follow Hermes into the afterlife (*Od.* 24.5): τῇ ῥ᾽ ἄγε κινήσας, ταὶ δὲ τρίζουσαι ἕποντο ("With [his wand, Hermes] roused and led [the suitors' souls], and they followed squeaking").[34] Vergil's phrasing in 12.952 is even closer to Theoclymenus' prediction of the suitors' deaths in *Odyssey* 20, which likewise describes mournful utterances and souls going to the underworld (20.353, 355–6): <u>οἰμωγὴ</u> δὲ δέδηε ... εἰδώλων δὲ πλέον πρόθυρον, πλείη δὲ καὶ αὐλή, / <u>ἱεμένων Ἐρεβόσδε ὑπὸ ζόφον</u> ("<u>Wailing</u> is kindled ... both the porch and the courtyard are full of ghosts <u>hastening down to Erebus beneath the darkness</u>"). Vergil's *gemitu* echoes οἰμωγὴ and *fugit ... sub umbras* echoes ἱεμένων ... ὑπὸ ζόφον.[35] Turnus' *gemitus*, more-over, in my view mirrors the *Odyssey*'s description that "an unseemly groan arose" when the suitors were massacred (στόνος ὄρνυτ᾽ ἀεικὴς, 22.308), a phrase that appears again when characters retell the story of the suitors' killing (24.184; cf. 23.40). The *Odyssey* depicts the violence between Odys-seus and the suitors as central to his success in his internal *nostos*. Given this Homeric precedent, Aeneas' killing of Turnus points towards Aeneas' completion of his *nostos* too. Yet the abruptness with which the *Aeneid* con-cludes also stresses the elements of an internal *nostos* that are absent from Vergil's epic.

Although the aspects of the ending of the *Aeneid* discussed above evoke the close of the *Odyssey*, Homer earlier shows Odysseus completing his internal *nostos* within his *oikos*. In contrast, the *Aeneid* does not present Aeneas completing anything akin to an internal *nostos* in Latium, except in predictions and prayers about events that occur after the end of the epic's narrative.[36] In particular Lavinia, one of the most critical figures for Aeneas' (re)establishment of an Italian home, remains a distant, silent presence.[37] Alongside these differences, to which I will shortly return, Lavinia's simi-larities to Penelope are signalled from the second line of the *Aeneid*, where her name appears in the adjective *Lauinia* (*A.* 1.1–3): *Arma uirumque cano, Troiae qui primus ab oris / Italiam fato profugus Lauiniaque uenit / litora* ... ("I sing of weapons and a man, who first from Troy's shores, exiled by fate, came to Italy and the Lavinian shores ..."). Although *Lauinia* is used as a toponym, until the reader reaches *litora* in the next verse, the phrasing suggests – phonetically though not syntactically – that Aeneas' *telos* in his journey is a land (*Italiam*) and a woman, a pairing evocative of an Odys-sean-style external and an internal *nostos*.[38] When Lavinia is first introduced into the narrative in *A.* 7, Vergil emphasizes her suitors, a situation that recalls Penelope in the *Odyssey* (7.54–5): *multi illam magno e Latio totaque petebant / Ausonia* ("Many wooed her from mighty Latium and from all of Ausonia"). The large number of Lavinia's suitors and the specification of their places of origin in my view echo the structure of Telemachus' initial description of Penelope's suitors as likewise being many in number and coming from throughout the region (*Od.* 1.245–50):

ὅσσοι γὰρ νήσοισιν ἐπικρατέουσιν ἄριστοι,
Δουλιχίῳ τε Σάμῃ τε καὶ ὑλήεντι Ζακύνθῳ,
ἠδ᾽ ὅσσοι κραναὴν Ἰθάκην κάτα κοιρανέουσιν,
τόσσοι μητέρ᾽ ἐμὴν μνῶνται τρύχουσι δὲ οἶκον.
ἡ δ᾽ οὔτ᾽ ἀρνεῖται στυγερὸν γάμον οὔτε τελευτὴν
ποιῆσαι δύναται …

As many leading men who hold sway on the islands of Dulichium and Same and wooded Zacynthus, and those who lord it over rocky Ithaca, they all woo my mother, and consume my household. And she neither declines a loathed marriage nor is able to bring the matter to an end.

While suitors are a common element in ancient narratives about women, both the *Odyssey* and the *Aeneid* describe suitors similarly, emphasizing their magnitude and their places of origin. Additionally, in both instances the suitors' courtships have encountered an obstacle, yet their pursuit continues.[39] In the quotation above, Telemachus attributes the obstacle to Penelope's indecision.[40] In the *Aeneid*, the suitors' courtship is blocked because Latinus has received a prophecy that his daughter must marry a foreigner (7.58–106).

Lavinia also shares with Penelope a future that will be distinguished by fame. In Lavinia's case her future fame is signalled by her hair catching fire (*A.* 7.71–7). Prophets "predict" (*canebant; OLD* s.v. 8) in response to this fiery omen that she will have renown through *fama* and fate (7.79–80). Penelope is the subject of a similar prediction in *Odyssey* 24, when Agamemnon proclaims that she will have undying *kleos* and that the gods will make her the subject of song (24.194–8). In Lavinia's case the "singing" is predictive. Yet Vergil's use of *cano* resonates with the song of Penelope that Agamemnon foresees, and evokes the close links between song and fame central to Homeric epic.

Alongside her similarities with Penelope in the *Odyssey*, Lavinia differs in several important respects. Penelope's reunion with Odysseus marks a culmination of the latter's internal *nostos*. The tradition stretching back to antiquity that makes the completion of their reunion at *Od.* 23.296 the conclusion of the epic reflects the significance of the event in Odysseus' *nostos*. By contrast, Lavinia is a silent figure, whose marriage to Aeneas is foretold but not depicted. This omission forms a major part of how the *Aeneid* leaves

Aeneas' internal *nostos* incomplete. Vergil does not depict Lavinia in a role analogous to Penelope in *Odyssey* 23, placing the conjugal aspects of her role beyond the narrative frame of his epic. Aeneas' final mention of Lavinia, which occurs at the conclusion of his vow about his actions should he defeat Turnus in one-on-one combat, omits an explicit reference to their marriage (12.187–94).[41] Instead, as in the opening lines of the *Aeneid*, Lavinia again becomes a mix of woman and land when Aeneas proclaims that he will found a city named after her (12.193–4).

The omission of Aeneas' marriage to Lavinia is one ramification of the *Aeneid*'s abrupt ending, which leaves off before depicting any of the foretold peace and reconciliation between the Trojans and Latins. The ending of the *Aeneid* and its divergence from the manner that either Homeric epic concludes may on one level resonate with Roman experiences of the aftereffects of internecine conflicts and the attendant complexities of returning home. The vivid memories of civil war and the political uncertainties of the 20s BCE, during which Vergil composed the *Aeneid*, speak to a very different post-war experience than does the close of the *Odyssey*, where divine intervention quickly ends internecine conflict and effects community reconciliation.

In addition to the cultural reflections in the *Aeneid*'s abrupt ending and in Aeneas' unfinished internal *nostos*, Vergil's move with Lavinia is consistent with his treatment of Aeneas' other lovers in the poem. Creusa disappears so thoroughly after Book 2 that she does not even reappear in the underworld.[42] Dido stands silently, before fleeing during her reunion with Aeneas in the *lugentes campi* (6.450–76), her silence presaging Lavinia's.[43] As I shall argue in the next section of the paper, Vergil's omission of an episode between Aeneas and Lavinia is structurally opposed to the practice of Propertius, who, in poems written in the shadow of the *Aeneid*, contorts *nostos* so that it can be fulfilled nearly entirely by the elegiac *puella*.

Propertian *Nostoi*

Propertius' engagements with Homeric epic are well established.[44] Here I focus on elegies 2.14 and 3.12, both of which interact with *nostos* traditions that go back to Homer. I also suggest that these two elegies have points of contact with one another. My discussion of 2.14 explores how Propertius repurposes Greek traditions about *nostos* and Roman notions of triumphal *reditus* in order to present the poet-lover returning to his *puella*'s good graces for a single night. In addition, I contend that the closing image of 2.14 engages with the opening of the *Aeneid* in a manner that suggests that the elegiac lover's journey towards *nostos* differs fundamentally from Aeneas' in Vergil's epic. Propertius 3.12 presents Postumus as a second Odysseus, but only thanks to his beloved Galla's virtue, which exceeds Penelope's. This claim leads to a reframing of the *Odyssey's nostos* that again heads in very different directions from Vergil's engagements with *nostos* in the *Aeneid*. In 3.12 Propertius also alludes to Odysseus' first words in the *Odyssey*, a speech to which Vergil likewise alludes with Aeneas' opening words. As noted above, the second and third books of Propertius date to the same years that Vergil was composing the *Aeneid*, and Propertius 2.34 displays familiarity with elements of Vergil's in-progress epic. I approach Propertius' treatments of *nostos* in these poems as responding to the *Aeneid's* receptions of *nostos* traditions, while also reshaping *nostos* to fit his own elegiac project.

As discussed at the opening of the chapter, Propertius links Cynthia to Penelope as early as 1.3. Propertius' second book evokes Homer from the opening elegy, in which the poet-lover proclaims that his *puella* inspires him to compose "long *Iliads*" (2.1.14). Two subsequent poems in Book 2 compare Cynthia to Penelope, providing more context for the *nostos* thematics of 2.14. Elegy 2.6 commences by lamenting that Cynthia's house is more thronged with lovers than Lais', Thais', and Phryne's (1–6). Cynthia's similarity to these famous courtesans is the opposite of the kinds of Greek *exempla* that the poet-lover wishes for her to emulate in 2.6, Alcestis and Penelope (23–4). Cynthia is once again an anti-Penelope in 2.9, which contrasts Penelope's twenty years of fidelity and Briseis' devotion to Achilles upon his death (3–18) with the *puella's* inability to stay faithful even for a day (19–20). In this elegy, the poet-lover's *nostos* after being absent for a single night is ruined by Cynthia's infidelity. Robbed of a successful reunion with his beloved, he ponders death (39–40) and vows to be alone (45–6). Elegy 2.9 signals what is made explicit in 2.14, and again in 3.12: that the poet-lover's *nostos* depends solely on reunion with the *puella*, to the exclusion of any rivals.

Before proceeding further in analysing Propertius' receptions of *nostos* traditions and how those receptions relate to Vergil's, I shall consider an episode in the *Odyssey* that offers a precedent for Propertius' elegiac *nostoi*, especially in 2.14. Propertius' focus on the reunion between poet-lover and *puella* in his treatments of *nostos* finds resonance in the *Odyssey's* description of Odysseus and Penelope directly after Odysseus passes Penelope's test regarding their marriage bed (23.231–40):

ὣς φάτο, τῷ δ' ἔτι μᾶλλον ὑφ' ἵμερον ὦρσε γόοιο·
κλαῖε δ' ἔχων ἄλοχον θυμαρέα, κεδνὰ ἰδυῖαν.
ὡς δ' ὅτ' ἂν ἀσπάσιος γῆ νηχομένοισι φανήῃ,
ὧν τε Ποσειδάων εὐεργέα νῆ' ἐνὶ πόντῳ
ῥαίσῃ, ἐπειγομένην ἀνέμῳ καὶ κύματι πηγῷ· 235

παῦροι δ᾽ ἐξέφυγον πολιῆς ἁλὸς ἤπειρόνδε
νηχόμενοι, πολλὴ δὲ περὶ χροῒ τέτροφεν ἅλμη,
ἀσπάσιοι δ᾽ ἐπέβαν γαίης, κακότητα φυγόντες·
ὣς ἄρα τῇ ἀσπαστὸς ἔην πόσις εἰσοροώσῃ,
δειρῆς δ᾽ οὔ πω πάμπαν ἀφίετο πήχεε λευκώ.   240

So Penelope spoke, and she aroused in Odysseus even more desire for lamentation. He wept as he held his beloved careful-hearted wife. Land is a welcome sight
to men swimming, whose well-built ship Poseidon smashes on the sea as it is
driven by the wind and swollen waves. And only a few have escaped, swimming
from the hoary sea to the shore, their bodies crusted thick with salt, but joyfully
they plant their feet on land, having escaped misery. So joyous now to Penelope
was the sight of her husband, and she did not loosen her white arms from around
his neck at all.

These verses move from Odysseus' weeping to a simile about the joy of
sailors surviving a shipwreck. While the passage initially gives the impression that the shipwreck simile applies to Odysseus, verse 239 reveals that it
describes Penelope, creating a parallel between Odysseus escaping dangers
at sea to achieve his *nostos* and what Penelope has undergone at home.[45]
Viewed through a Propertian lens, this passage also offers a parallel between
the reunion of lovers and Homeric *nostos*. Indeed, the phrase ἵμερον …
γόοιο ("desire for lamentation," 231) contains two major themes of love
elegy, thanks to the genre's amatory focus and putative derivation from the
expression of lament ἒ ἒ λέγειν.[46] In this sense, the *Odyssey*'s simile links
what occurs in the external world of the hero and what happens in the bed-
room, a connection that Vergil does not bring into Aeneas' *nostos*, but which
is central to Propertius 2.14 and 3.12.

In 2.14 Propertius forges parallels between *nostoi*, amatory unions, and
shipwrecks in his presentation of the poet-lover the night after he has
achieved rare amatory success with an unnamed *puella*, presumably Cynthia. Elegy 2.14 closes with a ship metaphor that has points of contact
with the shipwreck simile in *Odyssey* 23 as well as with the opening of the
Aeneid. I shall turn to these resonances after first considering other ways
that 2.14 engages with the theme of *nostos*. Propertius' treatment of *nostos*
in this elegy at once presents his night with his *puella* as the *telos* of his
amatory journey and, thanks to the myths and nautical imagery he uses,
imbues the poem with a sense of the impermanence of his *gaudia* and *nostos*
alike. Elegy 2.14 begins with a priamel comparing the poet-lover's amatory
gaudia to the joys of several mythical exemplars, in which returns are either
implicit or explicit (1–10):

Non ita Dardanio gauisus Atrida triumpho est,
   cum caderent magnae Laomedontis opes;
nec sic errore exacto laetatus Vlixes,
   cum tetigit carae litora Dulichiae;
nec sic Electra, saluum cum aspexit Oresten,   5
   cuius falsa tenens fleuerat ossa soror;
nec sic incolumem Minois Thesea uidit,
   Daedalium lino cum duce rexit iter,
quanta ego praeterita collegi gaudia nocte:
   immortalis ero, si altera talis erit.   10

Not thus did the son of Atreus rejoice in triumph over Troy, when the mighty power of Laomedon collapsed in ruin; nor so jubilant was Ulysses when, his wanderings over, he touched the shores of his beloved Dulichia; nor so Electra, when she beheld Orestes safe, having wept a sister's grief as she held his false bones; nor so Minos' daughter when she saw Theseus unharmed, having steered his course through Daedalus' maze, with thread for pilot: all their joys were nothing compared to those I garnered this past night: if there shall be another like this, I shall become immortal.

Although the primary elements of comparison in this passage are joy and happiness (*gauisus*, 1; *laetatus*, 3; *gaudia*, 9), return and reunion are explicit in the last three exempla and implicit in the first. *Nostos* becomes an overt theme in the second couplet when Propertius makes a comparison to Odysseus' joy at reaching his home.[47] Propertius' construction of a parallel between a night with a *puella* and Odysseus touching his home shores also resonates with the description of the shipwrecked sailors' joy at reaching land at *Odyssey* 23.236–8. Verses 5–6 present Orestes' *nostos*, focalized through Electra's happiness at the moment she sees him. The next couplet features another reunion: Ariadne's joy at Theseus' re-emergence from the labyrinth, which Propertius describes as an *iter* (8), and is the moment that marks the beginning of Theseus' return journey to Athens. Only the description in the first distich of the son of Atreus' joy at the sack of Troy does not have an explicit *nostos* or reunion element, instead initially conjuring the theme of *militia amoris*. Yet in the context of the other three exempla, the opening couplet may also invoke the initial moments of Agamemnon's return to his home, before things go terribly wrong.[48] In addition, Propertius' presentation of the sack of Troy combines with the next couplet's description of Odysseus, the last of the Greek heroes to reach home, to circumscribe the episodes in the Epic Cycle that fall in between these two events, including the post-war *nostoi*. In this sense, the first four lines of 2.14 also have similarities with

the opening verses of the *Odyssey*, where the narrative moves from the sack
of Troy to Odysseus' struggles to attain his *nostos*. Furthermore, Propertius'
placement of the description of the returns of Odysseus and Orestes directly
after his reference to Agamemnon evokes the disastrous conclusion of the
latter's unsuccessful *nostos*.

All of these *nostos*-related moments of joy, the poet-lover proclaims, fail
to equal the amatory *gaudia* he had the previous night (9–10), which he
spent at his *puella's* house (21–2, 28). Yet the examples in the priamel also
point to challenges subsequent to the moment described: Agamemnon's
joy at the sack of Troy is followed by Greek excesses that anger the gods
and make their *nostoi* difficult; when Odysseus and Orestes arrive at their
homelands, the trials of their internal *nostoi* still lie ahead; Ariadne's joy at
Theseus' return from the labyrinth evokes his eventual abandonment of her
on Naxos and Aegeus' death during Theseus' *nostos*. Similarly, the Propertian poet-lover qualifies his *gaudia*: more could make him immortal (10)
or, as he states at the close of the poem, like a ship, he could run aground
(29–32, see below). The ultimate outcome of the poet-lover's admittance
into his *puella's* affections is in doubt, but the opening of 2.14 lays out clear
links between his *puella* and *nostos*.

At 2.14.21–8 Propertius turns again to the theme of return, this time
presenting his amatory success in the Roman terms of a triumphal *reditus*:

> pulsabant alii frustra dominamque uocabant:
>   mecum habuit positum lenta puella caput.
> haec mihi deuictis potior uictoria Parthis,
>   haec spolia, haec reges, haec mihi currus erunt.
> magna ego dona tua figam, Cytherea, columna,   25
>   taleque sub nostro nomine carmen erit:
> HAS PONO ANTE TVAS TIBI, DIVA, PROPERTIVS AEDIS
>   EXVVIAS, TOTA NOCTE RECEPTVS AMANS.

Others were knocking in vain and calling our mistress: but my girl, at ease, kept her
head pillowed with me. This is a greater victory for me than defeating the Parthians!
These will be my spoils, my captive kings, and my chariot. I shall nail great offerings on your temple pillar, Cytherea, and this will be the poem posted in my name:
"I, Propertius, admitted as a lover for a whole night, place these spoils before your
temple, goddess."

The poet-lover proclaims that his night spent with the *puella* while his
excluded rivals called for her and knocked on the door is a greater victory
than defeating the Parthians. His amatory *gaudia* render him a triumphing

general. The sense of return in Propertius' triumphal imagery is emphasized in the dedicatory offerings and inscription that the poet-lover plans in verses 25–8. Like Odysseus, the poet-lover conquers his rivals as he returns to his *puella*. As a *triumphator*, their fruitless efforts are drawn into the train of his triumphal parade. The blending of return, conquest, and triumph in these verses also echoes the poem's opening where the poet-lover's *gaudia* (9) are compared to Agamemnon's *Dardanio … triumpho* (1). Yet the son of Atreus' failed *nostos* again casts a shadow over the poet-lover's celebration of his triumphal return here. This shadow grows in the final verses of the poem.

Elegy 2.14 concludes with a sailing analogy that resonates with the *nostos* theme that runs through the elegy, with the description of Odysseus at the beginning of the poem, with the shipwreck simile in *Odyssey* 23, and with the *Aeneid*'s opening (2.14.29–32):

> nunc a te <est>, mea lux, ueniatne ad litora nauis[49]
> > seruata; an mediis sidat onusta uadis.
> quod si forte aliqua nobis mutabere culpa,
> > uestibulum iaceam mortuus ante tuum!

Now, light of my life, it is up to you whether my ship comes safe to shore or founders overladen amid the shoals. And if any offence shall alter you towards me, then may I fall down dead before your entrance hall!

Like the simile in *Odyssey* 23, these verses present lovers in nautical terms. While the *Odyssey* uses a shipwreck simile to describe the reunion of lovers, in 2.14 it is up to the *puella* what sort of return voyage the poet-lover shall have. The final verse of 2.14 evokes a *paraklausithyron* but could also describe a returning sailor who fails in his attempt at an internal *nostos*.[50] Propertius' description of his ship that *ueniatne ad litora … seruata* (29–30) points back to his earlier presentation of Odysseus (*tetigit … litora*, 4). In addition, *ad litora … seruata* resonates with the sailors in *Odyssey* 23's shipwreck simile escaping the wreck and swimming to shore (23.236–7): παῦροι δ᾽ <u>ἐξέφυγον</u> πολιῆς ἁλὸς <u>ἤπειρόνδε</u> / νηχόμενοι ("And only a few <u>have escaped</u>, swimming from the hoary sea <u>to the shore</u>"). Elegy 2.14.31 gives the *puella* a role similar to Poseidon in the shipwreck simile (*Od.* 23.234): each determines whether the ship in their respective texts meets with trouble.

The closing verses of 2.14 also have points of contact with the opening of the *Aeneid*. Propertius' phrase *ueniatne ad litora* echoes Vergil's description of Aeneas as *qui … / Italiam, fato profugus, Lauiniaque <u>uenit</u> / <u>litora</u>

(1.1–3). This is the only time that Propertius uses the combination of *uenio* and *litus* in a phrase; Vergil only uses the combination once prior to the *Aeneid*, at *G*. 2.108.[51] Propertius confirms his knowledge of the opening verses of the *Aeneid* with another allusion to them at 2.34.63–4. This latter allusion occurs just prior to his comparison of Vergil's epic to Homer's (2.34.66), offering a similar triangulation of elegy, Vergil, and Homeric epic as in 2.14. The opening of the *Aeneid* is a particularly appropriate passage for 2.14 to allude to, since, as previously noted, in these verses Vergil engages with the opening of the *Odyssey*, while setting Lavinian *litora* as the *nostos*-like endpoint of Aeneas' travels. In addition, the metaphorical shores that the poet-lover hopes to reach in 2.14 are closely linked with his *puella*, much as Vergil's Lavinian shores, as discussed above, contain the name of the Penelope-like figure in the *Aeneid*. Yet where Vergil's phrase *Lauinia litora* embeds Aeneas' future wife in the landscape that is his fated goal to reach, Propertius' *puella* becomes akin to the *Aeneid*'s fates and the divine forces, in that she will determine whether the poet-lover's metaphorical journey will be a success. The centrality of the poet-lover's *puella* in the process of "coming to shore" in the closing verses of 2.14, when compared to the primacy of place in Vergil's first description of Aeneas' *nostos*, encapsulates the difference between Propertius' and Vergil's treatments of the theme of return: for the former everything depends upon the *puella*; for the latter the conjugal and amatory elements of *nostos* recede into the background.

For as much as 2.14 compares the Propertian lover's joy at his reunion with his *puella* to various *nostoi* from Greek myth and to the *reditus* of a triumphing Roman general, its final verses also present the Propertian poet-lover's *nostos* as unfinished, a natural result since a lasting reunion with a *puella* would mark an end to his elegiac poetry. Yet the unfinished state of his *nostos* also finds Homeric precedent: in order to appease Poseidon, Odysseus has further travel and separation from Penelope lying ahead of him at the end of the *Odyssey*. Indeed, both the *Odyssey* and Propertius 2.14 present the lovers at the centre of each text spending precisely one night together. Unlike the *Odyssey* and unlike Vergil's treatments of *nostos* in the *Aeneid*, however, 2.14's *nostos* is almost entirely dependent upon the *puella* alone. Aside from the brief mention of the exclusion of rival lovers, the poet-lover's *nostos* is disconnected from the broader community. Elegy 2.14 is often correctly noted as paired with 2.15, in which the poet-lover spends a happy night with Cynthia. Yet 2.14's emphasis on reunion and the exclusion of rival lovers also looks ahead to 2.16, in which the return of a *praetor* leads to the poet-lover's exclusion, a reminder that the *nostos* of a more epic figure can easily displace the elegiac lover, and that a *nostos* dependent upon a single beloved rather than an entire community is inherently unstable. Yet despite the instability of the *nostos* in 2.14, by focusing on the *puella* alone and omitting reclaiming a larger role in the community, the poet-lover is freed from the problems and dangers associated with return in the wake of Rome's civil conflicts.

Propertius' special focus on the role of women in his treatments of *nostoi* occurs not just in his presentations of poet-lover and *puella* but also, in the case of 3.12, when he depicts other figures.[52] Elegy 3.12 is a *propemptikon* for Postumus, often identified as Propertius' relative C. Propertius Postumus, who is departing on campaign against the Parthians (c. 21 BCE), leaving behind his beloved, Aelia Galla.[53] Postumus is decidedly not an elegiac lover, since by abandoning his beloved "to follow Augustus' brave standards as a soldier" (*miles … Augusti fortia signa sequi*, 2) he does what the poet-lover cannot do in elegy 1.6 when he refuses to accompany Tullus abroad as part of an imperial retinue. Propertius in turn presents Galla as possessing faithfulness that makes her unlike a typical elegiac *puella*, while also giving her an agency that recalls Penelope and differs from the *Aeneid*'s depiction of Lavinia.

Not only does Propertius devote the final section of 3.12 to a summary of Odysseus' travels that is occasioned by a comparison of Postumus to Odysseus and of Galla to Penelope, but the poem also has two points of contact with 2.14. These connections further facilitate reading the elegies in relation to one another. The first link to 2.14 is that Postumus is presented as on campaign against the Parthians (3.12.3), a detail that resonates with the poet-lover comparing his success with his *puella* in 2.14 to triumph over the Parthians (23–4).[54] Second, 3.12's description of Odysseus contains similar language to 2.14.3–4 (see below). In addition, through an intertext with the *Odyssey*, 3.12 interacts with Aeneas' first words in the *Aeneid*, offering another triangulation between Propertius, Vergil, and Homer.

I shall consider the latter connection first. Although the summary of Odysseus' travels begins later in 3.12, Propertius first alludes to the *Odyssey* at verses 13–15, where the poem finishes a list of Galla's fears for Postumus and praises Postumus' luck for having such a faithful wife: *neue aliquid de te flendum referatur in urna: / sic redeunt, illis qui cecidere locis. / ter quater in casta felix, o Postume, Galla!* ("… or that some part of you be brought home in an urn for her to mourn: in such a manner do they return, ones who perish in those lands. Three and four times, Postumus, are you blessed by chaste Galla!"). These verses echo a phrase first used at *Odyssey* 5.306–7 when Odysseus fears drowning at sea: τρὶς μάκαρες Δαναοὶ καὶ τετράκις, οἳ τότ᾽ ὄλοντο / Τροίῃ ἐν εὐρείῃ …

("Three and four times blessed were the Danaans who perished in those days in wide Troy ...") Propertius' *ter quater ... felix* corresponds to τρὶς μάκαρες ... τετράκις, and *qui cecidere* parallels οἳ ... ὄλοντο. Although similar phrases appear elsewhere, Propertius' description of dying on campaign in 3.12.13–14 specifically recalls the context of Odysseus' use of the phrase.[55] Vergil too alludes to this Homeric passage with Aeneas' first words. Yet in this instance Aeneas, reflecting a Trojan perspective, proclaims that those who died at Troy were "three and four times blessed" (*O terque quaterque beati, A.* 1.94) because they died at home. Both Vergil and Propertius reframe Odysseus' lament by turning the focus of being "three and four times blessed" to being at home, where in the *Odyssey* the phrase refers to dying at war. Propertius in addition links the phrase to the fidelity of Galla, which, as the elegy goes on to proclaim, will allow Postumus to have a return akin to Odysseus' *nostos*.

The Odyssean parallels in 3.12 become explicit in verse 23. After assuring Postumus that someday he will return to a faithful Galla, Propertius compares him to Odysseus (21–4):

> nam quocumque die saluum te fata remittent,
>   pendebit collo Galla pudica tuo.
> Postumus alter erit <u>miranda coniuge</u> Ulixes:
>   non illi longae tot nocuere morae

For whatever day the fates will send you safely home, chaste Galla will cling to your neck. Because of his <u>marvellous wife</u> Postumus will be a second Ulysses: Ulysses' long absences caused him no harm ...

As the syntax of verse 23 makes clear, it is because of Galla that Postumus is a second Odysseus, and he is no Odysseus until after she is a *miranda coniuge*. Furthermore, verse 24 compares Postumus to Odysseus because of his long absence, not because of his heroic deeds or adventures. Indeed, the events that the poem imagines Postumus experiencing on campaign are not anything like Odysseus'. In verses 7–14 Propertius describes Postumus exhausted, drinking from the Araxes, and, Galla hopes, not letting his *uirtus* get him killed. Postumus' activities while away are not Odyssean opportunities for glory. Instead they are only sources of fear for the Penelope-like Galla, who in turn renders him a second Odysseus.

After declaring Postumus a new Odysseus, Propertius describes the latter's travels. He dispenses with the Trojan war in a half line (*castra decem annorum*, 25), focusing on Odysseus' travails during his journey home (3.12.24–37).[56] The final verses of 3.12 move from the underworld and the Sirens directly to Ithaca, before concluding with a comparison between Galla and Penelope (33–8):

> nigrantisque domos animarum intrasse silentum,
>> Sirenum surdo remige adisse lacus,
> et ueteres arcus le[c]to renouasse procorum,   35
>> errorisque sui sic statuisse modum.
> nec frustra, quia casta domi persederat uxor.
>> uincit Penelopes Aelia Galla fidem.

… and Ulysses entered the dark halls of the silent dead, he was rowed by deaf oarsmen to the pools of the Sirens, and he brought his old bow to life with the slaughter of the suitors, thus putting an end to his wanderings. And not in vain, since his wife remained true to him at home. Aelia Galla bests Penelope's fidelity.

Propertius' Odyssean narrative jumps from the Sirens to Odysseus' slaughter of the suitors. Yet his phrasing in verse 36 points back to 2.14 and that poem's description of an episode absent from 3.12, Odysseus first setting foot on Ithaca. *Erroris … sic statuisse modum* (3.12.36) echoes 2.14.3: *nec sic errore exacto laetatus Vlixes*. 3.12 only makes indirect reference to the reunion of Odysseus and Penelope. Yet the obliquity is fitting, since the future reunion of Galla and Postumus spurs the poem's turn to the comparison with Homeric *exempla*, and so it stands in for the reunion of Odysseus and Penelope.

Galla's – and Penelope's – critical role in a successful Propertian *nostos* is confirmed in the final couplet (37–8). The declaration in verse 38 that Galla surpasses Penelope in *fides* confirms the claim in verse 23 that it is through Galla that Postumus will become an Odysseus.[57] Elegy 3.12 excludes all characters from its description of Odysseus' internal *nostos* except for Penelope and the suitors – and in this case even the suitors are defeated by Galla's fidelity: *Gallam non munera uincent* ("no gifts will conquer Galla," 19). Similar to 2.14, which likewise includes only a *puella* and amatory rivals, in 3.12 there is no Telemachus, Laertes, herders, slaves, or suitors' relatives. Nor is there a sense of home as a place or a polity, whether Ithaca or Rome.[58] As in 2.14, in the conception of *nostos* presented in 3.12, there is no return except for a return to the *puella*, precisely the element of *nostos* that is absent from the *Aeneid*.

Conclusion

How do Vergil's and Propertius' receptions of Greek *nostos* traditions reflect the literary and cultural milieu of 20s BCE? The *Aeneid*, as we have seen, ultimately offers a vision of both heroic epic and *nostos* that ends with violence between two men, with Lavinia's role as another Penelope left unfulfilled. Vergil's omission of the union between Aeneas and Lavinia is part of the *Aeneid's* broader scepticism of *amor*, but also suggests scepticism about the ease of transitions from conflict to peace. Propertius' focus on the *puella* in his treatments of *nostos* is not unexpected, as it reflects the larger theme in elegy that love is all-encompassing, and that Propertian elegy derives from *Cynthia prima*. Although place is not prominent in Propertian treatments of *nostos*, throughout much of his poetry Rome is constructed as the ideal space to pursue elegiac love, and in the poems considered here it is implicitly the location for *nostoi*, as the poet-lover's imagined triumph in 2.14 and the descriptions of Galla left alone at Rome in 3.12 indicate. Yet Propertius is from Assisi not Rome. In addition, elegiac *puellae* evoke women who were often trafficked from the Greek East.[59] Could Rome truly be the site of a *nostos* for either elegiac figure in these circumstances? Or was the *urbs* more akin to Calypso's island, a place where years could be spent and (poetic) immortality might be attained, but which could never be Ithaca?

Although in 2.14 and 3.12 the Propertian poet-lover and Postumus achieve *nostoi* centred on *puellae*, at the end of the *Monobiblos* Propertius points to a more fraught vision of home and *nostos*. Elegy 1.21 describes a *nostos* that is even starker than Vergil's in *B.* 1: one soldier's return is contrasted with another's death.[60] Propertius follows this *nostos* by defining his birthplace in 1.22 through its proximity to "the Perusine graves of the fatherland" (*Perusina … patriae … sepulcra*, 3). While elegies 1.21 and 1.22 recall internecine conflicts from the triumviral period, the dangers of return persisted under Augustus' regime. When Cornelius Gallus returned from Egypt to Rome and was driven to suicide in 27/26 BCE, his downfall may well have reinforced for Vergil and Propertius on a personal level the potential hazards of *reditus* in the Augustan age. Returns were also a theme that Gallus was interested in as a poet: fr. 2.2–5 concerns the triumphal *reditus* of "Caesar."[61] In addition, while the *Bucolics* open with a contrast between Tityrus' *nostos* and Meliboeus' forced departure from home, the collection closes with Gallus abroad in Arcadia, unable even to attempt a successful elegiac *nostos* since Lycoris has followed a rival lover to the Rhine frontier. The historical Gallus, however, did not return from Egypt as an elegiac lover bereft of his beloved, although Propertius tactfully represents his death along these lines (2.34.91–2): *et modo formosa quam multa Lycoride Gallus / mortuus inferna uulnera lauit aqua* ("And recently how many wounds did Gallus wash in the water of the underworld, dead from beautiful Lycoris"). Instead, Gallus returned as a former equestrian prefect who either already had or would lose the *amicitia* of the *princeps*, with deadly consequences.[62]

Within these social and literary contexts, Vergil and Propertius repeatedly engage with traditions about *nostos*. These traditions trace back to
Homer. Yet these two Roman poets take *nostoi* in divergent directions that
reflect the broader contemporary poetic conversation about the relationship between epic and elegy. As part of this conversation, the poets each
distil *nostos* down to the elements that suit generic conventions and their
different poetic projects, distinguish themselves from one another, and offer
implicit responses to the potential perils of return at Rome and in Italy.

NOTES

I would like to thank Alison Keith, Sharon James, Richard Martin, and Vince Tomasso
for their help at various stages of this essay. Any deficiencies that remain are my own.

 1 For travel as a cure for love: Plaut. *Merc.* 644–60; Ter. *Ad.* 274–5; Cic. *Tusc.*
    4.77; Prop. 1.17, 3.21; Ov. *Rem. am.* 213–48. Quotations of Propertius follow
    Fedeli 1984b; Vergil follows Mynors 1969; Homer follows Allen 1917–20.
    Translations are based on LCL with modifications.
 2 The reference to Ariadne in Prop. 1.3 also invokes Bacchus; see Heslin 2018:
    84–5 and 84n95 with further references.
 3 For links between Cynthia and Penelope in 1.3, see Reitzenstein 1936: 44;
    Wlosok 1967: 349–50; Hodge and Buttimore 1977: 97; Noonan 1991: 336;
    Tatham 2000: 44–6; Robinson 2013: 107, 112–14
 4 See Evans 1971; Hutchinson 2006a: 189; Fedeli, Dimundo, and Ciccarelli
    2015: 1012–13.
 5 See esp. Bright 1971.
 6 See esp. Stahl 1985: 180; J. Miller 2004; Heyworth 2007a: 275; O'Rourke
    2011b. Cf. Heslin 2018: 220, who argues that in the *Aeneid* Vergil may respond
    to Propertius 2.34's description of his epic.
 7 On Vergil's representations of *amor*, see Fedeli 1984a; Schafer 2014. For
    responses to elegy in the *Aeneid*, see Cairns 1989: 136–50; Heslin 2018;
    Myers 2020; McCallum in this volume.
 8 Bonifazi 2009, esp. 500–1. See also Frame 1978; Malkin 1998; Bonifazi 2008;
    Alexopoulou 2009; Hornblower and Biffis 2018.
 9 See Alexopoulou 2009: 7.
10 See Hornblower and Biffis 2018: 25–37 (who assume a second century BCE
    date for the *Alexandra*).
11 De Jong 2001: 313, following Schadewaldt 1970: 57.
12 For the equivalence between *nostos* and *reditus*, see Purcell 2018: 279–80. In this
    paper, *nostos* describes Vergil's and Propertius' receptions of Greek themes; *reditus*
    refers to representations of returns that emphasize specifically Roman elements.

13 On multiple *patriae*, see esp. Cic. *Leg.* 2.2–5; cf. Bonjour 1976: 1–112; Feldherr
    1997: 138–43; Fletcher 2014: 4–6. For *villeggiatura* around the Bay of Naples,
    see D'Arms 1970. On migration, see esp. Tacoma 2016.
14 Purcell 2018: 271–6.
15 Purcell 2018: 279–80.
16 On the theme of return in the *Aeneid*: Buchheit 1963: 151–63; Horsfall 1973, 1987,
    1989; Bonjour 1976: 481–5; Dekel 2012: 100–1; Fletcher 2014: esp. 26–7, 101–2.
    The recognition that the *Aeneid* divides into Odyssean and Iliadic halves is already
    implied in Servius ad *A.* 1.1 and explicit in Macrobius *Sat.* 5.2.6; see the recent
    discussion of Farrell 2021: 9, 41–2, who at 7–28 also offers a useful summary of
    scholarly approaches to Homeric elements in the *Aeneid*, especially from Knauer
    onwards.
17 Nelis 2001: 24–5.
18 Hornblower and Biffis 2018: 27–8, 35–6. On *nostoi* in the *Alexandra*, see also
    Hornblower 2015, esp. 57–8.
19 Lane Fox 2018: 193.
20 See esp. Horsfall 1987, 2000: 165–9 for discussion of Dardanus, with further
    references.
21 On Aeneas as oecist, see esp. Horsfall 1989. As Alessandro Barchiesi points
    out to me (*per litteras*), when the Trojans sail by the Sirens (*A.* 5.864–6), surely
    among them is Parthenope, whom Vergil prominently uses in the *sphragis* of
    the *Georgics* to mark his "pleasure home" at Naples (4.564). In this manner
    Vergil brings Aeneas by his own home en route to Latium.
22 The tradition preserved in Dionysius of Halicarnassus (*Ant. Rom.* 1.72.2), who
    attributes it to Hellanicus (*FGrHist* 4 fr. 84), that Aeneas founded Rome with
    Odysseus provides another intersection between Aeneas' *nostos* and Odysseus;
    cf. Lycoph. *Alex.* 1242–4. See Horsfall 1979: 378–82; Solmsen 1986; Wiseman
    1995: 50–1; Hornblower 2015: 443–4.
23 On Iliadic aspects of *A.* 7–12, see esp. Anderson 1957; Gransden 1984;
    Horsfall 1995: 203–6; Casali 2004; Barchiesi 2015. For Odyssean elements in
    the latter stages of the *Aeneid*, see esp. Knauer 1964b; Cairns 1989: 177–215;
    O'Hara 2010: 103–5; Dekel 2012: 109–15; Kelly 2014: 647.
24 Penelope is only one model with which Lavinia engages: see esp. Cairns 1989:
    151–76; Formicula 2006; Felici 2010.
25 Knauer 1964b: 76. Cf. Cairns 1989: 211, who notes that Vergil's description of
    Turnus as Lavinia's handsomest suitor (7.55) recalls Antinous' handsomeness
    in the *Odyssey* (17.381, 454; 21.277).
26 See esp. Barchiesi 2015: 83–91; Tarrant 2012: 341. Both also compare
    Adrestus' nearly successful plea to Menelaus at *Il.* 6.37–65. Quint 2018:
    180–90 explores parallels to Achilles and Memnon in the *Aithiopis*.
27 On Aeneas' final speech, see Esposito 2016 with further references.

28 For Turnus' motivation as a mix of marital and political ambitions, see Tarrant 2012: 12–13.

29 Conte 1986: 185–95 discusses another Odyssean connection here: Vergil's allusion to Heracles' baldric at *Od.* 11.609–12.

30 Fowler 1989: 100–1. For many of the parallels discussed in this paragraph, see further Knauer 1964a: 322–7; Cairns 1989: 211–14. Horsfall 1995: 194–216 and Tarrant 2012: 8–30 offer useful general summaries of the end of the *Aeneid*. See also O'Hara 2010 and Kelly 2014, both with further references.

31 12.943 and twice in 12.948. For the association between Pallas and Pallas Athena here, see Hornsby 1966: 358–9; Hardie 1993: 34; Spence 1999: 157–61, with further discussion of Athena/Minerva's presence at the end of the *Aeneid*.

32 Hardie 1997: 147n33.

33 Knauer 1964a: 431; these are the only parallels that he notes for *A.* 12.952. Vergil's use of this same line to describe the death of Camilla at *A.* 11.831 alludes to the appearance of the identical verse in the *Iliad* to describe the deaths of Patroclus (16.857) and Hector (22.363); see esp. the discussion of Tarrant 2012: 341.

34 *Odyssey* 24.6–8 compares the suitors' squeaks to sounds bats make; *gemitus* is also used to describe animal and bird sounds: *OLD* s.v. 1b.

35 The parallels between *A.* 12.952 and *Od.* 24.5 and 20.353–6 are not noted in Knauer 1964a or elsewhere to my knowledge. As De Jong 2001: 502 observes, οἰμωγή describes the sound of people dying in battle at *Il.* 4.450 = 8.64 and so at *Od.* 20.353 anticipates the suitors' violent deaths. Similar to *umbras* at *A.* 12.952, ζόφος is metonymy for the underworld at *Il.* 15.191. For Vergil's allusion at *A.* 12.952 back to his use of *umbra* at the close of *B.* 1 and 10, see esp. Hardie 1997: 144–5.

36 See *A.* 1.264–6, 6.763–6, 12.189–94.

37 See esp. Fratantuono 2008, with further references at 40n1. In this volume, see Papaioannou on Ovid's depiction of Aeneas and Lavinia in his Anna Perenna narrative (*F.* 3.523–696).

38 For the mixing of a land and woman here, see Keith 2000: 49–50; Syed 2005: 137–9; Fletcher 2014: 74–5. On the opening of the *Aeneid* and the opening of *Odyssey*, see esp. Hardie 1986: 302–3. Cf. the recent discussion of Iliadic and Odyssean elements in the opening of Vergil's epic in Farrell 2021: 41–8. On the textual issue of *Lauinia* or *Lauina*, see esp. Fratantuono 2008: 41.

39 Knauer 1964a: 399 parallels *A.* 7.54 with the description of "much wooed" (πολυμνήστη) Penelope at *Od.* 4.770. Horsfall 2000: 82 compares the presentation of Lavinia's suitors with Nausicaa's at *Od.* 6.34–5 and Barcé's suitors at Pind. *Pyth.* 9.107–9.

40 De Jong 2001: 29–31 summarizes the *Odyssey*'s varying depictions of the prospect of Penelope's remarriage.

41 See Tarrant 2012: 140

42 As Casali 2014: 312 observes, *A.* 2.788 may imply that Cybele detains the
   shade of Creusa in Troad, which would explain her absence from Book 6.
43 Fratantuono 2008: 42.
44 See Evans 1971; Berthet 1980, 1987; Dalzell 1980; Benediktson 1985; Dué
   2001; Brouwers 2006; Michalopoulos 2016; Kayachev 2018.
45 See further Russo, Fernández-Galiano, and Heubeck 1992: 338–9. Gardner
   and Murnaghan 2014: 2 discuss this passage in relation to modern receptions
   of the *Odyssey*.
46 On this etymology, see O'Hara 2017: xxin3 and xxiin4. On elegy and lament,
   see also Gladhill in this volume.
47 Propertius' substitution of Dulichia (elsewhere Dulichium; see Fedeli 2005:
   419) for Ithaca becomes common in Latin poetry (Coleman 1977: 200).
   Notably, Verg. *B.* 6.76 is the only instance prior to Prop. Book 2. For Odysseus'
   connection to Dulichium, see *Od.* 1.246, quoted above, with Heubeck, West,
   and Hainsworth 1988: 106.
48 I thank one of the anonymous reviewers for pointing out this element of *nostos* in
   2.14.1–2. In addition, Fedeli 2005: 416–17 notes the possibility that "son of Atreus"
   in 2.14.1 evokes Menelaus instead of or in addition to Agamemnon. In which case,
   Fedeli postulates that the couplet points to the former's reunion with Helen.
49 For verse 29, I follow Fedeli 2005, who prints the emendation of Luck 1962:
   338–40; the version transmitted in the manuscripts does not materially change
   my analysis.
50 More speculatively, Propertius' *uestibulum … ante* may be compared to the
   threshold (οὐδός) where Odysseus positions himself during the slaughter
   of the suitors (*Od.* 22.2), which Eurymachus exhorts his fellow suitors to
   push him from (22.70–8), and Odysseus fears they might succeed in doing
   (22.106–7).
51 Vergil also uses the combination at *A.* 3.186 and 3.651–2. Although
   uenio + *litus* seems prosaic, a PHI Latin yields few instances prior to Vergil and
   Propertius: Cic. *Verr.* 2.5.91 (*peruenio*); Varro *Rust.* 3.17.4 and *Antiquitates* 257;
   Catul. 64.121 (a contested supplement first suggested by Lachmann).
52 Cf. Prop. 4.3 with James 2012.
53 For the context and dating of this poem, as well as potential identifications of
   Postumus and Galla, the latter likely a relative of L. Aelius Gallus, the second
   prefect of Egypt, see esp. Fedeli 1985: 397–8; Cairns 2006: 16–21. Hor. *Carm.*
   2.14, which is also addressed to a Postumus, describes a *katabasis* with points
   of contact with the *Odyssey*; see Nisbet and Hubbard 1978: 223; Cairns 2006:
   19; Keith 2008b: 7.
54 On Propertius and Parthia, see also 3.4 with Fedeli 1985: 162–3.
55 On other instances of this phrase and on *makarismoi*, see Fedeli 1985: 403.
56 On the variations from the *Odyssey* in this passage, see Fedeli 1985: 405–11;
   Brouwers 2006.

57 Cf. Berthet 1980: 144.

58 Ithaca only appears in 3.12 in reference to the "Ithacan spits" upon which the cattle of the sun are roasted (29). Rome is only mentioned as a site of corrupting luxury that will not overcome Galla (18–19).

59 See Keith 2008b: 86–114, and 2011, esp. 29–31.

60 If we accept the interpretation of Du Quesnay 1992 that the speaker and addressee of 1.21 are brothers-in-law, the theme of *nostos* is further accentuated, since both figures had hoped to return to the same family.

61 Most scholars favour reading a reference to Julius Caesar in these verses: see Hollis 2007: 243.

62 Although Dio Cass. 53.23.5–6 and Amm. Marc. 17.14.5 attribute Gallus' downfall to misbehaviour while prefect (cf. Serv. ad *B.* 10.1), more chronologically proximate sources do not link his disgrace to Egypt. Instead they indicate that Gallus somehow offended the *princeps* (Suet. *Aug.* 66) or was falsely accused of doing something offensive (Ov. *Am.* 3.9.63–4). As Boucher 1966: 47 notes, Gallus may have come back from Egypt in 29 BCE well before his death, so he may have lost Augustus' *amicitia* after his return. See also Myers 2018: 217–18 and the reassessment of Gallus' stele at Philae by Hoffmann, Minas-Nerpel, and Pfeiffer 2009.

5

Lust in Lions and Lovers: Hunting for Civic Virtue in Vergil, Propertius, and Early Greek Elegy

EVA ANAGNOSTOU-LAOUTIDES

Introduction: Morality and Hunting in Vergil and Elegy

Scholars have long noted the influence of Vergil on Propertius,[1] although the various episodes of their intense poetic exchange remain elusive, with the dates for the publication of Propertius' *Monobiblos* still debated.[2] Nevertheless, Vergil's interest in the elegiac world of Propertius cannot be underrated, given Dido's elegiac investment, widely acknowledged in scholarship.[3] By allowing Dido to be smeared with the qualities ascribed to Roman elegiac mistresses, typically portrayed as tempestuous and extravagant creatures whose influence exemplifies the results of *turpis amor* (shameful love) on Roman men,[4] Vergil exploits the theme of moral decline that the Roman elegists systematically revised.[5] But while the Roman elegists renounce their duty towards the state in the name of unquenched passion,[6] answering not to Rome but to the dictates of their tyrannical mistresses,[7] Vergil defends traditional Roman values. Thus, Aeneas reinstates the Roman dedication to the state by managing to extricate himself from the shackles of *turpis cupido* ("shameful desire," *A.* 4.194) to the detriment of Dido, who is reduced from an inspiring leader (*A.* 1.340) to a raging Bacchant (*A.* 4.300–1), and more painfully, from a by-form of Diana, the divine huntress (*A.* 1.498–504), to hunted prey (*A.* 4.68–73). In an epic where hunting is "thematically important,"[8] Dido, an eastern queen, represents the chaotic forces of the East that must be subdued to the civilizing order of Augustus.

Hunting also offers a distinctive lens for examining Vergil's engagement with elegiac motifs, especially since erotic hunting is an(other) elegiac response to the old-fashioned aristocratic ideals of military prowess and commitment to the state. Propertius introduced his *Monobiblos* with a notable expression of the motif by depicting Milanion as hunting in the wilderness, more maddened by unrequited love than by the blows of his monstrous opponents, the Centaurs (1.12): *ibat et hirsutas saepe uidere feras* ("he [=Milanion] would often go and face shaggy wild beasts").[9] Vergil was evidently sensitive to this imagery, because in *B.* 10 (55–60) he portrayed Gallus,[10] the pioneer of Roman elegy, as burning with passion for Lycoris, while hunting on the slopes of Mount Parthenius in Arcadia (10.55–8): ... *Maenala ... Parthenios ... saltus* – the very location where Propertian Milanion received his wounds (1.11–14): *Partheniis ... antris ... saucius Arcadiis rupibus.*[11]

Hunting was hardly a traditional pastime of Roman aristocracy; in fact, the staging of *uenationes*, hunting games in the amphitheatre, was a relatively recent vogue which had taken root in Rome as a result of its expansion in the East and was frowned upon by traditionalists such as Cicero and Pliny,[12] while Augustus apparently tried to contain its popularity.[13] Hunting, however, is a ubiquitous theme in Greek initiation rites (and related narratives), overlaid with connotations of camaraderie in a military training context and sexual overtones in a metaphorical sense.[14] Despite its association with foreign monarchies, especially the Macedonian and the Carthaginian,[15] hunting as a sport originated with the competitive aristocrats of archaic Greek communities who sought to educate and entertain themselves with the epic reminiscences of Homer on one side, and the elegiac musings of Solon and Theognis on the pressing socio-political realities of their time on the other. While Homer intersperses his verses with numerous similes comparing mighty soldiers to lions,[16] Solon, who enjoyed a reputation as a sage and lawgiver among the Roman intelligentsia,[17] and Theognis, admired for his didactic verses,[18] used hunting as a *speculum uirtutis ciuilis* (mirror of civic virtue).

Thus, Solon discusses social injustice by comparing a tyrant devouring the property of the people (fr. 37.7–8) to a lion that "pounces upon the livestock in their pen,"[19] an image familiar to Theognis.[20] Solon also uses hunting as a metaphor for dealing with civil strife, by describing how he stood "like a wolf among many hounds" (ὡς ἐν κυσὶν πολλῆισιν ἐστράφην λύκος, fr. 36.27).[21] Statesmen or kings compared to wild animals hunting are typically invested in Greek tradition with connotations of tyranny (e.g., Pind. *Pyth.* 2.81–8; Hdt. 5.93; Pl. *Resp.* 565d–566a). The animalistic attributes of tyrants reflect their inability to control their emotions, especially their lustful urges.[22]

Therefore, here I expand on Dunkle's discussion of Aeneas as a hunter[23] by paying attention to similes of hunting warriors as wild animals in the *Aeneid*, including Volcens and Mezentius. I argue that, by drawing on Roman, mainly Propertian, and Greek elegiac (and lyric) poetry, Vergil associates the animalistic fury of hunting tyrants with the emotional exaggeration of elegiac mistresses, notably Dido and Camilla, destined to be killed as hunted prey. Thus, Vergil stages a battle of genders as much as a battle of genres.

1. Lovers and Tyrants Compared to Hunting Lions

This section discusses Vergil's use of hunting similes in the *Aeneid* and his Greek elegiac models, especially Theognis, to which Horace was also attracted. Vergil employs such similes to suggest that lovers and tyrants suffer from the same kind of emotional excess, which eventually emasculates them, leading them to their deaths, hunted rather than hunters.

Upon learning of Aeneas' decision to abandon Carthage, Dido complains bitterly against her unfeeling lover, whom she accuses of being cruel as befits one suckled by tigers (*A.* 4.365–7):[24] *nec tibi diua parens generis nec Dardanus auctor, / perfide, sed duris genuit te cautibus horrens / Caucasus Hyrcanaeque admorunt ubera tigres* ("Neither was your mother a goddess nor Dardanus the maker of your line, fickle man, but on its harsh rocks horrible Caucasus begot you and Hyrcanean tigresses suckled you"). Vergil's comparison of erotic aggression with that of wild animals hunting unavoidably draws on Homer's depiction of frenzied soldiers as wild animals, typically lions, as already noted.[25] Yet Vergil, known for his penchant for intertextuality, seems to further enrich his imagery here by alluding to Horace's comparison of tigers and the Gaetulean lion to a passionate lover (*Carm.* 1.23.9–10):[26] *atqui non ego te tigris ut aspera / Gaetulusue leo frangere persequor* ("Yet, I do not, as a harsh tiger or a Gaetulean lion, pursue you to break you"). In these lines, Horace's assurance to his beloved, that he does not wish any harm on her, echoes Theognis' lines 949–50, which were also copied in the second book of the *Theognidea* (= ll.1278cd):[27] νεβρὸν ὑπὲξ ἐλάφοιο λέων ὣς ἀλκὶ πεποιθὼς / ποσσὶ καταιμάρψας αἵματος οὐκ ἔπιον ("I did not drink, like a lion, confident in his strength, the blood of a fawn, having snatched it with his claws from the doe"). Although the simile has been understood in the context of early Greek political rivalries,[28] its erotic character is acknowledged already in Plato's *Charmides*, where Socrates employs the imagery of a lion attacking a fawn to describe (in a pederastic context) the passion inspired in him by Charmides' captivating beauty.[29] Given the prominence of lust as a tyrannical attribute in Greek elegiac and lyric poetry, it is likely that Theognis' verses were on the mind of both Horace and Vergil.[30] Furthermore, Vergil used a similar image of a lion attacking its victims in *A.* 9 for Nisus and Euryalus' attack on the sleeping Rutulian camp (9.339–41): *impastus ceu plena leo per ouilia turbans / (suadet enim uesana fames) manditque trahitque / molle pecus mutumque metu, fremit ore cruento* ("Just as a starving lion charging through packed sheepfolds – for raging hunger compels it – chomps and drags off the flock, soft and mute with fear, he roars with bloody mouth"). As Perkell has noted, although Vergil is aware of Homer's simile in *Il.* 10.485–6,[31] his adaptation here is considerably richer when it comes to describing the fear of the victims and the maddening hunger of the lion. In fact, the emphasis on the bloodstained mouth of the lion as well as the dragging of its victim recalls Theognis' verses.

Vergil reworks the simile twice in Book 10, first to describe the tyrannical Turnus when he is about to murder Pallas (*A.* 10.448: *tyranni*) as a lion attacking a bull (*A.* 10.455–7);[32] and second, a few hundred lines later, to describe Mezentius, Turnus' notoriously bloodthirsty ally (see n40 below), who attacks the Greek Acron, a soldier who left his wedding song half-sung (*A.* 10.720) to join the battle. The sudden transition from lover to soldier implies Acron's impending death (*A.* 10.723–9):[33]

> impastus stabula alta leo ceu saepe peragrans,
> suadet enim uesana fames, si forte fugacem
> conspexit capream aut surgentem in cornua ceruum,
> gaudet, hians immane, comasque arrexit et haeret
> uisceribus super accumbens, lauit inproba taeter
> ora cruor –
> sic ruit in densos alacer Mezentius hostis.

Then as a starving lion when he prowls about high pastures – for he is urged by maddening hunger – if perchance he sees a fleeing she-goat or tall-antlered stag, he rejoices, gaping wide, and lifts up his shaggy mane and clings to the victim's bowels lying on top of it, and foul gore bathes his cruel mouth – so Mezentius rushed fiercely into the thick of the enemy.

In this context of the ancient comparison between lust for power and erotic lust, a metaphor systematically renewed in Greek elegiac (and lyric) poetry, it is worth revisiting the other popular lion simile transmitted in the Theognidean corpus. Lines 293–4, possibly part of a longer fable, focus on the lion's hunger and have been interpreted as a metaphor designed a) to describe the beastlike cruelty of tyrants[34] but also b) to stress the value of self-control in pederastic relationships.[35] The erotic character of these lines is also palpable in the use of the word ἀμηχανίη, which becomes conventional of dumbstruck lovers in Hellenistic poetry:[36] οὐδὲ λέων αἰεὶ κρέα δαίνυται, ἀλλά μιν ἔμπης / καὶ κρατερόν περ ἐόνθ' αἱρεῖ ἀμηχανίη ("Not even a lion has always flesh to his supper; for all his might he is sometimes at a loss to get meat"). Unlike the Theognidean lover who recognizes the importance of self-control and is willing to endure hunger despite his might, Vergil's Mezentius cannot resist a chance victim; having surrendered to the most basic of his instincts, his hunger (for power), Mezentius alerts everyone to his ominous presence and superiority by staging a gory repast.

Notably, both Vergilian episodes discussed above include references to the glimmering or plumed helmets of the victims, which attract unwanted attention from their opponents.[37] The helmets impress Mezentius and Volcens (Turnus' lieutenant) in their search for victims in the way that tyrants rejoice in sparkling gifts and gold in Greek elegy. Bacchylides' *Epinician* 3 (7–14, 17–20), with its reference to Hieron's sparkling victory crown, furnishes a salient example.[38] Hieron does not know how to hide his wealth under black-cloaked darkness, an image that evokes Vergil's lines about the darkness of night which cannot hide the gleaming helmet of Euryalus:[39]

> ... τόθι Δ]εινομένεος ἔθηκαν
>   ὄλβιον τ[έκος στεφάνω]ν κυρῆσαι
> θρόησε δὲ λ[αὸς ◡ - -
>   ἁ τρισευδαίμ[ων ἀνήρ,
> ὃ παρὰ Ζηνὸς λαχὼν
>   πλείσταρχον Ἑλλάνων γέρας
> οἶδε πυργωθέντα πλοῦτον μὴ μελαμ-
>   φαρέϊ κρύπτειν σκότωι.
> ...
> λάμπει δ' ὑπὸ μαρμαρυγαῖς ὁ χρυσός
>   ὑψιδαιδάλτων τριπόδων σταθέντων
> πάροιθε ναοῦ, τόθι μέγι[στ]ον ἄλσος
> Φοίβου παρὰ Κασταλίας [ῥ]εέθροις
> Δελφοὶ διέπουσι. ...

... where they made the son of Deinomenes prosperous in the winning of crowns. And the [...] people cried out: O thrice-blessed man, who, allotted by Zeus the honour of ruling most people among the Greeks, knows not to hide his towering wealth under black-cloaked darkness ... And the gold shines under the gleam of the highly wrought tripods set up before the temple, where the Delphians tend the greatest grove of Phoebus beside Castalia's stream.

While Bacclylides praises Lydian Croesus, rewarded for his piety by Apollo, Vergil introduced Mezentius as a cruel tyrant overtaking a city of Lydian settlers in *A.* 8 (481–4):[40] *hanc multos florentem annos rex deinde superbo /*

imperio et saeuis tenuit Mezentius armis. / quid memorem infandas caedes, quid facta tyranni / effera? ("It prospered for many years, then by his arrogant rule / and cruel forces Mezentius got hold of it. / Why remember the unspeakable slaughters, the tyrant's cruel deeds?"). Similarly, Vergil described Volcens in *A.* 9 as enraged and determined to spill Euryalus' blood.[41] His attraction to gold, a symptom of Volcens' tyrannical character, complements Vergil's persistent association of gold with Dido's palace in the first book of the *Aeneid*.[42] Tyrants and lovers, it seems, are equally attracted to gold and its qualities, as Greek elegiac and lyric poets also remind us frequently.[43] Gold with its mesmerizing shine symbolizes the excess that rules both tyrants and lovers and, eventually, emasculates them.[44] Although the Homeric overtones of the Nisus/Euryalus episode have been recognized in scholarship,[45] its elegiac aspects are also worth noting.[46] Like Acron (cf. n50 below), Nisus is mainly characterized as a lover, and thus, upon realizing Euryalus' imminent death, he becomes *amens* (mindless; *A.* 9.424), an epithet that evokes Propertius' Milanion, mindlessly roaming the wilderness in 1.1.11.[47] In addition, Vergil portrays Nisus as unable to bear his pain (*A.* 9.425–6): *nec … tantum potuit perferre dolorem*, not unlike Dido, who had proclaimed, falsely (*A.* 4.419–20): *hunc ego si potui tantum sperare dolorem, / et perferre, soror, potero*, that she was strong enough to accept Aeneas' departure. Thus, throughout the *Aeneid* Vergil compares the affliction of lovers and tyrants (both likened to wild animals), pointing to emotional excess as the reason for their tragic ends and advancing all along the idea that the balanced ruler cannot be under the yoke of Eros.

2. Dido as Failed Huntress and a Propertian *domina*

Besides comparing wild animals to angry, tyrannical chieftains entering the battlefield, Vergil employed the motif of erotic hunting to describe Dido's capture and her rapid transformation from a worthy leader to an elegiac *puella*. An eastern queen, harbouring the ambition of replacing her husband as a ruler, and therefore of assuming the guise of victor and a hunter,[48] Dido becomes obsessed with Aeneas and is overwhelmed by her passion. Thus, she is instead identified with a deer which is hunted by a ferocious predator (*A.* 4.68–72):[49]

> uritur infelix Dido …,[50]
> 　　　… qualis coniecta cerua sagitta,
> quam procul incautam nemora inter Cresia fixit
> pastor agens telis liquitque uolatile ferrum
> nescius …

Unhappy Dido burns … like a deer, smitten by an arrow, which, all unwary, amid the Cretan woods, a shepherd hunting with darts has pierced from afar, leaving in her the winged steel, unknowing.

Vergil's rejection of the image of the *uenatrix*, which he finds problematic for civilized life and for the purpose of his poem,[51] is repeated in *A.* 11.780–2, where he represents his Amazonian Camilla "burning with feminine desire for prey and spoils" (*femineo praedae et spoliorum ardebat amore*, 782),[52] just before she is shot down. While the arrow that wounds Camilla drinks her maiden blood from her deep wound (*uirgineumque alte bibit acta cruorem, A.* 11.804),[53] Dido drinks deep draughts of love (*infelix Dido longumque bibebat amorem, A.* 1.749), a symbol of her impending doom. Vergil here equates military and erotic frenzy, both of which can be drunk like (or instead of) wine.[54]

Vergil casts Dido's erotic anguish, movingly detailed in *A.* 4.66–9, 72–3, in strikingly Propertian terms:

> … est mollis flamma medullas
> interea et tacitum uiuit sub pectore uulnus.
> uritur infelix Dido totaque uagatur
> urbe furens …
> … illa fuga siluas saltusque peragrat
> Dictaeos; haeret lateri letalis harundo.

Fire prevails in her tender soul all the while and deep in her breast lives the silent wound. Unhappy Dido burns and wanders throughout the whole city in frenzy … in flight she crosses glades and the Dictaean woods, but the deadly shaft clings to her side.

The image of falling in love to the marrow of one's bones (*est flamma medullas*) is found repeatedly in Catullus[55] and in Horace's *Epode* 5,[56] where the marrow and liver of a young boy, left to die from hunger, would be subsequently extracted and dried to be used in a love potion. If Vergil had Horace's *Epode* in mind, then Dido's falling in love with Aeneas could be understood as bewitchment,[57] offering a more consistent explanation of her (professed at least) turn to the witches at the end of *A.* 4. The witches are also invoked in Propertius' first poem to make Cynthia fall in love with her desperate suitor (Prop. 1.1.19–24).[58] Notably, Propertius also uses the motif of burning with love to the bones in elegy 1.9[59] as he warns his friend Ponticus, a former epic poet, now forced by an unexpected erotic wound to turn to Mimnermus' lyric verses thus (1.9.19–22):[60]

> tum magis Armenias cupies accedere tigres
> et magis infernae uincula nosse rotae,
> quam pueri totiens arcum sentire medullis
> et nihil iratae posse negare tuae.

Then you will rather tackle Armenian tigresses and experience the chains of Ixion's infernal wheel, than feel the boy's shaft strike all the way to your bones again and again, and be unable to deny a thing to your bad-tempered mistress.

Propertius rewords his warning a few lines later (29) noting that *qui non ante patet, donec manus attigit ossa* ("Love does not appear, until his hand has touched your very bones").[61] He returns to the motif in 2.12.17, where he wonders: *quid tibi iucundum est siccis habitare medullis?*[62] ("What is the pleasure in inhabiting dried bones?").

Propertius employs the image of the winged boy Eros who wounds his victims from afar in 2.12 in a way that further complements Dido's erotic wounding in *A.* 4.68–72. The arrow shot from a distance (*procul, A.* 4.70) clings to the side of the unsuspecting deer (*coniecta cerua sagitta, A.* 4.69), while its steely head remains in its body (*liquitque … ferrum, A.* 4.71), causing its demise slowly but surely. Propertius describes Eros as hunting in Cretan woods (*et merito hamatis munus est armata sagittis, / et pharetra ex umero Cnosia utroque iacet,* 2.12.9–10), which corresponds to the location where Vergil places the deer representing Dido (*nemora inter Cresia, A.* 4.70). Furthermore, he claims that no one will escape safe from this wound (*nec quisquam ex illo uulnere sanus abit,* 2.12.12), though I would be inclined to read here an allusion to the "sanity" of Eros' victims, who are often represented as suffering madness,[63] a notion that fits Vergilian Dido. Furthermore, Eros' shaft has stayed in him (*in me tela manent,* 2.12.13), as in the case of the Vergilian deer which is described as roaming away unaware of the persisting shaft in its side (*nescius, A.* 4.72). Propertius adds that the image of Eros also stays in his heart (*manet et puerilis imago*), mirroring thus Vergil's description of the image (and words) of Aeneas that remains infixed in Dido's heart (*haerent infixi pectore uultus uerbaque, A.* 4.4).[64]

Propertius also employs the motif of the erotic wound silently grieving the hearts of the enamoured (*tacitum uiuit … uulnus, A.* 4.67) in 3.21.31–2, where he hopes that "time and distance will soften the silent wound of his heart" (*et spatia annorum et longa interualla profundi / lenibunt tacito uulnera nostra sinu*).[65] As noted, he employs the hunting metaphor in his first poem, where he describes Milanion as hunting on mountaintops in search of real wounds that would soothe his erotic injury (*ille etiam Hylaei percussus uulnere rami,* 1.1.13).[66] Although the Propertian Milanion roams the wilderness in erotic frenzy (*nam modo Partheniis amens errabat in antris,*

1.1.11), while Dido is portrayed as roaming the city (*totaque uagatur / urbe furens*, *A*. 4.68–9), Propertius reworks the motif in 2.29a.1 (using the verb *uago*), where the lover admits that he was wandering the city streets drunk the night before (*hesterna, mea lux, cum potus nocte uagarer*).[67] An additional paradigm for this motif may be found in a little discussed iambic tetrameter by Archilochus (130.5 ap. Stob. 4.41.24, LCL 259), where the poet muses over the precariousness of human fortune, probably in a martial context; often, Archilochus says, well-established people have fallen, forced to "wander (in beggary so as to secure basic needs), bewildered in mind" (καὶ βίου χρήμη πλανᾶται καὶ νόου παρήορος). The phrase πλανᾶται καὶ νόου παρήορος matches strikingly Propertius' *amens errabat* (1.1.11),[68] while Aeneas arrives at the Carthaginian shores as a beggar (*egentem*, *A*. 4.373). Thus, suffering a blow, real or metaphorical, turns victims into hunted animals that frantically run away from their pursuers or the source of their misfortune, an image that suits the heartbroken lover in Propertius and the enamoured Dido in Vergil. Notably, although Dido and Aeneas have harboured similar misfortunes that saw them both wander in exile,[69] their love affair imposes a gendered hierarchy on their relationship which proves detrimental for Dido. By chasing happiness, Dido subjects herself to another blow,[70] while by remaining steadfast to his masculine pursuit of establishing a new state, Aeneas becomes the hunter.

Dido's erotic burning (*uritur*, 4.68) alludes to Catullus' 83.6, where Lesbia under the burden of passion is infuriated: *irata est*; that is, Catullus explains, *uritur et loquitur*. Although Dido initially suffers in silence, she rebukes Aeneas openly when she realizes his intention to abandon her.[71] The more she rebukes him, the more obvious her erotic suffering becomes to the reader. Propertius adapts the motif in 3.8, where Cynthia in rage throws things around, swears at the lover in a state of insanity (*insanae tot maledicta tuae*, 3.8.2), and threatens to set his eyes on fire (*tu minitare oculos subiecta exurere flamma*, 3.8.7), thus delighting the poet, who is assured of her love. As he says (3.8.10–14):[72]

> nam sine amore graui femina nulla dolet.
> quae mulier rabida iactat conuicia lingua,
>   haec Veneris magnae uoluitur ante pedes.
> custodum grege seu circa se stipat euntem,
>   seu sequitur medias, maenas ut icta, uias

for no woman suffers unless from a serious passion. The woman who hurls abuse with ranting tongue, she rolls around at the feet of mighty Venus. Whether, when going out, she surrounds herself with a throng of escorts, or rushes down the street like a possessed bacchante …

This image fits Vergilian Dido, who roams the city maddened by love, having hurled abuse at Aeneas because of his false promises. She is maenadic in her obsession with him and, also, in her zeal to exact revenge (*A.* 4.300–3):[73]

> saeuit inops animi totamque incensa per urbem
> bacchatur, qualis commotis excita sacris
> Thyias, ubi audito stimulant trieterica Baccho
> orgia nocturnusque uocat clamore Cithaeron

Helpless in mind she rages, and all aflame raves through the city, like some Thyiad startled by the shaken emblems, when she has heard the Bacchic cry: the biennial revels fire her and at night Cithaeron summons her with its din.

The notion is repeated in *A.* 4.666, where Vergil uses the verb *bacchantur* for the rumour that spreads through the city, just as the queen roamed all over the city (*concussam bacchatur Fama per urbem*).[74] In addition, like Propertius' mistress (*seu timidam crebro dementia somnia terrent*, 3.8.15), Dido has a terrifying dream, which she admits to her sister Anna (*Anna soror, quae me suspensam insomnia terrent, A.* 4.9; cf. n49).

Furthermore, Vergil systematically employs vocabulary alluding to Propertius' 1.1 to characterize Dido in *A.* 4.365–96. Here, we find references to Dido's erotic sighing (*ingemuit, A.* 4.369; *ingemuit*, Prop. 1.1.14),[75] the lover's unyielding glance (*lumina flexit, A.* 4.369; *lumina fastus*, Prop. 1.1.3), erotic madness (*demens, A.* 4.374; *amens*, Prop. 1.1.11), pain (*dolentem, A.* 4.393; *dolore mea*, Prop. 1.1.38) and sorrow (*curas, A.* 4.394; *cura*, Prop. 1.1.36), the shamelessness typical of Aeneas and Eros respectively (*improbe, A.* 4.386; *improbus*, Prop. 1.1.6), erotic lapsing (*labefactus amore, A.* 4.395; *sero lapsum reuocatis*, Prop. 1.1.25), erotic complaining (*sic accensa profatur, A.* 4.364; *quae uelit ira loqui*, Prop. 1.1.28), foreign travel as erotic remedy (*i, sequere Italiam uentis, pete regna per undas, A.* 4.381; *ferte per extremas gentes et ferte per undas*, Prop. 1.1.29), and erotic flames (*atris ignibus, A.* 4.384; *saeuos … ignes*, Prop. 1.1.27). There are also more generic references to the lover's misery (*miseratus amantem est, A.* 4.370; *miserum me*, Prop. 1.1.1) and to erotic fury (*furiis incensa feror, A.* 4.376; *furor … non deficit*, Prop. 1.1.7). By revising Dido's leadership ability, which Vergil praised early in the *Aeneid*,[76] to portray her as an ineffective hunter, and further as an erotic prey and an elegiac *puella*, unable to rise above her own emotional needs,[77] Vergil employs motifs stamped by Propertius' flair to explain Dido's political failure. Dido, like the tyrannical figures that threaten Aeneas' settlement in Latium, is too preoccupied with self-gratification and lacks the self-restraint that befits a Roman leader.

Thus, the magical fires of the witches in Propertius (1.19–24) will soon be replaced by the pyre that Dido asks Anna to raise on her behalf;[78] Vergil's description of the witches who can obstruct the flow of rivers and turn back the stars (*sistere aquam fluuiis et uertere sidera retro*, *A.* 4.489) with their spells (*carminibus*, *A.* 4.487) and magical arts (*magicis … artis*, *A.* 4.493) alludes to Propertius' witches, who rely on Thessalian spells to achieve the same spectacular feats (*tunc ego crediderim uobis et sidera et amnis / posse Cytinaeis ducere carminibus*, 1.1.23–4).[79] Notably, just as Propertius wishes his mistress to turn paler at his sight (*facite illa meo palleat ore magis*, 1.1.22), so Dido turns pale as soon as she concludes her address to her sister (*pallor simul occupat ora*, *A.* 4.499).[80] Propertius' poem finishes (*neque assueto mutet amore torum*, 1.1.36) with a warning against pursuing new love interests, which again evokes Dido's regrets for doing just that as she complains to Anna on the fateful night of her suicide (4.20–9); and, although the Propertian lover professes not to remember Love's ways (*nec meminit notas, ut prius, ire uias*, 1.1.18), Dido recognizes the symptoms of her fall only too well (*adgnosco ueteris uestigia flammae*, *A.* 4.23).

Conclusion

Investing his epic characters with elegiac traits allows Vergil to show empathy with their fall; Vergil is not unsympathetic to the suffering of Dido or Turnus or any of the other figures who fail to meet the punitive standards of Roman leadership.[81] Their examples serve as a warning about the dangers of uncontrolled passion for his audience, especially Augustus, who is now tasked with adhering to his own slogans.[82] Thus, Vergil seems to take a stance regarding the role of poetry in civic education: his engagement with elegy is an attempt to restore the debate on civic virtue by reminding his audience that the hunting games of their time, with all the gloss of neoteric elegiac poetry, originate in an epic past which Solon and Theognis were mostly aware of, already lamenting the loss of traditional (Homeric) values in their societies. By subjecting elegiac motifs to the superlative triumph of epic themes, Vergil appears to indicate to his intellectual circle that Dido, Turnus, and all their elegiac counterparts can only pave the way for the final, decisive battle that achieves Aeneas' objective. Equally, poetry ought to serve the greater good – a tenet very much in line with the major philosophical debates of his time about the role of poetry in society,[83] and certainly evocative of Augustus' nostalgia-filled campaign for moral rigour.

NOTES

1 For example, see Cairns 2003; O'Rourke 2011a; Heslin 2018, 11 with more bibliography.

2 See, for example, Heslin 2010.

3 On Dido's elegiac investment, see indicatively, Cairns 1989: 129–50; Desmond 1994: 31–3; Wyke 2002: 97–9; cf. Keith 1997; O'Rourke 2012: 401–2; cf. Farron 1993: esp. 74, where he discusses Donatus' and Servius' appreciation of the erotic (therefore, non-epic) character of Dido's episode; for Vergil's use of Apollonius Rhodius' Medea for his characterization of Dido as an enamoured witch, see Nelis 2001.

4 E.g., Prop. 2.16.36, 3.21.33. See Wyke 2002: 138–54; Bowditch 2006: 310; and cf. Desmond 1994: 33, on the reliance of Roman imperial power "on a depiction of the colonial enemy as a sexualised, racialised female other."

5 Nostalgia for an ideal past, superseded by a corrupt present, develops already in the late Republic; Harrison 2005.

6 There are numerous examples of the motif, often expressed as *militia amoris*, the worthy service in the name of Love (e.g., Prop. 1.6.29–30; 2.1.47; 2.7.13–14; 3.4.21–2; 4.2.3–4 and 51–4; Tib. 1.1.53–8, 75; Ov. *Am.* 1.9.1–10, 15–20 and 1.15.1–6; on *militia amoris*, see Murgatroyd 1975; Drinkwater 2013, esp. 195–9; cf. Fantham 2013: 118–23; Lyne 2002: 350–9; Gardner 2013: 88–92. Note especially Prop. 4.4.33–6, 51–2, 55–8, where the Vestal Virgin Tarpeia is invested with elegiac qualities that explain her betrayal of Rome to the Sabines on account of her love for Tatius. Propertius claims to turn to "loftier topics" and Augustus' praise in Book 4, yet his intentions remain debatable (i.e., whether this was a literary device designed to undermine Augustan policies; cf. Gale 1997a: 77–8).

7 See Bowditch 2006: 312–14 on the association of tyranny, luxury, and elegiac mistresses portrayed as decadent eastern queens. On luxury and tyrants, also see Griffin 1985: 15–36; cf. Wallace-Hadrill 1990: 87–90.

8 Dunkle 1973: 127; cf. his p. 140, which informs the second part of my statement here.

9 Text and trans. modified from LCL 18, Goold 1990: 38–9. Erotic hunting was also possible in urban places such as the theatre; Ov. *Ars Am.* 1.89; *Rem. Am.* 199–204. Also, see Janan 2001: 39; Mocanu 2012: 40n57.

10 Ross (1975: 90–2) suggested a common model for both poems, probably a poem of Gallus; cf. Servius ad *B.* 10.46: *hi autem omnes uersus Galli sunt de ipsius translati carminibus* ("but all these are Gallus' verses, adapted from his own poems"; my translation is informed by Lipka 2001: 88).

11 Vergil portrays Gallus as hunting boars; cf. Prop. 1.1, where Milanion woos Atalanta, the only female participant of the Calydonian boar hunt; Barringer

1996: 51–5 and 167–71; Anagnostou-Laoutides 2005: 23–4, 37–46, 69–73. Yet Homer makes no mention of Atalanta's role in the Calydonian hunt (*Il.* 9.529–99).

12 Cic. *Fam.* 8.2.2 (= LCL 205, Shackleton Bailey 2001: no. 78), 8.4.5 (= LCL 205, no. 81), 8.6.5 (= LCL 205, no. 88), and 8.9.5 (= LCL 205, no. 82); cf. Cic. *Fam.* 2.9.2 (= LCL 205, no. 85) and Pliny, e.g., *HN* 8.20, 8.64, 40.26.

13 Dio Cass. 54.1.3–4; cf. *RG* 22.

14 Barringer 2001: passim but esp. 9: "Hunters demonstrate the limits and norms of Greek society and sexuality"; cf. Barringer 1996: 62–6, on the erotic investment of the Calydonian hunt, which at first related a male initiation rite; cf. Green 1996: 222–5, discussing the role of Plato and Xenophon in promoting hunting as a prominent example of aspiring excellence in every manly endeavour; thus, not only is the metaphor of the hunter as a lover established in the visual arts as early as the sixth century but also Plato reinforces its educational value by comparing the pursuit of the beloved to a "legitimate kind of venery" that should be taught (*Leg.* 823b).

15 Carney 2015: 267–74; Sparreboom 2016: 42–5.

16 Clarke 1995: 140–59.

17 Hamilton 1977: passim; Yunis 1996: 223–4; Raaflaub 1993: 68–73; Hansen 1989: 71–99; cf. Cic. *Brut.* 27, 39; Plut. *Sol.*; *Cleom.* 18; *Phoc.* 7; see also Cic. *Tusc. Disp.* 46.3–4, where he recognizes the fame of Lycurgus and Solon as legislators and state organizers (*accipietur, Lycurgum, Solonem legum et publicae disciplinae ... gloria*).

18 See Thévenaz 2002: 878–9, on the relationship between Ennius, Theognis, and Horace with Erasmo 2006: 376; also see, e.g., Dio Chrys. *Or.* 2.18; Plut. *Quomodo adol. poet. aud. deb.*16c10 and 22a4–22a6; *de amic. mult.* 96f6–8; *max. cum princ.* 777c1; *Quaest. nat.* 916c2–916c4; *Terrest. an Aquat.* 978e5–978e7; *De Stoic. repug.* 1040a4–1040a6; *de Comm. Notit.* 1069d7–1069d10; Ath. *Deipn.* 364b and 632d; cf. DL, *Lives,* 6.16 and 10.1.26.

19 Noussia-Fantuzzi 2010: 492, discussing Hom. *Il.* 11.550 as a possible model.

20 See Thgn. 1181 on a people-devouring tyrant (δημοφάγον δὲ τύραννον); cf. Alcaeus, frs. 129.21–4 and 296a5.8.

21 Noussia-Fantuzzi 2010: 482–5, discussing Hom. *Il.* 12.41–2 as the possible model (ὡς δ᾽ ὅτ᾽ ἂν ἔν τε κύνεσσι καὶ ἀνδράσι θηρευτῆισι / κάπριος ἠὲ λέων στρέφεται, "as when, among hounds and huntsmen, a wild boar or a lion wheels about"; text and trans. LCL 170, Murray and Wyatt 1924: 58–9). For other instances of Solon's drawing on Homeric hunting similes, see fr. 4.27–9 (Noussia-Fantuzzi 2010: 255) and fr. 4c.1–2 (Noussia-Fantuzzi 2010: 275).

22 Tyrants were typically charged with the inability to control their sexual lust; e.g., Ar. *Pol.* 1374b30; Pl. *Resp.* 573d2–573d5; Polybius 6.7.5–8; also, Edwards 1993: 5, 28, 43, 91, 176–206.

23 Dunkle 1973; cf. Anagnostou-Laoutides 2020 on Turnus as a lion-like tyrant and different forms of violence in the second half of the *Aeneid*.

24 For Vergil's text and translation, I rely on Fairclough, rev. Goold 1999 throughout. Cf. Anagnostou-Laoutides 2017: 307, discussing Vergil's influence on Lucan and his portrayal of Pompey as a bloodthirsty tiger in *BC* 1.324–35.

25 E.g., Hom. *Il.* 11.113–14 (in Nisbet and Hubbard 1970: 278 s.v. 10 [*frangere*]) and 12.299–301; cf. n16 above.

26 Text from LCL 33, Rudd 2004; cf. Nisbet and Hubbard 1970: 278 s.v. 9 (*aspera*). On Vergil's familiarity with Horatian poetry, see Hor. *Sat.* 1.10.81; Harrison 2007a: 103, 204–6 with n22 citing Nisbet and Hubbard 1970: 107; cf. Austin 1971: 82.

27 See West 1974: 45. Text from LCL 258, Gerber 1999b. Nisbet and Hubbard 1970: 273–4 cite only Anacreon as Horace's Greek source; however, they do mention Theognis' influence on Horace at 1970: xlviii with n1, and 180.

28 Harrison 1902: 158–9.

29 Van Groningen 1966: 361 s.v. λέων cites Pl. *Charm.* 155d7–155e1 (text and trans. from LCL 201, Lamb 1927: 16–17: εὐλαβεῖσθαι μὴ κατέναντα λέοντος νεβρὸν ἐλθόντα μοῖραν αἱρεῖσθαι κρεῶν; "beware of coming as a fawn before the lion and being seized as his portion of flesh"); cf. n31 below.

30 Cf. Archilochus, fr. 19 ap. Plut. *tranq.* 10.470b–470c (LCL 259, Gerber 1999a); McGlew 1993: 26; Anderson 2005: 182–3, 187, 205, 208–9. Also, see Barringer 2001, 70–124, esp. 86 discussing Ibycus 287.

31 The text reads: ὡς δὲ λέων μήλοισιν ἀσημάντοισιν ἐπελθὼν / αἴγεσιν ἢ ὀίεσσι κακὰ φρονέων ἐνορούσῃ ("as a lion advancing on herds unshepherded, of sheep or goats, pounces on them with wicked intention," trans. Lattimore 1961: 229); text from LCL 170; see Perkell 1999: 170; also, cf. Hom. *Il.* 3.23–8 (where Menelaus is compared to a lion).

32 Anagnostou-Laoutides 2020: 151.

33 Cf. Apollonius' *Arg.* 1.985–1011 and 1030–3 where Jason kills Cyzicus, the newlywed king, by mistake; cf. Anagnostou-Laoutides and Konstan 2013: 123, reading Cyzicus as a double of Attis; in Greco-Roman belief, passionate lovers, whose prolonged obsession with sex effeminized them, were deemed inadequate soldiers or political leaders. See Ov. *Met.* 10.710–23, where Adonis, infatuated with Aphrodite, is portrayed as an ineffective hunter, drawing on Bion's pastoral elegy mourning the death of Adonis. Note that in *A.* 10.730 Acron is described as *infelix*, a typical elegiac adjective, also applied to Dido; cf. n50.

34 Van Groningen 1966: 118–19.

35 Lewis 1985: 218–19.

36 Ogilvie 1962: 108; Barringer 2001: 88; Anagnostou-Laoutides 2005: 131 with n107; cf. Pl. *Charm.* 155d2.

37 *A.* 9.373–4: *et galea Euryalum sublustri noctis in umbra / prodidit immemorem radiis aduersa refulsit* ("and in the faintly-lit shadow of the night, the helmet betrayed the thoughtless Euryalus as it shone back the light rays"); *A.* 10.721–2: *hunc ubi miscentem longe media agmina uidit, / purpureum pinnis et pactae coniugis ostro* … ("When he saw him from afar, stirring up trouble in the middle of the ranks, crimson with feathers and the purple of his pledged wife"); cf. Smolenaars 1994: 302 s.v. *Tyrio subtegmine.*

38 On Bacchylides' influence on Horace (esp. *Carm.* 1.15) and possibly Vergil, see Cairns 2010: 15; Nisbet and Hubbard 1970: 189; Kilpatrick 1969: 234 (on *Carm.* 3.21); cf. Wilkinson 1978: 114 (Bacchylides in Vergil's *Georgics*), and 2008: 182–5. Bacchylides was influenced by both Theognis and Solon; cf. Fearn 2007: 289 with n96.

39 Text and trans. Cairns 2010: 153. On the role of gold in this poem, see Carson 1984: 114–17.

40 The word tyrant has been linked etymologically to several Lydian names, including Turnus and Τυρσανοί, the alternative form of Τυρρηνοί (the Greek word for Etruscans). Whatmough 1937: 231, with White 1955: 2; Shell 1993: 12n7. On Lydian Gyges as the archetypal tyrant, see Archilochus' fr. 19; Anacreon (fr. 481 = schol. Aes. *Pers.* 42) coined the epithet λυδοπαθεῖς to describe the Lydians' excessive lifestyle. On Mezentius' impiety, see Verg. *A.* 7.648 and 8.7 as well as Serv. ad *A.* 7.648, all describing him as *contemptor deorum*; Bolt 2019: 303–4.

41 *A.* 9.420–1: *saeuit atrox Volcens nec teli conspicit usquam / auctorem nec quo se ardens inmittere possit* ("Fierce Volcens was enraged, but could not see who had hurled the shaft, nor where he could reply as he burned with anger").

42 Rimell 2015: 65–6, citing *A.* 1.343–64, 640–1, 728, 739, and 741; and 3.56–7.

43 Archilochus fr.19 described Gyges as πολύχρυσος, an epithet attributed to Aphrodite in *H. hymn Aph.* (5).1 (LCL 496, West 2003); cf. Anacreon fr. 358 (ap. Ath. *Deipn.* 599c) on χρυσοκόμης Ἔρως; *Anacreontea* 8.1–4 (LCL 143, Campbell 1988). For the use of the Vergilian Nisus/Euryalus episode by the anonymous panegyrist of *Lat. Pan.* 12(9), dedicated to Constantine the Great, see Anagnostou-Laoutides 2021: 77–81. In my view, the panegyrist appreciated Vergil's portrayal of the two young men as tyrannical, also encouraged by Vergil's reference to Euryalus' insistence on wearing a shiny helmet he had plundered from one of his victims, which eventually betrayed him to the Rutulians (*A.* 9.373–4). Notably, Servius also seems to have read the episode in this light and thus he comments on the young Trojans' common love for bloodshed (Serv. ad *A.* 9.182: *eodem studio flagrabat*).

44 E.g., Anacreon (fr. 388.10–12) castigates Artemon about his penchant for gold earrings, symptomatic of his effeminate behaviour (νῦν δ᾽ ἐπιβαίνει σατινέων χρύσεα φορέων καθέρματα / † παῖς Κύκης † καὶ σκιαδίσκην ἐλεφαντίνην φορεῖ / γυναιξὶν αὔτως <ἐμφερής>).

45 Meban 2009: 239 with n2 and 242–3; Makowski 1989 interprets Nisus and
   Euryalus as a homosexual couple modelled on Achilles and Patroclus; cf.
   Hardie 1994: 33–4; Crompton 2003: 84–6; and Fratantuono 2007: 139–40.
46 Hardie 1994: 150–1 ad 9.435–7 and 9.444 (also in Meban 2009: 244).
47 Cf. *B.* 2.69, where Corydon's erotic *dementia* distracts him from his duties.
48 In *A.* 1.192 and 196 Aeneas poses as *uictor* and *heros* while hunting stags; cf.
   A. 1.498–502 for Dido as a replica of Diana (Dunkle 1973: 131–5); *A.* 1.329
   for Venus disguised as Diana; and *A.* 11.857 for Camilla as Diana; on Dido's
   investment as an eastern queen, also see O'Rourke 2011a.
49 See *A.* 4.465–6 regarding Dido's dream of Aeneas as a savage hunter pursuing
   her; Dunkle 1973: 134–5. Also, see Cairns 1989: 129–50 and Desmond 1994:
   31–3 on Vergil's transformation of Dido from a strong political leader to a
   desperate woman in love. Cf. Alcaeus 10B (LCL 142, Campbell 1982), where a
   woman bemoans her situation, comparing herself to a maddened deer (ἰκνεῖται
   ἐλάφω δὲ] βρόμος ἐν σ[τήθεσι φυίει φοβέροισιν μ]αινόμενον [).
50 Propertian verse offers numerous instances where the lover is addressed as
   infelix (e.g., 1.5.2; 2.3.3; 2.23.20; 3.5.7; 3.7.13; 4.11.28; cf. Tib.1.2.4; 1.4.60
   and 3.6.37). In accordance with her elegiac investment, Dido is addressed four
   times as *infelix* in *A.* 4 (4.68; 4.450; 4.529 and 4.596). Notably, Acron is also
   characterized as *infelix* (*A.* 10.730 with n33 above).
51 See Nappa 2007: 308–12, discussing *A.* 4.551, where Dido wishes she had
   been allowed to live like a wild animal (*more ferae*). Nappa understands the
   verse as referring to Dido's dream of a world where she would avoid the
   institution of marriage and the pain it has caused her, opting instead for the
   life (not of a wild animal but) of the virginal huntresses in Diana's entourage
   and even of the goddess herself. This, however, would exclude Dido not only
   from the anguish of love but from Vergil's poem; cf. Green 1996: 228, 232–3,
   236, and esp. 242–9 on Ovid's reworking of the civic aspects of hunting in the
   first book of *Arts Amatoria*: since "taming" becomes as important as "pursuing"
   erotic prey already in fifth-century BCE vase representations, hunting as a
   metaphor of establishing civilized order requires male hunters to impose their
   superior judgment on the women they pursue. From this perspective, Dido's
   aspiration to be allowed to emulate Diana proves once more unrealistic: not
   only is she emotionally weak and hence unable to retain her status as a hunter
   but she does not fully subscribe to the *ratio* of the elegiac *puella*, who according
   to Ovid (and Green 1996, 251) is reduced to hunting for gifts. Dido's dream
   of an alternative world in which she would be allowed to rule without the
   guidance of a man is simply anomalous and, hence, she must die.
52 Mocanu 2012: 40–1; Camilla is compared to Amazons in *A.* 11.648, 660.
   Also, note the association of Atalanta, the huntress in Propertius' 1.1, with the
   (Scythian) Amazons; Barringer 2001: 149, 156–8, 166; also, see Anagnostou-
   Laoutides 2005: 27–8.

53 Camilla dies indignant, with a moan, just like Turnus (*A.* 11.831 and 12.952):
   uitaque cum gemitu fugit indignata sub umbras.

54 While wine is the drink of choice for lovers (e.g., Prop. 1.3 and 2.29
   with his Hellenistic models, including *AP* 5.136 and 137; 5.171, 5.190,
   etc.), blood is the drink tyrants have a predilection for; see Anagnostou-
   Laoutides 2017. Examples of both motifs, the lover bolstered by wine
   (e.g., Thgn. 261–6, 467–96; Anacr. frs. 4, 12, 357; Solon, fr. 26) and the
   bloodthirsty tyrant (see n20 above), abound in early Greek elegiac and lyric
   poetry.

55 Catull. 35.14–15; 66.23; cf. Austin 1986: 159 s.v. (6)442 (*peredit*); Fordyce
   1990: 207 s.v. 16, and 332 s.v. 23. For more Catullan examples, see
   Rosenmeyer 1999: 38–42; cf. ibid., 23–4 and 40–1 discussing Prop. 1.9.21–2
   and 2.12.15–17 but also Vergil's *G.* 3.271, *A.* 8.389–90 and, crucially, *A.* 4.66
   as adaptations of the Catullan motif.

56 *Ep.* 5.37–8: *exsecta uti medulla et aridum iecur / amoris esset poculum* (LCL 33).

57 Ogden 1999: 16–17, and Luck 1999: 121–2; also, Anagnostou-Laoutides
   2005: 67–101. This explanation does not discount Vergil's close reading of
   Apollonius Rhodius' *Argonautica*, as discussed by Nelis 2001, but offers an
   additional paradigm for the Roman understanding of love as bewitchment.

58 Anagnostou-Laoutides 2005: 81–3; cf. Watson 2003: 189n105.

59 Note that Lucan was also influenced by Horace's *Ep.* 5; see Watson 2003: 180,
   citing Ahl 1976: 133–7.

60 Text and trans. with my modifications from LCL 18.

61 Again, trans. modified from LCL 18.

62 Could *siccis* be a reworking of the Horatian *aridum* (n56 above) and possibly
   another allusion to love as magical affliction? Cf. Otis 1964: 72. Certainly,
   Horace was also familiar with Archilochus' compelling description of his erotic
   burning (fr. 193 ap. Stob. 4.20.45, LCL 259): see Harrison 2007a: 104–35;
   Watson 2007: 94–6.

63 Anagnostou-Laoutides 2005: 85–101.

64 Perhaps an allusion to the motif of falling in love through the eyes as in Prop.
   1.1.1 (*Cynthia, me prima cepit ocellis*) and 2.22a.7–9 (*interea nostri quaerunt
   sibi uulnus ocelli*, "meanwhile, our eyes search out their own wound").

65 Cf. 1.15.31, where Propertius claims that rivers will stop flowing to the sea and
   the seasons will run in reverse order before Cynthia leaves his heart (*quam tua
   sub nostro mutetur pectore cura*).

66 Cf. Prop. 3.24.17–18 describing the healing of his erotic wounds: *nunc demum
   uasto fessi resipiscimus aestu, / uulneraque ad sanum nunc coiere mea.*

67 The poem's urban setting is stressed by the reference to the slaves who lit the
   way with torches (1.2), the police force of Loves that arrest the lover (3–8), and
   Cynthia's Sidonian *mitra* (1.15).

68 If Archilochus draws on the tradition of Odysseus (Seidensticker 1978; Miller
   1994: 9–36), forced to beg on his way back from Ithaca, then Propertius chose
   perhaps to replace the Homeric Cyclops with the Centaurs of Atalanta's tale.
   Note the similarities in the description of the Centaurs (*hirsutas feras*, Prop.
   1.1.12) and the Cyclops (*hirsutus amictu*, Ov. *Met.* 14.165). Of course, the
   utopia in which the lover seeks to escape is in sharp contrast both with his own
   urban environment and the "real" battlefield in which Aeneas seeks to prevail.

69 Harrison 2007b: 130–1 with *A.* 1.628–30: *me quoque per multos similis fortuna
   labores / iactatam … / non ignara mali …* ("I was also thrown by a similar
   fortune into many toils / … / since I'm not unaware of misfortune …"). Text
   and trans. modified from LCL 63, Fairclough, rev. Goold 1999: 438–9.

70 Thus, she briefly airs the possibility of a second exile in *A.* 4.545–6: *quos
   Sidonia vix urbe revelli, / rursus agam pelago …?* ("shall I lead again over the
   sea, those I moved with difficulty from the Sidonian city …?") Text and trans.
   modified from LCL 63: 432–3.

71 Also note that Dido begins her complaint by calling Aeneas *perfidus* ("fickle," *A.*
   4.366), an adjective typically attributed to elegiac mistresses; e.g., Prop. 1.11.16;
   1.16.43; 4.7.13; for variations of the motif, see 1.5.1 (*inuide*); also, 4.7.31
   (*ingrate*).

72 Text and trans. modified from LCL 18, Fairclough, rev. Goold 1990: 246–7.
   Also, see Prop. 3./.18: *has didici certo saepe in amore notas* ("I have learned
   that these are often the signs of a sure love"). The line evokes Prop. 1.1.17–18,
   where the poet professes not to remember the ploys of love and its previous
   well-known paths (*in me tardus Amor non ullas cogitate artes / nec meminit
   notas, ut prius, ire uias*).

73 Trans. LCL 63: 443.

74 On Dido cast as a Euripidean Maenad, see Panoussi 2009: 134–8. Vergil also
   describes Turnus and his allies in strikingly Maenadic terms; see Mac Góráin
   2013: 142–3 (comparing Turnus and Pentheus); cf. Panoussi 2009: 201–2
   and 209 (for Turnus, Ajax, and their comparison with lions); also, Gale 1997b:
   182–3. For maenadism as a form of disorderly violence that Vergil wishes
   to juxtapose in the *Aeneid* with Aeschylean justice, in the context of which
   violence is deemed necessary in the struggle for establishing or restoring a
   kingdom, see Anagnostou-Laoutides 2020: 159–65.

75 Vergil also refers to Dido's crying (*fletu*, *A.* 4.369) and her tears (*lacrimas*, *A.*
   4.370); for *fletu*, see Prop. 1.4.23; 1.5.15; 1.15.40; 1.16.49; for *lacrimas*, Prop.
   1.3.46; 1.6.24; 1.9.7; 1.10.2; 1.12.16; 1.16.4.

76 Cf. Cairns 1989: 40 on *A.* 1.496–508, arguing that Dido's description (which
   parallels an earlier description of Aeneas) "establishes her firmly as a good king."

77 Cairns 1989: 44, noting that Dido's "claimed antipathy to marriage is a smoke-
   screen."

78 Cf. Prop. 3.13.15–22 on the eastern custom of adding the wife to the funeral
pyre of her husband. Being an eastern mistress, Dido sets up a pyre with all of
Aeneas' belongings, aware that her body will be added to it. This notion also
accords with the inglorious fate of tyrants who often throw themselves onto
fires (including Croesus, who was, nevertheless, spared because of his piety).
Harrell 2006: 124.

79 See n58 above.

80 On erotic pallor, see Sappho fr. 31, emulated by Catullus, poem 51. Cf.
Anagnostou-Laoutides 2005: 93–6.

81 When in *A.* 10.465–6 Hercules, aware of Pallas' impending death, is moved to
tears, Zeus points out to him the inescapability of human mortality by saying (*A.*
10.467–9): *breue et inreparabile tempus / omnibus est uitae: sed famam extendere
factis, / hoc uirtutis opus* ("Short and irreversible the span of life is for all. But to
prolong life's glory with great deeds, this is the power of virtue"). Vergil echoes
here Mimnermus' famous verses about the brevity of life (fr. 2.1–8), but also
Solon, whom Plutarch reports as having said (Plut. *Sol.* 3.2 = fr. 15 [LCL 258]:
ἀλλ᾽ ἡμεῖς αὐτοῖς οὐ διαμειψόμεθα / τῆς ἀρετῆς τὸν πλοῦτον / ἐπεὶ τὸ μὲν
ἔμπεδον αἰεί ("We will not exchange with them our virtue for their wealth since
virtue is ever abiding"). Cf. Cic. *Tusc.Disp.* 1.45.17 (LCL 141, King 1927): *Nemo
parum diu uixit, qui uirtutis perfectae perfecto functus est munere* ... ("No one has
lived too short a life who has discharged the perfect work of perfect virtue ...").
Cf. Hom. *Il.* 16.426–507, where Zeus, moved to pity for Sarpedon's impending
death, considers intervening to save him from the deadly spear of Patroclus but is
quickly dissuaded by Hera.

82 Cf. Green 1996: 226–7 and 256–61, on Ovid's pessimistic emphasis on the
deception that seems to be the main rule of hunting, a game where the roles
of the hunter and the prey are in a continuous flux, and which will eventually
affect the poet himself. In my view, Vergil responds to this threat by alluding
to the vicissitudes of the human condition as negotiated in Greek tragedy; see
Anagnostou-Laoutides 2020, esp. 146.

83 Cf. Nussbaum 1993: esp. 122–49. On Lucan's adaptation of Vergil's elegiac
motifs, see Hübner 1984: 229–35; Masters 1992: 188–92; Finiello 2005:
170–1; Arweiler 2006: 62–4, McCune 2014: 178–95. On his use of Roman
elegy in *De Bello Civili*, see Littlewood 2016: 163–8; on his use of Propertius,
Hübner 1984: 236–7 and McCune 2014: 173–9, 182, 189, 194 (also citing
Keith 2000: 68–9, 86–8; Fratantuono 2012: 94, 121–2, 129n68, and Heyworth
2007a: 9–10); cf. Anagnostou-Laoutides 2017: 307–8.

6

From Caieta to Erato: Vergil's Elegiac Program in *Aeneid* 7.1–45

SARAH MCCALLUM

Vergil initiates his *maius opus* with a series of interconnected panels that reveal his extraordinary vision for *Aeneid* 7–12. The framing elements of the entire sequence – an epitaphic address to Caieta (*A.* 7.1–4) and an invocation of Erato (*A.* 7.37–45) – are exceptionally unconventional. By starting with Caieta, Vergil inverts the traditional use of sepulchral imagery to mark moments of closure and finality. Erato, ousted from her rightful place by Caieta, must wait patiently for thirty-six lines to be called upon. Vergil's delay, as well as his choice of Muse, thwarts our expectations. Within the apostrophic frame, Vergil draws out the final stretch of Aeneas' journey to Italy with a lingering set of vignettes. From Caieta to Erato, the entire sequence consumes forty-five hexameter lines, far exceeding conventional limits and dwarfing the initial proem of *Aeneid* 1. What are we to make of such an introduction, which is as strange as it is magnificent? I propose to show how the various elements of the opening passage coalesce to produce a unified "proem in the middle," a complex articulation of the conceptual and poetic framework of Vergil's "Italian *Iliad*."[1] The central vignettes, rather than disrupting the proemial passage, enrich and reinforce the thematic and aesthetic significance of the surrounding frame. Through this elaborate nexus of images, Vergil creates an *exordium* of magnitude and scope that reflects the enormity of the task at hand.

The obvious structural correlation between Vergil's apostrophes of Caieta and Erato invites a consideration of how they operate as a linked pair of programmatic messages. Caieta and Erato emblematize *mors* and *amor*, respectively, starting with the epitaphic commemoration that marks the beginning of the end of Vergil's epic. In the four-line passage devoted to the *Aeneia nutrix*, Vergil appropriates expressions and themes conventionally found in Roman funerary inscriptions (*A.* 7.1–4):[2]

> Tu quoque litoribus nostris, Aeneia nutrix,
> aeternam moriens famam, Caieta, dedisti;
> et nunc seruat honos sedem tuus, ossaque nomen
> Hesperia in magna, si qua est ea gloria, signat.

You too, nurse of Aeneas, to our shores gave everlasting renown by dying, Caieta; even now your honour remains in your place of burial, and your name marks your bones in great Hesperia, if that be any glory.

The verses conform to the standard formula of Latin epitaphic inscriptions, which provide the name and status or occupation of the deceased, followed by the bestowal of praise.[3] The formulaic phrase *tu quoque*, as recognized, for example, by Nicholas Horsfall and Martin Dinter, appears frequently in funerary inscriptions and Latin literary epitaphs written for deceased poets.[4] When construed with *moriens, tu quoque* also evokes a common epitaphic motif that seeks to provide consolation for death through the contemplation that it is common to all.[5] In the next line, Caieta's *aeterna fama* echoes inscriptions that feature the notion of the eternal fame of the virtuous deceased.[6] The final two lines encapsulate the concept that "a conspicuous tomb or much-read epitaph ensures a sort of oblique immortality," thereby emphasizing Caieta's "everlasting renown."[7] Furthermore, they are a direct reflection of Latin funerary inscriptions that pervasively contain formulaic expressions that connect bodily remains, tomb, and place of burial – for example, the commonplace plea that the bones lie restfully in the earth.[8] Thus, Vergil creates an authentic epitaph that marks the tomb of Caieta in the realm of the imaginary. But in the realm of the text, the inscription carves out *mors* as something central to the narrative it introduces.

At the end of the frame, juxtaposed with Caieta, is Vergil's long-awaited invocation, in which he invokes Erato for assistance in recounting his narrative of war (*A.* 7.37–45):

> Nunc age, qui reges, Erato, quae tempora, rerum
> quis Latio antiquo fuerit status, aduena classem
> cum primum Ausoniis exercitus appulit oris,
> expediam, et primae reuocabo exordia pugnae.
> tu uatem, tu, diua, mone. dicam horrida bella,

> dicam acies actosque animis in funera reges,
> Tyrrhenamque manum totamque sub arma coactam
> Hesperiam. maior rerum mihi nascitur ordo,
> maius opus moueo.

Come now, Erato, who the kings were, what the times were, what the state of affairs in ancient Latium was, when the foreign army first landed on Ausonian shores, I will relate, and I will recall the commencement of the first battle. You, goddess, you remind your bard. I will tell of frightful wars, I will tell of battle arrays, and of kings driven by courage to their deaths, and of the Tyrrhenian host, and all of Hesperia assembled under arms. Greater is the series of events that arises for me, greater the work I set in motion.

The programmatic passage is a virtual catalogue of terminology related to warfare, including fleets, armies, battle arrays, courageous leaders, conflict, and casualties. By creating this elaborate expansion of the poem's initial *arma*, Vergil establishes with absolute clarity the overarching martial epic content and character of his *maius opus* (*A.* 7.45). Given the poetic program and elevated status of the forthcoming narrative, Vergil's invocation of Erato has proven to be a great source of interpretive consternation. In the Servian commentary, for example, bewilderment over the selection of Erato leads to the suggestion that Vergil must surely have simply used her as a proxy for Calliope or the Muse of epic in general: *sane ERATO uel pro Calliope, uel pro qualicumque musa posuit* ("Surely he put Erato either for Calliope or for any muse without distinction").[9] Bolstering this solution, which has continued to attract support in the scholarship,[10] are claims that the concretization of the Muses' specific roles occurred long after the composition of the *Aeneid*.[11] But the suggestion that Vergil would invoke Erato, stripped of any specific identity, is untenable for two reasons: first, it requires us to accept that Vergil, a poet not given to thoughtless imprecision, would make such a striking choice without significance; and, second, it fails to take into account the basic fact that by the first century BCE the Muses were conceptually linked to individual spheres of influence, some more concretely than others. Thus, there are two crucial questions. What was the precise identity of Erato for Vergil and his audience? And why would her divine expertise be sought by Vergil for recounting the events of *Aeneid* 7–12?

To answer the question of Erato's identity, literary sources confirm her long-established distinction as the Muse of the erotic sphere, a distinction which has its origins in the introductory hymn of the *Theogony* (Hes. *Theog.* 1–104). Hesiod begins his poetic genealogy of the gods by commemorating the nine Muses, each of whom he provides with a unique name etymologically derived from one of their shared activities (*Theog.* 76–80):[12]

ἐννέα θυγατέρες μεγάλου Διὸς ἐκγεγαυῖαι,
Κλειώ τ᾽ Εὐτέρπη τε Θάλειά τε Μελπομένη τε
Τερψιχόρη τ᾽ Ἐρατώ τε Πολύμνιά τ᾽ Οὐρανίη τε
Καλλιόπη θ᾽· ἡ δὲ προφερεστάτη ἐστὶν ἁπασέων.
ἡ γὰρ καὶ βασιλεῦσιν ἅμ᾽ αἰδοίοισιν ὀπηδεῖ.

The nine daughters born of mighty Zeus, Kleio and Euterpe and Thaleia and Melpomene and Terpsichore and Erato and Polymnia and Ourania and Kalliope: who is the most excellent of them all. For she is the attendant of venerated kings.

Through this poetic innovation, Hesiod lays the foundation for the subsequent differentiation of the Muses, whose names can be conceptually linked to the meaning of their etymological source words. In the case of Erato, the bestowal of a name formulated from cognates of ἔραμαι initiates her enduring association with the realm of the erotic.[13] Indeed, Plato further establishes Erato's conceptual identity by developing the Hesiodic model along more explicit lines in the *Phaedrus* (259c–259d):[14]

καὶ μετὰ ταῦτα ἐλθὸν παρὰ Μούσας ἀπαγγέλλειν τίς τίνα αὐτῶν τιμᾷ τῶν ἐνθάδε. Τερψιχόρᾳ μὲν οὖν τοὺς ἐν τοῖς χοροῖς τετιμηκότας αὐτὴν ἀπαγγέλλοντες [259d] ποιοῦσι προσφιλεστέρους, τῇ δὲ Ἐρατοῖ τοὺς ἐν τοῖς ἐρωτικοῖς, καὶ ταῖς ἄλλαις οὕτως κατὰ τὸ εἶδος ἑκάστης τιμῆς· τῇ δὲ πρεσβυτάτῃ Καλλιόπῃ καὶ τῇ μετ᾽ αὐτὴν Οὐρανίᾳ τοὺς ἐν φιλοσοφίᾳ διάγοντάς τε καὶ τιμῶντας τὴν ἐκείνων μουσικὴν ἀγγέλλουσιν, αἳ δὴ μάλιστα τῶν Μουσῶν περί τε οὐρανὸν καὶ λόγους οὖσαι θείους τε καὶ ἀνθρωπίνους ἱᾶσιν καλλίστην φωνήν.

And thereafter they went to the Muses to report who among those here honours which of them. And so to Terpsichore they report those who have honoured her in choral dances [259d] and make them more beloved to her, and to Erato those who have honoured her in erotic matters, and thus to the others, according to the nature of the honour belonging to each. But to Kalliope, the eldest, and to Ourania, who comes after her, they report those who spend their life in philosophy and honour the music that belongs to them, who of the Muses are especially concerned with heaven and discourses divine and human and utter the most beautiful voice.

Socrates, recounting the myth of the cicadas, differentiates Erato from three of her sisters – Terpsichore, Kalliope, and Ourania – by designating her as the Muse of τὰ ἐρωτικά, matters related to ἔρως.[15] Apollonius' invocation of Erato at the midpoint of his Hellenistic *Argonautica* bears further witness to her erotic significance (*Arg.* 3.1–5):[16]

εἰ δ᾽ ἄγε νῦν, Ἐρατώ, παρ᾽ ἔμ᾽ ἵστασο καί μοι ἔνισπε
ἔνθεν ὅπως ἐς Ἰωλκὸν ἀνήγαγε κῶας Ἰήσων
Μηδείης ὑπ᾽ ἔρωτι· σὺ γὰρ καὶ Κύπριδος αἶσαν
ἔμμορες, ἀδμῆτας δὲ τεοῖς μελεδήμασι θέλγεις
παρθενικάς· τῷ καί τοι ἐπήρατον οὔνομ᾽ ἀνῆπται.

Come now, Erato, stand beside me and tell me how from there Jason brought back the fleece to Iolcus with the aid of Medea's love. For you have a share also in Cypris' sphere of influence, and you bewitch unwedded maidens with your love-cares. And therefore to you is attached a name of love.

Apollonius invokes Erato precisely because her established erotic identity makes her uniquely qualified to assist with the story of Medea's love for Jason (Μηδείης ὑπ᾽ ἔρωτι, *Arg.* 3.3).[17] Apollonius, harking back to Hesiod, points out the etymological connection between Erato's name (ἐπήρατον οὔνομ᾽, *Arg.* 3.5) and specific erotic jurisdiction, which she shares with Aphrodite herself (σὺ γὰρ καὶ Κύπριδος αἶσαν / ἔμμορες, *Arg.* 3.3–4).[18]

Roman poets of the first century BCE are attuned to the Greek trend of ascribing special roles to different Muses, including Erato, and develop it with characteristically innovative imitation. In his third collection of elegies, Propertius creates a scene of poetic initiation in which he accompanies Apollo to a grotto inhabited by the Muses (Prop. 3.3.33–6):[19]

diuersaeque nouem sortitae iura Puellae
    exercent teneras in sua dona manus:
haec hederas legit in thyrsos, haec carmina neruis
    aptat, at illa manu texit utraque rosam.

And the nine Maidens having obtained by lot their provinces occupy their tender hands in their own gifts: this one gathers ivy for thyrsus wands, this one fits her songs to the strings, but that one weaves a rose with each hand.

Propertius conceives of the Muses as nine individualized goddesses, differentiated by the allotment of provinces and occupied with their own unique gifts. Furthermore, detailed descriptions of three unnamed Muses at lines 35–6 reflect the notion that the divine *Puellae* can represent specific types of poetic production.[20] The third, set in contrast to her Bacchic and lyric sisters by the phrase *at illa*,[21] appears in the emphatic final clause of the *tricolon crescens*. Her placement and signature activity identify her as the Muse of elegiac verse: she is the sole occupant of the pentameter line; and her weaving of roses, a flower that symbolizes both funerary and amatory poetics, evokes the two entwined facets of elegy.[22] In Ovid, we find the Roman incarnation of Erato herself, who retains the name and identity of her Greek antecedents in Hesiod, Plato, and Apollonius (Ov. *Ars* 2.15–16):[23] *nunc mihi, si quando, puer et Cytherea, fauete, / nunc Erato, nam tu nomen Amoris habes* ("Now, if ever, favour me, Cytherea and son, now favour me Erato, for you have the name of Amor"). When Ovid seeks Erato's assistance in *Ars Amatoria* 2, he, like Apollonius, associates her with Venus and underscores her erotic province by pointing out the etymological resonance of her name.[24] A second reference to Erato in *Fasti* 4 further emphasizes her share in Venus' month and the connection of her name with *amor* (Ov. *F.* 4.195–6):[25] *sic ego. sic Erato (mensis Cythereius illi / cessit quod teneri nomen amoris habet)* … ("So I spoke. So Erato replied – for the Cytherean month has passed into her care because she has the name of tender love – … ") What these examples from Propertius and Ovid clearly demonstrate is that Roman poets were accustomed to the differentiation of the Muses and Erato's conceptual connection to the erotic sphere. Thus, to answer the first crucial question, Vergil and his audience identified Erato precisely as the Muse of erotic themes and amatory poetics.[26]

Why, then, does Vergil seek Erato's assistance for recounting his martial *maius opus*? The simple answer, encoded in the opening line of Vergil's invocation, is that he, like Apollonius before him, enlists Erato because of her erotic expertise. With the phrase *nunc age Erato* (*A.* 7.37), Vergil repeats the opening phrase of Apollonius' invocation of the Muse in *Argonautica* 3 (εἰ δ'ἄγε νῦν, Ἐρατώ, *Arg.* 3.1).[27] The striking intertextual connection activates for the audience Erato's explicit erotic identity from the Apollonian model, without the need for further elaboration. In the *Aeneid*, just as in the *Argonautica*,[28] the invocation of Erato indicates the importance of amatory themes and poetics in the narrative to come.[29] As the counterpoint to the initial epitaph to Caieta, emblematic of *mors*, Vergil's call to Erato adds a further addendum to *arma* that identifies *amor* as another integral aspect of *Aeneid* 7–12.

Vergil's poetic gestures to Caieta and Erato, *mors* and *amor*, in the opening sequence have crucial programmatic implications. The clear structural correlation between the two framing devices unites *mors* and *amor* and sets the linked pair in productive tension with *arma*, the primary matrix outlined in the culmination of the proem. This design delineates, to borrow Conte's eminently useful formula, the *quid* and *quale* of Vergil's epic vision.[30] In terms of content, Caieta and Erato prefigure *mors* and *amor* as central themes that drive the martial narrative. Whereas Caieta anticipates the pervasive concepts of loss and lament, which exemplify the immense human cost of conflict, Erato looks ahead to the conflicting passions that ignite and sustain the violence of war throughout the "Italian *Iliad*." Within the larger schematic of *Aeneid* 7–12, Caieta and Erato correspond to the death of Turnus in the final lines of Vergil's epic: as one impassioned warrior dies at the hands of another, the poem reaches its appropriately funerary conclusion. In aesthetic terms, the interconnected gestures to Caieta and Erato introduce what I refer to in the title of this chapter as Vergil's "elegiac program." The programmatic juxtaposition of *mors* and *amor* emblematizes the two poetic facets of Roman elegy, the genre of love and lament.[31] Thus, the integration of Caieta and Erato within the opening sequence prefigures Vergil's incorporation of artistic materials from elegy throughout the overarching martial epic matrix, promising an innovative narrative that remains rooted in the epic tradition, yet engaged with current Roman poetic trends and sensibilities. Vergil thus lays programmatic claim to elegy, the genre which provides both the thematic and aesthetic means to articulate the tensions between love, death, and war that characterize his *maius opus*.

The tripartite importance of *amor*, *mors*, and *arma* established in the frame of the proem are further reinforced by a central panel of embedded vignettes. I aim to focus on two aspects from the series of images depicted therein; namely, the depiction of Circe, and the technicolour description of Aeneas' first Italian dawn. Whereas Circe underscores the epic roots of Vergil's conceptualization of love as a destructive and deadly force, the Italian sunrise exemplifies his transformative use of the specialized lexicon of elegy within the martial poetic matrix.

Opening the series of erotic and programmatic scenes is a depiction of the realm of Circe, which the Trojans sail past as they continue their voyage along the Italian coastline after the burial of Caieta (*A.* 7.10–20). As the ships graze the coastline, Vergil provides a glimpse of the goddess (*A.* 7.10–14):

> proxima Circaeae raduntur litora terrae,
> diues inaccessos ubi Solis filia lucos
> adsiduo resonat cantu, tectisque superbis
> urit odoratam nocturna in lumina cedrum
> arguto tenuis percurrens pectine telas.

Closely grazed are the shores of Circe's land, where the opulent daughter of the Sun makes the inaccessible woods echo with continuous singing, and in her sumptuous abode burns fragrant cedar to illuminate the night as she runs through the fine threads of the warp with a shrill comb.

The appearance of Circe, particularly given her roles in the *Odyssey* and the *Argonautica*, situates Vergil's "Italian *Iliad*" within the poetic tradition of epic verse.[32] Vergil's divine temptress is an intertextual conflation of the Odyssean accounts of both Circe and Calypso (*Od.* 10.220–2, 5.59–62):[33]

ἔσταν δ᾽ ἐν προθύροισι θεᾶς καλλιπλοκάμοιο,
Κίρκης δ᾽ ἔνδον ἄκουον ἀειδούσης ὀπὶ καλῇ,
ἱστὸν ἐποιχομένης μέγαν ἄμβροτον, οἷα θεάων
λεπτά τε καὶ χαρίεντα καὶ ἀγλαὰ ἔργα πέλονται.

They stood in the front entry of the goddess with beautiful hair, and heard Circe singing within in a beautiful voice, as she plied the great loom immortal, such as goddesses have, their works fine and graceful and splendid.

πῦρ μὲν ἐπ᾽ ἐσχαρόφιν μέγα καίετο, τηλόσε δ᾽ ὀδμὴ
κέδρου τ᾽ εὐκεάτοιο θύου τ᾽ ἀνὰ νῆσον ὀδώδει
δαιομένων· ἡ δ᾽ ἔνδον ἀοιδιάουσ᾽ ὀπὶ καλῇ
ἱστὸν ἐποιχομένη χρυσείῃ κερκίδ᾽ ὕφαινεν.

A great fire was blazing on the hearth, and the fragrance of cedar clefts and sweet wood burning suffused the island: she was singing within in a beautiful voice and plied the loom and wove with a golden shuttle.

Like her Homeric antecedents, Vergil's Circe occupies herself with weaving and song, burns fragrant cedar,[34] and dwells in a woodland setting.[35] Circe, like Erato, also connects Vergil's narrative to the story of Medea's deleterious passion for Jason in the *Argonautica*. Circe's epithet *solis filia* (*A.* 7.11) under-scores her genealogical connection to Medea,[36] whereas descriptions of her powers of sorcery emphasize the threatening magical ancestry and ability she shares with her mortal niece.[37] Vergil's Circe, evocative of her Homeric and Apollonian antecedents, conjures epic narratives in which destructive *amor* poses an enduring threat to the epic hero, whose erotic entanglements threaten homecoming through both delay and loss of life. In thematic and aesthetic terms, the image of Circe indicates that Vergil, like Homer and Apol-lonius before him, intends to grapple with *amor* in its most menacing aspect. His epic conceptualization of *amor*, unlike that of his elegiac contemporaries, identifies love as a powerful force that leads to real war and death. The image of Circe, resonating with Caieta and Erato, reinforces Vergil's tripartite design of *mors*, *amor*, and *arma* and situates it within the epic tradition.

But, as I have already suggested, Vergil's epic design for the "Italian *Iliad*" includes the incorporation of elegiac materials to create aesthetic moments that reinforce his central themes. The vibrant sunrise in the central panel of the proem provides a preview of the way in which Vergil punctuates his epic narrative by experimenting with the genre of *amor* and *mors* (*A.* 7.25–8):

Iamque rubescebat radiis mare et aethere ab alto
Aurora in roseis fulgebat lutea bigis,
cum uenti posuere omnisque repente resedit
flatus, et in lento luctantur marmore tonsae.

And now the sea was growing red with the rays of the sun and from high in the sky Aurora was blazing yellow in her chariot of rose, when the winds dropped and in an instant every breeze died off. The oars struggle in the marble stillness of the sea.

At first glance, Vergil conforms to epic tradition by utilizing a morning scene to mark an inaugural moment, namely Aeneas' first glimpse of the Tiber (*A.* 7.29–34).[38] But his integration of language and motifs from elegy, both erotic and funerary, poetically reinforces the tension between *amor* and *mors* established throughout the opening sequence from Caieta to Erato. When the morning rays hit the sea, it takes on the characteristic colours of erotic passion and sexual response. In the lexicon of amatory poetics, cognates of the verb *rubesco* signify the blush which arises from *pudor*, the sense of shame which marks the moment of erotic awakening.[39] This "blush" floods into the next line, colouring the horses of personified Dawn with a rosy hue (*in roseis … bigis, A.* 7.26).[40] The goddess herself is a vision of gleaming saffron (*Aurora … fulgebat lutea, A.* 7.26), the reddish-gold colour of the *flammeum* which veils the Roman bride.[41] Etymologically related to the Greek φλέγω (to burn),[42] the verb *fulgere* describes the radiance of Aurora in language evocative of fire, recalling the conventional elegiac association between love and consuming flame.[43] Surging with the colours of flushed skin and fire, the landscape evokes the concept of *amor* and resonates with the amatory implications of Erato.

A sudden change in tone, both chromatic and atmospheric, swiftly extinguishes the initial fervour of the landscape. Though the presence of elegiac language and motifs continues, the scene no longer conveys the heat of erotic awakening, but the chill of erotic refusal and the stillness of death. The dynamic undulation of crimson and saffron halts as a pale paralysis overtakes the landscape, the cessation of motion underscored by the shift from the imperfect (*rubescat, fulgebat, A.* 7.25–6) to the perfect tense (*posuere, resedit, A.* 7.27). Once aflame with the hues of erotic passion, the now tranquil sea resembles the smooth, white surface of marble (*lento … marmore, A.* 7.28), an image that recalls both the amatory and funerary aspects of elegy. The stony white sea calls to mind the elegiac lover-poet's descriptions of the beauty and coldness of the unresponsive *dura puella*: the exposed skin of the mistress is conventionally pale;[44] whiteness suggests the frigid absence of sexual feeling;[45] elegists use the term *lentus* to denote the withholding of affection;[46] and unyielding marble evokes the frequent elegiac topos that associates emotional hardness with stone.[47] But marble also evokes the materiality of epitaphs and the poetic expression of *mors* in funerary inscriptions. Through its striking chromatic shift, the Italian sunrise replicates the poetic dichotomy of *amor* and *mors* in elegy, thereby reinforcing the aesthetic and generic import of Caieta and Erato in the surrounding frame.

From beginning to end, the virtuosic opening sequence of *Aeneid* 7 provides a rich and complex introduction to Vergil's innovative artistic design for the "Italian *Iliad*." The conflation of *mors*, *amor*, and *arma* therein sets up a uniquely Roman epic, punctuated with elegiac moments that enrich Vergil's artistic program with electrifying interest and beauty. That Vergil shows such a deep investment in elegiac poetics within *Aeneid* 7–12 should come as no surprise: the genre rose to prominence during his lifetime; he had close personal and professional relationships with its star poets; and he experimented with elegy in the *Bucolics*, *Georgics*, and *Aeneid* 1–6. But despite the clear programmatic message of the first forty-five lines of *Aeneid* 7, elegy has largely been overlooked as a crucial component of Vergil's *maius opus*, due perhaps to its perceived incompatibility with martial epic. But the dissonance of elegy is precisely what makes it such a powerful addition to Vergil's narrative and artistic scheme. The conceptual metamorphosis of elegiac elements, transplanted from their original poetic context, is striking, transforming their meaning: the wounds of love become actualized in mortal combat; the lament of the rejected wooer becomes that of a bereaved soldier or mother; and the emotional ramifications of *amor* extend beyond weakening the constitution of the lover to threatening the very foundation of Rome. In essence, Vergil's engagement with elegy throughout the second half of the *Aeneid* is absolutely crucial to its poetic success, making it "something greater than the *Iliad*," indeed.

NOTES

I am grateful to Alison Keith and Micah Myers for their organization of the 2017 *Symposium Cumanum* and publication of this commemorative volume. I also wish to extend my thanks to the host of individuals who have shaped my contribution through their generous feedback and stimulating discussion: my fellow participants in Cuma; the anonymous readers; my graduate cohort at the University of Toronto; and my Thiasos gang, Zoa Alonso Fernández, Lauren Curtis, and Naomi Weiss.

1 For a discussion of the phenomenon of the "proem in the middle" in Latin
poetry, see Conte 1992: 147–59.
2 See Merkelbach 1971: 349–51; Barchiesi 1979: 3–11; Horsfall 1986: 44;
Hardie 1998: 108; Kyriakidis 1998: passim; Thomas 1999: 105; Horsfall
2000: 46 ad *A.* 7.1; Dinter 2005: 157–60. For the reception of these verses in
an epigram by the fifteenth-century humanist Francesco Patrizi, see Miletti in
this collection. All excerpts from Vergil's *Aeneid* in this chapter are cited from
Mynors 1969. All translations are my own.
3 See Lattimore 1962: 266 §76.
4 See Horsfall 2000: 45–6 ad *A.* 7.1–4 and Dinter 2011: 7–18, with further
examples and bibliography.
5 See Lattimore 1962: 250–6 §71 and Horsfall 2000: 45–6 on *A.* 7.1–4.
6 See Lattimore 1962: 241–3 §67.
7 See Lattimore 1962: 229 §62.
8 See *CCLE* s.vv. *ossa*.
9 On Calliope's epic associations elsewhere in the Vergilian *corpus*, see Coleman
1977: 147, on her appearance at *B.* 4.57; Hardie 1994: 171–2, on the
invocation at *A.* 9.525–8 prior to the *aristeia* of Turnus. The unnamed epic
Muse appears in the proem to each Homeric epic: θεά, Hom. *Il.* 1.1; μοῦσα,
Od. 1.1; θεά, θύγατερ Διός, *Od.* 1.10.
10 See, for example, Klingner 1967: 497; Basson 1975: 99–101; Toll 1989:
107–18; Kyriakidis 1998: 161–77. For a detailed summary of the scholarly
debate surrounding Erato, see Horsfall 2000: 69–71.
11 On the post-Augustan concretization of the specific designations of the Muses,
see Nisbet and Hubbard 1970: 282–3 on Hor. *Carm.* 1.24.3; Thomas 1999:
105 [= 1985: 72]; Kyriakidis 1998: 162–3; Nelis 2001: 268n6, with further
bibliography.
12 See West 1966: 180–1, on Hes. *Theog.* 77–9. All excerpts from Hesiod's
Theogony in this chapter are cited from West 1966.
13 The verb ἔραμαι refers properly to love in the sense of sexual passion and
desire: see *LSJ* s.v. ἔραμαι.
14 See Yunis 2011: 176 on Pl. *Phdr.* 259c6: "Plato borrows from Hesiod the names
of the Muses (*Theog.* 77–9) and the idea of connecting their names with the
activities they supervise (*Theog.* 63–74)." All excerpts from Plato's *Phaedrus*
are cited from Yunis 2011.
15 See Todd 1931: 217: "That Love is the province of Erato is quite certain. Plato,
Phaedr. 259c, says so."
16 The text I have used for Apollonius is Fränkel 1986.
17 See Hunter 1989: 96 ad *Arg.* 3.3–4.
18 See Hunter 1989: 97 ad *Arg.* 3.4–5; Nelis 2001: 268. The etymological
relationship between Ἐρατώ, ἔρως, and ἐπήρατος in the first, third, and final

lines further reinforces her erotic associations: see Hunter 1989: 97 ad *Arg.* 3.4–5; O'Hara 2017: 184–5 ad *A.* 7.37–40; Nelis 2001: 268.

19 Fedeli 1985: 143–5 on Prop. 3.3.33–6. Cairns 2006: 126–7 suggests that Gallus may have influenced this Propertian encounter with the Muses.

20 As Emma Scioli (2015: 155) observes, the verbs *legere* (Prop. 3.3.35), *aptere*, and *texere* (Prop. 3.3.36) all have secondary significance within the lexicon of literary production, signifying reading, adaptation, and writing, respectively.

21 *OLD* s.v. at 1.

22 For evidence of the importance of the rose in Roman funerary rituals and commemorative festivals (e.g., *Rosalia* and *Parentalia*), see Lattimore 1962: 135–41; Toynbee 1971: 62–4, 97–8; Brenk 1999: 87–90; Hope 2009: 99–100, 174. On the association of roses with Aphrodite, see Brenk 1999: 91–3. See also Postgate 1885: 156, on Prop. 4.3.36 [= 3.3.36]: "Perhaps Erato is meant. Love is crowned with roses." Note the use of *rosa* elsewhere in Propertius in programmatic passages related to *mors* and *amor*. See, for example, the poet imagining the beloved mingling his bones and roses in commemoration of his death (*molliter et tenera poneret ossa rosa*, Prop. 1.17.22); he wants to forever wear rose garlands, the symbol of amatory pursuits and poetry (*et caput in uerna semper habere rosa*, Prop. 3.5.22). Keith (2008b: 62–3) interprets Prop. 3.5.18–22 as the poet "sounding elegy's distinct, and distinctly conventional, disjunction from lyric." Cf. also Prop. 2.3.12, 4.2.40, 4.6.72, 4.7.60, 4.8.40.

23 Todd 1931: 217; O'Hara 1996b: 268–9.

24 Ovid here uses a bilingual wordplay that employs the Latin transliteration *Erato* with the noun *amor* to suggest the derivation of the Greek Ἐρατώ from ἔρως.

25 See Fantham 1998: 131 ad 195–6.

26 As Nelis (2001: 268) remarks, with supporting bibliography, "indeed it is impossible to believe that Vergil can allude to Apollonius' Erato but subtract any erotic associations which her name can carry."

27 On the Apollonian resonance of *nunc age*, see Fraenkel 1945: 1; Knauer 1964a: 227n1; Basson 1975: 96; Hunter 1989: 95 ad *Arg.* 3.1–5; O'Hara 2017: 184–5. ad *A.* 7.37–40. For discussion of the connection between Vergil's invocation of Erato and its Apollonian model, see Horsfall 2000: 67–8 on *A.* 7.37–45; Nelis 2001: 268, with further bibliography.

28 See Woodworth 1930: 178; Nelis 2001: 268.

29 Some associate Erato with erotic aspects of the narrative, looking forward to Lavinia and the theme of marriage, and/or backward to Aeneas' erotic affair with Dido: see Todd 1931: 217–18; Reckford 1961: 256–7; Williams 1973: 169 ad *A.* 7.37; Fordyce 1977: 64 ad *A.* 7.37; Pavlock 1992: 73; O'Hara 2017: 184–5 ad *A.* 7.37–40; O'Hara 1996b: 268–9; Nelis 2001: 268–75. Toll (1989: 113–15) proposes that Erato refers, not to erotic love, but rather to Aeneas'

amor patriae, which took precedence over his amatory attachment to Dido. Cf.
Aeneas' famous declaration to Dido regarding Italy: *hic amor, hic patria est* (*A.*
4.347). Others see the interrogative structure of Vergil's invocation as evocative
of the Callimachean technique of question and answer between Muses and the
poet which features prominently in the first two books of the *Aetia*: see Hunter
1989: 95 ad *Arg.* 3.1; and Kyriakidis 1994: 203–5. Yet another interpretation
connects Erato to the epithalamium, a suitable genre for the theme of
betrothal and marriage: see Todd 1931: 217; and Monteleone 1977: 184–91.
Interestingly, Erato may have been the muse of the *Achilleid*, a poem centred
upon the love affair between Achilles and Deidamia: see Coleman 1988: 198–9
ad Stat. *Silv.* 4.7.2.

30 Conte 1992: 147–9 differentiates between the proem's announcement of a
poem's *quid* (themes, contents, etc.), and *quale* (artistic character).

31 See Thomas 1998a; Dinter 2005; and Ramsby 2007. For examples of
epigrammatic material in Roman elegy, see Prop. 1.21–2, 2.1.78, 2.13.35–6,
4.7.85–6. 4.11.35–6; Tibullus 1.3.55–6.

32 See Hunter 1993: 175–82; Thomas 1999: 106–9; Nelis 2001: 259–62.

33 The text I have used for the *Odyssey* is Allen 1917–20.

34 For the burning cedar as a verbal echo of the Homeric description of Calypso's
cave, see Knauer 1964a: 137–8; Fordyce 1977: 55 ad *A.* 7.12; Thomas 1999:
107; Horsfall 2000: 55 on *A.* 7.12; Nelis 2001: 261.

35 This fusion may reflect post-Homeric moralizing interpretations of the
Odyssey in which these two goddesses come to represent the dangers of lust
and passion. For the moralizing interpretation of Circe, see Hunter 1993:
178–9, and Nelis 2001: 261. Perhaps one of the most famous moralizing
interpretations of the Homeric Circe occurs in Hor. *Epist.* 1.2.23–5: *quae si
cum sociis stultus cupidusque bibisset, / sub domina meretrice fuisset turpis et
excors, / uixisset canis immundus uel amica luto sus* ("If he had foolishly and
eagerly drunk Circe's cups along with his companions, he would have been
debased and void of reason under a prostitute mistress; he would have lived as
a filthy dog, or mud-loving sow"). Written in the period roughly contemporary
with the composition of the *Aeneid*, this epistle presents Homer as a superior
moral guide whose epics provide numerous morally instructive lessons and
illustrations: see Mayer 1994: 124. For Horace, Odysseus' encounter with
Circe illustrates both the dangers of female sexuality to male autonomy and
the importance of self-control in the face of desire – had Odysseus drunk the
magical concoction offered by Circe, he would have been shamefully unmanned
by a "prostitute mistress" (*domina meretrix*) and reduced to the status of a filthy
beast. Given the significance of the term *domina* in the lexicon of erotic elegy,
Odysseus' diminished status also resembles that of the submissive elegiac
lover.

36 Fordyce 1977: 55 ad *A.* 7.11 notes that Circe is traditionally the daughter of Helios and Perse, and the sister of Medea's father Aeetes. See also Hes. *Th.* 956–61; Hom. *Od.* 10.135–9; Ap. *Arg.* 3.309–13, 4.727, 4.743, 4.684. Cf. also Valerius Flaccus, who exploits the genealogy of Circe and Medea in his description of Venus, who adopts the guise of Circe to inflame Medea with love for Jason (V. Fl. 7.210–91).

37 See L-S s.v. *cantus* 2B; *OLD* s.v. *cantus* 3; and *TLL* 3.295.18–48 s.v. *cantus*. Papanghelis 1987: 40 notes that erotic enchantments, magic potions, and related motifs feature heavily in erotic literature, including elegy. The figure of the *saga* with powers over the universe and over love was well established among Vergil's elegiac contemporaries: see Cairns 1989: 145–6. Propertius includes the topos of the lover's search for *remedia amoris* through magic in the programmatic opening poem of his *Monobiblos*: see Cairns 1989: 146n73; Keith 2008b: 48–9. Cf. Prop. 1.1.19–24; Tib. 1.2.41–50, 1.6.43–54.

38 Temporal markers at the start of each section (*iam, A.* 7.25; *hic, A.* 7.29) indicate that the two aspects of the scene belong to the same moment in time: see Horsfall 2000: 62–3 ad *A.* 7.25–7 and 64 ad *A.* 7.29.

39 For the associations of colour red with sexual awakening or arousal, see Onians 1973: 153n2; Rhorer 1980: 79. See also Pichon 1902, s.vv. *pudor, rubere, rubor.*

40 For the erotic valence of *roseus*, see Pichon 1902, s.v. *roseus.*

41 Fordyce 1977: 59 ad *A.* 7.26. For the erotic symbolism of the colour yellow as signified by *luteus*, see Navarro Antolín 1996: 115 ad Lygd. 1.9. On Catullus' use of *luteus* in an epithalamic context to refer to Hymen's yellow slippers and the bride's blush, see Clarke 2003: 96–7. Among the elements of Roman bridal costume that might be coloured with *lutum* were the veil (*flammeum*), hairnet (*retinaculum luteum*), and footwear (*luteum soccum*): see La Follette 2001: 54–65; Sebesta 2001: 48; Edmondson 2008: 27.

42 For the etymological relationship between the Latin *fulgere* and the Greek φλέγω/φλεγέθω (to burn) and φλόξ (flame), see Ernout-Meillet 259 s.v. *fulgeo*; Frisk 1022–4 s.v. φλέγω; Halsey 140 φλεγ, *flag, fulg*; L-S s.v. *fulgeo*; *OLD* s.v. *fulgeo; TLL* 6¹.1507.46–8 s.v. *fulgeo.*

43 On the use of "fire" as an amatory image in elegy, see Pichon 1902, s.v. *ignes*; Cairns 1989: 149; Maltby 2002: 122n6, 418n6; Harrison 2007a: 211.

44 See Pichon 1902, s.vv. *candidus, marmoreus, niueus.*

45 See Rhorer 1980: 79.

46 See Pichon 1902, s.v. *lentus.*

47 On the various technical uses of *durus* (often in correlation with flint, stone, or iron), and its application in images of the beloved's insensitivity or unresponsiveness, see Pichon 1902, s.v. *durus*; Fedeli 1980: 73 on Prop. 1.1.10; Navarro Antolín 1996: 152 ad Lygd. 2.3; Maltby 2002: 142 ad Tib. 1.1.56 and 144 ad Tib. 1.1.63–4; James 2003b: 124.

7

Elegizing the Roman Dirge

BILL GLADHILL

The central argument of this paper asserts that Roman elegy contains an implicit and embedded non-literary genre, which falls under the heading *neniae*, a form of threnody sung by professional songstresses (*praeficae*) during a Roman *funus*. Roman genre and generic interplay are more than a feature of literature: they also intersect with songs of non-literary kinds, like *neniae*. While the argument here will stress generic embeddedness in understanding elegy, a sub-theme calls attention to problems of definition and classification of elegy more generally in the primary source material. The paper discusses Horace's thoughts on elegy in the *Ars Poetica* and *Odes*. Horace assumes a fundamental interplay between elegy and the *neniae*. The paper concludes with a brief exegesis on the Nisus and Euryalus episode in *Aeneid* 9, which demonstrates ways that epic too can embed the poetics of "nenian elegy" and the significance of this type of generic crossing.

Elegy, *Querimonia*, and *Neniae* in Horace

Horace's *Ars Poetica* 73–83 offers the most important evidence on Roman cataloguing of generic types of poetry. Horace's generic taxonomy frames conventions of poetic genres, while masking a deeper complexity and uncertainty as to the "purity" of genres, which allows us to tease out important distinctions when it comes to Roman conceptions of elegy (*AP* 75–8):

> uersibus impariter iunctis querimonia primum,
> post etiam inclusa est uoti sententia compos;
> quis tamen exiguos elegos emiserit auctor,
> grammatici certant et adhuc sub iudice lis est.

Verses yoked unequally first embraced lamentation, later also the sentiment of granted prayer: yet who first put forth humble elegiacs, scholars dispute, and the case is still before the court.[1]

It has long been recognized that Horace's phrase *uersibus impariter iunctis querimonia* gestures to funeral elegy.[2] *Grammatici* explicitly call elegy a *threnos*, or define it as having a threnetic metre or reflecting the sounds of those in mourning (ἔλεγος, ὁ θρῆνος, ὅθεν καὶ ἐλεγεῖον, μέτρον θρηνητικόν, Aelius Herodianus *Partitiones* 30.5; εὖ λέγειν in Orion's *Etymologicum* 58.7, ascribed to Didymus; ἒ ἒ λέγειν Suidas).[3] Scholars (with less certainty) too have suggested that *querimonia* may be alluding to *querelae* ("complaints/ plaintive sounds") of Roman love elegy, though one would have expected Horace to have used *querelae* if he had intended *querelae*.[4] His usage of *querimonia* here can be usefully filtered through Pseudo-Fronto's *De differentiis*, where we find the following distinction; *querimoniam et querelam: querimonia certae rei est, querela superuacua est. itaque prior grauitatis, posterior leuitatis est* ("complaint and whine: a complaint is for a particular reason, whining is pointless. And so the first consists of weightiness and the second of superficiality").[5]

The vast number of usages of *querimonia* in Latin literature suggests that Horace has something else in mind than *querela*, a difference in register that the later *De differentiis* appears to recognize. *Querimonia* is often found in contexts in which a state communicates a formal complaint to another polity through political channels, and is usually found in historical or oratorical works.[6] While we will complicate this definition of *querimonia* below, it is important to point out that the term could be linked to the sounds and expressions of grief and lamentation (what we might call *querelae*).[7] It is true that Propertius certainly did describe his elegiac output as *querelae*.[8] *Querela* too is found in overtly public and political contexts in a way entirely synonymous with *querimonia*.[9] While pseudo-Fronto can differentiate between *grauitas – querimonia/leuitas – querela* and Propertius could define his own elegiac program as *querelae*, the evidence overall suggests a distinction really without a difference.[10] In addition, the idea of dirge or funeral lament is not particularly the first thing that might come to mind when we encounter *querimonia* in the *AP*. Its application can be construed much more broadly in Roman literature. While *grammatici* and *commentaria* read Horace's *querimonia* in terms of threnodic elegy, the term is ambiguous enough to hint at Roman love elegy, a genre too in deep conversation with the epitaphic poetics of death.[11] While Horace could not have chosen a more lexically slippery term for elegy in the *AP*, Horace's usage of *querimonia* in the rest of his works strongly suggests that funeral lament is central to it.

In order to understand elegiac *querimonia* in the *AP* let us evaluate the cluster of words and concepts Horace connects to it. Horace's definition of elegy in terms of *querimonia* is marked; the term is never used by Roman elegists, and does not appear in poetry, aside from Horace's works, four usages in Plautus, and once in the *Appendix Vergiliana* (*Ciris* 461–2: *languida fessae / uirginis in cursu moritur querimonia longo* "the languid lament of the worn maiden perishes on the long journey"). Horace uses *querimonia* a total of four times (*Carm.* 1.13.19, 2.20.22, 3.24.33; *AP* 75), with one instance acting as a synonym for elegy (*AP* 75). Horace's description of elegy as *querimonia* is curious and it ought to cause one to ponder over its implications. Here one is confronted with a fundamental problem of Roman definition. Horace calls elegy *querimonia*; but this then begs the question, what does Horace mean by *querimonia*? As we will see below, Horace defines *querimonia* in terms of other words and expressions as he displays the "Matryoshka doll" approach to definition and lexicography: the definition of one word is embedded in another word which is then embedded in another word, etc. This is a process of associative definition; *querimonia* does define elegy, but only in so far as *querimonia* is a part of a cluster of other words and concepts within Horace's *opera* that, in turn, further delineate ideas of elegy. The problem of Horatian definition becomes more pointed upon reflection on his first usage of *querimonia* (*Carm.* 1.13.17–20): *felices ter et amplius / quos irrupta tenet copula nec malis / diuolsus querimoniis / suprema citius soluet amor die* ("three times lucky and more are those, whom the unbroken bond holds fast whom love, though torn asunder by awful complaints, does not too quickly set free until the final day"). Horace's first usage of *querimonia* in 1.13, in a poem closely linked to the poetics of love and jealousy (framed in Catullan terms), is associated with *amor* and death (*suprema die*).[12]

Querimonia's second occurrence (*Carm.* 2.20.22) is instructive; it builds on the death imagery of 1.13, while situating us in the poetics of a particularly Roman, threnodic lamentation, the *nenia*. In the final stanza of the final ode in Book 2, Horace embeds *querimonia* in an assemblage of funereal artefacts, linking the term to the Roman dirge (2.20.21–4):[13] *absint inani funere neniae / luctusque turpes et querimoniae; / conpesce clamorem ac sepulcri / mitte superuacuos honores* ("Let there be no lamentations or any ugly expressions of grief and mourning at my hollow funeral; restrain all cries, and do not trouble with the empty tribute of a tomb"). The biform *uates* commands that *neniae, luctus turpes*, and *querimoniae* be absent from his empty *funus*. He demands an implied *tu* to suppress their clamour and forget about the empty rites of the tomb. *Querimonia* is defined in terms of *neniae* and *luctus*, while, furthermore, participating in an elegiac soundscape around the ritual space of the *sepulchrum* and the *inane funus*. He hopes and commands that ritual and threnody not orbit his empty body and tomb (*inane funus*). Behind this line stands Sappho fr. 150, with *nenia* translating *thrēnos*: οὐ γὰρ θέμις ἐν μοισοπόλων †οἰκίᾳ† / θρῆνον ἔμμεν'· οὔ κ' ἄμμι πρέποι τάδε ("For it is not right that there should be lamentation in the house of those who serve the Muses. That would not befit us").[14]

It is possible that Horace's *querimonia* in the *Ars* is alluding to *Odes* 2.20 and the generic context of threnody that underlies it.[15] In fact, it is entirely possible that Horace's marked use of *querimonia* in the *Ars* is a function of its intertextual resonances with the *Odes* and the broader generic system that underlies the references. Horace is not alone in linking *querimonia* to *neniae*. Festus, for example, maps *querimonia* onto *neniae*; the *querimonia flentium* was similar to the *uox* (language) of *neniae* (*quod ei uoci sim<ilior querimonia flentium>*, "because the complaint of those weeping is quite similar to this sound," 161.55), while Diomedes Grammaticus emphatically links elegy to *neniae* (3.485.7–10): *nam et elegia extrema mortuo accinebatur sic uti nenia, ideoque ab eodem elegia uidetur tractum cognominari, quod mortuis uel morituris ascribitur nouissum* ("The elegy also was sung last to the dead in the same way as the *nenia*; and so elegy seems to be synonymous, drawn from the same place, namely the song most recently referring to the dead or those who are about to die").[16] When it comes to *Odes* 2.20 there is a sense of apprehension and dread that the poetics of *neniae* might intrude into the lyric world of Horace's *Odes*, causing it to become implicated in elegiac threnody. What impact might *neniae* have on the biform *uates* as he is in mid-flight through the liquid *aether*? We will answer this question below.

What are the implications in drawing a parallel between *neniae* and *querimonia*, and how do *neniae* colour our impression of Horace's definition of elegy in the *Ars*? Horace uses *nenia* two other times. In the first ode of Book 2 in the final stanza Horace refers to Simonides' lyric threnody to the fallen at Thermopylae, called here *Ceae … munera neniae*, which certainly anticipates the use of *nenia* in the final ode of Book 2 discussed above (2.1.39–42):[17] *sed ne relictis, Musa, procax iocis / Ceae retractes munera neniae; / mecum Dionaeo sub antro / quaere modos leuiore plectro* ("But steady, my impertinent Muse! Stick to frivolity, and do not rake up themes that call for the Cean dirge. Join me in the grotto of Dione's daughter and let us think of a tune for a lighter quill"). *Nenia* stands as the final word of *Odes* 3.28, in which *Nox* will be sung with a deserved *nenia*, usually translated here as "lullaby" (*Carm.* 3.28.9–16):[18]

> nos cantabimus inuicem
> Neptunum et uiridis Nereidum comas:
> tu curua recines lyra
> Latonam et celeris spicula Cynthiae:
> summo carmine, quae Cnidon
> fulgentisque tenet Cycladas et Paphon
> iunctis uisit oloribus,
> dicetur merita Nox quoque nenia.

We will sing in turn of Neptune and the green-haired Nereids; you will sing with your curved lyre of Latona and the arrows of swift-footed Cynthia. The last song will be of her who holds sway over Cnidos and the shining Cyclades, and visits Paphos with her team of swans. Night also will be celebrated in a well-deserved lullaby.

Beneath Horace's slippery definition of elegy in the *AP* are buried threnodic Roman songs in the *Odes*. Their lethal valence makes translating *nenia* as "lullaby" at 3.28.16 euphemistic. Arnold Bradshaw captures well the sense of the passage:

For the ageing Horace the sun is already past the zenith, and he feels a desperate urgency as his own evening approaches; prudence must be thrown to the winds and, before it is too late, the precious old wine must be snatched from store; it is time to sing the final hymns to the gods, the last ode to love, and at the end a dirge to darkness. The message is plain: soon the lyre and the songs which accompany it will be heard no more.[19]

In addition, the nominative *nox* is always connected to death in the *Odes*. At 1.4.16–17, *nox*, *Manes*, and the *Plutonia domus* will soon press upon Sestius. Likewise, at *Odes* 1.28.15, one night forever waits as the *carmen* moves in and through underworld images, shipwrecks, and a corpse asking for burial. Even at *Odes* 3.11.50, in which the Danaid Hypermnestra tells her new husband to flee while the night and Venus are favourable, the entire poem is an underworld reflection that concludes with her request that he inscribe a *querela* on her tomb (3.11.49–52). There is a dark resonance in Horace's *dicetur merita Nox quoque nenia*. The *nenia* is *merita* precisely because the subject of song is *Nox* itself, that moment when waking life slips into darkness. This is no lullaby; this is the eternal dirge.

Let us return now to *Ceae retractes munera neniae* at 2.1.40 and its connection to *absint inani funere neniae / luctusque turpes et querimoniae* at 2.20.21–2. At the end of 2.1 Horace asks the *Musa procax* to withdraw the *Ceae ... munera neniae* and to seek out with him song modes with a lighter tone (*leuiore plectro*). This comes at the end of an ode about dark topics, culled from Pollio's civil war *Historiae*, which is framed according to epic and tragic themes (2.1.1–10), followed by a martial clamour and content about Roman civil war in Africa (21–32).[20] Pollio's *Historiae* and, more importantly, Horace's conceptualization of this work in epic and tragic terms become the *Hesperiae sonitus ruinae* (2.1.32). The *Cea nenia* represents a dirge over Roman Civil War from Metellus (60 BCE) to Thapsus (46 BCE), a war that is then mapped onto a battle between Spartans and Persians. The epic and tragic content of this history becomes threnody by the end of the ode. This civil war dirge at the beginning of Book 2 gives way to funeral laments in the book's final ode when the *biformis uates* hopes that *neniae* are absent from his empty tomb. There is a sense of apprehension and dread that the poetics of *neniae* might intrude into the lyric world of Horace's *Odes*, causing it to become fully realized elegiac threnody (coloured with the poetics of Civil War). But this evidence too results in a rereading of *querimonia* in Horace's definition of elegy in the *AP*; the poet had already linked this term in deep and significant ways to the ritual contexts of *neniae*.

Neniae and Roman Lament

While studies of Greek lament and affiliated genres have received a great deal of scholarly attention, Roman funereal song culture has been comparatively understudied.[21] *Neniae* were part of women's emotional work in the singing of songs over the corpse during funeral rituals.[22] As de la Ville de Mirmont, Heller, Habinek, and Dutsch suggest, *neniae* were part of a cluster of ritual activities that both socially and psychologically aided in the transition of the corpse and the spirit from the world of the living to the realm of the dead.[23] While scholars have pointed to two examples of *neniae* in Roman literature (Catullus 3 and Seneca's *Apocolocyntosis* 12), there is an argument (one I am making elsewhere) that behind much of Catullus' poetry, Roman love elegy, and many episodes of lamentation in Roman tragedy and epic poetry stand the poetics of *neniae*. These songs are built into the psychosocial syntax of Roman belief in the performative efficacy of funeral songs on spirits of the deceased.[24] Dorota Dutsch characterizes these songs well:[25]

The *nenia* was embedded in an elaborate sequence of rites that accompanied the ultimate transition, the one between life and death. The Romans, it can be argued, conceptualised physical death as only the initial phase of a larger transformation, as the deceased person remained a member of the clan, either one of the friendly *di manes* or one of the hostile *lemures*, demanding annual propitiation. The funeral ritual thus involved the delicate task of driving the deceased away from the living without antagonizing him or her. It was a matter to be handled with extreme care, and all members of the community, both male and female, had their particular roles to play in this ritual.

The *neniae* were sung by a hired *praefica*, a professional singer of lament, as is noted by Lucilius[26] and Varro.[27] These songs would have been accompanied by flute and string music, and they would be broken by moments of *fletus* and *planctus*, weeping and wailing (*luctus* and *querimonia* in Horace). These hired women could be called mothers and sisters of the deceased, as Servius (ad *A.* 9.484) tells us. The songs too would not have ended until the body was wholly burned and placed in the urn. To quote Dutsch's reading of Servius here:[28]

According to Servius (ad *A.* 6.216), lamentations did not end until the body was burned, the ashes were collected, and the last word, *ilicet*, "you may go," was pronounced. Only then were the people standing around and responding to the lamentations (*fletibus*) of the *praefica* free to go. Because it was executed by the mourners, the *nenia* was associated with the traditional sounds and gestures of grief.

It takes upwards of five hours or more for a body to be cremated outdoors on a funeral pyre. These songs attended the corpse until the end. Every single reference or description of mourning over the dead – like those found throughout Ovid's *Metamorphoses* or Statius' *Thebaid* – imply the singing of *neniae*. Horace, Vergil, and Ovid all would have heard them when they buried their loved ones. We, however, cannot hear them. And when an author *does* include a song of lamentation, like those found throughout Seneca's *Tragedies* or even some of the generic posturing in Roman love elegy, these ought to be read as interfacing with and orbiting the songs of the *praeficae*. Horace wants *praeficae* nowhere near his *funus*.

There are demographic implications here, as well. The *praeficae* were hired. How many were needed to satisfy the needs of the Roman community? In a city of nearly one million inhabitants, there were countless burials per day, and it is likely that *neniae* could be heard in the course of the evening and night as the dead were taken out of the city, burned on funeral pyres, and then placed in a *columbarium* or tomb (if they were lucky enough). Such performances and songs are the dark matter of Roman culture; they are ubiquitous, but we simply cannot access them. We should not assume that only wealthy burials might include *praeficae*, but that these singers could be hired at various rates, and even that some could be paid through the cult of

Libitina. We might even imagine female relatives of the deceased attempting to sing these songs themselves. During the burial of Augustus, according to Suetonius, sons and daughters of the foremost members of Roman society sang *neniae* (*canentibus neniam principum liberis utriusque sexus, Aug.* 100). Marcellus (*De compendiosa doctrina* 2.145.24) says the song of the *praeficae* was *ineptum et inconditum* ("tasteless/inappropriate and artless/disordered"), while Aulus Gellius (*AN* 18.7.7) – in a curious passage in which he compares glossaries of foreign/antiquated vocabulary and little words (*lexidia*) to the *uoces* of *praeficae* – characterizes their voices as *taetrae* ("shameful"), *inanes* ("empty"), and *friuolae* ("silly"). This is in contrast to Varro, who remarks that the voice of the *praefica* was *optima* (*de uita populi Romani* 110.1). The evidence is contradictory, but there is a good argument to be made that *praeficae* performed in non-Greek metrical forms using marked and obscured language and vocabulary, perhaps in a way that would strike the ear as exotic, which to the learned ears of Gellius and Nonius might appear sloppy, uncouth, and foreign (perhaps even "Saturnian").

Neniae are lullabies and funeral dirges; they are sung at the moment of sleep and of death. They are sung at the beginning of life and at its end.[29] They invite the soul from the "spiritual" world into the body of the baby and they lead the soul out of the corpse – or rather accompany it to enter the underworld. *Neniae* represent very old (pre-Roman) beliefs concerning the soul's transition through non-corporeal domains in birth and death, and as such the word retains elements of meaning that appear like a strange appendage, as seen in Festus' definition of it as *extremum intestinum* (161.46–7).[30] Habinek can succinctly say of *nenia*, "[S]he is the end of the intestines, the last song, a lullaby, a farewell, a conclusion."[31] But she is more than this.

While in Festus the meaning of *nenia* as *extremum intestinum* reads like a lexical curiosity, Habinek is surely correct in prioritizing the word's connection to intestines: "[U]ses of *nenia* to refer to funeral song or to an ending of whatever sort are thus consistent with what I take to be an underlying, perhaps, original association with the last bit of the entrails, the last addition to the sacrifice."[32] These songs were intestinal at their origin.[33] The question, however, remains: what is the connection between songs of funeral lament and intestines? There is a broad range of cross-cultural evidence that links intestines to the underworld. To take one example, the "intestine man," in Rykwert's words, is a mask that represents the severed head of the monster Humbaba (Huwawa) in the *Epic of Gilgamesh*.[34] The lines that form the face of the mask are clearly intestinal, and this most likely reflects necromantic, intestinal prophetics, which are connected to narratives of katabasis as a journey through a metaphysical intestinal tract.[35] Scholars have long recognized that the Gorgon head and its semiology are ultimately influenced, if not derived from, the imagery of the Humbaba head.[36] Similar Gorgonic-intestine masks are found in Cyprus, Euboea, the Greek mainland, and Orvieto, Italy (fifth- to fourth-centuries BCE Temple of Belvedere).[37] Gorgons too are closely related to threnody (*polykephalos nomos*) as well, a type of song that "imitated the *threnos* sung by the heads of the Gorgons over the killing of Medusa by Perseus and it took its name from this episode."[38] Intestines, gorgons, masks, and songs all cluster around death.[39] The *pompa funebris* too included the wearing of masks, a winding journey through the city, and spiritually charged songs that are defined in terms of the intestinal tract (*neniae*). Even Vergil's underworld, which is refracted through many traditions, is entered through *fauces* (jaws), while in Catullus 3, which has been called a *nenia*, the *malae tenebrae Orci* devour (*deuoratis*) all beautiful things (3.13–14).[40] Many more examples can be found throughout Roman literature. Souls leave the corpse and are swallowed whole, as they move through the body of death. The metaphor does not stop at the jaws, but aligns the entire underworld along a digestive tract. Even the underworld river Phlegethon recalls an intestinal disease often discussed by medical writers, *phlegmon* (see Philumenus *De medicina* 1.105), while another river, the Cocytus, redirects us to lamentation and wailing. An inversion of the intestines' infernal connections is found in Suetonius' *Divus Augustus* (94.4), where *Atia, prius quam pareret, somniauit intestina sua ferri ad sidera explicarique per omnem terrarum et caeli ambitum* ("Atia, before she gave birth, dreamed that her intestines were brought up to the stars and were spread out through all the lands and the circuit of the sky"). The stretching and unfolding of her intestines around the earth and heaven resituates katabasis as an apotheosis.

That the meaning of *nenia* is localized at the *extremum intestinum* highlights the precise power of these songs; they are impactful at the end, the end of life, and at the end of the journey through the underworld (the Orphic golden leaves should be on our minds). *Neniae* are built into the cultural and religious syntax of Roman spirituality. It is for this reason, perhaps, that Horace demands that *neniae* be absent from his *inane funus*. These songs have the potential of pulling the *biformis uates* down from the *liquidus aether*. In this sense, lyric and *nenia* move along a vertical axis, ascent and descent, the *aether* and *tartarus*, wings and jaws. Surely, this idea stands behind Augustine's criticism of the Roman god Janus in the *City of God* (7.8):

Sed iam bifrontis simulacri interpretatio proferatur. Duas eum facies ante et retro habere dicunt, quod hiatus noster, cum os aperimus, mundo similis uideatur; unde et palatum Graeci οὐρανόν appellant, et nonnulli, inquit, poetae Latini caelum uocauerunt palatum, a quo hiatu oris et foras esse aditum ad dentes uersus et introrsus ad fauces. ecce quo perductus est mundus propter palati nostri uocabulum uel Graecum uel poeticum. quid autem hoc ad animam, quid ad uitam aeternam?

But now let the explanation of the two-faced image be produced. They say that he has two faces, one in front and one behind, because the space within our mouth, when it is open, seems similar to the universe. Hence the Greeks call the palate *ouranos*, or sky, and some Latin poets, Varro says, have called the sky *palatum*, or palate. From this hollow space in the mouth there are two passages, one outward toward the teeth, the other inward toward the throat. Now see what they have made of the world because of a word for our palate, whether it be Greek or poetical! But what does this have to do with the soul, or with eternal life?

From a Roman point of view, this has everything to do with notions of spiritual transition. It must be remembered that *neniae* would have been sung not only while the corpse was being transported out of the community as it was taken to a funeral pyre, but also, as noted earlier, while the corpse burned for hours on end. These songs perform the spiritual work of burial while the flame performs the physical work, and they continue to be sung until the flesh has been entirely consumed and the bones and ash placed in an urn. *Neniae* are built into the cultural and religious syntax of Roman elegy, as Horace's evidence suggests.

What does this analysis of *nenia* suggest about Horace's linking of elegy and *querimonia*? *Querimonia* in the *AP* then is something of an embedded genre; its elegiac contours include and contain *neniae*. I would like to end my analysis by situating this discussion of *querimonia* and *nenia* in epic, in order to think through the following questions: what is at stake in debates over genre, or generic mixing, crossing, miscegenation, or ambiguity? What does the mixing of generic principles and tones in texts mean in and of itself, and how do we assess them? What follows is something of a short case study that attempts to pose an answer to these questions.

Nenian Elegy and the *Aeneid*

Aeneid 9 is aware of its own epic-ness, its own *arma uirumque*-nicity. It is the first book in which something like Iliadic war occurs, but only after two youths have slaughtered drunken, sleeping soldiers and are themselves killed. In truth, martial epic in the *Aeneid* begins on the tip of a spear-point, in that vast maw between the forgotten bodies of Nisus and Euryalus and their spear-transfixed heads, in a passage where the iconicity of decapitation – seen in the hyperbaton – is accompanied by one of the half-lines in the *Aeneid* (9.465–7):[41] *quin ipsa arrectis (uisu miserabile) in hastis / praefigunt capita et multo clamore sequuntur / Euryali et Nisi* ("On uplifted spears (piteous sight!) they affix and follow with loud clamour the heads, the very heads, of Euryalus and Nisus." The great clamour of the Rutulians as they follow the heads of Nisus and Euryalus is an acoustic anticipation of another *clamor*, the blast of the war trumpet and the bellowing of the sky nearly forty lines later at 9.503–4 (*at tuba terribilem sonitum procul aere canoro / increpuit, sequitur clamor caelumque remugit*, "But the trumpet with brazen song rang out afar its fearful call; a shout follows and the sky re-echoes"), in a passage whose closest parallel occurs at 8.524–6, where Venus sends Aeneas a portent of war and of his divinely wrought *arma*: *namque improuiso uibratus ab aethere fulgor / cum sonitu uenit et ruere omnia uisa repente, / Tyrrhenusque tubae mugire per aethera clangor* ("For unexpectedly, launched from heaven, comes a flash with thunder, and everything seemed suddenly to reel, while the Tyrrhenian trumpet blast pealed through the sky"). *Remugit* in 9.504 is also linked to two other significant acoustic moments in the *Aeneid*: the bellowing of the Sibyl at *A.* 6.98–101 after she has finished telling Aeneas that a second *Iliad* awaits him in Italy; and the echo of groans of men rebounding off a mountain at the moment Aeneas' spear transfixes Turnus' *femur* at *A.* 12.926–9. In addition, the blast of the *tuba* at 9.503 (*at tuba terribilem sonitum procul aere canoro*) is an Ennian half-line (*at tuba terribili sonitu taratantara dixit, Ann.* 451). Vergil even replies to Ennius' epic battle cry – t-t-t-t-t-t-t – with c-c-t-qu-t-c-c-qu-t (*canoro / increpuit, sequitur clamor caelumque remugit*). Severed heads on spears, the epic bellowing of the *caelum*, and the terrible sound of an Ennian war trumpet break into the narrative, followed by "traditional" martial epic in an almost total retelling of the *Iliad*.[42] The momentum of this episode carries over through the final three books until Aeneas kills Turnus in the last lines of the epic after seeing the *arma* of Pallas.

There is a tension in *Aeneid* 9 – a near-pathological anxiety – over the commencement of epic (a tension we feel through all of Vergil's work), and there is an argument that this anxiety carries over into the final death of the *Aeneid* and our interpretation of it. There is a resistance to the genre that is more than a literary or generic game of a *poeta doctus*. The Nisus and Euryalus episode is a powerful transition here; the two heroes move through *Aeneid* 2 and the slaughter of the drunken, sleeping city (*inuadunt urbem somno uinoque sepultam*, 2.264); they replay the footrace of *Aeneid* 5; they are lost in the *errores* of labyrinthine woods that share a semiology with *Aeneid* 6; and their deaths are capped by an encomium that moves into an epitaphic tradition. They at once rework prior elements of the narrative, while Vergil offers a formal closure to the episode, but a false closure, nonetheless. It is as if the slaughtered Italians and the deaths of Nisus and Euryalus are a formal literary sacrifice to begin Vergil's *martial* epic.[43]

Almost immediately after Vergil addresses Nisus and Euryalus as *fortunati*, their severed heads are brought into focus and *Fama* reaches Euryalus' mother, who fills the *caelum* with *questus* (laments), a word etymologically connected to *querimonia* and *querela*.[44] In between the epic *clamor* of the Rutulians as they follow the heads of the young men and the *clamor* of the Rutulian *tuba* stands a marked generic shift, as epic is broken by a mother's lament (9.480–502):

> … caelum dehinc questibus implet:
> "hunc ego te, Euryale, aspicio? tune ille senectae
> sera meae requies, potuisti linquere solam,
> crudelis? nec te sub tanta pericula missum
> adfari extremum miserae data copia matri?
> *heu terra ignota canibus data praeda Latinis*
> *alitibusque iaces! nec te tua funere mater*
> *produxi pressiue oculos aut uulnera laui,*
> *ueste tegens tibi quam noctes festina diesque*
> *urgebam, et tela curas solabar anilis.*
> *quo sequar? aut quae nunc artus auulsaque membra*
> *et funus lacerum tellus habet?* hoc mihi de te,
> nate, refers? hoc sum terraque marique secuta?
> figite me, si qua est pietas, in me omnia tela
> conicite, o Rutuli, me primam absumite ferro;
> aut tu, magne pater diuum, miserere, tuoque
> inuisum hoc detrude caput sub Tartara telo,
> quando aliter nequeo crudelem abrumpere uitam."
> hoc fletu concussi animi, maestusque per omnis
> it gemitus, torpent infractae ad proelia uires.
> … corripiunt interque manus sub tecta reponunt.

Then she fills the sky with her plaints: "Is this you, Euryalus, that I see? You who were the last solace of my age, could you bring yourself to leave me alone, cruel one? And when you were sent on so perilous an errand, did you not give your poor mother a chance to bid you a last farewell? *Alas! You lie in a strange land, given as prey to the dogs and fowls of Latium! Nor did I, your mother, escort you to the grave, or close your eyes, or bathe your wounds, shrouding you with the robe which, in haste, night and day, I toiled at for your sake, beguiling with the loom the sorrows of age.*

Where am I to follow? What land now holds your mangled limbs and dismembered body? Is this all, my son, you bring back to me of yourself? Is it this I have followed by land and sea? Pierce me, if you have any feeling, on me hurl all your weapons, Rutulians; destroy me first with your steel; or you, great Father of the gods, be pitiful, and with your bolt hurl down to hell this hateful life, since in no other way can I break life's cruel bonds!" At that wailing their spirits were shaken, and a groan of sorrow passed through all; their strength for battle is numbed and crushed ... [they] catch her up and carry her indoors in their arms.

At the very moment Vergil emphatically begins the martial side of epic he introduces the raw, elegiac discharge of a mother's reaction to the severed head of her young, beautiful son.[45] Part of her lament intersects with laments for other notable dead men in the *Aeneid*, such as Priam and Palinurus (2.557–8; 5.870–1), one of whom lies headless, a body without a name, and the other of whom will lie a *nudus* in an *ignota harena*, unburied. The verb *iacere* is used of all three. Euryalus' mother too gestures to the opening of the *Iliad* (αὐτοὺς δὲ ἑλώρια τεῦχε κύνεσσιν / οἰωνοῖσί τε πᾶσι, 1.2–3) as Euryalus becomes the plunder of *Latin* dogs and birds (a line Statius recalls at *Thebaid* 10.352–3: *teneant quem iam fortasse uolucres / Thebanique canes*; "whom already perhaps birds and Theban dogs hold"). He will not enter the underworld through the *fauces* of Orcus, but through the jaws of animals. This heightens the impact of her lament, that she will be unable to perform the bundle of funerary rituals that allow her to ritualize the corpse for its transition. She does not even know where she might follow him, a reference to her place in the funerary procession directly behind the body as the movement of lamenters twist and turn out of the city for burial,[46] *neniae* at all times being sung. Her lament breaks the *animi* and *uires* of the Trojan men and they take her away.[47] This is precisely the sort of song Horace demands be absent from his *inane funus*.

However, Euryalus' mother's song breaks into the epic soundscape of *Aeneid* 9 and performs a broken elegy. In form her lament is structured by the hexameter. The content of her song emphasizes that it is severed from the psychosocial force that accompanied ritual burial. Epic results in the generic fracturing of elegy. Songs without bodies are empty threnody without any possibility of achieving final closure of the lament.[48] Elegiac *querimonia* (*nenia*) fails to merge with the requisite ritual contextualization because of the desecration of bodies, set emphatically in Iliadic terms. A severed head, the absence of burial, and the jaws of animals; within the matrices of spirituality in the poem, a Roman audience is left to wonder precisely what comes of Nisus and Euryalus in the underworld without heads and *neniae*; one requires the other. Standing behind the Greek term elegy is a cluster of Roman concepts such as *querimonia, querela,* and *neniae*. But these terms operate along Roman social and cultural vectors that complicate one's ability to define and understand the notion of elegy. Euryalus' mother epitomizes the deep cultural embeddedness of genre. For her, this instance of generic mixing (epic and a broken threnody) highlights a profound crisis that operates even at the level of the metaphysical.

NOTES

1 All translations are based on the Loeb Classical Library with minor modifications unless otherwise indicated.
2 See Rudd 1989 ad loc., and in particular see Page 1936: 209–10 on ἒ ἒ λέγειν in the scholiastic tradition of Horace and elegy; also Harvey 1955: 168–72. The fifteenth-century humanist scholar Aulo Giano Parrasio, who anticipates some of the discussion in this chapter, states: *hoc sane constat, defunctorum laudes hoc carmine celebrari solitas, unde sibi nomen elegia sumpsit. hinc et miserabilies uersus dicti ab Horatio ad Tibullum. crediderim ego, praeficas, quae conductae plorabant in funere, hoc carmine usas, lugubrem naeniam cecinisse* ("clearly it is established that the praises of the dead are accustomed to be celebrated by this song, from which elegy has taken up its name. And from this, verses have been called mournful from Horace to Tibullus. I tend to believe that *praeficae,* who lament in a funeral for payment, using this song, sang a mournful *naenia*"). Pseudo-Acro states: *Elegiacum significat … res tristes et lugubres primo elegiaco carmine scribebantur* ("This signifies an elegiac song … sad and mournful events were written first according to an elegiac song").
3 A discussion of elegiac *uotum* and *exigui elegi* is omitted here. See Faraone 2008; Swift 2010: 314–17; and Nobili 2011 (and bibliography therein) for a discussion of threnody, elegy, and epigram in Greece. On elegy and epigram in Rome, see Keith 2011a. On elegy more broadly, see Kennedy 2007.
4 Clark 1983: 3.
5 See Keil 1880: 517–19 on Giano Parrasio's attribution of *De differentiis* to Fronto. As to dating of *De differentiis,* Keil 1880, 518 states: *ceterum qua aetate libellus scriptus esset, quem omme antiquiorem esse puto, quam plurimos qui nunc supersunt commentarios de differentiis, certius definiri posset, siquid de Antonino grammatico p. 525.22 appellato compertum haberemus* ("Meanwhile during which period the book was written, which I think is a bit older than most of the commentaries on *De differentiis,* which survive to the present day, something more certain might be able to be determined if we knew something about the *grammaticus* Antoninus named on page 525.22").

6 For just a few of the many examples, see Cic. *Verr.* 2.1.50 (*querimonias, quae ad legatos populi Romani pertinerent*), 2.1.129 (*querimoniaque populi Romani*), 2.2.15 (*sociorum querimonias*); Livy *AUC* 7.9.2, 21.6.5 (*sociorum populi Romani querimonias deferrent*), 25.1.9 (*publicam querimoniam*, 39.46.7 (*crimina querimoniasque de Philippo*).

7 See Cic. *Verr.* 2.1.94 (*uocem cum dolore et querimonia emittere*), 2.3.52 (*totius Siciliae cotidie gemitus querimoniasque audires*), 2.3.207 (*luctum, lacrimas, querimonias*).

8 See, for example, Propertius 1.6.11, 1.16.13, 1.18.29 for the assimilation of his poetry to *querela*. On *querela* and mourning sounds, see Propertius 2.20.5, 3.7.55, 4.11.57, for example. The topic of *querela* requires a deeper study than I can give it here. On *querela* in Propertius as a "technical name for his elegy," see Saylor 1967.

9 See, for example, Cic. *Flacc.* 52.4, 70.3; *Sest.* 64.2, 74.10; *Marc.* 21.1, to name only a few.

10 The key demarcation between *querimonia/querela* as "official complaint through political channels" and "lament or plaintive tone" is really a distinction between public (communal) versus private (individual) expressions of grief.

11 On the usage of *querimonia* and its connection to love elegy, in particular, see Sellar 1899: 201–11; Otis 1945; Brink 1971: 165–7; Clark 1983; Freis 1993; James 2003a; Johnson 2012b (with bibliography therein). On love elegy and the conventions of funerary inscriptions, see McCallum 2015: 698n28.

12 Johnson 2012a: 195–6. Cf. the similar language describing love until death at Tib. 1.1.59 (*suprema … hora*).

13 On 2.20 see Schwinge 1965; Tatum 1973.

14 Spelman 2014: 27. See also Nisbet and Hubbard 1978: 30. *Querimonia* is used one other time at *Carm.* 3.24.33–4, where Horace refers to the uselessness of *tristes querimoniae* if crime is not pruned by punishment (*si non supplicio culpa reciditur*), in a stanza that criticizes the failure of law. This is the typical usage of the word we see in the majority of Latin texts (see above).

15 It is certainly possible that Horace is making a reference to 1.13.19, gesturing to the amorous *querimonia* there.

16 Keil 1857: 485.

17 For a succinct assessment of this *nenia Cea*, see Henderson 1996: 115–19.

18 Nisbet and Rudd 2004: 344.

19 Bradshaw 2002: 8. See also Habinek 2005: 236. Following Habinek, it is possible that *nenia* could be the sound of orgasm.

20 While the poem overtly addresses Pollio's civil war history, the language reads like standard epic poetics in the form of a *recusatio*.

21 On Greek lament, see Alexiou 1974; Holst-Warhaft 1992; Martin 2008; Swift 2010: 298–366 (with much not included here). For Roman lament,

see Treggiari 1993: 483–98; Corbeill 2004: 67–107; Keith 2008a and 2016; Richlin 2014. See also Suter 2008 and Bachvarova et al. 2016.

22 On the emotional work of mourning women in Roman society, see Richlin 2014.

23 de la Ville de Mirmont 1903: 361–406; Heller 1943; Habinek 2005: 233–56; Dutsch 2008. Much of what follows below is an addendum to Habinek's excellent discussion. Henri de la Ville de Mirmont is still the best entry point into *nenia*.

24 Gladhill 2018.

25 Dutsch 2008: 259.

26 *mercede quae conductae flent alieno in funere praeficae, multo et capillos scindunt et clamant magis* ("the *praeficae*, collected for a fee, weep at another's funeral, and they tear at their hair greatly and they cry out more," Lucil. Fr. 950).

27 <praefica> *dicta, ut Aurelius scribit, mulier ab luco quae conduceretur, quae ante domum mortui laudis eius caneret. Claudius scribit: "quae praeficeretur ancillis, quemadmodum lamentarentur, praefica est dicta … utrumque ostendit a praefectione praeficam dictam"* ("*Praefica* is defined, so Aurelius writes, as a woman who is collected from the sacred grove (Libitina?) and sings before the house of the dead man his praises. Claudius writes: 'she who is placed in charge of the maidservants, as they are lamenting, is called the *praefica*. Each shows that *praefica* is derived from overseeing/directing,'" Varro, *LL* 7.3.69).

28 Dutsch 2008: 262.

29 Habinek 2005: 244 suggests a connection between the poetics of beginnings (*Carmentis* and *Ianus*) and endings (*Nenia*). Endings and beginnings merge at moments of transition, as endings become new beginnings, which themselves eventually become endings.

30 On the old folk traditions of the *neniae*, see Heller 1943. On the connection between lullabies and the songs of *praeficae*, see Dutsch 2008: 263. See also Corbeill 2004: 67–106, on parallel rituals for birth and death. Heller 1939 expressed uncertainty on the precise connection of *nenia* to intestines.

31 Habinek, 2005: 244.

32 Habinek 2005: 236.

33 Ovid, *Fasti* 6.135–46, offers important evidence on the connection between *neniae* and intestines.

34 Rykwert 1976: 53–8. He connects intestinal prophetics to Etruscan and Roman haruspicy. For a historical reading of Humbaba, intestines, and prophecy, see Hansman 1976. On the frequency of diseased intestines in apparently healthy animals, see Temple 1982. Cross-cultural comparison with Aztec beliefs about intestines shows a similar cluster of ideas in prophecy, punishment, and the underworld (see Klein 1991). For an image of the mask, see: https://www.britishmuseum.org/collection/object/W_1883-0118-AH-2598.

35 Annus 2008; de Villiers 2010.

36 See Hopkins 1934; Croon 1955; Ogden 2013: 92–8.

37 The masks found at the sanctuary on Cyprus and at Ortheia are nearly replicas of the Assyrian Humbaba masks. See Carter 1987 and 1988; Averett 2015. For the "male" Etruscan gorgonic mask found in Orvieto, see Howe 1954: 215.

38 Nobili 2011: 29. Horace may have had this in mind at *Carm.* 2.13.33–6: *quid mirum, ubi illis carminibus stupens / demittit atras belua centiceps / auris, et intorti capillis / Eumenidum recreantur angues.* Lucan too at *BC* 9.620–35 clearly aligns Medusa with underworld poetics.

39 See Wilk 2000.

40 See also Lucretius *DRN* 3.1012; Vergil *G.* 4.467, *A.* 6.201, 6.241, 6.273, 7.570; Propertius 3.5.43; Ovid *Met.* 7.203, 8.819–20 (underworld language in which *Fames* moves through Erysichthon's *fauces* and body); Seneca *HF* 666, *Phoen.* 70, *Phaedra* 1201, *Thy* 782 (Atreus refers to Thyestes' *fauces* at the moment he is swallowing his children's flesh), *HO* 1772; Lucan *BC* 6.648; Martial 1.78.1; Sil. *Pun.* 5.618, 6.174. This underworld imagery extends through the medieval Hell's Mouth up through to the modern period whether we gesture to the whale Moby Dick, *Jaws*, or *Alien*.

41 The underworld resonances throughout the Nisus and Euryalus episode (see Putnam 1965: 48–63) end with a severed head of a boy who notably shares his name with a Gorgon (Fulg. Myth. 1.26, Myth. Vat. 1.130, 2.112f.l; see Zetzel 2005: 195). He shares the same fate as Medusa. The underlying implication is that a severed head is implicitly gorgonic.

42 See the introduction in Hardie 1994.

43 One would be hard pressed to argue that either *Aeneid* 7 or 8 is the true beginning of the *martial* epic that carries us through Books 9–12. I say this in spite of the invocation to Erato (*A.* 7.37–45), on which see also McCallum in this volume. Note that Vergil sets out his poetic agenda as *qui reges ... quae tempora, rerum / quis ... status* (7.37–8), which reflect the content of *A.* 7–8. He then states *dicam horrida bella, / dicam acies actosque animis in funera reges* (41–2). *Horrida bella* begin with the deaths of Nisus and Euryalus.

44 As the *OLD* s.vv. notes, all three words derive from *queror*.

45 See Sharrock 2011.

46 Treggiari 1991: 489.

47 On the significance of Euryalus' mother's lament for the Trojans, see Nugent 1992: 272–4.

48 This is precisely the implication of Euripides' *Alcestis*, that the entire social order will be subsumed in never-ending threnody.

PART TWO

Vergil in Ovidian Elegy

8

Pasiphaë in Vergil's *Bucolics* and Ovid's *Ars Amatoria*: A Bovine Lover's Discourse

MARIAPIA PIETROPAOLO

In the inherited mythological account, Pasiphaë was cursed to crave copulation with a bull, who impregnated her, siring the Minotaur. In his retelling of the myth in *B.* 6, Vergil concentrates compassionately on Pasiphaë's desperate longing and on Silenus, as reported by Tityrus,[1] consoling her for having been driven to such madness. In telling the story of how Pasiphaë was consumed with an unnatural desire for the bull, Silenus calls her passion a foul love, but sympathizes with her, suggesting a comparison with Calvus' *Io* (see discussion below) and hence prompting the reader to look for explanatory intertextualities. Ovid relates Pasiphaë's story in greater detail in the *Ars Amatoria,* a didactic poem on love and seduction, where he presents it, through his *praeceptor,* as a negative example of women's lust, which he articulates with biting humour and intertextual references to works in various genres. In particular, Ovid shows derisively how Pasiphaë makes use of the language and mannerisms of elegiac and bucolic poetry, including those in Vergil's account of her mad love, to interpret her passion for the bull in her pursuit of a mating strategy. Where Vergil focuses on her psychological situation, Ovid shows her drama unfolding in its fullness, including Pasiphaë's agency in the articulation of her pursuit. Ovid "mediates," as Rebecca Armstrong observes,[2] his account of Pasiphaë through Vergil. My purpose in this paper is to show that in his mediation Ovid makes strategic use of an ironic creative process, intent on foregrounding with mock seriousness the grotesque aspects of Pasiphaë's lust that undermine the expectations that readers of erotic elegy may bring to the elegiac form of the *Ars Amatoria.*

Ovid's account of Pasiphaë in the *Ars Amatoria* begins with her name, strategically given as the opening word of the first line of her story (*Ars* 1.295): *Pasiphaë fieri gaudebat adultera tauri* ("Pasiphaë was rejoicing to become a bull's adulteress").[3] As a verb of physical enjoyment, including sexual pleasure,[4] *gaudebat* indicates that, even before having sex with the bull, Pasiphaë fantasizes about it, enjoying her very desire of it. She devises ways of achieving her goal. She dresses in her best robes, follows the herd up the mountains, fixes her hair, checks her appearance in a mirror, orders the slaughtering of cows that could offer her competition for the bull's attention, and finally tricks the bull into mating with her by slipping into a wooden cow costume. Ovid expects his readers to be familiar with the details of the story that he is about to tell. *Nota cano* he observes immediately after introducing Pasiphaë (*Ars* 1.297), indirectly asking his readers to call to mind the events of the story even before he begins his account.

Ovid thus situates his narrative in his readers' literary memory, grounding the significance and aesthetic appeal of its details in the reader's consciousness of the larger background of the story. This compositional strategy presupposes that reading is expected to be a consciously creative act in which the reception of scripted words takes place in concomitance with the recollection of details from literary memory. For the *nota* mentioned by Ovid must be presumed to be present in the readers' consciousness from the beginning of the process, informing their apprehension of the scripted text as it unfolds before their eyes. If we consider the "aesthetic text" of the poem as the combination of the scripted words and the literary memory brought to presence in the reading experience, we can say that Ovid's aesthetic text of Pasiphaë is largely unwritten. Much of it must be contributed by the reader and integrated with the scripted words, not in the general sense in which all literary texts ask the reader to approach them with an active imagination, but in the special sense of a text that is purposely written in an incomplete form. This mode of composition imposes on the reader the responsibility of filling in the missing details, without which the work would lack fullness as a work of art. Such texts belong to the general category of aesthetic products called "open works" by Umberto Eco, a term that includes products in all the fine arts.[5] Many open works do not use language as their medium and can be read as texts only by a metaphorical operation. In the aesthetic appreciation and interpretation of literary open works, on the other hand, hermeneutics have no need for metaphor, since such terms as text, reading, misreading, literary memory, and poetic echoes can be taken in their normal literal sense. Considered from the perspective of the intended aesthetic experience, open texts are ontologically complex, consisting as they do of scripted words interwoven with unscripted echoes and literary memories, which at times are intentional distortions of their sources. The unscripted segments represent the mental images and narrative details that the readers contribute from their knowledge of the literary background that they bring to the text.

Among the *nota* in the readers' background knowledge, Vergil's treatment of Pasiphaë holds pride of place. The expectations raised by the narrative of *B.* 6 and the complex intertextualities that it incorporates constitute a recent and memorable chapter of Pasiphaë's literary memory. Through them Vergil tells a story in which the unhappy queen is worthy of commiserative language (whether that commiseration is genuine or not) designed to raise a feeling of ambivalent sympathy in the aesthetic experience of the reader, possibly oscillating between tenderness and irony. Much of that feeling derives from Vergil's use of Calvus' apostrophe to Io (Calvus fr. 20, Hollis):[6] *a uirgo infelix, herbis pasceris amaris* ("ah, unhappy girl, you will graze on bitter grasses"). Vergil famously quotes the apostrophe twice, but only the first half of the verse, *a uirgo infelix*, addressing it on both occasions to Pasiphaë, who is no *uirgo* (*B.* 6.47, 52),[7] and both times with the "neoteric *a*," suggestive of the rhetoric of emotional participation.[8] Io was unhappy because she had been undeservedly turned into a cow by Jupiter, so that Juno might not find him *in flagrante* with a nymph. The text here is profoundly ironic, since Vergil cites Io's story to console Pasiphaë, who is unhappy because she is not a cow and therefore cannot have sex with the bull.

Vergil completes the first quotation with the words *quae te dementia cepit!* ("what madness has seized you," *B.* 6.47) to underscore the reason for Pasiphaë's depravity and to justify the empathy expressed by Silenus. Textually, the vocative of emotional sympathy derives from the self-commiseration of Vergil's own Corydon, who laments his unrequited love for Alexis in *B.* 2.69 (*a, Corydon, Corydon, quae te dementia cepit!*).[9] But its meaning and its aesthetic quality resonate with echoes of Pasiphaë's passionate self-exculpation in Euripides' *Cretans*, high among the *nota* that the reader brings to the text, for Vergil no less than Ovid presupposes a reader with a vivid literary memory. In the *Cretans*, Pasiphaë says that she suffers, though her trouble is not of her doing (Eur. *Cretans* fr. 5.10): ἀλγῶ μέν, ἔστι δ' οὐχ ἐκο[ύσ]ιον κακόν ("I suffer, but my wickedness is not of my own volition").[10] She argues her innocence and blames Minos for the madness inflicted on her by Poseidon, which caused her to crave sex with a bull. In the process she raises difficult questions concerning innocence and culpability in the case of nefarious acts that result from a passion when that passion is a form of madness over which the person has no control.[11] Pasiphaë recognizes the gravity of her action but claims that she was forced into it by a god (Eur. *Cretans* fr. 5.9): ἐκ θεοῦ γὰρ προσβολῆς ἐμηνάμην ("I was driven to madness by the attack of a god"). Being the victim of a curse, Pasiphaë had lost her ability to restrain her behaviour. The conclusion to which her defence leads is that the logic of the readers' moral stance is faulty if they do not see her as an innocent victim worthy of compassion. The background presence of Euripides' tragedy lends *grauitas* and credence to Vergil's rhetoric of sympathy.

Vergil completes his second apostrophe to Pasiphaë with the words *tu nunc in montibus erras* ("now you wander in the mountains," *B.* 6.52), which cast Pasiphaë as a type of Gallus,[12] himself depicted as wandering by the streams of Permessus a few lines later, *errantem Permessi ad flumina* (*B.* 6.64). This description of Gallus echoes Vergil's own *mille meae Siculis errant in montibus agnae* ("a thousand of my lambs wander in the Sicilian mountains," *B.* 2.21), which itself includes echoes from Theocritus.[13] By this complex layering of intra- and intertextuality, Vergil pays tribute to his predecessors and prompts the reader to associate Pasiphaë with poets, as Margaret Hubbard and Rebecca Armstrong have argued.[14] More specifically, however, we could say that in *B.* 6 Pasiphaë's lust has potentially elegiac aspects that motivate the reader to associate her with poets only in so far as they are disconsolate lovers, like the Gallus of *B.* 10, that is to say *characters of elegy*, for this Gallus is not Cornelius Gallus the historical author but a fictional character who personifies for Vergil the spirit of his poetry. The same thing may be said of all the lovers of elegy, who are fictional personae for their authors. It is into their elegiac scenarios that Pasiphaë would like to fit her own narrative in order to make her desire appear less abominable. Her elegiac side remains visible even in the *Aeneid*, on the doors to the temple of Apollo, where Aeneas sees a depiction of her *crudelis amor* (*A.* 6.24), an expression of Gallan association and eminently elegiac.[15] Even after her death, moreover, Pasiphaë remained for Vergil a compassion-eliciting character, ending up as she does in the Fields of Mourning among those whom harsh love consumes with cruel languishing (*quos durus amor crudeli tabe peredit*, *A.* 6.442).

In montibus erras carries other layers of meaning, which bring the reader back to Pasiphaë's bucolic surroundings and to her culpability. For *errare* is both an elegiac and a pastoral term, equally applicable to humans and animals. In the elegiac world, it refers to the wandering of unrequited lovers and to the *malus error* of disastrous love,[16] whereas in the bucolic landscape, it may refer to the wandering of animals. As she wanders up the mountain like a disconsolate lover, the Vergilian Pasiphaë is imitating the cows moving in the meadow and getting closer to the bull grazing somewhere ahead of her. With reference to animals, *errare* often carries the implication of *pascere*,[17] in relation to which it denotes the apparently aimless search for areas of richer pasture. This double sense of the term suits Pasiphaë well, since it affords her the possibility of an analogy between her lust for the bull and the passion of an elegiac lover, superimposing the pastoral semantic field onto the elegiac one, while she constructs her narrative by wandering between genres. Wandering is an essential component of pastoral poetry, both thematically and metapoetically, since as animals and shepherds wander in the countryside, "the shepherd-poet wanders in subjects and topics."[18] Here, ironically, with her actions Pasiphaë also illustrates the meaning that *errare* has in logic, for in her analogy she falls prey to the *error* of interpreting her abominable lust in terms of the passion that moves elegiac lovers.

In contrast, the Ovidian Pasiphaë does not wander on the mountain. She goes with the cows as a companion, seeking out the mountain herds and venturing into the groves, like a Bacchant into the wilderness, beyond the boundaries of civilized norms (*Ars* 1.301–2, 311–12):

> it comes armentis, nec ituram cura moratur
>   coniugis, et Minos a boue uictus erat.
>
> …
>
> in nemus et saltus thalamo regina relicto
>   fertur, ut Aonio concita Baccha deo.

She goes as a companion of the herds, nor does concern for her husband delay her going, and Minos was surpassed by a bull … Having left behind her bedchamber, the queen is carried off into grove and glade, like a Bacchant incited by the Aonian god.

Nor does she do this without a plan, however myopic it may be not to think at all about the consequences of copulation with a bull.[19] Pasiphaë will not be an unrequited lover forever. Ovid does not use the term *errare* of her, and the *nota* induce the reader to bring into the picture the fact that she has a clever plan and the expertise of Daedalus to help her along. Rather than the *errare* resulting from unremitting love, the text emphasizes the place and life that she leaves behind in pursuit of the bull, namely her *uir* and his bedchamber. Nor is her going delayed by any *cura* – another conspicuously elegiac term – for her husband. She is impelled, rather, by her *cura* for the bull.

Ovid develops only a few aspects of the elegiac potential of *B.* 6 and omits the Calvan apostrophe altogether, thereby dismissing any possibility of compassion for Pasiphaë. For Ovid, Pasiphaë is not a passive victim of the passion to which she has been condemned. In his own *a, quotiens uaccam uultu spectauit iniquo* ("Ah, how often did she, with an unkind expression, look at a cow," *Ars* 1.313), he describes Pasiphaë with mock sympathy for her indignant jealousy, deriding her through his burlesque rendering of the expected emotional participation suggested by the neoteric *a*. Ovid directs the reader's empathy towards the real cows, all of which may be savagely slaughtered at Pasiphaë's request (*Ars* 1.318–20). The effect of this manipulation of the narrative is to bring the cows closer to the centre of the picture. This is tantamount to saying that Ovid temporarily shifts the hermeneutical and aesthetic focus from the human to the bovine world, changing the narrative tone from consolatory to derisive.

This attitude on Ovid's part is consistent with his own earlier apostrophe to Pasiphaë (*Ars* 1.303–4): *quo tibi, Pasiphaë pretiosas sumere uestes / ille tuus nullas sentit adulter opes* ("What good does it do you, Pasiphaë, to put on expensive clothes? That adulterer of yours does not notice any riches"). Here the poet addresses her without the participative *a* and for reasons that have nothing to do with commiseration. Her intended lover, the poet claims, does not care for enhanced female beauty quite simply because he is a beast. Yet Ovid calls the bull her *adulter*, using this decidedly elegiac word to suggest the idea of a love triangle comparable to that of the elegiac scenario.[20] The similarity is only a formal one, of course, since what Pasiphaë has in mind is not urbane elegiac love but bestiality. Ovid had already called her *adultera tauri* (at her introduction, *Ars* 1.295), combining an animal word with an elegiac one. Juxtaposed with the image of a bull, an animal without any sense of the human sentiments that inform the world of elegy, the image of *adultera* loses its elegiac patina and becomes shockingly grotesque.[21] The combination, in other words, brings to the fore Pasiphaë's attempt to make her bovine lust appear to fit the elegiac scenario while frustrating it at the same time.

In his presentation of Pasiphaë, Ovid uses language with clear elegiac overtones, but with mocking contempt and quick forays into nefarious eroticism. So, for example, women's *tam furiosa libido* (*Ars* 1.281) is, in its less frenzied mode, essentially elegiac because *furor* is a fundamental concept of the genre.[22] But in being envious of real cows in the herd (*inuida, Ars* 1.296), Pasiphaë is comically exhibiting an elegiac trait. To be sure, jealousy is a fundamental emotion of elegy, but here it is also ludicrous, because it shows no regard for the incongruity between human and bovine. Driven by animal instincts, she has transgressed the law of nature and, although she has not experienced any biological change, has undergone an intellectual metamorphosis, as Eleanor Leach observes.[23] She is unconcerned with human-bovine incongruity. That incongruity reaches a grotesque level when Ovid replaces Vergil's *aliquam [uaccam]* ("another [cow]," *B.* 6.55, also used in the plural by the Vergilian Pasiphaë herself at *B.* 6.60) with *paelices*, a term that explicitly casts the unfortunate cows as her rivals in love, as if she were the pursuing poet-lover of an elegy (*Ars* 1.320–1): *et tenuit laeta paelicis exta manu. / paelicibus quotiens placauit numina caesis* ("And she held her rival's entrails in her rejoicing hand. How often did she placate the gods with slain rivals"). These are not just other cows: for the Ovidian Pasiphaë they are *rival* cows.[24] But, inventing occasions for their sacrifice, she has them slaughtered, with a savagery reminiscent of the violent imagination of an elegiac witch.[25] Yet even this imagistic recollection reveals that Pasiphaë is not as perfect an elegiac fit as the language would appear to suggest, for in elegy the rival cannot be eliminated from the erotic scenario, and he often wins.

In addition to elegiac language, Ovid gives Pasiphaë the mannerisms of a lovelorn elegiac character, oscillating between the role of the *puella* and that of the *lover*. We see her trying to behave like a *puella*, when she repeatedly fixes her hair to make herself alluring and when she inspects herself in a mirror,[26] in which she hopes to see that she is growing horns (*Ars* 1.307–8): *crede tamen speculo, quod te negat esse iuuencam: / quam cuperes fronti cornua nata tuae!* ("Believe your mirror, which says you are not a heifer. How you would desire horns sprung from your forehead!"). Ovid here recasts Pasiphaë as an ironic inversion of Vergil's Proetides, who, having been driven mad into thinking they were cows, frequently felt their foreheads to see if they had sprouted horns; *et saepe in leui quaesisset cornua fronte* (B. 6.51).[27] Moreover, Ovid's Pasiphaë would like to be like Io or Europa, two of Jupiter's paramours, because, as she could recall from her literary memory in elegy, and especially as she could gather from Ovid's own *Amores*, though misunderstanding the text in this case, Jupiter changed Io into a cow and himself into a bull, thereby providing Ovid with another mythological opportunity to use bovine imagery in erotic poetry (*Am.* 1.3.21–4):

> carmine nomen habent exterrita cornibus Io
>   et quam fluminea lusit adulter aue
> quaeque super pontum simulato uecta iuuenco
>   uirginea tenuit cornua uara manu.

Io, terrified by her horns, and she whom the adulterer tricked while disguised as a river bird, have gained a name through song, as did she who, when she was carried over the sea by a counterfeit bull, held his curved horns in her maiden's hand.

Ovid's Pasiphaë desires the pleasure that, in her perception, comes with being the object of such lust. But she is mistaken in this regard, superimposing her own sexual instincts onto Io and Europa. Blinded by her lust to the psychology of these two unfortunate women, Pasiphaë imagines that

Io must have felt great pleasure in knowing that she was alluring to a god, while Europa must have been exceedingly gratified by the thought that in her human form her beauty was such as to provoke Jove's bovine desire.

Before resorting to a stratagem that would enable her to become the object of bovine desire, Pasiphaë pursues her beloved with gifts, in accordance with a literary memory of her background in *B.* 6. She brings the bull gifts that she knows he likes. Since for Vergil's Pasiphaë the bull was *herba captum uiridi* ("captivated by the green grass," *B.* 6.59), in the *Ars* Ovid's Pasiphaë now offers him *nouas frondes et prata tenerrima* ("new leaves and the most tender meadow grass," *Ars* 1.299) as a fine elegiac gift. Indeed, almost as if she were trying to push the elegiac convention to its limit, she brings her beloved the choicest grass, qualified by the superlative, *tenerrima*, making her grass gift that much more precious than the tender grass on which rival cows prance to impress the bull (*teneris … herbis, Ars* 1.315). Since *tener* is an elegiac word to begin with,[28] *tenerrima* makes Pasiphaë's gift of grass a superlatively elegiac gesture.

Pasiphaë's actions have clear analogies in the elegiac repertoire of mannerisms, and the resemblance is such as to lead to the conclusion that Ovid rewrote Vergil's Pasiphaë in accordance with elegiac conventions, however incoherent they may have been with her position as a queen and with her aberrant sexuality. Vergil's Pasiphaë appears refashioned by Ovid to give the impression of a character accustomed to reading elegy and to borrowing language and actions from its corpus, interpreting her own situation in literary terms. As Gian Biagio Conte reminds us, the modelling logic of a literary genre, including amatory elegy, has the power to turn everything "into an image of itself."[29] In yielding to this power, Pasiphaë enacts what we can describe – borrowing the title of the famous book by Roland Barthes – as a bovine lover's discourse in elegiac form.[30] The word discourse implies the existence of a community of poetic thought and erotic relations, an organization of the tropes and images of desire and its attendant passions, and a poetic language for their expression.[31] In many respects, Roman love elegy is a hybrid genre, with elements from various adjacent forms of poetry, but there can be no doubt that the corpus offers itself to the reader principally as a contained universe of discourse on love, coherently viewed from the perspective of the suffering lover. And the elegiac lover is always also a literary lover, an author and reader of love poetry, one who makes use of literary models to interpret and express his own passion. His erotic relations, motivated by a desire that cannot be fulfilled and propelled by the negative emotions that such desire naturally generates – emotions such as jealousy, indignation, and hatred[32] – are routinely articulated by means of language, imagery, and intertextual echoes that belong to a common poetic repertoire, which we may call the elegiac universe of discourse on love.

Ovid's Pasiphaë may be regarded as a lover with the traits of a reader who stands outside or, at most, on the *limen* of that discourse. The longer chapters of her literary memory are in the discourse of tragedy, which has come down to us in a fragment by Euripides, and in that of bucolic poetry, from Vergil's sixth eclogue. But by the time that Ovid wrote the *Ars*, Pasiphaë had also had three appearances in the elegies of Propertius, though these were quick appearances, in which she was never presented in a positive light.[33] Propertius had gone as far as to point to Pasiphaë as a prime illustration of the principle that women are more prone to lust than men (Prop. 3.19.11). In the *Ars Amatoria* the *praeceptor* behaves like Propertius, telling her story for a similar reason. Ovid's Pasiphaë thus finds herself already inscribed in elegy as a fiercely passionate woman, however negatively. She ignores Propertius' negative attitude towards her and decides to adapt elegiac models of behaviour to her action, advantageously, in a misreading of his poem, prompted perhaps by Silenus' sympathetic treatment of her in *B*. 6. For it is not in the context of Propertian elegy that she pursues the bull, but in Ovid's *Ars Amatoria*, which liberates the elegiac form from earlier thematic restrictions and gives it a didactic mode in order to teach the conventions of seduction.[34] There Pasiphaë can make new forays into the world of elegy, seeking to equip herself with imagery and vocabulary that she can use to articulate and enact her unnatural craving as love, camouflaging both its unconscionable nature and her strategy of seduction as aspects of an elegiac passion.

In elaborating a narrative for the realization of her bovine fantasy, Pasiphaë recycles images and motifs from the elegiac repertoire, imbuing herself with its language. Lovers who are also readers always succumb to the power of the literary language of love. Such lovers isolate themselves from reality, says Barthes, and surrender to imagery, allowing it to control their perspective on the world.[35] As a lover conceived on the analogy of a reader, Pasiphaë yields to the influence of the language of love and articulates her designs in accordance with it. She thus reconstructs her narrative of bovine love in elegiac terms, without apparent awareness of the incongruity, without, that is, realizing that her narrative is not a good elegiac fit. Though her story is told in the *Ars*, it takes place in a landscape that is remote from the urban setting of elegiac love affairs. She offers her intended beloved a gift of the choicest grass, in analogy to the refined poems of an elegiac poet-lover, reversing the gender of the giver and receiver of the gift. But her gift lacks the elegiac urbanity and refinement – the grass is cut by an *inassueta ... manu* (1.300) – suggested by the analogy because she is a queen and not a *puella* or an elegiac lover. As a queen she is alien to the bucolic genre as well. While following the herd, as in a bucolic narrative, she checks her appearance in a mirror, as in an elegy, but only to see if she has bovine erotic appeal. Pasiphaë both echoes and deforms the mannerisms of elegiac and bucolic poetry in order to apply them to her unnatural craving, which has nothing to do with the erotic desire of elegiac and bucolic lovers. Pasiphaë subjects both genres to a deforming misreading or a *cosciente deformazione*, a reading that both preserves and distorts the original model.[36] By presenting her situation as an echo of erotic behaviour in poetry, Pasiphaë overturns the imitation process basic to classical aesthetics, which is that poetry is ultimately an imitation of life and never the reverse. Poetry fictionalizes life, but life does not unfold as the realization of poetic fictions. Pasiphaë reverses the ontological order of life and art, in a manner reminiscent of Ovid's depiction of the creative process of nature in the regeneration of humanity after the great flood in Book 1 of the *Metamorphoses*. Nature makes human beings emerge from the stones cast by Deucalion and Pyrrha, slowly shaping them into human form just as a sculptor shapes a block of marble (*Met.* 1.403–6). In this portrayal of the creative process of nature, it is not art that resembles life, but life that resembles art.

Pasiphaë places her beloved bull in an elegiac aura, calling him *domino meo* (*Ars* 1.314), an expression that possessively recodes the gender of the elegiac *domina*. These are her own words, gleaned from the language of elegy and given a grotesque sense.[37] As for his appearance, Vergil presents the bull as snowy white, *niuei … iuuenci* (*B.* 6.46), and Ovid describes him as *candidus* (*Ars* 1.290). His being *candidus* is what made him attractive to the heifers in the herd, who hoped to have him on their backs (*optarunt tergo sustinuisse suo*, *Ars* 1.294). In the elegiac vocabulary the adjectives *niueus* and *candidus* are both used of the beloved,[38] and in Vergil's bucolic world Alexis himself, Corydon's beloved, is *candidus* (*B.* 2.15), all of which suggest that the bull has for Pasiphaë a function analogous to that of the beloved in the elegiac and bucolic erotic scenarios. In Vergil that possibility is made more plausible by the fact that *iuuencus* can mean both a young bull and a young man.[39] Vergil, moreover, consoles Pasiphaë for her love of the bull, *amore iuuenci* (6.46). Ovid does not go that far: he does not use the word *amor* of Pasiphaë's desire. In the twisted imagination of his Pasiphaë, the erotic appeal of the bull can be phrased in the literary language of love, but only mockingly so. Pasiphaë may lust for the bull like a heifer, but she is no *iuuenca* like her rivals in the field. Indeed, as discussed above, her mirror reminds her of this shortcoming whenever she inspects her forehead in the reflection (*Ars* 1.307). There, she does not see any horns to match the bovine beauty of her beloved. Moreover, elegiacally *candidus* though he may be for Pasiphaë, the bull is presented by Ovid as very much a bull, a *candidus taurus*, without ambiguity (*Ars* 1.290). He also has a black spot in the middle of his forehead (*Ars* 1.291–2): *signatus tenui media inter cornua nigro; / una fuit labes, cetera lactis erant* ("marked right between his horns

with delicate black: there was a single blemish, the rest was milky-white").
Though it is clearly an imperfection – Ovid calls it a *labes* – it is for Pasiphaë
a flaw with a positive aesthetic function.[40] The bull's *labes* marks him out as
somehow special.[41] Ovid, moreover, qualifies it as *tenuis*, an adjective that
associates the mark with both elegiac and bucolic poetry, recalling the *genus
tenue* of the former and delicate and slender pipes of the latter genre.[42]

The dramatic scenario in which Ovid's Pasiphaë visualizes herself is based
on vocabulary and forms of behaviour acquired from her reading of the elegists in addition to Vergil. Ovid contributes to her acquisition of elegiac
language, as we have seen, by designating the cows as her *paelices* or rivals.
In the elegiac discourse on love, *paelex* becomes a fundamental word only
with Ovid, who uses it frequently in the *Ars* and in the *Heroides* as part of
the vocabulary of the drama of women in love.[43] Pasiphaë appropriates it
from them, but in order to apply it to her own situation, she generates a
deformazione of the rival's elegiac role and aesthetic significance by filtering
it through her unnatural desire, which equates her anticipated bestial gratification with the erotic delight sought by elegiac and bucolic lovers. Ovid
makes use of the distorting power of Pasiphaë's desire to uncover the dark
animal instincts that may lie concealed under the conventionally refined
surface of erotic relations in elegiac and bucolic poetry.

Having made her partly elegiac, Ovid anchors his narrative perspective to Pasiphaë's bucolic context, where animals, unlike women, do not
conceal their lust. Eleanor Leach has demonstrated that in the *Ars* Ovid
celebrates the *mores* of Roman society while parodying the moral and patriotic ideals that inform Vergil's *Georgics*.[44] As far as Pasiphaë is concerned,
however, we can add that in the process Ovid fashions a bovine discourse
on love, conceived as both a parallel and a parody of the one discernible in
elegiac and bucolic poetry. In this discourse Pasiphaë moves in a bucolic
setting but immerses herself in an elegiac ethos. By interpreting her sexual
urges in the terms of this discourse, Pasiphaë unwittingly reveals that the
aesthetic of elegiac love to which she is drawn incorporates the possibility
of a sudden lapse into a dark region of the erotic imagination, where tropes
of monstrous transgression and a sneering mockery of conventions can
become a staple commodity. Especially in the case of Pasiphaë, we can say,
adopting J.P. Sullivan's descriptive terms, that Ovid replaces the "amorous
sensibility" of earlier elegists with "sexual cynicism."[45] Having walked into
that realm to pursue the object of her craving, Pasiphaë is puzzled by the
fact that the bull is attracted to a particular heifer, and she wonders *domino
cur placet ista meo?* ("Why is that one pleasing to my master?" *Ars* 1.314).
Here Pasiphaë forgets her station as a queen and courts her intended beastly
lover, addressing him in a manner that suggests a parodic reversal of the

elegiac relationship in the theme of *seruitium amoris*. The genuine tone of her reaction shows that Pasiphaë has already crossed the boundary between human and bovine and now readily interprets her erotic urges as the expression of an animal's readiness to mate.

In the elegiac tradition, tropes of animalization are used to degrade the Other and are motivated by indignation. Thus Catullus describes the foul smell of the lover's rival as an armpit goat (*alarum ... hircus*, 71.1), Propertius depicts his poet-lover's rival as a stupid animal (*stolidum pecus*, 2.16.8), and, more to our point, Tibullus describes Marathus as a young man capable of having sex with beasts (*cum trucibus ... feris*, 1.9.76), a phrase that seems almost to call out to Pasiphaë from within the core of erotic elegy. But what would happen to elegiac love itself and to the world that it governs, on the narrative and on the aesthetic planes, if, in a response to that call, the metaphorical language were literalized? The result would be an intentional manipulation of the logic of erotic elegy in an undertaking designed to invite the reader to think in graphic terms about a monstrous transgression and to savour the troubling aesthetic experience of its depiction in fantasy.

Pasiphaë's transgression into the realm of bestiality is for Ovid a narrative opportunity for a georgic reading of elegiac and bucolic erotic conventions. He transports the reader of the traditional myth into an ironically conceived poetic domain, in which the sense of amorous language can be reduced to a graphic and material representation of sexuality. At the same time, Ovid transports the reader of elegiac and bucolic poetry into a heinous region of erotic consciousness, where conventional aesthetic expectations can be undermined by nefarious fantasies of transgression. Acting under the impulse of such psychological hybridism, Pasiphaë behaves and speaks as if she were rereading the elegiac and bucolic discourse on love in a grotesque key, as a discourse on animals moved by the urge to mate. With Daedalus' help, she hopes to attract the bull by dressing up as a cow and by showing herself ready to mate. Neither Vergil nor Ovid describes how she might have envisaged the appearance of her cow costume, but a passage in Vergil's third *Georgic* on the breeding of cattle includes a few suggestive details (*G.* 3.56–9):

> nec mihi displiceat maculis insignis et albo,
> aut iuga detrectans interdumque aspera cornu
> et faciem tauro propior, quaeque ardua tota
> et gradiens ima uerrit uestigia cauda.

Nor would I find displeasing [a cow] marked with white spots, or one refusing the yoke and sometimes fierce with her horns, and with a face closer to a bull's, and one who is altogether tall and who, when she walks, sweeps her footprints with the very tip of her tail.

There Vergil observes that a well-formed cow has, among other features, a face that resembles that of a bull. This Vergilian detail must have suited Ovid well, since he pictured Pasiphaë assuming some mannerisms of an elegiac *puella* and yet exhibiting the aggressive behaviour of an *"amatrix."*[46] The facial similarity between bull and cow that Vergil describes could have been read by Ovid as an especially appealing opportunity for gender mixing and subject-object flipping in his fabrication of a bovine lover's discourse, in which to couch the story of Pasiphaë's union with the bull.

The offspring of that union is the Minotaur, by far the most famous of the *nota* in the story of Pasiphaë and the bull. Vergil leaves the Minotaur altogether out of *B.* 6. Even in the *Aeneid*, where he does name the Minotaur in his ecphrasis of the temple of Apollo at Cumae, he refers to him by the expressions *mixtum genus* and *proles biformis* ("the mixed offspring and double-formed issue," *A.* 6.25). His human-bovine hybridity is a worthy reminder of Pasiphaë's shameful sexual union, the *turpis concubitus* which Pasiphaë sought but which the Proetides did not (*B.* 6.49–50), in which the adjective *turpis* makes the poet's moral judgment momentarily visible through the veil of his compassion.

In his version, Ovid refers to the Minotaur only once, in the closing line of his account, *et partu proditus auctor erat* ("by the offspring the begetter was revealed," *Ars* 1.326). His readers, however, do not need more than that, as they are already familiar with the outcome of the story. The birth of the Minotaur haunts their reading teleologically and recollectively. From the future of the events in the story and from the past in the reader's literary memory, the Minotaur casts an ominous light on the aesthetic texture of the unfolding narrative.

We are given a graphic sense of that light later in *Ars* 2, in a famous line in which Ovid lingers over the Minotaur's hybridity by describing him as *semibouemque uirum semiuirumque bouem* ("both the half-bull man and the half-man bull," *Ars* 2.24). Ovid here prolongs the reader's interpretative and aesthetic focus on the Minotaur's hybridity for the duration of an entire verse, a "light and witty" pentameter, as Alison Sharrock describes it,[47] designed to convey mystery and monstrosity while displaying the poet's total control of symmetry, balance, and antithesis. This causes the reader to linger meditating on the magnitude of Pasiphaë's depravity (even in a story about Daedalus), visualizing the Minotaur's appearance by letting the eye of the imagination sweep over his body, first over his human half and then, backwards, over his bovine half, until his hybrid nature has been fully contemplated and the artistry of the verse fully appreciated.

Given the consolatory language with which Vergil describes her predicament, why does Ovid's Pasiphaë wish to give her plight an elegiac dimension? By stressing her state as a victim of an unfairly inflicted disease, Vergil offered her the possibility of eliciting a sympathetic reception, but virtually deprived her of volitional agency in the pursuit of her lust. The story of Pasiphaë, however, could be retold in a manner reminiscent of Io's and Europa's, using vocabulary and mannerisms from elegiac poetry. In such an account, her agency could emerge from the commiserative mantle of her madness and come to the foreground in the guise of an elegiac passion grown to horrible magnitude. Pasiphaë's narrative, however, is not compatible with some basic conventions and memories of elegiac eroticism. But it is fully consistent with the elegiac form of the *Ars Amatoria*, which makes use of conventions and memory to explore eroticism beyond the thematic limits of traditional elegy, breaking new generic ground. In Ovid's retelling of the story of Pasiphaë, the elegiac discourse on love is recast as a narrative of dark animal eroticism, which, conjoined with wry mockery, carries its own aesthetic fulfilment.

NOTES

1 On the complex relationship of the levels of narration in Silenus' song, see Breed 2006a: 74–94.

2 Armstrong 2006: 169.

3 All quotations of Vergil come from Mynors 1969 and all quotations of Ovid come from Kenney 1994. All translations are my own.

4 See Adams 1982: 198 and cf. *TLL* VI^2.1706.45–1707.72.

5 Eco 1976.

6 Cf. Courtney 1990: 102 on the somewhat inappropriate use of the Calvan allusion to address Pasiphaë.

7 *Virgo* is a high-register word. Cf. Clausen 1994: 195.

8 On the sense of pathos expressed by the neoteric exclamation, see Ross 1969: 30 and Ross 1975: 73, where he says that it is a distinctive trait of Gallus. Petrini 1997: 20, adds that it "typically occurs in erotic laments of stricken lovers," making explicit its elegiac potential. A very clear description of the expressive value of the neoteric *a* is given by Perutelli 2000: 93, who says that it conveys "un doloroso sentimento di solidarietà." Cf. also Hollis 1977: 95.

9 Moreover, *B*. 2.69 alludes to Theocritus *Id*.11.72, where the lovelorn Polyphemus asks himself ὦ Κύκλωψ Κύκλωψ, πᾷ τὰς φρένας ἐκπεπότασαι; Pasiphaë is not as bucolic a character as she might want to be, but this madness in love makes her reminiscent of one. Love is also linked to madness in *G*.

4.448 in the figure of Orpheus, a Gallan character, as Fabre-Serris 2016: 173, has shown. See also Keith in this volume. On *B.* 2 and its relationship to Vergil's Gallus, see also Fabre-Serris in this volume.

10 The text of the *Cretans* is from Jouan and van Looy 2000. On the textual issues involved in the interpretation of the pertinent fragments, cf. Cozzoli 2001 and Sansone 2013.

11 As Reckford (1974: 322) has argued in his study of the fragment, the Euripidean Pasiphaë here questions the philosophical soundness of "ordinary moral judgments."

12 Cf. Thomas 1979: 337–8.

13 Theocritus, *Id.*11.34 and cf. Thomas 1979: 338.

14 Hubbard 1975a: 61; Armstrong 2006: 176.

15 Cf. *B.* 10.29–30, where Pan speaks to Gallus: *nec lacrimis crudelis Amor nec gramina riuis / nec cytiso saturantur apes nec fronde capellae.*

16 Coleman 1977: 191.

17 Thomas 1988a: 40 ad 4.11, and Clausen 1994: 196.

18 Elder 1961: 118.

19 Significantly, Ovid does not speak of Pasiphaë's madness but of her foolishness (*inepta, Ars* 1.206), presenting her as a victim of her lack of judgment. On this point, see Fabre-Serris 2016: 175.

20 On the elegiac use of *adulter*, see Pichon 1902: 81–2.

21 But note that in *Am.* 1.3.22, Jupiter in animal form is described as *adulter*.

22 Cf., e.g., Prop. 1.1.7; 1.4.11; 1.5.1; Ov. *Am.* 1.2.35; 1.7.2–3. See also Pichon 1902: 157–8. On the Gallan association, see Cairns 2006: 127, 337–9; Fabre-Serris 2016: 173.

23 Leach 1968: 21.

24 Rightly, Hollis 1977: 93, remarks that Ovid turns the elegiac elements into farce and black humour.

25 In elegy, the *lena* is at times depicted engaging in gruesome witchcraft. Cf. Acanthis in Prop. 4.5 and Dipsas in *Am.* 1.8.

26 On the accoutrements of the *puella*, see Wyke 1994 and Olson 2008.

27 By recalling the story of the Proetides from within his account of Pasiphaë, Vergil is making use of the tale-within-a-tale narrative structure of the Alexandrian tradition, in which the enclosed and the enclosing tales had a "complementary relationship," as Coleman 1977: 190 observes. That relationship, however, is also ironic, since the Proetides thought they had been turned into cows against their will as a form of punishment, whereas Pasiphaë would very much like to be taken for a cow by the bull after which she lusts.

28 E.g., Prop. 1.8a.7; 1.18.22; Ov. *Am.* 1.13.5, 18; 2.1.4. See also Pichon 1902: 277–8.

29 Conte 1994: 37.

30 Barthes 1977.

31 As Duncan Kennedy (1993: 67) argues, when poets reduce love to discourse, they reveal (as they revel in) its "rhetoricity."

32 On the dependence of most negative emotions on jealousy and on the fundamental role of jealousy in elegiac love relations, see Caston 2012, especially chapter 2.

33 In Prop. 2.28.49–52, she is described as *nec proba*; in 3.19.11–12, she is the first example of uncontrolled, inappropriate, and excessive female lust; in 4.7.57–8 she is among the unfaithful in the underworld.

34 On the generic complexities of the *Ars*, pertaining to Ovid's melding of the elegiac and the didactic genres, see Volk 2007: 241; Volk 2002, chapter 5; Green 2007: 7; Thorsen 2013a: 213.

35 Barthes 1977: 90 and 148.

36 The Italian term is from D'Anna 1983: 52, for whom it describes Propertius' misreading of Vergil. For the use of *deformazione* as a designation of this type of misreading, see Cairns 2006: 32 and Cairns 2016: 127.

37 Hollis (1977: 95) remarks that *domino meo* is an endearing expression with an intentionally grotesque meaning.

38 For *candidus* and *niueus*, see, for example, Prop. 2.32, 3.6; Ov. *Am.* 2.4, 2.12, 2.16, 3.2, 3.7; Tib. 1.5.66. Cf. also Pichon 1902: 98–9. On *iuuencus*, cf. Horace *Carm.* 2.8.21 and Armstrong 2006: 174. See also *TLL* VII ^{2} 731.47–73.

39 See Horace *Carm.* 2.8.21 and cf. Armstrong 2006: 174. See also *TLL* VII ^{2} 731.47–73.

40 We know from Seneca the Elder that Ovid considered the presence of a mole on a woman's face an enhancement of her beauty (*Con.* 2.2.12): *aiebat interim decentiorem faciem esse, in qua aliquis naeuos fuisset.*

41 Cf. Moschus' bull with a silver circle between his horns (Mosch. *Eur.* 85): κύκλος δ' ἀργύφεος μέσσῳ μάρμαιρε μετώπῳ. This is evidence of his extraordinary nature (he *is* Zeus in disguise), but it also makes him beautiful and attractive to Europa.

42 As in *B.* 1.2 and 6.8.

43 See, for example, *Ars* 1.365, 2.377, 3.677, 3.684, 3.701, 3.739; *Her.* 5.60, 6.149, 6.81, 9.121, 9.132, 12.173, 14.95, 14.108, 19.102. The term also occurs in *Am.* 1.14.39.

44 Leach 1964: 154.

45 Sullivan 1962: 40.

46 Holzberg 1998: 104. Cf. Miller 2022: 287, who focuses precisely on the duality of Pasiphaë's role in his interpretation of her story as a pedagogical exemplum of both the lustful nature of women and the resolve of lovers who succeed in their erotic pursuits.

47 Sharrock 1994: 130. Lowe (2015: 187) notes that Ovid composed similarly structured lines elsewhere when he alludes to the Minotaur (e.g., *Her.* 2.70, *Ibis* 408), using the same stylistic "signature" to display his artistry.

9

Supprime, Musa, querellas: Ovid's Elegiac Aristaeus

BARBARA WEIDEN BOYD

1. Narrative and Bricolage

Ronald Syme's infamous view of Ovid's *Fasti* as "uncongenial" in subject matter, once the prevailing opinion, has long since been put to rest by a more recent generation of scholars working on Latin poetry.[1] The contemporary *aetas Ovidiana*, the origins of which can be dated to the 1980s, has witnessed a radical reassessment of Ovid's calendar poem, now rightly recognized as both the most Roman and most Callimachean of Ovid's marvellously abundant poetic corpus. His predecessor Propertius claimed for himself the title of "Romanus Callimachus" (4.1.64), but it is difficult not to see Ovid's *Fasti* as his entry into a poetic *armorum iudicium* with Propertius, asserting a persuasive claim to the title. Among the many advocates coming to Ovid's defence in this imaginary competition, I single out the studies of John Miller, Elaine Fantham, Alessandro Barchiesi, and Carole Newlands for the wholesale collective renovation of the *Fasti* initiated by Stephen Hinds' comparison of the Ceres and Proserpina episodes in the *Fasti* and the *Metamorphoses*.[2] In their wake have followed dozens of others, inspired by them almost as much as by Ovid himself to excavate and articulate the rich vein of poetic material running through the six surviving books of the poem.

A major source of the poem's fascination – as well as of its long relegation to the critical shadows – lies in its structure: Ovid's self-imposed purpose to catalogue and describe the occasions of the Roman calendar as they occur creates a narrative whose plot is neither less nor more than the passage of time itself.[3] The resulting effect is not that of a narrative at all, but rather of a concatenation of otherwise apparently unconnected events, commemorations, and astronomical phenomena;[4] but this appearance of randomness is itself undercut by abundant evidence for episodes linked by recurring characters, or by the evocation of particular genres or sources, or by repetitions on the level of diction, style, and tone. The general effect is of a mindful bricolage, neither narrative nor not-narrative, neither random nor linear, that constantly invites the reader to find the implied connections, or to make new ones.[5]

The sophisticated appreciation from which the poem has benefited in recent years has resulted not only in the publication of numerous critical studies, large and small, but also in the appearance of several commentaries on individual books that are informed to a great degree by the new contextualization of the poem.[6] Building on Franz Bömer's fundamental commentary on the entire six books, these newer works explore the complexities of Ovid's poem in great and perceptive detail, even as the "big picture" is also becoming clearer: the work of Alessandro Barchiesi and Carole Newlands in particular, along with a challenging essay by Dennis Feeney,[7] has helped to elucidate the political contexts for Ovid's calendar poem, even as it brings into stronger focus than ever before the complexities of Ovidian poetics.

The abundance of attention received by the *Fasti* in the last thirty years or so has not, however, illuminated all aspects of the poem with equal clarity, and I therefore propose to offer in this essay a necessarily modest but, I think, potentially far-reaching contribution to the discussion. I return momentarily to my earlier description of the poem as a sort of bricolage construction: the sequence of events in the poem, dictated at least ostensibly by the calendar rather than by any inherent structural rationale, has necessarily meant that some episodes and commemorations receive more attention from both Ovid and his readers than do others. The tendency to focus on some episodes more than others is both natural and necessary – the pursuit of one narrative pattern will always override and overwrite any other. But some parts of the poem are particularly susceptible to such segmentation because of the apparent evidence of revision by Ovid – that is, some parts of the poem can with convincing clarity be shown to be attributable not to the original period of composition, presumed to be before Ovid's exile in 8 or 9 CE, but to revisions made in exile.[8] The most obvious example is probably the apostrophe to Germanicus that appears in *Fasti* 4, as Ovid catalogues the many foreign travellers who made new homes for themselves in Italy, beginning with Evander and Hercules. The list works its way towards Aeneas (*F.* 4.77–8) but, rather than culminating with him, adds one last fellow traveller, Solymus, who is said to have come from Troy with Aeneas and to have founded Sulmo, Ovid's birthplace. This ostensibly straightforward mention becomes deeply personal, however, as the poet evokes both his loss and the elegiac Muse who inspires his lament (*F.* 4.79–84):[9]

> huius erat Solymus Phrygia comes unus ab Ida
> > a quo Sulmonis moenia nomen habent,
> Sulmonis gelidi, patriae, Germanice, nostrae.
> > me miserum, Scythico quam procul illa solo est!
> ergo ego tam longe – sed supprime, Musa, querellas;
> > non tibi sunt maesta sacra canenda lyra.

The sole companion of this man [i.e., Aeneas] from Phrygian Ida was Solymus, from whom the walls of Sulmo have their name – chilly Sulmo, my homeland, Germanicus. Poor me! How far that is from the Scythian land. I therefore from so far away – but, Muse, restrain your complaints; mournful songs should not be sung by your lyre.

The emotional epanalepsis of the place name Sulmo, together with the address to Germanicus and the allusion to Scythia, locate this passage explicitly in both time and place: the two place names juxtapose Ovid's beloved home and his far-distant place of relegation; and Ovid's appeals to Germanicus, as evidenced elsewhere in his work also,[10] all appear to postdate the death of Augustus, and to have been composed in the early years of the Tiberian principate.

Ovid's apostrophe to Germanicus here recalls a much more elaborate invocation of Tiberius' (and Augustus') adopted son earlier in the poem, in the proem to *Fasti* 1 (1–288).[11] Germanicus is addressed directly three times in the opening (at verses 3, 63, and 285), references interwoven with a detailed introduction of the poem's themes and a conversation with January's eponymous god, Janus. Next, Ovid launches into the calendar proper, with three couplets on the first major anniversary of the year involving the two temples on Tiber Island, those of Asclepius and Jupiter (*F.* 1.289–94). This beginning, however, is itself brought up short, as Ovid then introduces yet another passage of proemial character, explaining the rationale behind his inclusion of astronomical phenomena in the calendar (295–310); this justification comes to a close with three couplets (311–16) that take up the astronomical theme by identifying the constellation that will be rising at this time of year (Lyra) as well as the one that now disappears (Cancer). The obvious fragmentation of the narrative (or lack of narrative) here identifies much if not all of this first section, too, as part of a post-exilic revision, from a time when Ovid still had hopes of being recalled to Rome by a supportive and influential intermediary; indeed, it is sometimes thought that the section on astronomy is a gesture of fellowship directed toward Germanicus, who himself wrote an astronomical poem and might therefore be considered by Ovid a kindred soul.[12] Only at this point does the calendar narrative really establish itself as the dominant driver of the poem.

I draw attention to this opening sequence because it not only illustrates the challenges of working with the *Fasti's* narrative, but also exemplifies how the poem's segmentation can easily encourage one episode to be read apart from other sections of the same poem, even of the same book. The evidence for a second "edition" of the *Fasti* afforded by the prominence of Germanicus in this opening (together with what some have argued is the consequent displacement of the original proem to the beginning of *Fasti* 2)[13] has naturally garnered an abundance of critical attention; it has also invited readers to look less attentively than they might do otherwise at less explicit hints at revision in the poem. My purpose in this paper is to look at one segment in the subsequent narrative, Ovid's description of the Agon(al)ia, and to argue that its very subtlety and its engagements with the *Georgics'* descriptions of the Golden Age and Italy and with the culminating Aristaeus epyllion are crucial to a full understanding of Ovid's exilic poetics.

2. Slaughter or Sacrifice?

Ovid's description of the Agon(al)ia opens with an elaborate discussion, in nine couplets, of seven etymological possibilities behind the festival's name, all but one of which are linked in one way or another with animal sacrifice (*F.* 1.319–36). Ovid offers his opinion that the last on his list, *agonia = pecus*, is the one to which he subscribes (331–2); its predecessors include 1) the derivation of a term used for a priest (*minister = ago*, a rare noun elsewhere known only from Lact. *ap.* Stat. *Theb.* 4.463) from the formula used by the priest (*agatne*, 322) to inquire whether he should proceed with the sacrifice; 2) the action of driving the victims (*agantur*, 323) to sacrifice; 3) the orthography of the earlier name of the holiday, *Agnalia*, cognate with *agnus* (325); 4) the fear (*metus = agonia* [ἀγωνία]) of the sheep upon seeing the sacrificial knife; and 5) the relationship of holidays to *ludi*, or Greek *agones* (330).[14] Notably, in spite of the apparent overabundance of options,[15] most of them point to the same context: animal sacrifice and its origins. As if to bring this message home, Ovid concludes the list with a further two etymological extensions of the original inquiry, associating sacrifice with military victory by using military metaphors for other aspects of sacrifice: a *uictima* is so called because it is struck down by a victorious hand (*dextra uictrice*, 335); and the alternative name for a victim, *hostia*, constitutes an allusion to conquered enemies (*hostibus a domitis*, 336).[16]

All of this etymological speculation leads Ovid to remind his readers that, once upon a time, sacrifice did not involve bloodshed; the earliest sacrificial offerings were emmer wheat and salt (*F.* 1.338). The difference between past and present is then underscored by lingering reflection on the past and its innocence of blood sacrifice, a past basking in the reflection of the Golden Age (1.337–48):[17]

> ante, deos homini quod conciliare ualeret,
>   far erat et puri lucida mica salis.
> nondum pertulerat lacrimatas cortice murras
>   acta per aequoreas hospita nauis aquas,
> tura nec Euphrates nec miserat India costum,
>   nec fuerant rubri cognita fila croci.
> ara dabat fumos herbis contenta Sabinis,
>   et non exiguo laurus adusta sono;
> si quis erat, factis prati de flore coronis
>   qui posset uiolas addere, diues erat.
> hic, qui nunc aperit percussi uiscera tauri,
>   in sacris nullum culter habebat opus.

Previously, there was emmer wheat, which had the ability to reconcile gods with man, and the glistening grain of pure salt. Not yet had a visitor's ship, driven through watery seas, carried myrrh, wept by the tree's bark; the Euphrates had not sent incense, nor India, the fragrant root; nor had the threads of ruddy saffron been discovered. Content with Sabine shoots, the altar produced smoke, and with no small sound was the laurel burned; if there was anyone who could add violets to garlands made from the flowers of the field, he was wealthy. This knife, which now reveals the internal organs of the bull killed by a blow, formerly had no role in sacrifices.

The words opening each of the first two couplets (*ante*; *nondum*), together with a prominent reference to a time before seafaring (340), succinctly set the scene in the past, in particular, in the Golden Age.[18] Ovid uses the absence of seafaring to explain why in the early days there were no exotic and imported perfumes and incense to offer to the gods; native plants sufficed to make the gods happy when neither Asia (Euphrates) nor India was known (339–44). The contrast here between imported and native sources of burnt offerings clearly recalls, in compressed fashion, a much more extensive passage in Vergil's *laudes Italiae* laying out the difference between native and foreign resources (*G.* 2.109–76). Vergil begins by listing a number of substances not available in Italy, and to be gotten only in foreign lands, like ebony (*nigrum* / ... *hebenum*, 116–17), frankincense (*turea uirga*, 117), myrrh (*odorato* ... *sudantia ligno* / *balsama*, 118–19), the citron (*felicis mali*, 127), and a medicinal product similar (but not identical) to one derived from the Italian *laurus* (126–35).[19] The purpose of this catalogue is to serve as foil, for as Vergil asserts, no exotic foreign locales, however rich in resources, can compete with Italy (*G.* 2.136–9):[20]

> sed neque Medorum siluae ditissima terra
> nec pulcher Ganges atque auro turbidus Hermus
> laudibus Italiae certent, non Bactra neque Indi
> totaque turiferis Panchaia pinguis harenis.

But neither the forests of the Medes, a most wealthy land,[21] nor fair Ganges and Hermus, cloudy with gold, could compete with the praises of Italy, nor Bactria and the Indians, and all Panchaia, rich with its incense-bearing sands.

In recalling Vergil's *laudes*, Ovid thus suggests that the earliest inhabitants of Rome partook of a simplicity and innocence much like that operating, in at least some respects, in the idealized picture of Italy found in the second *Georgic*. But there is an important difference: What Vergil depicts as a timeless contrast between the perfection of Italy and the inferiority of all other locales is reconfigured by Ovid as a historically determined contrast between Italy past and Italy present, a contrast that culminates in the temporal adverb *nunc* (*F.* 1.347).[22] He underscores this difference by concluding his depiction of the past with an allusion to the sacrificial knife (*culter*, *F.* 1.348), the need for which did not exist in that simpler time. This notice not only sets a temporal boundary, but also reinforces the historically determined character of sacrifice, as mention of the sacrificial knife sends us back to the opening of the aetiological catalogue: the very first etymological option listed by Ovid includes use of the *culter* (*nominis esse potest succinctus causa minister* / … / *qui calido strictos tincturus sanguine cultros* / *semper agatne rogat*, "the reason for the name can be the girded priest, who always, when about to stain the unsheathed knife, asks whether he should act," 319–22).[23]

Elsewhere in the *Georgics*, Vergil does indicate that, as a consequence of history, the Golden Age is a thing of the past;[24] his reference at the close of the second *Georgic* to a time when people did not yet feast on slaughtered cattle is likewise marked by a sense of time's inevitable passage (*G.* 2.536–40):

> ante etiam sceptrum Dictaei regis et ante
> impia quam caesis gens est epulata iuuencis,
> aureus hanc uitam in terris Saturnus agebat;
> necdum etiam audierant inflari classica, necdum
> impositos duris crepitare incudibus ensis.

Indeed, before the sceptre of the Dictaean king and before an impious race dined on slaughtered cattle, golden Saturn led this life on earth; not yet had they heard the military trumpets being blown, not yet had they heard swords resound with a rattle when placed on hard anvils.

The strong differences between the two Vergilian passages, both central to the second *Georgic* yet at apparent odds with each other, are perplexing, and continue to provoke discussion: while the *laudes Italiae* presents the distinctive and seemingly timeless features of Italy in only the most glowing terms, the picture we are left with at the close of the second *Georgic* evokes a nostalgia for lost innocence. Ovid, on the other hand, unequivocally locates the days before Italy's cultural and economic sophistication in a past never to be seen again. Indeed, it would be possible to argue that Ovid's temporal specificity is an arch "correction" of Vergil's timeless Italy, meant to bring out the mutual contradiction found in the *Georgics*;[25] but I suggest that Ovid's purpose here is not simply to be seen as a learned or playful "correction," though it certainly is that. Rather, Ovid interweaves the two views of Vergil, even as he connects the end of the Golden Age with the invention of blood sacrifice. Ovid's emphasis on the past in the description of the time before the introduction of blood sacrifice (*ante, F.* 1.337; *nondum*, 1.339) can be seen as a direct borrowing of the temporal emphasis with which the second *Georgic* concludes (*ante* twice in *G.* 2.536; *necdum* twice in 2.539), even as he frames that past in terms that recall the timelessness of the *laudes Italiae*. Whereas the two Vergilian passages present readers with an unresolved conflict, and with a troubling uncertainty about the role of human agency in history, Ovid offers certainty and resolve; there is simply no timeless present in Ovid's version of the contemporary world, and blood sacrifice is essential to survival.

Finally, there is one other crucial difference: in Vergil's description of the slaying of cattle (*impia ... caesis gens est epulata iuuencis, G.* 2.537), the precise purpose for and context of the slaughter are unclear. Is he in fact describing the first sacrifice, albeit in purely suggestive terms, or is this slaughter entirely unmotivated by any religious rationale, and ascribable instead to human degeneracy, as suggested by the epithet *impia*? In Ovid's version, meanwhile, the connection is explicit, straightforward, and inescapable: the killing of animals is a fact of religious and ritual life. Again, it is tempting to think of the difference between the two poets as an instance of "correction," or at least, of Ovid's tendency to make explicit what Vergil leaves undefined. With unquestionable clarity, Ovid focuses on sacrifice as an – or the – essential key to survival in the world in which he lives.[26]

3. The Tears of Aristaeus

The position of the Agonalia passage so close to the beginning of the poem is
of course an accident of chronology – it is not my intent to suggest that Ovid
manipulates its timing to give it this position. He does, however, take advantage of its fortuitous appearance here, as the first major holiday to be celebrated
in the poem.[27] Furthermore, given the probability of extensive revision, the
prominence of this narrative has the potential to have a special significance.
And from at least one point of view, such significance is not hard to find: the
fact that this episode focuses on the invention of blood sacrifice might well be
thought to be of exceptional appropriateness to a poem that concerns itself with
the workings of Roman religion. This is, furthermore, a book all about beginnings: both the beginning of the calendar and the beginning of time, as is made
evident by the portrayal of Janus as the month's tutelary divinity. In identifying
himself with Chaos (*F.* 1.103): *me Chaos antiqui (nam sum res prisca) uocabant*
("the ancients called me Chaos (for I am the first thing)"), Janus locates himself
quite explicitly at the beginning of Hesiodic time; and when asked to explain
why the year does not begin with the spring, he explains with succinct authority the coincidence of the solstice with the end of one year and the beginning
of the next (163–4). There is thus an implicit logic in locating the aetiology for
blood sacrifice too at the beginning of the year and of the poem.

Ovid then offers what will turn out to be a very long catalogue of animals
that are sacrificed. Pigs and goats head the list (*F.* 1.349–60) and are quickly
followed by cattle and sheep (362): *quid bos, quid placidae commeruistis
oues?* ("What have you deserved, cow? and you, peaceful sheep?"). He then
focuses exclusively on cattle for the next nine couplets (363–80), followed
by a single couplet devoted to sheep (381–2), and closes with a framing
couplet in the form of a rhetorical question that echoes the earlier pairing of cattle and sheep (383–4): *quid tuti superest, animam cum ponat in
aris / lanigerumque pecus ruricolaeque boues?* ("What safety remains when
wool-bearing sheep and farming cattle give their lives on the altar?"). The
particular interest Ovid shows here in the sacrifice of cattle is in part a logi-
cal consequence of the transition he makes from describing the Golden Age
to illustrating contemporary religious practice: as we saw above, his Golden
Age depiction culminates in a reference to the earlier absence of any use
for a knife – the knife which is now employed for the slaughter of cattle
(347–8). But Ovid also uses the instance of cattle sacrifice to offer his own
version of the Aristaeus myth, a tale both his ancient readers and more
modern ones would immediately associate with the *Georgics* of Vergil (*G.*
4.317–558), where the loss of Aristaeus' bees and their rebirth through the
marvellous process of *bugonia* serves as the emotionally charged culmination of the entire poem.[28]

Surprisingly, given the enormous amount of attention paid in recent decades to the nature of *bugonia* in Vergil's Aristaeus epyllion, the Ovidian version has received little serious discussion.[29] I shall suggest, however, that it is possible to read Ovid's version of the Aristaeus epyllion as a prime example not only of how Ovid reads Vergil, but also of how he can so often go exactly to the heart of a difficult passage or idea to expose and interrogate its workings.[30] Secondly, I propose that it is no coincidence that with this episode Ovid "translates" Vergil into elegy: elegy's ancient function as the mode of mourning becomes for Ovid a means not only to celebrate the new Golden Age of the Augustan regime but also to acknowledge what has been lost, even as he struggles to survive in a brave new world. Finally, there is also, I think, a strong possibility that the alternative version of the Aristaeus story, along with its prominence in the *Fasti*, has personal implications for its poet; I shall return to that idea at the end of this essay.

As we turn to the Ovidian version, the differences from Vergil are as striking as the similarities; after quoting the *Fasti* version in full, therefore, I shall review both the numerous points of contact and the major variations (*F.* 1.363–80):

> flebat Aristaeus, quod apes cum stirpe necatas
>   uiderat inceptos destituisse fauos.
> caerula quem genetrix aegre solata dolentem
>   addidit haec dictis ultima uerba suis:
> "siste, puer, lacrimas! Proteus tua damna leuabit,
>   quoque modo repares quae periere, dabit.
> decipiat ne te uersis tamen ille figuris,
>   impediant geminas uincula firma manus."
> peruenit ad uatem iuuenis resolutaque somno
>   alligat aequorei bracchia capta senis.
> ille sua faciem transformis adulterat arte:
>   mox domitus uinclis in sua membra redit,
> oraque caerulea tollens rorantia barba,
>   "qua" dixit "repares arte, requiris, apes?
> obrue mactati corpus tellure iuuenci:
>   quod petis a nobis, obrutus ille dabit."
> iussa facit pastor; feruent examina putri
>   de boue: mille animas una necata dedit.

Aristaeus was weeping because he had seen that the bees, killed along with their offspring, had abandoned the honeycombs once begun. Having consoled him with difficulty as he grieved, his sea-blue mother added these final words to her speech: "Stop your tears, boy! Proteus will alleviate your losses, and will give you the means whereby you may restore what has perished. Nonetheless, lest he deceive you with his shapes transformed, let strong bonds hinder his two hands." The youth came to the prophet, and having seized the watery old man's arms, loosened by sleep, he binds them. That one, transforming, alters his appearance through his art; soon, restrained by bonds, he returns to his own limbs, and raising his mouth, dripping with its sea-blue beard, said, "You ask with what skill you may restore your bees? Cover the body of a slaughtered bull with earth; what you seek from me, that buried one will provide." The shepherd performs the orders; teeming swarms emerge from the rotting cow. One slaughtered cow gave forth a thousand souls.[31]

The first and most obvious difference between Ovid's Aristaeus and Vergil's is of course length – 18 lines in Ovid to Vergil's 242 hexameters. Numerous features of Ovid's Aristaeus narrative nonetheless show Ovid's involvement with the Vergilian model – in fact, the extreme disparity in the lengths of the two versions is, if anything, underscored by the many points of contact that often can themselves be read as drawing attention to or commenting on the disparity. First of all, Ovid follows much the same sequence of events: Aristaeus cries at the loss of his bees and approaches his mother for help; his mother consoles him and sends him to Proteus, with advice on how to handle the tricky *uates*; Aristaeus tames Proteus, who offers advice on how to regenerate the bees; Aristaeus slaughters the cow as instructed, and his bees are restored. Several aspects of Ovid's diction and descriptive style also show his close reading of Vergil: thus, his opening description of the bee-keeper, *flebat Aristaeus* (F. 1.363), succinctly summarizes the most striking feature of Aristaeus' presentation in the fourth *Georgic*. Vergil introduces Aristaeus as *multa querens* (G. 4.320), and has the nymph Arethusa echo this characterization when, after investigating the odd sound heard by the weaving nymphs (*luctus Aristaei*, "the grief of Aristaeus," 4.350), she reports the cause to Cyrene (4.355–6): *tristis Aristaeus ... / stat lacrimans* ("sad Aristaeus stands here crying"); in response, Cyrene welcomes the youth into her divine home in a reception redolent of Homeric hospitality.[32] In a breathtakingly brief summary of the lengthy Vergilian scene, Ovid's Cyrene consoles her son in one half of a single hexameter (*aegre solata dolentem*, F. 1.365); and she seems to comment metapoetically, on Ovid's behalf, upon the abundant tears shed by her son in the *Georgics* when she adds a few final words (*addidit haec dictis ultima uerba suis*, 366). Her first words of direct speech suggest that her son's tearfulness has gone on long enough – *siste, puer, lacrimas!* (367) – and so not only acknowledge her son's tears as described here but also, with an air of tendentious critique, look back to his self-pitying and reproachful address in Vergil (G. 4.321–32).[33] Ovid also reveals his confidence that his reader knows the Vergilian intertext in omitting Cyrene's name from his version of the scene; he simply calls her *genetrix* (F. 1.365) – and so echoes Vergil's only use of the word in the *Georgics*, to designate Cyrene (G. 4.363). Likewise, Ovid's Aristaeus and Proteus both receive designations which recall their identities in Vergil: Aristaeus is *iuuenis* (F. 1.371; cf. G. 4.360, 423, and 445), and Proteus is *uates* (F. 1.371; cf. G. 4.387, 392, and 450);[34] when Ovid gives the seer a blue beard (*caerulea …* *barba*, F. 1.375), he draws on the Vergilian description *caeruleus Proteus* (G. 4.388; Cyrene is speaking). Ovid also follows Vergil in having Cyrene describe how Proteus is to be bound (F. 1.370): *impediant geminas uincula* *firma manus* ("Strong bonds should restrict his two hands") ~ (G. 4.405): *correptum manibus uinclisque tenebis* ("you will catch and control him by means of hands and bonds").[35] The fact that, in Ovid, it is only possible to bind Proteus because he is sleeping (*somno*, F. 1.371) encapsulates the much fuller description of the sleeping Proteus given by Vergil (G. 4.403–14), who frames his description of the seer with the repetition of the word *somno* (404 and 415). Finally, Ovid closes his version of the story by referring to Aristaeus as *pastor* (F. 1.379) – thus employing at the end of this scene the very word with which Vergil had opened his version (*pastor Aristaeus*, G. 4.317).[36]

Clearly, then, Ovid takes a certain pleasure in drawing attention to the simultaneous repetition and compression of the Vergilian episode; indeed, such treatment is a hallmark of Ovidian intertextuality.[37] In other ways, Ovid revises details in Vergil's narrative to complement the much smaller scale of his own version: in the fourth *Georgic*, the information Aristaeus receives from Proteus to explain the death of his bees fills over seventy verses (G. 4.453–527) and offers no clear guidance. Rather, his speech must be interpreted in turn by Cyrene, who directs her son to perform a sacrifice of four bulls and four heifers to the Nymphs (4.534–43); it is from the carcasses of these slaughtered animals that the bees are to be regenerated. In the Ovidian version, the number of sacrificial animals is scaled down, in keeping with the smaller scale of the rest of the narrative: now the sacrifice of only one cow is called for, and the result is a thousand bees (*mille animas* *una necata dedit*, F. 1.380).[38] Most striking of all is the narrative economy with which Ovid's Proteus speaks: he himself tells Aristaeus quite clearly, and in three clipped verses (F. 1.376–8), that a sacrifice is required, and he assures Aristaeus of a positive result.

The most glaring difference, however, is not a question of compression or miniaturization, but of wholesale absence: Ovid excludes entirely the Orpheus story that provides the emotional centre of the *Georgics* version. In Vergil, Proteus' explanation of the source of Aristaeus' problem is the sole theme of his long speech; in it, he describes the death of Eurydice – caused by Aristaeus himself (*G.* 4.453–9); Orpheus' lamentation and eventual descent to the underworld to retrieve her (460–84); his fatal retrospection and her disappearance (485–503); his subsequent inconsolable mourning (504–20); and its abrupt end, brought about by the violent assault of the Bacchants rejected by the singer, whose severed head still calls Eurydice's name (520–7). The intricate relationship between this story and the demise of Aristaeus' bees is replicated in the very structure of Vergil's narrative: Proteus' speech is framed by descriptions of what at first appear to be an inexplicable loss and its eventual miraculous solution. Cyrene further clarifies the interrelationship by elucidating Proteus' opaque wisdom: it seems the Nymphs in sympathy with Orpheus have brought about the destruction of Aristaeus' bees (532–4);[39] and in addition to instructing her son to perform a sacrifice to them (534–6), Cyrene also tells him to offer a sheep to the spirit of Orpheus himself, and a calf to Eurydice (545–7). None of this complex inset narrative survives in the Ovidian version,[40] aside from the fact that, as we have seen, the bare frame around Ovid's Aristaeus, consisting of two rhetorical questions, makes mournful mention of sheep sacrifice alongside that of cattle (*F.* 1.362 and 383–4). The story of Orpheus and Eurydice – and of Aristaeus' implication in their tragedy – has not been miniaturized or compressed; rather, it is entirely gone.

4. No More Sorrow, No More Tears

The absence of any trace in the *Fasti* of the inset narrative about Orpheus and Eurydice – and about Aristaeus' complicity in it – can be explained in any number of ways: perhaps Ovid thought it would be too much of a distraction from his discussion of sacrifice; perhaps he wanted to downplay the miraculousness of the *bugonia*, and so reduced the story to a matter of clear instructions, succinctly given and effectively followed. The moral of Ovid's version of the story is clear: Aristaeus and we live in a world in which gods are wrathful and powerful, and humans can only obey.

I want to conclude this discussion with another possibility, however. I acknowledge at the outset that the possibility I propose is based on nothing more than a hypothesis, and one that I suspect can never be proved; but I offer it as one way to think about Ovid's poetic goals. I also recognize the risk involved in building a hypothesis on the basis of nothing, *nihil ex nihilo*, because that is certainly one way to think about the absence of Orpheus and Eurydice from Ovid's Aristaeus narrative; but I suggest instead that the absence we have just observed, along with the apparent clarity that results, are both effects created by Ovid precisely so that his readers will sense incomplete closure in his version. In other words, Ovid wants us to notice the absence of Orpheus and Eurydice, as well as the wholesale bowdleriza-tion of the Aristaeus story, and to seek his meaning in the choice.

The question of revision offers a potential solution – that is, if we under-stand the Aristaeus narrative in the *Fasti* as one of the changes Ovid made while in exile. In fact, a version of this argument has already, if inadvertently, been made, when in 1976 Eckhard Lefèvre published an article suggest-ing that the entire section on animal sacrifice, beginning immediately after the list of possible etymologies for the Agonalia and continuing through all the specific examples of animals appropriate for sacrifice (*F.* 1.336–456), is a late addition. Lefèvre's argument centres on two primary themes: 1) the reliance of the Golden Age–vegetarianism motif here on the speech of Pythagoras at *Met.* 15.96–142, indicative of the relative lateness of the composition of this section of the *Fasti*; and 2) the aetiological narrative that Ovid offers for ass sacrifice, consisting of a heretofore unattested myth about Priapus' attempted rape of the nymph Lotis (*F.* 1.391–440).[41] The latter of these is the focus of Lefèvre's analysis, as he argues for reading the similar frustrated rape story of *Fasti* Book 6, that of Vesta by Priapus, as the earlier of the two, and hypothesizes that Ovid considered while in exile removing the Vesta and Priapus episode because of its possible indelicacy, but salvaging much of the material in it by adding the Lotis and Priapus story to Book 1. We are left, suggests Lefèvre, with evidence of the incom-plete revision, presumably the result of Ovid's untimely death.[42] Lefèvre has relatively little to say about the Aristaeus narrative itself, aside from using it as part of his argument for dependence upon another part of the speech of Pythagoras: Pythagoras' description of the rebirth of bees through *bugonia* at *Met.* 15.364–6 is coherent with and fully motivated by the remainder of Pythagoras' speech, while in the *Fasti*, argues Lefèvre, the *bugonia* serves no meaningful function.[43]

Lefèvre does consider Ovid's Aristaeus narrative part of the post-exilic revision, then, but sees only its "negative image," so to speak – that is, he critiques its apparent lack of contribution to the aetiological passage, but does not question its very inclusion, which simply supports his argu-ment for the priority of *Metamorphoses* Book 15. What is missing here, I believe, is a fuller engagement with the dynamics of genre and Ovidian metatextuality. The suggestion by Servius that the Aristaeus epyllion is a substitute for an earlier "praises of Gallus" (*laudes Galli*, opening note on *G.* 4), and, thus, evidence of a revision intended to avoid the ire of Octa-vian, has been convincingly shown by modern scholars to evoke a phan-tom; instead, there is now a general consensus that the Aristaeus epyllion itself *is* in some sense the *laudes Galli*.[44] In its depiction of the erotic loss and lament of Orpheus, who is figured as the prototype of all poetry but of elegy in particular, we can trace the shadowy outline of Gallus himself;[45]

his failure to reanimate Eurydice and his own violent death are set out by Vergil in stark contrast to the eventual success of Aristaeus, who turns to powers greater and wiser than he, namely his mother and Proteus, for guidance. His achievement is apparently miraculous, at least insofar as his bees appear to be regenerated miraculously; but beneath this marvellous surface are remorse, submission, and piety, brought together to do the real work of atonement.

And Ovid? For the elegist Ovid, Gallus was clearly a model of fundamental importance, the author of the first *Amores* and the personification of erotic desire and its poetic expression. Though it is unlikely the two men ever met – Ovid was only about sixteen or seventeen at the time of Gallus' suicide – Ovid knew Gallus' work well, and knew as well the central role he played for Vergil, as a character in the *Bucolics* and as the inspiration behind unrequited poetic desire and tragic loss in the *Georgics*. For the exiled poet, no doubt, Gallus must have seemed an unfortunate forerunner, condemned to a fate even harsher than Ovid's own.[46] When challenged to revise the *Fasti* in exile, and in the hope of winning an imperial reprieve, I suggest, Ovid realized that the obedient success of Aristaeus could serve as a model for his own longing – that Aristaeus' miracle could prefigure his own. The inclusion of Orpheus, on the other hand, could be dangerous and self-defeating; after all, the death of the prototypical poet of erotic love and of lament could only remind his readers of Gallus' demise, no doubt deemed deserved by the powers of the age. Better, then, to exclude any hint of the dangerous poet entirely, and to focus attention on the unambiguous success of Aristaeus – unambiguous success that was never, in the end, to befall Ovid himself.[47]

NOTES

A much shorter and more tentative version of this paper was delivered at the Vergilian Society's 2017 *Symposium Cumanum*, on the theme of Vergil and elegy. I am deeply indebted to the organizers of the symposium, Micah Myers and Alison Keith, for bringing together a stimulating and exciting collection of papers, and for their encouragement regarding my contribution.

1 Syme 1978: 35.
2 Miller 1982, 1991, and 1992; Fantham 1983, 1985, and 1992; Barchiesi 1997b; Newlands 1995; Hinds 1987, following a course set seventy years before by Heinze 1919. (I list here only the seminal works; others by the same authors will be noted when relevant in subsequent notes).

3 Beard 1987.

4 Robinson 2011 uses a colourful metaphor to describe this view as a "conception of the *Fasti* as a chocolate-box of narratives, with each one separate and separable from the rest" (8).

5 I make a preliminary attempt to capture such phenomena as forms of "narrative patterning" in Boyd 2000. The segmentation of the narrative that I describe may well be the result, at least in part, of the work done by Merkel 1841 to impose the framework of the Roman calendar explicitly onto Ovid's poem, with the resulting visual breaks and the subtitle-like headings that appear in all subsequent editions. The benefit of Merkel's effort in this regard cannot be overestimated; at the same time, it is worth remembering that Ovid's first readers would probably have found such additions intrusive.

6 These include Green 2004 on Book 1; Robinson 2011 on Book 2; Heyworth 2019 on Book 3; Fantham 1998 on Book 4; and Littlewood 2006 on Book 6. Bömer 1958 is their indispensable predecessor.

7 Feeney 1992, developing some of the insights of Beard 1987; see also Hinds 1992.

8 And most likely in tandem with the *Metamorphoses*: see Fantham 1998: 3–4, following Hinds 1987a and Bömer 1958. The desire to identify precisely which parts of the *Fasti* can be dated to a revision, and the accompanying tendency to overvalue or discount some lines or references at the expense of others, has long exercised scholars: for an overview, see Bömer 1957: 17–20, expanded upon by Fantham 1985. Green (2004: 15–24) reviews the evidence and arguments, and proceeds with caution. On the dating of Ovid's exile, see now Hutchinson 2017.

9 I cite Ovid's *Fasti* from Alton, Wormell, and Courtney 1985, and Vergil's *Aeneid* from Mynors 1969. Translations are my own.

10 See, e.g., *Pont.* 2.1, 2.5, and 4.8. Bömer (1957: 17–18) details the evidence for the interrelated careers of Ovid and Germanicus; see also Fantham 1985; and cf. Knox 2004b: 15–17 and Myers 2014.

11 Most scholars limit the designation "proem" to the first twenty-six verses of *Fasti* Book 1, in yet another instance of arbitrary segmentation. Given the explicit references to Germanicus occurring well beyond this passage, however, I hope to demonstrate that a more expansive identification is appropriate here. See also Newlands 1995, 40, arguing for an association between the earlier addresses to Germanicus and the astronomical excursus.

12 See especially Fantham 1985, arguing for the possibility that Germanicus' poem was known to Ovid; also Barchiesi 1997b: 179. On the literary character of the passage, see Kenney 2002: 54–6.

13 See Miller 1991: 143–4, for an overview of the issue, together with Robinson 2011: 51–6, who defends the integrity of Book 2's opening to the composition of the book, framing it as a "delayed literary introduction."

14 On these etymologies, see Bömer 1958, ad loc.; Porte 1985: 209–13; Maltby
   1991 s.vv.; Miller 1992: 14–22; Green 2004 on *F.* 1.319–32.

15 Only the Parilia receives a comparable number of possible explanations (6): *F.*
   4.783–806.

16 Cf. Serv. ad *A.* 1.334: *hostiae dicuntur sacrificia quae ab his fiunt qui in hostem*
   pergunt, uictimae uero sacrificia quae post uictoriam fiunt.

17 Lefèvre (1976: 40–9) discusses the association between the Golden Age and
   sacrifice in this episode and shows that there is a close relationship between
   this passage and *Met.* 15.111–26; his primary aim is to demonstrate that the
   Metamorphoses passage is an earlier composition than that in the *Fasti*; see
   also Fantham 1992. Newlands 2020 revisits the similarities shared by the two
   passages, but her primary focus is on Ovid's intertextual engagement with
   Callimachus and Vergil in the creation of his own distinctive didactic program.
   She does not examine, however, the problems and possibilities of revision that
   I consider here, or the potential applicability of the episode to Ovid himself.

18 See Green 2004 ad loc. and cf., e.g., *B.* 4.37–9; *G.* 1.136–7; *Met.* 1.94–6; cf.
   Catull. 64.1–15; and see Thomas 1988a on *G.* 1.50. On the Golden Age in
   Vergil and Tibullus, see Gardner in this volume, similarly emphasizing the role
   of temporality in such depictions.

19 Cf. Thomas 1988a, ad locc.; Mynors 1990, ad locc.

20 Cf. Putnam 1979: 98–9; Thomas 1988a, ad loc.; Mynors 1990, ad loc.; Ross
   1987: 115–21.

21 See Thomas 1988a, ad loc. on the ambiguous syntax of the line; I follow his
   interpretation here.

22 Note also the proliferation of imperfect and pluperfect forms, in contrast to the
   present form *aperit* (347) used to describe sacrifice.

23 See also *F.* 1.327: *an, quia praeuisos in aqua timet hostia cultros …?* ("Or
   [is it] because the victim fears the knife seen beforehand [reflected] in the
   water?"). Miller (1992: 18–20) demonstrates how Ovid has here incorporated
   a Callimachean image (*Aet.* fr. 10–11 Pf.) into his depiction of the sacrificial
   animal's perspective on the knife.

24 See especially *G.* 1.125–46, with Thomas 1988a, ad loc.

25 On allusion as correction, see Thomas 1986: 185–9.

26 Myers (2014: 727–8) discusses the important role of sacrifice (and of imagery
   related to it) in Ovid's exile poetry. Green 2008, looking beyond this passage to
   others in both the *Metamorphoses* and the *Fasti*, argues for an ambiguous view
   of Ovid's treatment of sacrifice overall.

27 The Agonalia are celebrated three other times during the year, on 17 March, 21
   May, and 11 December; we do not have Ovid's discussion of the last of these,
   but it is worth noting that there is no mention of it at the appropriate time in
   Book 3, and in Book 5, he says only "He who seeks to know what the Agonia is
   should return to Janus; but this holiday has this time in the calendar, too" (*Ad*

Ianum redeat, qui quaerit Agonia quid sint / quae tamen in fastis hoc quoque tempus habent, F. 5.721–2).

28 For guidance to the vast bibliography on the significance of this episode (as well as of the questions surrounding its authenticity), see Griffin 1979; Jacobson 1984; Ross 1987, 214–33; Thomas 1988a, ad loc.; and cf. Conte 1986: 130–40, and Conte 2001. See also Nappa 2005: 191–218, and Thibodeau 2011: 191–201, for general discussion.

29 Feeney 2004a: 7–11, and Newlands 2020 are the exceptions. On the appearance of what is roughly the same mythological narrative in both Vergil and Ovid, Feeney 2004a: 11 (following an observation made by Zetzel 1983) notes that by making this episode the first mythological tale in the poem Ovid characteristically begins where Vergil had ended; see also Newlands 2020: 370. Other meaningful interaction between the two texts has generally been limited to a cataloguing of verbal similarities: in addition to Bömer, see Lefèvre 1976 and Fantham 1992. This lack of interest owes much to a scholarly debate about the Vergilian *bugonia*, beginning with Habinek 1990, arguing for *bugonia* as sacrifice, and countered by Thomas 1991; see also Dyson 1996, Morgan 1999. The most thorough treatment of sacrifice in the *Georgics* is by Gale 2000: 101–12. The best, and simplest, expression of the status quo is probably to be found in Nappa's words: "Here [i.e., at the end of the *Georgics*] … *bugonia* is a kind of sacrifice" (2005: 212). The simplicity of his words is belied by the measured ambiguity of the phrase "a kind of." For two recent general treatments that circumvent this debate, see now Glauthier 2020 and Osorio 2020.

30 On Ovid as Vergil's best reader, see O'Hara 1996b; Boyd 2002.

31 *una necata* is feminine in agreement with *boue* earlier in v. 380; in the preceding couplet, however, the gender of the animal to be sacrificed is masculine (*mactati corpus … iuuenci; obrutus ille*).

32 On the Homeric details in Vergil's description, see Thomas 1988a, on *G.* 4.376–9.

33 For another similarly matter-of-fact revision by Ovid of an emotional outburst in Vergil, see Boyd 1990; and cf. Boyd 2010: 230.

34 Vergil's use of *uates* to describe Proteus is a Callimachean touch: see Thomas 1988a, on *G.* 4.387; cf. also *Am.* 3.12.35, *Protea quid referam?* (in a list of stories illustrating the *fecunda licentia uatum*).

35 See also her words at *G.* 4.396, *hic tibi, nate, prius uinclis capiendus*.

36 Cf. Green 2004, ad loc. This is a nice inversion of the reciprocity observed by Feeney 2004a (above, n29).

37 For a more complex example of this technique, see Boyd 2017: 213–36.

38 On Ovid's play with scale in this episode, see also Newlands 2020: 375–6.

39 Thomas 1988a, on *G.* 4.532 explains that the Nymphs mentioned by Cyrene are to be identified with the Dryades who mourn Eurydice's death at *G.*

4.460–1; but it is tempting to think that Cyrene might also mean to include the Nymphs with whom she is weaving (as well as herself!) when he seeks her help.

40 Aristaeus is also absent from the Orpheus and Eurydice episode in the *Metamorphoses*, although Ovid does mention the Vergilian snakebite there (G. 4.457–9 ~ *Met*. 10.8–10). The allusion to different details in two different works in the Ovidian corpus may recall the distribution of originally connected narrative details by Vergil: see Hardie 1984.

41 At *Met*. 9.346–8, Ovid alludes to a very different version of the story, in which Lotis is transformed into a flower in order to escape Priapus.

42 Lefèvre 1976; see also Fantham 1983, esp. 201–6, for a survey of scholarly hypotheses about the relationship of these two episodes.

43 Lefèvre 1976: 46–7.

44 In addition to the selection of scholarly discussions listed in n27, see also Gagliardi 2013 for an exhaustive bibliography and catalogue of thematic connections between Gallus and Orpheus.

45 Havener 2019: 132–9, offers a persuasive discussion of the complex political manoeuvres surrounding Gallus' demise. For a measured assessment of Gallus' role in the creation of Roman love elegy, see Gibson 2012. My phrase "the shadowy outline of Gallus" is inspired by the title of Gagliardi 2013.

46 Barchiesi and Hardie (2010: 65–70) discuss Ovid's reception of Gallus' career, especially in *Tristia* Book 2; see also Claassen 2017 for a general discussion of Gallus' presence of Ovid's exile poetry.

47 Myers (2014: 733) notes Ovid's promise to compose "poems full of joy" (*carmina laetitiae … plena, Tr*. 5.1.42) if he is recalled from exile, and his comments elsewhere in the exile poetry on the challenge of giving up lament (e.g., *Pont*. 3.4.45–50).

10

Lamenting Tibullus as Literary Critique: Elegy and Vergilian Epic in Ovid, *Amores* 3.9

JUDITH P. HALLETT

In the first couplet of his epigram lamenting the death of the Roman elegist Tibullus, the Augustan poet Domitius Marsus indirectly acknowledges that Tibullus and Vergil died in the same year, which we can date precisely to 19 BCE. For he portrays them as sent simultaneously to Elysium, remarking: *Te quoque Vergilio comitem non aequa, Tibulle / Mors iuuenem campos misit ad Elysios, / ne foret aut elegis molles qui fleret amores / aut caneret forti regia bella pede*[1] ("Unjust Death also sent you, Tibullus, as a companion to Vergil while you were still a young man, to the Elysian fields, so that there would not be anyone to bewail sensitive love affairs in elegiac verses, nor to sing of kingly wars in epic metre"). *Amores* 3.9, Ovid's elegiac lament for Tibullus, similarly represents the dead Tibullus as bound for the Elysian fields, in its thirtieth couplet, 59–60, with "if however anything from us remains other than a name or a shade, Tibullus will be in the Elysian valley" (*in Elysia ualle*). But Ovid does not mention Vergil by name, much less observe that Vergil and Tibullus shared a death date, or a residence in the afterlife.

Yet in line 25 of Ovid's elegiac lament, a dactylic hexameter line like all of the lines in Homer's own epics, Ovid cites Homer among the poets who died in spite of their literary gifts, calling him by a metrically compatible toponymic (25–6): *adice Maeoniden, a quo ceu fonte perenni / uatum Pieriis ora rigantur aquis* ("Add Homer of Maeonia to the list, from whom, as if from an eternally flowing fountain, the mouths of bards are moistened with Pierian waters"). In two subsequent couplets, 29–32, Ovid alludes to Homer's *Iliad* and *Odyssey*, albeit without actually naming them either (29–32): *durant, uatis opus, Troiani fama laboris / tardaque nocturno tela retexta dolo. / sic Nemesis longum, sic Delia nomen habebunt, / altera cura recens, altera primus amor* ("They endure, the literary effort of the prophetic bard, the renown of the Trojan toil, and the slow weaving unravelled by a nightly trick. Thus Nemesis, thus Delia will have a long-lived name, one woman a recent desire, the other his first love"). In this characteristically learned way, and in a tone of humorous exaggeration, Ovid likens Homer's two monumental epics to Tibullus' two slender books of love elegies, the first featuring a female lover he calls Delia, the second her successor Nemesis.

My paper argues, however, that even though Ovid explicitly refers to Homer, and not to Vergil, in *Amores* 3.9, he nonetheless alludes to Vergil's *Aeneid*: hardly surprising in the light of Tibullus' and Vergil's deaths in the same year. I maintain, too, that Ovid seeks to critique – subtly, playfully, and at times subversively – aspects of this Augustan epic, much as he critiques, elsewhere in this poem, aspects of Tibullus' elegies: through intertextual evocations, presumably perceived by the literarily discerning members of his audience, that call attention to what both poets do not say. Ovid's Tibullan echoes, previously observed by other scholars, along with what I interpret as the message of these echoes, warrant our close scrutiny.[2] So do Ovid's allusions to Vergil's *Aeneid*. To my mind, Ovid is quoting Tibullus' actual words to point up Tibullus' own hyperbolic self-representation and lack of vatic veracity – and to rewrite Tibullus' own elegiac scenarios to underscore his other literary weaknesses. Similarly, he evokes Vergil's *Aeneid* to promote his literary agenda of equating the genres of epic and elegy, in part by calling attention to the shortcomings of what and how Vergil wrote.

In a single couplet, 33–4, Ovid addresses the dead Tibullus, anaphorically asking him three rhetorical questions in a tricolonic crescendo: *quid uos sacra iuuant? quid nunc Aegyptia prosunt / sistra? quid in uacuo secubuisse toro?* ("How do holy rites help you (plural)? How are your Egyptian rattles of profit now? How did it benefit to have slept apart in an empty bed?"). Ovid's interrogatively posed, tripartite assertion that the worship of the Egyptian goddess Isis has not protected Tibullus (and, with the plural *uos*, has not protected other bards) from death pointedly recall Tibullus 1.3.23–6. In these two couplets the poet/speaker Tibullus, representing himself as seriously ill in Phaeacia, similarly queries the worth of his beloved Delia's devotion to Isis; he also frames his inquiry as a tricolonic crescendo, albeit packed into one question, addressing Delia herself: *quid tua nunc Isis mihi, Delia, quid mihi prosunt / illa tua totiens aera repulsa manu, / quidue, pie dum sacra colis, pureque lauari / te memini et puro secubuisse toro?* ("How is your Isis now of profit to me, Delia, how do those bronze cymbals struck so often by your hand benefit me, or how, while you perform holy rites dutifully, did it help that you, I recall, washed yourself in an untainted fashion and slept apart in an untainted bed?").

Ovid's more tersely worded series of questions therefore shares rhetorical flourishes and sentence structure with Tibullus' single question. Ovid's words feature several identical verbal elements as well: the thrice-repeated interrogative pronoun *quid*, the noun *sacra*, the verb form *prosunt*, the adverb *nunc*, and the phrase *secubuisse toro*. So, too, Tibullus portrays Delia's devotion to Isis, particularly her ritual abstinence from sexual relations, which prevented their erotic couplings when they both dwelled in Rome, as of no avail to him in his illness while abroad in Phaeacia. Ovid likewise portrays such devotion, particularly the required sexual abstinence, as unable to prevent Tibullus' death. Nevertheless, merely to judge from the evidence of Tibullus' other poems in Books 1 and 2, and as Samuel Huskey has observed, Tibullus portrays himself as surviving this life-threatening disease while abroad, as returning to resume his affair with the woman he addresses in this poem, Delia, and as enjoying a second liaison with another woman, Nemesis.[3] Ovid thus spotlights the exaggerated, self-absorbed, and ultimately inaccurate nature of Tibullus' assertions in 1.3, exposing their content as anything but the veracity expected from a *uates* worthy of the name.

The next six lines, 47–52, evoke, again in briefer compass, eight lines (3–10) in Tibullus 1.3. Here Ovid opines that Tibullus' death at home in Rome was preferable to dying in Phaeacia apart from his mother and sister:

> sed tamen hoc melius, quam si Phaecia tellus
>   ignotum uili supposuisset humo.
> hinc certe madidos fugientis pressit ocellos
>   mater et in cineres ultima dona tulit;
> hinc soror in partem misera cum matre doloris
>   uenis inornatas dilaniata comas.

But nevertheless this situation is better than if the Phaeacian land had placed you, unknown there under cheap soil. Here indeed your mother closed your wet eyes as you were fleeing from life, and your mother brought the final gifts to your ashes, here indeed your sister, torn of uncombed tresses, came with your sorrowing mother to share the grief.

Ovid's strategically positioned reference to Phaeacia (as the fifth foot dactyl in the line, its position in line 3 of the Tibullan passage as well); his characterization of Tibullus as *ignotum*, unknown, in a Phaeacian burial site; and his mention of Tibullus' *mater*, *soror*, and sister's torn and uncombed hair recall Tibullus' own words. These echoes presume, too, that at least some members of Ovid's literarily sophisticated audience were expected to recall Tibullus' own words. Tibullus renders those words more powerful through significant repetition of phrases in a pentameter by the following hexameter line (1.3.3–8):

> me tenet ignotis aegrum Phaeacia terris:
> > abstineas auidas, Mors, precor, atra manus.
>
> abstineas, Mora atra, precor: non hic mihi mater
> > quae legat in maestos ossa perusta sinus.
>
> non soror, Assyrios cineri quae dedat odores
> > et fleat effusis ante sepulcra comis.

Phaeacia holds me, ill, in unknown lands, black Death, may you keep away your greedy hands, I pray, may you keep away, I pray, black Death: there is no mother here to gather my burnt bones in her sad embraces, no sister to bestow Assyrian scents on my ash, and weep before my tomb with dishevelled hair.

As he does when echoing Tibullus 1.3 earlier, Ovid acknowledges that Tibullus did not die in Phaeacia; here Ovid asserts in addition that Tibullus did die at home, accorded the rituals of mourning, performed by his mother and sister, that he feared would be denied him by his death abroad.

Ovid then builds upon these two intertextual evocations to set up a third, in this instance parodic, allusion to Tibullus' poetry in the next three couplets (53–8):

> cumque tuis sua iunxerant Nemesisque priorque
> > oscula nec solos destituere rogos.
>
> Delia discedens, "felicius" inquit "amata
> > sum tibi; uixisti, dum tuus ignis eram."
>
> cui Nemesis "quid" ait "tibi sunt mea damna dolori?
> > me tenuit moriens deficiente manu."

And, with your kinswomen, Nemesis and her predecessor had joined their own kisses, and did not abandon the lonely funeral pyres. Delia, departing, said, "I have been loved by you more happily; you were alive, as long as I was your fiery passion." To whom Nemesis responded, "Why are my losses a source of sorrow to you? Dying he held me with his weakening hand."

Here Ovid quotes Tibullus 1.1.59–60, in which the poet-speaker says to Delia: *te spectem, suprema mihi cum uenerit hora: / te teneam moriens, deficiente manu* ("May I look upon you when the final hour will have come to me. Dying may I hold you, with weakening hand").

By merely assigning words to Delia and Nemesis – a pentameter line plus two words in the preceding hexameter to Delia, a pentameter line plus six words in the preceding hexameter to Nemesis – Ovid breaks with Tibullus' practice of representing these two women in his elegies. For Tibullus never assigns any words of her own to either of them. It is noteworthy, too, that Tibullus only mentions Delia in his first book of elegies, and only mentions Nemesis in his second: they never appear in the same book, much less the same poem. Most significant, Ovid portrays the two women as verbally attacking one another over which of them Tibullus loved more and assigns Nemesis words that Tibullus employs at 1.1.60 when hoping to die with *Delia* at his side.

Ovid may well have had a serious artistic purpose in creating this fictitious conflict between these two female literary figures, scrupulously kept separate from one another in Tibullus' elegiac *corpus*, by inventing what we might call an amatory catfight at Tibullus' funeral. After all, this dispute between Delia and Nemesis provides a further rationale for elevating Tibullus' slight erotic *opus* to the literary level of Homer's epics about the mythic Trojan conflict and its contentious aftermath. But by placing the words Tibullus uses to express love for one of these women in the mouth of the other woman, to support her insistence that Tibullus loved her more, Ovid appears to be critiquing, subtly and humorously, Tibullus as a love elegist. For Ovid thereby highlights Tibullus' failure to endow the two women on whom many of his elegies centre with dramatic agency and energy, and indeed to differentiate his two female love objects from one another.

Ovid begins *Amores* 3.9 by personifying *Elegia* as a mourning mother, immediately after equating her loss of Tibullus to the loss of two male heroes from Homeric epic, Memnon and Achilles, by their own mothers (3.9.1–4): *Memnona si mater, mater plorauit Achillem, / et tangunt magnas tristia fata deas, / flebilis indignos, Elegia, solue capillos! / a, nimis ex uero nunc tibi nomen erit!* ("If his mother lamented Memnon, if his mother lamented Achilles, and sorrowful fates touch the great goddesses, tearful Elegy, loosen your unworthy hair! Oh, now your name will be extremely truthful!"). With these details, he seeks to compare and contrast the genres of elegy and epic, much as he does in earlier elegies such as *Amores* 1.9.

But I would contend that in this elegy about Elegy herself, and elegy itself, Ovid also critiques Vergil as an epic poet so as to elevate each genre to the level of the other, only to deflate them both. The workings of this abstract critical process thereby resemble the metrical operations of the half-epic elegiac couplet itself, as defined by Ovid in *Amores* 1.1 (27–8): *sex mihi surgat opus numeris, in quinque residat: / ferrea cum uestris bella ualete modis* ("Let my work rise in six measures, and let it fall again in five: farewell iron wars with your metres!"). I would argue, too, that Ovid does so by faulting

Vergil's epic, just as he does Tibullus' elegies, for its literary shortcomings: through playful, but unmistakable, allusions to Vergil's *Aeneid* that underscore its omissions and inaccuracies, not in the dramatic force of its narrative, but in its delineation of a major female character, Aeneas' mother Venus, and the values informing this portrait of Venus.

The allusions to Vergil's *Aeneid* in *Amores* 3.9 include Ovid's description at 7–14 of another character said to have mourned Tibullus, Venus' son Cupid, as well as two briefer descriptions of the grief displayed by Venus herself: first in the next couplet, 15–16, then in a later couplet, 45–6. Lines 7–14 culminate in an address to Aeneas' own sorrowing son, called, by name, *pulcher Iule*, while equating Cupid's grief over Tibullus' death with Cupid's earlier sorrow at the death of his "brother Aeneas." Significantly, Ovid does not use Cupid's actual name, merely labelling him "Venus' boy" (7–14):

> Ecce puer Veneris fert euersamque pharetram
> et fractos arcus et sine luce facem;
> adspice, demissis ut eat miserabilis alis
> pectoraque infesta tundat aperta manu!
> excipiunt lacrimas sparsi per colla capilli,
> oraque singultu concutiente sonant.
> fratris in Aeneae sic illum funere dicunt
> egressum tectis, pulcher Iule, tuis.

Look, Venus' boy carries an overturned quiver and broken bows and a torch without a light. Look at how he goes, pitiable with downturned wings, and pounds his bared chest with a troubled hand. His locks of hair, spread over his neck, absorb his tears, and his mouth resounds with a shaking sob. Thus they say that he left your house at the death of his brother Aeneas, beautiful Iulus.

In an essay on Augustan maternal ideology, I have argued that Vergil's *Aeneid* offers a sympathetic, but anomalous, portrayal of the goddess Venus in her role as mother so as to render her a fitting *Aeneadum genetrix*, mother of Aeneas' descendants. I contend that Vergil accomplishes this aim by stressing the similarities between his Venus and an admired historical woman of his own acquaintance who claimed descent from Aeneas: Augustus' sister Octavia. Wed successively to Gaius Claudius Marcellus and Augustus' fellow triumvir (and their cousin on the Julian side) Mark Antony, Octavia was remembered in Vergil's own biography for fainting, and only reviving with difficulty, when she heard Vergil read his tribute to her recently deceased son Marcellus at the end of *Aeneid* Book 6.[4]

Octavia was also remembered by ancient authors for her impressive if not totally successful efforts at rearing and fostering close bonds among the children of her own blended family, which numbered her two sons and a daughter by Marcellus, her two daughters by Antony, and four of Antony's offspring by other women – one by his previous wife Fulvia, three by his paramour Cleopatra – and thereby displaying exemplary devotion to her, notoriously unfaithful, husband.[5] I read Vergil's portrait of Venus as similarly emphasizing her endeavours at fostering familial connections between her offspring. Yet I regard Vergil's portrait of Venus as anomalous, since Vergil at the same time de-emphasizes Venus' non-marital sexual activities, accorded prominence by other Greek and Roman authors, in order to foreground her role as supportive mother of Aeneas, parent to his siblings Cupid and the Sicilian Eryx, and devoted wife to Vulcan.

At *Aeneid* 1.664–9, Vergil's Venus addresses Cupid as son, *nate*, twice, and specifically refers to Aeneas as Cupid's brother:

> nate, meae uires, mea magna potentia, solus
> nate, patris summi qui tela Typhoea temnis,
> ad te confugio et supplex tuo nomine posco
> frater ut Aeneas pelago tuus omnia circum
> litora iactetur odiis Iunonis acerbae,
> nota tibi, et nostro doluisti saepe dolore.

Son, source of my strength, my great might, you who alone, my son, scorn the Typhoean thunderbolts of my father Jupiter, I flee to you and make my demand in your name as a suppliant. That your brother Aeneas is tossed around from shore to shore by the sea, owing to the hatred of harsh Juno, is known to you and you have often grieved with my own grief.

So, too, at 5.23–4, Vergil has Aeneas' pilot Palinurus suggest they sail to Sicily by reminding him that Eryx, another son of Venus, lives there, referring to "the reliable shores of Eryx, belonging to a brother" (*litora ... fida ... fraterna Erycis*); in 412 he has the Trojan boxer Entellus recall for Aeneas that "your brother Eryx" (*germanus Eryx ... tuus*) formerly wore the arms of Hercules; in 630 he has the Trojan woman, Beroe, describe Sicily, where she would prefer the Trojans to settle, for Aeneas as "the territories of Eryx, belonging to your brother" (*Erycis fines fraterni*). Vergil's Venus, Palinurus, Entellus, and Beroe all characterize these two brothers as sources of personal and political support to Aeneas. Curiously, while the later Greek epic poet Nonnus claims Beroe was a daughter of Aphrodite and Adonis, and hence Aeneas' half-sister, Vergil does not include this detail.[6]

Nevertheless, Vergil does not depict Venus as entangled in adulterous liaisons of her own during the timeline of the *Aeneid* itself, contrasting her with both the god Mars and her divine husband Vulcan in that key regard.

Nor does he depict Venus as admitting to such relationships previously. Most important, the *Aeneid* never acknowledges Venus' illicit affair with Mars: even though it is related by Homer himself, in the *Odyssey*, as culminating in the capture of their Greek counterparts, Ares and Aphrodite, in chains by her cuckolded blacksmith husband; and even though it is celebrated in the opening lines of Lucretius' *De Rerum Natura*, where Venus is addressed as *Aeneadum genetrix*.[7]

Yet the *Aeneid* does identify Rome's founder Romulus and his twin Remus as Mars' own illegitimate offspring, violently sired on one of Venus' own female descendants. At *Aeneid* 1.273–4, Vergil portrays Jupiter as predicting that Ilia, a "priestess queen" (*regina sacerdos*), will bear twin offspring after being impregnated by Mars (*Marte grauis*). The name Ilia, rather than the more customary Rhea Silvia, indicates that this woman is a female descendant of Venus herself, through Ascanius/Ilus/Iulus.[8] What is more, at 8.630, when describing Aeneas' shield, Vergil alludes to Mars as the illegitimate father of Romulus and Remus, by stating that it portrays the twins as suckled by a she-wolf "in the green cave of Mars" (*uiridi … Mauortis in antro*).

By the same token, Vergil does not represent Venus as anything but faithful to Vulcan, even highlighting their mutual, physically expressed affection before Vulcan agrees to forge armour for Aeneas at the end of Book 8. At 8.373 Vergil describes her as "breathing divine love" (*diuinum adspirat amorem*) with her words to Vulcan, at 377 as calling Vulcan "dearest spouse" (*carissime coniunx*), and at 388 as "cherishing Vulcan with a soft embrace" (*amplexu molli fouet*). Earlier in that book, however, Vergil depicts King Evander relating to Aeneas how Hercules slew the fire-breathing monster Cacus and identifying Aeneas' stepfather Vulcan himself as having sired Cacus: first at 198, by remarking "Vulcan was the father to this monster" (*huic monstro Volcanus erat pater*); later, at 226, by describing an iron chain holding a large rock as forged by *arte paterna*, "his father's craftsmanship."

What is more, Vergil portrays Venus as saying nothing about her past sexual liaison with the Trojan mortal Anchises that resulted in the birth of Aeneas, although other characters identify both Venus and Anchises as Aeneas' parents. At *A.* 1.617–18, for example, Dido asks Aeneas if he is "the Aeneas whom kindly Venus bore (*alma Venus … genuit*) to Trojan Anchises; at 3.475 the seer Helenus addresses Anchises himself as "deemed worthy of proud union [*coniugio … superbo*] with Venus." At 2.594–8, Venus, addressing Aeneas with the vocative *nate*, urges him to depart from Troy and save his family members at home. But she merely refers to Anchises as Aeneas' male parent (*parentem*), without admitting that she and he have produced Aeneas together, as a couple. Similarly, while in *Aeneid* 5, as we have observed, Vergil thrice depicts characters as referring to the Sicilian

Eryx as Aeneas' brother, they do not identify Eryx' father, the Argonaut Boutes. As we noted, too, Vergil depicts Venus as referring to her son Cupid not only as *puer*, boy (much as Ovid does by calling him *puer Veneris* in *Amores* 3.9), but also as her son and Aeneas' brother. Even so, Vergil does not represent her or any other character in his epic as furnishing the identity of Cupid's father, much less indicating that Cupid and Aeneas are actually half, not full, brothers.[9]

But let us turn to the significance of Vergil's sexually sanitized Venus for Ovid *Amores* 3.9. At *A.* 1.267–8, Vergil depicts Jupiter as explaining that, and why, Aeneas' son Ascanius acquired the name Iulus. There Jupiter informs his daughter Venus that Iulus, through his descendants, will rule for three hundred years in Lavinium, and then move the kingdom to Alba Longa. He proclaims (1.267–8): *at puer Ascanius, cui nunc cognomen Iulo / additur, Ilus erat, dum res stetit Ilia regno* ... ("But the boy Ascanius, to whom now the surname Iulus is added – for he was called Ilus while the Ilian state stood ..."). Jupiter subsequently refers to Ascanius as Iulus again when prophesying, at 286–8, the birth of Augustus himself a millennium later: *nascetur pulchra Troianus origine Caesar, / imperium Oceano, famam qui terminet astris, / Iulius, a magno demissum nomen Iulo* ("A Trojan Caesar will be born of illustrious background, the kind of leader who will limit his power by the ocean, his glory by the stars, Julius, a name derived from great Iulus"). Vergil also refers to Ascanius as Iulus on several later occasions in the *Aeneid*, among them at 1.600–709, when narrating how Venus substitutes Cupid for Ascanius to make Dido become enamoured of Aeneas.

Consequently, I would maintain that at *Amores* 3.9.7–14, Ovid summons to mind Vergil's explanation for the name Iulus, with its reference to Augustus Caesar as *pulchra Troianus origine*: when addressing Aeneas' own son as *pulcher Iule*; and when representing Iulus as housing Cupid when the latter went forth to lament the loss of his brother Aeneas, sorrowing as deeply as he would, a millennium later, at the death of Tibullus.[10] Here Ovid wittily recalls the *Aeneid's* representation of Venus' sons Aeneas and Cupid as brothers, and of Venus herself as substituting Aeneas' son, her own grandson, for his uncle Cupid to achieve her amatory and ultimately political aims. Yet Ovid also, and with subversive humour, alludes to Vergil's failure to identify Aeneas as actually Cupid's half-brother by another father, as well as to provide information about who that father is, again whitewashing Venus' erotic track record.

Ovid's depiction of Venus herself at *Amores* 3.9.45–6 may playfully allude to the *Aeneid's* representation of the Sicilian Eryx as Aeneas' brother, without mentioning Venus as Eryx' mother or identifying Eryx' father. There he describes Venus at Tibullus' funeral pyre merely by stating, without mentioning her actual name: *auertit uultus, Erycis quae possidet arces; / sunt quoque qui lacrimas continuisse negant* ("She who controls the citadels of Eryx turned her face away; there are also those who say that she did not hold back tears"). While the name Eryx ordinarily refers to a Sicilian city, those familiar with the *Aeneid* would also associate it with another of Venus' sons.

Earlier in the *Amores*, we should note, Ovid also provides details about Venus' erotic dalliances, and their implications for her offspring, that Vergil does not, correcting Vergil in the process. At *Amores* 1.2.24, for example, Ovid refers to Vulcan as Cupid's stepfather (*uitricus*), providing a chariot for his triumph. Vergil never uses the noun *uitricus* for Vulcan, reserving the role if not the term itself for Vulcan's relationship to Aeneas. But Ovid is right to remind his readers that Vulcan enjoyed the same relationship with Cupid. Later, at line 51 of the same poem, Ovid characterizes Aeneas' descendant Augustus explicitly, and accurately, as Cupid's maternal kinsman (*cognati*). For Ovid, what matters about Venus' sons is that they are related, through their mother.

Unlike Vergil, Ovid does not take pains to suppress details of Venus' sexual history, even her illicit relationships that did not eventuate in offspring, so as to downplay what Augustan moral ideology would have regarded as her promiscuity. Indeed, in *Amores* 1.9, Ovid justifies according equal literary status to elegy and epic, representing the two genres by the figures of the lover and soldier respectively, and adducing erotic scenarios in the *Iliad* and *Odyssey* as evidence for generic equivalence. As the crowning example he notes (39–40): *Mars quoque deprensus fabrilia uincula sensit: / notior in caelo fabula nulla fuit* ("Mars, caught in adultery, also felt the chains of the smith: no story was better known in heaven").

To be sure, even here, when citing the popularity of Homer's story about Venus and Mars, Ovid does not mention Venus herself. Yet at *Amores* 3.9.15–16, Ovid explicitly recalls her extramarital erotic pursuits and passions, likening Venus' grief over the death of Tibullus to her sorrow when a wild boar fatally crushed her young lover Adonis in his groin (*Amores* 3.9.15–16): *nec minus est confusa Venus moriente Tibullo, / quam iuueni rupit cum ferus inguen aper* ("Venus was no less emotionally distraught by Tibullus' dying than when a savage boar crushed the groin of her beloved young man"). By emphasizing the location of Adonis' mortal wound as the bodily part of greatest value to Venus, Ovid of course also alludes, euphemistically, to the sexual subject matter of Tibullus' elegies, and all of elegy, as a convention of the genre, in refined and circumlocutory terms. But here again he reminds us of Vergil's lack of vatic veracity in his characterization of Venus herself, thereby critiquing the *Aeneid*'s sanitizing of sexually saturated Greek myths to promote Augustan moral ideology.

Ovid may also evoke and critique the *Aeneid* elsewhere in *Amores* 3.9. At lines 37 and 38, addressing Tibullus, he reflects: *uiue pius: moriere pius; cole sacra: colentem / mors grauis a templis in caua busta trahet* ("Live as a dutiful individual: you will die as a dutiful individual; perform holy rites; heavy death will drag you as you perform them from the temples into the hollow tombs"). The adjective *pius* recurs as a substantive in line 66, where he tells Tibullus: *auxisti numeros, culte Tibulle, pios* ("You, refined Tibullus, have increased the dutiful numbers"). Such applications of Aeneas' epithet *pius* to Tibullus may serve to equate this extramaritally amorous elegiac poet with Vergil's epic hero, who suffers and causes suffering from an illicit sexual liaison. Yet they also spotlight the differences between the repressive and hypocritical Augustan moral ideology informing the representation of erotic interactions in Vergil's epic and the more tolerant values of love elegy itself.

In positing that in *Amores* 3.9 Ovid is employing intertextual allusions to critique the poetry of both Tibullus and Vergil, and by extension how each poet represents his own literary genre, elegy and epic respectively, I do not claim that this Ovidian text is unique. I have, for example read Ovid's intertextual allusions to Sulpicia's elegies in *Amores* 3.14, the tale of Pyramus and Thisbe in *Metamorphoses* Book 4, and the story of Pygmalion in *Metamorphoses* Book 10 as critiquing her literary self-presentation and professed amatory values. *Amores* 3.14, apparently written in the mid-teens BCE, can be read as obliquely taking Sulpicia to task for her pride in openly celebrating and publicly sharing her transgressive sexual behaviour rather than keeping it under wraps, as well as Sulpicia's disregard for her *fama*, moral reputation. Ovid's implicit comparison between Sulpicia's erotic com-munications and those of Thisbe points up Sulpicia's demanding, complain-ing, self-absorbed modes of speaking to and about her lover. By linking the ivory statue created by Pygmalion to Sulpicia, Ovid spotlights and faults Sulpicia's preoccupation with her physical appearance and adornment. I have read Ovid's allusions to Horace *Odes* 3.30 in his narrative about Apollo and Daphne in *Metamorphoses* Book 1 as humorously criticizing Horace's self-aggrandizing vatic stance in that poem, too.[11]

Even while praising an illustrious group of Greek and Roman poets in *Amores* 1.15, Ovid explicitly recognizes the literary shortcomings of two on his list: indeed, a Greek elegist, Callimachus, and a Roman epic poet, Ennius. This roster includes Vergil in 25–6, followed by Tibullus in 27–8. Admittedly, Ovid extols both without reservation: he terms the former's *Bucolics, Georgics,* and *Aeneid* as to be read *Roma triumphati dum caput orbis erit* ("as long as Rome will be capital of the world she has triumphed over"); he addresses the latter as *culte Tibulle* (exactly as he does in *Amores* 3.9) while stating that *donec erunt ignes arcusque Cupidinis arma / discentur numeri, culte Tibulle, tibi* ("your metres will be learned as long as flames and bow will be the arms of Cupid").

But in his later autobiographical elegy *Tristia* 4.10, Ovid depicts self-criticism as central to his own poetic principles and identity. At 61–2, for example, he claims to have burnt his poems he thought full of flaws (*uitiosa*). It would be surprising if he did not regard the other Augustan poets whom he mentions there, Vergil and Tibullus among them, as deserving some criticism as well, subtly and wittily, subversively or seriously.[12]

NOTES

1 Ovid is cited from Kenney 1994, Domitius and Tibullus from Postgate 1915. All translations are my own unless otherwise noted. For the date of Vergil's death, see *VSD* 35–6: *obiit XI Kal. Octobr. Cn. Sentio Q. Lucretio cons.*

2 For these Tibullan echoes, see Huskey 2005 as well as Hallett 2009a; for Ovid's use of Tibullan language in *Amores* 3.9 and elsewhere, see Maltby 1999.

3 Huskey 2005.

4 Hallett 2020. For Octavia and Vergil, see *VSD* 32–3: *Cui tamen multo post perfectaque demum materia tres omnino libros recitauit, secundum, quartum et sextum, sed hunc notabili Octauiae adfectione, quae cum recitatione interesset, ad illos de filio suo uersus, "tu Marcellus eris," defecisse fertur atque aegre focillata est* ("However, much later, when his material had been finalized, Vergil finally read to Augustus three books in all, the second, fourth and sixth, but this last book exerted a remarkable emotional impact on Octavia, who, when she attended his reading, at those verses about her son, 'you will be Marcellus', is said to have fainted and was only revived with difficulty").

5 For Octavia and her blended family of nine children, see, for example, Suetonius, *Aug.* 63; Vell. 2.93, Plut. *Ant.* 54.2–3 and 87.

6 For the Argonaut Boutes/Butas as father of Eryx, see Diod. Sic. 4.83.1–4. On Beroe as a daughter of Aphrodite and Adonis, and hence Aeneas' half-sister, see Non. *Dion.* 41.155. It is, however, entirely possible that Nonnus' claim about Beroe does not go back as early as Vergil's day.

7 For Venus and Mars as illicit lovers, see Hom. *Od.* 8.266–366 and the proem to Lucretius, addressing Venus as *Aeneadum genetrix* (*DRN* 1.1) For "sexualized" interpretations of Venus in the *Aeneid*, see Gladhill 2012 and Lively 2012.

8 As observed by Hallett 2020: 119.

9 Indeed, despite her loving words to Vulcan, Venus is asking him to help a child of hers that she conceived with Anchises, an issue noted by Servius. See also Ov. *Tr.* 2.261–2: *sumpserit Aeneadum genetrix ubi prima, requiret /*

Aeneidum genetrix unde sit alma Venus ("As soon as [a respectable matron] will have taken up the *Aeneidum genetrix* [the first words of Lucretius' *De Rerum Natura*, depicting Venus as the lover of Mars], she will ask by whom nurturing Venus became the mother of the descendants of Aeneas"). Ovid implies that the paternity of Venus' offspring was of concern to his contemporary readers, owing to the literary testimony for her many lovers.

10 Boyd (1997: 182) notes that, aside from *Amores* 3.9, the epithet *pulcher* is only used in Latin literature to describe Iulus in the *Aeneid* and texts, such as Servius' commentary, related to the *Aeneid*.

11 Hallett 2009a, 2009b, 2010, and 2015.

12 See Ov. *Tr.* 4.10. 41–2, on his youthful encounters with Vergil and Tibullus: *Vergilium uidi tantum: nec auara Tibullo / tempus amicitiae fata dedere meae* ("I only saw Vergil: nor did the greedy fates give Tibullus time for my friendship").

11

The Hero and the Procuress: Anna and Her Elegiac Interface

SOPHIA PAPAIOANNOU

As soon as Dido realizes that she has fallen in love with Aeneas at the opening of *Aeneid* 4, she confides her feelings to her sister Anna. Anna's appearance in the epic is unanticipated. She features nowhere in the detailed account of Dido's Phoenician past, as reported by Venus in *Aeneid* 1, and Carthaginian present, as experienced by Aeneas in the same book. And yet, her presence in *Aeneid* 4 is notable: at the opening of the book, she becomes Dido's confidante and voices the queen's innermost desires as she urges Dido to give in to her feelings for Aeneas (31–53). Once the union between the two heroes is forged, Anna slips away, to appear again after Aeneas is directed by Mercury to break his relationship with Dido and resume his great mission. At this point Anna becomes Dido's intermediary: she transfers messages back and forth between the queen and Aeneas (416–38). And later on, when Dido gives up hope of keeping Aeneas in Carthage, Anna unknowingly becomes Dido's accomplice in helping orchestrate the queen's death (474–503) and stays by Dido's side to the very end: the queen will die in her arms, addressing her final words to her sister (672–92).

In the scholarly tradition, the association of Dido with a series of tragic heroines abandoned by their lovers has cast Anna in the role of the heroine's confidante and advisor in matters of the heart – her nurse or sister. One of the most prominent and commonly accepted tragic models proposed is the nurse in Euripides' *Hippolytus*.[1] This role of the nurse as an intermediary who facilitates an erotic communication has inspired A. Hollis to see Anna in a completely different generic light and discern behind Dido's sister the literary antecedent of the elegiac *ancilla* or trusty maid who carries back and forth the erotic correspondence between her mistress and the man she loves.[2] I will develop further Anna's association with the elegiac go-between, by showing that the elegiac side of Anna's role interacts dynamically with the comedic figure of the procuress (*lena*) who holds a no less prominent role in love elegy. My argument, to be presented in a series of five parts, will be aided by the reception of the Vergilian Anna as the goddess Anna Perenna in the *Fasti*, a poem which is often interpreted as Ovid's elegiac response to Vergil's *Aeneid*. Elegy is firmly in the subtext of Vergil's Anna, and this erotic generic interface behind the Vergilian heroine becomes the cornerstone for the characterization of Anna in the *Fasti*.

1.

Female (and male) servants in various capacities populate the household of the elegiac mistress already in Propertius and tend to her needs.[3] The first piece of evidence in my study to support the proximity of Anna to the elegiac *ancilla* is the distinct role of Dido's sister in the *Aeneid* as the exclusive intermediary between Aeneas and Dido. In the elegiac tradition, a trusted servant girl is typically chosen to facilitate the two lovers' communication via the exchange of written messages.[4] When Dido realizes that Aeneas is readying himself to depart from Carthage without notifying her, it is Anna she sends to him to try to change his mind, because, as the queen points out, Anna and Aeneas have a special understanding (4.421–3):[5] *solam nam perfidus ille / te colere, arcanos etiam tibi credere sensus; / sola uiri mollis aditus et tempora noras* ("For that treacherous man befriended you alone, to you he confided even his secret thoughts; only you knew the time to approach the man smoothly"). This special understanding between Dido's sister and the Trojan hero reaches back, according to Servius and Servius Danielis, who quote Varro, to an alternative tradition beyond the Vergilian epic. Anna was part of the Dido legend prior to Vergil, at least if we believe Varro.[6] Servius Danielis on *A.* 4.682 (*exstinxti te meque, soror*, "sister, you killed yourself and me") says that Varro wrote that Anna loved Aeneas, and that it was Anna who ultimately took the place of Dido on the funeral pyre:[7] *Varro ait non Didonem, sed Annam amore Aeneae impulsam se supra rogum interemisse* ("Varro said that not Dido but Anna, impelled by her love for Aeneas, took her own life on the pyre").[8] Servius, ad *A.* 4.9,[9] notes that Anna was part of the Dido tradition already in Naevius' *Bellum Poenicum* (*cuius filiae fuerint Anna et Dido, Naeuius dicit*),[10] a work generally considered to have influenced Vergil's Carthaginian episode.[11] The special bond between Anna and Aeneas, according to Vergil, and the erotic affair between the two in the pre-Vergilian tradition come together when one considers Anna in light of the *ancilla* of love elegy, the servant girl of the poet's mistress, who acts as intermediary but does not hesitate to take her mistress' place in the arms of the *amator* (*Ars* 3.665–6): *nec nimium uobis formosa ancilla ministret: / saepe uicem dominae praebuit illa mihi* ("Nor let a maid that is too pretty minister to you: often she has offered herself to me in place of her mistress").

2.

An elegiac *ancilla*, however, is never heard expressing an opinion or offering advice to the mistress (though, as a message carrier, she has the opportunity to rewrite the messages of her mistress and steal her voice; cf. *Am.* 1.11 and 1.12). The part of the *puella's* councillor in elegy is reserved for the old procuress. The *lena callida* is a stock character of Latin love elegy originating in the *palliata* and the mime, and plays a dominant role in at least four elegies (Tib. 1.5, 2.6; Prop. 4.5; Ovid *Am.* 1.8). In her article on the elegiac *lena*, Sara Myers has shown that, despite the distinct ways in which each elegist treats his own procuress character, all three poets invest the *lena* with certain characteristics that betray her comedic origin and at the same time underscore her common function in all three elegiac corpora. Yet, in Myers' analysis (embraced by later critics) the elegiac/comedic *lena* is consistently an opponent to the poet-lover: she preaches a different erotic code (one that ranks material benefits over genuine and mutual emotional fulfilment), and she also usurps the poet's role as instructor (*praeceptor*) and composer of the elegiac *puella*.[12]

This stereotypically elegiac portrait of the *lena*[13] seemingly harmonizes with Anna's conduct as her sister's advisor, but the advice Anna delivers is at odds with what she is expected to say. She begins her speech by chastising Dido's refusal to let go of her pathological grief for her husband's death and move on with her life (*A.* 4.31–4), by drawing on a topos of *consolatio* rhetoric, namely that there should be moderation in grief because excessive emotional suffering and depression are futile. This argument is articulated in Book 3 of the *Tusculan Disputations*, in a set of passages where Cicero comments on ways of assuaging grief for losing a loved one.[14] Subsequently, Anna successfully bends her sister's resistance by urging her *to follow* the promptings of her heart and dismiss concerns tied to material benefit (in Dido's case, her reputation and her royal title). The ease with which Dido, the inconsolable widow, is convinced to let go of her mourning is indicative of her likewise rapid transformation from an epic queen to an elegiac *puella*. At the same time, a more careful consideration of the encounter between Dido and Anna illustrates a more complex situation for the queen, which requires from her sister likewise a more complex – and contrary to the actions of a typical procuress – persuasion strategy. For the procuress never advises her trainee to choose love over interest, forbids emotional engagement with lovers, and recommends anger as a weapon. In this respect, Anna is called to perform at once the role of the elegiac *lena* AND the role of the poet-lover. She is partly the *lena*, who protects the *puella*'s material interest, and partly the *praeceptor* (inspired by the tragic nurse), who promptly sacrifices ethical principles for expediency. In order to convince Dido to give in to her attraction to Aeneas, Anna appeals to her sister's civic preoccupation. She relieves Dido's guilt over her late husband by insisting the dead have no interest in the living and advises her to consider a pact with the Trojans, who have suffered a similar fate, a politically suave move (*A.* 4.31–53). Civic duty is a good reason for Dido to convince herself to risk her *dux femina* status. By succumbing to the peculiar, that is, rationally determined erotodidactic instructions of an elegiac *praeceptor amoris*, she becomes convinced that her indulgence is as virtuous as Anna's advice.

3.

Linguistics, too, enforces the *lena* aspect of Anna's role: the etymology of Anna's name is far from certain. The para-etymology from *amnis perennis* suggested in one of Ovid's aetiologies (discussed below) seems to have been the most popular with the ancient scholars.[15] Radke etymologizes Anna's name from Oscan *amma*, a colloquial word for "mother" (something like "mama"), which is the term used in Roman comedy to refer to the *lena*.[16] Critics have also argued that this term might be a metaphor for the *nutrix*, the nurse. Specifically, Amma is the name of one of the seventeen divinities recorded by name on the Agnone tablet, a bronze inscription written in the Oscan alphabet that dates from the third century BCE found near Fonte Romito, between Agnone and Capracotta. The full name of the deity is Amma Cerealis, pointing to her identity as a mother goddess, a Ceres/Demeter, which is supported by Isidore of Seville's analysis of Amma as colloquial form for *mater* (Isid. *Etym.* 12.7.42): *strix uulgo amma dicitur ab amando paruulos unde et lac praebere fertur nascentibus* ("The screech owl in folk-language is called *mama* [*am*-ma], derived from loving [*am*-ando] her little ones, on account of which she is reported to provide milk for them").[17] Thus, already in the etymology of Anna's name her twofold role of the (tragic) nurse and the *lena/praeceptor* is firmly present.

Radke's etymological interpretation has been contested,[18] but a similar sounding name for a similarly functioning character in the *Fasti* speaks in favour of the association of Anna to the *lena* and the *nutrix* on the basis of her etymologically suggestive name. This character is Acca Larentia, who together with her husband Faustulus became the adoptive parents of Romulus and Remus. In the *Fasti*, Acca is associated with the Feralia, the

Larentalia, and the Lemuria, three festivals honouring the Lares, and she is honoured as, and identified with, the mother of the Lares.[19] A very strong argument for embracing this identification is that Romulus and Remus, Acca's foster children, became the "original" Lares posthumously.[20] Further, Acca, the mother and *nutrix* of the founders of Rome and the first Lares, on account of her pairing with the wolf led to a tradition casting her as a whore, aided by the equation *lupa* ("she-wolf")/*meretrix*.[21] Finally, the name "Acca" is related to the Sanskrit word for "mother."[22]

4.

The epic Anna's complex elegiac and comic interface is best illustrated in three of the aetiologies Ovid procures to explain the origin of the name and cult of Anna Perenna in *Fasti* 3.523–696.[23] The motifs of love elegy that distinguish these aetiological tales exhibit further elements of the Vergilian Anna's personality in a genuinely elegiac context. The aetiology Ovid reports first is the one most explicitly connected to the Vergilian text because in it he continues the Carthaginian unit of the *Aeneid*. In this story, Ovid associates the Roman deity Anna Perenna with Dido's sister Anna (*F.* 3.545–656). In Ovid's account, after Aeneas abandons Dido and she commits suicide, Iarbas and the Mauritanians attack Carthage. Anna escapes with some other Carthaginians and wanders in search of refuge. Eventually they are shipwrecked at Aeneas' settlement in Italy. This narrative forms both a sequel and a parallel to the first four books of the *Aeneid*. Ovid presents Anna as a counterpart of Vergil's Aeneas (and also of her sister, since one of Anna's persecutors is her brother Pygmalion, on account of whom the two sisters fled Tyre in the first place), who escapes from Troy and wanders the Mediterranean until he is shipwrecked at Dido's Carthage. Indeed, like Aeneas, Anna finds refuge at the home of the local ruler (Aeneas), only to be persecuted again, by a jealous Lavinia, who evidently had reasons – or rather the skills of an ingenuous and sensitive reader, and quite good intertextual memory of Anna's quasi-elegiac identity – to suspect that the love affair between Aeneas and Anna hinted in the *Aeneid* (4.42–53)[24] might be rekindled.

Lavinia, in fact, emphasizes the elegiac character of Anna's gifts to Aeneas, in her assumption that many gifts/messages were sent to the hero in secret, as lovers typically do (*F.* 3.635–6): *donaque cum uideat praeter sua lumina ferri / multa, tamen mitti clam quoque multa putat*[25] ("And though she saw many gifts given away openly, she suspected many more were sent secretly"). The portrayal of Aeneas, walking on the shore and along a secluded path (*secretum … iter*, 604), in the company of faithful Achates (a comedic *amicus fidelis* counterpart?), and barefoot, adds another colourful detail to Aeneas' elegiac portrait – a detail that points, according to Newlands, to "a condition more appropriate for a sorrowing elegiac lover than for a military hero."[26] Aeneas, in other words, is suggestively behaving like an elegiac lover who wanders aimlessly. Playfully, Ovid employs, in the line immediately following (605), the very word *errantem*, a typical modifier for the elegiac lover in distress.[27] The text in full runs as follows (*F.* 3.605–6): *aspicit errantem, nec credere sustinet Annam / esse* ("he saw [Anna] wandering, nor was he able to believe that she was Anna"). *Errantem*, in the accusative, actually modifies Anna, but the modifier, which comes first, has been split by the modified, in order to deceive the readers into identifying the wanderer with Aeneas.

Lavinia might even be thinking along the lines of the comedic *uxor dotata*[28] that she actually is. She is jealous (Barchiesi calls Lavinia's jealousy "vulgar") and vindictive, typically worrying about her husband's potential infidelities,[29] and, like the Plautine *uxor dotata* (e.g., Cleostrata in the *Casina*, about whom see below), is also shrewd (*callida*) and able to hide her actual feelings and thoughts under a deceptive facial expression (3.633–4): *falsum … uolnus / mente premit tacita dissimulatque metus* ("She hid an imaginary wrong within her silent heart, and concealed her fears"). The last line recalls similar behaviour by Dido in *Aeneid* 4, when she tries to deceive Anna and send her away so that she may plan her death more effectively (*A.* 4.477): *consilium uultu tegit ac spem fronte serenat* ("by her face she conceals her plan, making her brow serene with hope").

And so, Lavinia plots to destroy Anna. The episode seemingly ends with Anna's disappearance under the waves of the river Numicus, but the details of her escape from Lavinia's wrath evoke the plot of an adultery mime, either directly or indirectly through its reception in love elegy.[30] Warned by Dido's ghost (a ghost which exhibits traits that might assimilate it to the category of the so-called elegiac ghosts or even mimic ghosts),[31] Anna throws herself, scantily clothed, out of a "low window" (*F.* 3.643–6): *exsilit et uelox humili super ausa fenestra / se iacit (audacem fecerat ipse timor), / cumque metu rapitur tunica uelata recincta, / currit …* ("She leapt up and in haste she dared dive through a low window onto the ground: fear itself had made her daring, and with terror driving her, covered by a loose tunic, she runs …"). Window entrances and exits are recurrent features of love elegies and adultery mimes, and both Fantham and Barchiesi point to the adultery mime as the model behind the particular scene of Anna's escape.[32] And in *Ars Amatoria* 3, the *praeceptor amoris* advises his female pupils to prefer windows to doors as points of entry into their rooms (*cum melius foribus possis, admitte fenestra*, "though through the door it is potentially easier, let him in at the window," 605),[33] so that the lovers may be trained to use this escape route effectively when caught by surprise. *Humilis*, also, is used in Propertius as a technical term for elegy's characteristically "unpretentious" style (in contrast to the elevated genres of *epos* or tragedy).[34] Lavinia's wrath, finally, may originate in Propertian elegy as well: in 4.7 and 4.8 we learn from Cynthia's ghost that she was poisoned in order to be replaced by another woman, a *meretrix* named Chloris. In light of the fate of Propertius' Cynthia, an erudite Lavinia with her aforementioned intertextual memory, who may well have known of the amatory liaison between Aeneas and Anna, naturally feels insecure not simply about the fidelity of her husband but also about the safety of her own life!

Two of the remaining five Ovidian aetiologies for Anna Perenna likewise reach back to the Republican tradition and to Anna's role as go-between in an amatory relationship established in *Aeneid* 4. The fifth aetiology (*F.* 3.661–74), which Ovid seems to prefer above all the others (661–2), concerns a humble old hag of Bovillae named Anna, who, during the secession of the plebeians to the Mons Sacer outside Rome in 494 BCE, baked cakes every morning and brought them piping hot to the hungry rebels. In gratitude for her service, the plebeians afterwards worshipped her as a goddess. Anna's description in this story includes details that call to mind the elegiac and (comedic) performance of the procuress (*F.* 3.667–72):

> orta suburbanis quaedam fuit Anna Bouillis,
> pauper, sed multae sedulitatis anus;
> illa, leui mitra canos incincta capillos,
> fingebat tremula rustica liba manu,   670
> atque ita per populum fumantia mane solebat
> diuidere: haec populo copia grata fuit.

There was a certain Anna, born at suburban Bovillae, a poor old woman, but very industrious. She, with her grey hair bound up in a light cap, used to mould country cakes with tremulous hand, and it was her wont at morning to distribute them piping hot among the people: the supply was welcome to the people.

As Angeline Chiu has recently observed, "Anna's story has a Callimachean emphasis on the small, the humble, and the rustic."[35] Old Anna's fancy headdress (*mitra*) is distinctly foreign and bespeaks her foreign (oriental) origin inasmuch as it evokes the mitra-wearing Syrian tavern hostess (*copa*) of the first century CE pseudo-Vergilian *Copa* (*Copa* 1: *Copa Surisca, caput Graeca redimita mitella*, "A Syrian tavern girl, a Greek bonnet bound to her head ..."), who offers her customers cakes, love, and wine (*Copa* 20: *est hic munda Ceres, est Amor, est Bromius*). In fact, the offering of hot cakes on a daily basis strongly suggests that the industrious Anna of Bovillae might be a professional food provider, or more specifically, according to Chiu, a tavern keeper. What is more, "tavern keepers were occasionally regarded as brothel keepers, too, for their waitresses could double as prostitutes."[36] Intertextuality corroborates the procuress profile of Old Anna. The same oriental headband (*mitra*) is part of the disguise of an old procuress, which Vertumnus assumes last in a series of failed impersonations by means of which he tries (unsuccessfully) to win the love of Pomona (*Met.* 14.654–6): *ille etiam picta redimitus tempora mitra, / innitens baculo positis per tempora canis / adsimulauit anum* ("At length he had his brows bound with a *mitra* of colour, and then leaning on a stick, with white hair round his temples, he assumed the shape of an old woman").[37] In all, Anna of Bovillae, an old hag with the fancy foreign-looking headdress who is a professional baker (or brothel keeper) and caters to the plebeians, breathes life into the daily habits, activities, and preoccupations of the lower classes[38] – another expression of the *humilis* world celebrated in love elegy, as well as in Roman comedy and mime.

5.

The implicit elegiac-procuress identity of Anna of Bovillae becomes clear in the sixth and final aetiological story that, actually, in the *Fasti* narrative seems to be the continuation of the fifth. Anna of Bovillae is an *anus*, an old woman, as is the deified Anna of the sixth tale (Mars addresses her as *comis anus*, at 684).[39]

When Anna had just been made a goddess, Ovid reports, Mars asked her to procure Minerva for him as a bride. Ovid records in direct discourse Mars' appeal in order, among other things, to portray the god as an *amator*, who has fallen in love with Minerva, and Anna as the procuress and confidante to Minerva (*F.* 3.679–86):

> "mense meo coleris, iunxi mea tempora tecum;
>   pendet ab officio spes mihi magna tuo.   680
> armifer armiferae correptus amore Mineruae
>   uror, et hoc longo tempore uolnus alo.
> effice, di studio similes coeamus in unum:
>   conueniunt partes hae tibi, comis anus."
> dixerat; illa deum promisso ludit inani,   685
>   et stultam dubia spem trahit usque mora.

"You are worshipping in my month, I have joined my season to yours: I have great hope in the service that you can render me. An armed god myself, I have fallen in love with the armed goddess Minerva; I burn and for a long time have nursed this wound. She and I are deities alike in our pursuits; contrive to unite us. That office well befits you, kind old dame." So he spoke. She duped the god by a false promise and kept him dangling on in foolish hope by dubious delays.

Mars' lovelorn condition is reported at 682 (*uror, et hoc longo tempore uolnus alo*) in language previously employed by Vergil to describe the condition of the love-struck Dido at the famous opening of *Aeneid* 4 (1–2): *regina … iamdudum … uulnus alit uenis et caeco carpitur igni* (cf. 69 *uritur infelix Dido*). The verbal repetition is striking: Mars speaks in Dido's words, and addresses Anna Perenna, the deified version of the Vergilian Dido's sister! The evocation of the Vergilian subtext is more extensive. Mars' attraction to Minerva has been caused by the proximity of their identities as gods of war (681: *armifer armiferae correptus amore*, "an armed god myself, I have fallen love with the armed goddess [Minerva]"), and is acknowledged by the god himself (683): *di studio similes coeamus in unu* ("She and I are deities alike in our pursuits; let us become one"). Mars' words evoke what Dido said at *A.* 1.627–8, about the similarity between her plight and that of Aeneas: *me quoque per multos similis fortuna labores / iactactam hac demum uoluit consistere terra* ("Me, too, a like fortune has driven through many toils, and willed that in this land I should at last find rest"). Anna is called to perform the part of the Vergilian Anna to Mars' Dido, but the Vergilian part she embraces for herself is that of Dido's treacherous brother Pygmalion. The latter deceived Dido for a long time by hiding the death of Sychaeus (*multa malus simulans, uana spe lusit amantem, A.* 1.352). Vergil's phrasing is recalled by Ovid (685–6): *illa deum promisso ludit inani, / et stultam dubia spem trahit usque mora* ("She duped the god by a false promise and kept him dangling on in foolish hope by dubious delays").[40]

The rest of the story reads like an adultery mime in elegiac verse as it revolves around a love-triangle plot: Anna deceives Mars and takes the place of Minerva in bed herself, while Mars becomes a laughingstock. Indeed, in all likelihood, the plot follows an actual mime – a Republican play written by Decimus Laberius, entitled *Anna Peranna*, which dramatized for the stage the story of Anna Perenna.[41] The scant fragments surviving from this play do not allow the extraction of uncontested information about the storyline of this mime, but according to critical consensus, which the editor of Decimus Laberius, Costas Panayotakis, accepts,[42] the mime portrayed a certain Anna, who was an old hag and a *lena*-like character, undertaking to smooth Mars' path to the bed of Minerva, but ultimately taking Minerva's place herself (*F.* 3.687–94):

saepius instanti "mandata peregimus" inquit;
  "euicta est: precibus uix dedit illa manus."
credit amans thalamosque parat. deducitur illuc
  Anna tegens uoltus, ut noua nupta, suos.   690
oscula sumpturus subito Mars aspicit Annam:
  nunc pudor elusum, nunc subit ira, deum.
ridet amatorem carae noua diua Mineruae,
  nec res hac Veneri gratior ulla fuit.

When he often pressed her, "I have done your bidding," said she, "she is conquered and has yielded at last to your entreaties." The lover believed her and made ready the bridal chamber. Thither they escorted Anna, like a bride, with a veil upon her face. When he would have kissed her, Mars suddenly perceived Anna; now shame, now anger moved the god befooled. The new goddess laughed at dear Minerva's lover. Never did anything please Venus more than that.

Anna's impersonation of Minerva and the deception of Mars evoke the plot of Plautus' *Casina*.[43] The play features the most memorable *uxor dotata callida* in Roman comedy, who directs the staging of a transvestite adultery mime in order to humiliate and punish her husband.[44] Vergil, who knew Laberius well and was influenced by his works,[45] likely drew inspiration from this mime when he portrayed Anna, originally as a go-between, and subsequently as a trustworthy messenger, in light of the elegiac *lena* and *ancilla*.[46]

The bawdy amatory situations Ovid described in these actiologics are in a way anticipated by the particular opening of the Anna Perenna episode, which begins with a description of the festival for Anna Perenna that is celebrated on 15 March (*F.* 3.523–42). During this festival, the lower classes would pair off, lie about on the grass along the river Tiber (*plebs uenit ac uirides passim disiecta per herbas / potat, et accumbit cum pare quisque sua,* "the common folk come, and scattered here and there over the green grass they drink, every lad reclining beside his girl," 525–6), drink heavily (*sole tamen uinoque calent annosque precantur. / quot sumant cyathos, ad numerumque bibunt,* "they grow warm with sun and wine, and they pray for as many years as they take cups, and they count the cups they drink," 531–2), dance and sing obscene songs (*illic et cantant quicquid didicere theatris / et iactant faciles ad sua uerba manus,* "there they sing the ditties they picked up in the theatres, beating time to the words with nimble hands," 535–6), and eventually stagger home, "a spectacle for vulgar eyes" (*spectacula uolgi,* 539). The celebratory atmosphere of the festival calls to mind the settings of merriment, banqueting, and night-long revelry that frequent the world of love elegy, and also of Roman comedy, wherein they are associated with the houses of the courtesans.

Finally, the elegiac procuress was commonly found in conjunction with *witchcraft*, including the control of the sky and the moon.[47] And witchcraft is another theme that brings together Vergil's Anna and Anna Perenna. Love and witchcraft are juxtaposed in *Aeneid* 4, where Dido sends Anna to seek out a sorceress (4.509) who will be present and supervise the magic ceremonies the queen plans to conduct because this priestess knows how to relieve her thoughts of Aeneas' memory and cure her heart from the sickness of love (*A.* 4.489–91). Anna knows where to find her, and this suggestive acquaintance with magic corresponds to Anna Perenna's ties to magic. Excavations at the sanctuary of Anna Perenna just outside of the city walls of Rome have brought to light several *defixiones*, votive tablets with curses tied to magic. Let me note here, too, that in the second aetiology of Anna Perenna in the *Fasti* the Roman deity is equated with the moon.[48]

6.

In lieu of a conclusion, it is worth noting the survival of Anna's role as elegiac procuress in imperial literature, in Petronius' story of the widow of Ephesus – a story involving a widow, her loyal maid, the ghost of her husband, and a lover who is also a military man. Critics have pointed out[49] that the plot of this story is inspired by the love affair of Aeneas and Dido, with the maid of the widow acting the part of Anna in the story. What I would like to emphasize is that the Petronian *ancilla* is the only character who quotes nearly verbatim her Vergilian counterpart, Anna, and in doing so she consciously declares the model for her role as elegiac procuress: she alludes to Anna's words when the latter urges Dido to give in to her feelings of love for Aeneas (*Sat.* 111.12: *id cinerem aut manes credis sentire sepultos?* = *A.* 4.34, with *sentire* instead of the Vergilian *curare*; *Sat.* 112.2: *placitone etiam pugnabis amori?* = *A.* 4.38). This intertextual afterlife of Anna encapsulates the essence of her performance in the Vergilian epic and suggests that we may interpret Vergil's heroine as imported into a lofty generic environment from the lowly elegiac, even comedic world.

Vergil's *Aeneid* and love elegy traditionally form a binary association of sharp opposites conspicuously projected as such not least through poetological openings that cast epic as masculine, poetry singing of male deeds (*arma uirumque cano* ..., *A.* 1.1), and elegy as feminine, the dominion of the *puella* (*Cynthia prima* ... *me cepit*, Prop. 1.1). Yet, recent research has deconstructed this dichotomy of genre and gender in the works of the Augustan authors.[50] The complexity of experimenting with poetics, and by association with a variety of genres, is at the core of the *Aeneid*, one of the more sophisticated pieces of Latin literature, endorsing well-grounded arguments on the epic's many generic "voices." Dido's sister Anna dons such an epically congruent voice. Through her fleeting presence, confined inside a few lines in Book 4, Vergil engages with a long literary and mythological tradition that, on the one hand, reaches back to Naevius and corroborates the epic character of one of the least epic-coloured episodes of the *Aeneid*, and, on the other, reaches across the spectrum of lighter genres to elegy. The bond of mutual understanding and intimate communication between Aeneas and Anna casts the epic protagonist of Vergil's heroic narrative into the light of the elegiac male who deals and conspires through intermediaries, and learns to negotiate and be flexible. Vergil's ingeniously elliptic account of the Carthaginian sisters' relationship with Aeneas inspired Ovid's brilliantly entertaining construction of the legend behind the obscure Roman divinity of Anna Perenna, thus putting on the bones of the Vergilian Anna the elegiac flesh owed to her.

NOTES

1 The association of Anna with the tragic nurse in Hippolytus has already been proposed over a century ago, in De Witt 1907, and is noted repeatedly since, most recently in McIntyre and McCallum 2019: 19–21, offering a detailed overview of the bibliography on the tradition behind Vergil's Anna; also Harrison 2007a: 72–4, who actually believes that the leading tragic model behind Anna is Ismene, the Sophoclean Antigone's sister. Williams (1972: 335) considers Apollonius' Chalciope (Medea's sister) as Anna's model.

2 Hollis 1977: 100. In *Ars* 1.338 there is explicit reference to the Hippolytus exemplum (Hollis 1977: 98). Notice also that in Euripides' *Alcestis*, a female servant informs the audience, like a messenger, in the early part of the play (*Alces.* 141–212) about the state of mind and actions of her mistress, who has chosen to die on behalf of her husband. Still, in this case, the events described by the slave girl may be private, but the communication is not a secret confession to the slave to be transferred to a third party – rather, they are known to many members of the household who are all involved in the mourning (192–3).

3 The Propertian slaves Lygdamus, in 3.6, 4.7, and 4.8, and Lycinna in 3.15, and also Iole, Amycle, and Acanthis (4.5), Nomas, Petale, Lalage, Chloris, and Parthenie (4.7), and Phyllis and Teia (4.8) all have migrated into elegy from comedy. See the full list in Cairns 2006: 68–9. The elegiac *ancilla* calls to mind the comedic *ancilla* who likewise operates as go-between for her mistress (typically a courtesan) and her lover; a prominent such comedic *ancilla callida* is Milphidippa in the *Miles Gloriosus*, whose mission supposedly is to facilitate

the "illicit" amatory union between her mistress, the courtesan Acroteleution, and the soldier.

4 Ovid, *Am.* 2.19.41: [*quaerere*] … *quas ferat et referat sollers ancilla tabellas* ("[asking] … what messages the clever maid carries back and forth"); Tib. 2.6.46: *tabellas … portans itque reditque* ("back and forth she goes carrying messages"). Barchiesi (2001: 45) notes that "Anna's role as *messenger* of love is already a potential feature of *elegy*, one that the narrator, not by chance, immediately limits and reinterprets: *miserrima* is in fact a vigilant recall of the stern code of tragedy that hovers over the plot … *Miserrima … fert refertque soror* has a slight, but not unfelt, assonance with the stock elegiac formulas for the go-between through whom lovers keep in touch."

5 For the translation of Ovid's *Fasti* throughout, I have used Frazer 1976, with modifications; all other translations of ancient texts are mine, unless otherwise noted.

6 Detailed study of the available evidence in D'Anna 1975: 3–34. Recent discussion in McCallum 2019.

7 Thilo-Hagen 1881: 1.580.

8 Though Servius does not report whether, according to Varro, both sisters took their lives or Dido lived on after Anna's death. Also Servius ad *A.* 5.4: *sane sciendum Varronem dicere, Aeneam ab Anna amatum*; Barrett 1970 offers a linguistics-based study that suggests the interpretation of Anna as a lover to Aeneas during his stay at Carthage, and claims that Dido did know of this relationship, despite her mental state. Barrett too discusses Servius' annotations to the earlier tradition on Anna in the Dido legend. The evidence pointing to a suggestive amatory relationship between Anna and Aeneas is discussed also in Ahl 1985: 309–15. Casali (2008: 33–7) detects an allusion to Anna's own suicide atop a pyre in Varro also in the phrase *hoc rogus iste mihi* (*A.* 4.676), which according to Servius implies some historical reference (*adludit ad historiam*, Serv. ad *A.* 4.676); and also within *A.* 4.678–9 and 680.

9 Thilo-Hagen 1881: 1.462.

10 This fragment, 33 Baehrens, refutes Ahl's suggestion (1985: 346–7) that Vergil "reconciles" two different traditions, one holding that Dido was Aeneas' lover and another (the Varronian one, according to Servius on 4.682) holding that it was Anna who loved Aeneas, and so makes Anna Dido's sister and spiritual double. The fragment has survived out of context, in Servius' comments on *A.* 4.9; the name of the two sisters' father has not been preserved.

11 At the beginning of the fifth century CE, Macrobius (6.2.30–1) wrote that the first book of the *Bellum Poenicum* influenced Vergil considerably (Willis 1963: 365; Horsfall 1973–4: 6–13). See also D'Anna 1989: 159–96 (with bibliography), arguing for the credibility of Servius' testimony.

12 Myers 1996.

13 Lee-Stecum 2013: 77 calls the *lena callida* a stock character of love elegy.

14 E.g., *Tusc.* 3.28; 3.32. Also, Dido's unassuaged grief is contrary to what is introduced as another of Cicero's *consolatio* topoi, namely that the passage of time allows someone in grief to see one's condition in proportion. Despite what Anna considers the passing of ample time, Dido has not managed to appraise her situation rationally.

15 On Anna Perenna's etymology: Wissowa 1912: 241 states the Anna Perenna was the goddess of the year and the new year, and about her name, he cites Macr. *Sat.* 1.12.6 *ut annare perannareque commode liceat*; and Varr. *Sat. Men.* fr. 506 Buech., where she is called *Anna ac Perenna*. Her name, that is, would derive from *annare ac perannare*, referring to both the beginning and the end of the year (cf. Suet. *Vesp.* 5). Ovid at the end of the first aetiology etymologizes the name from *amnis perennis* (*F.* 3.655), the perennial river Numicus that received the body of the persecuted (by Lavinia) Anna.

16 Radke 1993: 134–6.

17 On the Agnone Tablets and the name of Amma thereupon, see Salmon 1967: 159 with n5. Le Bonniec (1958: 41) interprets *amma* in the phrase in Isidore's text as *nutrix* or something similar. Hesych. s.v. *Ammas* equates her with Demeter, the nourishing mother of all people.

18 Most recently by Forsythe 2012: 165n25.

19 On Acca Larentia as the mother of the Lares, see Tabeling 1932: 46–8; Altheim 1938: 133; Ogilvie 1965: 50; York 1988: 53–4.

20 Wiseman 1995: 70–1.

21 Cf. Ogilvie 1965: 50.

22 Martelli 2013: 138.

23 On Anna Perenna, the protecting goddess of the New Year, see Barchiesi 1997b: 123–30; Bömer 1958: 179–80; Littlewood 1980: 301–21; Miller 1991: 136–8; Wiseman 2004: 81, 84. Wiseman (1998: 65) offers a brief overview of the six aetiologies: (i) Anna is Dido's sister, eventually turned into a water nymph hiding in a perennial river (545–56); (ii) she is Luna, the moon, whose months fill the year (*annus*) (657); (iii) she is Themis or Io (658); (iv) she is an Arcadian nymph, who fed the infant Jupiter (659–60); (v) the most credible aetiology: she was an old woman from Bovillae, who fed the plebeians when they seceded to the Mons Sacer (661–74); (vi) after old Anna (of Bovillae?) was made a goddess, Mars asked her to procure Minerva for him as bride, but Anna took Minerva's place herself (675–96).

24 Notice also the suggestive phrase *consumpsi naufragus huius opes*, "shipwrecked I lived at her expense" (*F.* 3.630), by which Aeneas introduces Anna to his wife, his carefully avoiding spelling Anna's name and noting that her kingdom does not exist anymore, and his explicit remark that his relationship with

the Tyrian princess is "pious," *pia causa* (*F.* 3.628–32): *hanc tibi cur tradam, pia causa, Lauinia coniunx / est mihi: consumpsi naufragus huius opes. / orta Tyro est, regnum Libyca possedit in ora: / quam precor ut carae more sororis ames* ("Lavinia, my wife, I have a *pious reason* for entrusting this lady to you: shipwrecked, *I lived at her expense*. She's of Tyrian birth: her kingdom's on the Libyan shore: I beg you to love her, as your dear sister").

25 In a reversal of the elegiac stereotype, it is Anna, the unconfessed beloved – rather than the former lover and present host Aeneas – who sends Aeneas expensive gifts.

26 Newlands 2006: 361n15.

27 In Prop. 1.18, for example, the poet describes himself wandering through the countryside, longing for Cynthia, carving her name on trees and calling it out to the trees and the rocks. According to Heerink (2015, 194 n93), the term *error* as modifier of a lover's quest can function "as a kind of technical term denoting (the writing of) elegiac poetry"; and he cites Prop. 1.13.35; Ov. *Am.* 1.2.35, 20.9; Milanion in Prop. 1.1.11 (*Partheniis amens errabat in antris*); and Gallus' wanderings in *B.* 6 and Prop. 2.13. The association of *error* with a distraught lover at the very opening of Prop. 1.1, the programmatic poem of the genre of love elegy, suggestively designates wandering as the paradigmatic conduct of the elegiac lover. See also Pietropaolo in this volume on Pasiphaë's wandering in *B.* 6.

28 Newlands (2006: 361n15) notes that in the *Fasti* the shore is called *dotali* (603), an adjective suggestively acknowledging that Lavinia has the upper hand in their marriage: "Aeneas is not entirely his own master."

29 Barchiesi 1997b: 245, 165–7.

30 McKeown 1979: 76.

31 The two categories are interrelated in Propertius' categorization of ghosts in 4.7: see Knox 2004a: 157–9 (on elegiac ghosts), 160–7 (on mimic ghosts). For Knox, the circumstances of Cynthia's death by poison in order to be supplanted by Propertius' new mistress, Chloris, who is also a *meretrix*, presuppose the plot of some adultery mime.

32 Barchiesi 1997b: 245; Fantham 1983: 200.

33 Gibson 2013, ad loc. citing a series of elegiac passages, including *F.* 3.643–4.

34 See Fedeli 1981: 229.

35 Chiu 2016: 26. To Chiu, Anna of Bovillae harks back to the Callimachean *Hecale*.

36 Chiu 2016: 27. On the association of taverns and prostitution, see Wiseman 1998: 73; Kleberg 1957: 89–91; Chiu 2016: 27n17 listing *Digest* 23.2.43.*pref.* and 9, a legal provision by the jurist Ulpian, who aligned tavern keepers and waitresses with prostitution.

37 Contrary to the elegiac model, the pseudo-procuress gives sexual advice to the younger girl in favour of Vertumnus. On Vertumnus' disguise as that of an elegiac procuress, see Henderson 2002: 273.

38 As a result of her service to the plebeians, Anna Perenna was a deity particularly favoured by the Roman plebs, as exhibited by the freewheeling and pandemic character of her worship (Chiu 2016: 27–8), and her worship transcribed the memory of plebeian resistance to established civic authority.

39 On the *anus* as a mature version of the *puella*, see Gardner 2013: 181–218.

40 The intertextual relationship has been noted already in Bömer 1958: 192 ad 685.

41 According to Bonaria 1965: 105 (recorded in Panayotakis 2010: 117), the form Peranna was a coinage by Laberius in order to produce a homoeoteleuton between Peranna and Anna to amuse the Roman audience.

42 Panayotakis 2010: 116–23.

43 The similarity is remarked also in Panayotakis 2010: 119.

44 Another Plautine play with a similar plot is the *Menaechmi*. There the Epidamnian Menaechmus is married to a nagging *uxor dotata*, whom he dislikes as much as he fears, and he also has a lover in the courtesan Erotium (his monologue, 109ff., is a tirade to his wife, peppered with threats to divorce her if she keeps spying on him or asking him about his affairs).

45 Panayotakis 2010: 250–2, 320–4, *et alibi*, on adjectives first used in Laberius and afterwards found in Vergil. Wiseman 1998: 72–3, and Giancotti 1967: 61–3, speculate that Ovid's fifth and sixth aetiologies for Anna Perenna were the two acts of Laberius' mime *Anna Peranna*, with Anna the procuress performing her role as the landlady in the first part for the men, in the second part for the gods.

46 Giancotti (1967: 63–6), cited in Panayotakis 2010: 119, suggests that the love triangle of Laberius' *Anna Peranna* was between Anna, Aeneas, and the jealous Lavinia (pointing back to the first Ovidian aetiology for the festival).

47 Myers 1996: 6.

48 The remains of the sanctuary of Anna Perenna, including a fountain wherein twenty-six lead and copper tablets with curses inscribed on them had been deposited, came to light in 1999; on the excavation of the fountain of Anna Perenna, see Piranomonte 2002; on the *defixiones*, Blänsdorf 2015: 35–64; Piranomonte 2010, 2016.

49 Karakasis 2016b: 514f–515n40, with full record of earlier critics who read the tale of the Widow of Ephesus in light of the Vergilian Dido/Aeneas episode. Among the studies of note is Laird 1999: 244–5.

50 On the gender of epic, see notably Keith 2000 and Hinds 2000; on elegy and gender politics, see Wyke 2002: 155–91.

12

The Presence of Vergil in Ovid's *Epistulae ex Ponto* 1.8

GARTH TISSOL

Paul Alpers, in several influential works on pastoral, reacts against modern conceptions of pastoral as idyllic landscape, denying that Vergil's bucolics ought to be understood in terms of idealization, fantasy, and the Golden Age.[1] He denies that pastoral's "idyllic landscape represents a fantasy that is dissipated by the recognition of political and social realities," though he cites numerous authors for the view that it does indeed represent such a fantasy.[2] Whatever one may regard as a right and appropriate interpretation of Vergil, the process of idealizing pastoral is already underway in the early reception of Vergil's work. This paper concerns a case of engagement with Vergil near the end of the Augustan period in Ovid's last elegiac collection, the *Epistulae ex Ponto*. The exiled poet's thoughts turn to the first eclogue in *Pont.* 1.8, when his deeply felt separation from Rome generates idealizing fantasies about both the city of Rome and the Italian countryside. With Alpers in mind, one could conclude that modern misinterpretations of pastoral have a very old pedigree, one that goes back almost to Vergil's time; for in *Pont.* 1.8 pastoral pursuits do indeed represent "a fantasy that is dissipated by the recognition of political and social realities," which Ovid in exile cannot fail to recognize. Yet by showing us the process of his own effort at idealization, its origin in despair, its unsustainable nature, and the evanescence of the consolation that he seeks in it, Ovid makes clear that he is far from recommending a naïve, escapist, or otherwise discreditable interpretation of Vergilian pastoral.

The physical space in which Roman authors and their readers actually lived is a significant feature of the works that they wrote and read. Indeed, the exiled poet is preoccupied with the miseries resulting from his wretched location on the shores of the Black Sea and his separation from Rome; rarely does a Roman author make such an issue of his place or call his readers' attention so persistently to it. He customarily defines exilic space negatively, in terms of what it lacks. Tomis lacks everything that the city of Rome possesses: his friends, his wife, a liveable climate, a civilized and appreciative audience for his verse, the delights of the city. Unable to return to Rome physically, he sends his books of poetry, written in exile, in his place, so that their presence in Rome can in a sense restore him. In practical terms they can speak for him through the writing that they contain, but they also have a symbolic value as substitutes for their author. So important is their function as physical representatives of the exiled poet that he so defines his book in the opening line of the *Tristia* (1.1.1): *parue – nec inuideo – sine me, liber, ibis in urbem* ("Small book, you will go – and I don't begrudge it – without me to the city").

Ovid's separation from Rome also generates idealizing fantasies about the city, which are among the most powerful and moving features of the exilic poetry. In the *Epistulae ex Ponto* he gives up the hope of a recall to Rome and requests only a place of exile that is free from the imminent threat of war. The first poem of the collection sounds this note of diminished hope (*Pont.* 1.1.79–80), and later it is summarized as *spes exilii commodioris*, "the hope of a more convenient place of exile" (*Pont.* 2.8.72).[3] *Pont.* 1.8, to cite another example, ends with an expanded version such a request (*Pont.* 1.8.73–4): *terra uelim propior nullique obnoxia bello / detur: erit nostris pars bona dempta malis* ("I would like to be granted a land that is closer and not exposed to war: in that case a great part of my woes will have been removed"). One might expect that diminished expectations might be accompanied by a diminished longing for the city, but not so. In the same *Pont.* 1.8, for example, he goes well beyond nostalgia in the sense of longing for a return home: although he claims not to miss the conveniences or advantages (*commoda, Pont.* 1.8.29) of Rome, presumably because he desires only a safer place of exile, he proceeds to imagine the city's sites, buildings, gardens, public spaces, pools, canals, etc., in his mind's eye – *cunctaque mens oculis peruidet usa suis*, "and my mind surveys all those places with its own eyes" (*Pont.* 1.8.34) – recreating them in his imaginative vision so intensely that he seems to restore himself, conceptually at least, to the sites that he so lovingly invokes and describes (*Pont.* 1.8.29–38):

> nec tu credideris urbanae commoda uitae
>   quaerere Nasonem (quaerit et illa tamen).   30
> nam modo uos animo dulces reminiscor amici,
>   nunc mihi cum cara coniuge nata subit,

aque domo rursus pulchrae loca uertor ad Vrbis,
　　cunctaque mens oculis peruidet illa suis:
nunc fora, nunc aedes, nunc marmore tecta theatra,　　　　　　35
　　nunc subit aequata porticus omnis humo,
gramina nunc Campi pulchros spectantis in hortos
　　stagnaque et euripi Virgineusque liquor.

Nor should you believe that Naso seeks the conveniences of urban life (nevertheless he does seek them). For sometimes I call you, sweet friends, to mind; sometimes my daughter and my dear wife occur to my thought, and once again I turn from my house to the places of the beautiful City, and my mind surveys all those places with its own eyes: now the fora, now the temples, now the theatres covered in marble, now each portico with its levelled ground occurs to my thought, the green fields of the Campus Martius that faces lovely gardens, the pools, the canals, and the water of the Aqua Virgo.

The specific places mentioned in these lines are significant to the poet's effort to evoke in his readers' minds an image of a longed-for Rome that will engage them in his own imaginative undertaking. His list expands outward from his private home to public spaces of the city: initially buildings, then open spaces and water features. He mentions those urban buildings that an observer is most likely to consider beautiful – fora, temples, marble-covered theatres, and porticos. The last example receives some descriptive expansion (36): *aequata porticus omnis humo* ("each portico with its levelled ground").[4] The expansion, reminding a Roman reader that the attainment of architectural success sometimes requires considerable alteration of the natural site, ends the list of buildings. What follows is a marked contrast: more natural-looking, park-like features of the urban scene conclude the list – grassy fields, lovely gardens, pools, canals, and the water of the Aqua Virgo. All located in the Campus Martius, these features are characteristic examples of *rus in urbe*, no less artificial than the buildings that precede them in the list, but designed to reconstruct the countryside, at least to some extent, and to establish a link between the urban Roman's experience of the city and his or her recollection of the countryside surrounding it. That recollection, whether it be founded on a large or small experience of the actual countryside, is an imaginative leap invited by the semi-rural spaces of the Campus. It is comparable in kind, if not in scale, to the exiled poet's imaginative effort to cross the vast distance that separates him from city and country alike.

Ovid describes exile as separation not only from the city of Rome but also from the land of Italy; and as with the loss of Rome, so with that of Italy: the land of exile lacks all that defines the Italian landscape. Nature provides Italy with four seasons, but Tomis with winter alone (*Pont.* 1.2.24): *iners hiemi continuatur hiems* ("one lifeless winter is joined to another winter"). Whereas Italian agriculture flourishes, there is no agriculture at all in the land of exile: no crops, no fruit trees, no vines (*Tr.* 3.10.75). For his theme of *asperitas loci* Ovid draws on Vergil's description of the harsh climate of Scythia in the *Georgics* (*G.* 3.349–83) as well as his contrasting praises of Italy (*G.* 1.136–76).[5] Both are relevant to Ovid's experience of exile, for by presenting Italy as his idealized home, he can emphasize the unnatural displacement that he suffers in a harsh exilic landscape.

In *Pont.* 1.8 the contrast between his natural home, which is lost to him, and his actual place gives impetus to imaginative fantasy even more extreme than the urban fantasy mentioned above; for he goes on to dwell upon the agricultural life that he could undertake if the harsh conditions of Tomis did not prevent it (*Pont.* 1.8.39–62):

> at puto sic Vrbis misero est erepta uoluptas
>   quolibet ut saltem rure frui liceat: 40
> non meus amissos animus desiderat agros
>   ruraque Paeligno conspicienda solo,
> nec quos piniferis positos in collibus hortos
>   spectat Flaminiae Clodia iuncta uiae,
> quos ego nesciocui colui, quibus ipse solebam   45
>   ad sata fontanas (nec pudet) addere aquas,
> sunt ubi, si uiuunt, nostra quoque consita quaedam
>   sed non et nostra poma legenda manu,
> pro quibus amissis utinam contingere possit
>   hic saltem profugo glaeba colenda mihi.   50
> ipse ego pendentis, liceat modo, rupe capellas,
>   ipse uelim baculo pascere nixus oues.
> ipse ego, ne solitis insistant pectora curis,
>   ducam ruricolas sub iuga curua boues,
> et discam Getici quae norunt uerba iuuenci,   55
>   adsuetas illis adiciamque minas.
> ipse manu capulum pressi moderatus aratri
>   experiar mota spargere semen humo;
> nec dubitem longis purgare ligonibus herbas,
>   et dare iam sitiens quas bibat hortus aquas.   60
> unde sed hoc nobis, minimum quos inter et hostem
>   discrimen murus clausaque porta facit?

It's not that the pleasures of the city have been taken from me in my wretchedness in such fashion as to allow me at least to enjoy some country pleasures! My mind does not long for my lost fields and my estates, well worth seeing, in the

Paelignian country, nor for my gardens, lying on pine-covered hills, which the Via Clodia joined to the Via Flaminia faces – gardens that I tilled for I know not whom, in which I used to conduct spring water in person to the plants (and I am not ashamed of it); where there are as well, if they still live, certain fruit trees planted by my hand, but whose fruits are not also to be gathered by my hand. For their loss would that it could be my lot to have at least a clod to till here in exile! I in person, were it only allowed, would like to pasture goats hanging on a crag; I would like in person to pasture sheep, leaning on my staff. I would in person, lest my heart dwell on its usual cares, bring the country-dwelling oxen beneath the curved yoke and would learn the words that Getic bullocks recognize, and I would hurl the accustomed threats at them. I myself, having guided with my hand the handle of the pressed-down plough, would try to scatter seed in the furrowed soil. I would not hesitate to clear away weeds with a long mattock and to provide water for the soon-thirsty garden to drink. But whence shall this come to me? Between me and the enemy there is only a very small partition: a wall and a closed gate.

Just as he claims not to miss the sites of the city, so now his mind does not long for his estates near Sulmo, nor for his gardens near Rome. Their loss would be compensated if he could only cultivate a bit of ground in exile, he remarks; that reflection initiates the extended fantasy about himself as a farmer and herdsman in exile. Into this passage he incorporates several allusions to Tibullus, indeed casting himself in the role of Tibullus in the first of that poet's elegies, which opposes an idealized rural life to the harsh existence of the soldier. When, in the lines just quoted, Ovid repeats *ipse* at the beginning of three hexameters in close proximity (51, 53, 56), asserting that he in person would be content to pursue agricultural activities, the context and the emphatic *ipse* recall Tib. 1.1.7–8: *ipse seram teneras maturo tempore uite / rusticus et facili grandia poma manu* ("Let me, becoming a rustic, in person plant tender vines when the season is ripe and tall fruit trees with a skilful hand"). When Ovid, describing how he used to irrigate the plants of his garden, adds *nec pudet* (46), "and I am not ashamed of it," we are likely to think of the same poem of Tibullus (1.1.29–30): *nec tamen interdum pudeat tenuisse bidentem / aut stimulo tardos increpuisse boues* ("Yet let me not be ashamed at times to hold the two-pronged hoe and urge on the sluggish oxen with a goad"). Ovid expands upon the subject matter of Tibullus' couplet a few lines later, when he asserts that he would herd Getic bullocks and "would not hesitate to clear away weeds with a long mattock" (53–6, 59). The allusive context of Ovid's lines is enriched not only by Tibullus but also by an intervening passage of Ovid's own earlier poetry on amatory subjects, a "window allusion" through which we may view Tibullus' lines.[6] Ovid draws on his own *Remedia amoris*

169–96, where he recommends agricultural pursuits as a distraction from the cares of love. Here the activities of planting and irrigation, comparable to those of *Pont.* 1.8, serve as advice to the lover, and the anaphora of *ipse* links this passage to both its Tibullan predecessor and its Ovidian successor (*Rem.* 193–4): *ipse potes riguis plantam deponere in hortis; / ipse potes riuos ducere lenis aquae* ("You can in person set out plants in a well-watered garden; you can in person guide streams of gentle water"). When Ovid asserts that he "would bring the country-dwelling oxen beneath the curved yoke" (*ducam ruricolas sub iuga curua boues, Pont.* 1.8.54), he reuses language of Tibullus in 1.10, alluding to Tibullus' praises of Peace while in his own poem he laments the absence of Peace (Tib. 1.10.45–6): *Pax candida primum / duxit araturos sub iuga curua boues* ("Shining Peace first brought oxen beneath the curved yoke to plough").

The most striking allusions in this passage, however, are to that most influential poem of exile, Vergil's first eclogue.[7] The connections between *B.* 1 and *Pont.* 1.8 are worth pursuing not only because they are so conspicuous but also because they accentuate and heighten Ovid's sense of alienation from his natural place – or rather places, for he is separated from both city and country. In *Pont.* 1.8 Ovid calls to our minds the very features of *B.* 1 that mark it most strongly as a poem of exile. He exploits both the similarity between his own fate and that of Vergil's Meliboeus and the contrast between his fate and that of Vergil's Tityrus. Meliboeus opens the eclogue with a quick sketch of Tityrus at leisure in pastoral retirement, singing of his beloved Amaryllis, whereas Meliboeus himself is on his way to exile, abandoning his ancestral property, his "sweet fields," and his homeland (1–5). Not by remaining in the country, however, did Tityrus escape the land confiscations and attain his present good fortune. The city of Rome is where Tityrus' help lay. Hoping to add enough to his *peculium* to purchase his freedom, he travelled there to market his cheese. He was much impressed by the city's vast size (19–25) but did not prosper in business. Although his small hopes of financial success were unrealized, he gained a far greater benefit. In Rome he saw the *iuuenis* who granted his petition and whom Tityrus now worships as a god, for he has gained his freedom and has been allowed to keep his lands (40–5). For Tityrus both country and city are sites of divine favour and sources of happiness. In *B.* 1 there is no rejection of the city: we are far from the world of Horace, for whom the life of the city is commonly portrayed as wretched, and that of the country blessed. With *B.* 1 in mind, we should not be surprised that Ovid in *Pont.* 1.8 can first longingly celebrate the sites of Rome, then pass to a fantasy of agricultural life in the same poem. He lacks the advantages of both city and country as Vergil presents them. He is like Meliboeus in having to leave his *dulcia arua* and unlike Tityrus in that the city, where Augustus, no longer a *iuuenis*, still holds power, is closed off to him and refuses to offer him the help of which he is desperately in need.

Ovid makes his most specific allusions to a passage near the end of *B.* 1 (64–78). Meliboeus, dispossessed of his farm and going into exile, tells his goats that "I will no longer, lying stretched out in a green cave, watch you from afar hanging on a thorny crag" (*non ego uos posthac uiridi proiectus in antro / dumosa pendere procul de rupe uidebo, B.* 1.75–6). The image of Meliboeus in repose, *uiridi proiectus in antro*, "lying stretched out in a green cave," is meant to recall Tityrus at the beginning of the eclogue, *patulae recubans sub tegmine fagi*, "reclining under the shade of a spreading beech." Ovid, already in exile, wishes, in similar language, that he could personally pasture goats and sheep (*Pont.* 1.8.51–2): *ipse ego pendentis, liceat modo, rupe capellas, / ipse uelim baculo pascere nixus oues* ("I in person, were it only allowed, would like to pasture goats hanging on a crag; I would like in person to pasture sheep, leaning on my staff"). He chooses a more active image of repose, not *proiectus* but leaning on his staff; yet *liceat modo* makes clear that no pastoral activity at all is available to Ovid. In the allusion to Vergil's first eclogue, there is conspicuous irony: casting himself in the role of Meliboeus, he encourages us to remember what Meliboeus said and reminds us that he, Ovid, will never watch his goats from afar, even as he fantasizes about doing so. But he also changes what Meliboeus said, replacing a strong negative statement about the future (Meliboeus employs the future indicative) with hypothetical statements, saturated with hopeless longing and expressed in potential subjunctives. There is a further irony in Ovid's identification of himself with Meliboeus if we consider the etymology of his name. According to Servius, he is called Meliboeus "because oxen are his concern" (ὅτι μέλει αὐτῷ τῶν βοῶν, *id est quia curam gerit boum*, Servius, headnote to *B.* 1).[8] Ovid by contrast is emphatically not concerned with oxen; he only wishes that he could be.

Here again it is worth noting that lines of the *Remedia amoris* intervene between our reading of Ovid's exilic elegy and our memory of Vergil, for Ovid has already adapted the same passage of the first eclogue to an elegiac context (*Rem.* 177–80):

> aspice labentes iucundo murmure riuos;
>   aspice tondentes fertile gramen oues.
> ecce, petunt rupes praeruptaque saxa capellae;
>   iam referent haedis ubera plena suis.

Watch the streams gliding with a pleasant murmur; watch the sheep cropping the fertile grass. See, the she-goats seek the crags and the precipitous rocks; soon they will bring back full udders to their kids.

By combining reminiscence of Vergil with reminiscences of Tibullus, whose idealization of rural life suits Ovid's purposes so well, and by weaving them together into the same context, Ovid incorporates pastoral into elegy, reshaping pastoral along elegiac lines. As we observe him doing so, it is important to note that he has a significant predecessor in Tibullus himself. Because Tibullus too introduces reminiscences of Vergilian bucolic into love elegy, Ovid is alluding to texts that one can say are already in dialogue. In Tibullus 2.3, for example, he represents himself going to the country because he is in thrall to Nemesis, who has followed her new lover there. He establishes a parallel between his own *seruitium* and that of Apollo serving Admetus. At the same time Tibullus introduces reminiscences of Vergil's tenth eclogue, wherein Gallus is similarly stranded in the country as he follows Lycoris, and, as J.H. Gaisser shows, "It is Gallus who is Apollo's real counterpart in the eclogue. He, like Apollo, is alien to the countryside, for he is an elegiac poet sojourning in the bucolic world."[9] When in *Pont.* 1.8 we observe Ovid vainly struggling to imagine an agricultural life for himself in Tomis, we may well recall that Apollo and Vergil's Gallus are already linked with an elegiac poet, Tibullus himself, in 2.3; all are represented as "not at home in the countryside," as Gaisser writes of Apollo.[10] When she speaks of Gallus' "fantasy" and "imagined pastoral life" in Vergil's eclogue,[11] she could as well be speaking of Ovid in *Pont.* 1.8.[12] What contribution the actual poet Gaius Cornelius Gallus makes to the work of his successors will remain unclear unless more of his poetry comes to light, but there is no doubt that Tibullus adapted Gallan elegy to his own purposes and alluded to it.[13] In adapting bucolic themes to elegy, the Ovid of exile joins an interchange in which at least three poets are already engaged.

In Ovid's exilic elegy, pastoral becomes idealized and gains a consolatory function: indeed he explicitly states that the purpose of his imagined agricultural activity is to take his mind off his accustomed cares (*Pont.* 1.8.53–4): *ipse ego, ne solitis insistant pectora curis, / ducam ruricolas sub iuga curua boues* ("I would in person, lest my heart dwell on its usual cares, bring the country-dwelling oxen beneath the curved yoke"). When in *Pont.* 1.8 Ovid calls to our minds the same passage of *B.* 1 that he had used in the *Remedia amoris*, he invites us to contemplate its vastly different consolatory import in each context. In the *Remedia amoris* the poet purports to offer practical advice to the lover who is seeking relief from the cares of love: the lover can look after sheep and watch goats: pastoral activity, presented largely as an act of observation, will distract him from amatory distress. In *Pont.* 1.8 the consolation to be gained from agricultural pursuits is purely hypothetical: it would happen if the activity itself were possible; but there is no agriculture in Tomis. Earlier in *Pont.* 1.8 Ovid's recollection of the city offers consolation as well, but only as long as he dwells upon it; for in the *Epistulae ex Ponto* he acknowledges that he is unlikely ever to return there. It will exist for him now only through recollection and thought. In similar fashion he presents agriculture as an activity that is impossible in exile, and, as a result, the relief to his cares that it might have provided is not to occur as part of the activity itself. Instead, any relief is the result of fantasy and dependent on it; and so he expands and develops his agricultural fantasy as if to sustain it. Action is denied to Ovid in exile; he suffers a kind of paralysis. The poet as farmer becomes a figure for his impossible situation, for any action is available to him only through an attempt to imagine it, and only through his imagination can he attain some relief from his woes.

Even readers of *B.* 1 who have not been thinking about Ovid recently are likely to think of him when Meliboeus begins his last speech with a list of the places of exile to which he and others are headed (*B.* 1.64–5): *at nos hinc alii sitientis ibimus Afros, / pars Scythiam* ("some of us will go from here to thirsty Africa, others to Scythia"); for Ovid often hyperbolically conflates Scythia Minor, his actual place of exile, with the even more remote expanse of territory north of the Black Sea to which the name Scythia more properly applies. Beginning at an early date, Ovid's exilic elegies may have affected readers' understanding of Vergilian pastoral, since Ovid, the example *par excellence* of a Roman exile, so compellingly recalls the first eclogue when giving expression to his own experience.[14] Deprived of both city and country, Ovid seizes upon and exploits Vergil's poem for the parallels and contrasts to his own situation that are available in Tityrus and Meliboeus. He opportunistically reshapes the pastoral genre to his present purposes, just as he reshapes the elegiac genre, transforming the work of his elegiac predecessors and his own earlier elegy.

NOTES

I presented earlier versions of this paper at the Southern Section meeting of the Classical Association of the Middle West and South in Atlanta in 2016 and at the *Symposium Cumanum 2017* on Vergil and Elegy at Cuma, Italy. I am grateful to both audiences for their comments, and especially to Megan Drinkwater, Laurel Fulkerson, Alison Keith, and Micah Myers.

1 Alpers 1979, 1982.
2 Alpers 1982: 451; Putnam 1970 is among his representative examples.
3 Tissol 2014. All translations are mine unless otherwise indicated.
4 See Tissol 2014: 157 on *Pont.* 1.8.36: Ovid "has in mind such cases as the large and impressive Porticus Liviae … which, located on the Esquiline in hilly terrain, would have been conspicuous for artificial levelling of the site."

5 For the theme of *asperitas loci*, see Helzle 2003: 77; for Vergil on Scythia in the *Georgics*, see Mynors 1990, ad loc.

6 For window allusion, see Tissol 1992: 441, and the bibliography cited there.

7 On *B*. 1, see also Henkel in this volume.

8 Servius *apud* Thilo and Hagen 1881: 1.4. I am grateful to John Van Sickle for this observation.

9 Gaisser 1977: 135.

10 Gaisser 1977: 132–3.

11 Gaisser 1977: 143.

12 For Tibullus' use of Vergil, see Gaisser 1977 on Tibullus 2.3 and Gallus in Vergil's tenth eclogue. D'Anna 1986 argues that Tibullus knew *Aeneid* 8 and adapted features of it in 2.5, notably the myth of Aeneas. D'Anna 1990 addresses Tibullus' knowledge of Vergil's *Bucolics* and allusions to that collection. He then returns to the topic of Tibullus 2.5 in relations to *A*. 8. Fabre-Serris 2001 examines first the close relationship between Tibullus 2.1 and the *Georgics*, then that between Tibullus 2.5 and both the *Georgics* and *Aeneid*. Demonstrating the plasticity of love elegy, Tibullus unites elegy's erotic themes – both happy and unhappy love affairs – with the grander Roman themes of Vergil, "the praise of the *rus*, the valorisation of past times, the celebration of *pietas*, of military glory and Rome's destiny" (140). Fabre-Serris 2004 shows love elegy deeply engaged with Roman didactic poetry, especially Lucretius' *De rerum natura* and Vergil's *Georgics*, despite both predecessors' condemnation of erotic *furor*; see also Fabre-Serris in this volume. Fabre-Serris 2013a links Gallus, Tibullus, and Vergil in their use of the adjective *durus*, a term, like its opposite *mollis*, of wide application and rich significance in Roman elegy. For example, Gallus, as a character in Vergil's tenth eclogue, describes his Lycoris as *dura* (47), and Tibullus describes his Nemesis as *dura puella* (2.6.8). Houghton 2018: 197–200 discusses Tibullus' longing for the age when Saturn ruled (1.3.35–50) among the "early responses to Virgil's Fourth Eclogue."

13 For Tibullus' use of Gallus – both the elegist and the character in Vergil's tenth eclogue – see Gaisser 1977 on Tibullus 2.3 and Vergil's Gallus. Cairns (1979: 226–8) surveys various features of Gallus' elegies that may reasonably be deduced from Parthenius' *Erotika Pathemata* (dedicated to Gallus), Vergil's tenth eclogue, and the elegies of Tibullus and Propertius. O'Hara 2005 argues for reading *dulcis* at Tibullus 1.10.11 on the grounds that the poet thereby alludes to Gallus' use of the same adjective in the lines preserved in the Qaṣr Ibrîm papyrus. Fabre-Serris 2013a links Gallus in the tenth eclogue with Tibullus in their use of the adjective *durus*. Fabre-Serris 2017 aims "to show how the poetry of Sulpicia can contribute to clarify the way in which Gallus was read and used by his elegiac successors" (116), with reference to Gallus in the tenth eclogue, Tibullus, Propertius, and Ovid.

14 See Wheeler 2004–5 for the early reception of Ovid's exilic elegies.

Vergil and Elegy in Imperial Latin Literature

13

The Errant Flock: Calpurnius Siculus' Bucolic Response to Elegy

YELENA BARAZ

Pastoral is an unsettled genre, marked from its beginnings by intense generic interactions.[1] Love poetry is one of the most important generic interlocutors for bucolic poetry at its very origins in the work of Theocritus.[2] The erotic material in Theocritus is developed in the mythological erotic poetry of his Hellenistic successors, Bion and Moschus.[3] This prominence continues in Vergil's bucolic collection, in which the erotic forms a major thematic and generic strand.[4] But in the case of Vergil, it is more than that: elegy, personified as Gallus, is the one genre that enters into embodied dialogue with bucolic, and, in the end, fails to be contained within the collection. Gallus' departure from the pastoral landscape in *B.* 10 facilitates the poet's exit from the world of bucolic poetry, the world that is too full to embrace anything more.[5] This makes the question of how to accommodate love elegy a particularly challenging one for Calpurnius Siculus, an otherwise unknown poet whose name is attached to the first collection of eclogues after Vergil that has come down to us.[6] What complicates the matter even further is the simple fact that elegy as a genre, after its Augustan flowering, is no longer the same as it was for Vergil. Calpurnius has to face a much more complex and weighty generic inheritance when approaching a genre that was already presented as overwhelming and overflowing by Vergil.[7] In my discussion of Calpurnius' engagement with elegy in his *Ecl.* 2 and, more extensively, in *Ecl.* 3, I argue that his treatment not only represents a further step in the tradition of bucolic's entanglement with love poetry but also allows us to see how Calpurnius responds to and transforms the Vergilian paradigm of the bucolic in light of literary developments that postdate Vergil's *Bucolica* and in so doing creates his own version of pastoral. In my discussion of Calpurnius' *Ecl.* 3, I will focus on three features that he borrows from elegy: the prominence of writing, the development of an aesthetic sensibility and of a critical language among the shepherds, and the violence directed at the *puella*.

The challenge posed by the development of elegy as a post-Vergilian genre to Calpurnius' project of positioning himself as a successor both to Vergil and to the preceding literary tradition is significant, but not unique. Given the discontinuous nature of the pastoral tradition, Calpurnius' choice to write bucolic poetry creates a tension in his reception of what came before. On the one hand, he positions himself as a successor to the pastoral tradition and, of course, most particularly, to Vergil's bucolic collection.[8] On the other, he cannot situate himself as Vergil's immediate follower: inevitably, his poetry interacts with Latin literature as it developed after the *Bucolica*, including, significantly, Vergil's own later works. The distinctive pastoral poetics that Calpurnius develops are a direct response to this tension, this particular instantiation of the more general issue of belatedness.[9] In approaching the tradition of which he aims to become a part, Calpurnius targets features that can be seen as typical of the genre as he receives it, and then transforms them through rejection, distortion, or exaggeration. He does this by focusing on, and expanding, minor, often discordant, notes in the earlier tradition. A striking example is the breakdown in the exchange of song, both among shepherds and between nature and human singers, in Calpurnius' pastoral world, an essential part of the preceding tradition: unlike the shepherds in Theocritus and Vergil, his singers compete only when nature is silent and towards the end of the corpus (in his *Ecl.* 6), or they fail to engage in a traditional competition altogether, unable to extricate themselves from the preliminary squabbling.[10] Such changed features are present, and often developed, throughout the corpus, so that Calpurnius can be seen as staking out a distinctive poetic position on pastoral matters. In responding to the generic developments that stand between him and Vergil's *Bucolica*, Calpurnius employs a different strategy. Several poems can be read as dedicated to a full-scale exploration of a particular genre; such poems then represent an attempt to incorporate that genre within the framework of Calpurnius' new pastoral. The clearest example of this is *Eclogue* 5, which has a minimal bucolic frame, but whose didactic content is directed by an old shepherd to his *alumnus* on the georgic subject of raising sheep.[11] While it is useful for the purpose of analysis to separate these two strands – the comprehensive reworking of pastoral features throughout the corpus and the focused encounters with individual genres staged within one poem – in practice things are not quite as clear cut. Many genres are already integrated into pastoral in Vergil, and, conversely, Vergil's

Bucolica are an important influence on many texts in other genres that come after.[12] As a result, in Calpurnius' response, too, features of genres that he highlights in individual poems inevitably spread beyond their confines.

Elegy is a particularly important genre to consider in this light. We can read Vergil's *B*.10 and its engagement with elegy as the model for Calpurnius' own interactions with individual genres in *Ecl*. 3. But the genre of elegy with which Calpurnius engages is dramatically different, having undergone major developments and having been, in a certain sense, reviewed and closed by Ovid. Given that elegy can be said to end Vergilian pastoral, as Gallus is unable to settle into the bucolic world he encounters, Calpurnius' own encounter with the genre of elegy is also a setting in which he can measure his achievement against Vergil's as he seeks to give new life to the genre his predecessor left behind as the first step in what became a paradigmatic poetic career.[13] The very placement of Calpurnius' "elegiac" eclogue,[14] in the third position of the book – in contrast to Vergil's decision to close his collection with Gallus in *B*. 10 – is significant, and should be read as part of his response to Vergil, as a claim that he can do what Vergil could not. The fact that the poem is placed early in the collection announces that Calpurnius is able, contrary to Vergil, to contain the genre of elegy within his bucolic corpus. My reading of *Ecl*. 2 and 3 focuses on how Calpurnius deploys features of Augustan elegy that are not at home in Vergil's pastoral world but form an important part of the later poet's. I suggest that the effect of his use of elegy is twofold: on the one hand, Calpurnius' use of elegy can be understood as domesticating and containing the difficult genre, and in that way as surpassing his predecessor. On the other hand, we can see his use of elegy as productive: it provides building blocks for important characteristics of his pastoral poetics that are distinct from Vergil's; that is, the more fragmented, fractious, and belated atmosphere of his world. Calpurnius, I suggest, reframes developments derived from elegy so as to offer texture and pedigree to features of his own distinctive poetic world.

Calpurnius engages with elegy in an extended fashion in *Ecl*. 3, a poem which seems to exhaust his interest in the genre and in erotic matters more generally. Before I turn to it, I wish to look briefly at the poem that precedes it, Calpurnius' most Vergilian amoebaean competition poem that features an amatory thread running through it, but appears to avoid serious engagement with elegy. Love is highlighted as a theme at the start, when the competing singers are introduced as united in their love for the virgin Crocale (*Ecl*. 2.1–4):[15]

> intactam Crocalen puer Astacus et puer Idas,
> Idas lanigeri dominus gregis, Astacus horti,

> dilexere diu, formosus uterque nec impar
> uoce sonans.

The boy Astacus and the boy Idas have loved for a long time the virgin Crocale – Idas the master of a woolbearing herd, Astacus, of a garden, both beautiful and not unequal in the sound of their voices.

The boys' love for Crocale is one of the things that they share, and the singing contest between them can be read as a sublimation of their amorous competition for her affections. In this opening they are emphatically presented as well matched, and, in fact, this parity is what seems to undermine the possibility of a win: this is a contest that will be judged a tie. The singers invoke their love twice in the course of the competition: in the first exchange (2.51–9), they each appeal to the gods and pledge gifts should the girl be granted to them.[16] Another sequence, beginning at line 68, presents the respective gifts the boys' occupations (Idas is a shepherd, Astacus a gardener) allow them to offer to Crocale, then shifts to their description of their attractive appearance.[17] Each time Crocale is mentioned, she appears briefly, first as a pretext for the competition, then as a starting point for prayer, and finally as a recipient of gifts whose mention invites the singers' self-description. But she herself fades out from the narrative as soon as she is mentioned; the boys talk about their looks, but not hers. Her name, Κροκάλη, "sea-shore," marks her as an object of desire that is out of place in the pastoral environment, reminiscent of Polyphemus' misguided infatuation with the sea-nymph Galatea.[18] But unlike Polyphemus and the Vergilian lovers who struggle with their desire for distant love-objects (Corydon in *B.* 2 and Gallus in *B.* 10), the boys are presented by Calpurnius as removed from their predecessors' passions. Idas opens the last exchange by coming back to the underlying motivation for the competition (*Ecl.* 2.91): *carmina poscit amor, nec fistula cedit amoris* ("love demands songs, and the pipe does not yield to love"). Love is finally evoked here as the explicit motivation for the creation of bucolic song, the impetus for the competition. Yet, like all other references to the beloved Crocale, it is strikingly brief and fades quickly. More than that, the competition between the boys for Crocale is reconfigured as competition between *fistula*, pastoral song, and *amor*, love poetry, with the genre of erotic elegy on the losing side in the end. When *amor* reappears in the last line, in the judgment of Thyrsis, its meaning has changed (2.99–100): *este pares et ob hoc concordes uiuite; nam uos / et decor et cantus et amor sociauit et aetas* ("Be equal and for this reason live in concord; for grace and song and love have made you partners, and your age"). The poem, then, concludes as it began, with an emphatic assertion of the contestants' parity. But their love of Crocale, rather than leading one of them to victory, seems to have been displaced in the course of the competition. While *amor* in the last line can be taken to refer back to their shared love for the girl, it can also be interpreted as signifying their newly found *amicitia*, a homosocial relationship that sidelines the amatory one, turning it into a mere pretext.[19] I suggest that looking for the erotic allows us to read this poem as one response to the tension between the pastoral and the elegiac in the preceding pastoral tradition, and to Vergil's failure to contain elegy, especially in *B*. 10. Here Calpurnius strips the elegiac of its power by disempowering the beloved, who becomes a cipher, and by denying the lovers an opportunity for an unconstrained emotional expression by locating their singing within the confines of amoebaean exchange. The lack of definitive outcome in the competition is then an effect of the transferral of the emotional focus from the beloved to the rival.

But this victory of pastoral over elegy is only made possible by not allowing the full power of elegy to be present. The next poem, *Ecl*. 3, represents another attempt to tackle the same tension, but this time Calpurnius allows the emotional content of the genre in its Augustan manifestation into his text. What transpires then is a much more extensive exploration of the relative powers of the two genres. Unlike *Ecl*. 2, where love is a pretext and the passions are subdued, the third eclogue is preoccupied with love throughout, while its lover-character is in the grip of heightened emotions. The poem begins with a conversation between two shepherds, Iollas, who has lost a heifer, and Lycidas, whose beloved has left him after he beat her in a fit of jealousy. A slave is sent to look for the heifer while Iollas encourages Lycidas to send him as a messenger to win the girl back with a song. The song that follows occupies most of the poem, and, just as the two are about to set off on their mission to woo the girl, the heifer is brought back.

Calpurnius frames the poem by establishing a parallel between the situations of the two interlocutors, Iollas and Lycidas.[20] Iollas has lost a *iuuenca*, a heifer which, we learn, is often found grazing near the bulls that belong to Lycidas. Lycidas finds it difficult to show concern about his friend's bovine misfortune because he has also suffered a loss: his girlfriend, Phyllis, has left him for a new lover, Mopsus. The analogy between lovers and cattle itself has a long pedigree encompassing both Vergil and elegy. In *G*. 3, addressing the challenges that animal desire presents to the farmer, Vergil describes in highly anthropomorphizing language a heifer that watches two bulls battling for her affections.[21] The image returns in the *Aeneid*, with the tenor and vehicle now reversed, in a simile that compares Turnus and Aeneas fighting over Lavinia to the bulls in the *Georgics*.[22] It is then further transformed by Ovid, who uses it twice in the *Amores*. *Amores* 2.12, which presents his conquest of Corinna as a triumph, ends with a list of comparisons to great wars fought over women: the Trojan war, the battle between the Centaurs and Lapiths, the Trojans and the Italians in the second half of the *Aeneid*, and finally the Romans and the Sabines (*Am.* 2.12.17–24). But the final battle, true to the spirit of the poem, retrieves the simile from the *Aeneid* and puts the two sides of the comparison alongside each other: Ovid ends with the heifer watching the bulls.[23] The juxtaposition deflates both sides, and the poem ends with Ovid glorying in the bloodlessness of his victory.[24] But most important as a parallel for Calpurnius is Ovid's reuse of the image in *Amores* 3.5, a poem in which a dream about a heifer abandoning her bull-husband to pursue other bulls is read by a dream interpreter as an indication of the girl's unfaithfulness to the speaker.[25] It is this runaway heifer following someone else's bulls that serves as the closest link between this inter-textual strand and the starting point of Calpurnius' poem. At each step, the two sides of the comparison are articulated increasingly distinctly, and Calpurnius' reification of both the heifer and the girl completes the process.[26]

In structuring his poem around a parallel between the lost heifer and the lost girlfriend, Calpurnius encloses an amatory animal image from the *Georgics*, as developed in the *Aeneid* and in Ovid's elegies, within the frame of a bucolic poem on lost animals where, one might think, it properly belongs. But in fact, the image does not appear in Vergil's *Bucolica*: the closest we come is the opening of *B.* 7, in which Meliboeus is following a lost goat when he encounters Daphnis, who restores the animal to his owner and invites the shepherd to witness a singing contest.[27] Calpurnius' splitting of it into two parallel losses stages the encounter as one between the bucolic (the heifer) and the elegiac (the girl). The Ovidian versions, while playful and ironic, retain the connection to the higher generic register inherited from the *Aeneid*: *Am.* 2.12 through epic comparisons and *Am.* 3.5 through the act of dream interpretation.[28] Calpurnius' abandonment of these elevating generic features has the effect of lowering the poetic status of the elegiac conflict at the centre of the poem in the exploration of the reasons for Phyllis' abandonment of her lover and his efforts to win her back.

Within the opening section, Calpurnius also connects the affair between Lycidas and the now-lost Phyllis to Vergil's bucolic collection. As Iollas expresses his surprise at the breakup, he exclaims (*Ecl.* 3.10–12): *mobilior uentis o femina! sic tua Phyllis? / quae sibi, nam memini, si quando solus abesses, / mella etiam sine te iurabat amara uideri* ("O, woman, more change-able than winds! So your Phyllis? And she – for I remember – if ever you alone were absent, she swore that without you even honey seemed bitter to her"). The lover who grieves for her beloved's absence evokes the grief of *maesta* Amaryllis that Meliboeus recalls in recounting the effects of Tityrus'

absence in Vergil's first eclogue (*B*. 1.36–9). But the pathos is almost immediately undercut in Lycidas' response: ignoring the proffered sympathies,
Lycidas directs Iollas in searching for the lost heifer near his bull, describing
the animal in the words that recall the position in which Meliboeus found
Tityrus at the start of Vergil's poem. In Vergil's opening lines Meliboeus
describes coming upon Tityrus reclining in the shade (*recubans sub tegmine
fagi*, *B*. 1.1, *lentus in umbra*, *B*. 1.4) and playing his pipe. Lycidas describes
the leisure of his bull in similar terms (*Ecl*. 3.15–17): *nam cum prata calent,
illic requiescere noster / taurus amat gelidaque iacet spatiosus in umbra / et
matutinas reuocat palearibus herbas* ("For while the meadows are scorching,
there our bull likes to rest and he lies, stretched out in cool shadow, and
recalls the morning grass in his jaws"). While the woman who appears to
take the place of faithful Amaryllis has been turned into a faithless *puella*
(and analogized to a cow), the contented lover himself has been drawn even
further into the world of the pasture, and, in typical Vergilian fashion, his
features have been divided among characters in the new text. His posture
has been given to a bull, with rather a serious loss of dignity: instead of the
pastoral activity of singing, he is engaged, like Ovid's bull, in chewing the
cud.[29] But the name, Tityrus, appears soon after as that of the slave sent by
Iollas to search for the heifer while the master stays to listen to Lycidas'
talc of woe (*Ecl*. 3.19–21): *Tityre, quas dixit, salices pete solus et illinc, / si
tamen inuenies, deprensam uerbere multo / huc age; sed fractum referas has-
tile memento* ("Tityrus, go alone and look for the willows he described and
there, if indeed you find her, catch her and with many blows of the whip
drive her; but remember to bring back the broken rod"). In addition to intertextually mirroring and disrupting the iconic tableau at the start of Vergil's
first eclogue, Tityrus' presence here has another, metaliterary, meaning. As
is the case quite early in the reception of Vergil's *Bucolica*, Tityrus in Calpurnius stands for Vergil, most clearly in Calpurnius' *Ecl*. 4, where Vergil's
career and his relationship to Maecenas are recalled.[30] Thus, the dispatch of
Tityrus to look for the heifer and the bull can be read as a temporary removal
of the bucolic side of the encounter, a suspension of the bucolic frame which
gives room to the elegiac complaints of the lover Lycidas, in the same way
as the georgic monologue is given centre stage in *Ecl*. 5. The opening of the
poem makes connections between the elegiac and the bucolic that recall
Vergil, yet escape easy classification. The low register of the bucolic that
Calpurnius activates appears to compromise the seriousness of the elegy,
but the removal of Tityrus from the poem suggests that the elegiac might
be allowed to have its own circumscribed space to develop without explicit
input from the bucolic. The name of the girl, Phyllis, is also significant;
unlike watery Crocale, she is connected to φύλλα, "leaves," and so belongs

in the green world of the pastoral; indeed, the name appears several times in Vergil's *Bucolica*.[31] Jacqueline Fabre-Serris has read the Phyllises of the *Bucolica* and their successors in the poetry of Horace, Propertius, and Ovid to suggest that her prominence goes back to a treatment of the Phyllis myth by Gallus.[32] This is particularly attractive in light of Calpurnius' choice of the name as he re-enacts, with a difference, the encounter between the bucolic and the elegiac, which in Vergil is embodied by Gallus.

The central portion of the poem consists of Lycidas' account of his quarrel with Phyllis and Iollas' advice meant to bring about their reconciliation, advice that Lycidas accepts by producing a song to woo her back. Two strands can be distinguished in Calpurnius' presentation of elegiac material here: first, he imports stock features of the later elegiac tradition that are absent from Vergil, thus "updating" his version of elegy; second, despite the dismissal of Tityrus, he continues to contaminate the elegiac with the bucolic, drawing on the parallel between the girl and the heifer introduced in the opening conversation. These two directions interact to create the distinctive elegiac poetics within the poem, marked by use of writing, an aesthetic sensibility, and the presence of violence.

I begin with writing, which comes into the poem at the suggestion of Iollas. Iollas is a mediating figure, a conciliator and a *praeceptor amoris*. His approach to the lovers' disagreements is an Ovidian one: the lover should always yield to the girl, even if she is wrong.[33] He offers to take a message to the wounded Phyllis, and volunteers to write down the song that Lycidas addresses to her (*Ecl.* 3.43–4): *dic age; nam cerasi tua cortice uerba notabo / et decisa feram rutilanti carmina libro* ("Come, tell me; for I will mark down your words on cherry-tree bark and then cut the song off and bring it to her in a red-coloured book"). Written messages, letters conveyed through an intermediary, are a major feature of elegiac poetry; the separated lovers routinely communicate in this way, and the repertoire of Ovid's *Heroides* grows out of that practice.[34] While there are important gestures towards writing in Vergil's *Bucolica* (Mopsus in *B.* 5.13–15 and Gallus in *B.* 10.52–4 write their poems on tree bark), it is not as prominent a feature of his pastoral world,[35] and Gallus' writing can be attributed to his own elegiac provenance.[36] Yet for Calpurnius, whose book of eclogues opens with the singing of a prophecy found incised on a tree, the prominence of writing is an important marker that distinguishes his bucolic from Vergil's. The shepherd who offers to transmit his friend's song in written form, rather than memorizing it, lives in a world that is markedly post-Vergilian, and the elegiac strand in *Ecl.* 3 serves in part to provide a genealogy for this transition. Calpurnius adopts this expanded use of writing from elegy to supplement the failings of memory that are thematized towards the end of Vergil's bucolic book, in *B.* 9.[37] Iollas' offer borrows the language of Mopsus' carving in Vergil (*notare* and *cortex*) but adds *liber* and changes the colour.[38] The Vergilian Mopsus was writing on green bark (*in uiridi … cortice*, B. 5.13), the colour rooted in the pastoral environment. Iollas' *rutilanti libro* (*Ecl.* 3.44), by contrast, reads as a reference to a presentation copy of a papyrus roll. These shepherds are not just incising their songs on trees and reading them off; they are making books.

Another feature that is found elsewhere in Calpurnius, but in this poem is rooted in the elegiac context, is the emphasis on aesthetic qualities of both the shepherds' appearances and their songs. The girl's ability to appreciate the superior attractiveness of Lycidas is important to his appeal to her, but much more important is that she has recognized the superiority of his singing in the past (*Ecl.* 3.42): *solet illa meas ad sidera ferre Camenas* ("she is accustomed to carry my Muses to the stars"), he says as he makes the decision to take Iollas' advice and approach Phyllis through song. By contrast, Lycidas describes Mopsus' music as failing on all counts (*Ecl.* 3.59–62):

> a dolor! et post haec placuit tibi torrida Mopsi
> uox et carmen iners et acerbae stridor auenae?
> quem sequeris? quem, Phylli, fugis? formosior illo
> dicor, et hoc ipsum mihi tu iurare solebas.

Ah, pain! and after these [my songs] the parched voice of Mopsus pleased you and his unskilled song, and the hissing of his harsh pipe? Whom do you follow? Whom, Phyllis, do you flee? More beautiful than he I am said to be, and you used to swear that very thing to me.

Mopsus' voice is *torrida* ("hoarse"), his song *iners* ("lacking in craft"), and he is not a good pipe player: the pipe is *acerba* ("harsh"), and what it produces is *stridor* ("hissing"). Such explicit discussions of what makes music good are largely absent from Vergil. Calpurnius' *stridor* is derived from Menalcas' assault on Damoetas' piping in Vergil's third eclogue, but the connection helps clarify the difference (B. 3.25–7): *… aut umquam tibi fistula cera / iuncta fuit? non tu in triuiis, indocte, solebas / stridenti miserum stipula disperdere carmen?* ("… Did you ever even have a pipe joined by wax? Didn't you, ignoramus, use to destroy wretched songs in the crossroads, on your hissing pipe?"). *Stridenti* is the only one of the adjectives that Menalcas uses that is specific in describing the quality of Damoetas' art; the rest of his accusations are generic and vague. Vergilian contests are judged without explanation, and scholars have found few explicit clues in their attempts to analyse what makes Corydon the winner in *B.* 7.[39] Calpurnius develops the potential, present in *stridenti*, and gives his shepherds a critical language they can use in assessing each other's musical abilities. This language is unusual: *torridus* is not otherwise used for sound, and while there are *comparanda* for *iners*, used for verses by Horace, and for *acerba*, used of sound by Lucretius and Vergil, these are rare, and Calpurnius' particular collocations are unique.[40] Such precise and harsh criticism is on display in *Ecl.* 6, the failed competition poem,[41] but it is first found here in Lycidas' aesthetic assault on the absent Mopsus. In this case also, the elegiac background is a source from which Calpurnius derives the energy for his transmutation of Vergil.

One of the insults that Menalcas throws at Damoetas is that his opponent is *indocte*, "unskilled" (*B.* 3.26, quoted above). But unlike Vergil's shepherds, who seek approval from the judgment of their peers, Calpurnius makes clear that Lycidas focuses his desire for appreciation on his beloved, and it is her sudden inability to see the superior aesthetic quality of his song in comparison with that of his rival that deals a crushing blow to his self-esteem and to their relationship. This positioning of the beloved as learned and able to appreciate the quality of poetry, in contrast to the *indoctus* Damoetas, has as its antecedent the *docta puella* of elegy, whose genealogy goes back to Catullus but is fully developed in Augustan elegy, and especially in the corpus of Propertius.[42]

The centrality of the aesthetic to the amatory bond between Lycidas and Phyllis is closely connected to the most striking feature of this elegiac narrative, the presence of violence against the *puella* that critics have found shocking and that has led to the condemnation of the poem and the poet, beginning with Scaliger's damning *merum rus, idque inficetum* ("sheer country diction, and inelegant at that").[43] Instead of dismissing the violence as Calpurnius' inability to maintain proper generic decorum, we can now trace the origins of this violence to its elegiac precursors.[44]

What provoked the break between Lycidas and his beloved, Phyllis, was Lycidas' violent reaction to seeing Phyllis singing and piping together with his rival, Mopsus. Lycidas's reaction comes as a shock in the pastoral context: he tears the girl's clothes and beats her (*Ecl.* 3.26–30):

> en, sibi cum Mopso calamos intexere cera
> incipit et puero comitata sub ilice cantat.
> haec ego cum uidi, fateor, sic intimus arsi,
> ut nihil ulterius tulerim. nam protinus ambas
> diduxi tunicas et pectora nuda cecidi.

Look, she begins to cover reeds with wax together with Mopsus and, accompanied by the boy, under the holm-oak she sings. When I saw these things, I confess, I so burned inside, that I could bear nothing further. For instantly I ripped both her tunics and beat her naked breast.

The ripping of girls' clothing is a motive common in elegy, and once again the closest parallel comes from Ovid's account of beating his girlfriend in *Amores* 1.7.43–8:[45]

> denique, si tumidi ritu torrentis agebar,
>   caecaque me praedam fecerat ira suam,
> nonne satis fuerat timidae inclamasse puellae,
>   nec nimium rigidas intonuisse minas,
> aut tunicam a summa diducere turpiter ora
>   ad mediam? – mediae zona tulisset opem.

At last, if I were driven on like a swollen stream, and blind anger had made me its prey, wouldn't it have been enough to have shouted at the timid girl or to have thundered excessively harsh threats, or to have ripped the tunic from the top to the middle in a disgraceful manner? – the belt at her waist would have borne the attack.

Calpurnius has linked Lycidas' violent reaction to the importance of the girl's aesthetic judgment and his self-esteem as a singer. For Lycidas, it is not infidelity but an assault on his status as a superior musician, since so much of it is founded on the reinforcement it received from Phyllis, that causes him to lash out. But the violence also has an internal bucolic source within the poem, as it mirrors the gratuitous violence introduced by Iollas in his directions to Tityrus not simply to bring back the heifer but to beat her until the rod breaks (3.20–1, quoted above). Lycidas' attack on Phyllis also acquires further, metapoetic, meaning within the bucolic context. *Tunica* is a word that is used as a virtual synonym for bark by Vergil at G. 2.75. The word is also used by Pliny the Elder in the *Natural History* (16.65, 24.7), and his usage makes clear that technically it refers to a thin layer of membrane between the hard outer bark and the wood underneath. *Ambas*, which commentators have generally taken to refer to two layers of clothing,[46] can then likewise be read as referring to the outer and inner tree bark. In tearing off the tunics, then, Lycidas could be said to be stripping the songs, normally written on bark, just like the one he is about to send to Phyllis with Iollas, which he had entrusted to her judgment in the past. His violence is an attempt to recover his worth as a singer from the damage done by her betrayal.

The amatory burning of elegy, too, is transformed in the course of the assault into a different kind of passion: it becomes anger. *Arsi* ("I burned") in line 28 echoes Lycidas' first lines in the poem (3.7–8): *uror, Iolla, / uror, et immodice* ("I burn, Iollas, I burn, and without limit"). As Lycidas tells Iollas that he wants Phyllis to quarrel with her new lover more than he wants her back, this translation of emotion is further clarified: it is the burning for revenge rather than love that drives him. Lycidas' violence is connected in the poem with the quasi-bucolic treatment of women as property, women as cattle. When Lycidas expresses his fear that Phyllis will leave him for another (*ne forte uagetur*, "lest perchance she wander," 3.33), the verb he uses is one not unprecedented in elegy.[47] Propertius speaks contemptuously of *uagae puellae* in contrast to Cynthia, who takes passion seriously, in his warning to Gallus in poem 1.5, and Ovid describes all female worshippers of Cupid as *uaga turba, puellae* in *Amores* 2.9.[48] But this semantic cluster is more strongly associated with the aimless wandering of cattle, a meaning that is easily activated in the bucolic context.[49]

The violence and anger directed towards Phyllis are mediated and mitigated by the intervention of Iollas. As he involves Lycidas in the process of composition, the violence turns towards its true target. Since the fear that caused him to attack Phyllis is about his aesthetic competence, it surfaces again after he remembers her former admiration for his musical and poetic gift. Like a contrite elegiac poet (and, once again, most like Ovid in *Amores* 2.9), he acknowledges her justified fear of *uerbera* and offers to surrender his hands to be tied behind his back.[50] Even while evoking further violence, as he recalls having Tityrus tie up and hang his rival Mopsus in a past incident, in his appeal to Phyllis he develops the regret for his attack into a threat against himself. The rival was strung up as a warning, but Lycidas threatens suicide by hanging: he will hang from the very oak where he saw Phyllis together with Mopsus. The importance of song is made explicit here: her singing with Mopsus is described as a violation of their love (*uiolauit amores*, *Ecl.* 3.88) in language borrowed from Tibullus.[51]

This threat of suicide under the same tree where she betrayed his song further emphasizes the importance of the aesthetic to their bond, and his promise of an epitaph carved in the tree is a warning to future singers (*Ecl.* 3.89–91): *hi tamen ante mala figentur in arbore uersus: / "credere, pastores, leuibus nolite puellis; / Phyllida Mopsus habet, Lycidan habet ultima rerum"* ("First let these verses be carved on the evil tree: 'Shepherds, do not believe frivolous girls. Mopsus holds Phyllis; the last of all things holds Lycidas'"). The bucolic frame reveals how performative and manipulative this threat is: Lycidas is not about to go to the infamous tree to kill himself. He has just dictated the song that Iollas will sing for Phyllis and he hopes to achieve reconciliation. Just as the two shepherds are about to set off to woo Phyllis back, Iollas spots Tityrus coming back with the lost heifer and, in a reversal of the Ovidian dream reading, interprets her return as a good omen for the return of the girl.[52] On the metapoetic level, the parallel herding of the girl and the cow reinforces the precarious balance that the poet has achieved between the bucolic and the elegiac by integrating the features of the post-Vergilian elegiac poetry with the distinctive markers of his own pastoral world. Tityrus, to whose fame he aspires in the central poem of the collection, is here found doing Iollas' bidding. The taming of elegy and the enslaving of the bucolic Tityrus conclude the first half of the collection and form the foundation for the greater claims to come in *Ecl.* 4 and the bid to enclose Vergil's later works in the second half. Incorporating violence, giving the shepherds a language to express aesthetic judgment, and expanding the role of writing within the pastoral frame allow Calpurnius to present himself as having accomplished what Vergil appears to have given up on; that is, containing elegy inside a bucolic environment. It also helps him position himself not only as an imitator of Vergil but also as a poet who gives the bucolic genre a new life by locating his innovations in post-*Bucolica* literary history.

NOTES

1 A good starting point for the debate on treating pastoral in antiquity as a genre or a mode is Schmidt's 1998 review of Alpers 1996.

2 See, e.g., Acosta-Hughes 2006 on elegy and lyric.

3 Fantuzzi and Hunter 2004: 170–90.

4 On "generic enrichment" in Vergil's *Bucolica,* see Harrison 2007a: ch. 2, with further bibliography; cf. the Introduction of Karakasis (2011: 1–11) for an overview of "generic expansion" in pastoral more generally.

5 For a recent reading of the role of Gallus in closing the collection, see Seider 2016, with a different emphasis.

6 The date of Calpurnius is uncertain. Mayer 2006: 454–6 gives a concise overview of the debate. The Neronian dating proposed by Haupt in 1854, when he separated the corpus from Nemesianus, remains the majority view. The most important interventions proposing a different date are Champlin 1978 and 1986; Armstrong 1986; Courtney 1987; and Horsfall 1997.

7 Magnelli 2006.

8 Relationship to Vergil is central to Hubbard's (1998: 150–78) and Slater's (1994) readings of Calpurnius. See also Magnelli 2006 and Mayer 2006.

9 For the issue of belatedness, see, e.g., Hardie's 1993 treatment of post-Vergilian epic.

10 See Baraz 2015 and Baraz 2018 respectively.

11 See Becker 2012: 21–6 and 39–45 on georgic and epic strands in *Ecl.* 5 and 6 respectively. On *Ecl.* 5 and the georgic, see Esposito 2012; cf. Karakasis 2016a: 157–94.

12 E.g., Horace's *Satires*, on which see Van Rooy 1973; Zetzel 1980; Putnam 1995–6; Welch 2008; and Propertius, on which see most recently Heslin 2018; see also Tissol on Ovid in this volume.

13 On the Vergilian career and its influence, see Theodorakopoulos 1997; Putnam 2010; Barchiesi and Hardie 2010; cf. Farrell 2002.

14 See Fey-Wickert 2002: 22–9, for a list of elegiac features in that poem. For a different interpretation of the relationship between the bucolic and the elegiac in this eclogue, see Karakasis 2016a: ch. 4, who sees the two genres interacting in a mutually enriching, rather than competitive, manner.

15 I follow the text of Vinchesi 2014 except for *Ecl.* 3.33, discussed in n47. All translations are mine.

16 Idas begins with *o si quis Crocalen deus afferat!* ("oh, if any god should bring me Crocale!" 2.52); to which Astacus responds with *urimur in Crocalen: si quis mea uota deorum / audiat ...* ("We are on fire for Crocale: if any one of the gods should hear my prayers ..." 2.56–7).

17 In the first exchange of this sequence each singer ends his contribution with reference to Crocale, following the description of his gifts: Idas, *si uenias, Crocale, totus tibi seruiet hornus* ("if you should come, Crocale, the whole year will serve you," 2.71); Astacus, *si uenias, Crocale, totus tibi seruiet hortus* ("if you come, Crocale, the whole garden will serve you," 2.75). Another exchange continues the topic of gifts without reference to the recipient (2.76–83), and the following set (2.84–91), in which the boys praise their appearance, only contains one vague reference (*num, precor, informis uideor tibi?* "surely, I hope, I don't seem ugly to you?" 2.84) that can be taken as addressing the girl and alluding to Polyphemus and Galatea in Theocritus and Corydon and Alexis in Vergil's *B.* 2, but could also be read as directly engaging the opponent.

18 Theoc. *Id.* 6 and 11.

19 See Kosofsky Sedgwick 1985 for the foundational discussion of the triangulation of male homosocial bonds mediated through women in nineteenth-century English literature, esp. ch. 1, drawing on Girard and Freud.

20 Fey-Wickert 2002: 232, discusses the parallel as emerging in the closing lines of the poem.

21 *G.* 3.209–41. On the mixing of animal and human in Vergil's language, see Putnam 1979: 191–4.

22 *A.* 12.715–22. See Nelis 2001: 368–71, on the relationship between the *Georgics* and the *Aeneid* passages in light of their sources in Apollonius; cf. Tarrant 2012: 272–3.

23 *Am.* 2.12.25–6: *uidi ego pro niuea pugnantes coniuge tauros; / spectatrix animos ipsa iuuenca dabat* ("I have seen bulls battling over a snow-white mate; the watching heifer herself gave them courage").

24 On Ovid's use of Vergil in this poem, see Boyd 1997: 81–9.

25 See the introductory essay in Ingleheart and Radice 2011 for an overview of the poem, including the issue of its authenticity.

26 This is a technique that Calpurnius often uses in his treatment of the tradition; see Baraz 2018 for a reading of the breakdown of the song contest in *Ecl.* 6 as a result of the literalization of the underlying metaphors.

27 Verg. *B.* 7.6–7: *huc mihi … uir gregis ipse caper deerrauerat* ("Here my he-goat, the lord of the flock himself, had wandered").

28 Scioli 2015: 52–3 emphasizes how unusual it is that *Am.* 3.5 offers an interpretation of the dream and discusses the effect of the resulting "reviewing" of the dream on the reader.

29 *Am.* 3.5.17–18: *dum iacet et lente reuocatas ruminat herbas / atque iterum pasto pascitur ante cibo* ("While he lies down and slowly chews his cud, and feeds again on the food he has eaten").

30 See Küppers 1989: 37–44; Langholf 1990; Korenjak 2003.

31 On bucolic names, see Lipka 2001: 171–93; and Rumpf 2008.

32 Fabre-Serris 2013b; cf. Vinchesi 2014: 232–3 and Fey-Wickert 2002: 153 on the name in Calpurnius.

33 *Ecl.* 3.37–8: *decet indulgere puellae, / uel cum prima nocet*; cf. Ov. *Am.* 3.4.43–4: *si sapis, indulge dominae uultusque seueros / exue.*

34 Another important elegiac paradigm for the content of the letter-song is the *paraklausithyron*; see Fey-Wickert 2002: 184–5 for discussion.

35 But see Breed 2006a on writing more broadly understood in Vergil's *Bucolica.*

36 Cf. also Propertius' pastoral turn, writing Cynthia's name on trees, 1.18.19–22.

37 On poetic memory in *B.* 9, see Hubbard 1998: 117–27; Breed 2006a: 17–19; cf. Meban 2009 on social memory in the *Bucolica.*

38 On the difference between *cortex* and *liber*, cf. Coleman 1977: 157 ad Verg. *B.* 3.13.

39 See Clausen 1994: 210, for an overview; more recent attempts to answer the question are Egan 1996; Karakasis 2011: 54–86.

40 Cf. Vinchesi 2014: 258–69 ad loc.

41 Calp. *Ecl.* 6.22–4: *uel te certamine quisquam / dignetur, qui uix stillantes, aride, uoces / rumpis et expellis male singultantia uerba?*

42 Poetic competence of the beloved, e.g., Catull. 35.16–17: *Sapphica puella / musa doctior* and the use of the name Lesbia; Prop. 1.2.27–8: *cum tibi praesertim Phoebus sua carmina donet / Aoniamque libens Calliopea lyram*; 2.13.19–22; the need for her approval, e.g., Prop. 2.13.5–7: *non ut Pieriae quercus mea uerba sequantur, / aut possim Ismaria ducere ualle feras, / sed magis ut nostro stupefiat Cynthia uersu*; 2.26.25–6: *nam mea cum recitat, dicit se odisse beatos: / carmina tam sancte nulla puella colit*; Ov. *Am.* 2.4.19–20: *est, quae Callimachi prae nostris rustica dicat / carmina – cui placeo, protinus ipsa placet.*

For scholarly discussion, e.g., Wyke 2002: ch. 1 and 2; cf. Johnson 2012: 39–43.

43 Conington (1898: 129) cites Scaliger and then adds his own judgment: "though its coarseness may be paralleled from Theocritus, it is not what we would have expected from the imitator of Vergil."

44 On the role of violence in elegy, see Fredrick 1997; James 2003b: 184–97; O'Rourke 2018.

45 Other examples: Tib. 1.10.59–66, esp. 61: *sit satis e membris tenuem rescindere uestem*; Prop. 2.5.21: *nec tibi periuro scindam de corpore uestis*; Hor. *Carm.* 1.17.27–8: *et scindat haerentem coronam crinibus inmeritamque uestem*; cf., in the context of Ovid's advice against it, *Ars* 2.171: *nec puto, nec sensi tunicam luniasse.* A Theocritean parallel is the beating of Cinisca in *Id.* 14.

46 See Vinchesi 2014: 243–4 and Fey-Wickert 2002: 175–6 ad loc.

47 The most recent commentator, Vinchesi 2014: 245–6, prefers the alternate reading *negetur* (also printed by Fey-Wickert 2002) because she sees *uagetur* as inappropriate to the context. But the word is in fact perfectly suited to this poem with its conflation of the elegiac and the bucolic.

48 Prop. 1.5.5: *non est illa uagis similis collata puellis*; Ov. *Am.* 2.9.51: *accedant regno, nimium uaga turba, puellae!*

49 In singing of his own feelings of loss later in a message addressed to Phyllis, Lycidas uses the more expected *erro*, aligning himself to the elegiac lover, and in the same line calls her *domina* (3.50): *ut Lycidas domina sine Phyllide tabidus erro.*

50 Calp. *Ecl.* 3.70–1: *quod si dura times etiam nunc uerbera, Phylli, / tradimus ecce manus*; cf. Ov. *Am.* 1.7.1–2: *adde manus in uincla meas – meruere catenas – / dum furor omnis abit, siquis amicus ades!*

51 Calp. *Ecl.* 3.87–8: *laqueum miseri nectemus ab illa / ilice, quae nostros primum uiolauit amores*; cf. Tib. 1.3.81; 1.9.19.

52 Calp. *Ecl.* 3.96–8: *ibimus: et ueniet, nisi me praesagia fallunt. / nam bonus a! dextrum fecit mihi Tityrus omen, / qui redit inuenta non irritus ecce iuuenca.*

14

From *Militia Amoris* to *Amor Militiae*: Language of Rape in Lucan's Account of the Deforestation of the Sacred Grove of Massilia

GIULIO CELOTTO

Scholars of Latin elegy have long focused their attention on the motif of *militia amoris*, which consists in the description of love affairs in military terms.[1] As Murgatroyd notes, "in the Roman elegists there are over a hundred examples of its use."[2] It was not until recently, however, that the reverse trope of *amor militiae*, namely the description of martial activity in erotic terms, was brought to prominence. The first, to my knowledge, to use this definition is Kennedy, who observes that "the traffic, after all, can go both ways. If love can be described in terms applicable to war, then war can no less be eroticised."[3] In particular, he points out that when love and war are presented in similar terms, "we are invited to view aggression, domination and submission as aspects of the dynamics of erotic as much as of martial activity, and vice versa."[4]

Although elegy may be outwardly perceived as a non-violent genre on account of its focus on love, in contrast with epic's interest in war, the elegiac lover has a clear tendency toward violence. The metaphorical notion of *militia amoris* often finds practical application in the narrative world of elegy, as the poet assaults his *puella* as a soldier attacks his enemy.[5] Violence shatters the elegiac fiction of the poet as subjugated to his mistress and restores the traditional gender roles by allowing the male narrator to reaffirm his domination over the female protagonist.[6]

This violent and conventional aspect of elegy draws the attention of epic poets, who adapt the rape/onslaught analogy to the subject matter of their genre by reversing its terms, as they describe military aggression (toward places, as well as individuals) with the language of sexual assault.[7] Oliensis, for instance, argues that Vergil uses erotic language in his description of the death of the virgin warrior Camilla, whose breast is "penetrated" by a spear at *Aeneid* 11.803–4. This shows that "martial and marital wounds are consanguineous throughout the epic."[8] Similarly, Augoustakis draws a parallel between the story of Hercules' rape of Pyrene and Hannibal's crossing of the Alps in Silius' *Punica* 3, and demonstrates that "Hannibal follows in the footsteps of Hercules most closely by imitating the demigod's own inappropriate behavior."[9]

Following in the wake of recent studies on Lucan's engagement with elegy,[10] in this paper I argue that Lucan, who often uses the technique of *imitatio negatiua* to reverse single phrases, scenes, and ideas of his models, also uses it to reverse the elegiac trope of *militia amoris*, and turn it into that of *amor militiae*, more suitable for epic.[11] In particular, I suggest that an episode of military aggression, namely the deforestation of the sacred grove of Massilia at the hands of Caesar and his soldiers in Book 3, is portrayed by Lucan as an episode of sexual assault, namely the rape of a virgin. This scene has roused the interest of several scholars, who focus primarily on its literary models[12] – especially Vergil,[13] Ovid,[14] and Valerius Maximus[15] – and interpret it as a display of Caesar's impiety, and a prefiguration of Pompey's imminent death.[16] No one, however, has explored its sexual subtext.

Amor Militiae in Vergil and Lucan

The seeds of the notion of *amor militiae*, which fully germinate in the *Bellum Ciuile*, can be found in the *Aeneid*. However, both the extent of the use of this motif in the two poems and the way in which the two authors develop it are very different.[17] An analysis of Vergil's and Lucan's use of the noun *amor*, although not decisive, provides a significant hint of this discrepancy. The occurrences of the noun *amor* in the *Aeneid* are seventy-eight. Forty-five of these occurrences (58 per cent) refer to romantic love.[18] Among the remaining thirty-three occurrences, only two (3 per cent of the total) are directly related to war. Both of them are included in the second half of the poem, and refer to Aeneas' enemies: at 7.461 Turnus, who has just been stirred up by Allecto, rages with *amor ferri*;[19] a few lines later, Allecto herself tells Juno that she is ready to rouse the neighbouring towns against the Trojans with an insane love for war (*insano Martis amore*, 7.550).[20]

The occurrences of the noun *amor* in the *Bellum Ciuile* are only thirty-two,[21] less than half those in the *Aeneid*, which clearly shows the devaluation of the role of love in Lucan's *epos*. Furthermore, only twelve of these occurrences (38 per cent) refer to romantic love.[22] Among the several cases in which *amor* is not used with reference to a romance, it is directly related to war six times (19 per cent of the total). If the only two occurrences of the concept of love for strife in the *Aeneid* are found in the second half of the poem, the six occurrences of the same notion in the *Bellum Ciuile* are spread throughout the entire poem, so as to make clear that while Vergil devotes to war only half of his *epos*, Lucan wants conflict to dominate his work. Moreover, if in the *Aeneid* only Turnus and his men, stirred up by Allecto, are inflamed by an insane love for war, whereas Aeneas, the defender of order against chaos,[23] is never associated with this idea, in the *Bellum Ciuile* all parties involved in the civil war are affected by this madness. The first occurrence of this concept is in the proem of the *epos*, where Lucan blames the entire city of Rome for loving an execrable war: *tantus amor belli tibi, Roma, nefandi* (1.21).[24] This is also the first occurrence of the phrase *amor belli* in extant Latin literature. Lucan makes explicit a notion that Vergil only expressed through metonymies.

Caesar's *Amor Militiae*

Although in the *Bellum Ciuile* the whole state is prey to *amor militiae*,[25] Caesar and his men are often singled out on account of their dreadful love for war. By connecting Caesar to this utterly destructive type of love, Lucan seems to react against Vergil's flattering portrait of the Julio-Claudian dynasty. While the *Aeneid* emphasizes the descent of the *gens Iulia* from the goddess of love, Venus, in order to present Augustus as the restorer of peace after a century of civil conflicts, the *Bellum Ciuile* breaks this bond by claiming that Caesar's only true love is strife. On account of his warlike nature, Caesar can be considered the human alter ego of the other divine ancestor of Rome, Mars, to whom he is explicitly compared at 7.569. This shift suggests that in Lucan's view the *gens Iulia* is not responsible for the regeneration of Rome, but rather for its annihilation.

The Caesarians are first connected with *amor belli* in Book 1. Caesar has just concluded his speech, in which he exhorted his men to fight. At first the soldiers waver, but then they are recalled to duty by dreadful love for war: *diro ferri reuocantur amore* (1.355). Although this is the only case in which the description of the Caesarians features a direct association of the noun *amor* with war, Lucan alludes to their love for strife three other times by using words closely related to *amor*. First, in Book 4 Curio is about to attack Varus. His soldiers are scared and hesitant, so he tries to encourage them by saying that fear and hesitation can be overcome by audacity (4.705–7): *cum dira uoluptas / ense subit presso, galeae texere pudorem, / quis conferre duces meminit?* ("When the dreadful desire arises, the sword is drawn, and the helmets conceal the blush of shame, who remembers to compare the leaders?"). Here the longing for war, evoked by the presence of sword and helmet, is expressed with the noun *uoluptas*, which, especially after Lucretius' definition of Venus as *hominum divomque uoluptas* (*DRN* 1.1), is inextricably connected with love. This *uoluptas* is significantly defined as *dira*, which is the same adjective that modifies *amor ferri* at 1.355, so as to make clear that the two concepts are analogous. Furthermore, Vergil defines as *dira cupido*, itself a Lucretian phrase, the ominous lust for battle that characterizes Nisus at *A.* 9.185, and urges him and Euryalus to sortie into the enemy's camp.[26]

Second, in Book 5 Caesar has to face a desertion of his soldiers, who are tired of fighting. The leader cannot accept such behaviour, for he wishes that his soldiers demand of him that he allow them all atrocities, and love the rewards of war: *uult omnia certe / a se saeua peti, uult praemia Martis amari* (5.308). The symmetrical construction of the two sentences suggests that *saeua* and *praemia Martis* are on the same level: Lucan makes clear that in Caesar's view the primary reward of war is to commit atrocities, as in a sort of war for war's sake. Caesar loves war and its atrocities so much that he cannot understand why his men do not. He expects them to be like him. In fact, he immediately crushes the rebellion by killing the instigators (5.359–61).

Third, Caesar is associated again with love for war in Book 10. At 10.396 Pothinus, who is trying to persuade Achillas to assault and kill Caesar, argues that this is the right moment to act, for the leader has lowered his defences: he is sated with feasting, drunken with wine, and ready for love (*Venerique paratum*). The participle *paratus* is especially noteworthy, for in erotic contexts it often takes on a sexual connotation, meaning "aroused." Catullus in poem 15 warns Aurelius that he should stay away from his beloved boy (perhaps Juventius), and direct his penis, indicated by *paratus*, elsewhere (*quem tu qua lubet, ut lubet, moueto, / quantum uis, ubi erit foris, paratum*, 11–12).[27] Ovid uses the verb *paro* in this euphemistic sense at *Remedia amoris* 789–90, where he advises not to eat colewort – famous for its aphrodisiac properties – and all the other foods which "prepare" the body for love (*nec minus erucas aptum uitare salaces, / et quicquid Veneri corpora nostra parat*; note the construction with *Veneri*, as in Lucan), and at *Fasti* 1.437, where he describes Priapus as "aroused with that part of his body which is all too obscene"[28] (*obscena nimium quoque parte paratus*). Lastly, at *Priapea* 46.7–8 Priapus himself confesses that although he seems "up for it," he needs a huge amount of colewort (*nam quamuis uidear satis paratus, / erucarum opus est decem maniplis*). This interpretation of *paratus* seems to fit well with Lucan's scene: Caesar is aroused, and so "ready" for love. Interestingly, at 10.149–50 Caesar is defined by Lucan as *nefando / Marte paratus*. The symmetrical construction of the phrases *Veneri paratus* and *Marte paratus* and the use of metonymy in both cases prompt the reader to draw a parallel between the two *loci*:[29] as Caesar is "ready" for love, so he is "ready" for war; he is aroused by Cleopatra and civil war alike.[30]

An additional instance of love for war associated with a Caesarian soldier may be found in Scaeva's (attempted) *aristeia* in Book 6.[31] After he treacherously kills Aulus by pretending to ask him for mercy, Scaeva addresses the Pompeians, and affirms that their love for their leader and the cause of the Senate is weaker than his own love for death: *Pompei uobis minor est causaeque senatus / quam mihi mortis amor* (6.245–6). Scaeva's love for death may well be regarded as the expression of his love for war, for the death that he desires is unquestionably the one that comes from battle.[32] However, his *amor mortis* may also refer more specifically to his longing for fame, which is typical in the context of an *aristeia*, and his pursuit of an honourable death, which contrasts the humiliating life granted by pardon, rather than to a sheer love for war.[33]

Caesar and Rape

Since Caesar and (some of) his soldiers love fighting, it is natural for Lucan to describe them as lovers, and their military activity as love affairs. Considering the violent, harmful, and destructive nature of war, its episodes can only be associated with the most violent, harmful, and destructive type of sexual desire: rape. Besides, raping perfectly fits the character of Caesar. At the very beginning of the poem, Lucan sketches a brief but effective portrait of the two leaders. Pompey is described as "a passive character, tamed by declining years" (*uergentibus annis / in senium … tranquillior*, 1.129–30),[34] and "unable to support his former greatness with fresh power" (*nec reparare nouas uires*, 1.134). Thus, he is compared to a majestic yet static oak tree (1.135–43). Caesar, on the other hand, is introduced as an active character: "his energy is unable to rest" (*nescia uirtus / stare loco*, 1.144–5), he is "fierce and untamed" (*acer et indomitus*, 1.146), always "ready to move to action wherever hope and anger call" (*quo spes, quoque ira uocasset, / ferre manum*, 1.146–7); most importantly, he rejoices in clearing his way by destruction (*gaudensque uiam fecisse ruina*, 1.150). His dynamic and destructive nature is analogous to that of lightning (1.151–7). The difference between the two leaders becomes even more evident during the battle of Pharsalus, when Lucan explicitly says that Caesar's troops wage war, whereas Pompey's soldiers endure it: *ciuilia bella / una acies patitur, gerit altera* (7.501–2). Here Lucan uses for Pompey the verb *patior*, which Adams defines as "the technical term of the passive role in intercourse."[35]

Caesar's active, savage, and impious disposition explains his recurring association with rape throughout the *epos*. The first, although implicit, connection between Caesar and rape can be found in the episode that officially starts the war. As Caesar is standing on the bank of the Rubicon, the personification of Rome appears to him, and begs him to stop before crossing the river, lest he become an enemy of the country. Caesar flatly refuses and breaks the delay of war by invading Italy (1.183–205). Although Lucan does not use the language of rape in this episode of military aggression, it is still possible to perceive a slight sexual undertone.[36] Scholars, in fact, have associated this scene with the episodes of Cato and Marcia in Book 2, and of Pompey and Julia in Book 3. The mournful appearance of Rome, characterized by torn hair, bare arms, and a speech broken by sobs, recalls that of Marcia;[37] and the fact that she appears in a nocturnal vision is reminiscent of Julia's apparition to Pompey in a dream.[38] As Marcia is Cato's love, and Julia is Pompey's, Rome is here presented as Caesar's. In this light, Caesar's attack on Rome, in spite of her request to stop, invites interpretation as an allusion to sexual violence.

The connection between Caesar and rape becomes more explicit in the aforementioned scene of the mutiny in Book 5. Caesar's soldiers have just attempted to desert; the leader, who is used to enjoying the complete devotion of his men, is caught by surprise, and wishes that his men loved war and its atrocities as much as he does (5.305–8):

> non illis urbes spoliandaque templa negasset
> Tarpeiamque Iouis sedem matresque senatus
> passurasque infanda nurus. uult omnia certe
> a se saeua peti, uult praemia Martis amari.

He would have not forbidden them to sack cities and temples, even the Tarpeian dwelling of Jupiter, or to commit unspeakable acts on the mothers and the daughters-in-law of the senators. He wishes that they ask him the permission for all atrocities, and that they love all rewards of war.

Studies on sexual violence in the Roman world have demonstrated that abuses were frequently perpetrated during (foreign and civil) war: fighting was commonly followed by plunder and rape.[39] Roman soldiers could be prosecuted for *stuprum per uim* (i.e., forcible intercourse with a freeborn boy or woman) only in peacetime, whereas in wartime they enjoyed unrestrained licence.[40] However, although sexual violence during a city sack was not considered a crime, it surely evoked horror, to such an extent that it was used as a topos in portraits of tyrants.[41] By claiming that Caesar would allow his soldiers to rape Roman matrons, Lucan characterizes the leader as a ruthless despot.

In addition, in this passage Lucan openly associates rape with violation of sacred spaces, regarding them as two pleasures of war; then he makes clear that Caesar loves them both, whereas his soldiers do not (note the contrary-to-fact conditional sentence at 5.305–7).[42] These lines make explicit what the crossing of the Rubicon suggests in Book 1. Moreover, the combination of warfare, desecration, and sexual violence also characterizes the Massilia episode in Book 3, where the deforestation of a sacred wood, a true act of war, is described as a rape. There Lucan points out that while Caesar strongly desires it, his soldiers do not. The conclusions of the episodes in Books 3 and 5 are identical: if Caesar's soldiers end up cutting down the wood at Massilia, it is just because they are terrified by their leader's anger (*non sublato secura pauore / turba, sed expensa superorum et Caesaris ira*, 3.438–9); and they return to fight after the mutiny for the very same reason (*meruitque timeri / non metuens, atque haec ira dictante profatur*, 5.317–18). In this light, the Massilia episode can be rightly considered an anticipation and a miniature of the episode of desertion.

Caesar at Massilia

Bearing these considerations in mind, I turn to the analysis of the Massilia episode, in order to show that in the account of the deforestation Lucan uses the language of rape. The use of the language of rape in non-sexual contexts is not an *unicum* in the *Bellum Ciuile*. Scholars have long noticed that the scene of the prophetic possession of the Delphic priestess Phemonoe in Book 5 is described by Lucan with the language of rape.[43] This is not surprising, for the eroticization of prophetic experiences is quite common in Greek and Latin poetry: just like rape, prophetic possession entails a violent penetration, deprives the woman of her control and agency, and in extreme cases threatens her life.[44] The connection between deforestation and rape is not nearly as common. However, it is not startling, either. Adams[45] has noticed that when intercourse is intended as punishment or deflowering, it is often associated with actions like cutting and wounding, and the male organ is compared with weapons. In the case of the deforestation episode in *BC* 3, this pattern works in the opposite direction: instead of describing a rape as a wound, Lucan presents cutting down a forest as a rape.

The grove (*lucus*, 3.399) is a common setting for rape. In Ovid's *Metamorphoses*, rape scenes are often set in a grove,[46] and so is the episode of Phemonoe in Lucan (5.125–6). However, in Book 3 the grove is not simply the setting of the rape but also the victim. Adams notes that the female parts are often likened to "fields," not only on account of their external appearance but also on account of their fertility; as a consequence, the sexual act is often described in terms of ploughing or sowing.[47] Lucan reverses the situation by presenting the *lucus* as a metaphor of the female genitalia: the external appearance is the same; nevertheless, it does not possess a fertile soil, suitable for ploughing and sowing, but is rather a place unfit for cultivation, one that should remain untouched. Throughout the passage, in fact, Lucan insists on the idea of the "virginity" of the grove: in the very first line of its description the grove is defined as never violated (*numquam uiolatus*, 3.399), with a verb frequently used with reference to sexual violence.[48] Then Lucan says that the branches of its trees make it impenetrable to the rays of the sun (*obscurum cingens conexis aera ramis / et gelidas alte summotis solibus umbras*, 3.401–2). Soon after, he points out that it is inhabited by no Pan, no Silvanus, and no Nymphs (*hunc non ruricolae Panes nemorumque potentes / Siluani Nymphaeque tenent*, 3.403–4), all characters that are usually associated with sex and rape.[49] And when he specifies that neither wild beasts nor breezes and lightning have ever found space in this grove, he employs two compounds of the verb *cubo*, habitually employed with reference to intercourse[50] (*illis et uolucres metuunt insistere ramis / et lustris recubare ferae; nec uentus in illas / incubuit siluas excussaque nubibus atris / fulgura*, 3.407–10). Lastly, the grove, spared in earlier warfare, is described as very thick among hills already cleared (*nam uicina operi belloque intacta priore / inter nudatos stabat densissima montes*, 3.427–8): using explicitly sexual language, Lucan makes clear that unlike the other forests, which have been stripped of their trees, this impenetrable grove has never been touched before.[51]

Caesar asks his soldiers to cut down this grove with an axe (*inmisso ferro*, 3.426). As we have seen, in the representation of violent sex, love poetry tends to associate the male organ with cutting weapons. The fact that this phrase is immediately followed by lines 427–8, which allude to the virginity of the grove, corroborates its sexual connotation.

The soldiers hesitate. They are awed by the solemnity of the place (*uerenda / maiestate loci*, 3.429–30), and are afraid to hit the trunks (*robora sacra ferirent*, 3.430). The gerundive *uerendus* is often associated with virginity,[52] whereas the verb *ferio* is employed by the late elegiac poet Maximianus (5.97) to define violent intercourse, and its synonyms regularly occur in similar contexts. As soon as Caesar sees his soldiers so hesitant, he himself strikes the first blow, and he starts to speak while his sword is still buried in the violated trunk (*effatur merso uiolata in robora ferro*, 3.435).[53] If the grove is defined as *numquam uiolatus* at line 399, now its trunks are *uiolata* by Caesar. In the episode of Phemonoe, Lucan uses a similar technique: at the beginning of the passage he insists on the virginity of the priestess (*uirginei ... doli*, 5.141; *conterrita uirgo*, 5.161), whereas at the end he makes clear that Apollo has taken away her virginity (*domita ... uirgine*, 5.193).[54] Furthermore, the phrase *merso in robora ferro* resonates with the phrase *flamma in uiscera mergis*, used at 5.175 with reference to Phemonoe's possession by Apollo, and interpreted by Lovatt as a sexual allusion.[55]

What happens to the virgin-grove after the deforestation-rape is analogous to what happens to virgin-Phemonoe after the possession-rape. Phemonoe unwillingly receives Apollo in her breast for the first time, after the oracle had been silent for several generations (*inuito concepit pectore numen, / quod non exhaustae per tot iam saecula rupis / spiritus ingessit uates*, 5.163–5). Similarly, the grove, which used to be thick and impenetrable, loses its branches and admits the daylight for the first time (*tum primum posuere comas et fronde carentes / admisere diem*, 3.443–4). The parallel becomes even closer if one considers that Apollo is the sun-god, and therefore Phemonoe and the grove are admitting exactly the same thing. And as Phemonoe falls exhausted after the possession (*cadit*, 5.224), so the grove falls down (*cadens*, 3.445). Also, the phrase *posuere comas* may represent a veiled allusion to rape. In Ovid *Amores* 1.7, in which the poet admits that he used violence against his girlfriend, one of the most evident signs of rape is the girl's dishevelled hair. Early in the poem Ovid recounts that he tore at his girlfriend's hair, and enjoyed the sight (*ergo ego digestos potui laniare capillos? / nec dominam motae dedecuere comae*, *Am*. 1.7.11–12). Then at the end of the elegy he expresses his regret for his shameful deed, and begs the girl to put her hair back in place, so that the sad signs of his wickedness may not remain visible (*neue mei sceleris tam tristia signa supersint, / pone recompositas in statione comas*, *Am*. 1.7.67–8; note the use of the same verb *pono*, although with the opposite meaning).[56] Lucan may be playing here with the two meanings of *coma* to present the tearing of the leaves/hair as a sign of the violation of the grove/girl.

In conclusion, this analysis reveals that Lucan draws inspiration from the elegiac motif of *militia amoris*, particularly the description of sexual assault with the language of military aggression, and adapts it to the epic genre by reversing it into the trope of *amor militiae*, already employed, although more sparingly, by Vergil. This allusive strategy sheds light on Lucan's engagement with his models. First, by turning *militia amoris* into *amor militiae* Lucan suggests that, while elegy primarily deals with love and relegates war to a marginal role, as it merely provides the vocabulary to define the most violent aspects of desire, the narrative universe of the *Bellum Ciuile* is dominated by war, and love finds little space in it, to such an extent that sexual language is used to portray the contestants' insane lust for strife. In addition, by magnifying a motif evoked by Vergil only in the second half of the *Aeneid* to characterize Aeneas' enemies, Lucan makes it clear that all parties involved in the civil war are affected by an irrational desire for conflict, and therefore, Rome's fate is sealed.

A clear example of *amor militiae* is found in *BC* 3, where the deforestation of the sacred grove of Massilia is portrayed as the rape of a virgin. Caesar brings light to a dreadful place that should have remained dark.[57] His act can be compared with the violent deflowering of a virgin, who should have remained untouched. In other words, an instance of martial aggression is described as an instance of sexual aggression. By means of this literary device Lucan reaches two goals: on the one hand, he emphasizes the violent and impious nature of civil war; on the other hand, he adds a revealing touch to his dark portrait of Caesar by providing further evidence not only of his savage and sacrilegious disposition, which makes him the ideal leader in the context of civil war, and the exact antithesis of *pius* Aeneas, but also of his active and hyper-masculine attitude, in contrast with Pompey's passive and submissive behaviour.[58]

NOTES

1 See especially Spies 1930; Thomas 1964; Murgatroyd 1975; Lyne 1980: 71–8; Gale 1997a.
2 Murgatroyd 1975: 59.
3 Kennedy 2012: 189. Here Kennedy works out the implications of an insight mentioned, but not developed, in 1993: 53.
4 Kennedy 2012: 190.
5 See Tib. 1.10.55–66; Prop. 2.5.21–6, 2.15.17–20; Ov. *Am.* 1.7, 2.5.45–8.
6 Cf. Cahoon 1988: 297; Fredrick 1997: 189; Greene 1998: 67–8; Janan 2001: 82–4; James 2003b: 197; Witzke 2016: 267–8; O'Rourke 2018: 124.
7 Examples of military aggressions described as sexual assaults can also be found in elegy. Bowditch 2012: 122, suggests that in 2.10 Propertius "presents Augustus' current or intended geographic conquests in rhetoric suggestive of elegiac sexual relations": Arabia is portrayed as a fearful virgin ready to be assaulted by the *princeps* (2.10.16), and Britannia as a woman who will soon feel his hands on her (2.10.18).
8 Oliensis 1997: 308. On the allusions to defloration, marriage, and motherhood in the scene of Camilla's death, see also Fowler 1987.
9 Augoustakis 2003: 237.
10 Hübner 1984; Matthews 2008; Caston 2011; McCune 2014; Burns 2016; Littlewood 2016.

11 McCune 2014 has already argued that the *Bellum Ciuile* depicts the displacement of the elegiac notion of *militia amoris*. Her argument, however, goes in a different direction from mine. She analyses the figures of Julia, Erictho, Cleopatra, and Cornelia, and shows that although these characters are cast in elegiac roles, they are ultimately concerned with war, not with love.

12 Masters 1992: 27; Fantham 1996: 147–53.

13 Thomas 1988b; Panoussi 2003.

14 Phillips 1968; Degl'Innocenti Pierini 1987; Esposito 1988.

15 Augoustakis 2006.

16 Rowland 1969; Ahl 1976, 199; Narducci 1979: 110; Rosner-Siegel 1983; Loupiac 1998: 48.

17 Fantham 1995 argues that "the seeds of the devaluation of *uirtus* that will sprout sinister flowers in Lucan" are already visible in the *Aeneid*, and more precisely in the character of Turnus. Similarly, I suggest that the motif of *amor militiae*, which is only hinted at by Vergil in the description of Turnus and his allies, is magnified and taken to extremes by Lucan.

18 Verg. *A.* 1.344, 350, 663, 675, 689, 721, 749; 2.343; 3.298, 330, 487; 4.17, 28, 38, 54, 85, 171, 292, 307, 347, 395, 412, 414, 516, 532; 5.5, 296, 334, 538, 572; 6.24, 28, 442, 455, 474; 8.373; 9.182; 10.188, 191, 326, 614; 11.549; 12.70, 392, 668.

19 A similar phrase occurs at *A.* 12.282, where, after the Rutulians break the truce and resume the fight, all the soldiers are caught by the same desire to let the sword settle the dispute (*omnis amor unus habet decernere ferro*). I do not include this line among the instances of *amor militiae*, because the desire of the soldiers seems to be not simply to fight but to bring a definitive end to the conflict, in one way or another.

20 A third possible reference to *amor militiae* occurs at *A.* 11.583, where Vergil introduces Camilla by saying that she worships Diana, and therefore cultivates "eternal love for weapons and virginity" (*aeternum telorum et uirginitatis amorem*). Nevertheless, although Camilla actually takes part in the war between Trojans and Rutulians, the reference to Diana and the association of weapons with virginity suggest that the *tela* mentioned here are those used in hunting rather than in fighting. At *A.* 11.782 Camilla is also described as "inflamed by love for booty and spoils" (*femineo praedae et spoliorum ardebat amore*). A similar love for riches also characterizes Pygmalion (*auri caecus amore*, *A.* 1.349), and the generations of men after the Golden Age of Saturn (*amor successit habendi*, *A.* 8.327). Analogously, at *BC* 3.119, the tribune Metellus is said to be driven by love for gold (*auri … amor*) when he tries to prevent Caesar from robbing the temple of Saturn.

21 Tucker 1990 lists all the occurrences of the noun *amor* in the *Bellum Ciuile*. However, he restricts himself to summarizing these *loci*, without further comments.

22 Luc. *BC* 2.379; 3.26, 286; 5.729, 748, 763, 794; 6.455; 9.954; 10.70, 80, 363.

23 On this definition of Aeneas, see especially Galinsky 1966; Hardie 1986. This thesis is surely more in line with the "optimistic" reading of the *Aeneid*, which emphasizes Aeneas's achievements, than with the "pessimistic" reading, which focuses on what is sacrificed in pursuit of his goals. However, as Kallendorf (2007: vii) points out, this dichotomy "is more a matter of shades of grey than black versus white," for "no responsible 'optimist' would deny that Aeneas makes mistakes ... and no responsible 'pessimist' would argue that what was lost in founding Rome exceeds what was gained."

24 I cite the text of Shackleton Bailey 1988; translations are my own.

25 For the association of the trope of *amor militiae* with the Pompeians, see *BC* 4.236. For its association with the Catonians, see *BC* 2.325; 9.290.

26 On Nisus and Euryalus, see Gladhill and Ortiz in this volume.

27 Lafaye 1923 aptly translates *paratum* as "prête à l'action." *Contra* cf. Ellis 1876, ad loc., who interprets the phrase *ubi erit foris paratum* as impersonal, and Quinn 1970, ad loc., who considers *paratum* a neuter substantive adjective ("an opportunity"). It is interesting to note that *paratus* is used by Catullus with reference to Aurelius (and his friend Furius) also at 11.14 (*temptare simul parati*) in a context that according to Putnam 1974: 86 and Forsyth 1991: 462 has a clear sexual connotation.

28 Cf. Green 2004, ad loc.

29 The use of different grammatical cases for *Venus* and *Mars* is conditioned by the metrical context, and so does not invalidate my argument.

30 Lucan's depiction of Cleopatra and civil war as the two greatest passions of Caesar seems to be confirmed at 10.74–5, where the leader enjoys the queen's love while he is still drenched with the blood of Pharsalia: *sanguine Thessalicae cladis perfusus adulter / admisit Venerem curis*. This phrasing constitutes incontrovertible evidence of the sacrilegious and destructive nature of Caesar's relationship with Cleopatra in Lucan's view.

31 For a broader discussion of Lucan's perversion of the epic convention of the *aristeia* in the Scaeva episode, see Marti 1966; Conte 1974; Ahl 1976: 117–21; Johnson 1987: 57–60; Fantham 1995; Leigh 1997: 158–90; Gorman 2001: 277–9; Sklenář 2003: 45–58.

32 The phrase *amor mortis* occurs in a similar context with reference to the Celtiberians, who are defined at 4.146–7 as an untamed people, made eager for battle by their contempt for death: *indomitos ... populos et semper in arma / mortis amore feros*.

33 For a broader discussion of *amor mortis* in the *Bellum Ciuile*, see Rutz 1960.

34 It is worth noting that Pompey was only five years older than Caesar. So, the fact that Lucan emphasizes the age difference between the two leaders is all the more significant.

35 Adams 1982: 189.

36 Plut. *Caes.* 32 connects Caesar's invasion of Italy with an unlawful act of
   intercourse: the night before he crossed the Rubicon, Caesar dreamed that
   he had sex with his mother. Suet. *Iul.* 7 and Cass. Dio 41.24 also report this
   dream, but place it during Caesar's quaestorship in Spain.

37 Batinski 1993: 273. Roche 2009, ad 1.187–9, on the other hand, associates the
   description of Rome with that of Cato at the time of his second wedding with
   Marcia (2.372–8).

38 Morford 1967: 79; Roche 2009, ad 1.186.

39 Fantham 1991: 271; Williams 1995: 532; Vikman 2005: 27; Nguyen 2006:
   186; Gaca 2013, 2016, 2018a, and 2018b.

40 Phang 2001: 256. It is worth noting that the *stuprum per uim* was prosecuted
   according to the *Lex Iulia de ui publica*, most likely issued by Caesar in 45 BCE
   (see Gardner 1986: 119; Dixon 2001: 50; Nguyen 2006: 189).

41 See Dunkle 1967; 1971; Dixon 2001: 47; Phang 2001: 255. See also in this
   volume Anagnostou-Laoutides.

42 Rape and violation of sacred spaces are also associated at *Man.* 23.66, where
   Cicero praises Pompey's moderation and self-control by pointing out that
   the general "is capable of withholding his hands, eyes, and thoughts from
   the wives, children, and temple decorations" of the vanquished enemy (*qui
   ab eorum coniugibus ac liberis, qui ab ornamentis fanorum ... manus, oculos,
   animum cohibere possit*).

43 O'Higgins 1988, 212–13; Masters 1992: 140–1; Lovatt 2013: 146.

44 See the description of Cassandra in Aesch. *Ag.* 1202–13 (Lovatt 2013: 147–9),
   the episode of the Sibyl in Verg. *A.* 6.77–80 (Fowler 2002: 149; Sharrock 2002:
   211–12), and the scenes of Ocyrhoe (Heath 1994, 344) and the Sibyl (Lovatt
   2013: 148) in Ov. *Met.* 2.633–75 and 14.132–3, respectively.

45 Adams 1982: 14, 145–9.

46 Heath 1991.

47 Adams 1982: 83.

48 Adams 1982: 199.

49 Especially noteworthy is the parallel at *Met.* 14.634–40. The hamadryad
   Pomona only cares about gardening and has no interest in love. Fearing
   violence from peasants, she fences her orchard, and shuts herself in. In this
   way, she prevents the assault of lustful deities, such as Satyrs, Pans, Silenus,
   and Priapus. This Ovidian allusion seems to establish a connection between the
   garden of chaste Pomona and the virgin grove of Massilia.

50 Adams 1982: 177.

51 On the sexual connotation of *intactus*, see Adams 1982: 186.

52 Adams 1982: 54.

53 Phillips (1968: 298–9) notes the parallel at *Met.* 8.752–4, where Erysichthon
   orders his servants to cut down all trees in the sacred grove of Ceres. One
   mighty oak stands out, for it is covered with votive tablets and garlands. As the

servants hesitate to strike such a venerable tree, Erysichthon seizes the axe and gives the first blow, uttering impious words. The fact that the oak tree turns out to be a nymph corroborates the interpretation of the sacred grove cut down by Caesar in *BC* 3 as a maiden.

54 On the sexual connotation of this phrase, see Duplain Michel 1997: 113.

55 Lovatt 2013: 146–7.

56 On the (ostensible) contrast between lines 11–12 and 67–8, see Greene 1998: 91, who points out that although the two couplets seem to be antithetical, they both display Ovid's desire for domination, for they depict two different types of violence: the former, sexual aggression, the latter, subjugation.

57 So Ozanam 1990, who argues that Seneca uses the same metaphor of the impenetrable wood, where terrible things happen (see especially *Oedipus* and *Thyestes*), in order to illustrate the Stoic principle that knowledge is good only if such is its object; on the contrary, if its object is evil, knowledge is evil as well; evil should remain in the darkness. *Contra*, see Leigh 1999, who considers the deforestation an act of acculturation on the part of Caesar: he tames nature, and replaces superstition with rationality.

58 Part of this chapter is included in Celotto 2022. I express my gratitude to the University of Michigan Press for giving me permission to republish this material here. I am indebted to Professor L. Fulkerson and Professor T. Stover for advice on this paper.

15

Through the Looking Glass: Epic Exempla and Elegiac Mirrors in the *Argonautica*

JESSICA BLUM-SORENSEN

Introduction

From Homer onwards, love and lamentation are intrinsically part of the epic world. At the same time, however, elegy provides a sort of generic straw man in opposition to which Roman epicists define their poetic projects and measure their heroes' *uirtus*. Here as elsewhere, the *Aeneid* is the standard bearer, showing Aeneas' rejection of romantic love as necessary to the accomplishment of his epic mission, while demonstrating the deep-seated allure of that selfsame *amor* throughout its narrative.[1] Success lies in the correct choice between *amor* and *amor rerum*, a properly epic love that Aeneas achieves through his glimpse of the Roman future at *A.* 6.889: *famae uenientis amore* ("[Anchises inflamed Aeneas' mind] with love of glory to come"). For Vergil's successors, then, keeping one's eyes firmly fixed on the epic prize acts as a status marker in the competition-fuelled world of martial epic, measuring the fidelity of author and hero to Hinds' "essential epic."[2]

Writing his *Argonautica* in the late first century CE, Valerius Flaccus faced a truly Herculean dilemma: how to maintain an unrelenting focus on *arma uirumque* while accommodating the generic code-switch – from epic glory to elegiac romance to tragic downfall – at the core of the Argonautic story. To explore how the *Argonautica* achieves this, I use the Hylas episode of Book 3 as a case study to examine Valerius' integration of the turn towards elegy into the project of his epic *imitatio*. Heerink has shown how Apollonius, Theocritus, and Propertius employ Hylas as a character of generic differentiation, an elegiac counterpart to Hercules' role as the "symbol of epic poetry *par excellence*."[3] In Theocritus and Propertius, the story of Hercules and Hylas provides a sort of teaching moment: addressed to Nicias and Gallus respectively, these poems describe the universal dangers of love, which even Hercules cannot escape. Valerius' reworking of this episode, however, asserts Hylas' fidelity to *arma uirumque*, affirming the desire of both poet and cast to avoid the pitfalls of elegiac *amor*. And here, I think, is where we find Valerius' answer to the challenge posed by his myth. Hylas undergoes his generic metamorphosis through his too close *imitatio* of Vergil's Aeneas – in other words, by doing epic repetition too well, he finds himself in the world of elegiac *amor* instead of pursuing his *amor rerum*. Rather than an elegiac intruder into the epic landscape, Valerius' Hylas instead reflects on the generic dialogue of his Vergilian models. Even as he strives to disentangle himself from his tradition, Hylas finds himself caught in a web of poetic *aemulatio* that pulls him back into his elegiac persona.

One way of reading the contrast between epic and elegy is through the opposition between movement and stillness, heroic action and the passivity of the elegiac voice caught in love and lament – the performance of one's own story versus viewership of another's. In the *Aeneid*, Aeneas' romantic sojourn in Carthage threatens his forward progress to Rome, pitting – on the surface at least – his *amor rerum* against his *amor* for Dido.[4] For Aeneas, though, Carthage represents something slightly different, and it is here that I want to suggest a way that Valerius' reception of Vergil can help us tease out the implications of these two types of *amor*. In Carthage, Aeneas looks longingly back to the past world of Troy, and his digression into elegy is to some extent a manifestation of his desire to perform, or re-perform, Homeric epic.[5] As Sally Spence has suggested, feelings of loss and desire can operate as a motivating force, in terms of the longing for a different storyline.[6] By inhabiting the character's viewpoint, then, Vergil and Valerius illustrate how the desire to emulate an epic past can divert its future. Before diving into the *Argonautica*, I begin with a brief sketch of how this works in the *Aeneid*, and in the second part of the paper, demonstrate that Valerius' characters, through their epicizing *imitatio* of the cast of the *Aeneid*, end up confusing the categories of *amor* and *amor rerum*.

Vergil: Iliadic Mirrors

It is not Dido, at least initially, who lures Aeneas away from his mission. Throughout *Aeneid* 1, Aeneas repeatedly encounters his Trojan past, and, as he does so, is immobilized by his own idealized image.[7] While Aeneas is, as it were, looking the other way, re-performing or re-experiencing Homeric epic through images and stories of Troy, his narrative takes a sharp generic detour.

Aeneas' desire to re-enact a lost past is evident even before he reaches Carthage. In the midst of Juno's storm, facing a watery grave, Aeneas cries out his wish to have died gloriously on the Trojan battlefield (*A.* 1.94–6): *o terque quaterque beati, / quis ante ora patrum Troiae sub moenibus altis / contigit oppetere* ("O three- and four-times blessed, whom it befell to die before their fathers' eyes below the high walls of Troy!"). To Aeneas, a Hector-like death looks far more tempting than his own nebulous future. This lament is itself an act of *imitatio* of *Odyssey* 5 – a move backwards in the epic tradition. In a moment of *aporia*, both heroes view the stories they are enacting in terms of their reception as part of a normative, martial-epic tradition. Aeneas, like Odysseus, defines his epic project in terms of the self-image he sees reflected in the eyes of his audience, and through the creative refashioning of his epic models.

The intertwining of Homeric epic and self-reflection continues on Aeneas' arrival in Carthage. In the murals on Juno's temple, he sees illustrated the very battles for which he longs, and recognizes himself among the fighters (*A.* 1.488–9, 94–5):[8]

> se quoque principibus permixtum agnouit Achiuis,
> Eoasque acies et nigri Memnonis arma ...
> Haec dum Dardanio Aeneae miranda uidentur,
> dum stupet obtutuque haeret defixus in uno ...

Himself, too, he recognizes amidst the Greek leaders, and the eastern battle-lines and the arms of black Memnon ... While Trojan Aeneas surveys these wonders, while he stands agape and clings rapt to this sight ...

In effect, Aeneas becomes the audience he had envisioned in the storm, assembling the fragmented visual evidence before him into a (perhaps hyperbolic) vision of his own heroic past.[9] But the effect of this is, again, to divert Aeneas' attention in the wrong direction – towards Homer's *Iliad*, this time, and to a near-fatal misreading of his own storyline should he fail to escape the twin allurements of Carthage and Troy.

Dido and her city collude with Aeneas' longing for the Homeric past in more than one way.[10] Not only does Dido herself, by visually and behaviourally amalgamating the Homeric heroines Penthesilea, Calypso, Nausicaa, and Arete, suggest an Achillean or Odyssean role for Aeneas, but she also offers him the opportunity to narrate his Homeric narrative to an appreciative audience.[11] At her request, and despite his own grief, Aeneas tells the story of Troy's fall and his subsequent wanderings (*A.* 2.3–6):

> "Infandum, regina, iubes renouare dolorem,
> Troianas ut opes et lamentabile regnum
> eruerint Danai, quaeque ipse miserrima uidi
> et quorum pars magna fui … "

"An unspeakable grief, o queen, you bid me renew, how the Greeks overthrew Troy's riches and pitiable kingdom, heart-breaking events that I myself saw and in which I played a great part …"

Although the story is *infandum*, Aeneas nonetheless recounts it. The phrase *quorum pars magna fui* is telling – Aeneas presents himself as a main character, in a verbal complement to his visual reading of the temple murals. In both instances, Carthage offers a mirror in which Aeneas can re-envision his own story, a stage on which to give a truly epic performance that combines Achilles' physical prowess with Odysseus' poetic skill.[12] As he does so, he himself becomes an object of desire for his internal audience. Both he and Dido are immobilized by their longing for the hero he depicts, transforming their forward-looking foundation projects into an elegiac love story. And although Aeneas is forcibly drawn back into his own epic project by a different kind of image – that of his son and his father (*A.* 4.351–5) – the interactions of his desiring gaze, directed to the lost world of Troy, and Dido's, directed at him, demonstrate the generic consequences of looking too hard at the Homeric past.[13] And we could add in here Aeneas' brief visit to Buthrotum, in which *imitatio* of Troy has a similar freezing effect. As Vergil tells us, Helenus and Andromache's miniature replication of Troy is no material for epic achievement. Neither the muddy river nor the pure stream of Callimachus' *Hymn to Apollo* but a dried-up Homeric stream is what Aeneas sees instead in Buthrotum, the *arentem Xanthi cognomine riuum* ("parched stream named for the Xanthus," *A.* 3.350).[14] Throughout the opening books of the *Aeneid*, the protagonists' desire to replicate a Homeric, martial-epic past produces an elegiac future of love and lament.

Valerius Flaccus: Hercules' Reflection

Turning to the first generation of epic heroes, Valerius considers his own position in the epic tradition, and that of his protagonists, through the lens of epic *imitatio*. By following their normative models too closely, his Argonauts find themselves trapped in the same generic transposition as their predecessors. For our purposes, Valerius' version of the Hylas story – fertile ground for exploring the dynamics of poetic repetition, as Heerink, Barchiesi, and others have shown – illustrates and expands the precise mechanisms of this intergenerational and intergeneric transformation.[15]

Like Aeneas, Valerius' Hylas sees an opportunity to act out an epic story but ends up in a different generic world. Unlike Aeneas, he lacks the mythological imperatives that would allow him to escape. Within the *Argonautica*, furthermore, he functions as an adumbration for Jason in the epic's second half, thus offering a sort of case study for the dynamics of the poem as a whole.[16] Alongside his poet, Hylas attempts to evade the textual memory of his earlier iterations but ends up repeating it through his very engagement with epic exempla.

Valerius flags this episode for us as something to pay attention to right from the beginning.[17] Before the Argonauts set out, they hear two prophecies about their voyage from the seers Mopsus and Idmon. Mopsus' prophecy, intriguingly, follows the Apollonian, Theocritean, and Propertian stories of Hylas, in which the boy disappears while out looking for water (VF 1.217–26).[18] But Mopsus is wrong. As we will see, Valerius takes us – and Hylas – by surprise, casting Hylas as an epic actor who participates in *imitatio* of martial-epic models. By building in these traditional versions, Valerius flags his own departure, and his character's, from their predecessors. It is through his emulative relationship with Hercules – a figure who represents the norms of Homeric epic throughout the Argonautic tradition – that Hylas' divergence from the normative concepts of martial epic becomes most evident.[19] Valerius' generic reframing of this episode, therefore, flags it as a locus for exploring his own relationship to his authorial models.

Hylas' desire to imitate Hercules is clear from the very moment that the two join the Argonauts' expedition (VF 1.107–20):[20]

Protinus Inachiis ultro Tirynthius Argis
aduolat, Arcadio cuius flammata ueneno
tela puer facilesque umeris gaudentibus arcus
gestat Hylas; uelit ille quidem, sed dextera nondum
par oneri clauaeque capax. quos talibus amens
insequitur solitosque nouat Saturnia questus:
"o utinam Graiae rueret non omne iuuentae
in noua fata decus nostrique Eurystheos haec nunc
iussa forent. imbrem et tenebras saeuumque tridentem
iam iam ego et inuiti torsissem coniugis ignem … "
dixit et Haemonias oculos detorquet ad undas.

Straightaway from Inachian Argos the hero of Tiryns speeds unsummoned, whose arrows burning with Arcadian poison and pliant bow the boy Hylas bears on willing shoulders; indeed he is eager, but his right hand is not yet equal to the weight and size of the club. These frenzied Juno reproaches and breaks out anew into her former complaints: "If only all the glory of Grecian youth did not rush forth, and that these were now the orders of my Eurystheus! Already would I have hurled the rainstorm and fierce trident and fire of my unwilling husband ..." She spoke, and twisted her eyes to the Haemonian waves.

The word *nondum* emphasizes Hylas' youth and desire to follow in Hercules' footsteps – his eagerness to model himself on Hercules. As we shall see, while Hercules and Hylas' relationship is traditionally sexual, Valerius uses Vergilian allusions to suggest a father-son bond, reinforcing the sense of *imitatio* in and beyond the text.[21] Even as Hylas steps into this framework of heroic emulation, however, we see the alternate generic pathways down which this exemplum may lead him.

Hercules' entrance is viewed not through the Argonauts' eyes but through Juno's, who, far from welcoming Hercules' help, reinterprets his martial image as erotic insult.[22] The polyptoton *torsissem ... detorquet* evokes her storm in *Aeneid* 1, enacting the potential for *amor* and loss to disrupt the hero's forward progress. Furthermore, the scene hints that Juno's gaze is as much a weapon as her husband's lightning, pitting her visual reinterpretation of the story against Jupiter's plans.[23] And not only does Juno herself read epic material (Hercules) in elegiac terms (her jealousy), but she also uses Hylas' focus on epic exempla to lead him in a different direction.[24]

From this starting point, Valerius foregrounds the tensions between Hylas' epic aspirations and elegiac literary tradition throughout his brief career in the *Argonautica*. When, for instance, the Argonauts (mistakenly) join battle in Cyzicus, Hylas initially shows some promise in his quest to become an epic hero (VF 3.183–5):[25] *tum primum puer ausus Hylas (spes maxima bellis / pulcher Hylas, si fata sinant, si prospera Iuno) / prostrauitque uirum celeri per pectora telo* ("Then for the first time the boy Hylas (lovely Hylas, a great hope in war, if the fates allow, if Juno is kind) took aim and he laid the man low with a swift arrow through his breast"). His first taste of war echoes that of Iulus in Latium, carefully directing his *imitatio* to Vergilian rather than Apollonian models – a strong assertion of this *Argonautica*'s desire to follow through on its Homeric epic inheritance.[26] In his unfulfilled promise, too, Hylas evokes Marcellus in *A. 6*, a successor cut off before he can match the deeds of his epic ancestors, and Pallas, who dies prematurely in *A. 10*.[27]

Hylas' generic orientation comes to the fore in the passage on which we will focus in *Argonautica* 3. When Hercules accidentally breaks his oar (VF 3.474–9), the Argonauts put in at Mysia so that he can find a new one. As he heads off into the woods, Hylas mirrors his steps (VF 3.485–6): *petit excelsas Tirynthius ornos, / haeret Hylas lateri passusque moratur iniquos*

("The Tirynthian sought the lofty mountain ashes; Hylas clung to his side and delayed his outsize steps").[28] In this passage, the pair recalls Aeneas and Iulus' escape from the fall of Troy (*A.* 2.723–4): *dextrae se paruus Iulus / implicuit sequiturque patrem non passibus aequis* ("Iulus entwines his right hand with mine and follows his father with unequal steps").[29] Like Iulus, Hylas hovers on the cusp of an epic career, striving to follow the path of his hero-father.

Beyond this literary *imitatio*, Hylas shares Iulus' ambition to win glory as a hunter, an age-appropriate stand-in for the martial deeds of his paternal model. Compare, first, Iulus' pursuit of Silvia's stag at *A.* 7.493–7:

> hunc procul errantem rabidae uenantis Iuli
> commouere canes, fluuio cum forte secundo
> deflueret ripaque aestus uiridante leuaret.
> ipse etiam eximiae laudis succensus amore
> Ascanius curuo derexit spicula cornu …

The fierce dogs of the hunter Iulus roused this stag, as it wandered far off, when by chance it drifted down a flowing stream and cooled off from the heat on its green bank. Ascanius himself, aflame with desire for outstanding praise, aimed his arrow from a curved bow.

The phrase *eximiae laudis succensus amore* reveals the true object of Iulus' pursuit: the promise of epic glory.[30] But we, the audience, know that it is no such thing. Iulus' ambitions are instead the means by which Juno instigates war in Italy, a misdirection that embroils the Trojans in a bloody, civil-war-tinged re-enactment of the Trojan War. In his pursuit, Iulus follows too closely in his father's footsteps. He inhabits the same image in which Aeneas had brought about his own *amor*-oriented storyline during the hunt in Carthage (*A.* 4.141–50):

> ipse ante alios pulcherrimus omnis
> infert se socium Aeneas atque agmina iungit.
> qualis ubi hibernam Lyciam Xanthique fluenta
> deserit ac Delum maternam inuisit Apollo
> instauratque choros, mixtique altaria circum
> Cretesque Dryopesque fremunt pictique Agathyrsi;
> ipse iugis Cynthi graditur mollique fluentem
> fronde premit crinem fingens atque implicat auro,
> tela sonant umeris: haud illo segnior ibat
> Aeneas, tantum egregio decus enitet ore.

Aeneas himself, most handsome beyond all others, arrives and joins the lines. Just as when Apollo leaves wintry Lycia and the streams of Xanthus to visit his mother's Delos and renew the choruses; and the Cretans and Dryopes and painted Agathyrsi clamour, joined around the altar; he himself strides across the heights of Cynthus and binds his flowing hair with a soft frond and weaves it with gold, his weapons sounding on his shoulders: no less eagerly did Aeneas go, and just such beauty shines from his noble face.

Aeneas' epic simile provides a counterpoint not only to Dido's entrance as Diana (*A.* 1.498–504) but also to the deceptive effect of her Homeric framework. His beauty, like hers, dazzles its onlookers, an effect reflected in the simile comparing her to a wounded deer and Aeneas to the hunter who strikes her (*A.* 4.68–73).[31] The doubled visual emphasis on divinity and on radiance (*enitet*) links Dido's love-struck perception of Aeneas-as-Apollo with its misleading effect. Aeneas' enactment of a heroic role, and Iulus' re-enactment of his father's example, repeatedly threaten the project of Rome's foundation.

In the *Argonautica*, likewise, Juno diverts the story through Hylas' eagerness to follow in Hercules' footsteps.[32] While Hercules is busy refashioning his oar in the Mysian forest, Juno sends (another) stag across Hylas' path, luring him into giving chase (VF 3.545–51):[33]

> sic ait et celerem frondosa per auia ceruum
> suscitat ac iuueni sublimem cornibus offert
> ille animos tardusque fugae longumque resistens
> sollicitat suadetque pari contendere cursu.
> credit Hylas praedaeque ferox ardore propinquae
> insequitur, simul Alcides hortatibus urget
> prospiciens.

So she [Juno] speaks and rouses a swift stag among the trackless brush and presents it, tall-antlered, to the youth. Hesitating in flight and with long pause it provokes his spirit and invites him to contend in swift flight. Hylas falls for it, and pursues, wild with desire for the prey close at hand, while Hercules, watching, urges him on.

With Hercules cheering him on, Hylas does his level best to act an epic part, seeing the opportunity to prove himself.[34] Like Iulus, he is *praedaeque ferox ardore propinquae,* "wild with desire for the prey close at hand."[35]

What is intriguing about this episode, however, is that Hylas is not the only one lured into Juno's trap through the promise of an epic prize.[36] Before drawing the boy away from his companions, Juno first finds the right person to snatch him – the Dido to Hylas' Aeneas. Looking around the Mysian forest, she picks out a group of huntress nymphs (VF 3.521–5):

> haec ait et pariter laeui iuga pinea montis
> respicit ac pulchro uenantes agmine nymphas,
> undarum nemorumque decus. leuis omnibus arcus
> et manicae uirides et stricta myrtus habena,
> summo palla genu …

So she speaks, and at the same time looks among the pine-clad heights of the mountain and sees nymphs hunting in a pretty band, the pride of waves and woods. All have light bows and green cuffs, and bows drawn with myrtle, their robes bound at the knee …

One of these, Dryope, becomes her target. Like Hylas (and Dido), she is a huntress, and, furthermore, provides the raw material for Juno's restaging of the transformation from epic to elegy. While Dryope herself is a Valerian innovation in the myth, her name appears elsewhere in the tradition, recalling in particular Apollonius' story of Hercules' kidnapping of Hylas after the murder of his father, Theiodamas, king of the Dryopes.[37] Valerius thus again draws attention to the way in which his version of the story transforms his inherited models, figuring Hylas' own transformation from his (revamped) epic persona back to his elegiac tradition. The etymological play embedded in Dryope's name, as Heerink shows, emphasizes this poetic process: while he is ὕλη, the forest, she is δρῦς, wood, the substance of Valerius' metamorphic story.[38]

Like Hylas, too, Dryope follows Hercules into the story, giving her the same martial-epic orientation as Hylas and Dido. Hearing the sounds of Hercules' hunt, she comes away astonished at the sight (VF 3.529–42):

> e quibus Herculeo Dryope percussa fragore,
> cum fugerent iam tela ferae, processerat ultra
> turbatum uisura nemus fontemque petebat
> rursus et attonitos referebat ab Hercule uultus.
> hanc delapsa polo piceaeque adclinis opacae
> Iuno uocat prensaque manu sic blanda profatur:
> "quem tibi coniugio tot dedignata dicaui,
> nympha, procos, en Haemonia puer adpulit alno,
> clarus Hylas, saltusque tuos fontesque pererrat.
> uidisti roseis haec per loca Bacchus habenis
> cum domitas acies et eoi fercula regni
> duceret ac rursus thiasos et sacra mouentem.

> hunc tibi uel posito uenantem pectine Phoebum
> crede dari."

From whom Dryope, astonished at the crash made by Hercules, while wild animals flee his weapons, had come forward to see the disordered grove, and was now returning to her spring, her face dazed at the sight of Hercules. This one Juno calls, having slipped down from the sky and leaning against a dark pine, and, clasping her hand, addresses her with charming words: "He whom I so often promised you in marriage, nymph, see, comes here in the Haemonian ship, brilliant Hylas, and wanders among your groves and fountain. You saw when Bacchus with rosy reins led the conquered nations and chariots of the east through these regions, bringing his sacred bands and rites. Believe that this one is given to you, or the hunter Phoebus Apollo, with his lyre put aside."

Dryope's *attonitos uultus* suggest that she shares Hylas' admiration for Hercules' prowess. And Juno plays on this. She emphasizes Hylas' heroic appearance (*clarus*) and compares him to Bacchus and Apollo as *triumphator* and *uenator*, much as Aeneas had appeared to Dido in the passage above. But Juno also eroticizes these heroic qualities, turning Dryope's head from epic hero to erotic object, in a similar move to Aeneas' shifting gaze from Penthesilea to Dido-as-Diana.[39] Moving from Hercules' strength to Hylas' youth and beauty, therefore, she performs the same kind of generic translation that we saw both Dido and Aeneas do to each other – namely, that Hylas' epic qualities provide the material for his romantic recasting.

Hylas is blinded by his heroic self-image. In hot pursuit of the stag, he wanders far from his companions and, wearied, sinks down by a pretty spring (VF 3.551–7):

> … iamque ex oculis aufertur uterque,
> cum puerum instantem quadripes fessaque minantem
> tela manu procul ad nitidi spiracula fontis[40]
> ducit et intactas leuis ipse superfugit undas.
> hoc pueri spes lusa modo est nec tendere certat
> amplius; utque artus et concita pectora sudor
> diluerat, gratos auidus procumbit ad amnes.

And now both are carried out of sight, as the stag leads the boy, eager and brandishing weapons even with weary arm, far off to the mouth of a shining fountain and lightly springs over the untouched waters. Now the boy's hope deserts him and he pursues no further; but since sweat covers his limbs and eager breast, he eagerly sinks down by the welcome waters.

The scene situates the young hunter in an unexpectedly eroticized setting.[41] And like Carthage, the watery landscape presents an opportunity for visual reinterpretation, the same kind of mirror that Aeneas had confronted (VF 3.558–64):

> stagna uaga sic luce micant ubi Cynthia caelo
> prospicit aut medii transit rota candida Phoebi,
> tale iubar diffundit aquis: nil umbra comaeque
> turbauitque sonus surgentis ad oscula nymphae.
> illa auidas iniecta manus heu sera cientem
> auxilia et magni referentem nomen amici
> detrahit, adiutae prono nam pondere uires.

Just so do still pools gleam with shifting light when Cynthia looks down from the sky or the bright wheels of Phoebus in mid-course, such brilliance glitters on the waters; he notices neither the shadow nor the hair nor the sounds of the nymph rising up for a kiss. She, throwing eager hands about him, as he calls for help too late and cries the name of his great friend, drags him down, her strength helped by his falling weight.

The image of Phoebus links the dazzling surface that Hylas sees before him with the way he is perceived by Dryope's lustful gaze, and, in turn, by their joint re-enactment of Vergilian models.[42] The dazzling effect of the water suggests yet another Vergilian paradigm for Hylas, that of the huntress Camilla, who, blinded by her desire for Chloreus' shining armour, never hears the arrow that takes her life.[43] Like Camilla, Hylas and Dryope are eager hunters, both *auidus*, captivated by the image seen through and in the pool's water.[44] By drawing Hylas towards his epic reflection, Juno leads him, like Aeneas, into an elegiac trap, a detour from the narrative he wishes to write.[45]

But Aeneas and Iulus are not Hylas' only models.[46] As has been well shown, he follows a tradition of self-deceiving would-be heroes, foremost among them Ovid's Narcissus and Hermaphroditus.[47] Single-minded hunters like Hylas, they, too, are waylaid by their narrow view of *arma uirumque* and rejection of love, too dazzled by their self-fashioning projects to recognize their susceptibility to extra-generic rewriting. Hylas' alignment with Narcissus in particular suggests the role played by desire for his own self-image (*Met.* 3.413–24):[48]

> hic puer et studio uenandi lassus et aestu
> procubuit faciemque loci fontemque secutus,
> dumque sitim sedare cupit, sitis altera creuit,
> dumque bibit, uisae correptus imagine formae

spem sine corpore amat, corpus putat esse, quod umbra est.
adstupet ipse sibi uultuque inmotus eodem
haeret, ut e Pario formatum marmore signum;
spectat humi positus geminum, sua lumina, sidus
et dignos Baccho, dignos et Apolline crines
inpubesque genas et eburnea colla decusque
oris et in niueo mixtum candore ruborem,
cunctaque miratur, quibus est mirabilis ipse …

Here the boy sprawled, worn out with the effort of hunting and the heat, and enticed by the beauty of place and fountain, as he begins to slake his thirst, another thirst grows, and as he drinks, enraptured by the image of the beauty he sees, he loves a bodiless hope; he thinks it a body, which is only shadow. He gapes at his own image and unmoving sticks in the same expression, like a statue formed of Parian marble; stretched on the ground he gazes at a twinned star, his own eyes, and locks worthy of Bacchus, worthy too of Apollo, and his youthful cheeks and ivory neck and the beauty of his face and the blush mixed with snowy fairness, and he admires all …

The pool's shiny surface reveals a dazzling *umbra*, a shadow without substance. Narcissus' desire for his own idealized reflection renders him unable to move past this freeze-frame, while the image of Apollo once more activates the Vergilian role into which he reads himself – a warning, perhaps, of the dangers of looking too closely at models of the past as Aeneas had done.

Similarly, Ovid's story of Salmacis and Hermaphroditus shows the interaction of the hunter's epic object with the elegiac gaze of his internal audience. Like Narcissus and Hylas, Hermaphroditus is singularly focused on the hunt, and he, too, encounters a nymph who is both a huntress and the embodiment of elegiac inactivity (*Met.* 4.308–12):

nec iaculum sumit nec pictas illa pharetras,
nec sua cum duris uenatibus otia miscet,
sed modo fonte suo formosos perluit artus,
saepe Cytoriaco deducit pectine crines
et, quid se deceat, spectatas consulit undas …

She takes up neither spear nor painted quiver, nor disturbs her leisure with rough hunting, but she only washes her shapely limbs in her fountain, and often detangles her hair with a boxwood comb, and consults the reflecting waters as to what flatters her.

As she stares into the depths of the pool, Salmacis becomes the crystallization of a self-reflective gaze that renders both viewer and object immobile.[49]

Spotting Hermaphroditus, she turns her self-interested stare onto him. And he, too, is drawn to the mirror-like surface of her pool (*Met.* 4.347–9): … *flagrant quoque lumina nymphae, / non aliter quam cum puro nitidissimus orbe / opposita speculi referitur imagine Phoebus* ("The nymph's eyes are also aflame, not otherwise than when Phoebus shines most brilliantly with full orb, his image caught in a mirror opposite"). As Hermaphroditus strips off, Salmacis is overcome by lust, and, as soon as he enters the pool, she lays hold of the boy, who never sees her coming.[50] As with Dido and Dryope, her gaze reflects back onto Hermaphroditus the ideal image that he and his fellow hunters wish to project. All three see themselves in the guise of Apollo, in line with Aeneas' own dazzling performance in *A.* 1 and 4. But the image of the sun also figures their misguided self-perception. A too narrow focus on martial epic *imitatio* blinds them to the fact that they are raw material, ὕλη, in someone else's narrative.[51]

And this narrative, it turns out, is the reflection of Hylas' own elegiac past.[52] In Prop. 1.20, Propertius' Hylas demonstrates the dangers of pursuing his own dazzling *imago* (Prop. 1.20.41–7):

> et modo formosis incumbens nescius undis
> errorem blandis tardat imaginibus …
> cuius ut accensae Dryades candore puellae
> miratae solitos destituere choros
> prolapsum et leuiter facili traxere liquore …

And now reclining, distracted by the lovely waters, he delays his wandering with the charming images … enflamed by whose radiance the maiden Dryads in admiration abandoned their usual dances, and lightly drag the fallen youth through the yielding water …

Propertius uses Hylas' story to urge his friend Gallus to safeguard his love interest, a warning, in Heerink's reading, that elegy may be subsumed by Vergilian bucolic.[53] In the *Argonautica*, however, Valerius' substitution of a paternal dynamic between Hercules and Hylas for a sexual one figures a different relationship to his poetic forebears. For his Hylas, it is the desire to imitate his epic *imagines* that leads him to the mirror-like pool.

This blinding effect brings us back once more to the *Aeneid*, and Dido's elegiac impact on Aeneas' epic project. As he journeys through the underworld in Book 6, Aeneas encounters Dido once more, but here her radiance is muted, contained in the narrative past (*A.* 6.450–5):

> inter quas Phoenissa recens a uulnere Dido
> errabat silua in magna; quam Troius heros
> ut primum iuxta stetit agnouitque per umbras

> obscuram, qualem primo qui surgere mense
> aut uidet aut uidisse putat per nubila lunam,
> demisit lacrimas dulcique adfatus amore est …

Among whom Phoenician Dido, fresh from her wound, was wandering in a great forest. When the Trojan hero first stood close by her, and recognized her, obscure among the shades, just as one who sees, or thinks he has seen, the moon rising among the clouds early in the month, he shed tears and addressed her with sweet love …

Dido has become the moon, not the sun, and, lost in her elegiac *silua*, she no longer has the same blinding effect on the hero. Aeneas moves on to a clear view of his and his descendants' future, the ultimate realization of epic succession. Within the *Argonautica*, Valerius' protagonist is not as successful. As he looks at the image of his own tragic future on the doors of Sol's temple in *Argonautica* 5, Jason, too, is blinded by the pictures before him (VF 5.407–9): *non aliter quam si radiantis adirent / ora dei uerasque aeterni luminis arces, / tale iubar <per> tecta micat* ("not otherwise than if they should approach the very face of the shining god and the true citadels of his immortal light, such radiance shines from the palace"). He, like Hylas, fails to see the extra-generic future awaiting him beyond the end of his epic story.

Conclusion

As Valerius writes his belated precursor to the *Aeneid* – the Argo and its crew as exempla for future epic generations – he thus writes into his text a model of how *amor rerum* and *amor* can too easily become intertwined. Seeking to join the canon of epic heroes, Aeneas' epic successors look to him as an exemplar in and beyond his own text, but they only see a dazzling surface. As Aeneas shows, the *imitatio* of past generations of epic reveals its inextricable interconnections with elegy as it moves the hero backwards into the static world of longing and lament. Just as Aeneas' focus on the world of Homer raises the possibility that he will not complete his own project, so too does Hylas' *imitatio* of Vergilian and Herculean models transform him into the raw material of a far more multigeneric world.

NOTES

I am grateful to the organizers and participants of the *Symposium Cumanum* 2017, from whose feedback and papers this paper greatly benefited, and the Fondation Hardt for the opportunity of a research fellowship in June 2017.

1 Cf. Horace *Ars* 73. Hinds (2000: 223) describes how some of epic's most recurrent features (including female passion) are systematically treated as threatening the essence of the genre.

2 Hinds 2000: 221–7.

3 Heerink 2015: 6.

4 Heerink 2015: 18 discusses Vergil's construction of the Dido episode as "an elegiac delay in Aeneas' 'essential-epic' mission."

5 Heerink (2007: 606) discusses how "retrospective interpretation" can elucidate the generic dynamics of Vergil's and Valerius' poetry.

6 Spence 2017.

7 Keith (1999a: 217) discusses the contrast of mobile male hero and immobile female obstacle in Ovid.

8 Schiesaro (2015: 169–70) describes the dual processes of memory and invention in Aeneas' reading of the scenes on the doors. I quote the text of Vergil's *Aeneid* from Mynors 1969, and that of Valerius from Ehlers 1980; unless otherwise indicated, translations are my own.

9 Schiesaro (2015: 164) describes the frieze as a "theatre of memory" that prompts the activation of memory and provides a set of "ideological options" on which Aeneas must take a stance.

10 Most (2001: 163) has noted that Dido's allure is based in the fact that she offers Aeneas a clear alternative to his own murky future.

11 See Nelis 2001: 82–4; Austin 2004: xiii–xiv, 166–8.

12 See Schiesaro 2015: 167–8, on the doors as an opportunity for Aeneas to subjectively re-enact the Trojan past.

13 Most (2001: 151) discusses how the ending of the *Aeneid* illustrates the choice to prioritize one memory over another as a choice between possible courses of action in the present.

14 Call. *H. Ap.* 106–12; Horsfall (2006: 272) notes the echo of *G.* 3.555, and the "studied contrast" with Homeric δινήεις.

15 See especially Heerink 2015; Barchiesi 2000.

16 Hardie (1990: 5) describes how the first half of the *Argonautica* mirrors the second; Jason and Hylas are both young men in whose coming-of-age stories Juno intervenes.

17 Hershkowitz (1998: 27) discusses how Mopsus' version draws attention to Valerius' reworking of the myth; cf. Malamud and McGuire 1993: 197–207.

18 AR 1.1207–1362; *Id.* 13; Prop. 1.20.

19 See Heerink 2015: 8, on how the relationship between Hercules and Hylas represents the author's emulation of his literary predecessors; Malamud and McGuire (1993: 201) describe the *Aeneid* as an intermediary lens between Valerius and his elegiac models.

20 For Hylas carrying Hercules' weapons, Spaltenstein (2002: 68–9) cites *BC* 7.37, *Theb.* 5.443, *A.* 1.318.

21 Malamud and McGuire (1993: 208) describe how Hercules and Hylas' relationship is based on *pietas*. Wright (1998: 19) discusses the father-son framing of the relationship; this may play on the name Hyllus, the eldest son of Hercules and Deianira. In reference to Theocritus, Hunter (1999: 268) notes the evidence for the analogy between pederastic and parental relationships (cf. *Id.* 13.8–15; AR 1.1210–11).

22 Kleywegt 2005: 78 cites *A.* 7.286–91 for *Inachiis … Argis*. Buckley (2014: 321) shows how Valerius exploits the traditional element of Hylas' rape as a type of Senecan tragedy; while Hylas' disappearance is Ovidian-bucolic, Valerius' reworking of Hercules and Hylas' relationship, Juno, and Hercules' reaction are essentially tragic. Zissos (2008: 141) describes Valerius' departure from Apollonius in making Hylas' disappearance part of Juno's master plan.

23 Cf. Sen. *HF* 105–6: *acrior mentem excoquat / quam qui caminis ignis Aetnaeis furit.*

24 Heerink 2007: 117; Malamud and McGuire 1993: 201–2, note that Juno is a Valerian innovation in the episode.

25 Heerink (2015: 116) notes the echo between Hylas' description as *spes maxima bellis* (VF 3.183–5) and Iulus' as *magnae spes altera Romae* (*A.* 12.168), reflecting their shared goal of a heroic future.

26 Hershkowitz 1998: 152; Heerink 2007: 116. Hylas is not mentioned in the comparable Apollonian scene.

27 Cf. *A.* 6.868–86, 10.426–509.

28 The echo is reinforced by the description of Hercules' *pii amores* (VF 4.2). Heerink (2007: 141–2) points out that Hylas' unequal footsteps signal his elegiac orientation; the act of following behind Hercules is an image of poetic succession.

29 Buckley (2006: 72) and Wright (1998: 19) note that both Hylas and Iulus are described as *paruus* and *pulcher*; a similar instance may be found in Vergil's Euryalus, another youth of great beauty (*A.* 9.178–80) and heroic ambition (*A.* 9.197–8), who likewise provokes Iulus into taking on his father's role (*A.* 9.257–80), with disastrous consequences. Hershkowitz (1998: 150–2) describes their relationship as part of Valerius' Romanization of Hercules.

30 Horsfall (2000: 332) sees in Ascanius' eagerness the "heroic impulse," despite its tragic consequences.

31 Horsfall (2000: 322) highlights the complexity of interpreting agency and fault created by this connection. On hunting see also Anagnostou-Laoutides in this volume.

32 Putnam (2001: 168) shows how Silvia's stag and ecphrasis "anticipate the renewal of violence in the feminine form." Hylas' recreation of this scene likewise initiates a shift towards violence under Juno's aegis.

33 Zissos (1999: 293) notes the inconsistency of Mopsus' prophecy about Hylas' abduction; Hershkowitz (1998: 27) describes this as Mopsus' "meta-narrative awareness."

34 Cf. Callimachus *Ep.* 31 for the eroticized role of the hunter, creating a gap between Hylas' motive and context.

35 Cf. VF 1.107–11, 3.549–51, 4.30. Heerink (2007: 119–20) suggests that while hunting epicizes Hylas, *ardore* elegizes him.

36 Heerink (2007: 607) notes the echo of Prop. 1.20.23–4 in *processerat ultra*, a phrase that Valerius shifts from Hylas to Dryope; he describes Dryope as an elegiac figure (Heerink 2015).

37 AR 1.1211–18. For the name Dryope, cf. *Met.* 9.324–93 and Nicander *Heter.* Bk. 1 (*Ant. Lib.* 32). The name is also repeated from *Argonautica* 2, in which Venus assumes the form of Dryope to instigate the Lemnian massacre (VF 2.174). This intratextual echo links the two episodes in which Olympian goddesses divert an epic storyline into the worlds of tragedy and elegy.

38 Heerink 2015: 120–1, 131–40; 2007: 611. For the etymological play on ὕλη and *silua* as the material of poetic traditions, see Westerhold 2013: 900; Hinds 1998: 12. For the image of *silua* as specifically raw literary material, see Walters 2013: 427.

39 Malamud and McGuire (1993: 204) argue that one of Valerius' innovations is the lack of reference to Dryope's emotions, in parallel to Valerius' de-eroticized portrayal of the relationship between Hercules and Hylas. This is not strictly speaking true – we see the transfer of her gaze from Hercules (*attonita*) to Hylas, following the model of *A.* 1.490–7. Like Aeneas, Dryope carries over her response to the initial sight of Hercules to Hylas.

40 The phrase *spiracula fontis* evokes Allecto at *A* 7.568 (*saeui spiracula Ditis*), linking Juno's helpers and the consequent intrusion of *furor* into both epic narratives.

41 Segal (1969: 40) shows that the act of wandering in *auia* or *ignota loca* represents an active *dis*engagement with the world of love, reflecting the orientation of Hylas and his Ovidian models (see below).

42 Malamud and McGuire (1993: 206) note the water's blinding effect on Hylas.

43 Cf. *A.* 11.778–82, 799–804, with thanks to Kirk Freudenburg for his suggestion on this point.

44 Heerink (2007: 611) shows how this parallel develops Valerius' etymological play on the names of Hylas and Dryope; *auidus* anticipates the joining of the two.

45 Heerink (2007: 132) discusses how *iubar* evokes Ovid's Narcissus (see above) and Prop. 1.20.45.

46 Malamud and McGuire (1993: 203) describe how Valerius develops themes of the eroticism of hunting from the *Metamorphoses*.

47 Heerink 2015: 131–3.

48 Heerink 2015: 131.

49 Keith (1999a: 217, 220–1) shows how Salmacis embodies the landscape-as-obstacle for the hero. Discussing Valerius' response to Propertius and Ovid,

Robinson (1999: 218) notes that the flower-picking scene hints at rape before Salmacis takes over as focalizer and points out the inversion of Odyssean gender roles: while Salmacis' speech echoes Odysseus', it is overlaid with Nausicaa's hints at the possibility of marriage. Salzman-Mitchell (2005: 32–3) argues that Salmacis' gaze becomes performative through her speech, which echoes Odysseus' to Nausicaa in *Od.* 6; the episode illustrates the tension between female gaze and gender inversion in the characters' interaction. Stover (2012: 192–8) discusses the importance of Salmacis and Hermaphroditus for the first meeting between Medea and Jason in *Argonautica* 5. Hylas, therefore, anticipates the gender dynamics (and generic possibilities) of their relationship.

50 See Keith (1999a: 218) for Salmacis as a mirror; Malamud and McGuire (1993: 207) show how Dryope replaces Hylas' reflection.

51 Salzman-Mitchell (2005: 58) shows the intrusive quality of Narcissus' reflective gaze. Malamud and McGuire (1993: 205) cite AR 3.755–8 for Valerius' sun simile.

52 See Heerink (2015: 104n92) for Hylas' resemblance to Narcissus, reinforced by Ovid's "retrospective" intertext.

53 Heerink 2015: 102–3.

16

Epic and Elegy in the Poems of Statius

ALESSANDRA DE CRISTOFARO

The aim of this chapter is to demonstrate the presence of elegiac elements in Statius' epic *Achilleid* and in his epithalamion *Siluae* 1.2, in which he has recourse to the hexameter of epic, rather than the elegiac couplet, as was typical of lyric epithalamia. I argue that in both of these late works, Statius refines his hexameter poetic practice through the application of elegiac topoi in dialogue with the Augustan elegists and Vergil.[1] The first four books of *Siluae*, a collection of occasional poetry in a five-book set of various genres and metres, were published over the period from 92 to 95 CE, while the fifth appeared posthumously, probably after 96.[2] At the same time that Statius was collecting his occasional poetry into books of *Siluae*, he began work on his second hexameter epic poem, *Achilleid*, which was left unfinished (in one and a half books) at his death. The chronological overlap of both poetic projects, along with their overwhelmingly hexameter form and innovative poetics, invites scholarly study of their comparative use of elegiac materials.

The *Epithalamion in Stellam et Violentillam* (*Silv.* 1.2) is an early instance of the Flavian poet's genre-bending poetic practice, in which we can see the presence of both epic elements and elegiac interference. Dedicated to the nuptials of Stella and Violentilla, *Silv.* 1.2 was probably composed at the beginning of 90 or 91.[3] Statius employs the epic hexameter, rather than the expected elegiac couplet typical of the epithalamic tradition. He also inserts into his epithalamium epic *iuncturae* drawn from the fourth book of Vergil's *Aeneid*, itself an epic featuring a considerable presence of elegiac elements in the tale of Dido: love as wound and as a consuming fire, as well as an emotion beset by anxiety.[4] *Aeneid* 4 is devoted to the story of the all-consuming and devastating passion of Dido for Aeneas, a theme drawn from erotic lyric, elegy, and Hellenistic epyllion, and composed in the colours of

Greek tragedy. Vergil's engagement with the themes conventional to genres other than his own martial epic represents a great innovation in the history of Latin literature, since for the first time in an epic the poet probes the depths of passion in the human soul.

As noted by Giancarlo Abbamonte, Servius emphasizes that the content of the fourth book of the *Aeneid* lies "entirely in affection ... plans and intricacies" (*totus in affectione ... in consiliis et subtilitatibus*, Serv. ad *A.* 4.1).[5] This is a characteristic that determines the "comic style" (*comicus stilus*) of the book, since the theme of love accords with the generic propensity of comedies. It is also unlike the rest of the poem, characterized by the so-called elevated style (*stilus grandiloquus*) pursued by Vergil and thus defined by Servius (ad praef. *A.* 1; ad praef. *B.* 1):[6]

There's also the *stilus grandiloquus*, that it is found in high speech and great judgments. Indeed, we know there are three styles of speaking [*genera dicendi*]: humble, middle, and elevated. Vergil's intention is this: to imitate Homer and praise Augustus by means of his ancestors ... In fact, there are three registers: humble, middle, and elevated, all of which we find in this poet. For in the *Aeneid* he has the elevated style, in the *Georgics* the middle style, and in the *Bucolics* humble style.[7]

In particular, erotic motifs are strongly programmatic in the first lines of Book 4 (*A.* 4.1–6):[8]

> At regina graui iamdudum saucia cura
> uulnus alit uenis et caeco carpitur igni.
> multa uiri uirtus animo multusque recursat
> gentis honos; haerent infixi pectore uultus
> uerbaque nec placidam membris dat cura
> quietem ...

But the queen, wounded long since by intense love, feeds the hurt with her life-blood, weakened by hidden fire. The hero's courage often returns to mind, and the nobility of his race: his features and his words cling fixedly to her heart, and love will not grant restful calm to her body ...

Vergil's pervasive deployment of elegiac vocabulary in this passage can be illustrated by comparison with the poetry of the Augustan elegists. Thus, both Propertius and Tibullus employ the vocabulary of wounding in their elegies (*saucia, uulnus*), as well as of the erotic imagery of fire (*caeco carpitur igni*) and anxiety (*cura*).[9] Vergil resumes this imagery later in the book, where the elegiac metaphors become literal in Dido's epic suicide by the sword on the pyre (*A.* 4.642–66).[10]

The elegiac images of care, wound, and anxiety which Vergil draws on in the Dido narrative are present in Statius's epithalamium for Stella and Violentilla as well. Programmatically significant in this respect is *Silv.* 1.2.36–7, where Statius urges his friend Stella to enjoy a happy night with his bride, forgetting the cruelty of previous nights:[11] *amplexu tandem satiare petito / [contigit] et duras pariter reminescere noctes* ("take your fill at last of the embrace you sought [it has happened], and, as you do, remember the nights of discontent"). For the theme of nighttime suffering is, in fact, also an elegiac topos attested in Tibullus, Propertius, and Ovid.[12] Venus guarantees that Violentilla will be granted to young Stella because, while claiming not to wish to bear the yoke of a second marriage, she has begun to burn for the one who loves her (*Silv.* 1.2.137–40):

> sed dabitur iuueni cui tu, mea summa potestas,
> nate, cupis, thalami quamuis iuga ferre secondi
> saepe neget maerens. Ipsam iam cedere sensi
> inque uicem tepuisse uiro.

Yet shall she be granted to the young man you favour, my highest power, my son, though in her grief she often refuses to bear the yoke of a second marriage. Already I have seen that she herself is yielding, that she has warmed to him in her turn.

The verb *tepuisse* continues the metaphor of the fire of love already employed earlier to describe the ardent passion of Statius' friend Stella (1.2.81–4):

> ex illo quantos iuuenis premat anxius ignes,
> testis ego attonitus, quantum me nocte dieque
> urgentem ferat: haud ulli uehementior umquam
> incubui, genetrix, iterataque uulnera fodi.

Ever since, I am witness in my wonderment to what fires the tormented youth keeps down, how night and day he bears my urging. None, mother, did I ever lean upon harder, thrusting wound on wound.

It also recalls *tepefecit* in 104, referring to Cupid embracing his mother (*Silv.* 1.2.103–4): *Finis erat: tenera matris ceruice pependit / blandus et admotis tepefecit pectora pennis* ("He ended. Hanging fondly on his mother's tender neck, he warmed her bosom with his covering pinions"). The warmth of the god of love ends up being conveyed to Violentilla (1.2.79–80): *ast illam summa leuiter (sic namque iubebas) / lampade parcentes et inerti strinximus arcu* ("As for her, I but lightly grazed her with the tip of my brand – for such was your command – and a flaccid bow"), who now appears to be as wounded as Stella. That is to say that she is in the only possible condition to reciprocate the sentiments of her young lover.[13] The latter is explicitly described in 201 as *Latios inter placidissime uates* ("the sweetest of Latin poets"), a picture fully responsive to the conventions of the elegiac genre, whose lovers were often called soft, mild, and gentle. Such characteristics contrast starkly with the epic genre, in which the hero, even if shocked by love, is presented as strong and inflexible, while in epic women represent the most conventional female emotions. In this regard, we may compare in particular the descriptions of Aeneas in his encounters with the impassioned Dido.[14]

In lines 137–40, Statius engages, at least in part, in an inversion of the appropriation of an elegiac motif as performed by Vergil at *Aeneid* 4.529–32:

at non infelix animi Phoenissa, neque umquam
soluitur in somnos oculisue aut pectore noctem
accipit: ingeminant curae rursusque resurgens
saeuit amor magnoque irarum fluctuat aestu.

But the Phoenician woman, unhappy in spirit, did not relax in sleep, or receive the darkness into her eyes and breast: her cares redoubled, and passion, alive once more, raged, and she swelled with a great tide of anger.

In these lines Vergil describes the tormented and sleepless night of Dido, setting her mood in contradistinction to the splendid picture of the peace and silence of the night that unites all living things in the preceding verses (4.522–8). In elegy, however, it is almost always the man who is the tormented lover.[15] Here in the *Aeneid*, Dido is overwhelmed by a series of conventional female emotions, while Aeneas remains strong and unmoving in a manner that differs from the elegiac model in which male lovers are often seen as "soft," *mollis*, with all the term's connotations of "mildness," "gentleness," and "effeminacy."[16] Through his description of Violentilla's desire for Stella in *Silv.* 1.2 (*tepuisse uiro*, 140), Statius thus imports Vergil's inverted model into his elegiacizing epithalamium.

Another response to Vergilian precedent appears in Statius' comparison of the path taken by Stella, to reach Violentilla, to that taken by the river Alpheus from Elis to Sicily, without its waters mingling with those of the sea (*Silv.* 1.2.203–8):

... nitidae sic transfuga Pisae
amnis in externos longe flammatus amores
flumina demerso trahit intemerata canali,
donec Sicanios tandem prolatus anhelo
ore bibat fontes: miratur dulcia Nais
oscula nec credit pelago uenisse maritum.   205

So the renegade river of gleaming Pisa, on fire for a distant, alien love, draws on his inviolate stream in a sunken channel, until at last he comes to the surface and drinks the Sicilian fountain panting-mouthed. The Naiad marvels at his sweet kisses, nor believes that her lover has come from the sea.

This was a journey undertaken in order to reach Alpheus' beloved Arethusa, and the myth is recorded by the Augustan authors Strabo (6.270), Vergil (*B.* 10.1–5), and Ovid (*Met.* 5.572–641). Statius adapts the *iunctura* "*flammatus amores*," however, from Vergilian epic (*A.* 3.330): *ereptae magno flammatus amore* ("[Orestes,] inflamed by great love for his stolen bride ... ").

While Statius makes use of epic elements, he also inserts motifs inspired by elegiac style because Stella is an elegiac poet. Statius presents him as a poet (*Silv.* 1 *praef.* 1–2): *Stella iuuenis optime et in studiis nostris eminentissime*, "my excellent Stella, distinguished as you are in your chosen area of pursuit"), and colleague (*Silv.* 1 *praef.* 24): ... *at fortasse tu pro collega mentieris* ("and maybe you will tell a fib for a colleague").[17] Indeed, Statius describes not only conjugal love but also passionate love between Stella and Violentilla. The theme of love-passion appropriated here by Statius seems to violate the rules of the epithalamic genre, which conventionally addressed the legitimate aspects of the joys of marriage and referred to sex.[18] But this elegiac *deformazione* of Statius' lyric genre in *Silv.* 1.2 may be ascribed to the fact that the groom is an eloquent elegist and, therefore, his love for the bride conforms to elegiac conventions.

The motif of love is described in especially elegiac terms, as a consuming fire inspiring care and suffering in the lovers, when the young Cupid turns to his mother Venus, surrounded by a group of cupids, golden-winged children (*Silv.* 1.2.61–7):

> hic puer e turba uolucrum, cui plurimus ignis
> ore manuque leui numquam frustrata sagitta,
> agmine de medio tenera sic dulce profatur
> uoce (pharetrati pressere silentia fratres):
> "scis ut, mater," ait "nulla mihi dextera segnis   65
> militia; quemcumque hominum diuumque dedisti,
> uritur."

Then a boy from out the winged multitude, whose face had most of fire and whose light hands no shaft had ever failed, spoke up thus sweetly from the midst of the company in his childish tone (his quivered brethren kept mum): "Mother, you know," says he, "that my right hand is never slack in any service; whomsoever you give me, man or god, burns."

The expression *cui plurimus ignis / ore* (61–2) refers to the passion that shines through the eyes of Cupid, the god of the fire of love,[19] who will shoot his arrows at Stella a few lines later (74–5). Moreover, *cui plurimus ignis / ore* is, in and of itself, a meaningful *iunctura*, derived from the last book of the *Aeneid* (12.65): [sc. Lavinia] *cui plurimus ignem / subiecit rubor* ("while a deep blush kindled their fire").[20] Statius' verb *uritur*, in the emphatic position at the beginning of line 67, is a metaphor for the fire of love, evoking the *ignis* of line 62 to denote the image of the victims pierced by the arrows of Love (*Silv.* 1.2.54–6): *fulcra torosque deae tenerum premit agmen Amorum; / signa petunt quas ferre faces, quae pectora figi / imperet* ("A tender company of Loves presses the goddess' couch and cushions. They seek her sign: where does she bid them to carry their torches, what hearts are to be pierced?"). *Vritur* recalls, moreover, the elegiac theme of the cruelty of love (e.g., Prop. 1.1.27): *fortiter et ferrum saeuos patiemur et ignes* ("I will bravely endure the tortures of iron and fire"), and anticipates the moment in which Cupid will confide to his mother that he has pierced Stella to the quick (*Silv.* 1.2.74–8):

> hunc egomet tota quondam (tibi dulce) pharetra
> improbus et densa trepidantem cuspide fixi.
> quamuis Ausoniis multum gener ille petitus
> matribus, edomui uictum dominaeque potentis
> ferre iugum et longos iussi sperare per annos.

Him I once pierced with all my quiver – it was your pleasure – as he trembled in a hail of darts, no mercy. Much was he sought by Ausonian dames for their daughters, but I defeated and subjugated him, commanded him to bear the yoke of a potent mistress and hope through long years.

The participle *trepidantem* (75) clearly evokes the motif of the cares that upset the soul of the lover (cf. Prop. 2.3.49: *sic primo iuuenes trepidant in amore feroces*, "so at first the young people panic swaggering in love"). Statius' insistence (*Silv.* 1.2.77–8) on the sweet and bitter consequences of the cruelty of love draws on elegiac motifs such as the *seruitium amoris* of the poet to the *domina*.[21] The yoke to which Stella is forced to submit is conventionally "negative" in Roman erotic elegy,[22] but with marriage the yoke transforms into a "positive" burden because it is no longer illicit.[23] The expression *longos ... sperare per annos* ("hope through long years," 78) is also interesting. Although it is a typical wish formula of epithalamia, it may also recall another aspect of elegiac love, the poet's hope to meet his beloved mistress, such as we see, for example, in Tibullus: having fallen ill during a military expedition, the elegiac poet-lover anticipates with hope the happy moment when, coming home, he will find his Delia (1.3.88–94).

The image of an erotic fire that consumes the soul of a lover, along with that of the wounds and the anxiety of love, is also present in Statius' epithalamium (*Silv.* 1.2.81–4):

> ex illo quantos iuuenis premat anxius ignes,
> testis ego attonitus, quantum me nocte dieque
> urgentem ferat: haud ulli uehementior umquam
> incubui, genetrix, iterataque uulnera fodi.

Ever since, I am witness in my wonderment to what fires the tormented youth keeps down, how night and day he bears my urging. None, mother, did I ever lean upon harder, thrusting wound on wound.

Here Cupid tells his mother Venus about the moment immediately after Stella was struck by the torch thrown by his bow, drawing on the elegiac nexus of flame, wounds, and care.

Statius has composed an epithalamium with exceptional characteristics in the tradition of the genre, not only for the adoption of the hexameter instead of the elegiac couplet, but also for the insertion of epic and elegiac motifs. Certainly, the affinity between the two poets, Statius and Stella, is at the heart of the epithalamium, which does not celebrate the marriage of gods and heroes, but that of a friend. Statius revives the epithalamic genre, in a manner that reconfigures traditional elegiac elements through engagement with epic features drawn from *Aeneid* 4, which itself stands as an archetype for generic mixing within epic. Yet at the same time he deploys new elegiac elements previously unseen in the epithalamium. The poet anticipates the novelty of *Siluae* 1.2 already at the beginning of the composition with the meta-poetic claim implicit in the adjective *noua* (1.2.2), and he repeats the claim of novelty towards the end of the poem with the expression *intactum carmen* ("a new song," 238). These assertions confirm the proud tone of the *praefationes* to the *Siluae*, in which the poet presents his collections as constituting a new literary genre in the ancient tradition.[24]

If, in the opening lines of the epithalamium (*Silv.* 1.2.1–3), the image of Apollo with his lyre hanging from his hand is conventional and fully responds to the ecphrastic taste that dominates the *Siluae*, Statius innovates in the ecphrastic preface of his "epic" epithalamium, where he inserts current references to the ceremony, in order to make the mythological fiction, with both human and divine elements, more credible. Moreover, in lines 7–10, characterized by polysyndeton and caesuras in the hexameters almost mimicking the elegiac line, the poet inserts the personification of Elegy, already present in Ovidian elegy (*Am.* 3.1.7): *uenit odoratos Elegia nexa capillos* ("*Elegia* came with her perfumed hair bound up"). The personified genre's presence at the wedding of Stella and Violentilla must be considered another generic infraction because the elegiac code rejects the formality of marriage, to which an epithalamium is intended to offer poetic sanction as a legitimate and sacred bond (*Silv.* 1.2.7–10):[25]

> Quas inter uultu petulans Elegea propinquat
> celsior adsueto diuasque hortatur et ambit
> alternum fultura pedem, decimamque uideri
> se cupit et medias fallit permixta sorores.

Among them pert-faced Elegy draws near, taller than her wont; she urges the goddesses and courts them, concealing her alternate foot, wanting to be seen as a tenth and mingling among the Sisters unnoticed.

This is a nonconformist aspect of elegy as the genre is represented not only by Ovid but also by Propertius in his choice of *nequitia* as the subject of his elegy (e.g., 2.24a; cf. 1.6.25, 2.5.2). In this sense, Elegy's attempt to join the Muses suggests that she wants to transform herself, to break the principles of her own genre. The price she would have to pay is its substantial "liquidation" in the epithalamium, since, in the elegiac worldview, Stella cannot remain a poet-lover once he has married (cf. *Silv.* 1.2.31–7, 250, etc.).[26]

The unfinished *Achilleid*, begun towards the end of Statius' life, is a complementary instance of the Flavian poet's genre-bending poetic practice.[27] An epic prequel to Homer's *Iliad*, Statius' unfinished *epos* has a mixture of elegiac and epic elements: Achilles, a symbol of the heroic world celebrated by Homeric epic, exhibits traits far distant from the heroic code and the ethics of war. In Statius' hands, the hero is embroiled in events both erotic and sentimental that had not previously received the same treatment in the genre of epic as war.[28] Statius presents Achilles as the complete hero *and* lover by blending epic and elegiac motifs with the consummate learning of the classical *poeta doctus*.

Both Horace and Propertius supply the foundational precedents for the "reduction" of the heroic paradigm of Achilles to a more humane, elegiac dimension.[29] Horace's lyric Achilles has been treated extensively in the scholarly literature,[30] but Propertius' refashioning of Achilles is also of interest. For in 2.8.36, *tantus in erepto saeuit amore dolor* ("such great pain raged over his stolen love"), Propertius alludes to Achilles' tears over Agamemnon's theft of his beloved *puella* Briseis and his consequent elegiac suffering from their separation. Propertius' refashioning can be regarded as a kind of elegiac reinterpretation of Achilles' "heroic" tears at *Iliad* 1.348–56, elicited by the offence he suffered when Agamemnon took Briseis from him.[31] But above all Statius recurs to a stylistic scheme visible in Ovid, whereby the epic character of the *Achilleid* is weakened.[32] There are several Ovidian settings that portray Achilles as the passionate lover of Briseis, drawing on the elegiac lexicon of love, especially the metaphor of the fire of love activated in such terms as *ardeo, flebo,* and *flamma*.[33]

The pre-heroic image of Achilles as an elegiac *puer delicatus,* "tender youth," is also put into play by Statius in his emphasis on the hero's tender youth and sweet good looks (*Ach.* 1.161–2):[34] ... *dulcis adhuc uisu: niueo natat ignis in ore / purpureus fuluoque nitet coma gratior auro* ("... He was still sweet to look upon. A bright glow swims in his snow-white face and his hair shines fairer than tawny gold"). This image of Achilles associates him with feminine *mollitia* ("softness"), an unmanly effeminacy at odds with Achilles' Homeric stature.[35] Yet this highly marked elegiac portrait follows directly on the proto-hero's return from his training in arms, all sweaty and dusty (1.159–60): *ille aderat multo sudore et puluere maior, / et tamen arma inter festinatosque labores* ("The lad was there, much sweat and dust made him bigger, and yet amid weapons and hurried labours"). This striking juxtaposition introduces the elegiac background that offers a context for the subsequent behaviour of Achilles in love with Deidamia (1.301–6):

hanc ubi ducentem longe socia agmina uidit,
trux puer et nullo temeratus pectora motu
deriguit totisque nouum bibit ossibus ignem.
nec latet haustus amor, sed fax uibrata medullis
in uultus atque ora redit lucemque genarum   305
tinguit et inpulsam tenui sudore pererrat.

When the truculent boy, whose heart no stirring had ever assailed, saw her leading her attendant column from far ahead, he stiffened and drank novel flames in all his bones. Nor does his draught of love stay hidden; the brand waving in his inmost parts goes to his face and tinges the brightness of his cheeks, wandering over then with a light sweat as they feel the impulse.

In these lines Achilles is portrayed with the typically elegiac attitude of a lover who is overwhelmed by feelings of love. In particular, there is an emotional description of the effects of love, a common motif in ancient Greek poetics that has precedents in Sappho fr. 31. The metaphor of love's fire emerges especially clearly (*Ach.* 1.309–10): *sic uariis manifesta notis palletque rubetque / flamma repens* ("such is the sudden fire manifest in various signs, paling and blushing"), in combination with the colour contrast of white and red that conventionally signals erotic awakening in Latin literature.[36] Even earlier in the *Achilleid* (1.159–62), Statius evokes this fundamental motif of Achilles' sexual awakening in the vicissitudes of his stay at Skyros:

> ille aderat multo sudore et puluere maior,
> et tamen arma inter festinatosque labores   160
> dulcis adhuc uisu: niueo natat ignis in ore
> purpureus fuluoque nitet coma gratior auro.

The lad was there, much sweat and dust made him bigger, and yet amid weapons and hurried labours he was still sweet to look upon. A bright glow swims in his snow-white face and his hair shines fairer than tawny gold.

In these lines, in which Statius lingers over the soft beauty of a *puer delicatus*, the Flavian poet recalls Horace, *Carm.* 2.5.21–4: *quem si puellarum insereres choro, / mire sagacis falleret hospites / discrimen obscurum solutis / crinibus ambiguoque uoltu* ("If you put him in a choir of girls, the imperceptible difference of his loose hair and ambiguous face would wonderfully deceive the most shrewd guests").[37]

These are also the lines that Statius certainly recalls when he presents Achilles dressed as a woman by his mother Thetis, in order to be introduced into the *chorus puellarum* of Skyros' court (Stat. *Ach.* 1.325–37):[38]

> aspicit ambiguum genetrix cogique uolentem
> iniecitque sinus; tum colla rigentia mollit
> submittitque graues umeros et fortia laxat
> bracchia et inpexos certo domat ordine crines
> ac sua dilecta ceruice monilia transfert;
> et picturato cohibens uestigia limbo
> incessum motumque docet fandique pudorem.
> qualiter artifici uicturae pollice cerae
> accipiunt formas ignemque manumque sequuntur,
> talis erat diuae natum mutantis imago.
> nec luctata diu; superest nam plurimus illi
> inuita uirtute decor, fallitque tuentes
> ambiguus tenuique latens discrimine sexus.

His mother sees his indecision, sees that he would fain be forced, and throws the folds over him. Then she softens the stiff neck, lowers the weighty shoulders, loosens the strong arms; she subdues the unkempt hair, fixing and arranging, and transfers her necklace to the beloved neck. Constraining his steps with an embroidered hem, she teaches him how to walk and talk and how to speak with modesty. As wax that an artist's thumb will bring to life receives shape and follows fire and hand, such was the semblance of the goddess as she transformed her son. Nor did she struggle long. Charm is his in plenty and to spare, though manhood demur, and doubtful sex cheats the observer, hiding in a narrow divide.

Statius de-epicizes the young Achilles at his mother's hands here, stripping him of *colla rigentia, graues umeros, fortia bracchia,* and *inpexos crines* and imposing elegiac order (cf. *certo domat ordine*) on him by putting her own jewellery on his neck, checking his stride, and teaching him *fandi … pudorem.* However, it has been persuasively argued that Statius was again influenced above all by Ovid.[39] For in the *Metamorphoses,* Ovid devotes much attention to the theme of gender ambiguity, as in the cases of Hermaphroditus (4.378–9), and in myths of passage from one sex to the other, such as those of Tiresias (3.323): *Venus huic erat utraque nota* ("he had known the sex of each"); Iphis (*Met.* 9.711–13): *inde incepta pia mendacia fraude latebant. / cultus erat pueri; facies, quam siue puellae, / siue dares puero, fuerat formosus uterque* ("thence the lies, begun with pious deceit, lay hidden, and the child's dress was that of a boy; the face, whether you assigned it to a girl or boy, was beautiful for each"); Caeneus (*Met.* 12.171–5), who is specifically recalled by Statius (*Ach.* 1.264): *nec magnum ambigui fregerunt Caenea sexus* ("nor did his ambiguous sex weaken great Caeneus"); and Sithon (*Met.* 4.279–80): *nec loquor, ut quondam naturae iure nouato / ambiguus fuerit modo uir, modo femina Sithon* ("nor do I mention how once Sithon, with the law of nature renewed, became of doubtful sex, now a man, now a woman").[40] In particular, the myth of Iphis attracted Statius's interest, since the poet found in the story of a girl who was made to act as a man the functional opposite of Achilles' story. For Ovid too insists on the gender ambiguity and androgyny that makes the deception credible, both in the case of Iphis (*Met.* 9.712–13) and in that of Sithon (*Met.* 4.280).

Thus it has been argued that Statius' depiction of young love on the unwarlike island of Skyros, secluded from the outside world, with an uneasy mixture of courtship and rape, disguise, deception, cross-dressing, and ambiguities of sex, gender, and identity, derives fundamentally from Ovid's epic *Metamorphoses,* a mythological poem enriched by his earlier elegiac poetry.[41] All these characteristics enrich the genre Statius inherits from his predecessor with an innovative element. The influence of Ovid's epic upon the *Achilleid* is also evident in some formulaic expressions about Achilles' cross-dressing, as for example in *Ach.* 1.560–2: *At procul occultum falsi sub imagine sexus / Aeaciden furto iam nouerat una latenti / Deidamia uirum* ("But far away, Deidamia alone came to know, from his secret theft of her

virginity, that Achilles was a man beneath the guise of a false sex"). Statius'
locution *falsi sub imagine* clearly points to an Ovidian turn of phrase denoting metamorphosis, applied to the youth Actaeon at *Met.* 3.250 (*dilacerant
falsi dominum sub imagine cerui*, "the dogs killed their master beneath the
guise of a false deer"), and to a bullock at *Met.* 7.359–60 (*nati furta, iuuen-
cum, / occuluit Liber falsi sub imagine cerui*, "Bacchus concealed his son's
theft, a bullock, beneath the guise of a false deer").

Despite the insertion of these motifs, unknown to Homeric and Vergilian
epic, it cannot be said that Statius denies his adherence to the traditional
form of epic. Nonetheless, he delays the entry of his poem into the usual
topics of the epic genre, responding to the heroic paradigm of Achilles only
in the second book. There he refers to Achilles' departure for Troy in a preview of his heroic destiny, anticipated also in the concluding line of the first
book (*Ach.* 1.960): *inrita uentosae rapiebant uerba procellae* ("The airy gusts
swept his vain words away"). This verse has an important function in the
general economy of the poem, since it intimates to the reader that the promises made by Achilles to a weeping Deidamia (*Ach.* 1.956–9) are vain: this
allows us to anticipate his hero's destiny and the unrealized intentions of the
poet. Additionally, Statius had probably foreseen the experience of *eros* as
a constitutive and non-occasional element, linked precisely to the juvenile
story of Skyros. The poet thus radically modifies the Homeric epic tradition,
in which the hero was celebrated as the paradigm of martial heroism.[42]

The *Achilleid* should not be considered an un-epic poem because of the
presence of elegiac motifs opposed to Achilles' traditional bellicose heroism. Rather, it can be considered epic in all respects, since the patterns of
the genre to which Statius could refer were those not only of the traditional
martial epics of Homer and Vergil but also of the mythological epic of Ovid,
whose undeniable influence seems to characterize the *Achilleid* as a post-
metamorphic epic poem.[43] Such an interpretation of the *Achilleid* recognizes
and implicitly asserts Statius' originality in his deployment of various literary genres in the innovative representation of an ancient epic hero. Statius'
youthful Achilles, fashioned from the threads of classical epic and Latin
elegy, clearly responds to the author's own self-image as a contemporary
Roman *poeta doctus* and complements his fresh and sophisticated treatment
of Stella's elegiac artistry in the hexameters of *Siluae* 1.2.

NOTES

I thank Professors Micah Myers, Alison Keith, and Giancarlo Abbamonte for their
valuable suggestions on earlier versions of this chapter.

1 For Catullus' experimentation in the previous generation with the themes of elegy, epithalamium, and epic in his polymetrics, see Ross 1969; Skinner 2003; Keith 2011a; Schafer 2020.

2 More than date of publication should be considered in connection with the assembly of the *Siluae*, since the compositions were written at different moments. Then between 92 and 95 CE Statius returned to them, to assemble and publish them. See *Silv.* 1 praef. 1–5.

3 *Silv.* 1.2.35–6 refers to a *lex*, which, as Nauta suggests (2002: 298), may be the *lex Iulia de adulteriis coercendis*, the law on adultery originally promulgated by Augustus and reintroduced by Domitian at the end of 89. The resumption of the law by Domitian (as Nauta 2002: 298n22 suggests) is confirmed by Martial (6.2, 4, 7, 22, 45, 91), while the date of its re-promulgation is deducible from Mart. 5.75. The reference by Statius to the *lex* thus constitutes a *terminus post quem* for the composition of the epithalamium, as well as Cybele's post-eventum prophecy announcing the games organized by Stella at the triumph of Domitian over the Dacians in 89 CE (*Silv.* 1.2.180–1).

4 These are, of course, Lucretian amatory topoi, which Vergil adapts through the framework of the contemporary elegists. See Pichon 1902, s.vv. *amor, ignis*, and *uulnus*, for the evidence of their frequency in elegiac contexts; and see further Cairns 1989: 129–50, for the argument that the Dido narrative plays with elegiac frameworks. See further Nelis 2001 for Medea's passion in Apollonius' *Argonautica*, and Vergil's debt to Apollonius in his characterization of Dido.

5 Thilo-Hagen 1986: 1.459.2–4.

6 Thilo-Hagen 1986: 1.4.8–11; 3.1.16–2.3.

7 *est autem stilus grandiloquus, qui constat alto sermone magnisque sententiis. Scimus enim tria esse genera dicendi, humile medium grandiloquum. Intentio Vergilii haec est, Homerum imitari et Augustum laudare a parentibus … tres enim sunt characteres, humilis, medius, grandiloquus: quos omnes in hoc inuenimus poeta. Nam in Aeneide grandiloquum habet, in georgicis medium, in bucolicis humilem.*

8 I cite Vergil's *Aeneid* from the edition of Mynors 1969. All translations of the *Aeneid* are from Kline 2002.

9 See Harrison 2007a: 211, with n11. For *uulnus*, cf. Prop. 2.12.12, 2.22.7a; for *saucius*, cf. Tib. 2.5.109; for erotic fire, see Prop. 1.9.17, 3.6.39, 3.17.9; for *cura*, see Prop. 1.5.10, 1.10.17, 2.18.21, and 3.17.4.

10 Harrison 2007a: 211; cf. Lyne 1987: 121; Keith 2000: 113.

11 I cite Statius' *Siluae* from Traglia-Aricò 1980; translations are from Shackleton Bailey 2003a 15.

12 Tib. 2.4.11: *nunc et amara dies et noctis amarior umbra est* ("now day is bitter and the shadow of night is more so"); Prop. 1.1.33: *nam me nostra Venus noctes exercet amaras* ("for our Venus provokes me through bitter nights"); Ov. *Her.*

16.169–70: *non mihi grata dies, noctes uigilantur amarae / et tener a misero pectore somnus abit* ("day does not please me, bitter nights keep me awake, and tender sleep leaves my wretched breast"); cf. 16.69, *uiduas … noctes*, where the *iunctura* refers to the woman's "solitary nights." Cf. also Tib. 1.8.55–66, where the poet's sleeplessness is due to the love of a *puer*, on which see Pederzani 1995: 53 ad *Silv.* 1.2.37, *duras … noctes*.

13 Pederzani 1995: 94.

14 *A.* 4.331–2: *Dixerat. ille Iovis monitis immota tenebat / lumina et obnixus curam sub corde premebat* ("She had spoken. He set his gaze firmly on Jupiter's warnings, and hid his pain steadfastly in his heart"); 4.393–6: *At pius Aeneas, quamquam lenire dolentem / solando cupit et dictis auertere curas, / multa gemens magnoque animum labefactus amore / iussa tamen diuum exsequitur classemque reuisit* ("But dutiful Aeneas, though he desired to ease her sadness by comforting her and to turn aside pain with words, still, with much sighing, and a heart shaken by the strength of her love, followed the divine command, and returned to the fleet"); cf. 4.438–9.

15 Only in the female-authored poetry of Sappho, the Hellenistic female poets, and Sulpicia do we find first-person descriptions of lovesick women. Apollonius' portrait of the lovesick Medea in *Argonautica* 3 inaugurates a vogue in later Hellenistic Greek and Latin poetry for heroines tormented by love, such as Catullus' Ariadne, Cinna's Zmyrna, and Calvus' Io.

16 Edwards 1993: 63–97; Harrison 2007a: 212. For the conventions of Latin elegy, and their *deformazione* of Greek lyric, see also Wasdin 2018.

17 Cf. *Silv.* 1.2.257–8: *tecum similes iunctaeque Camenae, Stella mihi, multumque pares bacchamus ad aras* ("together with you, Stella, the Muses are similar and closely joined to me, and we revel equally at the divine altars of poesie"). The epic poet Statius lays claim to a kind of cultural and literary affinity with Lucius Arruntius Stella. Statius also tells us that his friend composed enchantments of love for his wife Violentilla in the central passage of *Silv.* 1.2 that celebrates their wedding and in which the woman is called *Asteris* (*Silv.* 1.2.96–102, 196–9). Yet it was probably not a generic and common love for poetry but a mutual preference for the elegiac genre that was the basis of the affinity between the two. As Traglia-Aricò 1980 explains, elegy may also be understood as a light poem with some preference for the theme of love, in which Martial and Statius say that Stella indulges.

18 On the genre of epithalamium, and its close relationship to elegy in the Latin literary tradition, see now Wasdin 2018.

19 Pederzani (1995, 65) notes, as Hellenistic precedents for this image, Moschus' Ἔρως δραπέτης 7–8: χρῶτα μὲν οὐ λευκὸς πυρὶ δ᾽εἴκελος ὄμματα δ᾽αὐτῷ / δριμύλα καὶ φλογόεντα (H. Beckby 1975, 268–71).

20 Pederzani 1995: 65. The expression also occurs in *B.* 7.60, *G.* 2.1.166; cf. Stat. *Theb.* 1.114; *Ach.* 1.164.

21 On the elegiac motif of *seruitium amoris*, the poet's enslavement to his woman, see Labate 1984: 212 and Garbarino 1987.

22 Tedeschi 1990, ad Prop. 3.24.

23 Pederzani 1995, ad 1.2.78; cf. *Silv.* 1.2.28–9: *fama tace: subiit leges et frena momordit / ille solutus amore* ("Rumour be silent: that love that ranged so widely now brooks control and takes the bridle"); 1.2.138–9: *thalami quamuis iuga ferre secundi / saepe neget maerens* ("though she often refuse with tears to bear the yoke of a second marriage").

24 Pederzani 1995: 94.

25 Pederzani 1995: 37, 38.

26 Pederzani 1995: 38.

27 Statius must have begun the *Achilleid* in the spring of 95, as some references in the *Siluae* indicate (Traglia-Aricò 1980, 24–5); *Silv.* 4.7 is dated precisely to that period, in which there is the first mention of the new *epos* at vv. 23–4: *et primis meus ecce metis / haeret Achilles* ("and look, my Achilles sticks at the first goalposts"); 4.4, from summer 95, which makes reference to the epic at vv. 93–4: *nunc uacuos crines alio subit infula nexu: / Troia quidem magnusque mihi temptatur Achilles* ("now a new fillet encircles my bare locks with another band: Troy indeed had great Achilles test me"). But Statius must have conceived the *Achilleid* before 95, as evidenced by the numerous references to the myth of Achilles in *Silv.* 1.2.216–17; 2.1.88–9, 90; 2.6.30–1, 54; 5.3.193–4 (Traglia-Aricò 1980: 26 and 48). Thus Traglia-Aricò (1980: 48–9) suggests the new poem should not be seen as the result of a sudden deliberation, but as a result of a decision made slowly over the years.

28 It must be acknowledged, however, that we do not have Hellenistic works on the theme, so we cannot be absolutely certain that Statius is innovating in this regard.

29 Hor. *Carm.* 1.8.13–16, 2.4.1–4, 2.5.21–4; Prop. 2.8. 29–36.

30 Rosati 1994; Feeney 2004b; Keith 2017.

31 Rosati 1994: 9.

32 Hinds 2000.

33 See especially *Heroides* 3; cf. Ovid *Am.* 1.9.33: *ardet in abducta Briseide magnus Achilles* ("great Achilles blazes for stolen Briseis"); *Am.* 2.8.11: *Thessalus ancillae facie Briseidos arsit* ("the Thessalian prince blazed with passion at the sight of his slave girl Briseis"); *Rem. am.* 777–8: *Hoc et in abducta Briseide flebat Achilles, / illam Plisthenio gaudia ferre uiro* ("Achilles wept over stolen Briseis, she endured the pleasures of Plisthenes' son Agamemnon"); *Trist.* 2.373: *quid prius est illi flamma Briseidos* ("What occurs earlier in the *Iliad* than [Achilles'] flaming passion for Briseis?").

34 I cite the text of Statius' *Achilleid* from Traglia-Aricò 1980; translations are those of Shackleton Bailey 2003b.
35 On the *puer delicatus* of elegy, see Maltby 2002; Zimmermann Damer 2014. On *mollitia*, see Edwards 1993: 63–97.
36 On the erotic valence of the red-white colour contrast, see Onians 1973: 153n2; Rhorer 1980: 79; Lateiner 1998.
37 On the relationship of this much-discussed Horatian passage to Statius' Achilles, see Dilke 1954: 103 ad loc.; Hinds 1998: 136; Ripoll/Soubiran 2008: 202 ad loc.; Uccellini 2012: 229 ad loc.; Keith 2017: 287–90.
38 Rosati 1994: 29.
39 Rosati 1994; Hinds 2000.
40 Rosati 1994: 29; Hinds 1998: 135–44.
41 Hinds 1998: 137. On Ovid's elegiacization of epic in the *Metamorphoses*, see Knox 1986; Hinds 1987a.
42 Rosati 1994: 57–8.
43 Hinds 1998: 143.

PART FOUR

Vergil's Elegiac Mode in Reception

17

Et in Arcadia Ego: Vergil the Elegist

NANDINI B. PANDEY

"A man who dies at the age of thirty-five," said Moritz Heimann once, "is at every point of his life a man who dies at the age of thirty-five." Nothing is more dubious than this sentence – but for the sole reason that the tense is wrong. A man – so says the truth that was meant here – who died at thirty-five will appear to remembrance at every point in his life as a man who dies at the age of thirty-five. In other words, the statement that makes no sense for real life becomes indisputable for remembered life.

Walter Benjamin, *The Storyteller*

Vergil, we all know, *was* an epic poet. But he *is* an elegiac one. Latin's foremost epic author has cut an elegiac profile since antiquity: in the circumstances of his death, the stories and pseudepigraphia that construct his remembered self, and the material contexts in which readers encounter his work. These include the prefatory epigrams that stand epitaphically over his book rolls, much like the grave inscription standing over his cenotaph in Naples. These posthumous accretions reify the elegiac sensibility that Vergil evinced in life when he imagined his voice receding into the perennial, yet perennially past-tense, world of his texts – beginning with the imperfect *canebam* and self-quotation from the *Bucolics* that close the *Georgics* (4.559–66). This paper inspects the paratextual palimpsest that encircles Vergil's poems like a winding-sheet, constructing his epic corpus as a kind of elegiac corpse that arrives to us today only through the interventions of countless undertakers.[1]

1. Generic Mixing in and around Vergil

As Justice Potter Stewart said of pornography, we know genre when we see it – through the ineffable interaction of formal patterns, aesthetic traditions, audience expectations, and performance situation. While any definition necessarily oversimplifies, one signature of a genre is the mutual positioning it implies among author, reader, text, and time. Epic sings eternal truths, sometimes mingled with falsehoods, in a public voice that exists in the "now" and claims to transcend the material world. Elegy, in contrast, trains a private gaze upon bodies (from the poet's dearly beloved to his literary corpus to his future grave) affected by the passage of time, often assuming what I call a "future perfect" stance in vocalizing what they will someday become. Elegy often therefore looks over its shoulder at epigram, a "distinctive type of elegy" that includes epitaphs, dedicatory epigrams, and other forms that struggle against time to speak to the living about the dead or other mute objects.[2] Elegy and *elogia* thematize loss both formally, with the "missing" foot of each alternate line, and etymologically, with their putative shared origin in the Greek *elegos*, derived onomatopoetically from cries of lamentation (*e e legein* or *eleleu*). More generally, they share an obsession with death, disenfranchisement, and the role of writing in preserving memory.

Generic distinctions like this, however, begin to disintegrate when it comes to Vergil, despite his epic insistence that he *sings* of arms and the man (*A.* 1.1).[3] Vergil did give occasional recitations and even, according to the biographical tradition, completed certain half-lines orally (*VSD* 33–4). But in *Georgics* 3.16–39, Vergil imagines his epic in monumental terms that prefigure its ultimate detachment from the author's voice.[4] So too did the *Georgics'* public debut over several days' recitation to Octavian; as Vergil's voice grew exhausted, Maecenas filled in to read from a script that divided and disembodied Vergil's *vox propria* at the poem's inception (*VSD* 27). The *Aeneid* itself partakes in the epitaphic tradition of speaking for and as those who lack a voice. Book 6.860–86 offers a eulogy for Marcellus through the persona of Anchises' ghost – words that, voiced by Vergil during an imperial reading, reportedly made Octavia faint.[5] The elegiacally tinged narrative of Nisus and Euryalus concludes at 9.446–9 with the poet's personal, epitaphic vow to immortalize the dead lovers as long as the Capitoline rock endures.[6] These interchanges between living voice and mute bodies replicate Aeneas' katabasis on a narratological level to confuse the boundaries among epic, elegy, epitaph, and eulogy. Vergil's poems drift into elegiac, even epitaphic, territory through their consciousness of their material survival of the poet.

2. Recapitulation and Decapitation in Epitaph and Elegy

Despite its "epic" claims to be public, oral, and eternalizing, then, the *Aeneid* already speaks in sepulchral tones. These are amplified by the *Aeneid's* origin mythos: the early and persistent rumour that the dying Vergil asked for his epic to be burned, only to be overridden on Augustus' authority (*auctore Augusto, VSD* 41).[7] I have argued elsewhere that this story ties the birth of the epic to the (literal) death of its author.[8] It also functions as a paratextual reminder of the perishability of Vergil's written poem, whose public survival nonetheless countervails its creator's private wishes. The *Aeneid* thereby becomes an epitaph of sorts. Instead of speaking *as* its author, it speaks in his place and against his will. As we read it, then, we view an object whose meaning (and very existence) are constructed by an audience, upon its supposed author, *in memoriam.*

In doing so, we occupy the same position as the viewers of grave inscriptions. The following elegiacs found at Rome (*CIL* I[2] 1222), for instance, call out to passers-by to mark the absence of the dedicator's daughter and make interpretive claims about her form and value.[9]

Sei quis hauet nostro conferre dolore[m]/adsit nec parueis flere quead lachrymis/ quam coluit dulci gauisus amore puella[m]/[hic locat] infelix unica quei fuerat/ [donec compleuit] fatorum tempora numphe/[nunc sublat]a domu cara sueis tegitur/[et candor uult]us et eo laudata figura/[umbra leuis nun]c est paruos et ossa cinis

If anyone cares to add his own grief to ours, here let him be; and with no scanty tears let him deign to weep. Here an unhappy parent has laid to rest his one and only daughter Nymphe whom he cherished in the joy of sweet love while the shortened hours of the Fates allowed it. Now she is torn away from home – earth covers her, dear to her own; now her fair face, her form too, praised as fair, – all is airy shadow and her bones are a little pinch of ashes.

Other epitaphs, like this first-century BCE inscription in senarii found near Cremona (*CIL* I[2] 2138), speak not just for but *as* the deceased, make possessive claims on his behalf, and highlight the separation between living and dead, even as they hint that the same fate awaits us all.

M[arcus] Statius/M[arci] l[ibertus] Chilo/hic/heus tu uiator las/se qu[i] me praete/reis/cum diu ambula/reis tamen hoc/ueniundum est tibi/in f[ronte] p[edes] X in ag[ro]/p[edes] X

Marcus Statius Chilo, freedman of Marcus, lies here. Ah! Weary wayfarer, you there who are passing by me, though you may walk as long as you like, yet here's the place you must come to. Frontage 10′, depth 10′.

These speaking stones on the margins of the city underline their material permanence vis-à-vis human life but also their reliance on readers to remember and give voice to the dead. Their extreme distillation of lives parallels the body's transformation into a handful of ash and all representations' miniaturization of reality. Or at least, such is the theme of the epitaph purportedly written by Ennius for Scipio:[10] *quam tantam statuam statuet populus Romanus / quamue columnam, quae teque et tua gesta loquatur* ("How great a statue will the Roman people raise to you, or how high a column, that may praise you and your deeds?"). These verses throw up their hands in despair at the inadequacy of any metonym, from image to text, to encapsulate the fullness of a great career.

By condensing a human life into a few synoptic words, epitaphs engage in a physical and temporal telescoping that is one generic hallmark of elegy. Elegists at least since Callimachus have fantasized about writing their gravestones in advance (*Epigrams* 35): Βαττιάδεω παρὰ σῆμα φέρεις πόδας εὖ μὲν ἀοιδήν / εἰδότος, εὖ δ᾽ οἴνωι καίρια συγγελάσαι ("By the tomb of Battus' son you bear your feet, a man well-skilled in song and at laughing in season over the wine"). In *Bucolics* 10, Gallus imagines how gently his bones will rest if the Arcadian shepherds sing his loves (33–4). As a highly wrought hexameter composition purporting to be sung by and about the first Roman elegist, this early poem of Vergil's already illustrates the generic mixing that would come to surround his corpus.[11] As Teresa Ramsby observes, Tibullus 1.3 preserves the first (and explicitly fictitious) epitaph in Roman literary elegy, as the poet imagines himself dying far from Delia in Messalla's service.[12] But it is Propertius who most insistently envisions his own death, developing a characteristically elegiac stance that would bleed over into his epic contemporary's reception.

By my reckoning, twenty of Propertius' elegies[13] anticipate, even pre-memorialize, the deaths of the poet or his beloved. At 2.13, for instance, Propertius envisions Cynthia and his books accompanying his funeral procession like heirs who will preserve his name after death (25–30). As the funeral flames miniaturize his body into ashes in a little urn (*paruula testa*, 32) for a tiny tomb (*exiguo ... busto*, 33), the poet crystallizes his life into a single epitaph: *QVI NVNC IACET HORRIDA PVLVIS, / VNIVS HIC QVONDAM SERVVS AMORIS ERAT* ("HE WHO NOW LIES HERE, COARSE DUST, / ONCE WAS THE SLAVE OF A SINGLE LOVE," 35–6). In asking Cynthia to mind his "remembering stones" (*lapides ... memores*, 40), unable to speak for themselves (57–8), Propertius collapses this epitaph with all his elegies to remind us that they continue to speak only through texts voiced by readers. This exemplifies elegy's future perfect vision of the poet's death as already past, often in terms of lapidary inscriptions that preserve his posthumous memory even as they eviscerate his inner life.

The cruellest twist is the deceased person's loss of control over the words that will resurrect her for posterity, sometimes in direct defiance of her own self-conception. At 4.7.83–6, Cynthia's ghost bids Propertius to inscribe a column with an epitaph that is "worthy" (*dignum*, 83), but brief enough that a traveller might read it as he hastens from the city (84):[14] *hic Tiburtina iacet aurea Cynthia terra: / accessit ripae laus, Aniene, tuae* ("Here in Tiburtine earth lies golden Cynthia: this glory, Anio, accrues to your banks"). The shining reputation that Cynthia here claims mismatches her now charred corpse (7–12) and Propertius' representations elsewhere. Indeed, her insistence that she has been faithful and he has failed to honour her in death (23–34) turns the tables on his earlier epitaphic profession of loyalty to a single mistress (2.13.35–6), as does the subsequent poem (4.8): a flashback to the night where she left town on another affair, only to discover Propertius entertaining other women in her absence. This latter poem's anti-chronological resurrection of the supposedly faithful mistress of 4.7 illustrates how memory continues to evolve after death, but also reminds us that the living (in this case, the poet) continue to control the mimetic purse strings.[15] In effect, then, these elegies stage a contest between writers and subjects over who controls posthumous summations and thereby perceptions of their lives. Though Cynthia returns from the dead to prick Propertius' conscience, and poke holes in his self-representation through her own attempted recapitulation of her life, she forever relies on him and his readers in order to speak. The point gains wider resonance when we regard Propertius' textually constructed *puella* as an emblem for his own poems. Vergil's corpus, too, would continue to speak as a corpse through the loving if refiguring embrace of his admirers.

We find a real-world example with John Keats' own lyre-topped grave in the Protestant Cemetery in the Roman *rione* of Testaccio (Figure 17.1). Keats, "half in love with easeful Death," carried the torch of elegy (and its future perfect stance) into English letters: he once wrote to his inamorata, Fanny Brawne, "I have two luxuries to brood over in my walks, your Loveliness and the hour of my death. O that I could have possession of them both in the same minute!"[16] As he lay dying far from home, he wished his tomb to say: "Here lies One Whose Name was writ in Water." This inscription transforms Catullus' lament at lovers' mutability (*sed mulier cupido quod dicit amanti, / in uento et rapida scribere oportet aqua*, 70.3–4) into a meditation on the ephemerality of poetic success. But what his friends Joseph Severn and Charles Brown actually had inscribed was:

This Grave / contains all that was Mortal, / of a / YOUNG ENGLISH POET, / Who, / on his Death Bed, / in the Bitterness of his Heart, / at the Malicious Power of his Enemies, /

17.1. John Keats' grave in the Protestant Cemetery in Rome. Image courtesy Wikimedia Commons.

Desired / these Words to be engraven on his Tomb Stone / "Here lies One / Whose Name was writ in Water.["] / Feb 24th 1821

Even in claiming to record the poet's intentions, this inscription defies them by editorializing and speaking in the poet's stead. It ventriloquizes Severn and Brown's own bitterness about Keats' early death onto the poet himself – as they themselves would come to regret. But in omitting the poet's name, and relying on faithful readers to supply it, the epitaph nonetheless proves Keats' fame and corrects his despair, even in English letters on the margins of Catholic Rome. Might this incident parallel Varius' and Tucca's evident defiance of their friend Vergil's behest that they publish "nothing that he himself had not revised" (*VSD* 40), under pressure from Augustus but also their own admiration?

3. Vergil, Following Ennius, as an Epic Elegist

The *genius* of Cynthia, Keats, and Vergil was thus paradoxically preserved by loving survivors' commemorative violence, in keeping with *elogia*'s secondary meaning as a codicil of disinheritance. Posterity also reshaped poets' remembered identities, embalming certain epic poets in the posture of elegists on their deathbeds. The funerary epigram (or two?) that Cicero attributes to Ennius (*Tusc. Disp.* 1.15.34 = Vahlen *Epigrammata* 1) constitutes a *sphragis* to the poet's works within the cultural memory of first-century BCE Rome:

> aspicite, o ciues, senis Enni imaginis formam.
>   hic uestrum panxit maxima facta patrum.
> nemo me lacrumis decoret nec funera fletu
>   faxit. cur? uolito uiuus per ora uirum.

Behold, citizens, the aspect of the image of old Ennius. He unfolded the great deeds of your forefathers. Let nobody honour me with tears or render funereal service with weeping. Why? I flit living through the lips of men.

These lines might have accompanied a book roll, frontispiece portrait, or statue of the poet, in a private library or the Scipios' tomb. Enhancing the ambiguity, *formam* (1) may either point deictically to an accompanying image or adumbrate the words that follow. Either way, Ennius' achievement has been transformed into an aesthetic object, viewable in one glance, that contains the "great deeds" of Rome's forefathers with little hint of the Scipionic epitaph's metonymic anxiety. The initial division between the dead author's past-tense image and its present audience (*o ciues*) finds resolution in the second couplet, whose first-person insistence that Ennius lives on through his readers imagines him in the elegiac position of envisioning and defying his mortality. Ironically, though, this last testament was likely written (certainly chiselled) by another's hand, and reappropriated by others to assert their own immortality – most memorably, Vergil in his "proem in the middle" at *Georgics* 3.9 and Ovid in his envoi at *Metamorphoses* 15.875–9.

    Of all Ennius' epic successors, Vergil takes on the most distinctly elegiac aspect. Not only is he too remembered in the elegiac stance of pre-memorializing his own death, but his poetic body has been transmitted through the millennia with prefatory material that stands over it like a headstone. The various epigraphs, dedications, biographies, and *accessus* that have accompanied Vergilian books since antiquity reflect successive generations' interpretive practices, continue to condition our receptions and transmissions, and encourage readers to approach Vergil's words with an elegiac appreciation for their mute monumentality.

According to various *uitae*, of which the *Vita Suetonii uulgo Donatiana* (*VSD*) and *Vita Focae* have received particular attention of late,[17] Vergil's first and last compositions were epitaphs. He is said to have cut his poetic teeth on a funerary distich for a brigand gladiator:[18] *monte sub hoc lapidum tegitur Ballista sepultus; / nocte die tutum carpe, uiator, iter* ("Under this mountain of rocks the buried Ballista is covered; safely by night and day, traveller, make your way"). As Ballista is smothered under stones, this couplet accreted countless imitations, of which the *Vita Focae* preserves no fewer than five (74–83). Other works attributed to Vergil's youth, Andrew Laird has noted, share a funereal tone. The *Culex*, for instance, concludes with the shepherd's *elogium* for the gnat who saved his life only to be killed with a smack (411–14):

> his tumulus super inseritur. tum fronte locatur
> elogium, tacita firmat quod littera uoce:
> PARVE CVLEX PECVDVM CVSTOS TIBI TALE MERENTI
> FVNERIS OFFICIVM VITAE PRO MVNERE REDDIT.

The tumulus is strewn with these [flowers] above. Then on its face is placed an elogium, which letters spell out with silent voice:

O LITTLE GNAT, A GUARDIAN OF FLOCKS REPAYS YOU, DESERVEDLY, THE OFFICE OF BURIAL IN RETURN FOR THE GIFT OF LIFE.

Flirting with elegiac pentameter through third-foot caesuras in alternate lines, these silently speaking letters share elegy's habit of finding magnitude in trivial events through a subjective lens, as well as the genre's characteristic irony, respect for the unidirectionality of time, and neglect of responsibility (nowhere does the epigrapher admit his guilt). This epitaph shares elements with the biographical incipit (*ille ego quondam …*) that Vergil supposedly intended for the *frons* of his epic, itself ironically probably authored by a third party to canonize Vergil's authentic corpus.[19]

The most famous of Vergil's elegiac epitaphs, however, is surely the one that still marks his cenotaph on the road from Naples to Pozzuoli: *Mantua me genuit, Calabri rapuere, tenet nunc / Parthenope; cecini pascua, rura, duces* ("Mantua gave birth to me; the Calabrians snatched me away; Parthenope now holds me; I sang of pastures, ploughlands, and leaders"). The *uitae* insist that Vergil personally authored these lines as he lay dying in

Brundisium.[20] The lines are, of course, almost certainly apocryphal. What matters, though, is that they put Vergil in the elegiac position of anticipating and memorializing his own burial far from home – and us in the equally elegiac position of reading alien words that speak for (and as) the dead. A proliferation of imitations, including ones commemorating Lucan and a dog named Margarita,[21] show that this distich circulated early and widely, and not just among superfans (though the latter certainly existed: Silius Italicus supposedly bought and restored Vergil's tomb, treated it like a temple, venerated the poet's bust, and honoured his birthday above his own).[22]

This epigram's lack of deictic markers and use of biographical formulae, Ahuvia Kahane has argued, suggest that it functioned not so much as an epitaph as a reproducible "epitaphic sign and ... biographical emblem of Vergil's life."[23] It also sculpts the poet's figure into elegiac shape for posterity. Much like the *Aeneid* incipit, this eulogy epitomizes Vergil's life and serves as a table of contents to his corpus, imposing an insistently tripartite chronological structure on both even as it recalls the tituli, *elogia*, and epitaphs mentioned above.[24] Like elegy, it reels time forwards and backwards, purporting to represent both the author's final premonition and his retrospective synopsis of his life. It also miniaturizes his hexameter *magna opera* into single words in the pentameter.[25] The violence of *Calabri rapuere* enhances our sense that Vergil's life and work were cut short, like elegy's catalectic distich: the epitaph thus functions as a paratextual seal to the epic, framing its half-lines as internal evidence of its "incompletion" upon the author's death.[26] *Parthenope*, an archaic name for Neapolis that refers to the "maiden-voiced" siren who died there when her songs failed to seduce Odysseus,[27] sets off a nostalgia trip back through Vergil's corpus to the *Georgics*, whose *sphragis* identifies Parthenope as the nourisher of Vergil's youthful *otium* (*dulcis alebat / Parthenope*, 4.563–4, discussed below). The poet's burial thus represents a homecoming, into the arms that nursed him in happier days, on a hill whose very name whispers freedom from care (Pausilypon, "respite from worry," now Posillipo).[28]

Through this epitaph, Vergil, like Ennius, oscillates between death and immortality. *Mantua, Calabria*, and *Campania* comprise a miniature verbal map, governing verbs that pin Vergil's singular body (*me*, 1) firmly to Italian earth like the stones that smother Ballista. *Campania* inscribes the dead poet, like his own creations Palinurus, Misenus, and Caieta,[29] into the same lugubrious landscape that *Aeneid* 6 conjoins with the underworld. In the distich's second half, though, the poet takes on new life as the first-person subject of one verb, *cecini*, with three different objects (*cecini pascua, rura, duces*). Shepherds, fields, and leaders serve as *tituli* to the books that generate the fame by which the poet continues to fly living through the lips of men. The plural form *duces* encompasses Aeneas along with his descendant Augustus, but reverses the latter's overwriting of the poet's dying wishes according to *VSD* 41; here, the *princeps* is merely one anonymous object of the poet's song. Might a coin of this same year featuring a crab grasping a butterfly (Figure 17.2), previously interpreted as a symbol of Cumae

17.2. Aureus of Augustus, c. 19 BCE. Oak-wreathed head of Augustus with legend CAESAR AVGVSTVS (obverse); crab holding butterfly with legend M DVRMIVS IIIVIR (reverse). RIC I² Augustus 316. Image files are licensed Public Domain Mark 1.0. Münzkabinett der Staatlichen Museen zu Berlin, 18206789. Photographs by Lutz-Jürgen Lübke (Lübke und Wiedemann).

holding the poet's body,[30] similarly hint at the transformative flight that liberated the poet from his body, books, and Augustus' grasp?

Cecini at once acknowledges and historicizes the poet's voice, above all his epic's clarion *cano* (*A.* 1.1). It also recalls closural motifs from earlier poems, engaging readers (and, before them, the inscribed author) in an elegiac backward glance from the future upon prior *scripta*. The perfect infinitive *cecinisse* had heralded the end of the *Bucolics* (10.70–4):

> haec sat erit, diuae, uestrum cecinisse poetam,
> dum sedet et gracili fiscellam texit hibisco,
> Pierides: uos haec facietis maxima Gallo,
> Gallo, cuius amor tantum mihi crescit in horas,
> quantum uere nouo uiridis se subicit alnus.

It will be enough for your poet to have sung these words, divine Pierides, while he sits and weaves a basket of supple hibiscus: you will make these songs great above all to Gallus, Gallus, for whom my love grows as much each hour as the green alder shoots up in the new spring.

The transition from pastoral songs (70) to woven basket (71) and growing tree (74) emblematizes the publication process itself; words the poet once rolled through his tongue are finally transcribed onto papyrus and circulated as books to replicate in others' hands. This image intertwines with Horace *Odes* 1.12, where the recently deceased Marcellus' fame grows like a young tree (45–6), to recall the Stoic conceptions of immortality that underwrote the *sidus Iulium* (46–8) and Augustus' own eventual deification.[31] Undercutting *cano*'s pretence of immanent performance, the perfect *cecini* and *cecinisse* remind us that the *uates* owes his fame over time to the perishable intermediary of his book – which was just as subject to neglect, encroachment, and destruction as the tomb inscriptions cited above. We glimpse Vergil's consciousness of this fact in his attempted burning of the *Aeneid* – an episode that itself became an object of elegiac lamentation, as poets like Sulpicius of Carthage mourned Troy's destruction for a second time had the poem not been snatched from the flames (*Calabri rapuere?*). As, before, and after "he" wrote his epitaph, Vergil was already felt to be a projection of his text, their fates and fames intertwined like Meleager's with the branch.

The *Georgics'* closural consciousness of its own materiality also crosses the katabatic boundary between song and text, poet and persona (4.559–66):

> haec super aruorum cultu pecorumque canebam
> et super arboribus, Caesar dum magnus ad altum

> fulminat Euphraten bello uictorque uolentes
> per populos dat iura uiamque adfectat Olympo.
> illo Vergilium me tempore dulcis alebat
> Parthenope studiis florentem ignobilis oti,
> carmina qui lusi pastorum audaxque iuuenta,
> Tityre, te patulae cecini sub tegmine fagi.

These things above on the care of fields and herds I was singing, and trees besides, while great Caesar thunders in war at the deep Euphrates and gives laws as a victor to willing peoples and pursues a path toward heaven. At that time sweet Parthenope nursed me, Vergil, flourishing in the pursuits of inglorious leisure, I who played with shepherds' songs and, bold in youth, sang you, Tityrus, under the shelter of the spreading beech.

The perfect *cecini* (566) "seals" the poem's authorship with an intertextual recollection of *Bucolics* 1.1.[32] But already at the start of the *sphragis*, *super* (559) marks the physical space "above" on the papyrus roll, breaking the illusion of continuous song. Likewise, the imperfect *canebam* abruptly transforms the lines above into a past-tense artefact, anchored in time to Caesar's campaign by the Euphrates. The name of this river, as Ruth Scodel and Richard Thomas have noted,[33] occurs six lines from the end of a book in *Georgics* 1.509, 4.561, and *Aeneid* 8.726. It thereby calls attention to the textual materiality and interallusivity of all these poems. The allusion also packs metapoetic heft: six lines from the end of Callimachus' *Hymn to Apollo*, the Euphrates stands in for the broad and muddy genre of epic, which the poet has rejected for the clearer streams of smaller forms (105–13). The Callimachean reference validates Vergil's choice to play with non-epic (if hexameter) forms while Caesar works at war. But it also unravels the poem's representational weft. Octavian was nowhere near the Euphrates at the time of composition and never conquered the river at all, despite its appearance on Aeneas' shield and perhaps his own triple triumph.[34] Vergil's recitation of the *Georgics* to Octavian at Atella (*VSD* 27), on his way home from the east, further argues that the poet knew fiction from fact.[35]

Why, then, does Vergil use this false report to anchor his poem to history? It puts the author in the elegiac pose of *appearing to have read* about Caesar's campaign – in keeping with contemporary poets' self-positioning as belated audiences of war's representations rather than direct participants.[36] The genre's originator, Gallus, envisions himself someday "surveying," or "reading about," the "temples of many gods, richer for being fixed with" Caesar's spoils (*multorum templa deorum / fixa legam spolieis deiuitiora tueis*, fr. 2.4–5).[37] Propertius fantasizes about "reading" triumphal *tituli* from the sidelines at 3.4.16; in *Ars* 1.219–28, Ovid urges his readers to invent referents for triumphal floats, naming one river the Tigris, another the Euphrates at will.[38] Not only are generals' representations of their victories tendentious and self-serving from the first; such distinctions, Ovid suggests, are also arbitrary and factually irrelevant to audiences in the city. *Georgics* 4's reference to a nonexistent Euphratic campaign footnotes the tendency of all mimeses, from the triumph to this very poem, to warp the facts they claim to distil.

This points in turn to all representations' inability, though their necessary metonymy, to encompass the full truth: of a leader's labours, a person's life, an epic's plot. This problem of omission comes to the fore with Servius' report that the second half of *Georgics* 4 originally sang the *laudes Galli* – until the elegist incurred Augustus' anger through epigraphic self-monumentalization in Egypt.[39] Vergil is said to have substituted his narrative of Orpheus' descent to the underworld, rendering Gallus' very absence from the *Georgics* a tacit *elogium in absentia* and a textual mirror for his erasure from the monumental landscape. Vergil's closural *haec ... canebam* thus misrepresents not just the circumstances but the content (*haec*) of poetic composition. Here at the borders of the book roll, Vergil's first-person song fades before readers' eyes into the mut(at)ed, past-tense embodiment of plural interactions and constraints.

4. Epitaphic Epigraphs

If this *sphragis* marks the *Georgics'* ultimate transformation into text, the dedications, *argumenta*, and other materials that have prefaced Vergil's books since antiquity accomplish this before he could even sing. They become epitaphs in advance, full of tombstones' metonymic anxiety even as they eulogize, package, and pre-digest the poems as objects for readers' consumption. The prevalence of elegiac dedications means that many ancient readers encountered Vergil's works in material contexts that were already generically chimerical, likely enhancing their appreciation for the hybridity of the poems. Such distichs also condition readers to approach Vergil's epics with an elegiac outlook. They detain us on the margins of the text, looking in from the outside; highlight the poem's material and temporal alienity; and (like Gallus viewing Caesar's spoils) beckon us to admire the past greatness of what Vergil has already written, rather than hear him sing in the present.

An epigram by Martial to accompany a Vergilian codex recalls Ennius' concern that any column could contain Scipio's deeds, even the "little pinch of ashes" or 10' x 10' plot to which Nymphe and Chilo have been reduced (Mart. 14.186): *quam breuis immensum cepit membrana Maronem / ipsius uultus prima tabella gerit* ("How thin, the skin that holds the great Maro; the first page wears his face"). These lines personify the physical book as a metonym for Vergil, a face (*uultus*) enclosed in skin (*membrana*), but like a tombstone transform the poet into a mute, third-person object and speak in his stead. Such non-authorial front matter, including portraiture, grafts an alien *caput* upon Vergil's *corpus*, sitting atop it but apart from it like a death mask.

Other prefatory elegiacs admire but anatomize Vergil's poems, like a butterfly dissected on a board. The magnificently produced fifth-century Vergilius Romanus (MS Vat. Lat. 3867) contains the following pseudo-Ovidian preface to the *Aeneid*, with ten-line hexameter *argumenta* epitomizing each book.[40]

> Virgilius magno quantum concessit Homero,
>   tantum ego Virgilio Naso poeta meo.
> nec me praelatum cupio tibi ferre poeta;
>   ingenio tantum si loquor, hoc satis est.
> argumenta quidem librorum prima notaui,   5
>   errorem ignarus ne quis habere queat.
> bis quinos legerent, feci, quos carmine uersus,
>   Aeneidos totum corpus ut esse putent.
> adfirmo grauitate mea, me crimine nullo
>   liuoris titulum praeposuisse tibi.   10

Vergil defers as much to the great Homer, as I, the poet Naso, defer to my Vergil. And I do not desire to hold myself preferable to you as a poet – if I speak with such talent, that is enough. Indeed I noted down the first arguments of the books, so that no-one unawares shall be able to make an error. I made twice five verses for each, for people to read with song, the whole corpus of the *Aeneid* so they would consider how it is. I declare that I, with my seriousness, and with no fault of envy, have laid out before you the summary.[41]

This preface, inserted between the closing *canebam* of *G.* 4 and the opening *cano* of *A.* 1, interpolates a disjunctive elegiac voice into the generic and genetic fabric of Vergil's corpus. Through his Ovidian persona (*ego … Naso*, 2), the elegist imports memories of the epic/elegy competitions at *Amores* 1.1 and *Metamorphoses* 1.452–65 to ironize the first couplet: *does* Vergil defer to Homer, and Ovid to Vergil, in all readers' judgment? In keeping with Ovid's didactic persona in the *Ars*, *Fasti*, and *Tristia* 2, the epitomizer reserves for himself the ability to "speak" (*loquor*, 4) while the *Aeneid* is a textual object to be dissected, taught, even corrected: he claims to provide summaries "so that no-one unawares shall be able to make an error" (6). But as every teacher knows, no summary can encompass an epic's Euphratic breadth; ignorance and error are no less part of the reading experience than they are central to Aeneas' journey.

In digesting "the whole corpus of the *Aeneid*" so readers might "consider how it is," this anonymous writer is performing an elegiac critique that prejudices readers' encounter with the text. In accordance with the Aristotelian dictum that a beautiful object must be visible at once (*Poetics* 7), the accompanying synopses not only radically condense each book but also strike an inverted elegiac relationship with it, like a pentameter that precedes the hexameter. The preface's final couplet recalls the legalism of Chilo's tombstone in defending the writer from charges of encroachment. But the mention of "Envy" recalls the latter's provocation of a contest between epigram and epic in Callimachus' *Hymn to Apollo* (105–13, quoted above), confirming the generic rivalries that re-emerge here via Ovid. This final couplet, for that matter, permits a sly ambiguity. On one reading, the poet has put *himself* forth at the head of the epic (*me … titulum praeposuisse*, 9–10), displacing the Vergilian incipit that served as its *titulus*, and forming an alliance with the reader (*tibi*) in "post-morteming" Vergil's epic text. Over the long history of the Vergilian book, many other scribal interventions would eulogize and etherize Maro's corpus, thus elegizing readers' approach to the text. One manuscript at the Bibliothèque Nationale, for instance, squeezes Vergil's hexameters into the left-hand column of the page, and divides each one at its caesurae into two uneven halves, in a *mise-en-page* that imitates the structure of the Psalms but also unconsciously replicates the unequal lines of elegy.

These elegiac prefaces, like the epitaphs with which this paper began, synopsize long stories into lapidary form, depend on readers to construct memory and meaning, and simultaneously lament and replicate the abbreviating force of death. Vergil's *uitae* imagine the epic poet participating in this elegiac process as he foresees his death, tries to define his legacy, and finally cedes control as others speak over and above his dead poetic body. His biographical and bibliographic paratexts also impose an elegiac temporality on readers: we already see the future as past, be it the span of the poet's life or his narratives. The emphatically *written* quality of Vergil's poems owes something to the elegiac epigraphs, which, for all their loving *pietas*, convey not the poet's living voice but rather his marmoreal *imago*.

NOTES

1 Genette's (1987) concept of paratexts has been gaining prominence in Roman studies; e.g., with Jansen 2014 and Laird 2016. Ancient biography's function as a form of literary criticism, and our inability to "get back to any originary meaning wholly free from subsequent accretions" (in the words of Martindale 1993: 7), are well recognized by Goldschmidt and other contributors to Powell and Hardie 2017.

2 Hutchinson 2008: 103; see also Keith 2011a on intermodalities between elegy and epigram, and Dinter 2013 on inscriptional intermediality in Latin literature.

3 See Lewis 1942, the classic discussion of primary vs. secondary epic, and Lowrie 2009 on orality and textuality.

4 In the sense that the temple representing the epic will have a separate existence from the poet (*G.* 3.13), will honour and belong to Caesar (*in medio mihi Caesar erit templumque tenebit*, 16), and will be subject to the same interpretive interventions as any speaking object (cf. Pandey 2018: 1–34).

5 *VSD* 32; this story is also attested in Servius (ad *A.* 6.861). Smolenaars 2017 and Ziogas 2018 have recently pushed against long-standing critical scepticism of the *VSD*, notably by Horsfall 2001. Norden (1957: 34–45) notes that *A.* 6.860–86 may echo Augustus' eulogy for his nephew.

6 Cf. Pandey 2017: 24–5, on Vergil's epigraphical appropriation by the September 11 Memorial in New York. On Nisus and Euryalus, see also Gladhill and Ortiz in this volume.

7 *Tristia* 1.7.13–16 is taken as the earliest evidence, though Laird (2017: 41) points out that Ovid could have back-formed the rumour. See also Krevans 2010.

8 Pandey 2017; see also the complementary argument in Laird 2016, unavailable at the time.

9 These two translations are by Warmington 1940, using his text; other translations are mine unless otherwise stated.

10 Vahlen 1854: 156, *Saturarum Reliquiae* III.7.

11 Servius claims that these lines rework Gallus into hexameter (ad *B.* 10.46); see Kennedy 1987 and Hollis 2007. On *B.* 10, see also Fabre-Serris in this volume.

12 Ramsby 2007: 73–87.

13 Prop. 1.7, 1.17, 1.19, 1.21, 1.22, 2.1, 2.8, 2.9, 2.11, 2.13, 2.14, 2.15, 2.20, 2.24, 2.26c, 2.27, 2.28, 2.34, 3.16, and 4.7.

14 Hutchinson (2008) views this as graffiti on a pillar rather than a tomb inscription and notes the echo of Gallus' *carmina … digna* (fr. 2.6–7).

15 At 2.20, Propertius hopes his parents' ghosts will come back to haunt him if he is unfaithful; Cynthia's revenant ghost at 4.7 seems to fulfil this self-imposed curse (cf. his identification of her with his home and parents at 1.12.23–4).

16 In a letter to her dated 25 July 1819, also quoted by Goold (1990: 183); the earlier quote is from "Ode to a Nightingale," line 52.

17 On the fourth-century *VSD*, based on an earlier Suetonian biography, see Horsfall 1995; Brugnoli and Stok 1997; Ziolkowski and Putnam 2008: 179–99, with text and translation; Stok 2010; Garrison 2017; and Laird 2016 and 2017.

18 This distich occurs in *VSD* 17, *Vita Seruii*, *Vita Focae*, *Vita Philargyrii* I, *Vita Gudiana* I, and many other interdependent biographies usefully catalogued by

Ziolkowski and Putnam (2008: 183, 203, 208, 213, 253, 285, 294, 308, 324, 347, 399–400), sometimes with the spelling Balista.

19 Brandt (1928) first suggested the incipit was on the *frons* of an early copy; see also Kayachev 2011 and Peirano 2013, with Kallendorf 2002 and Laird 2017: 44, on Vergilian title pages, and Wright 2001 on book design.

20 Pease (1940: 180) analyses these *uitae*'s variations on the phrase *quem ipse moriens dictauerat*. The present inscription is an expanded post-classical version. See Frings 1998.

21 See Pease 1940 and Kahane 2017. Lucan's is *Corduba me genuit, rapuit Nero, proelia dixi* (*Anth. Lat.* 668.1).

22 Martial 11.48 and 11.49; Pliny *Ep.* 3.7.8–9.

23 Kahane 2017: 53.

24 Theodorakopoulos 1997 discusses the perceived unity of Vergil's corpus and career.

25 Much as Domitius Marsus does in his epigram on Vergil and Tibullus, as Myers (2020: 112–13) observes.

26 On which see O'Hara 2010.

27 On Parthenope and Naples within the classical imagination, see Hughes and Buongiovanni 2015; an alternate Roman story holds that she was loved by the centaur Vesuvius.

28 DeWitt 1922 explores Vergil's time at Pausilypon and its Epicurean resonances. On homecoming, see also Myers in this volume.

29 Thomas 1985 and Kyriakidis 1998. Only twenty-five kilometres up the coast was the tomb of Scipio Africanus at Liternum, an object of pilgrimage for Augustus himself and supposedly inscribed with the self-composed epitaph *ingrata patria, ne ossa quidem habebis* ("ungrateful homeland, you will not have even my bones"). Seneca meditates on how small a space held the "terror of Carthage" (*Ep.* 86.4).

30 In the reading of Desnier 1995. Deonna 1954 interprets the type as an emblem of Augustus' dictum *festina lente*.

31 See Pandey 2018: 50–64.

32 Mynors (1990: 323–4) notes the possible Ennian touch in *fulminat* but takes the Euphrates as merely "representative of the Near East."

33 Scodel and Thomas 1984.

34 As Östenberg (2009: 230–2) suggests. If anything, Antony was associated with wars in this area; Augustus' best bid for eastern victory was the diplomatic return of the Parthian standards in 20 BCE.

35 Smolenaars 2017 argues that the episode, often dismissed, accords well with the events of summer 29 BCE.

36 As explored by Pandey 2018: 185–239; see also Beard 2007: 143–86 on the triumph as representation.

37 See Hollis 2007: 241–52 for commentary.
38 Among the copious bibliography, compiled by Pandey 2018: 185–239, see especially Putnam 1980 and Beard 2007: 184.
39 Serv. Dan. ad *B.* 10 *init.* and *G.* 4.1, with discussion, e.g., by Griffin 1979; Hollis 2007; and Pandey 2018: 205–6. See also Boyd in this volume.
40 For further description, see Wright 2001 and Lafferty 2018.
41 Edited and translated by Schodde 2014.

18

The Absence of the Elegiac Poets in Servius' Commentary on Vergil

GIANCARLO ABBAMONTE

Servius Honoratus (fifth century CE) was a renowned teacher, and his didactic activity in Rome is evidenced by some subscriptions on manuscripts containing Juvenal's *Satires*.[1] Accordingly, his famous commentary on Vergil's works was also written with an eye to his students, who represent his natural audience.[2] In the didactic context of the commentary, Servius rarely quotes the Latin love elegists, with the exception of Ovid.[3] Yet even he is either named without referring to his works[4] or represented by references only to the *Metamorphoses*. Moreover, in Servius' comments, where there are remarks on theoretical and functional aspects of literary genres,[5] Servius does not mention the elegiac genre. Through his silence on elegy Servius not only reinforces the marginalization of elegy in ancient literary critical traditions; he also ignores Vergil's elegiac tendencies. Given this situation, the purpose of the present paper is to explore instances where Servius comes closest to engaging with the realm of elegiac poetry by examining the passages of Servius' commentary where Ovid is quoted. I shall analyse these passages in order to understand how Servius makes use of and interprets Ovid's works. For my purposes I shall take into account Servius' commentaries on the three works of Vergil. I shall not consider the passages citing or considering elegiac poems which are in the part of Servius' commentary transmitted in his name, but actually written by a previous commentator and traditionally known as DS (*Danielis Servius*).[6] In fact, DS testifies to the slight, but significant presence of all three elegiac poets.[7]

As is well known, ancient literary criticism and the pre-Servian scholastic tradition did not pay too much attention to the elegiac poets in general.[8]

Accordingly, neither Ovid nor other elegiac authors were included in the school tradition or in the teaching programs of late antiquity: even if for Ovid there are some puzzling traces of a scholarly exegesis (a commentary?), it seems to have been confined to the field of scholarly criticism and not to have been used in the schools. We must accept that Ovid and the other elegiac poets were not read in classes or studied in schools.[9] Probably as a consequence of their absence from classrooms, we know of no tradition of continuous commentaries for the love elegists (with the disputed exceptions of Ovid), nor do any collections of glosses on them exist from late antiquity (see below).[10] By contrast, we can see that in the case of the epic poetry of Vergil, Lucan, and Statius, the comedies of Terence, the poems of Horace, and the satires of Juvenal and Persius, there is evidence already in late antiquity of a tradition of commentaries, often transformed into medieval glosses which were generated by the use of such works as school texts.

In fact, some doubt about the didactic utility of the elegiac poets appears already in Quintilian, who expresses a heavily critical judgment against Ovid in his work on the education of the orator (*Inst.* 10.1.88): *Lasciuus quidem in herois quoque Ouidius et nimium amator ingenii sui, laudandus tamen partibus* ("Ovid has a lack of seriousness even when he writes epic and is unduly enamoured of his own gifts, but portions of his work merit our praise").[11] In the famous passage where Quintilian presents the elegiac genre, he provides a cautious evaluation of Latin elegy.[12] In fact, although he admits that Latin elegy was an original product of the Latin literature and gives his preference for Tibullus, he is puzzled about the literary value of Propertius and repeats his criticism against the lascivious Ovid[13] and the excessively harsh Gallus. Whether or not Quintilian's attitude towards Ovid was justified on moral and/or stylistic grounds, his criticisms nevertheless provoked the exclusion of the whole elegiac genre from the educational program of the orators. Elegy was actually forbidden for young students (Quint. *Inst.* 1.8.6): *Elegia uero, utique qua amat<ur>, et hendecasyllabi, qui sunt commata Sotadeorum (nam de Sotadeis ne praecipiendum quidem est) amoueantur, si fieri potest, si minus, certe ad firmius aetatis robur reseruentur* ("Elegiacs, however, more especially erotic elegy, and hendecasyllables, which are merely sections of Sotadean verse (concerning which latter I need give no admonitions), should be entirely banished, if that can be done, or if not, certainly they should be reserved for pupils of a less impressionable age").

Quintilian's position was probably not unique, but represented a generally accepted view in the didactic-pedagogical field, as we can assume from the manuscript tradition of Ovid and the other elegists in the following centuries of antiquity and the middle ages. For instance, the first complete manuscript of Ovid's *Metamorphoses* dates to the eleventh century, while the oldest fragments to the ninth century:[14] no witness dates back to late antiquity. As it turns out, Ovid and in particular his *Metamorphoses* had to be first moralized by the French masters of arts of the twelfth century in order to be accepted, read, and commented on again across Europe.[15] For evaluating how effective the exclusion of Ovid from the late ancient schools was, it is noteworthy that the fourth-century CE grammarian Diomedes does not mention Ovid in the section of his *De poematibus* where he deals with elegy, while he confirms the preference for Tibullus already expressed by Quintilian (Diom. *Gramm.* 1.484.17–485.10):[16]

Elegia est carmen compositum hexametro uersu pentametroque alternis in uicem positis, ut: "diuitias alius fuluo sibi conserat auro/ et teneat culti iugera multa soli" [Tib. 1.1.1–2]. Quod genus carminis praecipue scripserunt apud Romanos Propertius et Tibullus et Gallus imitati Graecos Callimachum et Euphoriona. Elegia autem dicta siue παρὰ τὸ εὖ λέγειν τοὺς τεθνεῶτας (fere enim defunctorum laudes hoc carmine comprehendebantur), siue ἀπὸ τοῦ ἐλέου, id est miseratione, quod θρήνους Graeci uel ἐλεγῖα isto metro scriptitauerunt. Cui opinioni consentire uidetur Horatius, cum ad Albium Tibullum elegiarum auctorem scribens ab ea quam diximus miseratione elegos miserabiles dicit hoc modo: "neu miserabiles / decantes elegos" (C. 1.33.2–3). Apud Romanos autem id carmen quod cum lamentatione extremum atque ultimum mortuo accinitur nenia dicitur παρὰ τὸ νείατον, id est ἔσχατον: unde et in chordis extremus neruus appellatus est νήτη. Nam et elegia extrema mortuo accinebatur sic uti nenia ...

Elegy is a poem constituted alternatively by a hexameter and a pentameter, just as in the couplet *diuitias alius fuluo sibi conserat auro / et teneat culti iugera multa soli*. This poetic genre was used by the Roman writers Propertius and Tibullus, who imitated the Greeks Callimachus and Euphorion. The name "elegy" comes either from "to eulogize those who have passed away" (in fact, in these poems there were included eulogies of the dead) or from "commiseration," for Greeks used the couplets for the *threnos*, also called "elegy." Horace seems to be in favour of the latter opinion, when he writes to the elegist Albius Tibullus and calls elegiac verses "pitiable" because of the above-mentioned commiseration: *neu miserabiles / decantes elegos*. Romans called *nenia* the poem which is recited with many laments as last rites. The word *nenia* comes from νείατον, namely "the latest." In fact, the last nerve of the chords [in a musical instrument] is called νήτη. Thus, the elegy was the last song for the deeds just like the *nenia*.[17]

Diomedes' preference for Tibullus probably depends on Quintilian's judgment. But the fact that Horace addresses Tibullus in his poetry, and not Propertius, could also have been influential, while the elegiac production of Ovid is not taken into account.[18]

The scant attention paid by Diomedes and the other grammarians to Ovid is confirmed by Servius, who cites only Ovid's *Metamorphoses* and mostly for mythological issues, as one can see in the following list of the passages, where Servius mentions Ovid.

i. Serv. ad *B.* 5.10: Vergil tells of the metamorphosis of Phyllis into an almond tree. Servius describes the myth, mentioning Ovid's *Metamorphoses* at the end:

PHYLLIDIS IGNES Phyllis, *Sithonis filia*, regina Thracum fuit. Haec Demophoontem, Thesei filium, regem Atheniensium, redeuntem de Troiano proelio, dilexit et in coniugium suum rogauit. Ille ait, ante se ordinaturum rem suam et sic ad eius nuptias reuersurum. profectus itaque cum tardaret, Phyllis et amoris impatientia et doloris impulsu, quod se spretam esse credebat, laqueo uitam finiuit et conuersa est in arborem amygdalum sine foliis. postea reuersus Demophoon, cognita re, eius amplexus est truncum, qui uelut sponsi sentiret aduentum, folia emisit: unde etiam phylla sunt dicta a Phyllide, quae antea petala dicebantur. sic Ovidius in metamorphoseon libris.[19]

Fires of Phyllis Phyllis, daughter of Sithon, was queen of Thrace. She fell in love with Demophoon, son of Theseus, the king of Athens, when he was returning from battle at Troy, and she asked him to marry her. He said that he would attend to his affairs and return to for the wedding. Once he had left and was late in returning, Phyllis, because of the impatience of a lover and the impulse of grief, since she believed that she had been spurned, ended her life with a noose and was turned into an almond tree without leaves. Afterwards, when Demophoon returned, and discovered what happened, he embraced her trunk, which sent forth leaves as if it sensed the approach of its fiancée. Also for this reason phylla [almonds] are derived from the name Phyllis. Previously, almonds had been called "petala." So Ovid says in the books of his *Metamorphoses*.[20]

Ovid, however, never tells this myth of Phyllis in his works. For this reason, this passage cannot be taken into account for evaluating the presence of Ovid in Servius' commentary, although it shows that Servius had a meagre knowledge of Ovid's poems.[21]

ii. Serv. ad *A.* 3.34 (= *Met.* 8.738–76): In the eighth book of the *Metamorphoses* Ovid tells the episode of Erysichthon, who cut an oak consecrated to the Dryades and to the goddess Ceres. Immediately blood and cries went out from the tree, for the Amadryades, as Servius explains, are so interconnected with the trees that they live and suffer together with them:

MULTA MOVENS ANIMO ... Amadryades namque cum arboribus et nascuntur et pereunt: unde plerumque caesa arbore sanguis emanat. nam <ut> Ouidius ait, cum Erysichthon arborem incideret, primo sanguis effluxit, post ululatus secutus est: inde Statius "nec amplexae dimittunt robora nymphae" (*Theb.* 6.113). item cogitabam, ne forte ex terra Martis iure sanguis efflueret: nam quod dicit haec se ueneratum esse numina, illas constat praecessisse cogitationes.[22]

Pondering much in heart ... In fact the Hamadryads are both born and die together with the trees: therefore, the blood pours forth mainly through the cut-down tree. For, as Ovid says, when Erysichthon cut the tree, first blood started to flow, followed by a cry. From this description, Statius [says]: "By embracing it, the nymphs do not detach themselves from the wood." So I was pondering whether perhaps the blood flowed from the earth by the laws of Mars. Indeed it is evident that he had taken into consideration those thoughts, since he says that these were worshipped as deities.

iii. Serv. ad *B.* 10.62 (= *Met.* 8.738–76): Servius deals again with the myth of Erysichthon, distinguishing between the nymphs called Hamadryads, whose life is interdependent with the trees, and the Dryads, who are nymphs living close to, but independent of, the trees. The difference relies on the names of the two nymphs, for in the Greek word Hamadryads there is the preposition ἅμα, which means "together with," while the common part of the name "dryad" comes from δρῦς, which means "tree":

HAMADRIADES nymphae, quae cum arboribus et nascuntur et pereunt. qualis fuit illa, quam Erysichthon occidit: qui cum arborem incideret, et uox inde erupit et sanguis, sicut docet Ouidius. Dryades uero sunt quae inter arbores habitant.[23]

Hamadryads Nymphs who are both born and die together with the trees, like the one, whom Erysichthon killed: while he was cutting a tree, from there both a voice and blood flowed, as Ovid shows. The Dryads, however, are those who live in between the trees.

The two references by Servius to the same passage of Ovid's *Metamorphoses* have already been noticed by Haynes.[24] They seem to suggest that Servius used an intermediate source, which explained the difference between Dryads and Hamadryads by mentioning Ovid.

iv. Serv. ad *A.* 6.529 (= *Met.* 13.31): Servius interprets the attribute *Aeolides* given to Ulysses by Deiphobus on the basis of an episode in Ovid's *Metamorphoses*, where Ajax accuses Ulysses of actually being a natural son of Sisyphus, and not (as traditionally stated) of Laërtes:

AEOLIDES Vlixes, qui ubique talis inducitur: nam Anticliae filius est, quae ante Laertae nuptias clam cum Sisypho, Aeoli filio, concubuit, unde Vlixes natus est.

hoc ei et in Ovidio Aiax obicit "et sanguine cretus Sisyphio" (*Met.* 13.31). alii Oeliden legunt, de quo nusquam legimus.[25]

Descendant of Aeolus Ulysses, who everywhere was thus introduced: as a matter of fact, he is Anticlia's son, who, before her wedding with Laërtes, had secretly coupled with Sisyphus, Aeolus' son, from whom Ulysses was born. With this Ajax reproaches him in Ovid "and born from Sisyphian blood" (*Met.* 13.31.) Others choose "descendant of Oeleus," about which we have not read anywhere.

v. Serv. ad *A.* 12.405 (= *Met.* 1.521): Servius quotes Ovid in order to confirm that Aesculapius was originally a human physician, while Apollo is, for both Vergil and Ovid, the god who invented medicine:

NIHIL AVCTOR APOLLO medicinae inuentor: nam Aesculapius praeest medicinae, quam Apollo inuenit, qui in Ouidio de se ait "inuentum medicina meum est" [Met. 1.521].[26]

In no wise does Apollo's counsel The inventor of medicine. In fact, Aesculapius oversees medicine, which Apollo invented, who says of himself in Ovid, "Medicine is my discovery."

As these passages demonstrate, Servius makes use of Ovid especially in order to support or illustrate mythological explanations, as if the *Metamorphoses* were a sort of mythological handbook.[27] Yet he did not regard Ovid as an *auctoritas* even in the mythological field, where Ovid was generally considered an expert. The attitude of Servius could depend on the fact that he did not know the poems of Ovid directly, but took the Ovidian material from a mythological source.

Sometimes the commentator does not hesitate to make criticisms (even with a very polemical tone) against Ovid and his mythological choices, as we see in Servius' comment on a verse from *Georgics* 1 about the *Metamorphoses* episode in which a goddess transforms the inhabitants of Lycia into frogs after they have not allowed the thirsty goddess to drink water (Serv. ad *G.* 1.378):

ET VETEREM IN LIMO RANAE CECINERE QVERELLAM fabula duplex est: nam ut Ouidius dicit (*Met.* 6.339–85), Ceres cum Proserpinam quaereret, ad releuandam sitim accessit ad quendam fontem. Tunc eam Lycii rustici a potu prohibere coeperunt: et conturbantes pedibus fontem cum contra eam emitterent turpem naribus sonum, illa irata eos conuertit in ranas, quae nunc quoque ad illius soni imitationem coaxant. *Sed hoc non est ualde aptum*: nam illa magis insultatio fuerat, quam querella, et poenam sacrilegii iuste pertulerant. Unde magis Aesopus est sequendus, qui hoc dicit: cum Iuppiter reges omnibus animalibus daret et ranis dedisset colendum breuissimum lignum, illae questae et aspernatae sunt. Tunc eis hydrum iratus Iuppiter dedit, qui uescitur ranis (my emphasis).[28]

And in the mud the frogs sang of their ancient complaint: The myth is twofold: For, as Ovid says, when Ceres sought Proserpina, she came to a certain fountain to quench her thirst. Then, the Lycian farmers began to keep her from drinking, and when they stirred up the water with their feet while making an ugly noise at her through their noses, she became angry and turned them into frogs which now also croak in imitation of that sound. *But this is not particularly apt*, for that had been more of an insult than a complaint, and they had justly suffered the punishment of sacrilege. For this reason, Aesop must be followed here more. He says that when Jupiter gave out kingdoms to all the animals and he had given the frogs only a very short branch to live on, they complained and were contemptuous. Then Jupiter became enraged and gave them the water-serpent, which eats frogs.[29]

In commenting on this passage of the *Georgics*, Servius points out that multiple versions of the myth concerning the origin of the frogs existed. In the passage from the *Metamorphoses* to which Servius refers, Ovid maintains that they were originally human beings who inhabited Lycia and were transformed by Latona after they did not allow the goddess to drink and disturbed her by emitting awful noises. Servius refers the episode to Ceres, however, and observes that the Lycians were rightly punished, for they insulted the goddess. Therefore, the commentator says that he prefers the version of the myth given by Aesop: namely, after Jupiter gave a wooden bough to the frogs in search of a king, they were contemptuous. The behaviour of the frogs made Jupiter so angry that he decided to punish them by choosing a snake, the frogs' worst enemy, as their king.

In his criticism of the version of the myth given by Ovid, Servius seems to include Vergil, too. He describes the same version as Ovid when he refers to the *ueterem querellam*, namely the ancient lament of the Lycians, once they were transformed into frogs by Latona.[30] In a comment on *G*. 3.431 (*improbus ingluuiem ranisque loquacibus explet*) Servius confirms that the version of the myth accepted by Vergil refers to the frogs as previous human beings:

RANIS LOQVACIBVS clamosis. Et "loquacibus" ideo, quia ex hominibus factae sunt, ut dicit Ouidius[31]

Of croaking frogs garrulous. [He says] *croaking* since they were originally men, as says Ovid.

Although here Vergil describes the snake eating the frogs and seems closer to the Aesopian version of the myth, Servius interprets the expression *ranisque loquacibus* as a reference to the "Ovidian" version about the Lycians' transformation into frogs. Servius' mistake about the name of the goddess confirms his apparent lack of direct access to Ovid's poem.[32]

In the same field of mythological exegesis we can include some geographical comments, where Servius' explanations are often linked to mythological episodes and reveal his use of Ovid. Thus, in his comments on *A.* 7.715, Servius quotes Plautus and Ovid for the use of the river-name *Farfarus* (today, "Farfa" in Sabina) instead of the name *Fabarim* used by Vergil (Thilo-Hagen 1881: 187.11–14): *"Fabarim" autem quem dicit etiam ipse per Sabinos transit et "Farfarus" dicitur: Plautus "dissipabo te tamquam folia Farfari,"[33] Ouidius "et amoenae Farfarus umbrae"* [*Met.* 14.330 var.] ("He names here the river Fabaris, which flows through the territory of the Sabines and is called Farfarus. Plautus: 'I'll destroy you like the leaves of the Farfarus.' Ovid: 'the pleasant shadows of the Farfarus'").[34] However, Servius sometimes also criticizes Ovid for his geographical information, as in this comment on the etymology of the Rutulian name of the town *Ardea* (Serv. ad *A.* 7.412):

MAGNUM TENET ARDEA NOMEN bene adlusit: nam Ardea quasi ardua dicta est, id est magna et nobilis, licet Hyginus in Italicis urbibus ab augurio auis ardeae dictam uelit. Illud namque Ouidii in Metamorphoseos fabulosum est, incensam ab Hannibale Ardeam in hanc auem esse conuersam (cf. *Met.* 14.573–80). Sciendum tamen ardeam auem κατὰ ἀντίφρασιν dictam, quod breuitate pennarum altius non uolat: Lucanus "quodque ausa uolare ardea sublimis pennae confisa natanti." (5.553)[35]

Ardea holds a great name Well-done allusion: that is Ardea was called as if "lofty," that means great and noble, although Hyginus wants her to be named from the augury of a heron bird in Italian cities. The story told by Ovid in the *Metamorphoses* is too fictional, that is Ardea, set on fire by Hannibal, was turned into that bird. One must know however that the bird was called lofty by means of negation, because due to the shortness of its wings, it does not fly high: Lucan "[that] the heron dares to fly high/lofty trusting in his swimming wings."

Servius knows two versions concerning the name of *Ardea*: Vergil testifies to one and connects the name to the Latin attribute *arduus* ("lofty"), adding the expression *magnum nomen* in order to hint at this etymology. The second etymology, proposed by Hyginus and partially accepted by Ovid, refers the name to the bird *ardea* ("heron"), which gave a good omen to the town.

In the *Metamorphoses* Ovid specifies the version found in Hyginus by adding that the heron was born in *Ardea* after the town was burned down: thus, the name *Ardea* would be given to both the bird and the town, since it stems from the verb *ardeo* ("to burn").

In commenting on Ovid's explanation of the name, however, Servius sows some confusion. In fact, Ovid nowhere attributes the destruction of Ardea to Hannibal, but rather connects the ruin of the city to Turnus' war against the Trojans, his defeat, and death. However, we cannot exclude the possibility that Servius' passage transmitted by all the manuscripts is corrupted and needs correction: therefore, I quote the *apparatus criticus* of this passage: *ab Hannibale consens. codicum, sed Thilo in appar. adfirm.: "annibale reliqui. Aenea debuit scribere Servius. cf. Salmasius exerc. Plin."* Here we may note that in his edition of Servius, Georg Thilo rightly pointed out that the reading *Hannibale* is historically incongruous, and he proposed to emend it to *ab Aenea*, an emendation offered by the French humanist Salmasius (1588–1653). However, Giuseppe Ramires has informed me that, prior to Salmasius, the Italian humanist Guarinus from Verona (1374–1460), had already corrected *Hannibale* into *Aenea* in his copy of Servius.[36] In this case, Servius could be criticizing the Ovidian version where Aeneas would have burned Ardea after the end of the war with Turnus and the town was transformed into a heron.[37]

Sometimes Servius quotes Ovid when he discusses some grammatical subjects. Thus, in the comment on *A.* 4.2 Servius mentions Ovid's *Metamorphoses* in order to explain the meaning of the attribute *caecus* ("blind") referring to Dido's love as a hidden fire, which is the most dangerous. In fact, in the beginning of the love story, Dido, unwilling to recognize the symptoms of her love for Aeneas, is blind to her desire (Serv. *A.* ad 4.2):

CAECO CARPITUR IGNI ... agit Vergilius, ut inuentas frangat declamationes, ut hoc loco rem dixit sine declamatione: unde Ouidius "quoque magis tegitur, tanto magis aestuat ignis" (*Met.* 4,64). "caeco" ergo "igni" *possumus ut* ualidiore *accipere,* cuius *haec* natura est, ut conpressus magis conualescat.[38]

Consumed by blind fire ... wrote Vergil, in order to break free from creating a speech, so that in this passage he talked of the situation without the use of any speech: from here Ovid: "the more it is covered, the more the flame burns" (*Met.* 4.64). Therefore "blind" with "flame," we can take it to mean "more powerful," the nature of which is to grow stronger while being suppressed.

In the comment on *A.* 4.462 (*Solaque culminibus ferali carmine bubo*), Servius observes that, in the Vergilian phrase *sola bubo* ("the lonely owl"), *bubo* is regarded as feminine, whereas in Latin *bubo* is usually masculine, as evidenced by quotations from Lucan and Ovid's *Metamorphoses* (Serv. ad *A.* 4.462):

SOLA BUBO ... "sola" contra genus posuit. Lucanus: "et laetae iurantur aues bubone sinistro" (5.396), item Ouidius: "infandus bubo" (*Met.* 5.550). Et hoc est in usu; sed Vergilius mutauit, referens ad auem: plerumque enim genus relicta specialitate a generali sumimus, ut si dicas "bona turdus" referendo ad auem: item si dicas "prima est a," id est littera, cum "a" sit neutri generis.[39]

Alone the owl ... He used "sola" ("alone," fem.) contrary to its gender. Lucan: "The birds are in favour, although the owl is on the left," and again Ovid: "the unspeakable owl." And this is in use, but Vergil changed it by taking "auis" ("bird," fem.) as the gender of reference, and for that reason we tend to assume the gender of a noun from the gender (where it belongs) and not from the species, as if one said "the good thrush" in relation to auis, and again as if one said "the first is a," that means the letter "a," although "a" is of the neuter gender.

Interestingly, Haynes observes that Servius here quotes an entire line of Lucan, whilst he takes only the *iunctura infandus bubo* from Ovid.[40] This attitude could confirm that Servius did not read the *Metamorphoses* directly. As we have seen in the case of mythological and geographical problems, Servius also criticizes Ovid in relation to a grammar problem with the use of ablative plural of *mustum* ("the wine must"). According to Servius, *mustum* should be used in the singular and, in the rare cases we use the plural, only in nominative, accusative, and vocative cases (Serv. ad *G.* 2.7):

MUSTO NOVO mustum numero tantum singulari dicimus, sicut uinum, licet Ouidius abusiue dixerit "musta". sed hoc ille plus fecit, quod et "mustis" dixit (*Amor.* 1.15.11), cum, ut diximus (*Georg.* 1.210), de his nominibus tres casus tantum usurpari consueuerint.[41]

The new must We use "must" only in the singular number, like "wine," although Ovid had said inappropriately "musts." But this poet added more to this, because he said "with the musts," when, as I said (*G.* 1.210), for these nouns it is common to use only three cases.

In Ovid's poems there are many occurrences of the plural of *mustum*,[42] which is regarded by Servius as an improper use (*abusive*), namely a lack of elegance.[43] Servius only says here that Ovid uses *mustis*, but he does not refer to the *Amores*, where the word also appears, probably because he again derives this information from a grammar book or another Vergilian commentary,[44] which listed the words having only the direct cases of the plural form, like *uinum* (see *G.* 1.210) and *mustum*, and so he mentions

Ovid generically. Servius' opinion on the language of Ovid recalls here the judgment on Ovid's poetry expressed by Quintilian, who preferred Tibullus because of his clear and elegant language.[45]

In conclusion, Ovid did not play a pedagogical role in the scholastic world. That does not imply that Ovid was unknown to the culture of the imperial age and of late antiquity. As we know, thanks to the intertextual analysis of the Latin poems, his works were taken into account by Lucan, by the Flavian poets, and by the late antique cultivated poets (e.g., Ausonius, Paulinus of Nola, Sidonius, and especially Claudian). The same conclusion can be applied to the other elegiac poets.

In line with the scholastic trend, Servius seems to be uninterested in the elegiac poets: he quotes only once from Propertius and never from Tibullus, whilst Ovid is mentioned exclusively for his *Metamorphoses*. Ovid quotations are limited to the explanations of mythological, geographical, and grammatical subjects. Servius does not seem to know Ovid through a personal reading and therefore he does not regard the poet as an indisputable *auctoritas* (like Vergil, Lucan, Donatus, etc.). Instead, he sometimes shows a cautious, if not critical, attitude toward him, which is not far from what Quintilian said in order to disparage the poet from Sulmona. We do not have evidence of a direct connection between the opinion expressed by Quintilian on Ovid and his use by Servius, but there is among Roman schoolteachers a tendency to devalue Ovid for various reasons, and this determined Ovid's exclusion from the scholastic curriculum and from the list of the *auctores* used in scholastic works. The exclusion from the school curriculum made the late ancient scholars and grammarians free to criticize him openly.[46] As we have seen, however, Ovid is the only poet in the elegiac sphere that Servius quotes in his commentary, leaving Vergil's elegiac interfaces largely beyond the purview of Servius' work.

NOTES

I thank Giuseppe Ramires and Fabio Stok for their useful suggestions, and Georgia Ferentinou for her assistance with the English translations of both Servius' Latin and my Italian.

1 On Servius' life and works, see Kaster 2014.
2 On the teaching aspects of Servius' commentary on Vergil, see Abbamonte and Stok 2021.
3 Although Serv. ad *A.* 7.378 quotes Catullus for the use of the word *turben*, it is actually derived from a passage of Tibullus (1.5.3). Moreover, for the

expression *Testes sunt* Servius mentions Propertius (2.9.41) ad *B.* 5.21. There are obviously mentions of Gallus in Servius' commentary on the tenth eclogue.

4 See, e.g., below Serv. ad *G.* 2.7.

5 See, e.g., the difference established by Servius between the epic of Vergil and the historical poem of Lucan: Serv. ad *A.* 1.183. Quotations of Servius' commentary are taken from the edition of Thilo-Hagen 1881.

6 The name *Danielis Servius* stems from the French humanist Pierre Daniel (1530–1603), who first published in his edition of Vergil (Paris 1600) the additions he had found in some Servius' manuscripts: see Kaster 2014.

7 Ovid is mentioned in DS ad *Buc.* 6.54, *Aen.* 1.251 (and in Servius ibid. but in an abridged form), *Aen.* 4.462 (an unnamed quotation of Ovid), *Aen.* 10.145 about the etymology of *Campania*, where the attitude of DS towards Ovid is not so critical: for he accepts the etymology of Campania, given by Ovid. *F.* 4.45, from the name of Capys, the founder of Capua, regarded as a Trojan. In DS *Buc.* 7.22 and *A.* 11.457, the elegiac poet Valgius is quoted. Tibullus and Propertius are mentioned in the DS comment on *G.* 1.19, in order to identify the discoverer of the plough with Osiris: *ut dicit Propertius vel Tibullus*. In fact, whilst DS' reference to Tib. 1.7.29 is clear, Propertius did not refer to Osiris in his poems. The presence of the elegists in DS confirms the difference between these two commentaries.

8 See Scioli 2010: 761–2, on the fortune of Propertius in the imperial and late antique ages, and Sannicandro 2010: 1020–1. After the poetic success of Tibullus and Propertius in the first century CE, the two elegists are mentioned by Quintilian, who praises Tibullus, while limiting his views on Propertius to a famous *praeteritio* (*sunt qui Propertium malint, Inst.* 10.1.93), a perspective that probably played a role in the subsequent misfortune of Propertius during the second century CE and after. Tibullus, too, disappeared, probably because of the Archaistic movement, which did not appreciate the clear style of the Augustan poet. As one of the anonymous reviewers points out, however, Hubbard (1975b: 2) reads Quintilian's assessment of Propertius as more positive than other scholars. Interest in Tibullus appears still in Sidonius, while the fortunes of Propertius were revived at the end of the twelfth century CE by John of Salisbury.

9 Hollis (1996: 159–60) suggests that some commentaries on Ovid's *Metamorphoses* existed in late antiquity on the basis of the *Lactantianae Narrationes*, attributed to an unknown Lactantius and transmitted only in one group of the two families of manuscripts (see Tarrant 1983: 277–82). On Hollis' hypothesis, see Coulson 2011: 48–59. However, if a scholarly tradition on Ovid existed, it does not seem to have been used by the late antique Vergilian interpreters in general, or by Servius in particular. Already Haynes (2016: 216) has noticed that Servius did not read Ovid first-hand.

10 The first complete commentaries on Ovid's *Metamorphoses* that we know of were written in the twelfth century in the French school of Orléans: see Coulson 2011: 48–9, who points out that the titles and summaries known as

tituli and *narrationes Lactantianae* are too meagre to be evidence of a scholastic interest in Ovid's *Metamorphoses* during late antiquity. However, the origin and the date of the Lactantius material is still disputed.

11 Translations of Quintilian are cited from Butler 1922.

12 The passage is famous and the bibliography on it too large to be mentioned in a note. I limit myself here to quotation of the passage (Quint. *Inst.* 10.1.93): *Elegia quoque Graecos prouocamus, cuius mihi tersus atque elegans maxime uidetur auctor Tibullus. Sunt qui Propertius malint. Ouidius utroque lasciuior, sicut durior Gallus* ("We also challenge the supremacy of the Greeks in elegy. Of our elegiac poets Tibullus seems to me to be the most terse and elegant. There are, however, some who prefer Propertius. Ovid is more sportive than either, while Gallus is more severe").

13 Quintilian's charge of *lasciuia* against Ovid could refer not to morality, but rather to Ovid's choice of audience, viz. to write also for a female (and therefore lascivious) readership, as the poet proudly states in several passages. Clark 2011: 2–4 underlines Quintilian's words on Ovid, but he does not regard this episode as the origin of the scholastic misfortune of Ovid in late antiquity.

14 See the list in Tarrant 2004: viii–xiv and on the website of the Spanish project *Ovid's Metamorphoses Research Project* (http://www.uhu.es/proyectovidio/ing/).

15 The evidence for Ovid's presence in medieval Europe has been masterfully gathered in Coulson and Roy 2000 and Coulson 2002.

16 On *nenia*, see also Gladhill in this volume.

17 My translation.

18 Although there is a general preference for Tibullus among the elegists in the ancient commentaries, it has not extended to his inclusion in the scholastic programs: it is likely that ethical prejudices against the elegiac genre played a role in their exclusion: see Sannicandro 2010: 1020–1.

19 Thilo-Hagen 1881: 55.4–14.

20 I cite the English translation of Haynes 2016: 217–20.

21 See Haynes 2016: 219–20.

22 Thilo-Hagen 1881: 342.9–16.

23 Thilo-Hagen 1881: 125.27–126.3.

24 See Haynes 2016: 220–1.

25 Thilo-Hagen 1881: 75.17–21.

26 Thilo-Hagen 1881: 612.11–13.

27 Servius makes similar use of Euphorion in his commentary on the *Aeneid*. While he never quotes a verse, Servius mentions Euphorion, often with the expression *secundum Euphorionem*, in order to discuss rare variants of a myth: see, e.g., Serv. ad *A.* 2.32, 2.79, 2.201, 3.16, 6.618. It seems that Servius took the information on Euphorion not directly from the works of the Greek poet, but from a scholastic collection of myths where Euphorion was mentioned.

28 Thilo-Hagen 1881: 206.8–19.

29 English translation from Haynes 2016: 217–18.

30 Against Servius, Mynors (1990: 81) does not believe in a reference to the two versions of the myth in the expression *ueterem querellam* of Vergil, while Richter (1957: 168–9) and Erren (2003: 206–7) confirm the connection between the Vergilian *ueterem querellam* and the Ovidian version of the myth, derived from the Hellenistic poet Nicander.

31 Thilo-Hagen 1881: 310.9–10.

32 Haynes 2016: 217–18, comments on the same passages.

33 Frg. 72 Monda 2004 = 73 Goetz-Schoell. Thilo-Hagen 1881 ad loc. regards Plautus' text as a different version of Plautus' *Poenulus* l. 478: *eo praesternebant folia farferi* ("Within they laid leaves of coltsfoot," trans. Nixon 1980), while Ramires (2003 ad loc.) refers the phrase to a fragment of a lost Plautine play.

34 Notice that Tarrant prefers the reading *opacae Farfarus umbrae* ("the dull shadows of the Farfarus").

35 Thilo-Hagen 1881: 156.21–157.6 = Ramires 2003: 57.2–6.

36 Ramires *per litteras*.

37 See Haynes (2016: 218): "Certainly, Servius, with his well-established 'optimistic' reading, would be unlikely to see Aeneas as a *'barbarus ensis.'*"

38 Thilo-Hagen 1881: 460.17–23. The italics here distinguish the parts belonging to DS.

39 Thilo-Hagen 1881: 547.8–548.3.

40 Haynes 2016, 221.

41 Thilo-Hagen 1881: 218.15–18.

42 See Ovid. *Rem. am.* 190; *Met.* 14.146; *F.* 3.558, 4.888, 4.894; *Trist.* 3.10.72; *Pont.* 2.9.32.

43 On the concept of elegance, which is the quality consisting in a proper use of the Latin words, see Gell. 11.2.

44 See also Haynes 2016: 228.

45 See above n12. Ovid's *Amores* (3.5.18) are quoted in the commentary of DS: see DS ad *B.* 6.54 (Thilo-Hagen 1881: 75.16). DS mentions also the *Fasti*: see DS ad *A.* 10.145. The fact that DS mentions more works of Ovid confirms its different nature from Servius' commentary (see above n7). Here I shall not discuss whether DS transmits traces of Donatus' lost commentary on Vergil, but it is clear that DS' commentary is aimed at scholars in literary criticism, while Servius writes his works for pupils who hardly knew Ovid's *Metamorphoses*. On the presence of Ovid in DS, see Haynes 2016: 222–4 with his n18.

46 The attitude of DS towards Ovid is not so critical: see n7.

19

Ovidian Ghosts in Ausonius' Mourning Fields: Reading Vergil through Ovid in the *Cupido Cruciatus*

KENNETH DRAPER

Ausonius' *Cupido Cruciatus* is a fourth-century CE hexameter poem that describes Cupid's descent to the underworld, where he is tortured at the hands of women who died from love and are hungry for revenge. In the prose preface, Ausonius tells us that he has seen the episode in a wall painting in Trier that he has tried to put into verse, and he identifies the painting's heroines as in part those described by Vergil in the mourning fields (*lugentes campi*) of *Aeneid* 6: *quarum partem in lugentibus campis Maro noster enumerat*. The poem proper then begins with a description of the setting and its lovelorn heroines before moving on to an account of Cupid's arrival and punishment, the heroines' subsequent choice to pardon and release him, and, finally, Cupid's escape through the ivory gate, at which point the god of love wakes to find that it was all a dream.

In this essay, I focus on the first section of the poem proper (*CC* 1–44), in which Ausonius describes the denizens of his mourning fields, principally the heroines but also the boys-turned-flowers, like Narcissus and Hyacinthus, who grow along the banks of the underworld stream. Restating the debt expressed in the preface, Ausonius credits Vergil by name in the *incipit* (*Aeris in campis, memorat quos Musa Maronis*, "In the airy fields which Vergil's Muse calls to mind"), and he incorporates echoes of Vergil's text throughout.[1] But Ovid has his part to play too. In addition to Narcissus and his fellow flowers from the *Metamorphoses*, there are numerous Ovidian characters in the catalogue of heroines. While Laura Vannucci, Roger Rees, and Franca Ela Consolino have noted several of these reminiscences, no one has devoted attention to the metapoetic purpose of this insistent Ovidian presence or to how Ausonius self-consciously annotates the allusions.[2]

I will argue that by inserting these characters into a space that he explicitly marks as Vergilian, Ausonius dramatizes the way that Ovid intrudes into the experience of Vergil's post-Ovidian readers.[3] This is especially true for readers of Vergil's *lugentes campi*. In its original context, Vergil's account of the mourning fields was already generically hybrid, blending epic with tragedy and love poetry.[4] This is precisely the generic crossroads so often occupied by Ovid, both in his elegy and his epic. Vergil's lovelorn heroines now call to mind Ovid's suffering women – most notably those of the elegiac *Heroides*, but also those of his elegy-infused *Metamorphoses* and his other works.[5] To read Vergil's mourning fields after Ovid is to amplify their elegiac notes. We will see that at points in the catalogues of heroines and flowers Ausonius alludes to passages of Vergil and Ovid in which generic concerns are at the fore, either drawing on hybridity already present in his models or introducing it himself.[6] Meanwhile, in the poem as a whole, Ausonius responds to the generic blending of Vergil's *lugentes campi* by making Cupid – the elegiac god par excellence – the protagonist of an epicizing hexameter katabasis.

Ausonius' inclusion of Ovidian characters in this space might seem simply to document the phenomenon of reading Vergil through Ovid, but I believe that he self-consciously comments on it, deploying the tropes of memory, repetition, and afterlife to explore the intertextual relationship between Vergil and Ovid from the viewpoint of reception. In particular, he emphasizes the heroines' memory of their lives above ground and shows them repeating, in the Vergilian underworld, memorable actions from the lives they lived in Ovid's poetry. Ausonius shows that at the point of reception, Vergil's earlier text can be inhabited by "ghosts" from Ovid's subsequent works. Ausonius' Vergilian landscape is indelibly marked by Ovid's poetry.

This metapoetic commentary is a telling instance of late antique intertextual practice. Scholars such as Georgia Nugent and Aaron Pelttari have observed late antique writers' tendency to identify as readers, and Pelttari has suggested that in late antiquity there is a decrease in the competitive *aemulatio* that features so prominently in classical intertextuality.[7] Indeed, Ausonius' aim in the *Cupido Cruciatus* is not so much to compete with his models as to play with them, in the process exploring their interrelationship from his readerly point of view. Although in the preface he positions himself not as a reader but as a viewer, this difference collapses when we arrive at his description of the painting and find it is just as much an image of the literary past.[8] As we will see, the use of ecphrasis to explore intertextuality is itself an Ovidian touch.

The decrease in *aemulatio* does not mean a decrease in self-consciousness.[9] On the contrary, one aspect of the poem's ludic quality is its exuberant profusion of metapoetic signposting.[10] Ausonius draws on classical techniques for annotating allusion but deviates from classical models by deploying so many of them at once, making his text as much a patchwork of metaliterary metaphors as a patchwork of allusions. In the process, he plays with many aspects of the literary past but continually returns to the interplay between Vergil and Ovid.

Ovidian Allusions in the Catalogue

Before looking at some of Ausonius' metaliterary annotations, we should briefly examine the Ovidian character of the women in his underworld (*CC* 13–44):[11]

omnia quae lacrimis et amoribus anxia maestis
rursus in amissum reuocant heroidas aeuum.
exercent memores obita iam morte dolores: 15
fulmineos Semele decepta puerpera partus
deflet et ambustas lacerans per inania cunas
uentilat ignauum simulati fulguris ignem.
irrita dona querens, sexu gauisa uirili,
maeret in antiquam Caenis reuocata figuram.   20
uulnera siccat adhuc Procris Cephalique cruentam
diligit et percussa manum. fert fumida testae
lumina Sestiaca praeceps de turre puella,
et de nimboso saltum Leucate minatur
* * *
Harmoniae cultus Eriphyle maesta recusat,   26
infelix nato nec fortunata marito.
tota quoque aeriae Minoia fabula Cretae
picturarum instar tenui sub imagine uibrat:
Pasiphae niuei sequitur uestigia tauri,   30
licia fert glomerata manu deserta Ariadne,
respicit abiectas desperans Phaedra tabellas.
haec laqueum gerit, haec uanae simulacra coronae;
Daedaliae pudet hanc latebras subiisse iuuencae.
praereptas queritur per inania gaudia noctes   35
Laodamia duas, uiui functique mariti.

parte truces alia strictis mucronibus omnes
et Thisbe et Canace et Sidonis horret Elissa:
coniugis haec, haec patris et haec gerit hospitis ensem.
errat et ipsa, olim qualis per Latmia saxa   40
Endymioneos solita affectare sopores,
cum face et astrigero diademate Luna bicornis.
centum aliae ueterum recolentes uulnera amorum
dulcibus et maestis refouent tormenta querellis.

All these things [i.e., the mournful setting], troubled with tears and sad loves, recall the heroines back again to their lost lives. They indulge their unforgetting sorrows, although death is now past. Deceived Semele, as she gives birth, weeps over her lightning-struck delivery and destroys the burned cradle in the empty air as she attempts to put out the harmless fire of an imitation thunderbolt. Lamenting her gifts given in vain, having enjoyed her masculine sex, Caenis grieves, called back again to her ancient form. Procris still staunches her wounds, and loves the bloody hand of Cephalus even after being struck. The girl of Sestos carries the smoky light of her lamp headlong down from the tower, and threatening a jump down from cloudy Leucas * * * Sad Eriphyle refuses the necklace of Harmonia, unhappy in her son and unfortunate in her husband. The whole Minoan story of an airy Crete too shimmers beneath the thin image, like a series of pictures. Pasiphaë follows the footsteps of her snow-white bull. Deserted Ariadne carries wound-up thread in her hand; hopeless Phaedra looks back at her rejected tablets. This one bears a noose, that one the image of an empty crown; that one is ashamed to enter her hiding place in Daedalus' cow. Laodamia laments the pleasures of two nights carried off in the empty air, one with her husband living, one with him dead. Elsewhere, fierce with drawn blades, Thisbe and Canace and Sidonian Elissa stand terrible: this carries her husband's sword, that her father's, and that her guest's. She too is wandering, just as once upon a time over Latmus' rocks she often made attempts on Endymion's sleep – two-horned Luna with her torch and starry crown. A hundred others, renewing the wounds of their old loves, revive their torments with laments sweet and sad.

First, there is the question of the cast of characters itself. For comparison, here is Vergil's catalogue (*A.* 6.445–51):[12]

His Phaedram Procrinque locis maestamque Eriphylen
crudelis nati monstrantem uulnera cernit,
Euadnenque et Pasiphaen; his Laodamia
it comes et iuuenis quondam, nunc femina, Caeneus
rursus et in ueterem fato reuoluta figuram.
inter quas Phoenissa recens a uulnere Dido
errabat silua in magna …

In this place, [Aeneas] sees Phaedra and Procris and sad Eriphyle displaying the wounds from her cruel son, and Evadne and Pasiphaë; Laodamia accompanies them, and – once a young man, now a woman – Caeneus changed back into her previous shape by fate. Among these women Phoenician Dido, fresh from her wound, was wandering in a large wood.

Ausonius brings seven of these Vergilian characters back: Caenis, Procris, Eriphyle, Pasiphaë, Phaedra, Laodamia, and Dido. But the *Cupido*'s catalogue shares just as many names – also seven – with the roster of Ovid's *Heroides*: Hero, Sappho, Ariadne, Phaedra, Laodamia, Canace, and Dido. Especially noteworthy in Ausonius' catalogue is the presence of Sappho, whose name must have appeared in the text's lacuna at line 25, since the previous line describes the manner of her death: leaping from the Leucadian heights. She is the odd woman out in this group of mythological heroines, but her presence in Ovid's *Heroides* explains her inclusion here and prompts readers to think of Ovid's collection.[13] Other characters, such as Semele and Thisbe, are prominent in the *Metamorphoses*.

In addition to adding characters from Ovid, when Ausonius recycles heroines from Vergil's mourning fields who are also characters in Ovid, he tends to give them a distinctly Ovidian colouring. This reproduces on a smaller scale the effect of adding Ovidian characters to the catalogue: in both cases, Ausonius takes the Vergilian precedent and "Ovidianizes" it. Consider Phaedra. In the *Cupido Cruciatus*, she looks hopelessly back over her rejected letter (*respicit abiectas desperans Phaedra tabellas*, 32). Not only does Ausonius show her in her role as a letter writer, but he also echoes a line from the opening of her letter in the *Heroides* (*inspicit acceptas hostis ab hoste notas*, Her. 4.6), as well as Ovid's own imitation of this line in the similar tale of Byblis in the *Metamorphoses* (*proicit acceptas lecta sibi parte tabellas*, Met. 9.575).[14]

Another of Vergil's underworld heroines to get an Ovidian makeover is Procris. Ausonius writes that she still tries to staunch her wounds and loves Cephalus' bloody hand that struck her (*uulnera siccat adhuc Procris Cephalique cruentam / diligit et percussa manum*, 21–2). Here we find an echo of Cephalus' narrative of the tale in the *Metamorphoses* (7.849–50):[15] *uulnera saeua ligo conorque inhibere cruorem / neu me morte sua sceleratum deserat, oro* ("I bind the savage wounds and try to stop the blood, and I pray that she not leave me guilty of her death"). Ausonius imitates Ovid by beginning his own line with *uulnera* and ending it with *cruentam*, reminiscent of Ovid's *cruorem*. Ausonius' tweaking of this word, moreover, responds to the Ovidian intertext by emphasizing that Cephalus' wish not to be guilty of Procris' death was in vain: in Ausonius, her blood is now quite literally on his hands, with *cruor* converted into an adjective modifying *manum*. In describing Procris' love for Cephalus with a synecdochic reference to his hand (*diligit … manum*), Ausonius simultaneously recalls Ovid's version of the story in the *Ars*, in which the dying Procris' final words are a request that Cephalus close her eyes with his beloved hand (*cara … manu, Ars* 3.742).[16] The double allusion to the *Metamorphoses* and the *Ars* creates a composite Ovidian picture of the ill-fated pair.

And then of course there is Dido (*CC* 37–9): *parte truces alia strictis mucronibus omnes / et Thisbe et Canace et Sidonis horret Elissa: / coniugis haec, haec patris et haec gerit <u>hospitis ensem</u>*. In addition to demoting Dido from her central place in Vergil's account, Ausonius gives her an Ovidian epithet (*Sidonis, Met.* 14.80) and highlights a detail that Ovid emphasizes obsessively in his descriptions of her, namely that Aeneas supplied the sword with which she killed herself (*Her.* 7.195–6 = *F.* 3.549–50).[17] There is even a verbal echo of one of these passages (*Ars* 3.39–40): *et famam pietatis habet, tamen <u>hospes et ensem</u> / praebuit et causam mortis, Elissa, tuae* ("And he has the reputation of *pietas*, yet as a guest, he furnished both the sword and the cause of your death, Elissa"). Ausonius riffs on the Ovidian line-end *hospes et ensem* with his own *hospitis ensem*.

Furthermore, in grouping Dido with Canace and calling attention to their drawn swords (*strictis mucronibus*), Ausonius responds to Ovid's similar portraits of the "authors" of *Heroides* 7 and 11 in the act of composing their letters.[18] Dido writes (*Her.* 7.184–5): *scribimus, et gremio Troicus ensis adest, / perque genas lacrimae <u>strictum</u> labuntur in <u>ensem</u>* ("I am writing, and the Trojan sword is here in my lap, and tears slide down my cheeks onto the drawn sword"). Similarly, Canace says (*Her.* 11.3–4): *dextra tenet calamum, <u>strictum</u> tenet altera <u>ferrum</u>, / et iacet in gremio charta soluta meo* ("My right hand holds the pen, my other holds the drawn blade, and the unrolled paper lies in my lap"). Ovid's Dido writes as tears fall on her drawn sword, and Canace composes with the pen in her right hand, a drawn sword in her left. Likewise, Ovid's Hero, who calls herself *Sesti puella* (*Her.* 18.2), composes with the lamp at her side, as Ausonius' *Sestiaca puella* is described carrying the lamp.[19] In all these cases, Ausonius returns to emblematic pictures of these heroine-authors in Ovid.

Intertextual Memories

Now that we have surveyed the Ovidian texture of Ausonius' catalogue of heroines, we can turn to his meta-commentary on this intertextuality. Gian Biagio Conte, John Miller, and Stephen Hinds have shown how poets can signal allusion with references to memory, especially by having characters "remember" their experiences from past literary works.[20] I suggest that

Ausonius figures his engagement with the literary past in this way. The poem's opening fifteen lines, in which Ausonius sets the scene before the catalogue, are bookended by references to memory that signal the poem's double debt to Vergil and Ovid.

The first line cites Vergil as Ausonius' source for the poem's setting: *Aeris in campis, memorat quos Musa Maronis*. *Memorat* is a standard way to refer to the Muse's role of inspiring the poet. In one sense of the word, the Muse "reminds" the poet of the tale he is to tell.[21] But Ausonius' phrasing highlights the intertextual dimension of this act of remembering: by identifying the Muse specifically as Vergil's, he makes it clear that he is remembering not just the tale but also the telling. After all, the first half of the line, *aeris in campis*, is a direct quotation from *Aeneid* 6.887 (although there it is a description not of the mourning fields but of Elysium).[22] After this quotation, the relative clause, "which Vergil's Muse recalls to mind," effectively functions as a scholarly citation, with intertextuality represented as memory. The relative clause is thus a signpost of allusion, but Ausonius also playfully makes the signpost itself reminiscent of Vergil: its content, early position in the poem, and triple alliteration of "m" call to mind Vergil's instruction in the opening lines of the *Aeneid* – *Musa mihi causas memora* (1.8). The Muse reprises her role of activating the poet's memory at the beginning of his work, but this time she does not remind Vergil but reminds Ausonius *of* Vergil.

The final lines preceding the catalogue of heroines return to the theme of memory (13–15): *omnia quae lacrimis et amoribus anxia maestis / rursus in amissum reuocant heroidas aeuum. / exercent memores obita iam morte dolores* ("All these things [i.e., the mournful setting], troubled with tears and sad loves, recall the heroines back again to their lost lives. They indulge their unforgetting sorrows, although death is now past"). The reference to the heroines' unforgetting (*memores*) sorrows calls readers' attention to the intertextual reminiscences in the catalogue that follows. As we have seen, these reminiscences are in large part Ovidian ones, and Ausonius' use of the word *heroides* emphasizes this by suggesting the eponymous Ovidian intertext. The *heroides* in Ausonius' Vergilian underworld "remember" their lives in Ovid's poetry.

Just as the initial annotation of Vergilian allusion, *quos memorat Musa Maronis*, was an echo of Vergil, so too does this signpost of allusion (*exercent memores obita iam morte dolores*) itself rework a passage from Ovid (*Met.* 12.582–3): *mente dolet patria saeuumque perosus Achillem / exercet memores plus quam ciuiliter iras* ("[Neptune] grieves in his fatherly mind and, despising savage Achilles, fiercely indulges his unforgetting anger"). Both mentions of memory thus annotate nearby allusions but can also be read as playfully self-referential, since they are poetic reminiscences themselves. What is more, the references are connected in such a way as to highlight Vergil and Ovid's interrelationship. In the *Metamorphoses*, Neptune's anger over Cycnus' death makes him a driver of the archetypal epic plot, as he brings about Achilles' death. Fittingly, Ovid echoes Vergil's description of Juno's plot-driving anger in the *Aeneid* (*saeuae <u>memorem</u> Iunonis ob <u>iram</u>, A.* 1.4).[23] With the word *memores*, Ovid may give a sly, self-referential nod to the fact that Neptune's unforgetting anger is an intertextual memory of Juno's. Ausonius shows his awareness of this relationship by pairing this allusion with his earlier reference to *Aeneid* 1.8 (*Musa mihi causas memora*), in which Vergil asks the Muse to explain Juno's anger. However, the emotion that drives the action of Ausonius' poem, pushing the heroines to attack Cupid, will be more generically ambiguous. In substituting *dolores* for *iras*, and ascribing the emotion to *heroides* rather than an angered divinity, Ausonius takes epic rage in the direction of elegiac mourning in a way that suits the generic hybridity of the *lugentes campi*.[24]

With the opening and closing lines of this introductory section, then, Ausonius shows that his poem is marked by "memories" of both Vergil's and Ovid's texts. But there is a crucial distinction here between the memory of the setting and the characters' memories. The characters are situated in a setting that is specifically identified as a Vergilian space, and this creates a nesting effect: it is *within* Ausonius' memory of Vergil that the heroines "remember" Ovid's poetry. This disturbs the literary-historical chronology usually built into the memory-as-intertextuality trope. It illustrates how, at the point of reception, a reader's memory of an earlier text can be inhabited by memories of a later one.

Intertextual Repetitions and Re-presentations

A related trope with which Ausonius annotates his intertextuality is that of repeated action. In the *locus classicus* of memory as a trope for allusion, Ariadne's reminiscences in the *Fasti* (3.471ff) on her Catullan abandonment, memory coincides with repetition: Bacchus' desertion of her makes her think back to Theseus' similar actions, and Ovid calls attention to the reiterated nature of her plight with linguistic markers such as *iterum* (3.471–2) and the *re-* compound *relata* (3.473). In Ausonius' catalogue, the heroines likewise not only remember their old sufferings but also repeat them, and here too verbal markers of repetition and continuation call our attention to intertextual echoes. Procris still (*adhuc*, 21) staunches the wound that she had received in the similarly worded passage from the *Metamorphoses*. Phaedra looks back at (*respicit*, 32) her letter in the line that reworks *Her.*

4.6, reiterating its *inspicit*. In the final lines of the catalogue, Ausonius tells us that still more heroines are renewing (*recolentes*, 43) – or recalling, for this verb too can refer to memory – the wounds of their old loves and reviving (*refouent*, 44) their torments. It is not a requisite feature of underworld scenes that characters repeat episodes from their lives;[25] Ausonius works this pattern of repetition into his underworld as a way of representing poetic reception.

The first *re-* compound comes before the catalogue proper, in a line that we considered earlier, in which the mournful environment summons the heroines back (*reuocant*, 14) to their woeful lives. This *re-* compound sets the program for the ones that follow, explaining the coming repetitions. The verb *reuocant* suits iteration as a trope for intertextuality, for in addition to its most basic meaning, it has a common theatrical use: to summon an actor for an encore, or to call for a performance to be repeated (*OLD* s.v. 2). And the *heroides'* return to life does in fact take the character of an encore performance. They renew not only their suffering but also their Ovidian role as performers of lament, which Ausonius highlights with a series of verbs (and one verbal noun) of mourning: *deflet* (17), *querens* (19), *maeret* (20), *queritur* (35), and *querellis* (44). In contrast to the markedly silent denizens of Vergil's mourning fields, these women speak up, and the voice they raise is an echo of elegiac lament.

A dramatic performance is enhanced by props, and the heroines are indeed carrying objects that help tell their stories. On the one hand, in an ecphrasis of an underworld scene, it might seem fitting that Ausonius describes these objects in terms that apply both to ghostly doubles and to artistic imitations: Semele's *simulati fulguris ignem* (18); Ariadne's *uanae simulacra coronae* (33). On the other hand, it is precisely this ecphrastic context that makes the references to artistic imitation striking. In the conceit, after all, the whole scene is an artistic representation, so these references seem curiously recursive, as if describing images within an image.[26] But the recursive visual language dovetails with the emphasis on reiteration and re-performance.[27] It parallels in visual terms the nested intertextuality of the catalogue, in which (Ovidian) imitation is placed within a frame of (Vergilian) imitation. Bridging the gap between the visual and the verbal, Ausonius describes the heroines' props as *argumenta* (*leti argumenta gerebant*, 4), a term which can refer to literary plots as well as to the subjects of visual art.

Not only do Ausonius' heroines re-enact, and carry representations of, their lives in other literature. In certain cases Ausonius also exploits the metapoetic potential in these stories to further trope their poetic reappearances. Pasiphaë follows in the footsteps – another metapoetically loaded term – of her snow-white bull (*Pasiphae niuei sequitur uestigia tauri*, 30) in a line that itself follows in the footsteps of *B.* 6.46 (*Pasiphaen niuei solatur amore iuuenci*).[28] When Caenis is brought on for an encore (*reuocata*), she mourns her return to her previous *figura* (*maeret in antiquam Caenis reuocata figuram*, 20) in a line that returns to the *figura* (*OLD* s.v. 9c, "a manner of speaking or writing, literary style") of *A.* 6.449 (*rursus in ueterem fato reuoluta figuram*). In these cases, Ausonius tropes allusions to Vergil rather than to Ovid, but the fact remains that Ovidian "repetitions" are at least as prominent as the Vergilian ones in this supposedly Vergilian space.[29]

The Metapoetics of Setting: The Underworld and the *Silua*

This proliferation of figures for intertextuality extends to the afterlife itself, closely connected in this poem with the tropes of memory and repetition. Afterlife is of course a common metaphor for literary reception, but here the underworld setting allows Ausonius to literalize the metaphor: the heroines' *Nachleben* takes place in his poem. Or, to put it in another way, the Ovidian heroines' *Nachleben* takes place within Ausonius' Vergilian underworld, altering that space.

The use of the underworld to explore questions of reception is not alien to Vergil's own account of the *lugentes campi*. More specifically, Vergil employs the woods of the underworld to this effect, relying on the fact that *silua* can refer to literary source material. When he concludes his catalogue of suffering mythological heroines with the statement that *inter quas … Dido / errabat silua in magna* ("among them … Dido was wandering in a large *silua*," *A.* 6.450–1), he highlights the debt of his Dido to these other literary figures, who could be viewed as the "source material" from which she was constructed.[30] At the same time, by placing Dido among these tragic women in the underworld, Vergil anticipates and frames her reception. The juxtaposition shapes readers' interpretation not only of her and of the tragically coloured *Aeneid* 4, but also of her models, now associated with her. These heroines influenced her, and she in turn will have a *Nachleben* joined to theirs.

Ausonius takes such considerations further, advancing his project of exploring the intertextual relationship between Vergil and Ovid. He does so by adapting the Vergilian half-line *errabat silua in magna* and applying it to the Ovidian word *heroides*, so that these heroines too wander in a vast wood (*CC* 3–5):[31] *orgia ducebant heroides et sua quaeque, / ut quondam occiderant, leti argumenta gerebant, / errantes silua in magna* ("The heroines were conducting wild rites, and they were each bearing their own *argumenta* of death – how they had once upon a time died – wandering in a large wood …"). On the one hand, this describes the Ovidian heroines' debt to the quasi-elegiac figures of Vergil's *lugentes campi*, much as Vergil's use of the phrase described his Dido's debt to her tragic models. On the other hand, in Ausonius the metapoetic *silua* becomes self-referential, proving its own assertion: the phrase has literally become part of the source material through which his Ovidian heroines wander, as they assume the role of Dido in *A.* 6. Applying the borrowed phrase to the *heroides* at once describes and dramatizes this process. In the afterlife of poetic reception that Ausonius explores, the "influence" goes both ways. The Vergilian underworld is infiltrated by Ovid's heroines, and Ovidian heroines emerge from a *silua* of Vergil's making. The complementary tropes of the afterlife and the *silua* allow Ausonius to explore both sides of this exchange.

Flores of Mourning

Reversing course in the poem, I would like to turn now to the collection of flowers along the riverbanks (*CC* 8–12):

> quorum per ripas nebuloso lumine marcent
> fleti, olim regum et puerorum nomina, flores,
> mirator Narcissus et Oebalides Hyacinthus
> et Crocus auricomans et murice pictus Adonis
> et tragico scriptus gemitu Salaminius Aeas

Along the banks of these [streams] flowers of mourning languish in the misty light, once the names of kings and boys, Narcissus the admirer and Hyacinthus, son of Oebalus, and golden-haired Crocus and Adonis painted with purple and Ajax of Salamis inscribed with a tragic moan.

Once again, Ausonius dramatizes the act of reading Vergil through Ovid. By placing flowers from the *Metamorphoses* in Vergil's *lugentes campi*, newcomers to the space like the Ovidian heroines, Ausonius illustrates the way that Vergil's region of mourning now calls to mind these suffering figures from the *Metamorphoses*. For these Ovidian flowers similarly occupy a crossroads between epic, elegy, and tragedy, as we will see.

But let us first consider another way in which this passage illustrates Vergil's post-Ovidian reception. Ausonius introduces his list of flowers with an allusion to Vergil, mirroring on a smaller scale the intertextual strategy of his description of the *lugentes campi* as a whole: enclosing Ovidian material within a Vergilian frame. This allusion is to *Bucolics* 3, in which Menalcas presents the following riddle to Damoetus (*B.* 3.106–7): *dic quibus in terris inscripti <u>nomina regum</u> / nascantur <u>flores</u>, et Phyllida solus* *habeto* ("Tell me in which lands flowers inscribed with the names of kings grow, and you alone will have Phyllis"). In citing these verses from *B.* 3 and then drawing on Ovid, Ausonius is in line with the practice of Vergilian commentators. At least as far back as Servius, commentators have read this line of Vergil through Ovid, explicating Menalcas' riddle with reference to Ovid's two aetiologies for the hyacinth flower, whose petals appear to be marked with the letters AI.[32] In the first aetiology (*Met.* 10.196–216), the flower springs from the blood of Hyacinthus, accidentally killed by his lover Apollo, and the AI on its petals memorialize Apollo's lament. In the second (*Met.* 13.394–8), the flower arises from the blood of Ajax after his suicide, preserving the first two letters of his name on its petals. While Ausonius includes additional flowers in this section, he too draws on Ovid's accounts of Hyacinthus and Ajax as he elaborates on Vergil's reference. He recycles Hyacinthus' patronymic, *Oebalides*, used by Ovid in *Met.* 10.196. More significantly, his description of Ajax as inscribed with a moan (*scriptus gemitu*) echoes Ovid's description of the hyacinth imitating Apollo's moans with its script (*flosque nouus scripto gemitus imitabere nostros*, 10.206), rearranging the syntax of the two words but using them in the same portion of the hexameter.

Ovid is himself looking back to *B.* 3.106–7 in these two episodes, evoking Vergil's *inscripti ... flores* with his repeated use of the forms of *scribo* or *inscribo* (*Met.* 10.199, 10.206, 10.215, 10.216, 13.398). In citing Vergil and then Ovid's own allusion to Vergil, Ausonius shows how the two have become intertwined in literary memory.[33] In fact, we can perhaps see this intergrowth already in Ausonius' initial reference to the *Bucolics*: *fleti, olim regum et puerorum nomina, flores*. While the collocation of *regum*, *nomina*, and *flores* comes from Vergil, by expanding *regum* to *regum et puerorum*, Ausonius looks also to *Met.* 13.397–8, where Ovid seems to correct or elaborate on Vergil in saying that the hyacinth flower is doubly inscribed for a boy and a man: *littera communis mediis pueroque uiroque / inscripta est foliis, haec nominis, illa querelae* ("Shared lettering – both for the boy and for the man – was inscribed in the middle of the leaves, in the one case a name, in the other a cry of lament"). Ausonius responds in metaliterary terms to Ovid's emphasis on doubleness and shared lettering: like the hyacinth, Ausonius' line bears a double inscription, marked simultaneously by the words of Vergil and Ovid.

By placing these flowers in the *lugentes campi*, Ausonius is making a larger claim about reading Vergil through Ovid: not only do Ovid's Hyacinthus and Ajax colour our reading of Vergil's reference to the hyacinth in the *Bucolics*, but they and their fellow flowers intervene in readers' experience of this part of Vergil's underworld geography. A space dedicated to mourning brings to mind post-Vergilian instances of woe, including Ovid's flowers. In this sense, the phrase "flowers of mourning" (*fleti ... flores*) has a double meaning. The term *flores* is used of notable literary passages, sometimes with reference to their being gathered by other authors to decorate their texts, a use particularly common in late antiquity.[34] Vergil's grove is now full of other notable passages of mourning, plucked from the work of Ovid. As we have seen already with the words *silua*, *memorat*, and *memores*, the term *flores* is at once part of an allusion and a pointer to intertexuality. Each such metaliterary *double entendre* in Ausonius' poem increases the pressure on readers to see the others, strengthening the argument about literary memory that builds over the course of the poem.

For a post-Ovidian reader of Vergil's *lugentes campi*, it is not only the mode of mourning that might call Ovid's suffering lovers to mind, but also the generic hybridity of the space. As I noted above, Vergil's mourning fields bring epic into contact with elegy and tragedy, an intersection of genres that will become a signature feature of Ovid's poetry. Ovid's accounts of Hyacinthus and Ajax foreground these generic interactions. Extending Vergil's description of the hyacinth as "inscribed," Ovid uses a series of meta-generic terms in the final two lines of the Hyacinthus episode to identify the flower's text with elegy, the quintessential genre of mourning (*gemitus*), inscriptions (*inscribit*, *inscriptum*), and the combination of the two, the epitaph (*funesta littera*): *ipse suos gemitus foliis inscribit et AI AI / flos habet inscriptum funestaque littera ducta est* ("[Apollo] himself inscribes his own moans on the leaves, and the flower gets the inscription AI AI, and the funereal letter has been written," *Met.* 10.215–16). Then, by establishing direct cross-references between his accounts of Hyacinthus and Ajax, Ovid hints at the generic affinity between elegy and tragedy as genres of mourning, for the suicide of Ajax is one of the most emblematic scenes of tragedy. Ausonius responds to the generic valence of these episodes in describing Ajax as inscribed with a "tragic" moan (*tragico scriptus gemitu*). Elegiac epigram, tragedy, and mourning converge on the shores of these *lugentes campi*.

But no flower is better suited for themes of imitation and duplication, of course, than Narcissus. His presence in Ausonius' mourning fields is over-determined. As part of the group of Ovidian flowers, he is another story of woe that now haunts the *lugentes campi*. In addition, Ovid himself had already placed Narcissus in the underworld (*Met.* 3.504–5): *tum quoque se, postquam est inferna sede receptus, / in Stygia spectabat aqua* ("Even then, after he was received in his spot in the underworld, he was gazing at himself in the water of the Styx"). In so doing, Ovid provides a fitting end for a character who falls in love with an *umbra* (*Met.* 3.417, 434) at an eerily underworldly pool, repeatedly seeking to embrace this shade in a replay of Aeneas' attempts to embrace the underworld *imago* of Anchises (*Met.* 3.427–9; *A.* 6.700–1).[35] Ausonius makes Narcissus' return to his underworldly Vergilian source material more emphatic. As with Hyacinthus and Ajax, he takes a figure from Ovid that reworks Vergil's poetry and "completes the circle" by placing this figure in an explicitly Vergilian underworld.

Ovid's Narcissus narrative also shares with those of Hyacinthus and Ajax a thematics of duplication that plays into Ausonius' program of troping intertextuality. Narcissus' relationship with his reflection – at once him and not him – can be read as a figure for the unsettling resemblance between a text and its literary model(s).[36] Ovid's text refracts Vergil's as Narcissus is doubled by his reflection.[37] Ausonius' poem reflects both Vergil and Ovid, as well as their interrelationship, becoming a house of mirrors. In this respect, Narcissus is a programmatic choice for the poem's first named character. If Narcissus' fixation on an image tropes an author's relationship with his models, Ausonius' poem collapses the metaphor's tenor and vehicle: the poem purports to be an ecphrasis, but the deeply intertextual "image" is also explicitly a ghost of the literary past. Through "ecphrastic" description, Ausonius doubles this past, creating Vergilian fields that are at once his and not his. When Ausonius writes in the preface that he marvelled at (*miratus sum; mirandi*) the image, he resembles the *mirator Narcissus* (10) staring at his ghostly double.

We might compare Jaś Elsner's observations about a late antique Vergilian cento describing Narcissus.[38] Elsner argues that the anonymous author chooses passages from Vergil with careful attention to how Ovid himself comments on Vergil in his Narcissus episode. At the same time, Elsner suggests, the figure of Narcissus encapsulates late antique attitudes toward the classical past: simultaneous feelings of identification, difference, and longing. In Ausonius, too, the figure of Narcissus emblematizes the interrelationship between Vergil and Ovid while also evoking the author's own role as late antique spectator and imitator of this twofold shade.

Conclusion

Memories, repetitions, afterlives – the text obsessively thematizes and annotates its own engagement with literary tradition, and it is easy to get lost in the dizzying swim of signifiers, especially since, as we have seen, so many are self-referential: *memorat quas Musa Maronis* (1), *errantes magna in silua* (5), and *exercent memores obita iam morte dolores* (15), for example, are all simultaneously signposts and instances of allusion. Likewise, on a larger scale, the Vergilian underworld as a whole is both a trope for reception and itself the object of reception. This *mise en abyme* is all the more disorienting for the fact that in the poem as a whole, the nature and extent of our remove from "reality" are unclear: Are we in an ecphrasis, as the poem's preface suggests? Are we in a dream, as we might think from Cupid's sudden awakening at the end of the poem? A dream within an ecphrasis? Are the reminiscences of earlier poetic texts the recollections of ghosts in a dream within an image? However we look at it, Ausonius' relationship to the characters he describes is extensively mediated, just as his relationship to the literary past is metaphorically overdetermined.

But among all the echoes in the catalogue of heroines, Ovid's voice insistently makes itself heard; strikingly, given that Ausonius credits Vergil with the setting in the poem's first line. With this programmatic opening, Ausonius makes it clear that he is sharing ownership with Vergil: this is not simply Ausonius' underworld, or Vergil's underworld, but Ausonius' Vergilian underworld, the world that the Muse of Vergil recalls to his memory. This gesture highlights Ausonius' role as a reader and sets the tone for the exploration of intertextuality and reception that follows. The Ovidian echoes in the catalogues of heroines and flowers must then be understood against this backdrop – as part of Ausonius' Vergilian experience. From this vantage point, Ovid's and Vergil's texts mutually inform one another: reading Vergil through Ovid is inevitable. After Ovid, Vergil's mourning fields – with their blend of epic, tragedy, and elegy and their focus on lovelorn women – cannot help but seem partially Ovidian.

NOTES

1 On Ausonius' interpretation of the Vergilian gates at the end of the poem, see Davis 1994. On the katabasis of Cupid as a parody of Aeneas', see Gindhart 2006. For numerous echoes of Vergil and other authors, see Lucifora 1979; Vannucci 1989; Green 1991: 526–32; Franzoi 2002.

2 Vannucci 1989: 42–5; Rees 2011: 147–50; Consolino 2018: 89–113. Others mention Ovid's presence in passing. Consolino's treatment, published after the conference paper on which the present article is based, is the most extensive.

3 On the "couple" Vergil-Ovid, and its reception, see Clément-Tarantino and Klein 2015.

4 For epic and amatory poetry, see Norden 1957: 247; Feldherr 1999; Myers 2020. For tragedy, see, e.g., Panoussi 2002: 114–15.

5 On the elegiac characteristics of the *Metamorphoses*, see Knox 1986.

6 There is some debate about the extent to which elegy and epic were perceived as thematically distinct by late antiquity. Hinds (2016: 252–3) suggests that

the opposition is mostly obsolete by the time of Claudian. Fielding (2017: 11), however, notes that Isidore continues to explain the origin of elegy in mourning, and he argues that Ovid served as the late antique exemplar for elegiac form and content. At the least, Ovid's poetry would have been closely associated with erotic content, however the generic bounds were construed. Mattiacci (2018: 49–88) reads Ovid – both his elegy and his epic – as a programmatic model for the erotic and mythological subgenres within Ausonius' epigrams.

7 Nugent 1990; Pelttari 2014: 115–60.

8 Ausonius does draw on the traditional iconography of his heroines but always in close conjunction with literary allusion, which predominates. Cf. Rees (2011: 149): "The density of poetic allusion … deflates the ecphrastic pretensions of the passage." On Ovid's own use of verbal repetition in ecphrasis to destabilize the hierarchy of reality and representation, see Feldherr 2016: 28–34. On Ausonius' post-modern-style play with representation and the fool's errand of trying to reconstruct a "real" painting, see Nugent 1990: 31.

9 For the self-consciousness of Ausonius' allusions in his *Cento Nuptialis*, see Hinds 2014.

10 Helen Kaufmann (2017: 151) suggests that in late antique intertextuality, "Explicit markers of allusion … do not seem to be as common as in earlier poetry." This poem is a striking counter-example.

11 The Latin text follows Green 1991. All translations are my own, though for the *Cupido Cruciatus*, I have partially adapted that of Evelyn White (1919).

12 I cite Vergil from Mynors 1969.

13 Consolino 2018: 102. That Ausonius thought of Sappho alongside the other heroines of the *Heroides* is supported by Epigram 103.12–13 (*quod sibi suaserunt Phaedra et Elissa dabunt, / quod Canace Phyllisque et fastidita Phaoni*, "what they recommended to themselves, this advice will Phaedra and Dido give, and Canace and Phyllis and the woman scorned by Phaon"), even if the *Epistula Sapphus* was circulating separately at the time, as Peter Knox (1995: 7) suggests it may have been. Thea Thorsen (2014: 13–18), on the other hand, argues that the poem was part of the collection at Ausonius' time but that discomfort with its depiction of masturbation led to its excision in the Middle Ages, at which time references to the letter in Ausonius were also removed, hence our lacuna.

14 Vannucci (1989: 43) notes the verbal parallels with *Met.* 9.575 (and, citing Paratore 1970, the similarity of the Byblis and Phaedra tales) but curiously not those with *Her.* 4.6. The same is true of Franzoi (2002: 78) and Consolino (2018: 106).

15 I follow the text of Tarrant 2004.

16 Franzoi 2002: 69; Consolino 2018: 101.

17 This is the most frequently cited Ovidian reminiscence in the poem. See Green
(1991: ad loc.), Franzoi (2002: 82–3), O'Daly (2004: 142), Rees (2011: 149),
and Consolino (2018: 109). All mention the heroine's Ovidian epithet and
emphasis; Franzoi and Consolino also observe the reuse of the words *hospes*
and *enses* from *Ars* 3.39.

18 Consolino (2018: 109) notes the precedent for Dido's drawn sword but not
Canace's.

19 Consolino 2018: 102.

20 Conte 1986: 57–69; Hinds 1987b: 17–18 and 1998: 3–5; Miller 1993. Cf.
Solodow 1988: 227–8. See also Pietropaolo in this volume on Pasiphaë's
literary memory.

21 On Vergil's play in *A.* 1.8 with the shared etymology of *Musa, memoro,* and
other words of memory, see O'Hara 1996a: 115.

22 These are the only two regions of the underworld that Vergil describes with
the word *campi* in *A.* 6. Ausonius is borrowing a phrase from one locale and
applying it to the other, not placing his heroines in Elysium. *Pace* Consolino
2018: 89–90.

23 Austin 1971: 30; Bömer 1982: 185.

24 Grief is, of course, closely connected with epic rage (e.g., Juno's *dolores* in *A.*
1.25), but it is also emblematic of elegy.

25 But cf. Ov. *Met.* 4.444–6, esp. *antiquae imitamina uitae* (445).

26 On the way these phantom images problematize any notion of a "real" painting,
see Rees 2011: 144. Their recursive quality is also visible in Ausonius'
description of the Minoan *fabula* – the stories of Ariadne, Pasiphaë, and
Phaedra – as appearing "like pictures" (*picturarum instar*), on which see Davis
1994: 169–70 and Rees 2011: 142.

27 For parallels between ecphrastic imitation and verbal repetition in Ovid, see
Feldherr 2016: 28–34.

28 On following another author's *uestigia* (or deliberately avoiding doing so), see,
e.g., Lucretius 1.926–7 = 4.1–2, cf. 3.3–7; Vergil *G.* 3.289–94; Horace *Ep.*
1.19.21–2, *A.P.* 285–8; Quintilian 10.2.9–10. Cf. Pietropaolo in this volume.

29 We might even see a wink at Ovid in the description of Caenis. In *Met.*
12.522–35, Nestor narrates Caeneus' transformation into a bird and explicitly
casts doubt on accounts that place him in the underworld. In Ausonius, Caenis'
"return" is thus as much a return from her Ovidian form to her Vergilian one as
from male to female.

30 Similarly, Ioannis Ziogas (2013: 189) reads the *silua* in which Dido wanders as
the Hesiodic and Odyssean catalogues of women that precede Vergil's account.
The *locus classicus* on *silua* as a figure for intertextuality is Hinds 1998: 11–14.

31 *Pace* Aaron Pelttari (2014: 140), who cites these lines as an example of
nonreferential intertextuality.

32 Servius: *captiose "quibus in terris" dixit: hyacinthus enim ubique nascitur flos, qui natus primo est de Hyacinthi sanguine, postea de Aiacis, sicut etiam Ouidius docet* ("He says 'in which lands' deceptively, for the hyacinth flower grows everywhere, a flower that grew first from the blood of Hyacinthus and afterward from Ajax's, as Ovid also explains"). For the same phenomenon in modern commentaries see, e.g., Clausen 1994: ad loc.; Coleman 1977: ad loc. On Servius' use of Ovid's *Metamorphoses* to elucidate Vergil, cf. Abbamonte in this volume.

33 As he did with the allusions discussed above to Juno's anger in the *Aeneid* and Neptune's in the *Metamorphoses*. On this intertwined reception, see Clément-Tarantino and Klein 2015.

34 E.g., in Macrobius' *Saturnalia* (6.1.2), where Rufius Albinus introduces the discussion of Vergil's borrowings from other poets: *ostendere cupio quantum Vergilius noster ex antiquiorum lectione profecerit et <u>quos ex omnibus scriptoribus flores</u> uel quae in carminis sui decorem ex diuersis ornamenta liberauit* ("I desire to show how much our Vergil profited from the reading of his predecessors and to show the flowers which he took from all writers – or, if you will, the embellishments which he took from different sources for the decoration of his poem"). For this meaning of the term in general, see *TLL* s.v. 7. On the frequent use of the term in late antiquity to refer broadly to literary ornament, see Roberts 1989: 47–55.

35 Ovid's repeated *quotiens* outdoes Vergil's repeated *ter*. On other underworldly associations of Narcissus' pool, see Hardie 2002: 156–8.

36 On the metapoetic dimensions of Ovid's Narcissus tale, see Fulkerson and Stover 2016: 9–15.

37 See Hardie 2002 on the way that Ovid's Narcissus reworks Aeneas viewing himself in the reliefs of the Temple of Juno (146) and his viewing of Dido for the first time (148).

38 Elsner 2017. For Narcissus' position as the first named character in Ausonius' underworld, we can compare Elsner's observation on the placement of the Narcissus cento in the Latin Anthology: "the placement of the Narcissus poem, with all its metaliterary and self-reflexive potential as the first in the mythological sequence, looks like a deliberate and even programmatic act" (182).

20

Vergil's Renaissance Rebirth: Genre and Geography in Pontano, *Eridanus* 1.14

LUKE ROMAN

ME. Hac te nos fragili donabimus ante cicuta;
haec nos "formosum Corydon ardebat Alexin,"
haec eadem docuit "cuium pecus? an Meliboei?"[1]

I shall give you this fragile shepherd's pipe first. This taught me "Corydon was burning with desire for beautiful Alexis"; the very same taught me "whose flock is it? Meliboeus'?"

Verg. *B.* 5.85–7

Classical Latin poetry constitutes a tradition uniquely aware of the literary dynamics of its own continuation. In this passage from Vergil's fifth eclogue, the pastoral singer passes on his pipes to a fellow singer, and in doing so, alludes to the long-standing tradition of literary transmissions and successions. The present volume, which traces the history of interactions between Vergil and the Latin elegists *and* their successors and commentators, offers an ideal opportunity for reflecting on Latin poetry's unusually rich store of meta-discursive tropes for cultural transfer. The story of such interactions and continuations does not end with antiquity. The post-classical successors to the Latin poetic tradition are participants in a dialogue already begun in the classical period, the continuators of a continuation. This is clearly the case of the humanist poets of Renaissance Italy, who saw themselves as interlocutors in a conversation with the authors of the Greco-Roman past.

Giovanni Pontano (1429–1503), the leading humanist in fifteenth-century Naples and the head of the Neapolitan academy, was one such interlocutor.[2] Born in Cerreto di Spoleto in Umbria, he subsequently entered into the service of the Aragonese monarchy in Naples, where he lived for the remainder of his life. While Pontano's chief poetic model was Vergil, he wrote in a range of genres and metres, including elegiac couplets. His three-book collection, *De Amore Coniugali*, takes up the tradition of classical Latin love elegy, albeit with a crucial alteration: he writes about the satisfactions of married love as opposed to the un-conjugal desires and frustrations of classical elegy. In similarly un-classical fashion, he celebrates the birth and infancy of his son Lucio in a series of elegies called *Naeniae* or Lullabies (*De Amore Coniugali* 2.8–19). His later two-book elegiac collection, the *Eridanus*, has a very different erotic focus, a courtesan he calls Stella whom he met while on campaign in Ferrara in the 1480s and continued to maintain relations with after his wife's death in 1490. The title *Eridanus* refers to the mythic river, here identified with the Po, which flows past Ferrara and presides over the love of Pontano and Stella. The Po river valley also includes Mantua, the *patria* of Pontano's poetic predecessor, Vergil. The collection's conceptual geography is thus layered with associations at once autobiographical, mythic, and literary.

Eridanus 1.14, a striking example of Pontano's innovative engagement with classical poetry, offers a newly invented myth of Vergil's birth. At its opening, Cupid, dancing with swans and nymphs in a grove encircled by the Eridanus (1–4), plays with a flame-red arrow, which sends out sparks (5–8). An assembled crowd of rivers, including the Eridanus and the Mincio, are spectators of this performance (9–16). Suddenly, a swan seizes the arrow and carries it into the sky (17–20), where it catches fire (21); it falls into the lap of the Mincio, then strikes the nymph Pasyale. Wounded by Cupid's arrow, the two fall in love (23–6). The dancing then recommences, the power of love infuses the landscape, and the swan makes the grove reverberate with song (27–9). Pasyale becomes pregnant, and gives birth to Vergil (30). He is nurtured by Melissa, and bees smear his lips with honey (31–4); he then receives instruction in poetry from the Muses by the Neapolitan river Sebeto (35–60), and finally composes his three major poetic works while residing in Naples (37–44). Pontano then offers brief summaries of the *Bucolics* (38–40) and *Georgics* (41–4), and a longer account of the *Aeneid* (45–56). At the close, Pontano hails Vergil as the glory of the Italian race, asks Naples and Mantua to strew flowers in his honour, and directs his addressee, the humanist Antimachus of Mantua, to dedicate an altar to Vergil, the founder hero of the Latin poetic tradition (57–66).

As in Pontano's *De Amore Coniugali*, this elegy's focus on pregnancy, birth, and foundation deviates from the classical elegiac ideology of unfulfilled, non-procreative desire and social marginality. This oppositional gesture partly relies on non-conforming elements in classical elegy itself: for example, Ovid's references to pregnancy and abortion (*Amores* 2.13, 14), or the aetiologies and praises of married love in Propertius' fourth book. To push this point too far, however, would be to underestimate Pontano's substantial originality, the extent to which his poetics of *fulfilment* (sexual, marital, familial, and cultural) refashions the emphases of classical elegy. A further innovative aspect of Pontano's poetic project is the location of the site of such fulfilment in the Bay of Naples region. Liliana Monti Sabia has observed that Pontano's elegy represents Vergil as writing his poetic works, including the *Bucolics* and *Aeneid*, by the Neapolitan river Sebeto, "at the foot of green Vesuvius' cliff" (1.14.46–7).[3] Pontano did not have to insist on a Neapolitan *locus* of composition for the *Georgics*, because Vergil himself, in the poem's closing *sphragis*, already did so: *illo Vergilium me tempore dulcis alebat / Parthenope* ("in that period, I, Vergil, was nurtured by sweet Parthenope," 4.563–4). Therefore, in Pontano's account, Mantua was Vergil's birthplace, but *only* that: Naples was the site of his entire poetic career. This geographical sleight-of-hand makes Vergil into an ideal prefiguration of Pontano himself, who was born in Umbria, but produced his major poetic works in Naples. It also identifies the fertile land of Naples as the place where the poet's birth ultimately bears literary and cultural fruit. The place of physical conception and pregnancy yields to the place where poetic composition, a more enduring mode of parturition, occurs. Naples becomes the site of lasting outcomes and the foundation of a new cultural order.

The locative dimension of *Eridanus* 1.14 can be better appreciated through an examination of Pontano's Vergil from the perspective of a series of observations that draw on, but also complement and extend, Monti Sabia's arguments about the Neapolitanization of Vergil. These involve two key elements: first, the importance of ideas of place and space in Vergil's and Pontano's poetics; and second, the teleological discourse of prophecy in Vergil as received by Pontano. These two ideas are combined in a third conceptual matrix that goes back to the medieval period and that found renewed expression and took on new emphases in the Renaissance: *translatio studii et imperii*, cultural and civilizational transfer from one location to another. Consideration of this broader set of themes will provide the background necessary for evaluating *Eridanus* 1.14 and the elegy's dialogue with both Vergilian poetry and classical elegy.

Aduena et ipse: *Vergilian Prophecy and Humanist* translatio

While full consideration of the significance of place in Vergilian poetics would exceed the bounds of this essay,[4] we might consider, as an example pertinent to Pontano's elegy, Vergil's references to the river Mincio.

Vergil mentions the river in all three of his major works in metapoetic contexts that signal Mantua's status as the author's region of origin. In the seventh eclogue, the Mincio provides the setting for the song contest between Corydon and Thyrsis (*B.* 7.12–13): *hic uiridis tenera praetexit harundine ripas / Mincius, eque sacra resonant examina quercu* ("Here Mincio fringes his green banks with tender reeds, and from the sacred oak tree swarms of bees resound with buzzing"). The appearance of *Mincius* as the delayed subject of *praetexit* in verse-initial position comes as the culmination of a series of deictics (*huc … huc … huc … hic*: 6–12): the author's Mantuan *patria* thus receives conspicuous emphasis. A comparable focus on authorial fame and land of origins marks the opening of *Georgics* 3, where Vergil proclaims that the metapoetic *templum* he plans to build in Octavian's and his own honour will be located by the Mincio (*G.* 3.12–15).

> primus Idumaeas referam tibi, Mantua, palmas,
> et uiridi in campo templum de marmore ponam
> propter aquam, tardis ingens ubi flexibus errat
> Mincius et tenera praetexit harundine ripas.

I shall be the first, Mantua, to bring back to you Idumaean palms, and establish a temple of marble by the water on the green field, where vast Mincio wanders with slow windings and fringes his banks with tender reeds.

With very similar phrasing, Vergil now combines authorial fame with ruler-panegyric, and imposes a more architectonic figure for poetic activity by contrast with the natural setting of pastoral dialogue. Finally, in the catalogue of Etruscan forces near the beginning of *Aeneid* 10, the personified Mincio, clothed in reeds (*harundine*), makes an appearance as a hero leading warriors into battle (*A.* 10.198–206).

> ille etiam patriis agmen ciet Ocnus ab oris,
> fatidicae Mantus et Tusci filius amnis,
> qui muros matrisque dedit tibi, Mantua, nomen,
> Mantua diues auis, sed non genus omnibus unum:
> gens illi triplex, populi sub gente quaterni,
> ipsa caput populis, Tusco de sanguine uires.
> hinc quoque quingentos in se Mezentius armat,
> quos patre Benaco uelatus harundine glauca
> Mincius infesta ducebat in aequora pinu.

Ocnus too, son of prophetic Manto and the Etruscan river, who gave you, Mantua, walls and his mother's name, summons a troop from his native shores – Mantua, rich in ancestors, but not all the same lineage: her race is threefold, and under each race four peoples, herself head of the peoples, her strength from Tuscan blood. From here, too, Mezentius arms against himself five hundred men, whom Mincio, son of Benacus, wreathed in grey reeds, was leading over the sea in hostile ships of pine.

The repetition *Mantus … Mantua … Mantua* (10.199–201), culminating in *Mincius*, again highlights the author's *patria*, while Manto, like other prophetic figures in the *Aeneid*, functions as metapoetic marker of Vergil's prophecy-driven epic. The river Mincio thus links Vergil's poetry and city of origin across his three major poetic works. At the same time, the changing contexts of the river's mention trace the poet's evolving generic orientation, from the "natural" world of the *Bucolics* (the *locus amoenus*), to the constructive *labor* of the *Georgics* (the *templum*), to the foundation of cities and conflicts between them (the origins of Mantua; warfare). As we move from pastoral *locus amoenus* to commemorative architecture to the praises of a land rich in heroic genealogy, the river Mincio comes to encapsulate the power and range of Vergilian poetry.

Such passages would have spoken with special force to an Italian humanist poet such as Pontano with a profound interest in the places of the classical past. The rediscovery of antiquity by Italian humanists was informed by awareness of their proximity to the classical places that were at once tantalizingly "present" and unattainable because of temporal distance and the ruined state of physical structures. Both humanist intellectuals and Renaissance princes participated in the project of restoration (*instauratio*) of the architectural and textual glories of antiquity.[5] This impulse to restore or replace the lost places of the classical past had particular importance in Aragonese Naples.[6] As the "land of the Siren," Naples harboured the divine power of classical song in its very soil. These associations were further strengthened by the so-called tomb of Vergil and the region's archaeological remains. The Aragonese monarchs took advantage of this rich classical patrimony by making the revival of antiquity on Neapolitan soil a major component of their ideology of rule. This revival was embodied by public building projects such as the restoration of the Bolla aqueduct system, the classicizing triumphal arch inserted into the medieval façade of Castel Nuovo, and the immense classicizing villa at Poggioreale.[7]

Pontano, a trusted minister of the Regno, celebrated the places of Naples in his poetry, especially places associated with the architectural achievements of the Aragonese monarchy. He also linked his poetry to places of importance in his own life, such as his villa at Antignano, personified in his poetry as the nymph Antiniana.[8] This villa on the Vomero, where the poet cultivated citrus orchards, comes into focus in Pontano's *De hortis Hesperidum*, a Vergilian didactic poem on the cultivation of citrus fruit, including orange and lemon trees, which were unknown to classical authors.[9] The poem closes with the praises of his garden villa at Antignano, which, he says, surpasses the famous gardens and vineyards of antiquity (*Hort. Hesp.* 2.577–81).

> nec mihi Naiades in tanti parte laboris
> abnuerint uiridem salicis de fronde coronam,
> nec mihi culta suos neget Antiniana recessus,
> quis superat uites Hermi atque rosaria Pesti
> quaeque et Idumeas mittunt palmaria bacas.

Neither may the Naiads, for their part in so great a labour, deny me a green garland made from foliage of willow, nor may cultivated Antiniana deny me her retreats, with which she outstrips the vineyards of the Hermus, the rose beds of Paestum, and the palm groves that produce the fruit of Idumaea.

In a passage dense with allusions to Vergil's *Georgics*,[10] the toponym "Idumaean" stands out: Pontano recalls Vergil's metapoetic monument by the Mincio in *Georgics* 3 (*Idumaeas … palmas*, 3.12), yet replaces Mantua with Naples and his villa at Antignano. Even as he imitates the Vergilian gesture of transferring poetry to a new place, he replaces Vergilian places with his own.

Humanist poets often viewed this process of replacing the literary topographies of antiquity with their own sites of cultural prestige within a conceptual framework informed by Vergilian ideas of prophecy and destiny.[11] Pontano's Florentine contemporary, Angelo Poliziano, exemplifies this viewpoint in his *Silua* entitled *Manto*, in which the prophetess Manto predicts Vergil's future career.[12] Poliziano begins by telling how Greek civilization, after great successes, was humbled by Nemesis (1–32). Greece came under the yoke of Roman arms; then was surpassed in eloquence by Cicero, and finally, challenged even in poetry by Vergil (29, 32): *Editus ecce Maro, quo non felicior alter … / Hesiodum premit et magno contendit Homero* ("Behold, Maro appeared, than whom no one else is more successful … He overwhelms Hesiod and competes with great Homer"). Vergil's and Rome's triumphs are presented here according to a Renaissance understanding of cultural transmission: a new civilization rises from the ruin of its predecessor. The culminating words of the prophecy of Vergil's greatness drive this point home: "antiquity, astonished, will yield all its glory to him" (*cui decus omne suum cedet stupefacta uetustas*, 308). Vergil outstripped his predecessors; by implication, modern Italian writers can now occupy the same position in relation to antiquity that Vergil held in relation to *his* past. With the marvellous phrase *stupefacta uetustas*, Poliziano dramatizes the power of the dominant modern poet to amaze and subjugate antiquity. Just as Greece was humbled by Nemesis in being subordinated to Rome, so Rome, in turn, was destroyed, making way for the cultural renewal of Renaissance Italian cities. This distinctly Renaissance conception of cultural *translatio* highlights the ruin and restoration of civilizations and the successor poet's supremacy over the past.[13] This is not so much a seamless transfer of cultural authority as a discontinuity or fracture followed by deliberate acts of reappropriation and competitive imitation.

Significantly, Poliziano's articulation of cultural *translatio* comes from the mouth of Manto, a goddess whose very name evokes both prophecy and Vergil's *patria*. Humanist poets, like W.H. Auden, enjoyed subjecting Vergil to the implications of his own prophetic discourse: just as Aeneas was destined to transfer his *penates* from ruined Troy to Italy and found a new, greater civilization, so Vergil himself was destined to surpass Homer, but also, eventually, to be surpassed by others according to the relentless logic of *translatio*. Pontano offers his own reflections on this process in his eclogue *Lepidina*, which celebrates the mythic marriage of Parthenope (personification of the city of Naples) and the river Sebeto. The poem is an encomium of the places of the Bay of Naples, including rural localities and urban neighbourhoods.[14] This monumental eclogue, comprising over eight hundred lines, begins with a conversation between the title character Lepidina and her husband Macron, and continues through seven *pompae* ("processions"), in which the personified places of Naples engage in extended dialogue. Drawing on both Vergilian pastoral and the urban settings and spectacles of Theocritean mime, Pontano's innovative pastoral opus offers a panoramic overview of the region's places, including places important to the Aragonese regime such as the royal villa at Poggioreale (*Ecl.* 1.30).

Near the eclogue's close, in the seventh and final *pompa*, Antiniana, Pontano's villa-nymph, predicts the future greatness of the *proles* that will issue from the marriage of Parthenope and Sebeto, including two poets of unusual greatness. In a passage woven from Vergilian *loci*,[15] Antiniana predicts that the first poet, a stranger from Mantua, will come to Naples and sing pastoral poetry (*Ecl.* 1.745–8):

> nascetur qui longinquis procul aduena terris
> haec adeat pastor pauper loca, cuius ab ore
> arida uicini resonent et saxa Veseui,
> ipsae quem pinus, ipsa haec arbusta uocabunt.

There will be born one who will come from afar, a stranger, from faraway lands, to these parts, a poor shepherd, with whose words the parched rocks of neighbouring Vesuvius will resound, whom these very pine-trees, these very orchards will invoke.

This stranger is Vergil himself and the resounding rocks and responsive landscape are reminiscent of Vergilian pastoral, but the location is now emphatically Neapolitan (*Veseui*, 747). In subsequent lines, Antiniana goes on to predict that this shepherd-poet will recite the poetry of the shepherds Damon and Alphesiboeus (750); Tityrus, she proclaims, will give him his sheep and Menalcas his she-goats (751–2), and the "rivers, in amazement, will bring their currents to a stand-still" (*mirata suos requiescent flumina cursus*, 753). The names cited by Antiniana correspond to the familiar shepherds of Vergilian pastoral, while the rivers spellbound by pastoral song echo yet another Vergilian trope (*B.* 8.5). Adapting an intertextual strategy from the classical tradition,[16] Pontano inserts the Vergilian author amid the characters and figurative matrix of his own poetry.

Pontano has carefully designed this scenario to combine motifs of Vergilian embedded autobiography and pastoral place with the themes of prophecy and destined *proles* that pervade both Vergil's *Aeneid* and his fourth eclogue. Just as in Vergilian prophecies, moreover, the earlier founder-figure foreshadows, and functions as a prelude to, a latter-born scion who is both a continuator and new founder in his own right. In the next lines, following the above cited "prophecy" of Vergil's arrival in the Bay of Naples, Antiniana predicts the emergence of another shepherd-poet in a much later time period (*alius longo post tempore pastor*, 757), also a "stranger" (*aduena*, 758), accompanied by the Muse Urania. This latest poet in the pastoral landscape is Pontano himself, author of the didactic poem *Urania* (*Ecl.* 1.762–6).

> hic pascet niueos herbosa ad flumina cygnos,
> misceat ipsa suos pascenti Amaryllis olores;
> hic et populea uacuus cantabit in umbra,
> Uranie intactam cantanti iunget auenam,
> et cantum argutae referent ad sidera ualles.

He will pasture snow-white swans by the grassy river banks; let Amaryllis herself mingle her own swans with his as he pastures them, and he will sing, at leisure, in the shade of poplars; Urania will accompany him on an untouched oaten pipe as he sings, and the clear-sounding valleys will convey his song to the stars.

The underlying point of this story of parallel (and competing) poetic careers is the Neapolitan adoptive *patria* common to Vergil and Pontano: both are enumerated among the future *proles* who will inhabit, and contribute to the glory of, the city symbolized by the marriage of Parthenope and the river Sebeto. Even as Pontano both situates Vergil in a Neapolitan setting and inserts himself within the landscape of Vergilian pastoral, he hints at his own superiority, boldly appropriating Vergilian figures for poetic supremacy: his songs will be conveyed "to the stars," and he too will pasture swans, signified by both the Greek-derived Latin word *cygnus* (*cygnos*, 762) and the Latin word *olor* (*olores*, 763).[17] Pontano thus signals an intention to occupy Vergilian terrain in more senses than one. As in Vergil's poetic reimaginings of the Mincio, Antiniana's prophecy intertwines strands of authorial autobiography with geography and place-centred conceptions of poetic fame. Indeed, Pontano develops the Vergilian poetics of place in newly explicit ways, "out-Vergiling" Vergil himself. To take one striking example, the Vergilian figure Manto is a female place-divinity imbued with prophetic powers and associated with the author's *patria*. Pontano's Antiniana renews this role, yet belongs to an even more intensely personalized location: the personified place of the author's own villa property.

One final detail here deserves further attention: the word *aduena*. The paradigm of the glamorous stranger who comes from afar to fulfil his cultural destiny in his adoptive *patria* is exemplified by the Vergilian character of Aeneas.[18] Reading this aspect of Aeneas' identity into the present passage further sharpens Pontano's point. If *translatio loci*, the replacement of an earlier place with a new one, is a paradigm for cultural change, then Vergil and Pontano embody this paradigm in the pattern of their own lives. What interests Pontano, at least as much as Naples as a final destination, is the paradigm of cultural transmission itself, the act of transfer to a new place, which Pontano and Vergil achieved in their biographies and their poetics.[19]

Eridanus *1.14: Birth, Burial, and Foundation*

Returning now to *Eridanus* 1.14, we are in a position to appreciate the comparable combination of biographical change of location and cultural *translatio* in Pontano's narrative of Vergil's life and career. The opening mythological vignette, in which Cupid dances with the flame-red arrow (1.14.1–8) near the collection's eponymous river (*Eridanus placidis qua nemus ambit aquis*, "where Eridanus encircles a grove with his calm streams," 1.14.2), suggests a suitably erotic and elegiac theme. The subsequent description of the rivers in attendance broadens the generic scope by recalling the prophetic Tiber of the *Aeneid*,[20] the previously cited martial role of the Mincio, and the Po's regal status in the first *Georgic* (*Eridanus* 1.14.9–16):[21]

> Eridanus spectat flauenti crine superbus,
> > populeo madidum cinctus honore caput,
> Mincius et spectat uarianti laetus amictu,
> > Mincius Ausoniae clarus honore tubae,

> spectat harundineo formosus Mela galero,
>> diues et undosis Abdua gurgitibus,
> quique amnes socii regem uenerantur, et ipsi
>> quique scatent fontes, quaeque palustris aqua.

Eridanus, haughty with his golden hair, his perfumed head enwreathed with poplar leaves, was watching, as was Mincio, happy in his garb of many colours, famed for the renown of the Ausonian clarion; and the Mella handsome in cap of reeds, and Adda, opulent in flowing waters – all the allied streams that show reverence to the king, the gushing springs, and all the waters of the fens.

Pontano incorporates into his elegiac vignette Vergil's cross-generic interest in rivers along with their aesthetic, political, and patriotic associations. From the aetiological perspective of this origins story, the presence of elaborately garbed rivers at the scene of Vergil's conception, in combination with the claim that he was sired by a river god, has the anticipative function of "explaining" the key roles that will be occupied by symbolic rivers in Vergilian poetry, including his recurrent foregrounding of the Mincio. Vergil's rivers thus flow intertextually into Pontano's, which then, in a recursive loop, explain the origins of Vergil's.

This tactic of incorporating Vergilian intertexts into the story of Vergil's birth, even while reactivating the aetiological framework of Vergilian prophecy, continues in the next scene, where a very Vergilian swan seizes Cupid's arrow and carries it aloft, where it catches fire (*Eridanus* 1.14.17–21):

> ecce autem niueis cycnus se sustulit alis,
>> cycnus olorini duxque decusque chori,
> deque manu pueri rostro plaudente sagittam
>> eripit et cantu sidera summa petit.
> concepit flammas ferro stridente sagitta …

But look! A swan, the leader and the glory of the flock of swans, on snow-white wings rose up, with snapping beak plucked the arrow from the boy's hand, and singing, sought the starry heights. The arrow caught flame as the iron point hissed …

The details of this story are "prophetic" of the future Vergil's preeminent fame: the Greco-Roman swans employed as intertextual emblems of poetic superiority in Pontano's *Lepidina* return here in emphatic juxtaposition (*cycnus olorini … chori*, 18) along with ascent to the stars as a Vergilian figure for poetic glory (*cantu sidera summa petit*, 20). What follows is a mutual love-wound (*Pasyale uulnus sensit et ipsa suum*, "Pasyle herself felt her own wound," 26) that recalls both Vergilian[22] and elegiac figuration of erotic suffering, resulting in a very un-elegiac pregnancy and birth

(1.14.30): *infantem decimo sidere nympha parit* ("In the tenth month, the nymph brought forth a baby boy"). At this point, however, there is a geographical shift, as Pontano documents the poet's early poetic career in the land of the Sebeto and Vesuvius (*Eridanus* 1.14.35–6): *Hinc Musae placidis salicum docuere sub umbris, / Sebethus liquidis qua fluit uber aquis* ("The Muses taught him in the tranquil shade of willow trees, where Sebeto, who abounds in watery streams, flows by"). The role of the Sebeto both here and in the *Lepidina* exemplifies Pontano's highly focused reworking of the Vergilian poetics of place: he moves from being fathered by the river Mincio to the composition (or parturition) of his own poetry by the Neapolitan river Sebeto. This story of changing rivers follows the contours of Pontano's project of poetic *translatio*: he merges his authorial profile with Vergilian autobiography, even as he rewrites his predecessor's *uita* by emphatically resituating it in his own adoptive city of Naples.

The paradigm of changing places and locations can be retraced immanently in the very content of the Vergilian oeuvre. When, in subsequent lines, Pontano offers a summary of Vergil's *Bucolics* and *Georgics* in densely allusive language,[23] there are changes of literary place (pastoral to georgic: *salicum … sub umbris … segetes … ager*, 35, 41–2), paradigms of stasis and displacement (Tityrus and Meliboeus, 38–40), and at the meta-discursive level, movement between generic terrains and remembered *loci*. Such spatio-literary play culminates in the foundational and territorial themes Pontano highlights in his extended discussion of the *Aeneid* (*Eridanus* 1.14.45–56):

> felix aruorum cultu, felicior armis,
> dum profugum Aeneam, dum canit arma uirum:
> illi Vulcanus clipeum, sua Mulciber arma
> aptat et in classem corruit omne nemus.
> illi fatorum seriem gentisque togatae
> Deiphobe Glauci monstrat et omne genus;
> inde sedens ebore in niueo Sebethida ad undam,
> colligit Etruscas Marrubiasque manus:
> agmen agit Lausus, magnique ipse agminis instar,
> attrituque pedum terra Sabina tremit,
> et, quotiens raucum gemuit caua buccina, matres
> presserunt natos pectora ad ipsa suos.

He is happy in his cultivation of the fields, and even happier in arms, when he sings of exiled Aeneas, when he sings the arms of men: for him, Vulcan supplies a shield, Mulciber furnishes arms, and a whole grove is felled to make a fleet. To him Deiphobe, Glaucus' daughter, shows the sequence of destiny, the history of the toga-wearing people, and the entire lineage. Then, sitting on a snow-white ivory chair by Sebeto's stream, he musters Etruscan and Marrubian troops. Lausus leads a squadron, and is like a great squadron unto himself, and at the tread of his feet the Sabine land shudders,[24] and whenever the hollow horn groans its hoarse war cry, mothers press their sons to their breasts.

Pontano refers to the shield episode in Book 8, the transformation of Aeneas' fleet into sea goddesses in Book 9, the prophecy of Rome's future destiny in Book 6, the catalogue of Italian heroes in Book 7, and the Etruscan forces allied to Aeneas in Book 10.[25] The emphasis falls heavily on the latter half of the *Aeneid*, especially episodes relating to the prophesied destiny of the Italian people: *fatorum seriem gentisque togatae ... et omne genus* (49–50). Pontano's *Aeneid* is one almost wholly focused on outcomes and fulfilment of destiny – Aeneas' victories in war, the lineage and accomplishments of the Romans – as prophesied by the Shield and the Sibyl. The accomplishment of *fata* is privileged over wanderings, aporetic uncertainty, and elegiac delay (*mora*). This coheres both with Pontano's interest in the emergence of newly powerful and prestigious Italian places in his own time and with the Aragonese ambition to revive the authority of Roman *imperium*. The Aragonese dynasty, which came to power in 1442 through conquest, was a relatively new monarchy in Naples, and accordingly sought to bolster its prestige by appealing to classical antiquity.[26] This effort included the recruitment of a stable of talented humanists such as Antonio Beccadelli (1394–1471), Lorenzo Valla (1407–1457), and Pontano himself. Pontano's summary of Vergil's foundation epic privileges elements related to Rome's genealogy of power and cultural authority. Pontano's *Aeneid* thus coheres with the ideological concerns of a dynasty that founded and maintained its reign in Naples through martial force.

The less warlike dimension of Vergil's epic receives considerably less emphasis. The single word *profugum* encapsulates the Odyssean wanderings of Books 1–5, while all overt mention of Dido is excluded. This might seem a surprising choice for an elegiac reading of the *Aeneid*, but it coheres with Pontano's teleological vision of Italian destiny that Vergil both expresses in his work's content and embodies through his contributions to Roman civilization. Dido represents an anti-foundational, anti-teleological force in the *Aeneid*: she threatens to undermine Aeneas' foundational destiny, and abandons the building of her city for self-destructive immersion in love-driven frenzy. She is thus sometimes read as a tragic or elegiac figure within Vergil's epic.[27] From a proto-Roman perspective, she does not correspond to any positive outcome, cultural or genealogical. She was not truly married to Aeneas and did not conceive a child from him; hence, the relationship lacked meaningful and enduring fulfilment.

Pontano's elegy, by contrast, emphasizes procreation as the final outcome of desire and the generative mechanism of Roman destiny. Erotic pleasure leads to *proles* and helps perpetuate the *genus*. This emphasis, while coherent within the elegy, becomes problematic in the broader framework of Pontano's *Eridanus*, where he plays the role of *senex amator*, tarrying, like Dido's lover, in a place that is not his *patria* with a woman not his wife. Support for this line of thought comes from the hint of an intertextual link between Pontano's flaming arrow (1.14.21, quoted above) and the simile of the deer shot by an unknowing shepherd's arrow near the opening of *Aeneid* 4. Dido, in that passage, suffers from a *flamma* and *uulnus*, as Pasyale does here; lexical similarities strengthen the link.[28] Perhaps Dido and the futility of elegiac desire are not so far away, after all.

The shepherd of Book 4, however, is not the only conspicuous archer in the epic. A more overt Vergilian model for Pontano's arrow is the one shot by Acestes that catches fire and vanishes in the archery contest in Book 5 (500–44).[29] That arrow, with its suggestions of divinely sanctioned destiny, shot by a hero whose mother was Trojan and whose father was a Sicilian river-god, suits the context of Vergil's miraculous birth, changing locations, and literary apotheosis. In this elegiac poem that traces Vergilian poetics across different genres and geographies, the allusive texture that emerges is suitably cross-generic in literary terms and spatially guided by the trajectories of cultural transfer. The intertextual path of Pontano's *stridens sagitta* ("whizzing arrow"), following the route of the *Aeneid* itself, leads from the non-procreative love-wound of Dido in North Africa to the intimations of heroic immortality in the Sicilian interlude of Book 5. The destructive erotics of the Dido episode are discreetly downplayed, and resolved in favour of the productive genealogy of Rome and a focus on *proles* as synecdoche of cultural increase.[30] Such a resolution cannot wholly erase the tension between productive and destructive models of desire that is at issue both here and in Vergil's *Aeneid*. In both instances, however, the narrative follows an instructive spatial arc. Pontano's elegy and Vergil's epic trace a path toward the production of *proles* and the foundation of enduring cultural institutions, even as the poems' heroes move from their places of origins (Troy/Mantua) to their destinations of teleological fulfilment (Italy/Naples).

Missing from Pontano's elegiac narrative of cultural transfer is the overt element of prophecy prominent in Pontano's *Lepidina* and Poliziano's *Manto*. Closer inspection, however, reveals the implicit presence of the Vergilian prophetic paradigm. Like Vergil's fourth eclogue, Pontano's elegy hails the birth of a world-changing individual whose greatness is already evident in his birth:[31] in viewing the poet's origins, we are witnessing the foundation of a literary *imperium* that will endure for centuries. Like Poliziano, Pontano constructs a foundational discourse that absorbs Vergilian poetry within the

Vergilian framework of destiny and cultural change. This becomes explicit at the close, where the hero Vergil receives an altar and cultic honours (*Eridanus* 1.14.57–66):

> o salue, Italidum gentis decus, in Latium qui
>   Aonio ducis uertice Pieridas,
> salue et Idumaeas debet cui Mantua palmas,
>   cui Phoebus Latio uestit honore comam;
> sparge, Charis, roremque tuum Syriosque liquores,
>   Parthenope, uiolas, Mantua, funde rosas.
> ipse aram statuens uati uenerare Camoenas,
>   Antimache, et patriae concine grata tuae,
> quae puerum genuit, cuius sub uoce locutae
>   Pierides nostrum constituere decus.

Hail, O glory of the Italian race, who lead the Pierides to Latium from the Aonian peak, and hail again, to whom Mantua owes the Idumaean palms, whose hair Apollo decks with Latian crown of bay. Strew, Grace, your dew, and Syrian incense; Parthenope, strew violets, and Mantua, roses. And you, Antimaco, dedicate an altar to the bard, venerate the Muses, and sing songs pleasing to your fatherland, which brought to birth that boy, through whose voice the Pierides have spoken and established our renown.

"Idumaean palms" yet again evoke the opening of *G.* 3, where Vergil claims to have led the Muses from Helicon to his own *patria*. Pontano ends with the declaration that Vergil "established our renown" (*nostrum constituere decus*, 66). The verb *constituo*, often used by Vergil in ritual and foundational contexts such as establishing an altar or founding a rite,[32] here puts a capstone on ideas developed throughout the elegy: Vergil is the founder of the strand of poetic Latinity that connects humanist poets to the classical past and allows them to achieve their own glory in Latin verse in places such as contemporary Naples. Pontano's assimilation of Vergil to the heroic pattern of his own epic protagonist is complete: like Aeneas, Vergil is a founder hero of divine birth who established his cultural legacy through transfer to a new location.

Me ... tenet nunc / Parthenope: *The Poetics of Tombs*

Pontano does not overtly mention the poet's death and burial, but the silence is deafening. Both the elegy's geographical itinerary from Mantua to Naples and its plotting of Vergil's works in order of magnitude follow the blueprint of Vergil's epitaph in the Donatan *uita* (*VSD* 36):[33]

Ossa eius Neapolim translata sunt tumuloque condita qui est in uia Puteolana
intra lapidem secundum, in quo distichon fecit tale:
>   Mantua me genuit, Calabri rapuere, tenet nunc
>   Parthenope; cecini pascua rura duces.

His bones were transported to Naples and buried in a tomb which is on the Via
Puteolana inside the second milestone, on which he made the following distich:
>   *Mantua bore me; the Calabrians snatched me away; now Parthenope pos-*
>   *sesses me; I sang pastures, fields, leaders.*

This sequence of places informs both the present poem and the claims of
the Neapolitan humanists to ownership of Vergil's literary inheritance.
Puerum genuit ("[Mantua] bore the boy," 65) in the present elegy echoes
Mantua me genuit in the Vergilian epitaph, prompting thoughts of the
words that follow: *tenet nunc / Parthenope* ("Naples holds [me] now").
Mantua and "Parthenope," the personified places of Vergil's birth and
death, will give him offerings – almost certainly funereal ones, as even
a brief intertextual survey will confirm.[34] In Pontano's works, metapoetic
offerings and rites in honour of Vergil typically occur at the classical poet's
so-called tomb on the slopes of Posillipo. Pontano also appears to have
owned a villa in this area, which he personifies as the nymph Patulcis.
Granting Vergil's birthplace to Mantua confirms Naples' ownership of his
tomb, the more important and permanent possession. Near the opening
of *De hortis Hesperidum* Book 2, Pontano addresses Patulcis along with
his own metapoetic place-nymph, Antiniana, and imagines that the urn
containing Vergil's remains will put forth new flowers – a symbol of his
perpetuation of Vergil's poetic lineage (*De hortis Hesperidum* 2.12–16):

>   … tuque o mihi culta Patulci,
>   prima assis primosque mihi, dea, collige flores,
>   impleat et socios tecum Antiniana quasillos:
>   sic tibi perpetuum spiret rosa, floreat urna,
>   scilicet urna tui qua conditur umbra Maronis …

May you, my cultivated Patulcis, come first, gather the first flowers for me, goddess, and may Antiniana fill shared baskets with you: so may the rose breathe its
fragrance perpetually for you, the urn put forth flowers, no doubt the urn in which
the shade of your own Maro is buried.

This pairing of place-nymphs elegantly links Posillipo and Antignano, the spatial domains, respectively, of Vergil and his Neapolitan poetic successor. In a
similar gesture of locative association, Pontano's fellow Neapolitan humanist,

Jacopo Sannazaro, constructed his villa and tomb at Mergellina, not far from Vergil's tomb on the slopes of Posillipo.[35] As for Silius Italicus and the Neapolitan Statius,[36] so for Pontano and Sannazaro, returning to Vergil's tomb is a return to the source, the catalyst of new poetry: the poet's *monumentum* is a site of memory and thus also of emulative regeneration of the classical past.

This point returns us to the thematic matrix with which we began: literary succession, continuation, and the perpetuation of the Latin poetic tradition. The image of the "passing of the pipes" suggests continuity, an emblem of intact inheritance, but, as we have seen throughout this examination of Pontano's relocation of Vergil's poetic legacy, the dynamics of literary succession are marked at least as much by discontinuities, displacements, and migrations. *Eridanus* 1.14, which begins by narrating Vergil's birth and ends with his funeral rites, hinges on polarities and transitions that are deeply enmeshed in Renaissance *translatio* and the replacement of the classical past: life and death, burial and resuscitation, ruin and restoration, origin and destination, movement and stasis, the "whizzing arrow" of desire and the monumental solidity of the tomb. The urn that hold Vergil's ashes is the site of new growth. The tomb itself is an unmoving place marker, yet it provides a point of departure for new creations and renewed traditions. Perhaps to a unique extent, Naples is a city where tombs are viewed with a sense of aesthetic excitement and possibility. This makes sense if we recall the legendary associations of the tomb of the Siren with the earliest formation of the city. The poet's tomb, from this perspective, is even more important than his birthplace. Beyond simply marking an end, it is also a beginning, an origin, and a foundation.

NOTES

1 Citations of Vergil are from Mynors 1969. All translations are my own. I have mostly followed Italian instead of Latin spelling conventions for proper names that are viewed in terms of their fifteenth-century context – Pontano instead of Pontanus, Mincio instead of Mincius, Sebeto instead of Sebethos, and so forth – with the exception of Eridanus, the name of the mythic river that came to be identified with the Po.

2 On Pontano, see Monti Sabia et al. 2010; Kidwell 1991. For the *Eridanus*, I cite Oeschger 1948 as modified in Roman 2014.

3 See Monti Sabia 1983; on Eridanus 1.14, 1127–30. Note also a variant myth of Vergil's birth in Pontano's *Urania* (2.1286ff.): Mincio is the father; the mother is the toponymic nymph "Andes."

4 For geography and space in Vergil, see, for example, Thomas 1982; Jones 2011; Skempis and Ziogas 2014.

5 On the restoration of antiquity, see Weiss 1969; McCahill 2009.

6 On Renaissance Naples and Neapolitan humanism, see Bentley 1987; on the city's memories of antiquity, Hughes and Buongiovanni 2015.

7 On Aragonese building, see De Divitiis 2007; Beyer 2000; on the villa at Poggioreale, Modesti 2014.

8 See Percopo 1921; Kidwell 1991: 104–5.

9 On the *De hortis Hesperidum*, see Caruso 2013; Iacono 2015; Ludwig 1982. The text cited is my own (Roman 2022), based on the 1505 Aldine *editio princeps* and an apograph in the Biblioteca Communale di Avellino: see De Nichilo 1977.

10 Cf. *G.* 4.118, 19 (Paestum); 3.12 (Idumaean palms); 2.136–8 (Hermus). *Hermus* simultaneously refers to the *mons sancti Hermi*, i.e., the present-day Vomero hill: see the explanatory commentary appended to Summonte 1512.

11 On Renaissance receptions of Vergilian prophecy, see Wilson-Okamura 2010: 187–90, 71–2.

12 For Poliziano's *Siluae*, I follow Bausi 1996.

13 On Poliziano and *translatio imperii et studii*, cf. Mengelkoch 2010: 85–6.

14 On the *Eclogae*, see Monti Sabia 1973; Casanova-Robin 2011b; Tufano 2015; Roman 2022. The text cited is that of Monti Sabia 1973.

15 Verg. *B.* 1.39, 56; 2.34; 4.46–7; 5.72; 7.3; 8.1, 4–5; *G.* 2.199; for *nascetur, A.* 1.286, *B.* 4.5, 8; cf. Catull. 64.338.

16 For a discussion of how poems of the *Appendix Vergiliana* reflect "the curiosity of Roman readers about the early and otherwise undocumented phases of the poet's life" (76), and the ways in which biographical fiction and literary imitation inform each other, see Peirano 2012: 74–116, 173–204.

17 On stars and fame: *B.* 5.51–2; 6.84; on swans as singers: *B.* 8.55; 9.29; *cycni*, with stars (*olores*, 9.36); cf. *G.* 2.199 (in Mantua).

18 *A.* 4.591; 7.38; 10.460 (Hercules); 10.516; 12.261.

19 Compare a passage in the fourth *pompa* of the *Lepidina* describing the fountain personified as Formellis, corresponding to the monumental fountain in front of Castel Capuano in Naples (*Ecl.* 1.324–6): *non aduena fontem, / Nauita non sitiit, auido quin captus amore / Deserat et patriam et fessos aetate parentes* ("No foreigner, no sailor ever slaked his thirst at that fountain who did not fall passionately in love and desert his fatherland and his parents weary with years"). The *aduena* is implicitly Pontano himself, as noted by Monti Sabia 1973: 46 ad loc.

20 Cf. *A.* 8.31–4: *populeas … frondes … amictus … harundo.*

21 *G.* 1.482: *fluuiorum rex Eridanus*; cf. *G.* 4.365–73, where the Eridanus comes at the culmination of a catalogue of rivers, and is described as having the greatest force (*quo non alius … uiolentior*, 372–3).

22 *A.* 4.2, 67; 6.450 (literally, Dido's physical wound). See further discussion below.

23 Cf. *B.* 3.20, 7.9, 10.77; *G.* 1.1–5, 2.228–9, 4.140–1.

24 *A.* 7.707: *agmen agens Clausus magnique ipse agminis instar.* It is not clear

whether Pontano has confused Lausus with Clausus, or deliberately substituted the more prominent character.

25 Cf. *A.* 1.282, 641–2; 6.36; 7.519–20, 734, 750; 11.474–6.

26 See, for example, Bentley 1987.

27 See, for example, Hardie 1993: 36. Many readers have seen Vergil's Dido as a highly sympathetic character – a line of interpretation, which, while important on its own terms, does not appear to be prominent in Pontano's reception of the *Aeneid*. Dido's exclusion from this summary of the epic penned by Pontano, who was normally keen to cite classical erotic exempla, seems significant.

28 Cf. *A.* 4.66, 69, 71: *flamma ... sagitta ... ferrum*. Also compare *pastor agens cecini* ("Living as [*sic*, intransitive] a shepherd, he sang ... ," *Eridanus* 1.14.38; cf. Arnaldi et al. 1964, "uiuendo da pastore"), with *A.* 4.70–1: *quam ... fixit / pastor agens* ("whom the shepherd, hunting, struck [with his darts]").

29 Cf. *A.* 5.501: *neruo stridente sagitta*; for the arrow catching flame, *A.* 5.525–6.

30 Compare the opening *pompa* of Pontano's *Lepidina*, which highlights two elements that are highly unusual within the generic frame of classical pastoral: one of the principal interlocutors, and the title character, is female, and not only that, she is also pregnant (*Ecl.* 1.1). This pregnancy functions as a humble correlate of the civilizational *proles* that will arise from the marriage of Parthenope and Sebeto.

31 On Renaissance interpretation of the *puer* in the fourth eclogue as Christ, see Wilson-Okamura 2010: 70–3.

32 *G.* 4.542; *A.* 5.237, 6.217, 6.244, 6.506, 11.6, 11.185, 12.194.

33 On Vergilian epitaphs, see also Pandey in the present volume.

34 Cf. Statius' *consolatio* in *Siluae* 3.3 (211–12): *semper odoratis spirabunt floribus arae, / semper et Assyrios felix bibet urna liquores* ("Always will your altars exhale the scent of flowers, always will your happy urn drink Assyrian perfumes").

35 On Vergil's "tomb," see Trapp 1984 and Pandey in this volume. On Sannazaro's villa and tomb, Croce 1892; Deramaix and Laschke 1992. Sannazaro's spatial/ literary "proximity" to Vergil is thematized in two epitaphic epigrams by Pietro Bembo: 1. "Give flowers to the holy ash. Here lies Sincerus [=Sannazaro], closest to Maro in his poetry as in his tomb" (*Da sacro cineri flores*: *Hic ille Maroni / Sincerus musa proximus ut tumulo*); 2. "Why do I delay? The shade of immortal Maro admires you, and allows you to have a place near him" (*Quid moror? aeterni te suspicit umbra Maronis, / et tibi uicinum donat habere locum*).

36 Stat. *Silv.* 4.51–5; on Silius, see Martial 11.48, 50, which similarly play on the idea of literary property or terrain. The Capella Pontano, which still stands today on the Via dei Tribunali in Naples, is a classicizing funeral monument built by Pontano for his family: De Divitiis 2012. Pontano also wrote two books of epitaphic epigrams entitled *De Tumulis*: Monti Sabia 1974.

21

Vergil and Antiquarian Poetry in Distichs in the Kingdom of Naples: Four Case Studies (Fifteenth–Sixteenth Centuries)

LORENZO MILETTI

From the second half of the fifteenth century on, an antiquarian culture flourished in the Kingdom of Naples, as in several areas of the Italian peninsula, which aimed to explore and investigate the past of the most ancient and prestigious towns, and to celebrate their foundations, origins, monuments, etc. This phenomenon, far from concerning the capital of Naples alone, touched all the main centres of the kingdom, especially the ones which could boast ancient origins and mythical ancestors.[1]

As elegy and epigram were among the most common and versatile poetic forms in Renaissance Italy, the humanists who composed works about their city's past often recurred to distichs.[2] If Latin classical poems in elegiac couplets were indeed the main models for this humanistic production, other authors were often sources of inspiration, above all Vergil, since many cities of the Kingdom of Naples are explicitly mentioned by Vergil in his verses. Influence by Vergil cannot constitute a surprise at all: having been the most inspiring poet of the entire Middle Ages did not prevent Vergil from being one of the main pillars of education for the entire Renaissance period as well.[3] This is all the more true for southern Italy and Naples, the city which Vergil loved and chose as his burial place: the humanistic culture of the whole Kingdom of Naples was imbued with a deep Vergilianism, which resonates in the works of all the most prominent poets of this area, including Giovanni Pontano and Iacopo Sannazaro.[4]

In this chapter I furnish a few examples of this poetic-antiquarian production in distichs from southern Italy in a discussion of the dialectic between Vergilian matters and elegiac and/or epigrammatic solutions and reinterpretations. I also investigate Vergil's role (both as poetic model and as antiquarian source) in the light of these poems' specific aims and purposes. In my discussion I omit poems devoted to the city of Naples, which is celebrated, for instance, in many works by Antonio Beccadelli Panormita, Pontano, and Sannazaro, in order to discuss verses by humanists who dealt with other centres of the kingdom that have been only partially studied until today, or are almost unknown. I will focus, following chronological order, on four humanists in particular: Francesco Patrizi, Elisio Calenzio, Aurelio Serena, and Francesco Peto.

1. Francesco Patrizi of Siena, Bishop of Gaeta

Francesco Patrizi (1413–1494) was a cultivated nobleman of Siena, who was made bishop of Gaeta in 1461 by his childhood friend Enea Silvio Piccolomini, when the latter became Pope Pius II.[5] Despite the habit, common for many bishops of the late medieval period, of not residing in the diocese, Patrizi lived consistently in Gaeta, while also encouraging the development of the local cultural life.[6] As a humanist, he was a prolific writer, whose work is still largely unpublished or has received no modern edition.[7] I focus here only on a few examples of his production in distichs, namely his mostly unpublished poetic collection to which he gave the name of *Epigrammata*. This collection is witnessed by a sole manuscript, which once belonged to Phyllis Goodhart Gordan and is today conserved in the library of Bryn Mawr College.[8] In 1968 Leslie Smith published an edition of 28 of these poems, together with a full index of the manuscript's contents.[9] The listed poems (the first verse of each of which is also transcribed by Smith) amount to 345, so the number of the unpublished epigrams is about the 92 per cent of the total.[10]

As far as is possible to infer from the 28 published poems, and consistent with the title of the collection, the epigrams gathered in this collection are influenced by both Augustan elegiac poetry and Martial, whose rediscovery ignited an intense debate throughout the whole fifteenth century and beyond.[11] Like many humanists of his time, however, Patrizi also nurtured historical and antiquarian interests.[12] According to Smith's list of the titles of the collection, many poems deal with the city of Gaeta.[13] Only a complete edition will show to what extent these testify to an antiquarian reading of the ancient sources on this city. Relying on Smith's work, I will discuss here, as a specimen of Patrizi's antiquarian taste, the title and first verse of one among the unpublished poems (Epigram 84), and the first four couplets of a published one (Epigram 188), both dealing with Gaeta.

The title and incipit of Epigram 84 seem to merge Martial audaciously with Vergil: the authorial voice addresses "Caieta," a personification of the city, in order to defend a girl named Marulla, who has a reputation for being unchaste: *Ad Caietam exagitantem Marullam impudicam* – *Casta nimis mollem spernis, Caieta, Marullam* ("To Caieta, chastizing wanton Marulla – Chaste Caieta you spurn Marulla, who is too soft"). The girl is said to be *impudica* and *mollis*, in opposition to Caieta, who is emphatically described as *casta*. The epigram apparently aims to refute or mitigate Caieta's (the citizens'?) moralistic reprobation of this girl, a theme which definitely recalls Martial, especially because of the presence of the *"impudicitas* theme" and of the name Marulla, a protagonist of a licentious epigram in Martial (10.55). Vergil's influence is, however, undeniable if we only consider the opening of *Aeneid* Book 7 (1–4):

> Tu quoque litoribus nostris, Aeneia nutrix,
> aeternam moriens famam, Caieta, dedisti;
> et nunc seruat honos sedem tuus, ossaque nomen
> Hesperia in magna, si qua est ea gloria, signat.

You too, Caieta, Aeneas' nurse, gave eternal fame to our shores with your death; and now your honour preserves your resting place, and in great Hesperia – if that be glory – your name marks your bones.[14]

Like Vergil, Patrizi directly addresses Caieta, and places the vocative in the same metrical position as Vergil does in 7.2.[15] The Vergilian episode was famous to such an extent that no cultivated Renaissance poet dealing with Gaeta could avoid mention of it. Although Epigram 84 still awaits full publication and study, a certain humoristic purpose is nonetheless perceptible in the daring union of a solemn Vergilian verse and an obscene epigram by Martial.

In Epigram 188 (fully published by Smith), addressed to a Fra Romanus who comes to visit Gaeta, we can better observe how Patrizi alludes to and even incorporates Vergilian phrases. Here I quote the first four couplets:

> 188. *Caieta ad F. Romanum hospitem* (vv. 1–8)
> Aeneadum soboles magna de stirpe nepotum,
>   hospes ades nostris, en, modo littoribus.

Urbis in amplexum curuatum respice portum
   quo residet pontus Nereidesque silent.
Hic discunt omnes mitescere Tethyos undae
   saeuaque Neptuni concidit ira dei.
Securi ludunt nautae somnosque priores
   instaurant, nullo concutiente Noto.

Gaeta to the visitor F. Romanus: Offspring from the great lineage of Aeneas' descend-ants, there, just now you approach our coasts as a visitor. Behold in the city's embrace, the curved harbour where the sea lingers and the Nereids hold silence. In this place all Tethys' waves learn to grow calm and the fierce anger of the god Neptune subsides. Carefree the sailors play and renew their former slumber, since no South wind blows violently.[16]

In these verses Caieta herself is speaking to her guest. If compared with the previous example, this composition has apparently nothing to do with Martial, but displays a certain solemnity, which evokes Latin hexametric poetry. The first verse, in which the exordial term *Aeneadum* is an ostenta-tious homage to Lucretius 1.1, ends with the expression *magna de stirpe nepotum*.[17] This phrase is drawn *litteratim* from the underworld prophecy on Marcellus (*A.* 6.865), a passage which has, in itself, no connection with Gaeta, but is located very close to a meaningful mention of this city: a few lines after, at 6.900, Vergil reports how Aeneas, after exiting the underworld through the ivory gate, leaves the coasts of Campania and goes directly to Gaeta: *Tum se ad Caietae recto fert litore portum*. The expression *recto litore* is generally interpreted as referring to the straightness of the direc-tion. So it is very interesting how Patrizi, in v. 3 of his epigram, takes this phrase and modifies it in order to produce another sense: in describing the Gulf of Gaeta, he writes *Urbis in amplexum curuatum respice portum*, where *curuatum* and *urbis … portum* clearly oppose, respectively, *recto* and *Caietae … portum* in Vergil. In sum, Caieta's episode in the *Aeneid* is largely present in Patrizi's Epigram 188, but the Vergilian expressions are adapted by the humanist to his purposes.

A last remark concerns v. 5: the expression *Tethyos undae* appears in the same form and position in Priscian, *De situ orbis*, 688, a Latin translation in verse of Dionysius Periegetes' geographical work. This does not seem a coincidence, since Patrizi wrote an epitome of Priscian's *Institutiones gram-maticae* and it is probable that he also read other works by this author, who had great diffusion throughout the whole Middle Ages and beyond, and whose translation of Dionysius was printed no less than seventeen times before the end of the fifteenth century.[18]

2. Elisio Calenzio's Elegies on Taranto

Elisio Calenzio was born in 1430 in a small village in southern Lazio, within the Kingdom of Naples.[19] Thanks to his refined education, he came to be appointed tutor of King Ferrante's son Federico, who would be the last king of Naples. At the Neapolitan court, Calenzio, who befriended Giovanni Pontano and many humanists of the *Academia Pontaniana*, wrote several works, both in verse and prose. He was preparing their publication in 1503 when he died. The final revision of his works was probably close to being finished, since they were collected and printed posthumously by his son Lucio, in the same year of the author's death, under the title of *Opuscula*, and dedicated to Angelo Colocci.[20] The prose section of the book is a collection of letters, while the poems include a Latin version of the *Batrachomyomachia* entitled *Croacus* and a "cycle" of erotic elegies addressed to a woman called Aurimpia.[21]

Some of the compositions which open Book 2 of the collection of elegies are unified by a specific antiquarian interest in the city of Taranto. Calenzio's attention to this city was due to the fact that, in the mid-1460s, after the end of the so-called Succession War (or First *Congiura dei Baroni*) in 1465, Federico, who was still a teenager, was sent by his father, King Ferrante, to govern the Principality of Taranto. Calenzio followed as adviser and mentor. After being ruled for a long time as a sort of "state within the state" by a fierce opponent of the king, namely Giovanni Antonio Orsini, the Principality of Taranto was incorporated into the Crown's direct control at the end of the war. Federico thus had an important political task in both controlling the Principality's local policy and facing the cultural challenge of endowing the region and its capital Taranto with a new "personality," loyal to the king. This effort entailed abandoning the late medieval and Anjou-oriented identity promoted by Orsini, in order to embrace a full humanistic identity which relied on the prestige of the ancient past of Taranto.

As a humanist and a counsellor, Calenzio had a prominent role in supporting Federico in this challenge. Thus, he wrote an elegy to Federico as governor of Taranto (*Ad Hiaracum*), another elegy in praise of the city (*Laus Tarenti*), and one on the girls of Taranto (*De puellis Tarentinis*);[22] he also wrote an epistle to the Tarantini and one in which the city is accurately described.[23] The first of these elegies, *Ad Hiaracum*, is a sort of *propemptikon* addressed to Federico (here hidden under the literary name of Hiaracus); in the first part of the poem, Calenzio inserts a sort of mythic-antiquarian profile of the Principality, mentioning Taranto and several other centres. Here I transcribe the first four couplets:

<*Ad Hiaracum*>
Ibis Leucadias foelix dominator ad urbes
   ultimaque Hesperiae terra petenda tibi est.
ad populous alios alisque uocaris ad artes.
   iamque puer leges et noua iura dabis,
ubi uecta mari primum Neptunia proles
   dicitur optatos composuisse lares
atque urbem dixisse suo de nomine uirgo
   et fontem structa non procul urbe Taram.[24]

<*To Hiaracus*>: You will come a happy conqueror to the cities of Lefkada and you are to travel to the remotest land in Hesperia. You will be summoned to different peoples and to different skills. And already as a young boy you will administer precepts and new laws, where it is said that first the Neptunian offspring, carried on the sea, raised the desired abodes, and that a maiden called the city and a fountain, close to the constructed city, "Taras," after her own name.[25]

In the first two distichs, Hiaracus/Federico's new role (*dominator*) in Apulia is celebrated also through the evocation of specific toponyms: *Leucadias … urbes* / *ultimaque Hesperiae terra*. The first verse cites a non-elegiac model, namely Horace *Ep.* 1.1: *Ibis Liburnis inter alta nauium …* , a famous *propemptikon* to Maecenas. It is also interesting that, in this first verse, *Leucadiae urbes*, which refers to the southern part of Salento (see the modern toponym S. Maria di Leuca), is reminiscent of the *Leucadia* of several Latin sources (see, e.g., Lucan, 5.479), which refers to the island of Lefkada and hence to the Battle of Actium, with all the ideological burden this mention carries.[26] See also the expression *iura dabis*, which recalls, among other sources, Jupiter's prophecy of Rome in Vergil's *Aeneid* (*A.* 1.293). After these four verses, Calenzio mentions the mythical foundation of Taranto, describing the city as a place where the "Neptunian offspring" arrived. The expression *Neptunia proles* is drawn from a Vergilian passage, namely from the epithet of the Apulian hero Messapus, featuring in a verse reoccurring three times in the *Aeneid*: *at Messapus equum domitor, Neptunia proles*.[27] But here Calenzio refers this epithet to Taras, not to Messapus. He could find the connection between Taras and Neptune in a passage of Servius' commentary on *A.* 3.551, where Aeneas' arrival in Italy is described.[28] Servius tries to explain a quite obscure expression used by Vergil (*Hinc sinus Herculei, si uera est fama, Tarenti*) that alludes to the mythical "Herculean" foundation of the city by Phalantus:

HERCULEI, SI UERA EST FAMA, TARENTI *fabula talis est*: Lacones et Athenienses diu inter se bella tractarunt, et cum utraque pars adfligeretur, Lacones, quibus iuuentus deerat, praeceperunt ut uirgines cum quibuscumque concumberent. Factum est ita, et cum post sedata bella iuuentus incertis parentibus nata et patriae [erubesceret] et sibi esset obproprio – nam partheniatae dicebantur – accepto duce Phalanto, octauo ab Hercule, profecti sunt delatique ad breue oppidum Calabriae quod Taras, Neptuni filius, fabricauerat, id auxerunt et prisco nomine appellauerunt Tarentum.[29]

"Of the Herculean Tarentum, if the tradition is true": *and this is the story*: The Lacedaemonians and the Athenians were waging war between them for a long time, and although both sides were weakened, the Lacedaemonians, who were lacking in young warriors, ordered that the virgins should sleep with everyone. Thus it was done, and after the wars were diffused, when the young men born from spurious parents were feeling both ashamed in their fatherland and that this was a disgrace for them – for they were called "born from virgins" – after Phalas became their accepted leader, an eighth descendant to Hercules, they set forth and were carried to a small town in Calabria, which Taras, Neptune's son, had built, and which they enlarged and called by its ancient name, Tarentum.[30]

Here Calenzio receives Servius' expression *Taras, Neptuni filius* and modulates it in *Neptunia proles* by borrowing the epithet from the Vergilian passage related to Messapus. Thus, the epithet continues to refer to an Apulian hero, though not the same one mentioned by Vergil. It is striking that the humanist does not insert any reference to the Spartan colonization of Phalantus described by Servius, to which Vergil alludes through the epithet *Herculeus*. The reasons for the humanist's silence on this episode are unclear: I wonder if we may assume that Calenzio aims to underline the Apulian (i.e., truly "local," almost "autochthonous") origins of the city, setting aside the role of the Greeks.

Compared to Servius, Calenzio offers something "less" (i.e., Phalantus), but also something "more": in the verses of the elegy quoted above we find mention of a "maiden" (*uirgo*) and a "fountain" or "source" (*fontem*), neither of which is mentioned by Servius. Here Calenzio apparently has in mind one among the sources referring to a young woman named Satyria, who is in general considered the mother or, alternatively, the wife of Taras.[31] The main Latin source reporting this myth is Ps.-Probus' commentary to Vergil's *Georgics*, in which the episode is described as follows:

Dicitur autem Tarentus, Neptuni filius, Lacedaemonia ciuitate ex Saturia, Minois Cretensium regis filia, procreasse filium … A Saturia uxore eum locum Saturium appellasse fertur et postea ei loco ex suo nomine nomen Tarentum imposuisse.[32]

But it is said that Tarentus, the son of Neptune from the Lacedaemonian state, bore a son from Saturia, daughter of Minos, the king of Cretans … From Saturia, his wife, the tradition claims that he called this place Saturium, but later to the same place he imposed the name "Tarentum" after his own name.[33]

Calenzio probably consulted this source, although he seems to use it very selectively. The name Saturia is omitted, and no reference to Crete is present (but this may be explained, as noted above, by the humanist's concern to highlight only the "autochthonous" side of the city's identity). Some expressions seem to coincide: see, for instance, Calenzio's *dicitur optatos composuisse lares / atque urbem dixisse suo de nomine uirgo* and Ps.-Probus' *ex suo nomine nomen Tarentum imposuisse*.

Calenzio's words, and in particular his use of the term *uirgo*, may recall another source, namely Pausanias' version of the foundation myth of Taranto (Paus. 10.10.6–8). After reporting how Phalantus conquered the city according to an oracle, Pausanias adds (10.10.8): Τάραντα δὲ τὸν ἥρω Ποσειδῶνός φασι καὶ ἐπιχωρίας νύμφης παῖδα εἶναι, ἀπὸ δὲ τοῦ ἥρωος τεθῆναι τὰ ὀνόματα τῇ πόλει τε καὶ τῷ ποταμῷ· καλεῖται γὰρ δὴ Τάρας κατὰ τὰ αὐτὰ τῇ πόλει καὶ ὁ ποταμός ("They say that Taras the hero was a son of Poseidon by a nymph of the country, and that after this hero were named both the city and the river. For the river, just like the city, is called Taras).[34] The reference to a nymph (νύμφη: "nymph" but also "young girl") and the expression "both the city and the river" (τῇ πόλει τε καὶ τῷ ποταμῷ) seem to be recalled by Calenzio's *uirgo* and *urbem et fontem*, but the question of whether Calenzio could or could not read the text of Pausanias should receive a separate investigation. Here we limit ourselves to concluding by pointing out Calenzio's ability in rewriting myths according to his own taste and purposes, and in "dissimulating" his sources.[35]

3. Aurelio Serena of Monopoli

A third example of an elegiac poet from southern Italy profoundly imbued with Vergilian poetics is Aurelio Serena. This humanist was born in Monopoli, in central Apulia on the seaside, and passed most of his life in his hometown, until he went to Rome, about at the age of forty. There he published some poems and prose works in praise of Popes Julius II and Leo X, and other members of the papal milieu.

Out of all the works by this humanist – for which I refer the interested reader to the essays by Domenico Defilippis[36] – I would only like to present briefly a passage from a curious elegy, in which the humanist maintains that Vergil's famous description of the port of Carthage in *Aeneid* 1.159–69 is entirely inspired by the real form of the port of Brundisium, which is shaped like a pair of deer antlers. Brundisium is a port which, of course, Vergil would know well, largely before his final and "fatal" visit. Verses 1–4 of Serena's *Descriptio portus Brundusii quem intellexit Vergilius in primo Aeneidos* are as follows:

> Brundusii pulchrum cupiens descriuere portum
> non sensisse alium censeo Vergilium.
> Inveniuntur in hoc quae describuntur ab illo
> de portu Aeneas quem profugus petiit.[37]

Wishing to describe the beautiful harbour in Brundisium, I judge that Vergil did not think of a different one. The characteristics which he describes of the harbour which the exiled Aeneas sought are found in this [harbour].[38]

As one can see from this short specimen, it is clear that Aurelio Serena's purpose is demonstrative and even didactic. Moreover, the rest of the text constitutes a virtuoso attempt to manage rhetorical and literary-critical problems in elegiac couplets. Serena, after all, was a rhetorician and a private teacher of rhetoric at Rome. Between the lines, furthermore, it is possible to read a sort of "Apulian pride" in celebrating Brindisi as a Vergilian place *par excellence*; Serena's acquaintance with the ancient Apulian topography and geography is clear from other poems. For instance, he inserts an extended and erudite description of this region in his *Theatrum Capitolinum*, a hexameter poem celebrating the arrival at Rome, in 1514, of Giuliano and Piero de' Medici, respectively brother and nephew of Pope Leo X.[39] In both poems, the reading of classical authors is merged with the direct observation of local landscape and local antiquities; while, however, in the *Theatrum Capitolinum* the hexameter form implies a more ambitious connection with the Vergilian model, in the case of the *Descriptio portus Brundisii* the author chose elegiac couplets, apparently because the hexameter is felt as too elevated for a merely "grammatical" or "exegetical" (albeit deeply Vergilian) poem.

4. Francesco Peto of Fondi

Francesco Peto was born in Fondi, in southern Lazio, one of the most northern places in the Kingdom of Naples, and moved while very young to Naples in order to meet an elderly Giovanni Pontano, probably in 1501.[40] He also was under the protection of a powerful Roman *condottiero* and baron, Prospero Colonna, who was Count of Fondi and friend and advisor of Gonzalo de Cordoba, El Gran Capitán, who had conquered the Kingdom of Naples during the Franco-Spanish war of 1500–4.

At the beginning of 1504, Peto dedicated two elegiac poems to a lieutenant of Prospero Colonna, Ettore Fieramosca, a nobleman who had led a squad of Italian cavaliers in an "official" duel (the so-called *Disfida di Barletta*) against the Frenchmen, which took place near the Apulian city of Barletta in 1503.[41] This poem in praise of the Italian winner of the duel is also in praise of the dedicatee's hometown, the city of Capua, whose mythological founder was the Vergilian hero Capys, friend of Aeneas. Vergil himself makes a connection between this hero and the city by claiming *et Capys hinc nomen Campanae ducitur urbis* (*A.* 10.145). Peto develops his poetic *laudatio* by passing through several rhetorical topoi and by playing with the homonymy between the dedicatee and the Trojan hero Hector:[42]

Militiae pacisque insignis laudibus Hector,
    qui Capyn Iliacos quique reducis auos,
cum tua uel mutis benefacta silentia rumpant
    ne dum doctorum clara per ora sonent
certatimque sacro plaudent tibi carmine uates   5
    quique pede et numero liberiore canunt.
Nonne reus Phoeboque uocer Pindique Puellis
    nulla ego si ingenii dem monumenta mei?
Quinetiam moneor tacitas prope natus Amyclas
    saepe parum tacitos consuluisse sibi.   10
Namque ferunt bellis uexatam tristibus urbem
    finitimi infensam Marte fugasse manum,
sed cum dira mali durarent semina belli,
    interdum uanas extimuisse minas,
nunciat hostileis dum rumor adesse cateruas   15
    moenibus urbs falso concut<it>urque metu.
Hinc cautum nequis uenientem nunciet hostem,
    et pietas poenam sedulitasque tulit.
Venit, et incautis nudatam ciuibus urbem
    repperit, obsessa ui potiturque ferox.   20
Diruit Oebaliis constructaque tecta colonis
    unde rear patriae ducta elementa meae.
Nam lares dum pulsi latis noua moenia fundis
    ponunt Fundanis nomina facta locis.

Distinguished with praises during wartime and peacetime, Hector, you who restore Capys and the forefathers of Ilion, since your acts of benevolence even to the mute break the silence, may they resound glorious, all the more, through the mouths of the learned, in turn poets, who sing using a more free metre and rhythm, will applaud you with sacred song. Is it not the case that I should be summoned to answer to Phoebus and the girls of Pindus, if I don't offer any monuments of my talent? Indeed born next to the silent city of Amyclae, I am reminded that the similarly silent were often unable to take care of themselves. For indeed the tradition goes that the city, disturbed with deplorable wars, pushed back, in a battle, the hostile army of its neighbours. But it is said that since the cruel seeds of evil war persevered, in the meantime the city grew afraid of empty threats, during a time in which rumours claimed that crowds from an enemy town were approaching, and the city was shaken with false fear. Hence no one announced that a cautious enemy was coming, but religious piety and persistency suffered punishment. He came, and indeed he discovered a city exposed by its heedless citizens, and, after he besieged it with force, fiercely he conquered it. He also tore down the houses built by the Oebalian settlers, from where I believe the first principles were brought to my fatherland. Since the expelled household gods set new fortifications to a broad land [*fundi*], the names for the places of Fundi were created.[43]

The mention of Hector and Capys contributes to the evocation of a Vergilian scenario, but the use of Vergil becomes more original in vv. 9–24, where Peto inserts a long account of the myth of Amyclae, a legendary city of southern Lazio, an account opened up by the autobiographical remark *tacitas prope natus Amyclas* (v. 9), according to which the poet was born in a place (i.e., Fondi) "next to the silent city of Amyclae," an expression drawn from *A.* 10.564 *tacitis regnauit Amyclis*. The obscurity of this Vergilian phrase garnered the attention of Servius, who explained it by reporting two interpretations of why Amyclae is called *tacitae* by Vergil: first, the inhabitants of this city followed the Pythagorean religion, which implied a ritual silence; second, the city imposed a silence on their own sentinels after a series of false alarms, so when the enemies really arrived, the city was invaded and destroyed.[44] Peto develops his account of Amyclae by making reference to the latter anecdote only, describing it in detail and in an elevated style. In order to praise his own birthplace, furthermore, he modifies (or better, integrates) Servius' explanation by establishing an explicit connection between the fall of Amyclae and the foundation of Fondi, an episode which is not reported by any ancient source, and is clearly invented by the humanist.[45] Peto could, however, find an explicit connection between Amyclae and Fundi (though not relating to myth, but to the cultivation of vines) in Martial 13.115: *Caecuba Fundanis generosa cocuntur Amyclis, / uitis et in media nata palude uiret* ("Generous Caecuban grapes grow ripe at Amyclae near Fundi. The vine born in the midst of the swamp grows green"). The use of Vergil as a source, here, enables Peto to engage encomiastic and antiquarian motifs by narrating an ancient myth and by modifying it in order to fulfil his purposes. It is worthy of note that, also here, the commentary of Servius plays a fundamental role as source, and that, as in the epigrams of Francesco Patrizi with which this survey began, allusions to Vergil and Martial may peacefully coexist.

5. Conclusions

We have seen four examples of humanists from southern Italy who engage with Vergilian themes by writing epigrams and elegies, four different cases of how poems in elegiac couplets absorb themes, words, and longer expressions from a hexameter model as fundamental as Vergil. The four authors apparently know Vergil by heart and are eager to "dialogue" with him when possible. They not only make Vergilian formulas resonate within their distichs, but also draw from Vergil, as from an encyclopaedia, myths, notions, names, places, etc. in order to enrich the style and content of their poems. Aurelio Serena goes so far as to write a poem which is a textual interpretation of a Vergilian passage. It is, however, noteworthy that if, on the one hand, the Vergilian presence in such works as Pontano's didactic poem *Urania*, Sannazaro's bucolic *Arcadia*, or (at a lower scale) Porcelio de' Pandoni's epic *De proelio apud Troiam* is unavoidable and fully predictable,[46] on the other hand, four examples discussed here testify to how Vergil was felt as a major model also by humanists who nurtured a particular penchant for elegiac and/or epigrammatic poetry, and who probably considered (as also happened in antiquity) the hexameter suitable only when dealing directly with *pascua, rura, duces,* according to Vergil's famous funeral epigram.

The four cases discussed can possibly enrich our overall understanding of the elegiac and epigrammatic production of Renaissance Italy, since the rise of these genres, which was impressive between the fifteenth and the sixteenth centuries, constitutes a phenomenon which has been only partially explored, especially as regards the literature that flourished across the entire Kingdom of Naples.[47] Undoubtedly, Patrizi, Calenzio, Serena, and Peto are to be considered four different ways of dealing with poetry in distichs, and also four different ways of receiving the Roman elegiac and epigrammatic poets in the Renaissance. The lack of editions, commentaries, translations, and studies prevents us from going deeper into this investigation, and from fully understanding to what extent Propertius, Tibullus, Ovid, and other *auctores* have been used by these humanists. These issues notwithstanding, it seems possible to state that, thanks to their profound classical education, Patrizi, Calenzio, Serena, and Peto make the most of the intrinsic ductility of the poetry in elegiac couplets, and meld in their verses, not without a certain originality, different sources deriving from different genres – Vergil, as we have seen, but also other poets and even commentators and prose authors, as in the case of Francesco Peto, who amply draws material from Servius for his encomiastic elegy.

We have also seen how, in these poems, antiquarianism and erudition oriented towards local antiquities merge with encomiastic purposes. According to these humanists' attitude towards the past, it is not possible to celebrate a place, a city, or a region without studying its ancient myths, histories, and the Greek or Roman celebrities who were born or lived there. So Taranto cannot be praised without mentioning Taras, Fondi without Amyclae, Capua without Capys, Gaeta without Caieta, or Brundisium without Vergil himself. In this sense, these poets are "faithful followers" of their Latin models, and were perfectly aware of how Latin poetry in distichs could be perfect for encomia, if we think, for instance, of Ovid's production from exile or of Claudian's prefaces, but also for antiquarianism, if we think, for instance, of Propertius' Books 3 and 4 or Ovid's *Fasti*. To sum up, although these four cases indeed constitute heterogeneous material, they are fully understandable only within the frame of at least three issues relating to Renaissance literary culture, namely the reception of Vergil, the diffusion of elegy as a major poetical form, and the rise of antiquarianism. The poetic experience of these humanists is thus to be set at the crossroads of these three phenomena.

NOTES

This paper starts from the achievements of the recently completed ERC project HistAntArtSI (2011–16), coordinated by Bianca de Divitiis at the University of Naples Federico II, which has dealt, among other things, with the antiquarian culture developed in the centres of the Kingdom of Naples in the Renaissance period. I wish to express my gratitude to the members of the project staff, and to the colleagues who discussed with me a first sketch of this paper at the *Symposium Cumanum: Vergil and Elegy* (Cuma and Naples, 27–30 June 2017). My warmest thanks to Claudio Buongiovanni for his friendly suggestions and to Alison Keith and Micah Myers for inviting me to participate in this volume and also to them and to Georgia Ferentinou for supporting me in writing these pages in English.

1 In the centres of southern Italy, in the late Quattrocento, an antiquarian interest grew up which increased significantly throughout the sixteenth century, at the end of which nearly all the major centres of the kingdom could boast the production of local histories which were based, with more or less reliability, on antiquarian and often "proto-archaeological" inquiries. A general profile, with several examples, of this literature devoted to local

antiquity in Renaissance southern Italy, both in prose and in verse, is in Miletti 2023.

2 If elegy and epigram are genres whose reciprocal boundaries were perceived as blurred already in antiquity, this is all the more true for Renaissance poetry: See Coppini 2009; Pieper 2009: 165–6; Moul 2016: 45–7; see also Ijsewijn and Sacré 1998: 111–16. The essays collected in Catanzaro and Santucci 1999 are useful attempts to approach the multifaceted humanistic production in elegiac couplets by furnishing case studies; on the transformation of elegy in the Italian Quattrocento, see Casanova-Robin 2011a. De Beer 2014 and Houghton 2017 are useful, though synthetic, profiles of Renaissance Latin elegy. A recent collection of essays on Renaissance epigram is that of De Beer, Enenkel, and Rijser 2009; see also Cummings 2017.

3 For an overview of the Vergilian tradition between the Middle Ages and the early modern period, see Comparetti 1896, Zabughin 1921–3, and Ziolkowski and Putnam 2008. See also recent studies on Vergil's reception in the Renaissance: Wilson-Okamura 2010, Houghton and Sgarbi 2018, and numerous publications by Craig Kallendorf (e.g., Kallendorf 1989; 2007; 2019), who is also preparing the entry *Virgil* for the *Catalogus Translationum et Commentariorum*.

4 See the collection of essays dedicated to Vergil's reception in the Kingdom of Naples in Deramaix and Germano 2018. On Sannazaro's "Vergilianism" in his most famous work, *Arcadia*, modelled on Vergil's *Bucolics*, see Vecce 2013. On Pontano and Vergil, see Roman's chapter in this volume, with further references. On Vergil at Naples in the Middle Ages (especially during the "Golden Age" of Frederick II), see Delle Donne 2015; on how the fifteenth-century rediscovery of Statius made it possible for this Neapolitan poet to complement (and sometimes be preferred to) Vergil at Naples in the Quattrocento, see Abbamonte 2015.

5 Biographical details on Pius II in Quintiliani 2014.

6 The cultural life of Gaeta in the second half of the fifteenth century is not without interest, if we think, for instance, of the fact that no less than eleven books (according to the *Incunable Short Title Catalogue*) were printed between 1484 and 1485 by the German typographers Andreas Freitag (eight editions) and Jodocus Hohenstein (three editions). It is clear that Gaeta benefited from its strategic position between Rome and Naples.

7 For Patrizi's letters, see de Capua 2014. On his poems, see below. On his political works (*De regno* and *De institutione reipublicae*), which were printed more than once in the early modern period (but have benefited from no modern critical edition and/or translation), see Chiarelli 1932; Cappelli 2004; Schiera 2007; Rossi 2015. A useful *status quaestionis* on Patrizi's manuscripts and printed works is Chiti n.d.

8 Bryn Mawr Library, ms. Gordan 153.

9 Smith 1968.

10 Smith 1968. As far as I know, there is no edition available of these poems, though I am ignorant of whether some scholar is currently working on it.

11 In the second half of the Quattrocento, Martial was at the core of a polemical debate which involved several commentators of his verses, and above all Angelo Poliziano, Domizio Calderini, and Niccolò Perotti. An accurate overview of the Renaissance studies on Martial is offered by Rutger-Hausmann 1980, updated with Pade 2016.

12 Before becoming bishop of Gaeta, Patrizi wrote a history of his hometown of Siena, *De origine et uetustate urbis Senae*, which is still unpublished and conserved in Siena, Biblioteca Comunale degli Intronati, mss. A.III.10; B.III.3; C.I.19.

13 See, e.g., Epigrams 130, 172, 180, 274 in Smith 1968.

14 Trans. adapted from Fairclough, rev. Goold 1999.

15 On Caieta in *A.* 7, see McCallum in this collection.

16 I am grateful to Georgia Ferentinou for the translation of Patrizi's epigram into English.

17 The collocation of *Aeneadum* at the beginning of the verse is also a homage to the impressive fortune of this expression in several post-Lucretian authors (but not in Vergil, who uses the term but avoids inserting it in this metrical position): see, for instance, Ov. *Tr.* 2.262 or, more meaningfully, Sil. 1.2; 2.295; 13.500; 14.4. Silius Italicus was often read by humanists from the Kingdom of Naples, since he makes several references (not unlike his source, Livy) to places and persons connected to ancient southern Italy: see Miletti 2013: 728–30, and Miletti 2018a: 19–21, for examples of use of this author by, respectively, the poet Cosma Anisio and the humanist and doctor Ambrogio Leone.

18 Data drawn from the *Incunable Short Title Catalogue*. Patrizi's epitome of Priscianus is still unpublished: see Chiti n.d., nr. 9.

19 Biographical details in Foà 1998; Caruso 2018, with ample bibliography.

20 Calenzio 1503.

21 On Calenzio's poems, see Iacono 2014; Germano 2015; and Germano 2016. On the letters (*Epistulae ad Hiaracum*), see Caruso 2016; Mongelli 2017.

22 Calenzio 1503: *Elegiae*, respectively fols. C^{1}r–C^{2}r; C^{2}v–C^{3}r; C^{4}r–v.

23 Calenzio 1503: *Epistolae*, respectively fols. B^{5}v; C^{2}v–C^{3}r.

24 Calenzio 1503: II.1, fol. C^{1}r. The title is a simple integration, since in the printed edition the title is omitted, probably because it was "obliterated" by the general dedication of Book 2 to Angelo Colocci. I am grateful to Giuseppe Germano for confirming that this portion of the *Opuscula* is not witnessed by any manuscript, but only by the edition of 1503.

25 I thank Georgia Ferentinou for the English translation.

26 This verse is, however, also reminiscent of Ov. *Her.* 16.333: *Ibis Dardanias ingens regina per urbes*. More generally, several *propemptika* seem to resonate

with Calenzio's verses, especially the ones written by Propertius (1.6) and
Tibullus (1.3), who were among the humanist's main models in regard to his
love elegies for Aurimpia.

27 Verg. *A.* 7.691 (= 9.523; 12.128).

28 Throughout, by "Servius" we mean, of course, the so called *Seruius minor*, since
the extended version of *Seruius auctus* or *Danielinus* was rediscovered only
by the French scholar Pierre Daniel, who published it in 1600. On Servius'
reception from late antiquity to Renaissance, see Méniel, Bouquet, and Ramires
2011.

29 Serv. ad *A.* 3.551, Thilo-Hagen 1881: 435–6.

30 I am grateful to Georgia Ferentinou for the English translation.

31 For the literary sources on ancient Taranto, see Nafissi 1995.

32 Ps.-Probus, ad *G.* 3.197.

33 English translation by Georgia Ferentinou.

34 The translation is from Jones 1918–35.

35 At the turn of the fifteenth century, Pausanias' *Periegesis* was far from easy
to gain access to (useful *status quaestionis* in Parks 1971). The Greek text,
edited by Marco Musuro, was printed for the first time in 1516. A sort of Latin
paraphrase of the whole work was published in Milan in 1517 by a pupil of
Demetrius Chalcondylas, Sebastiano Negri, while a full Latin translation of
his text appeared only in 1547, done by Romolo Quirino Amaseo, since the
translation that Domizio Calderini had begun in the early 1470s was never
completed, and only reached part of Book 2 (full discussion in Vairo 2021). If
neither a printed Greek text nor a Latin translation was available to Calenzio,
he could have drawn this reference directly from a Greek manuscript (though
it is not clear how refined his competence in Greek was), or from a second-
hand reference found, e.g., in printed commentaries of other classical authors:
we know, for instance, that Angelo Poliziano and Domizio Calderini used
Pausanias in writing their commentaries to Statius' *Siluae*. The Greek text
of this author, after all, circulated in the late Quattrocento, through a certain
number of copies, all derived from a codex possessed by Niccolò Niccoli and
now lost (Diller 1956 and Diller 1957). As regards the Kingdom of Naples,
a few witnesses of Pausanias' presence can be mentioned: during the reign of
Ferrante, the humanist and secretary Marco Cinico mentions Pausanias as one
of the geographers not owned by the king's library (Corfiati and Sciancalepore
2009: 102), a fact which testifies that the topic of the *Periegesis* was known
at Naples, but also that the text was not owned by the greatest library in the
kingdom, at least until Ferrante's death (1493). The humanist Giano Parrasio
of Cosenza possessed a manuscript copy of the Greek text of Pausanias (BNN
III.Aa.16bis) and largely used it to study ancient topography, but this activity
dates to the second decade of the sixteenth century, when Parrasio had come

back to Cosenza after being a pupil, among others, of the aforementioned Demetrius Chalcondylas in Milan.

36 See especially Defilippis 1987; Defilippis 1988; Defilippis 2008. On Serena's poems dedicated to Pope Julius II's "antiquarian" policy of monumental restoration in Rome, see Miletti and Tuccinardi 2017.

37 Serena 1512: fols. C^{1}v–D^{1}r. Transcription and Italian translation in Defilippis 1987: 26–32.

38 I am grateful to Georgia Ferentinou for the English translation.

39 Serena 1514: fols. F2r–v. On this poem, see Defilippis 1988.

40 Biographical details in Miletti 2015.

41 These two elegies are part of a collection of poems, on whose genesis see Miletti 2019. On the Disfida di Barletta, see the essays collected in Delle Donne and Rivera Magos 2017, and in Delle Donne and Rivera Magos 2019.

42 Damiani 1547: fol. L^{1}r–v. The text of this elegy is only witnessed by a sixteenth-century edition edited by the Capuan notary Giovan Battista Damiani. *Status quaestionis* in Miletti 2015 and Miletti 2018b. The etymology of Capua from Capys is one among the many attested in antiquity: see Heurgon 1984.

43 I am grateful to Georgia Ferentinou for the English translation.

44 Serv. ad *A.* 10.564, Thilo-Hagen 1881: 449–50.

45 Full discussion in Miletti 2018b.

46 On Pontano's *Urania* and his connection with Vergil, see Germano 2018 and Roman in this volume; for the influence of Vergil on Sannazaro's *Arcadia* I refer to the detailed commentary of Vecce 2013 (while on Vergil in Sannazaro's *De partu Virginis*, see Deramaix 2018); on Porcelio de' Pandoni's *De proelio apud Troiam*, see Iacono 2011.

47 Some poems in distichs written by authors from the Kingdom of Naples (Giovanni Pontano, Antonio Galateo, Gabriele Altilio, Girolamo Carbone) are discussed in the essays collected in Catanzaro and Santucci 1999. See also the bibliography cited above, n4.

22

Elegiac Loss and the Poetics of Translation in Vergil's *Aeneid* and Ariosto's *Orlando Furioso*

JOSEPH M. ORTIZ

Near the midpoint of *Aeneid* 9, Vergil inflects his account of Nisus and Euryalus' nighttime raid with an elegiac strain. Here, Vergil poignantly sums up the predicament of Nisus, who at this moment sees his lover Euryalus in the hands of the enemy (*A.* 9.399–400): *quid faciat? qui ui iuvenem, quibus audeat armis / eripere* ("What can he do? With what force, what arms dare he rescue the youth?").[1] For Vergil's reader, these desperate questions are both arresting and disorienting, in large part because their voice is not easy to identify. As J.D. Reed has carefully shown, Vergil's representation of Nisus' confusion ambiguously hovers between the perspectives of Vergil and Nisus, and this ambiguity is especially pronounced in the interjected question, which is positioned in the middle of the passage's gradual shift from poetic speaker to focalizing character.[2] The same passage also constitutes a brief but important modulation into the elegiac mode, drawing on both elegy's mournful register (in the sense that Euryalus is already fatally lost) and its erotic one (in the sense that Euryalus' body is conventionally eroticized).[3] In addition, Nisus' (or Vergil's) terse question – *quid faciat?* – unexpectedly echoes two distinct moments in the *Bucolics* in which a shepherd laments his current predicament.[4] In a sense, Nisus wanders the dark woods in search of Euryalus, only to find himself in a landscape redolent of elegy and pastoral.

Recent criticism has begun to pay more attention to the elegiac strains in the Nisus and Euryalus episode, and in the second half of the *Aeneid* more generally. Reed shows in careful detail how Vergil repeatedly employs the *sermo amatorius* to eroticize the bodies of fallen warriors in the poem, most notably Euryalus and Pallas.[5] Sarah McCallum and Deborah Beck likewise identify elegiac aspects in the Nisus and Euryalus episode, which they show to be part of a larger pattern of elegiac moments in the *Aeneid*. In particular, McCallum persuasively argues that Vergil's experimentation with elegy in the second half of the *Aeneid* taps into both elegy's erotic and funerary registers, "creat[ing] a productive tension between war and love, and public duty and private loss."[6] Reading the Nisus and Euryalus passage with an eye toward Renaissance elegiac traditions, Stephen Guy-Bray suggests that elegy (which he construes as lament) and Vergilian pastoral overlap in their capacity to register a sense of loss. Accordingly, the double generic enrichment of the episode with elegy and pastoral works to articulate a complex of amatory, funerary, and nostalgic impulses that are motivated by epic's systematic destruction of young warriors. As Guy-Bray puts it, "the nostalgia for country life that pervades so much pastoral is an extension of the regret for the loss of so many young men."[7] Put another way, Vergil's generic experimentation in the Nisus and Euryalus section intensifies the episode's representation of loss while simultaneously whetting desire for the very object of loss.

This essay builds on recent work on elegy in the *Aeneid*, and it focuses on the complex relationship between desire and loss that Vergil highlights in the Nisus and Euryalus episode. However, I want to suggest that Vergil is also interested here in a different kind of loss – not of country life or young men, but of something we might characterize as more *literary*. What is at stake here, I think, is an older poetic tradition. Vergil uses the episode to figure self-reflexively his own relationship to Greek poetic models, chief among them Homeric epic. Vergil figures this relationship on more than one occasion in the *Aeneid*, but perhaps nowhere as pessimistically as in the middle of Book 9, where the dense imitation of Homeric material erupts in an expression of futility. Reading the Nisus and Euryalus episode as a drama of Vergilian intertextuality helps to explain the presence of elegy, but it also illuminates the appeal of pastoral at this moment in the poem. As Thomas Hubbard suggests, to write pastoral is already to engage in an intensely self-reflexive intertextuality: "the Alexandrian bucolic tradition evolved as a genre always already conscious of its literary past, ever concerned with framing the poet's relationship to his precursors."[8] Eleanor Winsor Leach also recognizes the intertextual self-consciousness of Vergilian pastoral, but she detects in it a cynical attitude, noting that Vergil's first eclogue "measures the distance between … Vergilian and Theocritean pastoral [and] shows the impossibility of maintaining an old pastoral ideal in a new world."[9] With these ideas about intertextuality in mind, I will argue in the following pages that Vergil's pastoral-elegiac *Doloneia* figures a pessimistic view of his larger "translation" project, which attempts to revivify Greek forms in

Latin. Moreover, as I will show in the second half of the essay, at least one Renaissance poet seems to have read the *Aeneid* in a similar way: the Italian epicist Ludovico Ariosto. In his *Orlando Furioso* (1532), Ariosto imitates Vergil's Nisus and Euryalus as a way of figuring his own translation of classical material. But he also – unexpectedly – suggests the impossibility of such translation, and he does so partly by modulating from epic into elegiac and pastoral registers – or, as later Renaissance poets would (somewhat anachronistically) term it, into the register of pastoral elegy.[10]

Barbaric Spoils

We may as well begin with the preparations for the nighttime raid by Nisus and Euryalus. The raid has received considerable attention, particularly in critical debates over the moral implications of the Trojans' actions, which include killing several soldiers in their sleep and taking their armour.[11] I will not intervene in these debates here, but I do want to draw attention to the episode's repeated references to barbaric *arma* – which can be read as figures of translation. In terms of spoils, criticism has tended to focus on the armour taken from the slaughtered Rutulians, but it is worth remembering that these spoils are preceded by the gifts that Ascanius generously promises to Nisus and Euryalus as a reward for their mission.[12] In particular, Ascanius gives a set of artistic objects previously acquired through Trojan conquest (*A.* 9.263–6):

> bina dabo argento perfecta atque aspera signis
> pocula, deuicta gentior quae cepit Arisba,
> et tripodas geminos, auri duo magna talenta,
> cratera antiquum, quem dat Sidonia Dido.

A pair of goblets will I give, wrought in silver and rough with chasing, that he took when Arisba was vanquished; and two tripods, two great talents of gold, and an ancient bowl that Dido of Sidon gave.

Interestingly, although Ascanius indirectly reveals that the goblets contain figures (*signa*), no information about these images is ever given. Vergil forgoes the opportunity for an ecphrasis, even a characteristically brief one, and instead depicts the physical, material texture of the goblets. He also emphasizes the antiquity of the objects: the goblets are from a city no longer extant, and the bowl is *antiquum*. These are relics in the most literal sense. Thus, by giving the objects to Nisus and Euryalus, Ascanius symbolically gives them access to a cultural past that is nearly lost. In fact, the idea of recovery is made explicit and amplified in the preceding two lines, when

Ascanius defines the aim of the mission by using three different terms for "recover" (*A.* 9.261–2): *reuocate parentem, / reddite conspectum; nihil illo triste recepto* ("Recall my father, give him back to sight; with him recovered all grief vanishes"). This is a strange way for Ascanius to frame his request, since it is the Trojans in Latium, not Aeneas, who are in immediate danger. In effect, Ascanius casts the raid as a recovery mission, which has as its object a set of ancient, foreign artefacts – and Aeneas, a "lost father" who at the moment is surrounded by Greeks while learning ancient Greek and Trojan history.[13] Critics who argue that Nisus and Euryalus are primarily motivated by the pursuit of objects may be right, but this pursuit looks very different in the context of the symbolic meaning that Ascanius gives it.[14]

The second example of foreign spoils has a more prominent role in the narrative, though here again Vergil suggests the idea of a recovered artefact. We are told first that Nisus and Euryalus leave alone *multa arma* as they pass through the hordes of sleeping Rutulians. When Euryalus finally takes up a set of armour, Vergil takes the opportunity to describe its origins (*A.* 9.359–64):

> Euryalus phaleras Rhamnetis et aurea bullis
> cingula, Tiburti Remulo ditissimus olim
> quae mittit dona, hospitio cum iungeret absens,
> Caedicus; ille suo moriens dat habere nepoti;
> post mortem bello Rutuli pugnaque potiti:
> haec rapit atque umeris nequiquam fortibus aptat.

Euryalus takes the trappings of Rhamnes and his gold-studded swordbelt, gifts that of old wealthy Caedicus sent to Remulus of Tibur, when plighting friendship far away; he when dying gave them to his grandson for his own; after his death the Rutulians captured them in war and battle. These he tears away, and fits upon his valiant breast – all in vain.

In this condensed history, Vergil reveals that the armour was originally from Etruria before it was taken as spoils by the Rutulians.[15] In this light, there is something very poignant about Euryalus's attempt to fit on himself (*aptat*) Etruscan armour – especially after the revelations of Dardanus's Etruscan origins. Here, Euryalus mirrors Aeneas, who in Book 8 is also pondering Etruscan artefacts (8.310–12). At the same time the moment also recalls the end of Book 8, where another *dona parentis* is made the centre of attention. Aeneas's placement of the shield on his shoulder is mirrored by Euryalus' similar handling of Etruscan armour (*attollens umero*, 8.731; *umeris ... aptat*, 9.364), and both sets of armour arrest the viewer's attention with gleaming plumes (*terribilis cristis galeam*, 8.620; *galeam ... cristisque decoram*, 9.365). All three episodes are thus linked by the discovery of a dazzling, historical (in the fullest sense of the word) object.

I read these artefactual objects as figures of translation in the *Aeneid*. Such a figural significance for Aeneas' shield is clear enough in light of its conspicuous intertextual relationship to Homeric epic. The figural dimension of Euryalus' spoils is less explicit, but Vergil imbues the episode with several details that suggest a self-reflexive meaning. For example, Vergil gives a long description of the forest that momentarily hides Nisus and Euryalus – a landscape that generates the poem's most harrowing image of maze-like wandering (*A.* 9.381–93):

> silua fuit late dumis atque ilice nigra
> horrida, quam densi complebant undique sentes;
> rara per occultos lucebat semita calles.
> Euryalum tenebrae ramorum onerosaque praeda
> impediunt fallitque timor regione uiarum.
> Nisus abit. iamque imprudens euaserat hostis
> atque locos, qui post Albae de nomine dicti
> Albani (tum rex stabula alta Latinus habebat),
> ut stetit et frustra absentem respexit amicum:
> "Euryale infelix, qua te regione reliqui?
> quaue sequar, rursus perplexum iter omne reuoluens
> fallacis siluae?" simul et uestigia retro
> obseruata legit dumisque silentibus errat.

The forest spread wide with shaggy thickets and dark ilex; dense briers filled it on every side; here and there glimmered the path through the hidden glades. Euryalus is hampered by the shadowy branches and the burden of his spoil, and fear misleads him in the line of the paths. Nisus gets clear; and now, in heedless course, he had escaped the foe to the place afterward styled Alban from Alba's name – at that time King Latinus had there his stately halls – when he halted and looked back in vain for his lost friend. "Unhappy Euryalus, where have I left thee? Or where shall I follow, again unthreading all the tangled path of the treacherous wood?" Therewith he scans and retraces his footsteps, and wanders in the silent thickets.

Stephen Hinds persuasively and provocatively reads such landscapes as troping metaphors for intertextuality: "the landscape of ancient Italy serves to metaphorise a literary encounter between the poet of the *Aeneid* and his archaic predecessor in the Roman epic tradition." As Hinds explains, the self-reflexive dimension of these landscapes is registered (or "self-annotated," as he puts it) by Vergil's reference to *silua*, which "is used metaphorically in various contexts in Latin to represent ὕλη, in the sense [of] 'raw material.'"[16] In the specific case of the *silua oscura* in the middle of Book 9, I would argue that this "raw material" is Homeric epic, not least because of the unusually dense pattern of allusions to Homeric epic in this part of the poem – which many critics have noted, typically citing the *Doloneia* episode in Book 10 of the *Iliad*.[17] Vergil further intensifies the episode's metapoetic register by focusing the perspective of Nisus, who experiences the forest as the vestiges of a lost antiquity. Nisus' lament that he has left Euryalus in an unknown place (*qua te regione reliqui?*) activates one of the poem's most frequently used words for something lost in place or time, while his diligence in "reading footsteps" (*uestigia*) suggests the study of ancient material. In the metapoetic perspective, the *uestigia* that Nisus studies are thus the "traces" (*traccie*) of Homeric poetry that Alessandro Barchiesi sees scattered throughout the Vergilian text.[18] Put simply, Nisus is mired in ancient Greek epic. If, as Don Fowler has proposed, the Nisus and Euryalus episode is a *mise en abyme* for Vergil's literary project as a whole, then I would suggest that it frames this project – the imitation and transformation of Homeric epic models – as a profoundly ambitious exercise in literary and cultural translation.[19]

As a figure for a Hellenistic Vergil, Nisus (and, to a lesser extent, Euryalus) represents one of the poem's most pessimistic visions of translation. For Nisus does not only get lost in the wood – he gets supremely lost, finding only a lover's death at the moment he recovers Euryalus. Vergil's description of Nisus as "wandering" in the woods (*dumis silentibus errat*, 9.393) echoes the image of Aeneas wandering in the first half of the poem (*siluis … errat*, 1.578), and it also echoes Dido's scene of wandering in Book 4 (*illa fuga siluas saltusque peragrat*, 4.72). In this way, the figure of the wandering Nisus is linked to other elegiac gestures in the poem – as well as to gestures that incline toward pastoral. For example, the Dido passage echoed by Nisus is part of a larger simile that centres on the strangely hybrid figure of a "shepherd bearing weapons" (*pastor agens telis*, 4.71); Nisus himself will play the role of this armed shepherd, when, after wandering, he throws weapons of his own (*tela*, 9.409; *telum*, 9.417). The pastoral undercurrents in the scene of Nisus' wandering are signalled by echoes of the *Bucolics* (which I noted earlier) and even more so by echoes of Theocritus – notably *Idyll* 13, in which Hercules, searching for his beloved Hylas, is similarly described as wandering in the woods.[20] It is significant that Theocritus' Hylas himself has elegiac potential: he appears as the central object of desire in Propertius' Elegy 1.20, a poem which Jennifer Ingleheart singles out as being concerned with Hellenistic reception.[21] By translating Theocritus' Hylas into a context marked by generic mixing, Vergil looks also to Propertius' elegiac appropriation of the figure. In the larger picture, the multiple pastoral and elegiac episodes evoked in the Nisus and Euryalus episode – and the generic complexity of *those* episodes – suggests that the *silua oscura* in which Nisus loses himself is a landscape of generic confusion as well as of Greek intertextuality.

This dense pattern of allusion, along with the complex generic modulations that inflect it, enables Vergil to construct what I call a "poetics of translation" distinguished by its sense of loss. By this I mean a set of figures of loss that Vergil takes from pastoral and elegy and "activates" at crucial, intensely self-reflexive moments in the *Aeneid*. The epic mode, with its emphasis on foreign spoils and geographical movement, in turn refracts these figures of loss as a pessimistic commentary on the poem's own relationship to ancient Greek models – in other words, a commentary on the poem as a failed translation. That Vergil pessimistically figures his own poem is interesting in itself, but also significant is the fact that some Renaissance poets also recognized Vergil's poetics of translation and used it to think through their own relationship to antiquity. These poets also read the *silua oscura* in Book 9 as a figure for intertextuality, and they apprehend the elegiac and pastoral markers of loss that permeate this metapoetic forest. Above all, they remember that the *silua* that undoes Nisus and Euryalus is a *labyrinth*. In this way, it evokes the labyrinth that appears in Daedalus' engraving in the temple of Apollo in Book 6 – a work that also suggests a translation, an archaeological artefact, and an artistic failure. At the same time, these Renaissance poets remember that Vergilian labyrinths are visually resplendent. Whether marked by gleaming boys (*ante ora parentum … lucent*, 5.553–4), gleaming gold (*aurea tecta*, 6.13; *effingere in auro*, 6.32), or glittering spoils and glimmering trails (*radiisque aduersa refulsit*, 9.374; *rara per occultos lucebat semita calles*, 9.383), the poem's labyrinths are distinguished by their ability to confuse and dazzle simultaneously.[22] A translation failure may still stupefy its audience, and – for some poets – stupefaction is the very index of such a failure.

Elegiac Orlando

One of the earliest Renaissance poets to imitate the Nisus and Euryalus episode at length was Ludovico Ariosto, whose *Orlando Furioso* was completed in 1532. Almost as soon as it appeared, Ariosto's poem generated a fierce debate over the definition of epic, including whether or not *Orlando* should be considered an epic at all.[23] In this context, Ariosto's imitation of Nisus and Euryalus was pivotal. Defenders of the Italian poem argued for its epic status by pointing out its many imitations of Vergil. Not surprisingly, Ariosto's defenders almost always cite the Nisus and Euryalus episode, since it is the source of the longest Vergilian imitation in the *Orlando*, and since the episode was already known as "a topos in the epic tradition."[24]

Such defences were not limited to Italian critics. When John Harington published his English translation of the *Orlando Furioso* in 1591, he defended it by claiming that "whatsoever is praiseworthy in *Vergil* is plentifully to be found in *Ariosto*" and cited among others the Nisus and Euryalus episode.[25]

However, Ariosto does not make things easy for his defenders. While there is no question that his imitation of Nisus and Euryalus constitutes an "epic anchor" in the *Orlando Furioso*, his incorporation of the episode undercuts many of the arguments for the poem's epic status. Most notably, Medoro (the poem's Euryalus figure) does not die in Ariosto's poem. Instead, he is rescued from the brink of death by Angelica, who immediately falls in love with the eroticized Medoro. (Cloridan, the poem's Nisus figure, does not escape death.) At this point the narrative moves abruptly from a focus on warring armies to an elaborate account of Medoro and Angelica's love affair. In generic terms, Ariosto's poem veers from epic to love elegy. The unexpectedness of this generic shift is amplified by the fact that, up until Angelica's intervention, Ariosto also imitates Statius' Hopleus and Dymas episode in the *Thebaid*, another (and more generically faithful) imitation of Vergil's Nisus and Euryalus.[26] In effect, Ariosto undercuts both his Vergilian imitation and his "imitation of imitations," as Daniel Javitch terms Ariosto's keen attention to the Vergilian tradition.[27] Indeed, the Medoro and Angelica episode not only moves the poem into the elegiac mode – it alludes to *other* poems similarly contaminated by elegy. Eventually, Medoro and Angelica start carving their names on the bark of trees, an image that derives (as Ariosto's sixteenth-century commentators recognized) from *B.* 10, in which the elegiac poet Gallus carves his poems on slender trees (*tenerisque meos incidere amores / arboribus*, 53–4).[28]

Ariosto's striking revision of Vergil's Nisus and Euryalus is periodically cited as evidence of a preference for romance over epic, or a preference for Ovid over Vergil, or some other literary affiliation. This may all be true, yet discussions of Medoro and Angelica that emphasize their love affair sometimes take too little notice of the ramifications that follow in the poem. For, as I will show in the remainder of this essay, Ariosto circumscribes his account of Cloridan and Medoro, and his account of Medoro and Angelica, within a larger narrative arc that at many points evokes a self-reflexive commentary on humanist ideas about reading and translation.[29] Moreover, in taking this opportunity to figure his poem's relationship to its classical models, Ariosto also recalls the pessimistic view of translation that the Vergilian episode more subtly suggests. In this way, Ariosto's turn to the elegiac mode represents not so much a whimsical abandonment of epic as it does a very serious understanding of the uses to which Vergil puts elegy and pastoral in *Aeneid* 9.

Ariosto's imitation of the Nisus and Euryalus episode begins in Canto 18 of the *Orlando Furioso*, with the death of the African commander Dardinel. At the moment of Dardinel's death, Ariosto makes a brief but clear allusion to the *Aeneid* (*OF* 18.153):

> Como purpureo fior languendo muore,
> che 'l vomere al passar tagliato lassa;
> o come carco di superchio umore
> il papaver ne l'orto il capo abbassa:
> cosí, giú de la faccia ogni colore
> cadendo, Dardinel di vita passa.

As a purple flower fades and dies if the ploughshare has severed it in passing; or as a poppy in a meadow hangs its head if it be weighed down with overmuch moisture: so, as all colour drained from Dardinel's face, he departed this life.[30]

As Javitch and others have noted, the Vergilian passage imitated here – the description of Euryalus' death in *Aeneid* 9 – is itself an imitation of Homer's *Iliad* and Catullus' eleventh poem.[31] The densely layered intertextuality of the allusion, along with Ariosto's reference to "human creativity" (*umano ingegno*, 18.154) in the first line of the next stanza, provokes questions about poetic imitation and originality. Accordingly, the allusion sets the stage for Ariosto's Cloridan and Medoro, easily recognized as an imitation of Vergil's Nisus and Euryalus. The two are African soldiers who, in their attempt to recover the dead body of their commander, perform a nighttime raid on the Christian army. The soldiers slaughter several sleeping Christians before they find Dardinel, at which point they are seen and pursued by returning Christian knights. Cloridan manages to escape, but Medoro (who is carrying Dardinel's body) is hindered and caught by the Christians. Cloridan makes a futile attempt to rescue Medoro and ends up dying on the pierced, bleeding body of Medoro.

Before Cloridan's death (and Medoro's revival), Ariosto closely follows Vergil's description of the wood in which the soldiers lose themselves (*OF* 18.192):

> Era a quel tempo ivi una selva antica,
> d'ombrose piante spessa e di virgulti,
> che, come labirinto, entro s'intrica
> di stretti calli e sol da bestie culti.

In those days there was an ancient wood there, thickly planted with shady trees and shrubs; it formed a labyrinth of narrow paths and was frequented only by wild beasts.

Ariosto's *selva antica* echoes Vergil's *antiqua silua*, while his description of the wood as a labyrinth recalls Vergil's association of the *silua* with Daedalian labyrinths. In effect, Ariosto tropes the *selva antica* as a poetic encounter with antiquity – and thus a figure for his own relation to Vergil.[32] Moreover, even when Ariosto strays from the Vergilian model and focuses on Medoro and Angelica's love affair, he makes it clear that Vergilian topography still dominates the scene. Medoro and Angelica consummate their relationship in a cave that is lifted directly from Book 4 of the *Aeneid* (*OF* 19.35): *un antro li copriva, / forse non men di quel commodo e grato, / ch'ebber, fuggendo l'acque, Enea e Dido* ("A cave enclosed them, hardly less comfortable and welcoming than that which received Aeneas and Dido fleeing the storm").

This densely Vergilian – and generically layered – landscape is Ariosto's carefully orchestrated setting for the entrance of Orlando, the poem's eponymous figure, who, like most of the knights in the poem, is also in love with Angelica. In Canto 23, soon after entering the wood, Orlando learns about Angelica's affair and loses his mind as a result. Self-reflexive as the earlier moments are, the scene of Orlando's discovery is even more so. For one thing, Ariosto represents Orlando's discovery as an act of *reading*. First, Orlando sees and reads the names "Angelica" and "Medoro" carved hundreds of times on trees in the wood. He then sees the same names, along with a poem by Medoro, inscribed on the cave where Angelica and Medoro consummated their relationship. The scene is rife with typical Ariostan humour (at Orlando's expense), though more striking is the emphasis that Ariosto places on the graphic, material quality of the inscriptions. The names carved on the trees and cave are "tied together in a hundred knots" (*con cento nodi / legati insieme*, 23.103) and carved into the tree's "bark" (*scorza*, 23.103). Ariosto describes the effect of the inscriptions on Orlando with a simile that also suggests visually the jagged shape of the individual letters: "There were as many letters as there were nails with which Amor stung and wounded his heart" (*Quante lettere son, tanti son chiodi / coi quali Amore il cor gli punge e fiede*, 23.103). Likewise, Ariosto's description of the cave's inscriptions dwells on the sensuous perception of their textural, pigmentary features: they are written "some with coal and some with chalk, and some with the point of a knife inscribed" (*qual con carbone e qual con gesso, / e qual con punte di coltelli impresso*, 23.106), and they have evidently been "freshly carved" (*parean scritta allotta*, 23.107).[33] Ariosto elides this graphic sense of the inscriptions with the surrounding landscape, and it is here for the first time that he specifies the topographical layout of the wood's prominent features (*OF* 23.105–6): *Orlando viene ove s'incurva il monte / a guisa d'arco in sua la chiara fonte. / Aveano in su l'entrata il luogo adorno / coi piedi storti edere e viti erranti* ("Orlando came to where a bow-shaped curve in the hillside made a cave overlooking the clear spring. Twisting on their stems, ivy and rambling vines adorned the entrance"). The artfulness of this landscape makes its description sound like an ecphrasis – and essentially it is. As he does so often in the *Furioso*, Ariosto pushes the boundaries of ecphrasis. Here, inscription and landscape are treated as ecphrastic objects, while for Orlando, reading Angelica's and Medoro's writing becomes inseparable from seeing their writing *as* image.

Many of the details that Ariosto adds to his *selva antica* are also designed to emphasize the visuality of reading, or to represent reading in visual terms. For example, his placing of a "clear spring" (*chiara fonte*) below the fateful cave activates a common humanist metaphor for poetic inspiration, though in a way that transforms the metaphor into an unusually literalizing emblem: the poetic source (*fonte*) at the base of his epic imitation (Dido's cave). The encircling ivy further evokes the border of a tapestry or the decorative border of a title page. In a sense, Ariosto renders the "raw matter" of Vergilian poetry *as* topographical matter. Put another way, he represents the Vergilian text as the object of a literal *translation* – that is, a physical transferral.

The climax of this metapoetic tour occurs when Orlando enters the cave and discovers a complete poem carved by Medoro. At this moment Ariosto moves even more resolutely into elegiac and pastoral registers (*OF* 23.108):

> Liete piante, verdi erbe, limpide acque,
> Spelunca opaca e di fredde ombra grata,
> Dove la bella Angelica che nacque
> Di Galafron, da molti in vano amata,
> Spesso ne le mie braccia nuda giacque …

Happy plants, verdant grass, limpid waters, dark, shadowy cave, pleasant and cool, where fair Angelica, born of Galafron, and loved in vain by many, often lay naked in my arms …

The poem goes on for nine more lines. Both Ariosto's sixteenth-century commentators and modern critics have noted the passage's imitation of Vergilian pastoral (along with its debts to Ovid and Petrarch), including the prominence of *B*. 10 with its incorporation, or translation, of Gallus' elegy.[34] Indeed, in imitating a Vergilian mode of elegiac pastoral, Ariosto seems to confirm Propertius' view of Vergilian pastoral as having an "elegiac sensibility" (as Donncha O'Rourke has put it).[35] Likewise, Medoro's poem confirms that this *selva antica*, for all of its epic signposts, was elegiac pastoral all along. If the inclusion of Gallus in *Bucolics* 10 is designed to assert Vergil's superiority over his poetic models (as Servius and others argued),[36] then Ariosto's inclusion of both Vergilian elegy and pastoral in his *Orlando Furioso* might likewise be read as a triumphalist feat of imitation – as the translation of all three Vergilian registers into Italian ottava rima.

Except that Medoro's poem is not in Italian. Ariosto builds the noise of Vergilian intertextuality to a fever pitch before dropping a bombshell about Medoro's poem (*OF* 23.110): *Era scritto in arabico* ("It was written in Arabic"). What first appears to be an Italian transcription is revealed to be translation from Arabic. By placing this information after the poem, Ariosto creates an elaborate bait-and-switch game which goads his humanist reader to see familiar Vergilian matter, only then to be *alienated* from that matter. At this point other details about the *selva* become more meaningful. Ariosto had previously told his reader that the inscriptions on the trees and cave "were inscribed a thousand times ... tied together in various ways in varying knots" (*in mille luoghi scritto ... in vari modi / Legati insieme di diversi nodi*, 19.36). Describing the inscriptions a second time, he again notes that they are "tied together in a hundred knots" (*con cento nodi*). Ariosto frequently represents writing as image in his poem, but this is the only instance where he does so twice, and with so much detail. The point, I believe, is to make Medoro's writing look like an arabesque. Put another way, Ariosto material-izes Vergilian matter in his Italian landscape and then "orientalizes" it. As a result, the foreignness, or inscrutability, of this text is inextricably bound with its status as a visual, material, ecphrastic object.

The idea that Ariosto intends his figuration of Vergilian matter as a com-mentary on humanist philology and translation is bolstered by the fact that he puts Orlando, rather than any other character in the poem, at the centre of this *selva oscura*. It is Orlando whom Ariosto repeatedly identifies as the poem's chief linguist – as when Orlando uses his linguistic training to infil-trate a Moorish camp with ease (*OF* 9.5):

> e ben lo potea far sicuramente,
> avendo indosso l'abito arabesco;
> et aiutollo in questo parimente,
> che sapeva altro idioma che francesco,
> e l'africano tanto avea espedito,
> che parea nato a Tripoli e nutrito.

This he could safely do, dressed as he was in Arab costume. He was also aided by the fact that French was not his only tongue: he spoke African with such fluency that he could have passed for a native of Tripoli.

Ariosto reminds his reader of Orlando's linguistic fluency again when he reveals that Medoro's poem is in Arabic (*OF* 23.110): *Era scritto in arabico, che 'l conte / intendea cosí ben come latino, / Fra molte lingue e molte ch'avea pronte, / Prontissima avea quella il Paladino* ("It was written in Arabic, which the count understood as well as Latin. He knew many and many a tongue, but Arabic is one with which he was most familiar"). In this respect, Orlando is the poem's quintessential figure of a humanist, able to read the *uestigia* embedded in the landscape and reconstruct an accurate history of the past, recovering not only the meaning of foreign inscriptions but also the feelings and sensations of its writers (as Poliziano urged his students to do).[37] Given this building up of Orlando's philological credentials, it is all the more surprising when his expert reading – and rereading – of Medoro's poem leads to a debilitating stasis (23.111–18):

> Tre volte e quattro e sei lesse lo scritto
> quello infelice, e pur cercando invano
> che non vi fosse quel che v'era scritto;
> e sempre lo vedea piú chiaro e piano:
> et ogni volta in mezzo il petto afflitto
> stringersi il cor sentia con fredda mano.
> Rimase al fin con gli occhi e con la mente
> fissi nel sasso, al sasso indifferente.

Three and four times the unfortunate man re-read the inscription, trying in vain to wish it away, but it was more plain and clear each time he read it. And each time, he felt a cold hand clutch his heart in his afflicted breast. Finally he fell to gazing fixedly at the stone – stone-like himself.

Ariosto here plays on the term *chiaro*, a word which, for humanists like Petrarch, signals classical eloquence. As Orlando goes from *reading* the poem to merely *looking* at it, the meaning of *chiaro* changes from "intelligible" to "visually gleaming." That is, Ariosto wittily literalizes the humanist term before our eyes, making Medoro's poem crystalline in the most literal sense. Further, Orlando's visual stupefaction is magnified as he himself begins to resemble the stone that he scrutinizes (*fissi nel sasso, al sasso indifferente*). It is no coincidence that this moment marks the first stirrings of Orlando's madness and his alienation from the reader. The palindromic structure of the stanza's final line foregrounds the visual quality of Ariosto's own text, as if to suggest that the reader of the *Orlando Furioso* is also seeing, rather than understanding, a work of translation. The poem's meaning – whatever it is or was – has vanished behind the graphic material of its inscription.

Taken all together, Ariosto's representation of Orlando's reading constitutes a profoundly pessimistic vision of the humanist project. This image is a self-incriminating figure that calls into question Ariosto's own effort to translate Vergilian epic to Renaissance Italy – a project whose humanist credentials are stated more confidently by Ariosto's defenders than by Ariosto himself. While Orlando eventually recovers his sanity, his descent into madness – which Ariosto places deliberately at the very centre of his poem – raises lingering, ineradicable doubts about what it means to try to read and understand an ancient or foreign text.[38] It is supremely ironic, then, that Ariosto seems to have learned this pessimism from Vergil: Orlando gazing stonily at Arabic inscriptions is an imitation of Aeneas gazing at Daedalian labyrinths. Ariosto recognizes Vergil's figures of translation and amplifies their pessimistic potential. In a word, Ariosto's deeply philological reading of Vergil teaches him the limitations, if the not the futility, of philology. Likewise, in sensitively apprehending and imitating Vergil's modulation between epic and elegiac registers, Ariosto seems to have understood that Vergil's poetics of translation was always already a poetics of loss.

There is a final, less conspicuous, irony in the idea that these pessimistic figures of translation in Vergil and Ariosto are marked by turns to the elegiac mode, given that the meaning of elegy itself undergoes a transformation in Renaissance Europe. While Vergil and Ariosto enmeshed pastoral with elegiac strains, later Renaissance poets would come up with a different notion of elegiac pastoral – one that had little to do with the erotic poetry of Ovid, Propertius, or Gallus, but much to do with the poetics of loss. When Ariosto's contemporary, the Italian poet Jacopo Sannazaro, wrote his *Arcadia*, he drew on Vergilian and Theocritean pastoral while amplifying their sense of mourning. This convention of a pastoral elegy caught on, and nowhere more so than in England, where poets from Spenser to Donne used the term "pastoral elegy" to denote a poem about lamenting shepherds, often funereal in tone. The instability of the term across languages is put into relief by John Milton, whose classical learning had few equals. In his Latin *Elegia* 1, he mixes Vergilian pastoral with Ovid's *Amores* while calling attention to his elegiac couplets; yet it is his English *Lycidas*, a pastoral-funeral poem, that immediately becomes the model for "pastoral elegy."[39] Even now, the situation is such that classical scholars are likely to call *Lycidas* a "pastoral lament," while Renaissance scholars comfortably place it in a "pastoral elegy" tradition that begins with Theocritus and Vergil.[40] Proponents of the funereal "elegy" at times will say the usage recuperates an older Hellenistic meaning – even an ancient etymology – though there remains the nagging possibility that the early modern "elegy" is fundamentally an anachronism, if not a mistranslation.

NOTES

1 All quotations and translations of Vergil's works are taken from Fairclough, rev. Goold 1999.

2 Reed 2007: 25–6.

3 The funerary associations of elegy are more prominent in Hellenistic poetry than in Latin poetry, though, as many critics have pointed out, Latin poets were well aware of the funerary origins of elegy and of Latin elegy's capacity to speak in this register. See Papanghelis 1987; Yardley 1996; Ramsby 2007; Houghton 2011; Keith 2011a; Gladhill in this volume, who also discusses Nisus and Euryalus.

4 See *B*. 1.41–2: *Quid facerem? neque seruitio me exire licebat, / nec tam praesentis alibi cognoscere diuos* ("What could I do? I could neither leave my slavery nor elsewhere find gods of such ready aid"); *B*. 7.14–15: *Quid facerem? neque ego Alcippen, nec Phyllida habebam / depulsos a lacte domi quae clauderet agnos* ("What could I do? I had neither Alcippe nor Phyllis at home to pen my lambs, newly weaned from their mother's milk"). In the first instance Tityrus' lament is sincere, though in the second Meliboeus is being rhetorical.

5 See Reed 2007: 16–23.

6 McCallum 2015: 703. Although her essay does not discuss the Nisus and Euryalus episode, she does note the episode's elegiac aspects. See also McCallum in this volume and forthcoming. Beck 2015 and Griffith 1985 detect a mixing of epic and lyric allusions in Euryalus' flower simile. As McCallum 2015 and Beck note, studies of elegy in the *Aeneid* have tended to focus on Dido in Book 4. See Harrison 2007a: 210–14 and Cairns 1989: 129–50.

7 Guy-Bray 2002: 19. On the pervasiveness of elegy in the *Bucolics*, see Kenney 1983; cf. Henkel, Pietropaolo, and Fabre-Serris in this volume.

8 Hubbard 1995: 38. Hubbard refers here to an argument he makes at length in the first chapter of Hubbard 1998.

9 Leach 1974: 113.

10 The potentially anachronistic nature of the term "pastoral elegy" points more to a change in the meaning of "elegy" rather than "pastoral," particularly between classical Latin and English Renaissance poets. It also points to the fact that Renaissance poets did not generally use metrical schemes to make generic distinctions. For more on the Renaissance reworking of these classical genres, see Hanford 1910 and Alpers 1996.

11 Makowski 1989 recounts most twentieth-century criticism of the episode, which is often critical of the Trojans, arguing that Vergil intends Nisus and Euryalus as *erastes* and *eromenos* in a Platonic (not platonic) relationship that ends nobly in an *aristeia*. More recently, Casali 2004 argues that the divergent critical reactions to the episode are an effect of the text itself, which is marked by contradictory motifs and imitations.

12 See, however, Casali 2004: 327–35, who discusses at length the spoils
promised by Ascanius to Nisus and Euryalus, focusing on the dense
intertextual relationship between this passage and both Homer's *Iliad* and
ancient criticism of Homer. See also Pavlock 1985: 212, who argues that
the allusions to Euripides' *Rhesus* in the episode contribute to the sense that
Ascanius's gift giving is an appeal to material greed.

13 Casali 2004: 334 notes that the idea of recovering a lost father or homeland
may be suggested in the passage in another way, since Ascanius' mention of
Arisba (a reference which has confounded modern critics) may call to mind
Hyrtacus of Arisba (mentioned in the *Iliad*) and since Nisus is called *Hyrtacides*
earlier in the *Aeneid* (9.234).

14 The association of historical recovery with Ascanius, Nisus, and Euryalus is
suggested twice earlier in Book 5, during the foot-race and the *lusus Troiae*.
In both of these instances, the figurative significance of the event is signalled
by references to *uestigia*, which the three Trojans either successfully or
unsuccessfully retrace: *hic iuuenis iam uictor ouans uestigia presso / haud tenuit
titubata solo* (5.330–1); *haud alio Teucrum nati uestigia cursu / impediunt
texuntque fugas et proelia ludo* (5.592–3).

15 Hardie 1994: 138–9 notes that the specific chain of acquisition outlined in
the passage has been an "insoluble problem" for Vergilian critics since Servius,
though there seems to be little doubt about Etruria as a starting point.

16 Hinds 1998: 13.

17 For example, Hardie 1994: 8–10 reads Book 9 as the poem's most sustained
imitation of Homer. Reed 2007: 16 includes Euryalus among a handful of
characters in the poem who "embod[y] a quintessentially Greek and essentially
Oriental stereotype." See also Rabel 1974, who argues that the imitation of
Homer in Book 9 extends beyond character or plot. Taking a different (though
very influential) approach, Schlunk 1974: 59–81 emphasizes the differences
between the episode and its Iliadic models, though he suggests these
differences stem partly from Vergil's engagement with ancient scholarship
on Homer. Schmit-Neuerberg 1999: 23–65 also sees Vergil as responding
to ancient Homeric scholarship, though he argues that Vergil's revision is
designed to make Nisus and Euryalus more sympathetic than their Homeric
forebears.

18 See Hinds 1998: 101.

19 Fowler 2000: 90.

20 See Blum-Sorensen in this volume.

21 See Ingleheart 2015.

22 See Doob 1990: 28–9, who also comments on the disorienting and self-reflexive
aspects of Vergilian labyrinths. As Theodorakopoulos 2000: 129–34 shows,
Vergil's use of the labyrinth as a figure for intertextuality and literary imitation
owes much to the representation of the Daedalian labyrinth in Catullus 64.

23 The definitive account of the sixteenth-century debates over Ariosto is Javitch 1991.

24 Whittington 2010: 593n15.

25 Harington 1591: Sig. 3¶iiii(r).

26 On Statius' engagements with epic and elegy, see De Cristofaro in this volume.

27 Javitch 1985.

28 Ariosto's imitation of Nisus and Euryalus, which occupies much of Cantos 18 and 19, has generated much critical discussion for the ways in which it revises and diverges from Vergil. See, for example, Feinstein 1990.

29 The landmark study of the poem as a response to Renaissance humanist education is Ascoli 1987. For an overview of the kind of humanist education with which Ariosto was likely most familiar, see Looney 2003.

30 All quotations of Ariosto are from Papini 1957. Translations are from Waldman 1974 unless otherwise noted.

31 See Javitch 1985: 217–19. Javitch notes that this genealogy of Ariosto's simile was recognized as early as 1584, and he notes a possible fourth source in Ovid.

32 If the intertextual nature of the terrain were not evident enough, Ariosto cheekily suggests the presence of Vergil through a clever wordplay on *uirgulti*.

33 See Marcus 1993, who offers a perceptive reading of the material qualities of the inscriptions in relation to Angelica's bodily experience.

34 See Shapiro 1988: 132–5; Looney 1996: 19–21; Bigi 1982: 995.

35 O'Rourke 2011a.

36 See Perkell 1996: 132–3.

37 See Grafton 1991: 8, 25.

38 Interestingly, when Orlando is restored, he speaks only Vergilian Latin – as if to underscore the idea that one cannot truly inhabit two worlds, or two languages.

39 On the unstable meanings of "elegy" and "pastoral elegy" over time, see also Miller 2010 and Watterson 2010. On Sannazaro, see also Fabre-Serris, Roman, and Miletti in this volume.

40 See Reed 2014.

WORKS CITED

Abbamonte, G. 2015. "Naples – a Poet's City: Attitudes towards Statius and Virgil in the Fifteenth Century." In Hughes and Buongiovanni, 170–88.

Abbamonte, G., and F. Stok. 2021. "Teaching Strategies in Servius' Commentary." *Maia* 73: 365–84.

Acosta-Hughes, B. 2006. "Bucolic Singers of the Short Song: Lyric and Elegiac Resonances in Theocritus' Bucolic *Idylls*." In Fantuzzi and Papanghelis, 25–52.

Acosta-Hughes, B., and S. Stephens. 2012. *Callimachus in Context*. Cambridge.

Adams, J.N. 1982. *The Latin Sexual Vocabulary*. Baltimore.

Ahl, F.M. 1976. *Lucan: An Introduction*. Ithaca.

Ahl, F.M., trans. 1985. *Virgil, Aeneid*. Oxford.

Alexiou, M. 1974. *The Ritual Lament in Greek Tradition*. Oxford.

Alexopoulou, M. 2009. *The Theme of Returning Home in Ancient Greek Literature: The* Nostos *of the Epic Heroes*. Lewiston, NY.

Allen, T., ed. 1917–20. *Homeri Opera*. 4 vols. Oxford.

Alpers, P. 1979. *The Singer of the Eclogues: A Study of Virgilian Pastoral*. Berkeley.

– 1982. "What Is Pastoral?" *Critical Inquiry* 8.3: 437–60.

Altheim, F. 1938. *A History of Roman Religion*. London.

Alton, E.H., D.E.W. Wormell, and E. Courtney. 1985. *P. Ovidi Nasonis Fastorum libri sex*. Leipzig.

Anagnostou-Laoutides, E. 2013 [2005]. *Eros and Ritual in Ancient Literature: Singing of Atalanta, Daphnis and Orpheus*. Piscataway, NJ.

– 2017. "Drunk with Blood: The Role of Platonic Baccheia in Lucan and Statius." *Latomus* 76.2: 304–23.

– 2020. "Vergil on Tyrants and Suppliants: Greek Tragedy and the End of the *Aeneid*." *GIF* 72: 137–78. https://doi.org/10.1484/j.gif.5.121458.

– 2021. "Tyrants and Saviours in Pan. Lat. XII(9): Pro-Constantinian Readings of the Aeneid." *JLA* 14.1: 75–96. https://doi.org/10.1353/jla.2021.0005.

Anagnostou-Laoutides, E., and D. Konstan. 2013. "Apollonius Rhodius, Cyzicus and the Near East." *GIF* 65: 30–72.

Anderson, G. 2005. "Before Turannoi Were Tyrants: Rethinking a Chapter of Early Greek History." *CA* 24.2: 173–222. https://doi.org/10.1525/ca.2005.24.2.173.

Anderson, R.D., P.J. Parsons, and R.G.M. Nisbet. 1979. "Elegiacs by Gallus from Qaṣr Ibrîm." *JRS* 69: 125–55. https://doi.org/10.2307/299064.

Anderson, W.S. 1957. "Vergil's Second *Iliad*." *TAPhA* 88: 17–30. https://doi.org/10.2307/283889.

– 1958. "Juno and Saturn in the *Aeneid*." *Studies in Philology* 55: 519–27.

André, J.-M. 1949. *La vie et l'oeuvre d'Asinius Pollion*. Paris.

Angeli, A., and M. Rispoli. 1996. "La ricomposizione del quarto libro del trattato di Filodemo sulla musica." *ZPE* 114: 67–95.

Ankarloo, B., and S. Clark, eds. 1999. *Witchcraft and Magic in Europe: Ancient Greece and Rome*. Philadelphia.

Annus, A. 2008. "The Soul's Journey and Tauroctony: On Babylonian Sediment in the Syncretic Religious Doctrines of Late Antiquity." In M.L.G. Dietrich, T. Kulmar, and T. Münster, eds., *Body and Soul in the Conceptions of the Religions*. 1–46. Ugarit.

Armstrong, D. 1986. "Stylistics and the Date of Calpurnius Siculus." *Philologus* 130: 113–36. https://doi.org/10.1524/phil.1986.130.12.113.

Armstrong, D., J. Fish, P.A. Johnston, and M.B. Skinner, eds. 2004. *Vergil, Philodemus and the Augustans*. Austin, TX.

Armstrong, R. 2006. *Cretan Women: Pasiphaë, Ariadne, and Phaedra in Latin Poetry*. Oxford.

Arnaldi, F., L.G. Rosa, and L. Monti Sabia, eds. 1964. *Poeti latini del Quattrocento*. Milan.

Arweiler, A. 2006. "Erichtho und die Figuren der Entzweiung. Vorüberlegungen zu einer Poetik der Emergenz in Lucans *Bellum Civile*." *Dictynna* 3: 3–69. https://doi.org/10.4000/dictynna.202.

Ascoli, A.R. 1987. *Ariosto's Bitter Harmony: Crisis and Evasion in the Italian Renaissance*. Princeton.

Augoustakis, A. 2003. "*Lugendam Formae Sine Virginitate Reliquit*: Reading Pyrene and the Transformation of Landscape in Silius' *Punica* 3." *AJP* 124: 235–57. https://doi.org/10.1353/ajp.2003.0027.

– 2006. "Cutting Down the Grove in Lucan, Valerius Maximus, and Cassius Dio." *CQ* 56: 634–8. https://doi.org/10.1017/s0009838806000711.

Austin, R.G. 1971. *P. Vergili Maronis Aeneidos Liber Primus*. Oxford.

– 1986. Aeneidos: *Liber Sextus*. Oxford.

– 2004. Aeneidos: *Liber Primus*. Oxford.

Averett, E.W. 2015. "Masks and Ritual Performance on the Island of Cyprus." *AJA* 119: 3–45. https://doi.org/10.3764/aja.119.1.0003.

Bachvarova, M., D. Dutsch, and A. Suter, eds. 2016. *The Fall of Cities in the Mediterranean: Commemoration in Literature, Folk-Song, and Liturgy.* Cambridge.

Ball, R.J. 1975. "Tibullus 2.5 and Vergil's *Aeneid.*" *Vergilius* 21: 33–50.

Baraz, Y. 2015. "Sound and Silence in Calpurnius Siculus." *AJP* 136: 91–120. https://doi.org/10.1353/ajp.2015.0003.

– 2018. "*Certare alterno carmine*: The Rise and Fall of Bucolic Competition." In C. Damon and C. Pieper, eds., *Eris vs. Aemulatio: Valuing Competition in Classical Antiquity*, 78–97. Leiden.

Barchiesi, A. 1979. "Palinuro e Caieta. Due 'epigrammi' Vergiliani (*Aen.* VI 870 sg.; VII 1–4)." *Maia* 31: 3–11.

– 1994. "Alcune difficoltà nella carriera di un poeta giambico. Giambo ed elegia nell'*Epodo* XI." In R. Cortés Tovar and J.C. Fernández Corte, eds., *Bimilenario de Horacio*, 127–38. Salamanca.

– 1997a. "*Elegia.*" In S. Mariotti, ed., *Orazio: Enciclopedia Oraziana*, 2.42–4. Rome.

– 1997b. *The Poet and the Prince: Ovid and the Augustan Discourse.* Berkeley.

– 2000. "Genealogie letterarie nell'epica imperiale. Fondamentalismo e ironia." In *L'Histoire Litteraire Immanente dans la Poesie Latine*, 315–54. Entretiens Hardt Tome XLVII. Geneva/Vandoeuvres.

– 2001. *Speaking Volumes: Narrative and Intertext in Ovid and Other Latin Poets.* London.

– 2015. *Homeric Effects in Vergil's Narrative.* Princeton.

Barchiesi, A., and P. Hardie. 2010. "The Ovidian Career Model: Ovid, Gallus, Apuleius, Boccaccio." In Hardie and Moore, 59–88. https://doi.org/10.1017/cbo9780511778872.006.

Barrett, A.A. 1970. "Anna's Conduct in *Aeneid* 4." *Vergilius* 16: 21–5.

Barringer, J.M. 1996. "Atalanta as Model: The Hunter and the Hunted." *CA* 15.1: 48–76.

– 2001. *The Hunt in Ancient Greece.* Baltimore.

Barthes, R. 1977. *Fragments d'un discours amoureux.* Paris.

Basson, W.P. 1975. *Pivotal Catalogues in the* Aeneid. Amsterdam.

Batinski, E. 1993. "Julia in Lucan's Tripartite Vision of the Dead Republic." In M. DeForest, ed., *Woman's Power, Man's Game: Essays on Classical Antiquity in Honor of Joy K. King*, 165–93. Wauconda.

Bausi, F., ed. 1996. *Angelo Poliziano: Silvae.* Florence.

Beard, M. 1987. "A Complex of Times: No More Sheep on Romulus' Birthday." *PCPS* 33: 1–15. https://doi.org/10.1017/s0068673500004892.

– 2007. *The Roman Triumph.* Cambridge, MA.

Beck, D. 2015. "Elegy and Epic in the *Aeneid.*" Presented at the Society for Classical Studies Annual Meeting. 8–11 January 2015. New Orleans.

Beckby, H. 1975. *Die griechischen Bukoliker.* Meisenheim am Glan.

Becker, G. 2012. *Titus Calpurnius Siculus: Kommentar zur 5. und 6. Ekloge.* Trier.

Benediktson, D.T. 1985. "Propertius' 'Elegiacization' of Homer." *Maia* 37: 17–26.

Bentley, J.H. 1987. *Politics and Culture in Renaissance Naples*. Princeton.

Berthet, J.F. 1980. "Properce et Homère." In A. Thill, ed., *L'élégie romaine: enracinement, thèmes, diffusion*, 141–55. Paris.

– 1987. "Encore Properce et Homere." *BFLM* 75: 55–62.

Beyer, A. 2000. *Parthenope: Neapel und der Süden der Renaissance*. Munich.

Bigi, E., ed. 1982. *Ludovico Ariosto*, Orlando Furioso. Milan.

Blänsdorf, J. 2010. "Dal segno alla scrittura. Le defixiones della fontana di Anna Perenna." In *Fattura scritta. Tecnica grafica e rituali magici nel mondo antico. Atti Convegno Università La Sapienza di Roma (Roma 2009)*, 35–64. Rome.

– 2015. "Gods and Demons in Texts: Figures and Symbols of the Defixion Inscriptions of the Nymphaeum of Anna Perenna at Rome." In F. Carlà and I. Berti, eds., *Ancient Magic and the Supernatural in the Modern Visual and Performing Arts*, 19–37. London and New York.

Bolt, T.J. 2019. "Theomachy in Greek and Roman Epic." In C. Reitz and S. Finkmann, eds., *Structures of Epic Poetry, vol. II.1: Configuration*, 283–316. Berlin and Boston.

Bömer, F., ed. 1957. *P. Ovidius Naso. Die* Fasten. *Band I: Einleitung, Text und Übersetzung*. Heidelberg.

– ed. 1958. *P. Ovidius Naso. Die* Fasten. *Band II: Kommentar*. Heidelberg.

– ed. 1982. *P. Ovidius Naso*, Metamorphosen. *Buch XII–XIII*. Heidelberg.

Bonaria, M. 1965. *I Mimi Romani*. Rome.

Bonfante, L., and J.L. Sebesta, eds. 2001. *The World of Roman Costume*. Madison.

Bonifazi, A. 2008. "Early Greek Explorations across the Mediterranean and the Semantics of *Nostos* in Homer." In E. Cingano and L. Milano, eds., *Papers on Ancient Literatures: Greece, Rome, and the Near East*, 105–33. Padua.

– 2009. "Inquiring into *Nostos* and Its Cognates." *AJP* 130: 481–510. https://doi.org/10.1353/ajp.0.0078.

Bonjour, M. 1976. *Terre Natale: Études sur un Composante Affective du Patriotisme Romain*. Paris.

Boucher, J.P. 1966. *Caius Cornélius Gallus*. Paris.

Bowditch, P.L. 2001. *Horace and the Gift Economy of Patronage*. Berkeley.

– 2006. "Propertius and the Gendered Rhetoric of Luxury and Empire: A Reading of 2.16." *CLS* 43: 306–25. https://doi.org/10.2307/complitstudies.43.3.0306.

– 2012. "Roman Love Elegy and the Eros of the Empire." In Gold, 119–33. https://doi.org/10.1002/9781118241165.ch8.

Bowie, E. 1985. "Theocritus' Seventh *Idyll*, Philetas and Longus." *CQ* 35: 67–81. https://doi.org/10.1017/s0009838800014580.

Boyd, B.W. 1990. "*Non hortamine longo*: An Ovidian 'Correction' of Virgil." *AJP* 111: 82–5. https://doi.org/10.2307/295262.

– 1997. *Ovid's Literary Loves: Influence and Innovation in the* Amores. Ann Arbor.

– 2000. "'*Celabitur auctor*': The Crisis of Authority and Narrative Patterning in Ovid, *Fasti* 5." *Phoenix* 54: 64–98. https://doi.org/10.2307/1089091.

– 2002. "'When Ovid Reads Vergil …': A Response and Some Observations." *Vergilius* 48: 123–30.

– 2010. "Island Hopping: Ovid's Ariadne and Her Texts." In Boyd and Fox, 225–33.

– 2017. *Ovid's Homer: Authority, Repetition, and Reception.* Oxford.

Boyd, B.W., and C. Fox, eds. 2010. *Approaches to Teaching the Works of Ovid and the Ovidian Tradition.* New York.

Boyle, A.J., ed. 1990. *The Imperial Muse.* Victoria.

Bradshaw, A. 2002. "Horace's Birthday and Deathday." In T. Woodman and D. Feeney, eds., *Traditions and Contexts in the Poetry of Horace*, 1–16. Cambridge.

Brandt, E. 1928. "Zum Aeneis-prooemium." *Philologus* 83: 331–5. https://doi.org/10.1524/phil.1928.83.14.335.

Braund, S. 2019. "Virgil and the Cosmos: Religious and Philosophical Ideas." In Mac Góráin and Martindale, 279–98.

Breed, B.W. 2006a. *Pastoral Inscriptions: Reading and Writing Vergil's* Eclogues. London.

– 2006b. "Time and Textuality in the Book of *Eclogues*." In Fantuzzi and Papanghelis, 333–67.

Brenk, F.E. 1999. *Clothed in Purple Light: Studies in Vergil and in Latin Literature.* Stuttgart.

Bright, D. 1971. "A Tibullan Odyssey." *Arethusa* 4: 197–214.

Brink, C.O. 1971. *Horace on Poetry: The* Ars Poetica. Cambridge.

Brink, C.O., ed. 1982. *Horace on Poetry:* Epistles *Book II: The Letters to Augustus and Florus.* Cambridge.

Brouwers, J.H. 2006. "On the Summary of the Adventures of Odysseus in Propertius 3.12." In A. Lardinois, M. van der Poel, and V. Hunink, eds., *Land of Dreams: Greek and Latin Studies in Honour of A.H.M. Kessels*, 215–28. Leiden.

Brugnoli, G., and F. Stok, eds. 1997. *Vitae Vergilianae Antiquae: Scriptores Graeci et Latini.* Rome.

Buchheit, V. 1963. *Vergil über die Sendung Roms: Untersuchungen zum* Bellum Poenicum *und zur* Aeneis. Heidelberg.

– 1965. "Tibull II 5 und *die Aeneis*." *Philologus* 109: 104–20. https://doi.org/10.1524/phil.1965.109.14.104.

Buckley, E. 2006. "Valerius Flaccus' *Argonautica*: Post-Vergilian Literary Studies." PhD Dissertation, University of Cambridge.

– 2014. "Valerius Flaccus and Seneca's Tragedies." In Heerink and Manuwald, 307–25.

Burns, P.J. 2016. "*Amor Belli*: Elegiac Diction and the Theme of Love in Lucan's *Bellum Civile*." PhD Dissertation, Fordham University.

Butler, H.E. 1922. *Quintilian with an English Translation.* 4 vols. Cambridge, MA, and London.

Cahoon, L. 1988. "The Bed as Battlefield: Erotic Conquest and Military Metaphor in Ovid's *Amores*." *TAPA* 118: 293–307. https://doi.org/10.2307/284173.

Cairns, D. 2010. *Bacchylides: Five Epinician Odes (3, 5, 9, 11, 13)*. Cambridge.

Cairns, D., and L. Fulkerson, eds. 2015. *Emotions between Greece and Rome*. London.

Cairns, F. 1979. *Tibullus: A Hellenistic Poet at Rome*. Cambridge.

– 1983. "Propertius 1,4 and 1,5 and the 'Gallus' of the Monobiblos." *PLLS* 4: 61–103.

– 1989. *Virgil's Augustan Epic*. Cambridge.

– 1999. "Virgil, *Eclogue* 1.1–2: A Literary Programme?" *HSCP* 99: 289–93. https://doi.org/10.2307/311486.

– 2003. "Propertius 3.4 and the 'Aeneid' Incipit." *CQ* 53.1: 309–11. https://doi.org/10.1093/cq/53.1.309.

– 2006. *Sextus Propertius, the Augustan Elegist*. Cambridge.

– 2008. "C. Asinius Pollio and the *Eclogues*." *PCPS/CCJ* 54: 49–79. https://doi.org/10.1017/s1750270500000579.

– 2016. *The Hellenistic Epigram: Contexts of Exploration*. Cambridge

Calenzio, E. 1503. *Opuscula*. Rome.

Cameron, A. 1995. *Callimachus and His Critics*. Princeton.

Campbell, D.A. 1982. *Greek Lyric, Volume I: Sappho and Alcaeus*. LCL 142. Cambridge, MA.

– 1988. *Greek Lyric, Volume II: Anacreon, Anacreontea, Choral Lyric from Olympus to Alcman*. LCL 143. Cambridge, MA.

Cappelli, G.M. 2004. "*Ad actionem secundum virtutem tendit*. La passione, la sapienza, la, prudenza. *Vita activa e vita* contemplativa nel pensiero umanistico." In F.L. Lisi, ed., *The Ways of Life in Classical Political Philosophy*, 203–30. St. Augustine.

Capron, L., and D. Delattre. 2007. *Sur la musique, livre IV. Philodème de Gadara*. Paris.

Carney, E. 2015. *King and Court in Ancient Macedonia: Rivalry, Treason and Conspiracy*. Swansea.

Carson, A. 1984. "The Burners: A Reading of Bacchylides' Third Epinician Ode." *Phoenix* 38.2: 111–19. https://doi.org/10.2307/1088895.

Carter, J.B. 1987. "The Masks of Ortheia." *AJA* 91: 355–83. https://doi.org/10.2307/505359.

– 1988. "Masks and Poetry in Early Sparta." In R. Hägg, N. Marinatos, and G.C. Nordquist, eds., *Early Greek Cult Practice: Proceedings of the Fifth International Symposium of the Swedish Institute at Athens*, 89–98. Stockholm.

Caruso, C. 2013. *Adonis: The Myth of the Dying God in the Italian Renaissance*. London.

Caruso, P. 2016. "*Nostri ordinis homo*: per una nuova interpretazione dell'epistolario di Elisio Calenzio." *Vichiana* 53.1–2: 113–18.

– 2018. "Calenzio, Elisio." In Data Base HistAntArtSI, on line at http://
db.histantartsi.eu/web/rest/Famiglie e Persone/222 (last revision 23 March
2018; consulted 10 July 2018).

Casali, S. 2004. "Nisus and Euryalus: Exploiting the Contradictions in Virgil's
Doloneia." *HSCPh* 102: 319–54. https://doi.org/10.2307/4150045.

– 2008. "'Ecce ἀμφιβολικῶς dixit:' allusioni 'irrazionali' alle varianti scartate della
storia di Didone e Anna secondo Servio." In S. Casali and F. Stok, eds., *Servio:
stratificazioni esegetiche e modelli culturali*, 24–37. Brussels.

– 2014. "Creüsa." In R.F. Thomas and J.M. Ziolkowski, eds., *The Virgil Encyclopedia*,
1: 312–13. Malden, MA. https://doi.org/10.1002/9781118351352.wbve0567.

Casanova-Robin, H. 2011a. "La notion de nouveauté dans l'élégie, de Properce à
Giovanni Pontano. Une revendication de modernité poétique?" In L. Chappuis
Sandoz, ed., *Au-delà de l'élégie d'amour Métamorphoses et renouvellements d'un
genre latin dans l'Antiquité et à la Renaissance*, 187–208. Paris.

Casanova-Robin, H., ed. 2011b. *Pontano:* Églogues = Eclogae. Paris.

Caston, R.R. 2011. "Lucan's Elegiac Moments." In P. Asso, ed., *Brill's Companion to
Lucan*, 132–52. Leiden.

– 2012. *The Elegiac Passion: Jealousy in Roman Love Elegy.* Oxford.

Catanzaro, G., and F. Santucci, eds. 1999. *Poesia umanistica latina in distici elegiaci.
Atti del convegno internazionale, Assisi, 15–17 maggio 1998.* Assisi.

Celotto, G. 2022. Amor Belli: *Love and Strife in Lucan's* Bellum Ciuile. Ann Arbor.

Champlin, E. 1978. "The Life and Times of Calpurnius Siculus." *JRS* 68: 95–110.
https://doi.org/10.2307/299629.

– 1986. "History and the Date of Calpurnius Siculus." *Philologus* 130: 104–12.
https://doi.org/10.1524/phil.1986.130.12.104.

Chiarelli, G. 1932. "Il *De Regno* di Francesco Patrizi." *Rivista Internazionale di
Filosofia del Diritto* 12: 716–38.

Chillet, C. 2016. *De l'Étrurie à Rome: Mécène et la foundation de l'empire.* Rome.

Chiti, E. n.d. "Franciscus Patricius Senensis, Caietanus episcopus." Online at
http://www.mirabileweb.it/calma/franciscus-patricius-senensis-caietanus-
episcopus-/2416 (consulted 9 July 2018).

Chiu, A. 2016. *Ovid's Women of the Year: Narratives of Roman Identity in the* Fasti.
Ann Arbor.

Claassen, J.-M. 2017. "The Exiled Ovid's Reception of Gallus." *CJ* 112: 318–41.
https://doi.org/10.1353/tcj.2016.0016.

Clark, J.G. 2011. "Introduction." In Clark, Coulson, and McKinley, 1–25.

Clark, J.G., F.T. Coulson, and K.L. McKinley, eds. 2011. *Ovid in the Middle Ages.*
Cambridge.

Clark, M.E. 1983. "Horace, *Ars Poetica* 75–78: The Origin and Worth of Elegy."
CW 77: 1–5. https://doi.org/10.2307/4349487.

Clarke, J. 2003. *Imagery of Colour and Shining in Catullus, Propertius and Horace*. New York.

Clarke, M. 1995. "Between Lions and Men: Images of the Hero in the *Iliad*." *GRBS* 36.2: 137–59.

Clausen, W. 1964. "Callimachus and Latin Poetry." *GRBS* 5: 181–96.

– 1976. "*Cynthius*." *AJP* 97: 245–7.

– 1977. "*Cynthius*: An Addendum." *AJP* 9: 362. https://doi.org/10.2307/293798.

– 1987. *Virgil's* Aeneid *and the Tradition of Hellenistic Poetry*. Berkeley.

Clausen, W., ed. 1994. *Virgil:* Eclogues. Oxford.

Clauss, J.J. 2004. "Vergil's Sixth Eclogue: The *Aetia* in Rome." In M.A. Harder, R.F. Regtuit, and G.C. Wakker, eds., *Callimachus II*: 71–93. *Hellenistica Groningana* 7. Leuven.

Clément-Tarantino, S., and F. Klein, eds. 2015. *La représentation du "couple" Virgile-Ovide dans la tradition culturelle de l'Antiquité à nos jours*. Villeneuve-d'Ascq.

Coleman, K.M. 1988. *Statius:* Silvae *IV*. Oxford.

Coleman, R., ed. 1977. *Vergil*, Eclogues. Cambridge.

Comparetti, D. 1896. *Virgilio nel Medioevo*. 2 vols. Florence (repr. Florence 1981).

Conington, J. 1898. *The Works of Virgil, vol. I:* Eclogues *and* Georgics. 5th ed., rev. 2007 by H. Nettleship and F. Haverfield. London.

Consolino, F.E. 2018. "Flowers and Heroines: Some Remarks on Ovid's Presence in the *Cupido Cruciatus*." In F.E. Consolino, ed., *Ovid in Late Antiquity*, 89–117. Turnhout.

Conte, G.B. 1974. *Saggio di commento a Lucano:* Pharsalia *VI 118–260*. Pisa.

– 1984. *Il genere e i suoi confini*. Milan.

– 1986. *The Rhetoric of Imitation: Genre and Poetic Memory in Virgil and Other Latin Poets*. Ithaca.

– 1992. "Proems in the Middle." In F.M. Dunn and T. Cole, eds., *Beginnings in Classical Literature*, 147–60. Cambridge.

– 1994. *Genres and Readers: Lucretius, Love Elegy, Pliny's Encyclopedia*. Trans. G.W. Most. Baltimore and London

– 2001. "Aristaeus, Orpheus, and the *Georgics*: Once Again." In S. Spence, ed., *Poets and Critics Read Virgil*, 44–63. New Haven.

Coppini, D. 2009. "Premessa." In R. Cardini and D. Coppiniv, eds., *Il rinnovamento umanistico della poesia: l'epigramma e l'elegia*, vii–xviii. Florence.

Corbeill, A. 2004. *Nature Embodied: Gesture in Ancient Rome*. Princeton.

Corfiati, C., and M. Sciancalepore. 2009. "'Et non se trova in libraria': note sull'Elencho historico del Cinico." In C. Corfiati and M. de Nichilo, eds., *Biblioteche nel Regno fra Tre e Cinquecento*, 89–117. Lecce.

Coulson, F.T. 2002. "Addenda and Corrigenda to *Incipitarium Ovidianum*." *Journal of Medieval Latin* 12: 154–80. https://doi.org/10.1484/j.jml.2.304175.

– 2011. "Ovid's *Metamorphoses* in the School Tradition of France, 1180–1400. Texts, Manuscripts Traditions, Manuscripts Settings." In Clark, Coulson, and McKinley, 48–82. Cambridge.

Coulson, F.T., and B. Roy, eds. 2000. *Incipitarium Ovidianum: A Finding Guide for Texts in Latin Related to the Study of Ovid in the Middle Ages and Renaissance.* Turnhout.

Courtney, E. 1987. "Imitation, chronologie littéraire et Calpurnius Siculus." *REL* 65: 148–57.

– 1990. "Vergil's Sixth *Eclogue*." *QUCC* 34: 99–112. https://doi.org/10.2307/20547031.

– 1993. *The Fragmentary Latin Poets.* Oxford.

Cova, P.V. 1989. *Il poeta Vario.* Milan.

Cozzoli, A.-T. 2001. *Euripides, Cretesi, Introduzione, testimonianze e commento.* Pisa and Rome.

Croce, B. 1892. "La Tomba di Jacobo Sannazaro e la chiesa di Santa Maria del Parto." *Napoli Nobilissima* 1: 68–76.

Crompton, L. 2003. *Homosexuality and Civilization.* Cambridge, MA.

Croon, J.H. 1955. "The Mask of the Underworld Daemon: Some Remarks on the Perseus-Gorgon Story." *JHS* 75: 9–16. https://doi.org/10.2307/629162.

Crump, M.M. 1931. *The Epyllion from Theocritus to Ovid.* Oxford.

Cummings, R. 2017. "Epigram." In V. Moul, ed., *A Guide to Neo-Latin Literature,* 83–97. Cambridge.

Dahlmann, H. 1977. *Über Helvius Cinna.* Mainz Akademie der Wissenschaften und der Literature. Wiesbaden.

Dalzell, A. 1980. "Homeric Themes in Propertius." *Hermathena* 129: 29–36.

Damiani, G.B. 1547. *Successo de lo combattimento delli tredeci Italiani.* Capua.

D'Anna, G. 1975. "Didone e Anna in Varrone e in Virgilio." *RAL* 30: 3–34.

– 1983. "I rapporto di Properzio con Virgilio: una sottile polemica col classicismo augusteo." In S. Vivona, ed., *Colloquium propertianum (tertium),* 45–57. Assisi.

– 1986. "Qualche considerazione sui rapporti di Tibullo con Virgilio e Orazio." *Atti del Convegno internazionale di studi su Albio Tibullo (Roma-Palestrina, 10–13 maggio 1984), Ciceroniana Suppl.,* 29–45. Rome.

– 1989. *Virgilio. Saggi critici.* Rome.

– 1990. "Virgilio e Tibullo." In Marcello Gigante, ed., *Virgilio e gli Augustei, Pubbl. virgiliane promose dal Comitato virgiliano della Regione Campania,* 87–110. Naples.

D'Arms, J.H. 1970. *Romans on the Bay of Naples: A Social and Cultural Study of the Villas and Their Owners from 150 B.C. to A.D. 400.* Cambridge, MA.

Davis, G. 1994. "Cupid at the Ivory Gates: Ausonius as a Reader of Vergil's *Aeneid*." *Colby Quarterly* 30: 162–70.

– 2012. *Parthenope: The Interplay of Ideas in Vergilian Bucolic.* Leiden.

De Beer, S. 2014. "Elegiac Poetry." In P.J. Ford, J. Bloemendal, and C. Fantazzi, eds., *Brill's Encyclopaedia of the Neo-Latin World.* 2 vols., through-paged, 387–97. Leiden.

De Beer, S.K., A.E. Enenkel, and D. Rijser, eds. 2009. *The Neo-Latin Epigram: A Learned and Witty Genre.* Leuven.

De Capua, P. 2014. *Le lettere di Francesco Patrizi*. Messina.

De Divitiis, B. 2007. *Architettura e committenza nella Napoli del Quattrocento*. Venice.

– 2012. "*Pontanus Fecit*: Inscriptions and Artistic Authorship in the Pontano Chapel." *California Italian Studies* 3.1: 1–36. https://doi.org/10.5070/c331009008.

Defilippis, D. 1987. "Brindisi tra poesia e storia nelle descrizioni di A. Serena e A. De Ferrariis Galateo." *Brundisii res* 13: 3–32.

– 1988. "Interessi geografici ed esperienze letterarie di un umanista monopolitano alla corte papale. Gli *Opuscula* di Aurelio Serena." In D. Cofano, ed., *Monopoli nell'età del Rinascimento*, 3:949–84. Fasano.

– 2008. "Retorica e pedagogia in Aurelio Serena." In M. Spedicato, ed., *Tra letteratura e storia. Studi in onore di Rosario Jurlaro*, 53–64. Galatina.

Degl'Innocenti Pierini, R. 1987. "Erisittone prima e dopo Ovidio." *Prometheus* 13: 133–59.

De Jong, I.J.F. 2001. *A Narratological Commentary on the* Odyssey. Cambridge.

Dekel, E. 2012. *Virgil's Homeric Lens*. New York.

Delattre, D. 2001. "Vers une reconstruction de l'esthétique musicale de Philodème." In C. Auvray-Assayas and D. Delattre, eds., *Cicéron et Philodème, Polémique en philosophie*, 371–84. Paris.

– 2004. "Vergil and Music, in Diogenes of Babylon and Philodemus." In Armstrong et al., 244–63.

De La Ville de Mirmont, H. 1903. *Études sur l'ancienne poésie latine*. Paris.

Della Corte, F. 1980. *Tibullo: le elegie*. Verona.

Delle Donne, F. 2015. "Virgiliana Neapolis Urbs. Receptions of Classical Antiquity in Swabian and Early Angevin Ages." In Hughes and Buongiovanni, 152–69.

Delle Donne, F., and V. Rivera Magos, eds. 2017. *La Disfida di Barletta. Storia, fortuna, rappresentazione*. Rome.

– 2019. *La Disfida di Barletta e la fine del Regno. Coscienza del presente e percezione del mutamento tra fine Quattrocento e inizio Cinquecento*. Rome.

De Nichilo, M. 1977. "Lo sconosciuto apografo avellinese del *De hortis Hesperidum* di G. Pontano." *Filologia e Critica* 2: 217–46.

Deonna, W. 1954. "The Crab and the Butterfly: A Study in Animal Symbolism." *Journal of the Warburg and Courtauld Institutes* 17.1: 47–86. https://doi.org/10.2307/750132.

Depew, M., and D. Obbink, eds. 2000. *Matrices of Genre: Authors, Canons, and Society*. Cambridge, MA.

Deramaix, M. 2018. "*Synceromastix nescio quis*. Théorie et pratique de l'exemplum virgilien chez Sannazar dans sa correspondance et dans le *De partu Virginis*." In Deramaix and Germano, 65–100.

Deramaix, M., and G. Germano, eds. 2018. *L'Exemplum virgilien et l'Académie napolitaine à la Renaissance*. Paris.

Deramaix, M., and B. Laschke (A. Virey-Wallon, tr.) 1992. "*Maroni musa proximus ut tumolo*: L'église et le tombeau de Jacques Sannazar." *Revue de l'Art* 95: 25–40. https://doi.org/10.3406/rvart.1992.347962.

Deratini, N. 1931. "Virgile et l'age d'or." *RP* 57: 128–31.

Desmond, M. 1994. *Reading Dido: Gender, Sexuality, and the Medieval* Aeneid. Minneapolis.

Desnier, J.-L. 1995. "*Tenet nunc Parthenope*." *Latomus* 54: 298–304.

De Villiers, G. 2010. "The Origin of Prophetism in the Ancient Near East." *HTS* 66: 1–6. https://doi.org/10.4102/hts.v66i1.795.

De Witt, N.W. 1907. "The Dido Episode as a Tragedy." *CJ* 2: 283–8.

– 1922. "Virgil at Naples." *CP* 17.2: 104–10. https://doi.org/10.1086/360406.

Dilke, O.A.W., ed. 1954. *Statius*, Achilleid. Cambridge.

Diller, A. 1956. "Pausanias in the Middle Ages." *TAPA* 87: 84–97. https://doi.org/10.2307/283874.

– 1957. "The Manuscripts of Pausanias." *TAPhA* 88: 169–88. https://doi.org/10.2307/283902.

Dinter, M. 2005. "Epic and Epigram – Minor Heroes in Virgil's *Aeneid*." *CQ* 55.1: 153–69. https://doi.org/10.1093/cq/bmi011.

– 2011. "Inscriptional Intermediality in Latin Elegy." In A. Keith, ed., *Latin Elegy and Hellenistic Epigram: A Tale of Two Genres at Rome*, 7–18. Newcastle upon Tyne

– 2013. "Inscriptional Intermediality in Latin Literature." In P. Liddell and P. Low, eds., *Inscriptions and Their Uses in Greek and Latin Literature*, 303–16. Oxford.

Dixon, S. 2001. *Reading Roman Women: Genres and Real Life*. London.

Doob, P.R. 1990. *The Idea of the Labyrinth from Classical Antiquity through the Middle Ages*. Ithaca.

Drinkwater, M.O. 2012. "'His Turn to Cry': Tibullus' Marathus Cycle (1.4, 1.8 and 1.9) and Roman Elegy." *CJ* 107: 423–48. https://doi.org/10.1353/tcj.2012.0030.

– 2013. "*Militia Amoris*." in Thorsen, 194–206.

Ducrot, O., and T. Todorov. 1972. *Dictionnaire encyclopédique des sciences du langage*. Paris

Dué, C. 2001. "*Sunt Aliquid Manes*: Homer, Plato, and the Alexandrian Allusion in Propertius 4.7." *CJ* 96: 401–13.

Dunkle, J.R. 1967. "The Greek Tyrant and the Roman Political Invective of the Late Republic." *TAPA* 98: 151–71. https://doi.org/10.2307/2935871.

– 1971. "The Rhetorical Tyrant in Roman Historiography: Sallust, Livy and Tacitus." *CW* 65: 12–20. https://doi.org/10.2307/4347532.

– 1973. "The Hunter and Hunting in the *Aeneid*." *Ramus* 2.2: 127–42. https://doi.org/10.1017/s0048671x00004653.

Duplain Michel, N. 1997. "*Bacchatur demens aliena per antrum*: Les modèles littéraires de la Pythie chez Lucain." In D. Knoepfler, ed., *Nomen Latinum*:

Mélanges de langue, de littérature et de civilisation latines offerts au professeur André Schneider à l'occasion de son départ à la retraite, 109–19. Geneva.

Du Quesnay, I.M.Le.M. 1979. "From Polyphemus to Corydon: Virgil, *Eclogue* 2 and the *Idylls* of Theocritus." In D. West and T. Woodman, eds., *Creative Imitation in Latin Literature*, 35–70. Cambridge.

– 1981. "Vergil's First *Eclogue*." *PLLS* 3: 29–182.

– 1992. "*In memoriam Galli*: Propertius 1.21." In T. Woodman and J. West, eds., *Author and Audience in Latin Literature*, 52–83. Cambridge.

Dutsch, D. 2008. "*Nenia*: Gender, Genre, and Lament in Ancient Rome." In Suter, 258–79. Oxford.

Dyson, J.T. 1996. "*Caesi Iuvenci* and *Pietas Impia* in Virgil." *CJ* 91.3: 277–86.

– 2001. *King of the Wood: The Sacrificial Victor in Virgil's* Aeneid. Norman, OK.

Eck, W. 2007.[2] *The Age of Augustus*. Trans. D.L. Schneider. Malden, MA. [Originally published in German as *Augustus und seine Zeit*. Munich 1998].

Eckerman, C. 2016. "Freedom and Slavery in Vergil's *Eclogue* 1." *WS* 129: 257–80.

Eco, U. 1976. *Opera aperta*. Milan.

Edmondson, J. 2008. "Roman Dress and Social Control." In Edmondson and Keith, 21–46.

Edmondson, J., and A.M. Keith, eds. 2008. *Roman Dress and the Fabrics of Roman Culture*. Toronto.

Edwards, C. 1993. *The Politics of Immorality in Ancient Rome*. Cambridge.

Egan, R.B. 1996. "Corydon's Winning Words in *Eclogue* 7." *Phoenix* 50: 233–9. https://doi.org/10.2307/1192651.

Ehlers, W.-W. 1980. *Gai Valeri Flacci Setini Balbi Argonauticon libros octo*. Stuttgart.

Elder, J.P. 1961. "*Non Iniussa Cano*: Virgil's Sixth Eclogue." *HSCP* 65: 109–25. https://doi.org/10.2307/310834.

Ellis, R. 1876. *A Commentary on Catullus*. Oxford.

Elsner, J. 2017. "Late Narcissus: Classicism and Culture in a Late Roman Cento." In Elsner and Lobato, 176–204.

Elsner, J., and J.H. Lobato, eds. 2017. *The Poetics of Late Latin Literature*. Oxford.

Erasmo, M. 2006. "Birds of a Feather? Ennius and Horace, 'Odes' 2,20." *Latomus* 65.2: 369–77.

Erren, M. 2003. *P. Vergilius Maro, Georgica, Band 2 Kommentar*. Heidelberg.

Esposito, J. 2016. "Who Kills Turnus? 'Pallas' and What Aeneas Sees, Says and Does in *Aeneid* 12.939–52." *CJ* 111.4: 463–81. https://doi.org/10.1353/tcj.2015.0060.

Esposito, P. 1988. "Il bosco disabitato (*Phars.* 3.402–3 e i suoi modelli)." *Orpheus* 9: 306–11.

– 2012. "Interaction between *Bucolics* and *Georgics*: The Fifth Eclogue of Calpurnius Siculus." *Trends in Classics* 4: 48–72. https://doi.org/10.1515/tc-2012-0004.

Evans, R. 2008. *Utopia Antiqua: Readings of the Golden Age and Decline at Rome.* London and New York.

Evans, S. 1971. "Odyssean Echoes in Propertius IV.8." *G&R* 18.1: 51–3. https:// doi.org/10.1017/s0017383500017678.

Evelyn White, H.G., tr. 1919. *Ausonius.* London and New York.

Fabre-Serris, J. 2001. "Deux réponses de Tibulle à Virgile: les élégies II, 1 et II, 5." *REL* 79: 140–51.

– 2004. "Tibulle, 1,4: L'élégie et la tradition poétique du discours didactique." *Dictynna* 1: 29–43. https://doi.org/10.4000/dictynna.162.

– 2005. "L'élégie et les images romaines des origins." In J.P. Schwindt, ed., *La représentation du temps dans la poésie augustéenne/ Zur Poetik der Zeit in augusteischer,* 141–57. Heidelberg.

– 2008. *Rome, l'Arcadie et la mer des Argonautes.* Lille.

– 2010. "La réception des *Amores* de Gallus dans un *lusus* horatien: lectures de l'*Épode* 11." In J. González Castro and J. de la Villa Polo, eds., *Perfiles Grecia y Roma II* (Actas del XII Congreso Español de Estudios clásicos), 881–95. Madrid.

– 2013a. "Genre et gender: usages et enjeux de l'emploi de '*durus*' chez les élégiaques." *Eugesta* 3: 209–39.

– 2013b. "Onomastics, Intertextuality and Gender; 'Phyllis' in Roman Poetry (Gallus, Vergil, Horace, Propertius and Ovid)." In D. Lateiner, B.K. Gold, and J. Perkins, eds., *Roman Literature, Gender and Reception:* Domina Illustris, 119–35. New York.

– 2016. "The ars *rhetorica*: An Ovidian *remedium* for Female *furor*?" In P. Hardie, ed., *Augustan Poetry and the Irrational,* 170–86. Oxford.

– 2017. "Sulpicia, Gallus et les élégiaques: propositions de lecture de l'épigramme 3.13." *Eugesta* 7: 115–39.

– 2018. "Love and Death in Propertius 1.10, 1.13 and 2.15: Poetic and Polemical Games with Lucretius, Gallus and Virgil." In S. Frangoulidis and S. Harrison, eds., *Life, Love and Death in Latin Poetry,* 37–50. Berlin and Boston.

Fairclough, H.R., rev. G.P. Goold. 1999. *Virgil.* Eclogues. Georgics. Aeneid: *Books 1–6.* LCL 63.

– *Virgil. Aeneid: Books 7–12.* Appendix Vergiliana. LCL 64. Cambridge, MA.

Fantham, E. 1983. "Sexual Comedy in Ovid's *Fasti*: Sources and Motivation." *HSCP* 8: 185–216. https://doi.org/10.2307/311258.

– 1985. "Ovid, Germanicus and the Composition of the *Fasti*." *PLLS* 5: 243–81.

– 1991. "*Stuprum*: Public Attitudes and Penalties for Sexual Offences in Republican Rome." *EMC* 35: 267–91. https://doi.org/10.1515/9783110229349.115.

– 1992. "Ceres, Liber and Flora: Georgic and Anti-Georgic Element in Ovid's *Fasti*." *PCPS* 38: 39–56. https://doi.org/10.1515/9783110229349.409.

– 1995. "The Ambiguity of *Virtus* in Lucan's *Civil War* and Statius' *Thebaid*." *Arachnion* 3. http://www.cisi.unito.it/arachne/num3/fantham.html.

– 1996. "*Religio … dira loci*: Two Passages in Lucan *de Bello Civili* 3 and Their Relation to Virgil's Rome and Latium." *MD* 37: 137–53. https://doi.org/10.2307/40236165.

– ed. 1998. *Ovid, Fasti Book IV*. Cambridge.

– 2009. *Latin Poets and Italian Gods*. Toronto.

– 2013. *Roman Literary Culture: From Plautus to Macrobius*.[2] Baltimore.

Fantuzzi, M., and R. Hunter, eds. 2004. *Tradition and Innovation in Hellenistic Poetry*. Cambridge.

Fantuzzi, M., and T. Papanghelis, eds. 2006. *Brill's Companion to Greek and Latin Pastoral*. Leiden.

Faraone, C. 2008. *The Stanzaic Architecture of Early Greek Elegy*. Oxford .

Farrell, J. 1991. *Vergil's* Georgics *and the Traditions of Ancient Epic*. Oxford.

– 1997. "The Vergilian Intertext." In Martindale, 222–38.

– 2002. "Greek Lives and Roman Careers in the Classical *Vita* Tradition." In P.G. Cheney and F.A. De Armas, eds., *European Literary Careers: The Author from Antiquity to the Renaissance*, 24–46. Toronto.

– 2021. *Juno's* Aeneid*: A Battle for Heroic Identity*. Princeton.

Farrell, J., and M. Putnam, eds. 2010. *A Companion to Virgil's* Aeneid *and Its Traditions*. Malden, MA, and Chichester.

Farron, S. 1993. *Vergil's* Aeneid*: A Poem of Grief and Love*. Leiden.

Fearn, D. 2007. *Bacchylides: Politics, Performance, Poetic Tradition*. Oxford.

Fedeli, P. 1972. "Sulla prima bucolica di Virgilio." *GIF* 3: 273–300. https://doi.org/10.4000/italique.461.

– ed. 1980. *Sesto Properzio: Il Primo Libro Delle Elegie*. Florence.

– 1981. "Elegy and Literary Polemic in Propertius' *Monobiblos*." *PLLS* 3: 227–42.

– 1984a. "*Amor*." In *Enciclopedia virgiliana*, 1:143–7. Rome.

– ed. 1984b. *Sexti Properti: Elegiarum Libri IV*. Stuttgart.

– ed. 1985. *Properzio. Il libro terzo delle elegie*. Bari.

– ed. 2005. *Properzio, Elegie Libro II: Introduzione, testo e commento*. Cambridge.

Fedeli, P., R. Dimundo, and I. Ciccarelli, eds. 2015. *Properzio: Elegie Libro IV*. 2 vols. Nordhausen.

Feeney, D.C. 1986. "History and Revelation in Vergil's Underworld." *PCPS* 3: 1–24. https://doi.org/10.1017/s0068673500004806.

– 1992. "*Si licet et fas est*: Ovid's *Fasti* and the Problem of Free Speech under the Principate." In A. Powell, ed., *Roman Poetry and Propaganda in the Age of Augustus*, 1–25. London.

– 2004a. "Interpreting Sacrificial Ritual in Roman Poetry: Disciplines and Their Models." In A. Barchiesi, J. Rüpke, and S. Stephens, eds., *Rituals in Ink: A Conference on Religion and Literary Production in Ancient Rome*, 1–21. Stuttgart.

– 2004b. "*Tenui … latens discrimine*: Spotting the Differences in Statius' *Achilleid*." *MD* 52: 85–106. https://doi.org/10.1017/9781108680226.014.

– 2007. *Caesar's Calendar: Ancient Time and the Beginnings of History*. Berkeley.

Feinstein, W. 1990. "Ariosto's Parodic Rewriting of Virgil in the Episode of Cloridan and Medoro." *South Atlantic Review* 55.1: 17–34. https://doi.org/10.2307/3199870.

Feldherr, A. 1997. "Livy's Revolution: Civic Identity and the Creation of the *Res Publica*." In T. Habinek and A. Schiesaro, eds., *The Roman Cultural Revolution*, 136–57. Cambridge.

– 1999. "Putting Dido on the Map: Genre and Geography in Vergil's Underworld." *Arethusa* 32: 85–122. https://doi.org/10.1353/are.1999.0002.

– 2016. "Nothing Like the Sun: Repetition and Representation in Ovid's Phaethon Narrative." In Fulkerson and Stover, 26–46.

Felici, C. 2010. "Lavinia, al margine: strategia matrimoniale e insediamento troiano nel Lazio." *I Quaderni del Ramo d'Oro Online* 3: 267–91.

Fey-Wickert, B. 2002. *Calpurnius Siculus: Kommentar zur 2. und 3. Ekloge*. Trier.

Fielding, I. 2017. *Transformations of Ovid in Late Antiquity*. Cambridge.

Finiello, C. 2005. "Der Bürgerkrieg: Reine Männersache? Keine Männersache! Erictho und die Frauengestalten im Bellum Civile Lucans." In C. Walde, ed., *Lucan im 21. Jahrhundert*, 155–85. Munich.

Fletcher, K. 2014. *Finding Italy: Travel, Nation, and Colonization in Vergil's* Aeneid. Ann Arbor.

Foà, S. 1998. "Gallucci, Luigi." In *Dizionario Biografico degli Italiani* 51: 743–5. Rome.

Fordyce, C.J., ed. 1977. Aeneidos: *Libri VII–VIII*. Oxford.

– 1990. *Catullus: A Commentary*. Oxford.

Formicula, C. 2006. "Dark Visibility: Lavinia in the *Aeneid*." *Vergilius* 52: 76–95.

Forsyth, P.Y. 1991. "The Thematic Unity of Catullus 11." CW 84: 457–64. https://doi.org/10.2307/4350911.

Forsythe, G. 2012. *Time in Roman Religion: One Thousand Years of Religious History*. London.

Fowler, D.P. 1987. "Virgil on Killing Virgins." In M. Whitby, P. Hardie, and M. Whitby, eds., Homo Viator: *Classical Essays for John Bramble*, 185–98. Bristol.

– 1989. "First Thoughts on Closure: Problems and Prospects." *MD* 22: 75–122. https://doi.org/10.2307/40235930.

– 2000. "Epic in the Middle of the Wood: *Mise en Abyme* in the Nisus and Euryalus Episode." In Sharrock and Morales, 89–113.

– 2002. "Masculinity under Threat? The Poetics and Politics of Inspiration in Latin Poetry." In Spentzou and Fowler, 140–59.

Fraenkel, E. 1945. "Some Aspects of the Structure of *Aeneid* VII." *JRS* 35: 1–14. https://doi.org/10.2307/297274.

Frame, D. 1978. *The Myth of Return in Early Greek Epic*. New Haven.

Fränkel, H. 1986. *Apollonius Rhodius:* Argonautica. Oxford.

Franzoi, A. 2002. *Cupido messo in croce: introduzione, testo, traduzione e commento.* Naples.

Fratantuono, L. 2007. *Madness Unchained: A Reading of Virgil's* Aeneid. Lanham, MD.

– 2008. "*Laviniaque venit litora*: Blushes, Bees, and Virgil's Lavinia." *Maia* 60: 40–50.

– 2012. *Madness Triumphant: A Reading of Lucan's* Pharsalia. Lanham, MD.

Frazer, J.G. 1976. *Ovid*, Fasti. Cambridge, MA.

Fredrick, D. 1997. "Reading Broken Skin: Violence in Roman Elegy." In Hallett and Skinner, 172–93.

Freis, R. 1993. "*Exiguos Elegos*: Are *Ars Poetica* 75–78 Critical of Love Elegy?" *Latomus* 52: 364–71.

Freudenburg13, K. 1993. *The Walking Muse: Horace on the Theory of Satire.* Princeton.

Frings, Irene. 1998. "*Mantua me genuit*: Vergils Grabepigramm auf Stein und Pergament." *ZPE* 123: 89–100.

Fulkerson, L., and T. Stover, eds. 2016. *Repeat Performances: Ovidian Repetition and the* Metamorphoses. Madison, WI.

Gaca, K.L. 2013. "Girls, Women, and the Significance of Sexual Violence in Ancient Warfare." In E.D. Heineman, ed., *Sexual Violence in Conflict Zones: From the Ancient World to the Era of Human Rights*, 73–88. Philadelphia.

– 2016. "Continuities in Rape and Tyranny in Martial Societies from Antiquity Onward." In S.L. Budin and J.M. Turfa, eds., *Women in Antiquity: Real Women across the Ancient World*, 1041–56. New York.

– 2018a. "Ancient Warfare and the Ravaging Martial Rape of Girls and Women." In M. Masterson, N.S. Rabinowitz, and J. Robson, eds., *Sex in Antiquity: Exploring Gender and Sexuality in the Ancient World*, 278–97. New York.

– 2018b. "The Martial Rape of Girls and Women in Antiquity and Modernity." in F. Ní Aoláin, N. Cahn, D.F. Haynes, and N. Valji, eds., *The Oxford Handbook of Gender and Conflict*, 305–15. Oxford.

Gagliardi, P. 2013. "Orfeo e l'ombra di Cornelio Gallo nei poeti augustei." *WS* 126: 101–26. https://doi.org/10.1553/wst126s101.

– 2014. "L'ecloga 10 di Virgilio e la poesia post-teocritea." *REL* 92: 123–36.

Gaisser, J.H. 1977. "Tibullus 2.3 and Vergil's Tenth Eclogue." *TAPA* 107: 131–46. https://doi.org/10.2307/284031.

Gale, M.R. 1997a. "Propertius 2.7: *Militia Amoris* and the Ironies of Elegy." *JRS* 87: 77–91. https://doi.org/10.1017/s0075435800058093.

– 1997b. "The Shield of Turnus (*Aeneid* 7.783–92)." G&R 44.2: 176–96. https://doi.org/10.1093/gr/44.2.176.

– 2000. *Virgil on the Nature of Things: The* Georgics, *Lucretius and the Didactic Tradition.* Cambridge.

Galinsky, G.K. 1966. "The Hercules-Cacus Episode in *Aeneid* VIII." *AJP* 87: 18–51. https://doi.org/10.2307/292975.

– 1996. *Augustan Culture: An Interpretive Introduction*. Princeton.

Garbarino G. 1987. "Properzio e la «domina»: l'amore come dipendenza." In R. Uglione, ed., *Atti del convegno nazionale di studi su la donna nel mondo antico: Torino 18–19–20 Aprile*, 169–93. Turin.

Gardner, H.H. 2013. *Gendering Time in Augustan Love Elegy*. Oxford.

Gardner, H.H., and S. Murnaghan, eds. 2014. Nostos: *Odyssean Identities in Modern Cultures*. Columbus, OH.

Gardner, J.F. 1986. *Women in Roman Law and Society*. London and Sydney.

Garrison, I.P. 2017. "Between Biography and Commentary: The Ancient Horizon of Expectation of *VSD*." In Anton Powell and Philip Hardie, eds., *The Ancient Lives of Virgil: Literary and Historical Studies*, 1–28. Bristol.

Gauly, B.M. 1990. *Liebesfahrungen: Zur Rolle des elegischen Ich in Ovids* Amores. Frankfurt.

Genette, G. 1987. *Seuils*. Paris. Trans. 1997 as *Paratexts: Thresholds of Interpretation* by Jane Lewin. Cambridge.

Gerber, D.E. 1999a. *Greek Iambic Poetry: From the Seventh to the Fifth Centuries BC*. LCL 259. Cambridge, MA.

– 1999b. *Greek Elegiac Poetry: From the Seventh to the Fifth Centuries BC*. LCL 258. Cambridge, MA.

Germano, G. 2015. "Alcune considerazioni su tradizione, costituzione e struttura degli *Elegiarum Aurimpiae ad Colotium Libri* dell'umanista Elisio Calenzio." *Bollettino di Studi Latini* 45.2: 549–65.

– 2016. "Un canzoniere umanistico ed i suoi modelli strutturali: le *Elegiae Aurimpiae* di Elisio Calenzio." In G. Matino, F. Ficca, and R. Grisolia, eds., *Il modello e la sua ricezione*, 69–90. Naples.

– 2018. "Allusioni virgiliane nell'*Urania* di Giovanni Pontano." In Deramaix and Germano, 217–41.

Giancotti, F. 1967. *Mimo e Gnome. Studio su Decimo Laberio e Publio Siro*. Messina and Florence.

Gibson, R.K. 2012. "Gallus: The First Roman Love Elegist." In Gold, 172–86.

– 2013. *Ovid:* Ars Amatoria *Book 3*. Cambridge.

Gibson, R.K., S. Green, and A. Sharrock, eds. 2007. *The Art of Love: Bimillennial Essays on Ovid's* Ars Amatoria *and* Remedia Amoris. Oxford.

Gindhart, M. 2006. "*Evolat ad superos portaque evadit eburna*: Intertextuelle Strategien und Vergilparodie im *Cupido cruciatus* des Ausonius." *RM* 149: 214–36.

Gladhill, C.W. 2012. "Post Scriptum: Sons, Mothers and Sex: *Aeneid* 1.314–20 and the *Hymn to Aphrodite* Reconsidered." *Vergilius* 58: 159–68.

– 2018. "Women from the Rostra." In C. Gray, A. Balbo, R.M.A. Marshall, and C.E.W. Steel, eds., *Reading Republican Oratory: Reconstructions, Contexts, Receptions*, 297–308. Oxford.

Glauthier, P. 2020. "*Bugonia* and the Aetiology of Didactic Poetry in Virgil, *Georgics* 4." *CQ* 69: 745–63. https://doi.org/10.1017/s0009838820000038.

Gold, B.K., ed. 2012. *Blackwell Companion to Roman Elegy*. Malden, MA, and Oxford.

Goold, G.P. 1990. *Propertius. Elegies*. LCL 18. Cambridge, MA.

Gorman, V.B. 2001. "Lucan's Epic *Aristeia* and the Hero of the *Bellum Civile*." *CJ* 96: 263–90.

Gow, A.S.F., ed. 1952. *Theocritus*. 2 vols.² Cambridge.

Gowers, E., ed. 2012. *Horace: Satires Book I*. Cambridge.

Grafton, A. 1991. *Defenders of the Text: The Traditions of Scholarship in an Age of Science, 1450–1800*. Cambridge, MA.

Gransden, K.W. 1984. *Virgil's Iliad: An Essay on Epic Narrative*. Cambridge.

Green, C.M.C. 1996. "Terms of Venery: *Ars Amatoria* I." *TAPA* 126: 221–63. https://doi.org/10.2307/370178.

Green, R.P.H., ed. 1991. *The Works of Ausonius*. Oxford.

Green, S.J., ed. 2004. *Ovid*, Fasti *I: A Commentary*. Leiden and Boston.

– 2007. "Lessons in Love: Fifty Years of Scholarship on the *Ars Amatoria* and *Remedia Amoris*." In Gibson, Green and Sharrock, 1–20. Oxford.

– 2008. "Save Our Cows? Augustan Discourse and Animal Sacrifice in Ovid's *Fasti*." *G&R* 55: 39–54. https://doi.org/10.1017/s0017383507000307.

Greene, E. 1998. *The Erotics of Domination: Male Desire and the Mistress in Latin Love Poetry*. Baltimore.

Griffin, Jasper. 1979. "The Fourth *Georgic*, Virgil and Rome." *G&R* 26: 61–80. https://doi.org/10.1017/s0017383500026711.

– 1985. *Latin Poetry and Roman Life*. Chapel Hill.

Griffith, R.D. 1985. "Literary Allusion in Virgil, *Aeneid* 9.435ff." *Vergilius* 31: 40–4.

Gutzwiller, K.J. 1991. *Theocritus' Pastoral Analogies: The Formation of a Genre*. Madison, WI.

– 1996. "Vergil and the Date of the Theocritean Epigram Book." *Philologus* 140: 92–9. https://doi.org/10.1524/phil.1996.140.1.92.

Guy-Bray, S. 2002. *Homoerotic Space: The Poetics of Loss in Renaissance Literature*. Toronto.

Habinek, T. 1990. "Sacrifice, Society, and Vergil's Ox-Born Bees." In M. Griffiths and D. Mastronarde, eds., *Cabinet of the Muses: Essays on Classical and Comparative Literature in Honor of Thomas G. Rosenmeyer*, 209–23. Atlanta.

– 2005. *The World of Roman Song: From Ritualized Speech to Social Order*. Baltimore.

Hallett, J.P. 2009a. "*Corpus Erat*: Sulpicia's Elegiac Text and Body in Ovid's Pygmalion Narrative (*Metamorphoses* 10.238–297)." In T. Foegen and M. Lee, eds., *Bodies and Boundaries in Graeco-Roman Antiquity*, 111–24. Berlin.

– 2009b. "Sulpicia and Her Resistant Intertextuality." In D. van Mal-Maeder, A. Burnier, and L. Nunez, eds., *Jeux de voix: Énonciation, intertextualité et intentionnalité dans la littérature antique*, 121–55. Bern.

– 2010. "Ovid's Thisbe and a Roman Woman Love Poet." In Boyd and Fox, 414–33.

– 2015. "*Omnia Movet Amor*: Love and Resistance, Art and Movement in Ovid's Daphne and Apollo Episode (*Metamorphoses* 1.452–567)." In C.A. Clark, E. Foster, and J.P. Hallett, eds., *Kinesis: The Ancient Depiction of Gesture, Motion and Emotion*, 207–18. Ann Arbor.

– 2020. "Augustan Maternal Ideology: The Blended Families of Octavia and Venus." In A. Sharrock and A. Keith, eds., *Maternal Conceptions in Classical Literature and Philosophy*, 113–26. Toronto.

Hallett, J.P., and M.B. Skinner, eds. 1997. *Roman Sexualities*. Princeton.

Hamblin, F.R. 1922. "The Development of Allegory in the Classical Pastoral." PhD Dissertation, University of Chicago.

Hamilton, R. 1977. "Solon 13.74 ff. (West)." *GRBS* 18: 185–8.

Hanford, J.H. 1910. "The Pastoral Elegy and Milton's *Lycidas*." *PMLA* 25.3: 403–47. https://doi.org/10.2307/456731.

Hansen, M.H. 1989. "Solonian Democracy in Fourth-Century Athens." *Class. Mediaev.* 40: 71–99.

Hansman, J. 1976. "Gilgamesh, Humbaba, and the Land of the Erin-Trees." *Iraq* 38: 23–35.

Harder, A., ed. 2012. *Callimachus*, Aetia. 2 vols. Oxford.

Harder, M.A., R.F. Regtuit, and G.C. Wakker, eds. 1998. *Genre in Hellenistic Poetry*. Groningen.

Hardie, A. 2017. "The Formation of an Augustan Elegist: Empedocles and Propertius' 'Monobiblos'." In A.J. Woodman and J. Wisse, eds., *Word and Context in Latin Poetry: Studies in Memory of David West*, 61–87. Cambridge Classical Journal Supplement 10.

Hardie, P.R. 1984. "The Sacrifice of Iphigeneia: An Example of 'Distribution' of a Lucretian Theme in Virgil." *CQ* 34: 406–12. https://doi.org/10.1017/s0009838800031037.

– 1986. *Virgil's Aeneid: Cosmos and Imperium*. Oxford.

– 1990. "Flavian Epicists on Virgil's Epic Technique." In Boyle, 3–20.

– 1993. *Epic Successors of Virgil: A Study in the Dynamics of a Tradition*. Cambridge.

– 1994. *Virgil: Aeneid Book IX*. Cambridge.

– 1997. "Closure in Latin Epic." In F.M. Dunn, D.P. Fowler, and D.H. Roberts, eds., *Classical Closure: Reading the End in Greek and Latin Literature*, 139–62. Princeton.

– 1998. *Virgil*. Oxford.

– 2002. *Ovid's Poetics of Illusion*. Cambridge.

– 2006. "Cultural and Historical Narratives in Virgil's *Eclogues* and Lucretius." In Fantuzzi and Papanghelis, 275–300.

Hardie, P.R., A. Barchiesi, and S. Hinds, eds. 1999. *Ovidian Transformations: Essays on Ovid's* Metamorphoses *and Its Reception*. Cambridge.

Hardie, P.R., and H. Moore, eds. 2010. *Classical Literary Careers and Their Reception*. Cambridge.

Harington, J. 1591. Orlando Furioso *in English Heroical Verse*. London.

Harrell, S.E. 2006. "Synchronicity: The Local and the Panhellenic within Sicilian Tyranny." In S. Lewis, ed., *Ancient Tyranny*, 119–34. Edinburgh.

Harrison, E. 1902. *Studies in Theognis*. Cambridge.

Harrison, E.L. 1972–3. "Why Did Venus Wear Boots?" *PVS* 12: 10–25.

– 1989. "The Tragedy of Dido." *EMC* 33: 1–21.

Harrison, S.J. 1990. "Review of F. Cova, Il poeta Vario." *CR* 40: 487.

– 1991. *Vergil,* Aeneid *10*. Oxford.

– 2005. "Decline and Nostalgia." In S.J. Harrison, ed., *A Companion to Latin Literature*, 285–99. Malden, MA.

– 2007a. *Generic Enrichment in Vergil and Horace*. Oxford.

– 2007b. "Exile in Latin Epic." In J.F. Gaertner, ed., *Writing Exile: The Discourse of Displacement in Greco-Roman Antiquity and Beyond*, 129–54. Leiden.

– ed. 2017. *Horace,* Odes *Book II*. Cambridge.

Harvey, A.E. 1955. "The Classification of Greek Lyric Poetry." *CQ* 5: 157–75. https://doi.org/10.1017/s0009838800011411.

Haupt, M. 1854. *De Carminibus Bucolicis Calpurnii et Nemesiani*. Berlin (=1875. *Opuscula* I: 358–406. Leipzig: Hirzel).

Havener, W. 2019. "Egyptian Victories: The *Praefectus Aegypti* and the Presentation of Military Success in the Age of Augustus." In K. Morrell, J. Osgood, and K. Welch, eds., *The Alternative Augustan Age*, 130–46. Oxford.

Hawkins, J.N. 2017. *Therapoetics after Actium: Narrative, Medicine, and Authority in Augustan Epic*. Baltimore.

Haynes, J. 2016. "Citations of Ovid in Virgil's Ancient Commentators." In C.S. Kraus and C. Stray, eds., *Classical Commentaries: Explorations in a Scholarly Genre*, 216–32. Oxford.

Heath, J. 1991. "Diana's Understanding of Ovid's *Metamorphoses*." *CJ* 86: 233–43.

– 1994. "Prophetic Horses, Bridled Nymphs: Ovid's Metamorphosis of Ocyroe." *Latomus* 53: 340–53.

Heerink, M. 2007. "Going a Step Further: Valerius Flaccus' Metapoetical Reading of Propertius' Hylas." *CQ* 57.2: 606–20. https://doi.org/10.1017/s0009838807000584.

– 2015. *Echoing Hylas: A Study in Hellenistic and Roman Metapoetics*. Madison, WI.

Heerink, M., and G. Manuwald, eds. 2014. *Brill's Companion to Valerius Flaccus*. Leiden and Boston.

Heinze, R. 1915. *Vergils epische Technik*. Leipzig.

– 1919. *Ovids elegische Erzählung*. Leipzig.

Heller, J.L. 1939. "Festus on *Nenia*." *TAPA* 70: 357–67. https://doi.org/10.2307/283095.

– 1943. "Nenia: πίγνιον." *TAPA* 74: 215–68. https://doi.org/10.2307/283601

Helzle, M. 2003. *Ovids* Epistulae ex Ponto: *Buch I–II Kommentar*. Heidelberg.

Henderson, C., Jr. 1955. "A Lexicon of the Stylistic Terms Used in Roman Literary Criticism." PhD Dissertation, University of North Carolina at Chapel Hill.

Henderson, J. 1996. "Polishing Off the Politics: Horace's Ode to Pollio, 2, 1." *MD* 37: 59–136. https://doi.org/10.2307/40236164.

– 2002. "Corny Copa: The Motel Muse," In Spentzou and Fowler, 253–78.

Henkel, J. 2011. "Nighttime *labor*: A Metapoetic Vignette Alluding to Aratus at *Georgics* 1.291–296." *HSCP* 106: 179–98.

– 2014a. "Vergil Talks Technique: Metapoetic Arboriculture in *Georgics* 2." *Vergilius* 60: 33–66.

– 2014b. "Metrical Feet on the Road of Poetry: Foot Puns and Literary Polemic in Tibullus." *CW* 107: 451–75. https://doi.org/10.1353/clw.2014.0032.

Henry, W.B. 2005. "*Editio Princeps* of *P. Oxy.* 4711: Elegy (*Metamorphoses?*)." *The Oxyrhynchus Papyri* 69: 46–53. https://doi.org/10.1163/9789004331815_006.

Hershkowitz, D. 1998. *Valerius Flaccus'* Argonautica: *Abbreviated Voyages in Silver Latin Epic*. Oxford.

Heslin, P. 2010. "Virgil's 'Georgics' and the Dating of Propertius' First Book." *JRS* 100: 54–68. https://doi.org/10.1017/s0075435810000055.

– 2018. *Propertius, Greek Myth, and Virgil: Rivalry, Allegory, and Polemic*. Oxford.

Heubeck, A., S. West, and J.B. Hainsworth. 1988. *A Commentary on Homer's* Odyssey: *Volume 1: Introduction and Books I–VIII*. Oxford.

Heurgon, T. 1984. "Capua," *Enciclopedia Virgiliana* 1: 656–68.

Heyworth, S.J. 2007a. *Cynthia: A Companion to the Text of Propertius*. Oxford.

– ed. 2007b. *Sexti Properti Elegi*. Oxford.

– ed. 2019. *Ovid,* Fasti *Book III*. Cambridge.

Heyworth, S.J., and J.H.W. Morwood, eds. 2011. *A Commentary on Propertius Book 3*. Oxford.

Hinds, S. 1983. "*Carmina digna*, Gallus P. Qaṣr Ibrîm 667 Metamorphosed." *PLLS* 4: 43–54.

– 1987a. *The Metamorphosis of Persephone: Ovid and the Self-Conscious Muse*. Cambridge.

– 1987b. "Generalising about Ovid." *Ramus* 16: 4–31. https://doi.org/10.1017/s0048671x00003234.

– 1992. "*Arma* in Ovid's *Fasti*, Part II: Genre, Romulean Rome and Augustan Ideology." *Arethusa* 25: 113–53. https://doi.org/10.1017/9781108635806.006.

– 1998. *Allusion and Intertext: Dynamics of Appropriation in Roman Poetry.* Cambridge.

– 2000. "Essential Epic: Genre and Gender from Macer to Statius." In Depew and Obbink, 221–44.

– 2014. "The Self-Conscious Cento." In M. Formisano and T. Fuhrer, eds., *Décadence: Decline and Fall or Other Antiquity*, 171–97. Heidelberg.

– 2016. "Return to Enna: Ovid and Ovidianism in Claudian's *De raptu Proserpinae*." In Fulkerson and Stover, 249–78.

Hodge, R.I.V., and R.A. Buttimore. 1977. *The "Monobiblos" of Propertius.* Cambridge.

Hoffman, F., M. Minas-Nerpel, and S. Pfeiffer. 2009 *Die dreisprachige Stele des C. Cornelius Gallus.* Berlin and New York.

Hollis, A.S. 1977. *Ovid:* Ars Amatoria I, *Edited with Introduction and Commentary.* Oxford.

– 1996. "Traces of Ancient Commentaries on Ovid's *Metamorphoses*." *PLLS* 9: 159–74.

– ed., 2007. *Fragments of Roman Poetry c. 60 BC–AD 20.* Oxford.

Holst-Warhaft, G. 1992. *Dangerous Voices: Women's Laments and Greek Literature.* London and New York.

Holzberg, N. 1998. *Ovid: Dichter und Werk.* Munich.

Hope, V.M. 2009. *Roman Death: The Dying and the Dead in Ancient Rome.* London.

Hope, V.M., and J. Huskinson, eds. 2011. *Memory and Mourning: Studies on Roman Death.* Oxford.

Hopkins, C. 1934. "Assyrian Elements in the Perseus-Gorgon Story." *AJA* 38: 341–58. https://doi.org/10.2307/498901.

Hornblower, S. 2015. *Lykophron:* Alexandra. Oxford.

Hornblower, S. and G. Biffis, eds. 2018. *The Returning Hero:* Nostoi *and the Traditions of Mediterranean Settlement.* Oxford.

Hornsby, R. 1966. "The Armor of the Slain." *PhQ* 45: 347–59.

Horsfall, N. 1973. "Corythus: The Return of Aeneas in Virgil and His Sources." *JRS* 63: 68–79. https://doi.org/10.2307/299166.

– 1973–4. "Dido in the Light of History." *PVS* 13: 1–13.

– 1979. "Some Problems in the Aeneas Legend." *CQ* 29: 372–90. https://doi.org/10.1017/s0009838800036004.

– 1986. "Virgil and the Inscriptions: A Reverse View." *LCM* 11: 44–5.

– 1987. "Corythus Re-Examined." In J. Bremmer and N. Horsfall, eds., *Roman Myth and Mythography*, 89–104. London.

– 1989. "Aeneas the Colonist." *Vergilius* 35: 8–27. https://doi.org/10.1093/oso/9780198863861.003.0022.

– 1995. *A Companion to the Study of Virgil*. Leiden.

– 1997. "Criteria for the Dating of Calpurnius Siculus." *RFIC* 125: 166–96.

– 2000. *Virgil, Aeneid 7: A Commentary*. Leiden.

– 2001. "Vergil Reads; Octavia Faints: Grounds for Doubt." *PVS* 24: 135–7.

– 2006. *Virgil, Aeneid 3: A Commentary*. Leiden and Boston.

Houghton, L.B.T. 2011. "Death Ritual and Burial Practice in the Latin Love Elegists." In Hope and Huskinson, 61–77.

– 2017. "Elegy." In V. Moul, ed., *A Guide to Neo-Latin Literature*, 98–112. Cambridge.

– 2018. "Early Responses to Virgil's Fourth Eclogue." *Greece and Rome* 65.2: 189–204. https://doi.org/10.1017/s0017383518000141.

Houghton, L.B.T., and M. Sgarbi, eds. 2018. *Virgil and Renaissance Culture*. Turnhout.

Howe, T.P. 1954. "The Origin and Function of the Gorgon-Head." *AJA* 58: 209–21. https://doi.org/10.2307/500901.

Hubbard, M. 1975a. "The Capture of Silenus." *PCPS* 21: 53–62. https://doi.org/10.1017/s0068673500003692.

– 1975b. *Propertius*. New York.

Hubbard, T. 1995. "Allusive Artistry and Vergil's Revisionary Program: *Eclogues* 1–3." *MD* 34: 37–67. https://doi.org/10.2307/40236051.

– 1998. *The Pipes of Pan: Intertextuality and Literary Filiation in the Pastoral Tradition from Theocritus to Milton*. Ann Arbor.

Hübner, U. 1984. "Episches und Elegisches am Anfang des dritten Buches des *Pharsalia*." *Hermes* 112: 227–39.

Hughes, J., and C. Buongiovanni, eds. 2015. *Remembering Parthenope: The Reception of Classical Naples from Antiquity to the Present*. Oxford.

Hunter, R.L., ed. 1989. *Apollonius of Rhodes*, Argonautica *Book III*. Cambridge.

– 1993. *The* Argonautica *of Apollonius: Literary Studies*. Cambridge.

– ed. 1999. *Theocritus: A Selection*. Cambridge.

– 2014. *Hesiodic Voices: Studies in the Ancient Reception of Hesiod's* Works and Days. Cambridge.

Huskey, S.J. 2005. "In Memory of Tibullus: Ovid's Remembrance of Tibullus 1.3 in *Amores* 3.9 and *Tristia* 3.3." *Arethusa* 38.3: 367–86. https://doi.org/10.1353/are.2005.0016.

Hutchinson, G.O. 2006a. *Propertius: Elegies Book IV*. Cambridge.

– 2006b. "The Metamorphosis of Metamorphosis: P. Oxy. 4711 and Ovid." *ZPE* 155: 71–84.

– 2008. *Talking Books: Readings in Hellenistic and Roman Books of Poetry*. Oxford.

– 2017. "Some New and Old Light on the Reasons for Ovid's Exile." *ZPE* 203: 76–84.

Iacono, A. 2011. "Epica e strategie celebrative nel *De proelio apud Troiam* di Porcelio de' Pandoni." In G. Abbamonte, J. Barreto, T. D'Urso, A. Perriccioli

Saggese, and F. Senatore, eds., *La battaglia nel Rinascimento meridionale. Moduli narrativi tra parole e immagini*, 269–90. Rome.

– 2014. "Le *Elegiae ad Aurimpiam* tra tradizione e novità." *Bollettino di Studi Latini* 44.2: 505–31.

– 2015. "Il *De hortis Hesperidum* di Giovanni Pontano: tra innovazioni umanistiche e tradizione classica." *Spolia* 1: 188–237.

Ijsewijn, J., and D. Sacré, eds. 1998. *Companion to Neo-Latin Studies: Literary, Linguistic, Philological and Editorial Questions*. Leuven.

Ingleheart, J. 2015. "'Greek' Love at Rome: Propertius 1.20 and the Reception of Hellenistic Verse." *Eugesta* 5: 124–53.

Ingleheart, J., and K. Radice, eds. 2011. *Ovid* Amores *III: A Selection: 2, 4, 5, 14*. Bristol.

Jacobson, H. 1984. "Aristaeus, Orpheus, and the *Laudes Galli*." *AJP* 105: 271–300. https://doi.org/10.2307/294992.

James, S. 2003a. "Her Turn to Cry: The Politics of Weeping in Roman Love Elegy." *TAPA* 133.1: 99–122. https://doi.org/10.1353/apa.2003.0006.

– 2003b. *Learned Girls and Male Persuasion: Gender and Reading in Roman Love Elegy*. Berkeley, CA.

– 2012. "Re-reading Propertius' Arethusa." *Mnemosyne* 65: 425–44. https://doi.org/10.1163/156852511x547839.

Janan, M. 2001. *The Politics of Desire: Propertius IV*. Berkeley and Los Angeles.

Jansen, L., ed. 2014. *The Roman Paratext: Frame, Texts, Readers*. Cambridge.

Javitch, D. 1985. "The Imitation of Imitations in *Orlando Furioso*." *Renaissance Quarterly* 38.2: 215–39. https://doi.org/10.2307/2861663.

– 1991. *Proclaiming a Classic: The Canonization of* Orlando Furioso. Princeton.

Jocelyn, H.D. 1984. "The Annotations of M. Valerius Probus." *CQ* 34.2: 464–72.

Johnson, T.S. 2012a. *Horace's Iambic Crticism Casting Blame (Iambikē Poiēsis)*. Leiden and Boston.

– 2012b. "Horace's Elegiac Criticism and the Open-Ended Door (*C.* 3.10)." *CJ* 107: 165–88. https://doi.org/10.1353/tcj.2011.0013.

Johnson, W. 1987. *Momentary Monsters: Lucan and His Heroes*. Ithaca.

– 2012. "Propertius." In Gold, 39–52.

Johnston, P. 1980. *Vergil's Agricultural Golden Age: A Study of the* Georgics. Leiden.

Jones, F. 2011. *Virgil's Garden: The Nature of Bucolic Space*. London and New York.

Jones, W.H.S. 1918–35. *Pausanias, Description of Greece*. 6 vols. Cambridge, MA.

Jouan, F. and H. van Looy, eds. 2000. *Euripide, vol. 8: Fragments.*[2] Paris.

Kahane, A. 2017. "Biography and Virgil's Epitaph." In Powell and Hardie, 51–72. https://doi.org/10.2307/j.ctt1z27gqg.7.

Kallendorf, C. 1989. *In Praise of Aeneas: Virgil and Epideictic Rhetoric in the Early Italian Renaissance*. Hannover and London.

– 2002. "The Virgilian Title Page as Interpretive Frame." *Princeton University Library Chronicle* 64: 15–50. https://doi.org/10.25290/prinunivlibrchro.64.1.0015.

– 2007. *The Other Virgil: "Pessimistic" Readings of the* Aeneid *in Early Modern Culture.* Oxford.

– 2019. *Printing Virgil. The Transformation of the Classics in the Renaissance.* Leiden.

Karakasis, E. 2011. *Song Exchange in Roman Pastoral.* Berlin.

– 2014. "Servius." In R. Thomas and J. M. Ziolkowski, eds., *The Vergil Encyclopedia,* .3: 1153–4. Malden, MA.

– 2016a. *T. Calpurnius Siculus: A Pastoral Poet in Neronian Rome.* Berlin.

– 2016b. "Petronian Spectacles: The Widow of Ephesus Generically Revisited." In S. Frangoulidis, S.J. Harrison, and G. Manuwald, eds., *Roman Drama and Its Contexts,* 505–32. Berlin.

Kaster, R.A. 2014. "Servius." In R. Thomas and J. M. Ziolkowski, eds., *The Vergil Encyclopedia,* .3: 1153–4. Malden, MA.

Kaufmann, H. 2017. "Intertextuality in Late Latin Poetry." In Elsner and Lobato, 149–75.

Kayachev, B. 2011. "*Ille ego qui quondam*: Genre, Date, and Authorship." *Vergilius* 57: 75–82.

– 2018. "The *Aura* of Homer in Propertius. 1.1." *CP* 113.4: 482–5. https://doi.org/10.1086/699479.

Keil, H. 1857. *Grammatici Latini,* vol. 1. Leipzig.

– 1880. *Grammatici Latini,* vol. 7. Leipzig.

Keith, A.M. 1994. "*Corpus Eroticum*: Elegiac Poetics and Elegiac *Puellae* in Ovid's *Amores.*" *CW* 88: 27–40. https://doi.org/10.2307/4351614.

– 1997. "*Tandem venit amor.* A Roman Woman Speaks of Love." In Hallett and Skinner, 295–311.

– 1999a. "Versions of Epic Masculinity in Ovid's *Metamorphoses.*" In Hardie, Barchiesi, and Hinds, 214–39.

– 1999b. "Slender Verse: Roman Elegy and Ancient Rhetorical Theory." *Mnemosyne* 52: 41–62. https://doi.org/10.1163/1568525991560972.

– 2000. *Engendering Rome: Women in Latin Epic.* Cambridge.

– 2008a. "Lament in Lucan's *Bellum Civile.*" In Suter, 233–57.

– 2008b. *Propertius: Poet of Love and Leisure.* London.

– ed. 2011a. *Latin Elegy and Hellenistic Epigram: A Tale of Two Genres at Rome.* Newcastle upon Tyne.

– 2011b. "Lycoris Galli/Volumnia Cytheris: A Greek Courtesan in Rome." *Eugesta* 1: 23–53.

– 2015. "Elegiac Women and Roman Warfare." In J. Fabre-Serris and A. Keith, eds., *Women and War in Antiquity,* 138–56. Baltimore.

– 2016. "City Laments in Latin Epic." In M. Bachvarova, D. Dutsch, and A. Suter, eds., *The Fall of Cities in the Mediterranean: Commemoration in Literature, Folk-Song, and Liturgy,* 156–82. Cambridge.

– 2017. "Lyric Resonances in Statius' *Achilleid.*" In F. Bessone and M. Fucecchi, eds., *The Literary Genres in the Flavian Age,* 283–95. Berlin.

– 2018. "*Pascite boues, summittite tauros*: Cattle and Oxen in the Virgilian Corpus." In S.J. Harrison, S. Frangoulidis, and T.D. Papanghelis, eds., *Intratextuality and Latin Literature*, 99–130. Berlin.

– 2020. *Virgil*. Understanding Classics. London.

Kelly, A. 2014. "Apollonius and the End of the *Aeneid*." *CQ* 64.2: 642–8. https://doi.org/10.1017/s0009838814000214.

Kennedy, D.F. 1987. "*Arcades Ambo*: Virgil, Gallus and Arcadia." *Hermathena* 143: 47–59.

– 1993. *The Arts of Love: Five Studies in the Discourse of Roman Love Elegy*. Cambridge.

– 2007. *Elegy*. New York and London.

– 2012. "Love's Tropes and Figures." In Gold, 189–203.

Kenney, E.J. 1983. "Virgil and the Elegiac Sensibility." *ICS* 8: 44–59.

– 1994. *P. Ovidi Nasonis*: Amores, Medicamina faciei femineae, Ars amatoria, Remedia amoris. Oxford.

– 2002. "Ovid's Language and Style." In Boyd, 27–89.

Kidwell, C. 1991. *Pontano: Poet and Prime Minister*. London.

Kilpatrick, R.S. 1969. "Two Horatian Poems: *Carm.* 1.26 and 1.32." *YCS* 21: 213–40. https://doi.org/10.1017/cbo9780511933721.008.

King, J.E. 1927. *Cicero*. Tusculan Disputations. LCL 141. Cambridge, MA.

Kleberg, T. 1957. *Hotels, restaurants et cabarets dans l'antiquité romaine: études historiques et philologiques*. Uppsala.

Klein, C.F. 1991. "Snares and Entrails: Mesoamerican Symbols of Sin and Punishment." *RES: Anthology and Aesthetics* 20: 81–103.

Kleywegt, A.J. 2005. *Valerius Flaccus*, Argonautica, *Book 1: A Commentary*. Leiden.

Kline, A.S. 2002. *The Aeneid. A Translation into English Prose*.

Klingner, F. 1967. *Virgil:* Bucolica, Georgica, Aeneis. Zurich.

Knauer, G.N. 1964a. *Die Aeneis und Homer: Studien zur poetischen Technik Vergils, mit Listen der Homerzitate in der* Aeneis. Göttingen.

– 1964b. "Vergil's *Aeneid* and Homer." *GRBS* 5: 61–84. https://doi.org/10.1093/oso/9780197531594.003.0009.

Knox, P.E. 1986. *Ovid's* Metamorphoses *and the Traditions of Augustan Poetry*. Cambridge.

– ed. 1995. *Ovid:* Heroides, *Select Epistles*. Cambridge.

– 2004a. "Cynthia's Ghosts in Propertius 4.7." *Ordia Prima* 3: 153–69.

– 2004b. "The Poet and the Second Prince: Ovid in the Age of Tiberius." *MAAR* 49: 1–20. https://doi.org/10.2307/4238815.

– ed. 2006. *Oxford Readings in Ovid*. Oxford.

Korenjak, M. 2003. "*Tityri sub persona*: Der antike Biographismus und die bukolische Tradition." *A&A* 49: 58–79. https://doi.org/10.1515/9783110176070.58.

Korn, M., and H.J. Tschiedel, eds. 1991. *Ratis omnia vincet: Untersuchungen zu den* Argonautica *des Valerius Flaccus*. Zurich and New York.

Kosofsky Sedgwick, E. 1985. *Between Men. English Literature and Male Homosocial Desire*. New York.

Krevans, N. 2010. "Bookburning and the Poetic Deathbed." In Hardie and Moore, 197–208.

Kroll, W. 1924. *Studien zum Verständnis der romischen Literatur*. Stuttgart.

Kronenberg, L. 2016. "Epicurean Pastoral: Daphnis as an Allegory for Lucretius in Vergil's *Eclogues*." *Vergilius* 62: 25–56.

Küppers, J. 1989. "Tityrus in Rom – Bemerkungen zu einem vergilischen Thema und seiner Rezeptionsgeschichte." *ICS* 14: 33–47.

Kyriakidis, S. 1994. "*Inuocatio ad Musam (A. 7.37)*." *MD* 33: 197–206. https://doi.org/10.2307/40236045.

– 1998. *Narrative Structure and Poetics in the* Aeneid: *The Frame of Book 6*. Bari.

Labate, M. 1984. *L'arte di farsi amare*. Pisa.

Lafaye, G. 1923. *Catulle: Poèsies*. Paris.

Lafferty, M. 2018. "Vergil and the Changing Mise-en-Page from Late Antiquity to the Middle Ages." Paper delivered at the 2018 CAMWS Annual Meeting in Albuquerque.

La Follette, L. 2001. "The Costume of the Roman Bride." In Bonfante and Sebesta, 54–65.

Laird, A. 1999. *Powers of Expression, Expressions of Power*. Oxford.

– 2016. "Recognizing Virgil." In J. Hanink and R. Fletcher, eds., *Creative Lives in Classical Antiquity: Poets, Artists and Biography*, 75–99. Cambridge.

– 2017. "Fashioning the Poet: Biography, Pseudepigraphy and Textual Criticism." In Powell and Hardie, 29–50.

Lamb, W.R.M. 1927. *Plato*. Charmides. Alcibiades *I and II*. Hipparchus. The Lovers. Theages. Minos. Epinomis. LCL 201. Cambridge, MA.

Lane Fox, R. 2018. "Macedonians and *Nostos*." In Hornblower and Biffis, 193–212.

Langholf, V. 1990. "Vergil-Allegorese in den *Bucolica* des Calpurnius Siculus." *RhM* 133: 350–70.

Lateiner, D. 1998. "Blushes and Pallor in Ancient Fictions." *Helios* 25: 163–89.

Lattimore, R. 1961. *The* Iliad *of Homer*. Chicago.

– 1962. *Themes in Greek and Latin Epitaphs*. Urbana.

Lawall, G. 1967. *Theocritus' Coan Pastorals: A Poetry Book*. Washington, DC.

Leach, E.W. 1964. "Georgic Imagery in the *Ars Amatoria*." *TAPA* 95: 142–54. https://doi.org/10.2307/283788.

– 1968. "The Unity of *Eclogue 6*." *Latomus* 27.1: 13–32.

– 1974. *Vergil's* Eclogues: *Landscapes of Experience*. Ithaca.

Le Bonniec, H. 1958. *Le culte de Cérès à Rome des origines à la fin de la République*. Paris.

Le Doze, P. 2014. *Mécène: Ombres et flamboyances*. Paris.

Lee, A.G., ed. 1984. *Virgil: The* Eclogues. London.

Lee, M.O. 1989. *Death and Rebirth in Virgil's Arcadia*. Albany.

Lee-Stecum, P. 1998. *Powerplay in Tibullus: Reading Elegies Book One*. Cambridge.

– 2013. "Tibullus in First Place." In Thorsen, 68–82.

Lefèvre, E. 1976. "Die Lehre von der Entstehung der Tieropfer in Ovids *Fasten* I, 335–456." *RhM* 119: 39–64.

Leigh, M. 1997. *Lucan: Spectacle and Engagement*. Oxford.

– 1999. "Lucan's Caesar and the Sacred Grove: Deforestation and Enlightenment in Antiquity." In P. Esposito and L. Nicastri, eds., *Interpretare Lucano. Miscellanea di Studi*, 167–205. Naples.

Lewis, C.S. 1942. *A Preface to* Paradise Lost. Oxford.

Lewis, J.M. 1985. "Eros and the Polis in Theognis Book II." In T.J. Figueira and G. Nagy, eds., *Theognis of Megara: Poetry and the Polis*, 197–222. Baltimore.

Lightfoot, J.L. 1999. *Parthenius of Nicaea*. Oxford.

Lipka, M. 2001. *Language in Vergil's* Eclogues. Berlin and New York.

Littlewood, C. 2016. "Elegy and Epic in Lucan's *Bellum Civile*." In A. Keith and J. Edmondson, eds., *Roman Literary Cultures: Domestic Politics, Revolutionary Poetics, Civic Spectacle*, 159–84. Toronto.

Littlewood, R.J. 1980. "Ovid and the Ides of March." In C. Deroux, ed., *Studies in Latin Literature and Roman History II*, 301–21. Brussels.

Littlewood, R.J., ed. 2006. *A Commentary on Ovid's* Fasti, *Book 6*. Oxford.

Lively, G. 2012. "*Mater Amoris*: Mothers and Lovers in Augustan Rome." In L. Hackworth Peterson and P. Salzman-Mitchell, eds., *Mothering and Motherhood in Ancient Greece and Rome*, 105–203. Austin, TX.

Looney, D. 1996. *Compromising the Classics: Romance Epic Narrative in the Italian Renaissance*. Detroit.

– 2003. "Ariosto and the Classics in Ferrara." In D. Beecher, M. Ciavolella and R. Fedi, eds., *Ariosto Today: Contemporary* Perspectives, 18–31. Toronto.

Loupiac, A. 1998. *La poétique des éléments dans La Pharsale de Lucain*. Brussels.

Lovatt, H. 2013. *The Epic Gaze: Vision, Gender and Narrative in Ancient Epic*. Cambridge.

Lovatt, H., and C. Vout, eds. 2013. *Epic Visions*. Cambridge.

Lowe, D. 2015. *Monsters and Monstrosity in Augustan Poetry*. Ann Arbor.

Lowrie, M. 2009. *Writing, Performance, and Authority in Augustan Rome*. Oxford.

Lucifora, R.M. 1979. "I loci similes del *Cupido Cruciatus*." *Atti della Accademia Peloritana dei Pericolanti* 55: 261–71.

Luck, G. 1962. "Beiträge zum Text der römischen Elegik." *RhM* 105: 337–51.

– 1999. "Witches and Sorcerers in Classical Literature." In Ankarloo and Clark, 91–158.

Ludwig, W. 1982. "Neulateinische Lehrgedichte und Vergils *Georgica*." In D. H. Green, L.P. Johnson, and D. Wuttke, eds., *From Wolfram and Petrarch to Goethe and Grass: Studies in Literature in Honour of Leonard Forster*, 151–80. Baden-Baden.

Lyne, R.O.A.M. 1979. "Servitium Amoris." *CQ* 29: 117–30. https://doi.org/10.1017/s0009838800035229.

– 1980. *The Latin Love Poets: From Catullus to Horace*. Oxford.

– 1987. *Further Voices in Vergil's* Aeneid. Oxford.

– 1995. *Horace: Behind the Public Poetry*. New Haven.

– 1998a. "Introductory Poems in Propertius: 1.1 and 2.12." *PCPS* 44: 158–81. https://doi.org/10.1017/s006867350000225x.

– 1998b. "Propertius 2.10 and 11 and the Structure of Books '2A' and '2B.'" *JRS* 88: 21–36. https://doi.org/10.2307/300803.

– 2002. "The Life of Love." In P.A. Miller, ed., *Latin Erotic Elegy: An Anthology and Reader*, 348–65. London and New York.

Mac Góráin, F. 2013. "Virgil's Bacchus and the Roman Republic." In J. Farrell and D. Nelis, eds., *Augustan Poetry and the Roman Republic*, 124–45. Oxford.

Mac Góráin, F., and C. Martindale, eds. 2019. *The Cambridge Companion to Virgil*.[2] Cambridge.

Mack, S. 1978. *Patterns of Time in Vergil*. Hamden, CT.

MacKay, L.A. 1956. "Saturnia Juno." *G&R* 3: 59–60. https://doi.org/10.1017/s0017383500013048.

Magnelli, E. 2006. "Bucolic Tradition and Poetic Programme in Calpurnius Siculus." In Fantuzzi and Papanghelis, 467–77.

Makowski, J.F. 1989. "Nisus and Euryalus: A Platonic Relationship." *CJ* 85.1: 1–15. https://doi.org/10.1002/9781118351352.wbve1458.

Malamud, M., and D. McGuire, Jr. 1993. "Flavian Variant: Myth. Valerius' *Argonautica*." In Boyle, 192–217. https://doi.org/10.4324/9780203439463-16.

Malkin, I. 1998. *The Returns of Odysseus: Colonization and Ethnicity*. Berkeley.

Maltby, R. 1991. *A Lexicon of Ancient Latin Etymologies*. Leeds.

– 1999. "Tibullus and the Language of Latin Elegy." *Proceedings of the British Academy* 99: 377–98.

– 2002. *Tibullus: Elegies. Text, Introduction, and Commentary*. Chippenham, Wiltshire.

Marcus, M. 1993. "Angelica's Loveknots: The Poetics of Requited Desire in *Orlando Furioso* 19 and 23." *Philological Quarterly* 72.1: 33–48.

Martelli, F.K.A. 2013. *Ovid's Revisions: The Editor as Author*. Cambridge and New York.

Marti, B. 1966. "Cassius Scaeva and Lucan's *Inventio*." In L. Wallach, ed., *The Classical Tradition: Literary and Historical Studies in Honour of Harry Caplan*, 239–57. Ithaca.

Martin, R. 2008. "Keens from the Absent Chorus: Troy to Ulster." In Suter, 118–38.

Martindale, C. 1993. *Redeeming the Text: Latin Poetry and the Hermeneutics of Reception*. Cambridge.

Martindale, C., ed. 1997. *The Cambridge Companion to Virgil*. Cambridge.

Masters, J. 1992. *Poetry and Civil War in Lucan's* Bellum Civile. Cambridge.

Matthews, M. 2008. *Caesar and the Storm: A Commentary on Lucan* De Bello Civili, *Book 5 lines 476–721*. Bern.

Mattiacci, S. 2018. "'*An vos Nasonis carmina non legitis?*': Ovid in Ausonius' *Epigrams*." In F.E. Consolino, ed., *Ovid in Late Antiquity*, 49–87. Turnhout.

Mayer, R. 2006. "Latin Pastoral after Virgil." In Fantuzzi and Papanghelis, 451–66.

Mayer, R., ed. 1994. *Horace* Epistles *Book I*. Cambridge.

McCahill, E.M. 2009. "Rewriting Vergil, Rereading Rome: Maffeo Vegio, Poggio Bracciolini, Flavio Biondo, and Early Quattrocento Antiquarianism." *MAAR* 54: 165–99.

McCallum, S. 2015. "Elegiac *amor* and *mors* in Virgil's 'Italian *Iliad*': A Case Study (*Aeneid* 10.185–93)." *CQ* 65.2: 693–703. https://doi.org/10.1017/s0009838815000403.

– 2019. "Rivalry and Revelation: Ovid's Elegiac revision of Virgilian Allusion." In McIntyre and McCallum, 19–36. London.

–. Forthcoming. *Taking Love Seriously: Elegiac Love and Death in Vergil's* Aeneid. Oxford.

McCune, B.C. 2014. "Lucan's *Militia Amoris*: Elegiac Expectations in the *Bellum Civile*." *CJ* 109: 171–98.

McGlew, J.F. 1993. *Tyranny and Political Culture in Ancient Greece*. Ithaca.

McIntyre, G., and S. McCallum, eds. 2019. *Uncovering Anna Perenna: A Focused Study of Roman Myth and Culture*. London.

McKay, A.G. 1970. *Vergil's Italy*. Greenwich, CT.

McKeown, J.C. 1979. "Augustan Elegy and Mime." *PCPS* 25: 71–84. https://doi.org/10.1017/s0068673500004132.

– 1987–98. *Ovid:* Amores, Text, *Prolegomena and Commentary*. 3 vols. Leeds.

Meban, D. 2009. "Virgil's *Eclogues* and Social Memory." *AJP* 130: 99–130. https://doi.org/10.1353/ajp.0.0035.

Mengelkoch, D. 2010. "The Mutability of Poetics: Poliziano, Statius, and the *Silvae*." *Modern Language Notes* 125.1: 84–116. https://doi.org/10.1353/mln.0.0230.

Méniel, B., M. Bouquet, and G. Ramires, eds. 2011. *Servius et sa reception de l'Antiquité à la Renaissance*. Rennes.

Merkel, R., ed. 1841. *P. Ovidii Nasonis* Fastorum *Libri Sex*. Berlin.

Merkelbach, R. 1971. "*Aeneia Nutrix*." *RhM* 114: 349–51.

Michalopoulos, A.N. 2016. "Homer in Love: Homeric Reception in Propertius and Ovid." In A. Efstathiou and I. Karamanou, eds., *Homeric Receptions across Generic and Cultural Contexts*, 289–300. Berlin.

Miletti, L. 2013. "Classicismo ed élites locali nel Rinascimento meridionale. Il caso di Lelio Gentile di Capua." *Aevum* 87.3: 713–31.

– 2015. "Peto (Poetus, Paetus), Francesco (Franciscus)." In *Dizionario Biografico degli Italiani* 82, 665–7. Rome.

– 2018a. "Ambrogio Leone's *De Nola* as a Renaissance work. Purposes, Structure, Genre, and Sources." In B. de Divitiis, F. Lenzo, and L. Miletti, eds., *Ambrogio Leone's De Nola, Venice 1514: Humanism and Antiquarian Culture in Renaissance Southern Italy*, 11–44. Leiden.

– 2018b. "*Tacitis regnavit Amyclis*. Francesco Peto da Fondi su Virgilio *Aen*. X 563–4." In Deramaix and Germano, 145–61.

– 2019. "Prospero Colonna e la silloge di poesie latine per Ettore Fieramosca." In Delle Donne and Rivera Magos, 169–86.

– 2023. "Writing of Cities in Renaissance Southern Italy: Local History, Antiquarianism, and Classical Sources." In B. de Divitiis, ed., *A Companion to Renaissance in the Centres of Southern Italy (1350–1600)*. Leiden.

Miletti, L., and S. Tuccinardi. 2017. "Una celebrazione poetica del Cortile delle Statue e della Cleopatra in Vaticano: Aurelio Serena da Monopoli." *Prospettiva* 165–6: 3–19.

Miller, J.F. 1982. "Callimachus and the Augustan Aetiological Elegy." *ANRW* 2.30.1: 371–417. https://doi.org/10.1515/9783110844108-006.

– 1991. *Ovid's Elegiac Festivals: Studies in the* Fasti. Frankfurt and New York.

– 1992. "The *Fasti* and Hellenistic Didactic: Ovid's Variant Aetiologies." *Arethusa* 25: 11–31.

– 1993. "Ovidian Allusion and the Vocabulary of Memory." *MD* 30: 153–64.

– 2004. "Propertian Reception of Virgil's Actian Apollo." *MD* 52: 73–84. https://doi.org/10.2307/40236445.

– 2009. *Apollo, Augustus and the Poets*. Cambridge.

– 2022. "Teaching through Exempla in the *Ars Amatoria*: The Case of Pasiphae." In J.S. Clay and A. Vergados, eds., *Teaching through Images: Imagery in Greco-Roman Didactic Poetry*, 272–89. Leiden.

Miller, P.A. 1994. *Lyric Texts and Lyric Consciousness: The Birth of a Genre from Archaic Greece to Augustan Rome*. London.

– 2004. *Subjecting Verses: Latin Love Elegy and the Emergence of the Real*. Princeton.

– 2010. "'What's Love Got to Do with It?': The Peculiar Story of Elegy in Rome." In Wiseman, 46–66.

Moatti, C. 1997. *La raison de Rome. Naissance de l'esprit critique à la fin de la République, IIe-Ier siècles av. J.-C.* Paris.

Mocanu, A. 2012. "Hunting in Seneca's *Phaedra*." *Past Imperfect* 18: 27–52. https://doi.org/10.21971/p7x88g.

Modesti, P. 2014. *Le delizie ritrovate: Poggioreale e la villa del rinascimento nella Napoli aragonese*. Florence.

Mongelli, M. 2017. "Editori e lettori dell'epistolario *ad Hiaracum* di Elisio Calenzio." In D. Canfora and C. Corfiati, eds., *Roma, Napoli e altri viaggi per Mauro de Nichilo*, 325–31. Bari.

Monteleone, C. 1977. "*Eneide, 7, 37*: L'invocazione Ad Erato Come Segnale." *AC* 46: 184–91. https://doi.org/10.3406/antiq.1977.1855.

Monti Sabia, L., ed. 1973. *Ioannis Ioviani Pontani* Eclogae. *Testo critico*. Naples.

– ed. 1974. *Iovannis Iovani Pontani:* de Tumulis. Naples.

– 1983. "Trasfigurazione di Virgilio nella poesia del Pontano." In *Atti del Convegno virgiliano di Brindisi nel Bimillenario della Morte: Brindisi, 15–18 ottobre 1981*, 47–63.

Monti Sabia, L., S. Monti, and G. Germano. 2010. *Studi su Giovanni Pontano*. Messina.

Morford, M.P.O. 1967. *The Poet Lucan: Studies in Rhetorical Epic*. Oxford.

Morgan, L. 1999. *Patterns of Redemption in Virgil's* Georgics. Cambridge.

Most, G. 2001. "Memory and Forgetting in the *Aeneid*." *Vergilius* 47: 148–70.

Moul, V. 2016. "Lyric Poetry." In S. Knight and S. Tilg, eds., *The Oxford Handbook of Neo-Latin*, 41–56. Oxford.

Murgatroyd, P. 1975. "*Militia Amoris* and the Roman Elegists." *Latomus* 34: 59–79.

Murray, A.T., and W.F. Wyatt. 1924. *Homer*. Iliad. *Books 1–12*. LCL 170. Cambridge, MA.

Myers, K.S. 1994. *Ovid's Causes*. Ann Arbor.

– 1996. "The Poet and the Procuress: The *Lena* in Latin Love Elegy." *JRS* 86: 1–21. https://doi.org/10.1017/s0075435800057403.

– 2014. "Ovid, *Epistulae ex Ponto* 4.8, Germanicus, and the *Fasti*." *CQ* 64: 725–34. https://doi.org/10.1017/s0009838814000329.

Myers, M.Y. 2018. "Import/Export: Empire and Appropriation in the Gallus Papyrus from Qasr Ibrim." In M.P. Loar, C. MacDonald, and D. Padilla Peralta, eds., *Rome, Empire of Plunder: The Dynamics of Cultural Appropriation*, 214–36. Cambridge.

– 2020. "Vergil's Underworld and the Afterlife of Lovers and Love Poets." In B. Gladhill and M.Y. Myers, eds., *Walking through Elysium: Vergil's Underworld and the Poetics of Tradition*, 111–33. Toronto.

Mynors, R.A.B., ed. 1969. *P. Vergilii Maronis Opera*. Oxford.

– ed. 1990. *Virgil*, Georgics. Oxford.

Nafissi, M. 1995. "La documentazione letteraria ed epigrafica." In E. Lippolis, S. Garraffo, and M. Nafissi, eds., *I Culti greci in Occidente. I: Taranto*, 155–334. Taranto.

Nappa, C. 2005. *Reading after Actium: Vergil's* Georgics, Octavian, and Rome. Ann Arbor.

– 2007. "Unmarried Dido: *Aeneid* 4.550–52." *Hermes* 135.3: 310–13.

Narducci, E. 1979. *La provvidenza crudele: Lucano e la distruzione dei miti augustei*. Pisa.

Nauta, R.R. 2002. *Poetry for Patrons: Literary Communication in the Age of Domitian*. Leiden.

– 2006. "Panegyric in Virgil's *Bucolics*." In Fantuzzi and Papanghelis, 301–32.

Navarro Antolín, F., ed. 1996. *Lygdamus: Corpus Tibullianum III. 1–6*. Leiden.

Nelis, D. 2001. *Vergil's Aeneid and the* Argonautica *of Apollonius Rhodius*. Leeds.

Néraudau, J.-P. 1983. "Asinius Pollion et la poésie." *ANRW* 2.30.3: 1732–50.

Newlands, C. 1995. *Playing with Time: Ovid and the* Fasti. Ithaca.

– 2006. "Ovid's Narrator in the *Fasti*." In P.E. Knox, ed., *Oxford Readings in Ovid*, 351–64. Oxford.

– 2020. "Ovid's Aristaeus (*Fast.* 1.363-80)." *CJ* 115.3–4: 268–81.

Newman, J.K. 1998. "*Saturno Rege*: Themes of the Golden Age in Tibullus and Other Augustan Poets." In A.E. Radke, ed., *Candide Iudex: Beiträge zur augusteischen Dichtung*, 225–46. Stuttgart.

Nguyen, N.L. 2006. "Roman Rape: An Overview of Roman Rape Laws from the Republican Period to Justinian's Reign." *MJGL* 13: 75–112.

Nikoloutsos, K.P. 2007. "Beyond Sex: The Poetics and Politics of Pederasty in Tibullus 1.4." *Phoenix* 61: 55–82.

– 2011. "The Boy as Metaphor: The Hermeneutics of Homoerotic Desire in Tibullus 1.9." *Helios* 38.1: 22–57. https://doi.org/10.1353/hel.2011.0000.

Nisbet, R.G.M. 1987. "Pyrrha among Roses: Real Life and Poetic Imagination in Augustan Rome." *JRS* 77: 184–90.

Nisbet, R.G.M., and M. Hubbard. 1970. *A Commentary on Horace's Odes Book I*. Oxford.

– 1978. *A Commentary on Horace. Odes Book II*. Oxford.

Nisbet, R.G.M., and N. Rudd. 2004. *A Commentary on Horace. Odes Book III*. Oxford.

Nixon, P. 1980. *Plautus with an English Translation*. 5 vols. Cambridge, MA.

Nobili, C. 2011. "The Threnodic Elegy in Sparta." *GRBS* 51: 26–48.

Noonan, J.D. 1991. "Andromeda Is Missing." *CJ* 86.4: 330–6.

Norden, E. 1957. *P. Vergilius Maro: Aeneis Buch VI*. Stuttgart.

Noussia-Fantuzzi, M. 2010. *Solon of Athens: The Poetic Fragments*. Leiden.

Nugent, S.G. 1990. "Ausonius' 'Late-Antique' Poetics and 'Post-Modern' Literary Theory." *Ramus* 19: 26–50. https://doi.org/10.1017/s0048671x00002940.

– 1992. "Vergil's 'Voice of the Women' in *Aeneid* V." *Arethusa* 2: 255–92.

Nussbaum, M. 1993. "Poetry and the Passions: Two Stoic Views." In J. Brunschwig and M. Nussbaum, eds., *Passions and Perceptions: Studies in Hellenistic Philosophy of Mind*, 97–149. Cambridge.

O'Daly, G. 2004. "*Sunt etiam Musis sua ludicra*: Vergil in Ausonius." In R. Rees, ed., *Romane Memento: Vergil in the Fourth Century*, 141–54. London.

Oeschger, J., ed. 1948. *Ioanis Iovanni Pontani: Carmina: ecloghe, elegie, liriche*. Scrittori d'Italia 198. Bari.

Ogden, D. 1999. "Binding Spells: Curse Tablets and Voodoo Dolls in the Greek and Roman Worlds." In Ankarloo and Clark, 1–90.

– 2013. *Drakon: Dragon Myth and Serpent Cult in the Greek and Roman Worlds*. Oxford.

Ogilvie, R. 1962. "The Song of Thyrsis." *JHS* 82: 106–10. https://doi.org/
  10.2307/628546.
– 1965. *A Commentary on Livy, Books 1–5*. Oxford.
O'Hara, J. 1996a. *True Names: Vergil and the Alexandrian Tradition of Etymological
  Wordplay*. Ann Arbor.
– 1996b. "Vergil's Best Reader? Ovidian Commentary on Vergilian Etymological
  Wordplay." *CJ* 91: 255–76.
– 2005. "War and the Sweet Life: The Gallus Fragment and the Text of Tibullus
  1.10.11." *CQ* 55.1: 317–19. https://doi.org/10.1093/cq/bmi029.
– 2007. *Inconsistency in Roman Epic: Studies in Catullus, Lucretius, Vergil, Ovid,
  and Lucan*. Cambridge.
– 2010. "The Unfinished *Aeneid*?" In Farrell and Putnam, 96–106.
– 2017. *True Names: Vergil and the Alexandrian Tradition of Etymological
  Wordplay*. Ann Arbor.
O'Higgins, D. 1988. "Lucan as *Vates*." *CA* 7: 208–26. https://doi.
  org/10.2307/25010888.
Oliensis, E. 1997. "Sons and Lovers: Sexuality and Gender in Virgil's Poetry." In
  Martindale, 294–311.
Olson, K. 2008. *Dress and the Roman Woman: Self-Presentation and Society*.
  London and New York.
Onians, R.B. 1973. *The Origins of European Thought: About the Body, the Mind, the
  Soul, the World, Time, and Fate*. Cambridge.
O'Rourke, D. 2011a. "'Eastern' Elegy and 'Western' Epic: Reading 'Orientalism' in
  Propertius 4 and Virgil's *Aeneid*." *Dictynna* 8: 2–23. https://doi.org/10.4000/
  dictynna.699.
– 2011b. "The Representation and Misrepresentation of Virgilian Poetry in
  Propertius 2.34." *AJP* 132: 457–97. https://doi.org/10.1353/ajp.2011.0030.
– 2012. "Intertextuality in Roman Elegy." In Gold, 390–409.
– 2018. "Make War Not Love: *Militia amoris* and Domestic Violence in Roman
  Elegy." In M.R. Gale and J.H.D. Scourfield, eds., *Texts and Violence in the Roman
  World*, 110–39. Cambridge.
Osorio, P. 2020. "Vergil's Physics of *Bugonia* in *Georgics* 4." *CP* 115: 27–46.
  https://doi.org/10.1086/706565.
Östenberg, I. 2009. *Staging the World: Spoils, Captives, and Representations in the
  Roman Triumphal Procession*. Oxford.
Otis, B. 1945. "Horace and the Elegists." *TAPA* 76: 177–90. https://doi.
  org/10.2307/283335.
– 1964. *A Study in Civilized Poetry*. Norman, OK.
Ozanam, A.M. 1990. "Le mystère et le sacrè dans le stoicism romain à l'époque
  néronienne." *BAGB* 3: 275–88. https://doi.org/10.3406/bude.1990.1441.

Pade, M. 2016. "Martialis. Addenda et Corrigenda." In G. Dinkova-Brun, J. Gaisser, and J. Hankins, eds., *Catalogus Translationum et Commentariorum*. Mediaeval and Renaissance Latin Translation and Commentaries 11: 371–82. Toronto.

Page, D.L. 1936. "The Elegiacs in Euripides' *Andromache*." In C. Bailey et al., eds., *Greek Poetry and Life*, 693–703. Oxford.

Panayotakis, C. 2010. *Decimus Laberius: The Fragments*. Cambridge.

Pandey, N.B. 2017. "Sowing the Seeds of War: The *Aeneid*'s Pre-History of Interpretive Contestation and Appropriation." *CW* 111.1: 7–25. https://doi.org/10.1353/clw.2017.0062.

– 2018. *The Poetics of Power in Augustan Rome: Latin Poetic Responses to Early Imperial Iconography*. Cambridge.

Panoussi, V. 2002. "Vergil's Ajax: Allusion, Tragedy, and Heroic Identity in the *Aeneid*." *CA* 21: 95–134. https://doi.org/10.1525/ca.2002.21.1.95.

– 2003. "Virgil and Epic Topoi in Lucan's Massilia." In P. Thibodeau and H. Haskell, eds., *Being There Together: Essays in Honor of Michael C.J. Putnam on the Occasion of His Seventieth Birthday*, 222–39. Afton.

– 2009. *Greek Tragedy in Vergil's* Aeneid: *Ritual, Empire, and Intertext*. Cambridge.

Papanghelis, T.D. 1987. *Propertius: A Hellenistic Poet on Love and Death*. Cambridge.

– 1999. "Eros Pastoral and Profane: On Love in Virgil's *Eclogues*." In S.M. Braund and R. Mayer, eds., *Amor: Roma. Love in Latin Literature*, 44–59. Cambridge.

Papini, P., ed. 1957. *Ludovico Ariosto:* Orlando Furioso. Florence.

Paratore, E. 1970. "L'influenza delle *Heroides* sull'episodio di Biblide e Cauno nel l. IX delle *Metamorfosi* ovidiane." In *Studia Florentina Alexandro Ronconi sexagenario oblata*, 291–309. Rome.

Parks, G.B. 1971. "Pausanias." In P.O. Kristeller, ed., *Catalogus Translationum et Commentariorum:* Medieval and Renaissance Latin Translations and Commentaries 2, 215–20. Washington, DC.

Parry, A. 1972. "The Idea of Art in Vergil's *Georgics*." *Arethusa* 5: 35–52.

Paturzo, F. 1999. *Mecenate, il ministro d'Augusto: politica, filosofia, letteratura nel period augusteo*. Cortona.

Pavlock, B. 1985. "Epic and Tragedy in Vergil's Nisus and Euryalus Episode." *TAPA* 115: 207–24. https://doi.org/10.2307/284198.

– 1992. "The Hero and the Erotic in *Aeneid* 7–12." *Vergilius* 38: 72–87.

Pease, A.S. 1940. "*Mantua Me Genuit*." *CPh* 35.2: 180–2. https://doi.org/10.1086/362354.

Pederzani, O. 1995. *Il talamo, l'albero e lo specchio. Saggio di commento a Stat. Silv. I 2, II 3, III 4*. Bari.

Peirano, I. 2012. *The Rhetoric of the Roman Fake: Latin Pseudepigrapha in Context*. Cambridge.

– 2013. *Ille ego qui quondam*: On Authorial (An)onymity." In A. Marmodoro and J. Hill, eds., *The Author's Voice in Classical and Late Antiquity*, 251–85. Oxford.

Pelttari, A. 2014. *The Space That Remains: Reading Latin Poetry in Late Antiquity*. Ithaca.

Percopo, E. 1921. "Ville ed abitazioni di poeti in Napoli. I. La villa del Pontano ad Antignano." *Napoli Nobilissima* 2.2: 1–7.

Perkell, C.G. 1996. "The 'Dying Gallus' and the Design of *Eclogue* 10." *CP* 91: 128–40. https://doi.org/10.1086/367503.

– 1999. *Reading Vergil's Aeneid: An Interpretative Guide*. Norman, OK.

– 2002. "The Golden Age and Its Contradictions in the Poetry of Vergil." *Vergilius* 48: 3–39.

Perutelli, A. 2000. *La poesia epica latina: dalle origini all'età dei Flavi*. Rome.

Petrini, M. 1997. *The Child and the Hero: Coming of Age in Catullus and Vergil*. Ann Arbor.

Phang, S.E. 2001. *The Marriage of Roman Soldiers (13 BC–AD 235): Law and Family in the Imperial Army*. Leiden.

Phillips, O.C. 1968. "Lucan's Grove." *CP* 63: 296–300. https://doi.org/10.1086/365420.

Pichon, R. 1902. *De sermone amatorio apud Latinos elegiarum scriptores*. Paris; reprinted as *Index Verborum Amatorium* (Hildesheim 1966).

Pieper, C. 2009. "Genre Negotiations: Cristoforo Landino's *Xandra* between Elegy and Epigram," In De Beer, Enenkel, and Rijser, 165–90.

Piranomonte, M. 2002. *Il santuario della musica e il bosco sacro di Anna Perenna*. Rome.

– 2010. "Religion and Magic at Rome: The Fountain of Anna Perenna." In R.L. Gordon and F.M. Simón, eds., *Magical Practice in the Latin West*, 191–213. Leiden.

– 2016. "The Discovery of the Fountain of Anna Perenna and Its Influence on the Study of Ancient Magic." In G. Bąkowska-Czerner et al., eds., *The Wisdom of Thoth: Magical Texts in Ancient Mediterranean Civilisations*, 71–85. Oxford.

Porte, D. 1985. *L'Étiologie religieuse dans les Fastes d'Ovide*. Paris.

Postgate, J.P. 1885. *Select Elegies of Propertius*. London.

– 1915.[2] *Tibulli aliorumque Carminum Libri Tres*. Oxford.

Powell, A., and P. Hardie, eds. 2017. *The Ancient Lives of Virgil: Literary and Historical Studies*. Bristol.

Purcell, N. 2018. "Mediterranean Perspectives on Departure, Displacement, and Home." In Hornblower and Biffis, 267–86.

Putnam, M.C.J. 1965. *The Poetry of the* Aeneid: *Four Studies in Imaginative Unity and Design*. Ithaca.

– 1970. *Virgil's Pastoral Art*. Princeton.

– 1974. "Catullus 11: The Ironies of Integrity." *Ramus* 3: 70–86. https://doi.org/10.1017/s0048671x00004616.

– 1979. *Virgil's Poem of the Earth: Studies in the* Georgics. Princeton.

– 1980. "Propertius and the New Gallus Fragment." *ZPE* 39: 49–56.

– 1995. *Virgil's Aeneid: Interpretation and Influence*. Chapel Hill, NC.

– 1995–6. "Pastoral Satire." *Arion* 3rd series 3.2/3: 303–16.

– 2001. "The Ambiguity of Art in Virgil's *Aeneid*." *Proceedings of the American Philosophical Society* 145: 162–83.

– 2010. "Some Virgilian Unities." In Hardie and Moore, 17–38.

Quinn, K. 1970. *Catullus: The Poems*. London.

Quint, D. 2018. *Virgil's Double Cross: Design and Meaning in the* Aeneid. Princeton.

Quintiliani, M.M. 2014. "Patrizi, Francesco." In *Dizionario Biografico degli Italiani* 81: 732–8. Rome.

Raaflaub, K.A. 1993. "Homer to Solon: The Rise of the Polis. The Written Evidence." In M.H. Hansen, ed., *The Ancient Greek City State*, 7–29. Copenhagen.

Rabel, R.J. 1974. "The Iliadic Nature of *Aeneid* 9." *Vergilius* 24: 37–44.

Radke, G. 1993. "Römische Feste im Monat März." *Tyche* 8: 129–42. https://doi.org/10.15661/tyche.1993.008.17.

Ramires, G., ed. 2003. *Servio, Commento al libro VII dell'Eneide di Virgilio. Con le aggiunte del cosiddetto Servio Danielino*. Bologna.

Ramsby, T. 2007. *Textual Permanence: Roman Elegists and Epigraphic Tradition*. London.

Reckford, K.J. 1961. "Latent Tragedy in *Aeneid* VII, 1–285." *AJP* 82.3: 252–69. https://doi.org/10.2307/292368.

– 1974. "Phaedra and Pasiphae: The Pull Backward." *TAPA* 104: 307–28. https://doi.org/10.2307/2936095.

Reed, J.D. 2007. *Virgil's Gaze: Nation and Poetry in the* Aeneid. Princeton.

– 2014. "The Pastoral Lament in Ancient Greek and Latin." In M. Tuhkanen and E.L. McCallum, eds., *The Cambridge History of Gay and Lesbian Literature*, 51–67. Cambridge.

Rees, R. 2011. "Nailing Down the Poet: Ausonius' *Cupid Crucified*." In P. Millett, S.P. Oakley, and R.J.E. Thompson, eds., Ratio et Res Ipsa: *Classical Essays Presented by Former Pupils to James Diggle on His Retirement*, 135–49. Cambridge.

Reitzenstein, E. 1936. *Wirklichkeitsbild und Gefühlsentwicklung bei Properz*. Leipzig.

Rhorer, C.C. 1980. "Red and White in Ovid's *Metamorphoses*." *Ramus* 9: 79–88. https://doi.org/10.1017/s0048671x00040029.

Richlin, A. 2014. *Arguments with Silence: Writing the History of Roman Women*. Ann Arbor.

Richter, W. 1957. *Vergil*, Georgica. Munich.

Rimell, V. 2015. *The Closure of Space in Roman Poetics: Empire's Inward Turn*. Cambridge.

Ripoll, F., and J. Soubiran, eds. 2008. *Stace, Achilléide*. Leuven.

Roberts, M. 1989. *The Jeweled Style: Poetry and Poetics in Late Antiquity*. Ithaca.

Robinson, M. 1999. "Salmacis and Hermaphroditus: When Two Become One (Ovid, *Met*. 4.285–388)." *CQ* 49: 212–23. https://doi.org/10.1093/cq/49.1.212.

– ed. 2011. *A Commentary on Ovid's* Fasti, *Book 2*. Oxford.

– 2013. "Propertius 1.3: Sleep, Surprise, and Catullus 64." *BICS* 56: 89–115. https://doi.org/10.1111/j.2041-5370.2013.00052.x.

Roche, P. 2009. *Lucan: De Bello Civili, Book 1*. Oxford.

Roman, L., trans. 2014. *Giovanni Gioviano Pontano:* On Married Love. Eridanus. Cambridge, MA.

– ed. and trans. 2022. *Giovanni Gioviano Pontano: Eclogues. Garden of the Hesperides*. Cambridge, MA.

Rosati, G. 1994. "L'*Achilleide* di Stazio, un'epica «en travesti»." In G. Rosati, ed., *Stazio, Achilleide*, 5–61. Milan.

Rosen, R., and J. Farrell. 1986. "Acontius, Milanion and Gallus: Vergil, *Ecl*. 10.52–61." *TAPA* 116: 241–54. https://doi.org/10.2307/283919.

Rosenmeyer, P.A. 1999. "Tracing *Medulla* as a *Locus Eroticus*." *Arethusa* 32.1: 19–47. https://doi.org/10.1353/are.1999.0005.

Rosner-Siegel, J.A. 1983. "The Oak and the Lightning: Lucan *Bellum Civile* 1.135–157." *Athenaeum* 61: 165–77.

Ross, D.O., Jr. 1969. *Style and Tradition in Catullus*. Cambridge, MA.

– 1975. *Backgrounds to Augustan Poetry: Gallus, Elegy, and Rome*. Cambridge.

– 1987. *Virgil's Elements: Physics and Poetry in the* Georgics. Princeton.

Rossi, G. 2015. "L'umanista senese Francesco Patrizi e la lezione etico-politica degli antichi: il trattato *De institutione reipublicae* (ante 1471)." In A. Steiner-Weber and K.A.E. Enenkel, eds., *Acta Conventus Neo-Latini Monasteriensis. Proceedings of the Fifteenth International Congress of Neo-Latin Studies (Münster 2012)*, 440–9. Leiden.

Rothstein, M. 1920–4. *Die Elegien des Sextus Propertius*. 2 vols. Berlin.

Rowland, R.J. 1969. "The Significance of Massilia in Lucan." *Hermes* 97: 204–8.

Rudd, N. 1989. *Horace* Epistles *Book II and* Epistle to the Pisones (Ars Poetica). Cambridge.

– 2004. *Horace*. Odes *and* Epodes. LCL 33. Cambridge, MA.

Rumpf, L. 2008. "Bucolic *nomina* in Virgil and Theocritus: On the Poetic Technique of Virgil's *Eclogues*." In K. Volk, ed., *Oxford Readings in Virgil's* Eclogues, 64–78. Oxford.

Russo, J., M. Fernández-Galiano, and A. Heubeck. 1992. *A Commentary on Homer's* Odyssey: *Volume III: Books XVII–XXIV*. Oxford.

Rutger-Hausmann, F. 1980. "Martialis, Marcus Valerius." In F.E. Cranz and P.O. Kristeller, eds., *Catalogus Translationum et Commentariorum*. Mediaeval and Renaissance Latin Translation and Commentaries 4, 250–96. Washington, DC.

Rutz, W. 1960. "*Amor mortis* bei Lucan." *Hermes* 88: 462–75.

Rykwert, J. 1976. *The Idea of a Town: The Anthropology of Urban Form in Rome, Italy and the Ancient World*. Princeton.

Salmon, E.T. 1967. *Samnium and the Samnites*. Cambridge.

Salzman-Mitchell, P. 2005. *A Web of Fantasies: Gaze, Image, and Gender in Ovid's Metamorphoses*. Columbus, OH.

Sannicandro, L. 2010. "Tibull (Albus Tibullus)." In Walde, coll. 1019–26.

Sansone, D. 2013. "Euripides, *Cretans* frag. 472e.16–26 Kannicht." *ZPE* 184: 58–65.

Saylor, C. 1967. "*Querelae*: Propertius' Distinctive Technical Name for His Elegy." *Agon* 1: 142–9.

Schadewaldt, W. 1970. *Hellas und Hesperien: Gesammelte Schriften zur Antike und zur neueren Literatur.*[2] Zurich.

Schafer, J. 2014. "Love." In R.F. Thomas and J.M. Ziolkowski, eds., *The Virgil Encyclopedia*, 2: 759–60. Malden, MA.

– 2020. *Catullus through His Books: Dramas of Composition*. Cambridge.

Schiera, P. 2007. "L'amicizia politica in Francesco Patrizi, senese." In G. Angelini and M. Tesoro, eds., *De Amicitia. Scritti dedicati a Arturo Colombo*, 61–72. Rome.

Schiesaro, A. 2015. "Emotions and Memory in Virgil's *Aeneid*." In Cairns and Fulkerson, 163–76.

Schlunk, R.R. 1974. *The Homeric Scholia and the* Aeneid: *A Study of the Influence of Ancient Homeric Literary Criticism on Vergil*. Ann Arbor.

Schmidt, E. 1998. "Ancient Bucolic Poetry and Later Pastoral Writing: Systematic and Historical Reflections: Paul Alpers, *What Is Pastoral?*" *IJCT* 5: 226–51. https://doi.org/10.1007/bf02688424.

Schmit-Neuerberg, T. 1999. *Vergils Äneis und die antike Homerexegese: Untersuchungen zum Einfluß ethischer und kritischer Homerrezeption auf imitatio und aemulatio Vergils*. Berlin.

Schodde, C. 2014. "Publius Ovidius Naso: Decastich arguments of the *Aeneid* with the monostich arguments of Herennius Modestinus." Online at https://foundinantiquity.files.wordpress.com/2014/09/the-mini-aeneid.pdf.

Schwinge, E.-R. 1965. "Horaz, *Carmen* 2.20." *Hermes* 93: 438–59.

Scioli, E. 2010. "Properz (Sextus Propertius)." In Walde, coll. 759–72.

– 2015. *Dream, Fantasy, and Visual Art in Roman Elegy*. Madison, WI.

Scodel, R.S., and R.F. Thomas. 1984. "Virgil and the Euphrates." *AJP* 105: 339. https://doi.org/10.2307/294999.

Sebesta, J.L. 2001. "Symbolism in the Costume of the Roman Woman." In Bonfante and Sebesta, 46–53.

Segal, C.P. 1969. *Landscape in Ovid's* Metamorphoses: *A Study in the Transformation of a Literary Symbol*. Wiesbaden.

Seidensticker, B. 1978. "Archilochus and Odysseus." *GRBS* 19: 5–22.

Seider, A. 2016. "Genre, Gallus, and Goats: Expanding the Limits of Pastoral in *Eclogues* 6 and 10." *Vergilius* 62: 3–23.

Sellar, W.Y. 1899. *The Roman Poets of the Augustan Age: Horace and the Elegiac Poets*. Oxford.

Serena, A. 1512. *Aurelii Sereni Monopolitani* Opuscula. Rome.

– 1514. *Theatrum Capitolinum Magnifico Iuliano institutum per Aurelium Serenum Monopolitanum. Et De elephante carmen eiusdem*. Rome.

Shackleton Bailey, D.R., ed. 1988. *M. Annaei Lucani* De bello civili *libri X*. Stuttgart.

– ed. and trans. 2001. *Cicero*. Letters to Friends, *vol. 1*. LCL 205. Cambridge, MA.

– ed. and trans. 2003a. *Statius*, Silvae. Cambridge, MA.

– ed. and trans. 2003b. *Statius*, Thebaid *Books 8–12, Achilleid*. Cambridge, MA.

Shapiro, M. 1988. *The Poetics of Ariosto*. Detroit.

Sharrock, A. 1994. *Seduction and Repetition in Ovid's* Ars Amatoria 2. Oxford.

– 2002. "An A-Musing Tale: Gender, Genre, and Ovid's Battles with Inspiration in the *Metamorphoses*." In Spentzou and Fowler, 207–27.

– 2011. "Womanly Wailing? The Mother of Euryalus and Gendered Reading." *Eugesta* 1: 55–77.

Sharrock, A., and H. Morales, eds. 2000. *Intratextuality: Greek and Roman Textual Relations*. Oxford.

Shell, M. 1993. *The Economy of Literature*. Baltimore.

Skempis, M., and I.V. Ziogas, eds. 2014. *Geography, Topography, Landscape: Configurations of Space in Greek and Roman Epic*. Berlin.

Skinner, M.B. 2003. *Catullus in Verona*. Columbus, OH.

Sklenář, R.J. 2003. *The Taste for Nothingness: A Study of* Virtus *and Related Themes in Lucan's* Bellum Civile. Ann Arbor.

Skutsch, F. 1901. *Aus Vergils Frühzeit*. Leipzig.

– 1906. *Gallus und Vergil: aus Vergils Frühzeit*. Leipzig.

Slater, N. 1994. "Calpurnius and the Anxiety of Vergilian Influence: *Eclogue* I." *SyllClass* 5: 71–8. https://doi.org/10.1353/syl.1994.0000.

Smith, L.F. 1968. "A Notice of the *Epigrammata* of Francesco Patrizi, Bishop of Gaeta." *Studies in the Renaissance* 15: 92–143. https://doi.org/10.2307/2857006.

Smolenaars, J.J.L. 1994. *Statius* Thebaid *VII: A Commentary*. Leiden.

– 2017. "The Historical Truth of Vergil's Recitation of the *Georgics* at Atella (VSD 27)." In Powell and Hardie, 153–72.

Solmsen, F. 1986. "'Aeneas Founded Rome with Odysseus.'" *HSCP* 90: 93–110. https://doi.org/10.2307/311463.

Solodow, J.B. 1986. "*Raucae, tua cura, palumbes*: A Study of Poetic Word Order." *HSCP* 90: 129–53. https://doi.org/10.2307/311465.

– 1988. *The World of Ovid's* Metamorphoses. Chapel Hill, NC.

Spaltenstein, F. 2002. *Commentaire des* Argonautica *de Valerius Flaccus (livres 1 et 2)*. Brussels.

Spanoudakis, K. 2002. *Philetas of Cos*. Leiden.

Sparreboom, A. 2016. "*Venationes Africanae*: Hunting Spectacles in Roman North Africa: Cultural Significance and Social Function." PhD Dissertation, University of Amsterdam.

Spelman, H. 2014. "Alcman 3 'PMGF' and Horace *C*. 2.8." *ZPE* 192: 23–8.

Spence, S. 1999. "The Polyvalence of Pallas in the *Aeneid*." *Arethusa* 32: 149–63. https://doi.org/10.1353/are.1999.0011.

– 2017. "'Love's Labors Lost'? Mapping the Elegiac in the *Aeneid*." Paper presented at *Symposium Cumanum* 2017, Cuma.

Spentzou, E., and D. Fowler, eds. 2002. *Cultivating the Muse: Struggles for Power and Inspiration in Classical Literature*. Oxford.

Spies, A. 1930. "*Militat Omnis Amans*: Ein Beitrag zur Bildersprache der antiken Erotik." PhD Dissertation, University of Tübingen.

Stahl, H.-P. 1985. *Propertius: "Love" and "War." Individual and State under Augustus*. Berkeley.

Stephens, S.A. 2004. "Whose Rituals in Ink?" In A. Barchiesi, J. Rüpke, and S. Stephens, eds., *Rituals in Ink*, 157–60. Stuttgart.

Stephens[JL30] , S.A., ed. 2015. *Callimachus: The Hymns*. Oxford.

Stok, F. 2010. "The Life of Virgil before Donatus." In Farrell and Putnam, 107–20.

Stover, T. 2012. *Epic and Empire in Vespasianic Rome*. Oxford.

Sullivan, J.P. 1962. "*Cynthia Prima Fuit*: A Causerie." *Arion* 1: 34–44.

Summonte, P. 1512. *Pontani De fortuna*. Naples.

Suter, A., ed. 2008. *Lament: Studies in the Ancient Mediterranean and Beyond*. Oxford.

Swift, L.A. 2010. *The Hidden Chorus: Echoes of Genre in Tragic Lyric*. Oxford.

Syed, Y. 2005. *Vergil's Aeneid and the Roman Self: Subject and Nation in Literary Discourse*. Ann Arbor.

Syme, R. 1978. *History in Ovid*. Oxford.

Tabeling, E. 1932. *Mater Larum: Zum Wesen Der Larenreligion*. Frankfurt.

Tacoma, L.E. 2016. *Moving Romans: Migration in Rome in the Principate*. Oxford.

Tarrant, R. 1983. "Ovid's *Metamorphoses*." In L.D. Reynolds, ed., *Texts and Transmission*, 276–82. Oxford.

– 2004. *P. Ovidi Nasonis* Metamorphoses. Oxford.

– 2012. *Virgil*. Aeneid *Book XII*. Cambridge.

Tatham, G. 2000. "'Just As Ariadne Lay … ': Images of Sleep in Propertius 1.3." *Scholia* 9: 43–53.

Tatum, J. 1973. "Non Usitata Nec Tenui Ferar." *AJP* 94: 4–25. https://doi.org/10.2307/294035.

Tedeschi, A. 1990. "Il giogo imperfetto e lo scarto in amore. A proposito di Properzio 3, 24." *Aufidus* 10: 53–67.

Temple, R. 1982. "An Anatomical Verification of the Reading of a Term in Extispicy." *Journal of Cuneiform Studies* 34: 19–27.

Theodorakopoulos, E. 1997. "Closure: The Book of Virgil." In Martindale, 155–65. https://doi.org/10.1017/ccol0521495393.011.

– 2000. "Catullus, 64: Footprints in the Labyrinth." In Sharrock and Morales, 115–41.

Thévenaz, O. 2002. "Le cygnet de Venouse: Horace et la metamorphose de l'Ode II,20." *Latomus* 61.4: 861–88.

Thibodeau, P. 2011. *Playing the Farmer: Representations of Rural Life in Vergil's Georgics.* Berkeley and Los Angeles.

Thilo, G. and H. Hagen.1881 (= 1986). *Servii grammatici qui feruntur in Vergilii Carmina Commentarii.* 3 vols. Leipzig (= Hildesheim, Zürich, and New York, 1986).

Thomas, E. 1964. "Variations on a Military Theme in Ovid's *Amores.*" *G&R* n.s. 11: 151–65. https://doi.org/10.1017/s0017383500014169.

Thomas, R.F. 1979. "Theocritus, Calvus, and *Eclogue* 6." *CP* 74: 337–9. https://doi.org/10.1086/366521.

– 1982. *Lands and Peoples in Roman Poetry: The Ethnographical Tradition.* Cambridge.

– 1983. "Callimachus, the *Victoria Berenices,* and Roman Poetry." *CQ* 33.1: 92–113. https://doi.org/10.1017/s0009838800034327.

– 1985. "From *Recusatio* to Commitment: The Evolution of the Vergilian Programme." *PLLS* 5: 61–73.

– 1986. "Vergil and the Art of Reference." *HSCP* 90: 171–98.

– ed. 1988a. *Virgil,* Georgics. 2 vols. Cambridge.

– 1988b. "Tree Violation and Ambivalence in Virgil." *TAPA* 118: 261–73. https://doi.org/10.2307/284171.

– 1991. "The 'Sacrifice' at the End of the *Georgics,* Aristaeus, and Vergilian Closure." *CP* 86: 211–18. https://doi.org/10.1086/367256.

– 1998a. "'Melodious Tears': Sepulchral Epigram and Generic Mobility." *Hellenistica Groningana* 3: 205–23.

– 1998b. "Voice, Poetics, and Virgil's Sixth Eclogue." In J. Jasanoff, H.C. Melchert, and L. Oliver, eds., *Mír Curad: Studies in Honor of Calvert Watkins,* 669–76. Innsbruck.

– 1999. *Reading Virgil and His Texts: Studies in Intertextuality.* Ann Arbor.

Thorsen, T.S. 2013a. "Ovid the Love Elegist." In Thorsen, 114–29.

– 2014. *Ovid's Early Poetry: From His Single* Heroides *to His* Remedia Amoris. Cambridge.

Thorsen, T.S., ed. 2013b. *The Cambridge Companion to Latin Love Elegy.* Cambridge.

Tissol, G. 1992. "An Allusion to Callimachus' *Aetia* 3 in Vergil's *Aeneid* 11." *HSCP* 94: 263–8.

– 2002. "Ovid and the Exilic Journey of Rutilius Namatianus." *Arethusa* 35: 435–46. https://doi.org/10.1353/are.2002.0027.

– 2014. *Ovid,* Epistulae ex Ponto, *Book 1.* Cambridge.

Todd, F.A. 1931. "Vergil's Invocation of Erato." *CR* 45: 216–18. https://doi.org/10.1017/s0009840x00057152.

Toll, K. 1989. "What's Love Got to Do with It? The Invocation to Erato, and Patriotism in the *Aeneid*." *QUCC* 33: 107–18. https://doi.org/10.2307/20547016.

Toynbee, J.M.C. 1971. *Death and Burial in the Roman World*. Baltimore.

Traglia, A. and G. Aricò, eds. 1980. *Publio Papinio Stazio, Opere*. Turin.

Traina, A. 1965. "*Si numquam fallit imago*. Riflessioni sulle *Bucoliche* e l'Epicureismo." *Atena e Roma* 10: 72–8.

Tränkle, H. 1960. *Die Sprachkunst des Properz und die Tradition der lateinischen Dichtersprache*. Hermes Einzelschrift 15. Wiesbaden.

Trapp, J.B. 1984. "The Grave of Vergil." *Journal of the Warburg and Courtauld Institutes* 47: 1–31. https://doi.org/10.2307/751436.

Treggiari, S. 1991. *Roman Marriage:* Iusti Coniuges *from the Time of Cicero to the Time of Ulpian*. Oxford.

Tucker, R.A. 1990. "Love in Lucan's *Civil War*." *CB* 66: 43–6.

Tufano, C.V. 2015. *Lingue, tecniche e retorica dei generi letterari nelle* Eclogae *di G. Pontano*. Naples.

Uccellini, R. 2012. *L'arrivo di Achille a Sciro. Saggio di commento a Stazio* Achilleide *1, 1–396*. Pisa.

Vahlen, I. 1854. *Enniae Poesis Reliquiae*. Leipzig.

Vairo, V. 2021. "La riscoperta di Pausania nel Rinascimento. Stephanus Niger e l'eredità di Demetrio Calcondila." *Rivista di cultura classica e medioevale* 63.2: 551–75.

Van Groningen, B.A. 1966. *Theognis: le Premier Livre*. Amsterdam.

Van Noorden, H. 2015. *Playing Hesiod: The "Myth of the Races" in Classical Antiquity*. Cambridge.

Vannucci, L. 1989. "Ausonio fra Virgilio e Stazio: A proposito dei modelli poetici del Cupido cruciatus." *Atene e Roma* 34: 39–54.

Van Rooy, C.A. 1973. "Imitatio of Vergil, *Eclogues* in Horace, *Satires*, Book I." *Acta Classica* 16: 69–88.

Van Sickle, J. 2000. "Virgil vs. Cicero, Lucretius, Theocritus, Plato, and Homer: Two Programmatic Plots in the First Bucolic." *Vergilius* 46: 21–58.

– 2004. "Virgil *Bucolics* 1.1–2 and Interpretive Tradition: A Latin (Roman) Program for a Greek Genre." *CP* 99: 336–53. https://doi.org/10.1086/429940.

Vecce, C., ed. 2013. *Iacopo Sannazaro. Arcadia*. Rome.

Vikman, E. 2005. "Ancient Origins: Sexual Violence in Warfare, Part I." *Anthropology and Medicine* 12: 21–31. https://doi.org/10.1080/13648470500049826. Medline:28135871.

Vinchesi, M.A. 2014. *Calpurnii Siculi* Eclogae. Florence.

Volk, K. 2002. *The Poetics of Latin Didactic: Lucretius, Vergil, Ovid, Manilius*. Oxford.

– 2007. "*Ars Amatoria Romana*: Ovid on Love as a Cultural Construct." In Gibson, Green, and Sharrock, 235–51. Oxford.

Volk, K., ed. 2008. *Oxford Readings in Classical Studies: Vergil's* Georgics. Oxford.

Walde, Chr., ed. 2010. *Der Neue Pauly Supplemente 7. Die Rezeption der Antike Literatur.* Stuttgart.

Waldman, G., trans. 1974. *Ludovico Ariosto:* Orlando Furioso. Oxford.

Wallace-Hadrill, A. 1982. "The Golden Age and Sin in Augustan Ideology." *Past and Present* 95: 19–36. https://doi.org/10.1093/past/95.1.19

– 1990. "Pliny the Elder and Man's Unnatural History." *G&R* 37: 80–96. https://doi.org/10.1017/s0017383500029582.

Walters, B. 2013. "Cicero's *Silva* (A Note on *Ad Atticum* 12.15)." *CQ* 63.1: 426–30. https://doi.org/10.1017/s0009838812000869.

Warmington, E.H., ed. 1940. *Remains of Old Latin, vol. 1: Archaic Inscriptions.* Cambridge, MA.

– ed. 1967. *Remains of Old Latin, vol.1, Ennius and Caecilius.* Cambridge, MA.

Wasdin, K. 2018. *Eros at Dusk: Ancient Wedding and Love Poetry.* New York.

Watson, L.C. 1982. "Cinna and Euphorion." *SIFC* 54: 93.

– 1990. "Rustic Suffenus (Catullus 22) and Literary Rusticity." *PLLS* 6: 13–33.

– 2003. *A Commentary of Horace's* Epodes. Oxford.

– 2007. "The Epodes: Horace's Archilochus." In S.J. Harrison, ed., *The Cambridge Companion to Horace*, 93–104. Cambridge.

Watterson, W.C. 2010. "Nation and History: The Emergence of the English Pastoral Elegy." In Wiseman, 135–52.

Weiss, R. 1969. *The Renaissance Discovery of Classical Antiquity.* Oxford.

Welch, T. 2008. "Horace's Journey through Arcadia." *TAPA* 138: 47–74. https://doi.org/10.1353/apa.0.0006.

Wendel, C. 1966. *Scholia in Theocritum uetera.* Stuttgart.

West, M.L. 1966. *Hesiod:* Theogony. Oxford.

– 1974. *Studies in Greek Elegy and Iambus.* New York.

– 2003. *Homeric Hymns. Homeric Apocrypha.* Cambridge, MA.

Westerhold, J. 2013. "Ovid's Epic Forest: A Note on *Amores* 3.1.1–6." *CQ* 63.2: 899–903. https://doi.org/10.1017/s0009838813000402.

Whatmough, J. 1937. *The Foundations of Roman Italy.* London.

Wheeler, S.M. 2004–5. "Before the *Aetas Ovidiana*: Mapping the Early Reception of Ovidian Elegy." *Hermathena* 177/8: 9–26.

White, M. 1955. "Greek Tyranny." *Phoenix* 9.1: 1–18. https://doi.org/10.2307/1085948.

White, P. 1993. *Promised Verse: Poets in the Society of Augustan Rome.* Cambridge, MA.

Whittington, L. 2010. "Vergil's Nisus and the Language of Self-Sacrifice in *Paradise Lost*." *Modern Philology* 107.4: 588–606. https://doi.org/10.1086/652531.

Wilk, S.R. 2000. *Medusa: Solving the Mystery of the Gorgon.* Oxford.

Wilkinson, L.P. 1978. *The* Georgics *of Virgil: A Critical Survey.* Cambridge.

– 2008. "Pindar and the Proem to the Third Georgic." In K. Volk, ed., *Vergil's Georgics*, 181–8. Oxford and New York.

Williams, C.A. 1995. "Greek Love at Rome." *CQ* 45: 517–39. https://doi.org/10.1017/s0009838800043597. Medline:16437843.

Williams, G. 1972. *Virgil: The Aeneid I-VI. A Commentary*. London.

Williams, R.D., ed. 1973. *The Aeneid of Virgil: Books 7-12*. London.

Willis, J.A., ed. 1963. *Ambrosii Theodosii Macrobii Commentarii in Somnium Scipionis*. Leipzig.

Wilson-Okamura, D.S. 2010. *Virgil in the Renaissance*. Cambridge.

Wimmel, W. 1961. "Tibull 2,5 und das elegische Rombild." In ΑΠΑΡΧΑΙ 4: *Gedenkschrift für G. Rohde*, 227–66. Tübingen.

Wiseman, T.P. 1974. *Cinna the Poet*. Leicester.

– 1995. *Remus: A Roman Myth*. Cambridge.

– 1998. *Roman Drama and Roman History*. Liverpool.

– 2004. *The Myths of Rome*. Exeter.

Wissowa, G. 1912. *Religion und Kultus der Roemer*.[2] Munich.

Witzke, S.S. 2016. "Violence against Women in Ancient Rome: Ideology versus Reality." In W. Riess and G.G. Fagan, eds., *The Topography of Violence in the Greco-Roman World*, 248–74. Ann Arbor.

Wlosok, A. 1967. "Die dritte Cynthia-Elegie des Properz (Prop. 1.3)." *Hermes* 95: 330–52.

– 1976. "Vergils Didotragöedie. Ein Beitrag zum Problem des Tragischen in der *Aeneis*." In H. Görgemanns and E. Schmidt, eds., *Studien zum antiken Epos*, 228–50. Meisenheim am Glan.

Woodworth, D.C. 1930. "Lavinia: An Interpretation." *TAPA* 61: 175–94. https://doi.org/10.2307/282800.

Wright, D. 2001. *The Roman Vergil and the Origins of Medieval Book Design*. London.

Wright, J.R.G. 1983. "Virgil's Pastoral Programme: Theocritus, Callimachus and *Eclogue* 1." *PCPS* 29: 107–60. https://doi.org/10.1017/s0068673500004557.

Wright, T.L. 1998. "Valerius Flaccus and the Poetics of Imitation." PhD Dissertation, University of Virginia.

Wyke, M. 1994. "Woman in the Mirror: The Rhetoric of Adornment in the Roman World." In L.J. Archer, S. Fischler, and M. Wyke, eds., *Woman in Ancient Societies*, 134–51. London.

– 2002. *The Roman Mistress: Ancient and Modern Representations*. Oxford.

Xinyue, B. 2019. "Divinization and Didactic Efficacy in Virgil's *Georgics*." In B. Xinyue and N. Freer, eds., *Reflections and New Perspectives on Virgil's Georgics*, 93–104. London.

Yardley, J.C. 1996. "Roman Elegy and Funerary Epigram." *EMC* 40.15: 267–73.

York, M. 1988. "Romulus and Remus, Mars and Quirinus." *JIES* 16: 153–72.

Yunis, H. 1996. *Taming Democracy: Models of Political Rhetoric in Classical Athens.* Ithaca.

– ed. 2011. *Plato: Phaedrus.* Cambridge.

Zabughin, V. 1921/3. *Vergilio nel Rinascimento italiano da Dante a Torquato Tasso. Fortuna, studi, imitazioni, traduzioni e parodie, iconografia.* 2 vols. Bologna (repr. Trento 2000).

Zanker, P. 1988. *The Power of Images in the Age of Augustus,* tr. H.A. Shapiro. Ann Arbor.

Zarker, J.W. 1969. "Amata: Vergil's Other Tragic Queen." *Vergilius* 15: 2–24.

Zecchini, G. 1982. "Asinio Pollione: dall'attività politica alla riflessione storiografica." *ANRW* 2.30.2: 1265–96. https://doi.org/10.1515/9783110839685-009.

Zetzel, J. 1977. "Gallus, Elegy, and Ross." Review of Ross 1975. *CP* 72: 249–60. https://doi.org/10.1086/366360.

– 1980. "Horace's *Liber Sermonum*: The Structure of Ambiguity." *Arethusa* 13: 59–77.

– 1983. "Catullus, Ennius, and the Poetics of Allusion." *ICS* 8: 251–66.

– 2005. *Marginal Scholarship and Textual Deviance: The* commentum Cornuti *and the Early Scholia on Persius.* London.

Zicàri, M. 1978. *Scritti catulliani.* Urbino.

Zimmermann Damer, E. 2014. "Gender Reversals and Intertextuality in Tibullus." *CW* 107.4: 493–514. https://doi.org/10.1353/clw.2014.0040.

Ziogas, I. 2013. *Ovid and Hesiod: The Metamorphosis of the Catalogue of Women.* Cambridge.

– 2018. "Singing for Octavia: Vergil's *Life,* Marcellus' Death, and the End of Epic." *HSCP* 109: 428–81.

Ziolkowski, J.M., and M.C.J. Putnam, eds. 2008. *The Virgilian Tradition. The First Fifteen Hundred Years.* New Haven and London.

Zissos, A. 1999. "Allusion and Narrative Possibility in the *Argonautica* of Valerius Flaccus." *CP* 94: 289–301. https://doi.org/10.1086/449443.

– 2008. *Valerius Flaccus'* Argonautica: *Book 1.* Oxford.

CONTRIBUTORS

Giancarlo Abbamonte, University of Naples

Eva Anagnostou-Laoutides, Macquarie University

Yelena Baraz, Princeton University

Jessica Blum-Sorensen, University of San Francisco

Giulio Celotto, University of Virginia

Alessandra De Cristofaro, University of Naples

Kenneth Draper, University of Indiana

Jacqueline Fabre-Serris, Charles De Gaulle University – Lille III

Hunter H. Gardner, University of South Carolina

Bill Gladhill, McGill University

Judith P. Hallett, University of Maryland

John Henkel, Georgetown College

Alison Keith, University of Toronto

Sarah McCallum, University of Arizona

Lorenzo Miletti, University of Naples

Micah Y. Myers, Kenyon College

Joseph Ortiz, University of Texas at El Paso

Nandini B. Pandey, Johns Hopkins University

Sophia Papaioannou, University of Athens

Mariapia Pietropaolo, McMaster University

Luke Roman, Memorial University of Newfoundland

Garth Tissol, Emory University

Barbara Weiden Boyd, Bowdoin College

INDEX LOCORUM

Aelius Herodianus
Partitiones
30.5, 140

Aeschylus
Agamemnon
1202–13, 263n44

Alcaeus
10B, 121n49
fr. 129.21–4, 118n20
fr. 296a.5.8, 118n20

Ammianus Marcellinus
17.14.5, 105n62

Anacreon
fr. 4, 122n54
fr. 12, 122n54
fr. 357, 122n54
fr. 358 (= Ath. *Deipn.* 599c), 120n43
fr. 388.10–12, 120n44
fr. 481 (=schol. Aes. *Pers.* 42), 120n40

Anthologia Latina
668.1, 317n21

Anthologia Palatina
5.136, 122n54
5.137, 122n54
5.171, 122n54
5.190, 122n54
6.336, 33
7.196, 33
9.205, 44n10
12.117, 56

Antigonus of Carystus
19.23 (=Fr.14a Spanoudakis),
  21n33

Antoninus Liberalis
32, 281n37

Apollonius of Rhodes
Argonautica
1.451–2, 43
1.985–1011, 119n33
1.1030–3, 119n33
1.1207–1362, 279n18
1.1210–11, 280n21
1.1211–18, 281n37
2.500–27, 21n36
3, 296n15
3.1–5, 128–9, 136n27
3.1, 130, 136–7n29
3.3, 129
3.3–4, 129, 135n17
3.4–5, 135–6n18
3.5, 129
3.309–13, 137–8n36

Quintilian

Sallust

Sannazaro, Jacopo

Sappho

Scholia Veronensis

GENERAL INDEX

Poseidon, 92, 95, 96, 161, 376. *See also*
Neptune
Posillipo, 309, 365–6
Postumus, C. Propertius, 91, 97–100,
104n53
praeceptor amoris, 58–9, 159, 167, 208,
209, 211, 242
praefica, 139, 145–6, 152n2, 154n26,
154n27, 154n30
Priapus, 52, 187, 192n41, 254, 263n49
principate: first, 64, 65, 75, 78;
Tiberian, 177
Priscian, 372; *Institutiones grammaticae*,
372
Procne, 5, 7. *See also* Philomela
Procris, 335–8, 340
profectio, 85
Prometheus, 66, 79n7
Propertius, 6, 7, 8, 16–18, 21n16,
23n50, 27, 31, 39, 44n4, 46n51,
58–9, 61–2n19, 62n31, 62n32,
82–4, 90–101, 101n1, 101n12,
104n47, 104n50, 104n51, 104n54,
106–7, 111–16, 117n6, 122n65,
123n68, 124n83, 129–30, 136n22,
138n37, 140, 153n8, 167, 170, 174n36,
175, 207, 212, 220n31, 231n13, 242,
244, 246, 248n12, 249n36, 260n7,
265–6, 277, 281–2n49, 284–5, 290,
291, 304–5, 312, 316n15, 320,
321–2, 329, 329–30n3, 330n7,
330n8, 331n12, 353, 380, 391, 396,
399; *Monobiblos*, 58, 100, 106, 107,
138n37
Proteus, 12–14, 183–6, 188, 191n34
puella(e), 34, 40, 42, 54, 62n20, 73, 75,
83, 90, 91, 92, 93, 94, 95, 96, 97, 99,
100, 111, 115, 121n51, 129, 132,
165, 167, 171, 173n26, 208, 209,
216, 221n39, 231n12, 236, 241, 244,
246, 251, 290, 305, 338

puer delicatus, 15, 24n61, 291–2,
298n35
Pygmalion (in the *A.*), 210, 214,
261n20; (in the *Met.*), 203
Pyrene, 252

Quattrocento, 381–2, 382n4, 383n11,
384–5n35
querela, 140–3, 150, 152, 153n8,
153n10
querimonia, 139–45, 148, 150–2, 153n7,
153n10, 153n11, 153n14, 153n15
Quintilian, 22n29, 320–2, 329, 330n8,
331n11, 331n13

rape, 19, 22n36, 187, 252, 255–9,
260, 263n42, 280n22, 281–2n49,
293; and deforestation, 259;
as possession, 259
recusatio, 27, 30–2, 39, 43–4n2,
153n20
reditus, 84–5, 90, 94, 96, 100, 101n12.
See also *nostos*; return
Remus, 68, 76, 200, 209, 210. *See also*
Romulus
Renaissance, 353, 355, 356, 357,
366, 367n11, 368n31, 369, 371,
380, 381, 382n2, 382n3, 383n11,
384n28, 387, 388, 398, 399, 400n10,
402n29; Italy, 19, 351, 357, 369, 380,
381–2n1, 392, 399; Naples, 367n6
renuntiatio amoris, 54, 57, 60
return, 14, 18, 40, 55, 56, 63, 64, 65,
66, 72, 79n6, 82, 83, 84, 85–6, 90,
92, 93, 94, 95, 96, 97, 98, 99, 100,
101, 101n12, 102n16, 105n60,
105n62, 223, 230, 246, 247, 291,
296n14, 305, 317n34, 322, 349n29,
366, 394. See also *nostos*; *reditus*
Rhea Silvia, 200. *See also* Ilia
rhetoric, of sympathy, 162